Management Information Systems

A User Perspective

Third Edition

Management Information Systems

A User Perspective

Third Edition

James O. Hicks Jr.

Virginia Polytechnic Institute
and State University

West Publishing Company

Minneapolis/St. Paul   New York   Los Angeles   San Francisco

PRODUCTION CREDITS

Copyediting	*Sheryl Rose*
Text Design	*John Rokusek*
Cover Design	*Diane Beasley*
Cover Image	*David Bishop*
Artwork	*Alexander Teshin and Associates*
Composition	*American Composition & Graphics, Inc.*

Production, Prepress, Printing and Binding by West Publishing Company.

Photo Credits follow index.

WEST'S COMMITMENT TO THE ENVIRONMENT

In 1906, West Publishing Company began recycling materials left over from the production of books. This began a tradition of efficient and responsible use of resources. Today, up to 95 percent of our legal books and 70 percent of our college and school texts are printed on recycled, acid-free stock. West also recycles nearly 22 million pounds of scrap paper annually—the equivalent of 181,717 trees. Since the 1960s, West has devised ways to capture and recycle waste inks, solvents, oils, and vapors created in the printing process. We also recycle plastics of all kinds, wood, glass, corrugated cardboard, and batteries, and have eliminated the use of styrofoam book packaging. We at West are proud of the longevity and the scope of our commitment to our environment.

Library of Congress Cataloging-in-Publication Data
Hicks, James O.
    Management information systems: a user perspective/James O. Hicks, Jr.—3rd ed.
        p. cm.
    Includes index.
    ISBN 0-314-93367-0 (hard)
    1. Management information systems.   I. Title
T58.6.H49 1993
658.4'038—dc20   92-26260
                                                      ∞ CIP

To
My Wife Eva
and
My Son Kevin

Brief Table of Contents

Table of Contents

Chapter 8   Artificial Intelligence and Expert Systems, 167

Chapter 23   Information Systems and Society, 618

Preface

Information Systems (IS) is a dynamic and changing field. Perhaps the most important driving force behind this field is the computer. Computers are everywhere. This is particularly true in business. The student who learns to use this powerful tool to gain a competitive advantage and provide the information needed in his or her career, regardless of whether that career is finance, marketing, management, accounting, economics, or another business area, will be far ahead of those who do not master this tool.

In information systems we study how computer hardware and software are combined to build efficient and effective information systems for business professionals. Computer hardware and software are, however, only tools. Too often people mistakenly feel that computer information systems are mysterious, complex, and hard to understand. This is an unfortunate misconception. In this text, we take the approach that management information systems are logical, interesting, essential for a business career, and can be mastered with a reasonable degree of effort by any student.

The text takes a user orientation. I have covered the topics that are important for a manager, an accountant, a marketing person, and other business professionals to know. The hardware and software for information systems are usually readily available. It is the application and use of these tools that is important. Accordingly, this text's primary thrust is to cover the fundamental concepts concerning the development and use of information systems, from alignment of the information system with business strategy to the ongoing use and management of IS. Within this user orientation, contemporary IS topics are emphasized, including:

1. Managing international information systems

2. Information systems ethics

3. Business strategy and the use of information systems for competitive advantage

4. Information strategy planning

5. Artificial intelligence, including expert systems and neural networks

6. End-user computing

7. Outsourcing

8. Connectivity, including communications, networks, and client-server computing

9. Decision support systems and executive information systems

10. Information systems and individual human behavior

11. Information systems and organizational behavior

12. Structured systems development and computer-aided software engineering (CASE)

13. Information systems security, including computer viruses.

It is essential that users be directly involved in the information systems development process. Certainly, information systems professionals such as systems analysts and programmers are important to this process. They have the technical expertise in the area. Research has shown, however, that the most successful information systems applications are those in which users are directly and heavily involved in their development and maintenance. A business professional simply cannot take the attitude that it is not necessary to have knowledge in the information systems area, and that application development should be left to information systems professionals. Only you know what information you need from a system. If you do not understand information systems, it will be impossible to translate your need for information into an operational information system.

The first part of this book is designed to give you an overview of the conceptual foundations of information systems. In this part, we discuss information systems and their interactions with individuals and organizations. Business strategy and the use of information systems for competitive advantage are also covered. The second part of the book, "Information Systems Applications," provides an introduction to the information systems used by the various functions of a business. Then a chapter is devoted to each of the following three areas: decision support and executive information systems; artificial intelligence; and office automation systems. Part Three, "Information Systems Technology," provides a basic understanding of the hardware, software, and communications technology used in information systems. Topics covered are information processing hardware, systems software and programming languages, data storage and processing, database management systems, and communications/distributed data processing. While a basic understanding of information systems technology is essential to effective utilization of computers, it is not the most important topic in this book. Therefore, only five chapters, about 20 percent of the text, is devoted to the technology subjects. You will also find that it is not necessary to cover these technology topics prior to covering the material in the first two parts of the book. Part Four, "Development of User Applications," begins with information strategy planning which deals with tying the information system into a business strategy and then follows with five chapters dealing with the development of information systems, their acquisition, and their control and security. Part Five, "Information Systems, Management, Society and You," covers information resource management, managing international information systems, information systems and their relationships to society, and how information systems may affect you and your career.

This book contains several features designed to assist you in learning and reinforcing the materials contained in the text. Each chapter contains the following:

1. A detailed chapter outline, which provides you with an overview of the chapter so that you can see where we are going before you begin reading.

2. Two or three short application cases per chapter showing how the concepts and technology discussed are being applied in real-world business. Examples: Chapter 5, "Being the Best in Business"; and Chapter 1, "Stanley Hammers on Quality: Tool Maker Focuses Resources on Applications to Improve Quality."

3. A point-by-point chapter summary, which summarizes the major topics introduced in the chapter.

4. A list of key terms. I have found that learning the terminology is an important part of studying information systems. I suggest that you review these key terms, and if there are any that you do not understand, refer back to the chapter or to the comprehensive glossary at the end of the text.

5. Review questions are provided so that you can independently test your knowledge of the chapter.

6. Short discussion questions and cases apply the chapter material to real-world situations. Often these cover controversial topics. Your instructor is likely to use these questions and cases for class discussion purposes.

7. Information Systems Strategies provide a case at the end of each chapter to illustrate the ways in which various firms use information systems technology. They can give unique insights into the thoughts of managers and information systems professionals concerning materials presented in the text. Discussion questions are included at the end of each Information Systems Strategy.

8. A glossary of industry-standard definitions at the end of the text. Understanding terminology is essential to an understanding of information systems. Students should learn standardized definitions.

I am sure you will find this an enjoyable and useful course. In fact, if you master the material in this course and apply it in your career, there is no doubt in my mind that you will find this course one of the most useful of your collegiate program.

To the Instructor

This text employs a user-perspective approach, emphasizing information systems topics that are important for a manager, an accountant, a marketing person, and other business professionals to know. The intent of the text is to provide a business student with the information systems fundamentals necessary to operate effectively in a computerized business environment.

The text was specifically developed to cover the material that satisfies the American Assembly of Collegiate Schools of Business (AACSB) requirement for MIS coverage in business programs. The text assumes that a student has little or no prior background in information systems. However, it is also often used at the higher level where students have had a previous course in business data processing or computer literacy. At this level, I would simply skip some of the chapters containing material covered in the previous course, such as the hardware chapters in Part Three. I have attempted to put enough materials in the text to facilitate skipping previously covered material and yet have ample material for a full semester or quarter-long information systems course.

As with previous editions of the text, fundamental concepts of information systems are covered. However, in this edition technology is de-emphasized and managerial issues related to information systems are emphasized. Many contemporary and evolving information systems topics are covered, including:

1. Managing international information systems (Chapter 22)

2. Information systems ethics (Chapter 3)

3. Business stragegy and the use of information systems for competitive advantage (Chapter 5)

4. Information strategy planning (Chapter 15)

5. Artificial intelligence, including expert systems and neural networks (Chapter 8)

6. End-user computing (Chapter 18)

7. Outsourcing (Chapter 19)

8. Connectivity, including communications, networks, and client-server computing (Chapter 14)

9. Decision support systems and executive information systems (Chapter 7)

10. Information systems and individual human behavior (Chapter 3)

11. Information systems and organizational behavior (Chapter 4)

12. Structured systems development and computer-aided software engineering (CASE) (Chapters 16, 17, & 18)

13. Information systems security, including computer viruses (Chapter 20)

These topics are also integrated throughout the discussion in the remainder of the text.

Approximately 75 percent of the text is new to this edition. These revisions direct the emphasis of the text strongly towards the role that information systems play in business enterprises and away from technical hardware and programming topics. In addition to the revised material in chapters that appeared in the second edition, there are eight new chapters in the third edition. These include:

Chapter 3   Information Systems and Individual Behavior

Chapter 4   Information Systems and Organizational Behavior

Chapter 5   Business Strategy and the Use of Information Systems for Competitive Strategy

Chapter 8   Artifical Intelligence

Chapter 9   Office Automation

Each chapter of the text is written as independently as possible, so that you can rearrange the sequencing of the material coverage if you prefer.

The teaching and learning tools in each chapter include the following:

1. Chapter Outline: A detailed outline at the beginning of each chapter, providing an overview of the chapter.

2. Applications: Two or three short examples per chapter of how the concepts and technology being discussed are being applied in real-world business. Examples: Chapter 5, "Being the Best in Business"; and Chapter 1, "Stanley Hammers on Quality: Tool Maker Focuses Resources on Applications to Improve Quality."

3. Chapter Summary: A point-by-point summary of the major topics of the chapter.

4. Key Terms: A list of the key terms of the chapter, which can be used for review of terminology.

5. Review Questions: Fifteen to twenty review questions, which can be used by the students on their own or in class to review the chapter.

6. Short discussion questions and cases: These provide situations, related to the chapter material, that are often controversial, to stimulate student interest and class discussion. There are five to eight of these per chapter.

7. Information Systems Strategies: These provide a case at the end of each chapter to illustrate the ways that various firms use information systems technology. They can give unique insights into the thoughts of managers and information systems professionals concerning materials presented in the text. Discussion questions are included at the end of each Information Systems Strategy. Examples: Chapter 3, "The Ethics Gap"; and Chapter 5, "An Illuminating CEO-CIO Alliance."

At the end of the text is a comprehensive glossary. Understanding terminology is essential to understanding information systems. Quite often I have had students purchase a paperback dictionary of information systems terms. This should not be necessary with this text owing to the comprehensive nature of the glossary. Furthermore, I think the definitions in the glossary should be standardized, since teaching students standardized definitions enhances their ability to understand and communicate information systems concepts. Therefore, when possible I have used American National Standards Institute definitions from *The American National Standard for Information Systems-Dictionary for Information Systems*. Also used are definitions from the IBM publication *Dictionary of Computing* and from the *International Organization for Standardization's Vocabulary—Information Processing*.

The supplements to this text include the following:

1. *Instructor's Resource Manual with Test Bank* By James O. Hicks, Jr.: This manual contains author's notes, chapter overviews, lecture outlines, and suggested answers to the review questions, discussion questions, discussion cases, and information systems strategies. This manual contains approximately 1,500 multiple-choice test bank questions. These test questions are also available in the Westest© computerized form.

2. Computerized Instructor's Manual: These are text files on disk containing the same material as in the *Instructor's Resource Manual with Test Bank*. They are available in both the IBM PC and Apple Macintosh formats.

3. Transparency Masters: A large set of transparency masters containing all the diagrams used as figures in the text and many additional illustrations not used in the text.

Acknowledge-ments

I would like to thank the following professors for reviewing the manuscript for this book.

Barbara Denison
Wright State University

Efrem G. Mallach
University of Massachusetts
    at Lowell

James Gips
Boston College

Lawrence McNitt
College of Charleston

Thomas M. Harris
Ball State University

Mary R. Meredith
The University of Southwestern
    Lousiana

Thomas Hilton
Utah State University

Ron Pedigo
Emporia State University

Jack T. Hogue
The University of
    North Carolina at Charlotte

Floyd Ploeger
Southwest Texas State
    University

Elizabeth Megalski
Marquette University

Ronald L. Thompson
The University of Vermont

1

Introduction to Information Systems

Introduction

Information systems have become crucial to the functioning of modern organizations and businesses. Firms are using information systems technology to gain competitive advantages over their rivals. In fact, many basic business processes are now being redesigned to take advantage of the productivity increases that are available through the use of information systems. Many believe that computer-based information systems will have profound impacts on the way we organize to do business and on the processes we use in carrying out business functions. In this chapter we will first look at an information system, then we will discuss the impact of information systems on business. Next, we will cover some of the contemporary information systems issues. By this time you should have a good understanding of why the study of information systems is crucial to an individual contemplating a business career. Finally, we will provide an overview of this textbook.

What Is an Information System?

An **information system** (IS) is a formalized computer information system that can collect, store, process, and report data from various sources to provide the information necessary for management decision making. Not all information systems and organizations are formal. There are informal information sources such as the office grapevine, gossip, and so on. Neither do information systems have to be computer-based. Information is often gathered and stored through manual processes, although manual information systems are becoming relatively less important. The information systems covered in this book are those that have been planned in a structured way and are managed for the benefit of the organization. Although many of the concepts covered in this book also apply to manual information systems, the focus of this book is on computer-based information systems.

The Parts of an Information System

Figure 1–1 illustrates the six parts of an information system: inputs, processes, data files, outputs, personnel, and hardware. All systems, including information systems and computer systems, have inputs, processes, and outputs. Processes transform inputs (data) to outputs (management information). Processes can be subdivided into computer programs and procedures. Computer programs are executed by computer hardware, and procedures are executed by people. For example, sometimes data must be collected and checked manually before they are input to the information system. An information system also contains data files, which can be either computer-based or manual.

Personnel are without a doubt the most important component of an information system. System analysts and programmers design, implement, and maintain the programs and procedures, while computer operators run the computer-based portion of the system. Accounting, finance, marketing, and manufacturing personnel operate other aspects of an information system, sometimes, in fact, without the use of computer hardware. Furthermore, management personnel set the overall policies that govern the operation of an information system.

In summary, the core of an information system is made up of inputs, processes, data files, and outputs. These components are executed and controlled by hardware and personnel.

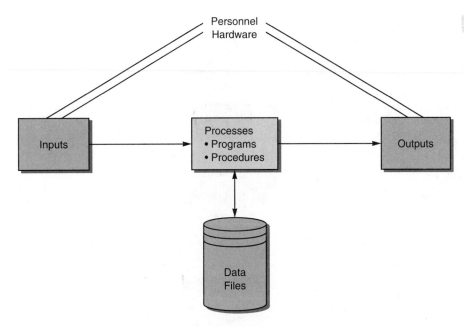

FIGURE 1–1
The Parts of an
Information System
The portions of an
information system that
are computer based are
executed on a computer
system. However, as we
will see in this chapter,
much of an IS depends on
highly skilled personnel.

The Types of Information Systems

Prior to the 1980s, information systems were usually classified as data processing systems or management information systems (MIS). **Data processing systems** were oriented toward capturing, processing, and storing data whereas MIS is oriented toward using data to produce management information. The relationship between data processing and management information systems is illustrated in Figure 1–2. The data processing system performed transaction processing. It was very much involved with processing orders, sales, payments on account, and so on. In the course of processing these transactions, the data processing system collected and stored a large amount of detailed information. This information was the database for the management information system.

In the 1980s the term *data processing system* went out of style and was replaced with the term **transaction processing system**. Also, several new types of information systems began to be used widely. Some authors have modified the definition of the term MIS while others have grouped these new types of systems as a part of a management information system. Figure 1–3 lists the contemporary types of information systems.

Transaction Processing Systems

A **transaction** is a business event such as a sale to a customer. Other transactions include payment to an employee for work performed, purchase of raw materials, and payment of an accounts payable. Transaction processing systems keep track of these daily business events. Examples of typical transaction processing systems include accounts receivable systems, payroll systems, accounts payable systems, airline reservation systems, and order processing systems. Transaction processing systems have three basic objectives. First, they must collect and store data concerning business events. Second, they provide the information necessary for the day-to-day control of business events. And finally, they serve as

4

FIGURE 1–2
The Relationship between Data Processing and Management Information Systems
Most firms implement data processing systems first since processing of transactions with customers is a necessity. As the data are collected through data processing, they also become available to produce the reports required by a management information system.

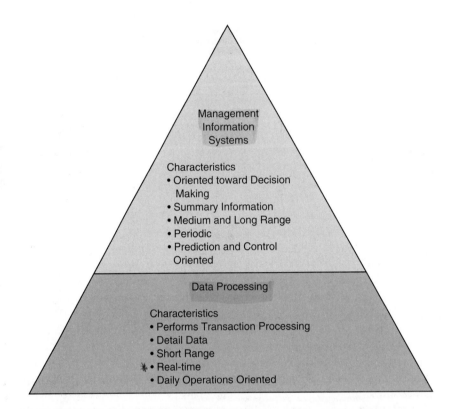

the database for higher-level information systems that are used by managers and executives at the middle and upper levels of an organization.

Office Automation Systems

Office automation systems (OAS) use the computer to automate many of the routine tasks that are performed in a typical office. Perhaps the most widespread type of office automation system is word processing. But there are many other applications in the office including desktop publishing, electronic mail, facsimile transmission, and image processing.

Executive Information Systems

Executive information systems (EIS) provide for the communication of summary-level information to executives. These systems typically have high-resolution graphics so that the information can be displayed in graphic form. The information is updated frequently, such as on a daily basis, and the systems also provide the capability to display more detailed information if an executive wants to look at it. Many executives use these systems to keep track of information concerning the factors that they consider most critical to the success of their firm.

Expert Systems

An **expert system** is a computer program that enables a computer to make (or give advice concerning) an unstructured decision normally made by humans with special expertise. These systems store facts and

Transaction Processing Systems
Office Automation Systems
Executive Information Systems
Expert Systems
Decision Support Systems
Management Information Systems

FIGURE 1-3
Types of Information
Systems
The types of information
systems increased
dramatically in the
1980s. To a large extent
this can be attributed to
the increase in the
capabilities of computer
hardware. As these
capabilities continue to
develop, you can expect
new types of information
systems to emerge.

rules that are used in reaching a judgment in a particular case. Examples of decisions that have been made or supported by expert systems are loan approvals, the diagnosis of malfunctions in diesel-electric locomotives, and the sizing of computer systems based on a customer's anticipated workload. Applications 1–1 and 1–2 illustrate additional applications of expert systems.

Decision Support Systems

A **decision support system** (DSS) is an integrated set of computer tools that allow a decision maker to interface directly with computers to create information useful in making semistructured and unstructured decisions. These decisions may involve, for example, mergers and acquisitions, plant expansions, new products, stock portfolio management, or marketing. Management information systems in the past have been most successful in providing information for routine, structured, and anticipated

APPLICATION 1-1

Expert System Used by the French America's Cup Entry

By Justin Kestelyn

Few sporting events have been as profoundly affected by technology as yacht racing. An America's Cup challenge is usually synonomous with publicity for advanced spaceage hulls, computer-designed spinnakers, and other cutting-edge innovations. The French entry for the 1992 America's Cup race features yet another high-tech yachting application: an on-board, workstation-based expert system. Nemo-America, which was developed by Developpement of Paris and runs on a Sun SparcStation 1, captures the sailing expertise of hundreds of yachtsmen.

Yacht racing is a subtle and intricate chess game of tactical moves, countermoves, and parries. Each boat battles for position, trying to steal the adversary's wind and force it to

change course and speed. Formulating and countering these tactics can be a baffling task, especially if the navigator is unsure of his or her own boat's exact position (which is a common problem). Furthermore, the crew may be unfamiliar with the waters and prevailing winds.

Nemo-America, which comprises two modules, is designed to work closely with the skipper, navigator, and tactician. The system's Positioning Expert module is crucial in determining the boat's position; it monitors radio waves from the shore and verifies position to within three meters. The system then feeds the radio-wave data into the Tactic Expert module, which contains Nemo-America's knowledge base. The Tactic Expert provides tactical analysis and recommendations on a graphical, diagrammed screen.

As an additional benefit, the system captures knowledge about the America's Cup racing rules and notifies users of rule infractions. Furthermore, the system's memory serves as an audit trail for any potential investigations.

In one demonstration, tactician Marc Bouet and a colleague simulated a race in the waters outlying San Diego harbor. The system instantly loaded the wind, current, and tidal features of the course. (It keeps such data on many well-known courses in its memory.) As the simulated race progressed with Bouet's boat in the lead, the system analyzed the situation and made recommendations in about three seconds.

Adapted with permission of *AI Expert*, June 1991, v. 6, n. 6, p64(1). COPYRIGHT Miller Freeman Publications 1991.

6

APPLICATION 1–2

Texas Air's GateKeeper Airport Gate Scheduling

By Justin Kestelyn

If you think you've got a complicated scheduling problem, try coordinating all the gates with their respective flights at a major airport. As if the coordination weren't difficult enough, a single delayed or canceled flight can have repercussions for the entire airport and its gate schedule. Strangely enough, this facet of airport management is one of the most underautomated processes in the friendly skies.

Texas Air has a better way to solve the problem. Its GateKeeper system, which is written in Common LISP and runs on VAXs and 386-based PCs, helps personnel design and maintain gate schedules in real time. GateKeeper's database has access to flight arrival/departure, passenger, maintenance, and routing data, and features a knowledge base that captures information about gate layout, airplane prep, and other constraints. It formulates a gate-schedule scheme, typically for a single airport day. GateKeeper's most valuable feature, however, is its ability to modify schedules in real time.

Adapted with permission of *AI Expert*, June 1991, v. 6, n. 6, p64 [1]. COPYRIGHT Miller Freeman Publications 1991.

types of decisions. In addition, they have succeeded in acquiring and storing large quantities of detailed data concerning transaction processing. They have been less successful in providing information for semistructured or unstructured decisions, particularly those that were not anticipated when the computer information system was designed. The basic idea underlying decision support systems is to provide a set of computer-based tools so that management information systems can produce information to support semistructured and unanticipated decisions.

Management Information Systems

The meaning of the term *management information systems* has changed over the past twenty years and in fact, there is still some confusion about what an MIS is. Today the term generally refers to a system that provides recurring information about routine and anticipated business events. These systems produce summary information about normal business activities to middle- and upper-level management. They are also called management reporting systems. Developed in the 1960s, management information systems are still in widespread use today. They form the backbone of information systems in business.

Traditionally the complete information system of a business has been called a management information system. Under this definition, all the other types of information systems, transaction processing, decision support, expert systems, and so on are parts of the management information system. Thus, the field and discipline of information systems is often called MIS. However, the trend today is to relegate the term MIS to its more restricted meaning as defined at the beginning of this section and to refer to the discipline, field, or complete information system of the business as simply information systems. In this text we will use the term *MIS* to refer to the more restricted meaning and the term *information systems* to refer to the collection of all the information systems of an organization.

Alphabet Soup, DSS, EIS, OAS, MIS, etc.

Sometimes it seems that information systems professionals are very adept at coming up with new names for both existing and new systems. It can be confusing, but we must recognize that information systems is a quickly evolving field. Computers are being applied to new applications, thus creating new types of systems. Older terms such as MIS may be used in different ways and applied to more restricted areas of systems. The domains of the types of information systems discussed above certainly overlap. For example, all of these systems are used to support decisions, yet all of them are not decision support systems. An executive information system is used for reporting information to executives, as is a management information system.

In summary, the above types of information systems are the major types in business today. However, you will certainly find other types of systems. And in some cases it will be difficult to classify an individual system as an MIS, an executive information system, or a decision support system. Some systems combine elements of two or more of these types of systems. As you continue through this text you will begin to understand the distinctions between the types of systems and also the lack of distinction between certain systems.

The Impact of Computer Information Systems on Business

All businesses, large or small, must perform transaction processing. They perform it either manually or with computers and other machines such as calculators and adding machines. Even the smallest business must perform data processing to keep records for income tax purposes, as required by federal tax law.

Often, though, small business managers depend less on a formal information system and more on informal information sources for decisions. A small business manager is intimately familiar with all aspects of the business. Therefore, he or she has less need for a formal information system. However, as a business grows larger, managers depend much more on formal information systems for their information. Imagine the managers of General Motors depending on informal sources for information about the operations of the company. Such an approach would be a disaster since the higher-level managers are not close enough to day-to-day operations to have the information necessary to make decisions.

Information is truly the lifeblood of a business. A business simply could not service its customers or make high-level decisions without information. The use of computers in information systems has had an impact on business in many areas. Among these are competitive advantage, increased product quality, shorter product cycles, easier business growth, productivity, automation of some decisions, and the availability of different types and greater quantities of information.

Competitive Advantage

In the early 1980s many business firms began to view information systems as tools with which to gain advantages over their competitors. The use of information systems to support management planning and control has always been directed at making business operations more effective

Not on Test

and efficient. But the emphasis on using information systems to gain **competitive advantage** is new.

Several major firms have gained significant competitive advantages through the strategic use of information technology. For example, American Airlines' Sabre System and United Airlines' Apollo System are used by reservation agents to book flights on all airlines. Each system was designed to show the owner's (American's or United's) flights first on the computer screen when agents check for available flights. Thus, agents are more likely to book passengers on an American or United flight. These systems gave such a competitive advantage to their owners that competing airlines successfully appealed to both courts and the government to change the order in which flights appear on these systems' screens.

Increased Product Quality

The quality of products and services has become the major concern of businesses. Much of the emphasis on quality has occurred because of the increased competition of foreign firms, especially in the automobile and electronics areas. Companies realize that unless they produce quality products and services, they will lose the market to competitors. Computer information systems can provide substantial improvements in product quality. For example, computer-aided design and computer-aided manufacturing systems assist engineers in producing quality designs and in controlling the quality of manufacturing. Simply maintaining information about the quality demands of consumers in general and about individual consumers can significantly improve product quality and perceptions of product quality. Application 1-3 illustrates how the toolmaker Stanley Works uses information systems to improve quality.

Shorter Product Cycles

Today, the firm that gets a product to market early will capture a significantly greater portion of the market than those who come along later. Thus, there is a large premium on the ability to design and manufacture

---

APPLICATION 1–3

Stanley Hammers on Quality: Tool Maker Focuses Resources on Applications to Improve Quality

By Catherine Marenghi

The firm of Stanley Works believes quality management is an every day component of work life. It does not have a formal quality program, but all departments, including its information systems (IS) operation, are focused on ways to improve. The IS department uses its $30 million yearly budget and personnel resources to create important applications to enhance quality. Stanley just invested in a warehouse management system to improve shipping. The system utilizes weight-verification systems, barcode readers, and other technologies to enhance accuracy and cut down on manual errors. The firm also is putting money towards improving the manufacturing planning process so that the process responds better to client needs. Stanley takes advantage of electronic data interchange to create 65 percent of its orders via direct connections with customers, reducing manual errors because of less reliance on paper.

Adapted with permission from *Computerworld*, January 6, 1992, v. 26, n. 1, p63 (1). Copyright 1992 by CW Publishing, Inc., Framingham, MA 01701.

products quickly. Computer-aided design and manufacturing systems have significantly decreased product cycles from the time of initial product concept until delivery to the first customers.

Easier Business Growth

Once computer information systems are installed, most businesses find that they can expand their operations without substantial changes in the information system they have chosen. For example, if the information system is designed correctly, it will have excess capacity. Therefore, it can easily accommodate a growth in the number of customers with perhaps only small changes, such as the addition of a more powerful central processing unit, or no changes at all. Furthermore, a significant factor in the growth of today's large businesses is the very existence of computer information systems, which provide managers with the information to control these enterprises.

Improved Productivity

Productivity is a measure of the amount of outputs that can be produced with a given amount of inputs, outputs being goods and services and inputs being human labor, material, and so on. The productivity we are normally interested in is the amount of output that can be produced by a given amount of human labor. In manufacturing, computers have produced very significant increases in output through the use of machines such as robots. In white-collar, professional areas such as engineering, accounting, marketing, and finance, computers have certainly increased the productivity of individuals engaged in these professions. One only has to look at electronic spreadsheets to see the impact of the computer on the productivity of accountants.

The use of computers has also reduced the need for clerical workers in business. In the past, these workers were the individuals who did the information processing with a manual system. However, as the demand for clerical workers has decreased, demand has increased for people who are technically trained in the use of the computer, such as systems analysts and programmers. Demand has also increased for other information workers, such as accountants, whose disciplines are closely linked with information processing.

Computers can process information at a much lower cost than humans can. Therefore, the cost of processing information in relation to the amount of output generated from the information system has declined drastically.

Automation of Decisions

Many businesses have used the computer to automate certain low-level decisions. Examples of decisions that have been automated are when to reorder goods to replenish inventory stocks, how much fuel to carry on a specific airline flight, and what mix of raw materials to use to produce paint that meets certain specifications.

More and Better Information

Computers have substantially increased the quantity of information available to management. Much information now available would have been impossible to produce in the past with manual systems simply because the amount of calculation necessary to produce it would have been prohibitive. Examples of this type of information include the output from linear programming, forecasting, and simulation models.

To illustrate this point, consider a simulation example. Using a computer program with mathematical formulas, one can build a model of a real-world system, such as an aircraft. Through a large number of manipulations of these mathematical formulas the computer simulates the performance of the aircraft. If a manufacturer is considering developing and producing a new type of passenger aircraft, it may decide to simulate that aircraft before committing millions or billions of dollars to its development. The manufacturer can simulate many factors concerning the aircraft, including fuel consumption and passenger load in relation to specific airline route structures. The output of such a simulation would enable the manufacturer to judge how profitable the aircraft would be. This is useful information considering the large amount of resources that would be committed to build the proposed aircraft.

Increased quantities of information are not always useful to managers, however. In today's environment, with computers producing large quantities of information, many managers suffer from information overload. So much information is available that they have difficulty sorting out and using information that is truly relevant. However, more sophisticated computer users have designed ways that managers can use the computer to select only the information that will be used to make a specific decision.

Contemporary Information Systems Issues

Information systems is a dynamic field where issues and ideas emerge almost daily. The vast increases in computer power that have occurred over the past few decades has opened up an almost unlimited number of applications for computers. This process produces many interesting issues. This textbook covers most of the current information systems issues. However, certain major issues are currently in the forefront of the field. We will briefly cover some of these issues now so that you can be aware of them as you study the material in this book.

Using Information Systems for Competitive Advantage

This issue was introduced above under "The Impact of Computer Information Systems on Business." We bring it up again here because it is perhaps the most important information system thrust today. Businesses have discovered that they can use information systems as a competitive tool. Thus, when they put together a strategic plan to map out their future, businesses also consider how the computer can be used to further their strategic objectives. For example, a multinational firm must have an international computer network that coordinates information from various widespread locations. A body of literature is beginning to evolve that defines how businesses can use information systems for competitive advantage. We will cover this in depth in Chapter 5.

Connectivity

Connectivity is the tying together of individual computers through communication networks. Today the most widely used computer is the personal computer (PC). As more individuals began using personal computers there arose a demand for connecting these personal computers not only to each other, but to minis and mainframes so that data contained in files on other computers could be accessed and so that individuals using these personal computers could exchange files with one another.

Ideally, one should be able to sit at a personal computer and communicate with any other computer in a transparent fashion (that is, without knowing that the PC is communicating with another computer). This transparent communication between computers is often called a **single system image**. That is, to the user there is only one computer system. Of course, in reality there are many computer systems connected to one another. Advances in communications such as *fiber-optic communications* is making this connectivity possible.

The connectivity between personal computers through networks will almost certainly make minicomputers and mainframes obsolete, at least as far as the way they are being used today. In the future, mainframes are likely to be used as if they are very large personal computers storing large amounts of data and providing this data to personal computer users over a network. Thus, mainframes will become *file servers* for networks of personal computers.

Globalization

Business firms are increasingly becoming global in scope. It is widely believed that in the future nations will compete with one another within the economic and business arenas instead of the military arenas. Computer information systems are necessary to this internationalization of business. Computer information systems and communication advances now enable firms to perform tasks even when individuals who contribute are located in many different countries or geographical locations. For example, in the production of a new aircraft some of the engineering may be done in Europe, the manufacturing of subassemblies could be performed in several different countries, and the final aircraft assembled in the United States.

Standards have been established for the electronic interchange of transaction processing data on a global basis. Thus, orders for goods and payment for these orders can be transmitted globally on an instantaneous basis.

Expert Systems and Artificial Intelligence

Artificial intelligence is a broad field that attempts to apply computers to tasks that normally take human intelligence to perform. Some of the fields of artificial intelligence are robotics, computer vision, and expert systems. Expert systems promise to have profound effects through the augmentation or replacement of human judgment. Human judgment along with human creativity has long been considered one of the highest forms of human intelligence. Using computers through expert systems to augment and/or replace human judgment obviously has profound implications. It has the possibility of greatly increasing human productivity and also of rendering obsolete the skills of many people. However, most people believe that regardless of how competent expert systems become there will always be interesting tasks for humans to perform. One thing is certain, though—the development, application, and adjustments to expert systems will be a most interesting challenge.

Computer-Aided Software Engineering

Traditionally large, complex information systems were developed through the process of first developing a model of the system. This model, a description of the system, was developed on paper through manual drawings such as data flow diagrams. Computer-aided software engineering (CASE) automates the process of developing this model of an information system. Data flow diagrams, structure charts, pseudocode, and data dictionaries have all been automated with CASE tools. These models of information systems are largely graphical and thus are easily understood by users of information systems. CASE tools can produce executable program code and thus automate the programming process to some extent. CASE tools promise to greatly increase the productivity of information systems professionals in developing new information systems.

Information Systems Ethics

There are many ethical issues in the information systems area. Some of the more prominent are the copying and use of personal computer software without paying for it, the use of computers to monitor the performance of human beings, and the collection and storage of confidential data, particularly data about individuals.

Information Strategy Planning

As firms begin to view information as a strategic resource that can be used to gain competitive advantage, they are spending increasing amounts of money on managing the information resource. The primary objective of information strategy planning is to align information resources with the competitive strategy of the organization. To do this firms must plan their information systems strategy, particularly in the area of gathering and sharing data among the organizational units. Building a common database that can be shared by organizational units requires that a firm decide on its objectives and then develop a data model that supports these objectives. One method by which this can be accomplished is through focusing on the critical success factors of the firm. **Critical success factors** are a limited number of factors that determine the success of a firm. Data that constantly measure the status of these critical success factors form the structure of the data model for the firm.

End-User Computing

End users are the persons who ultimately use application software. **End-user computing** is the direct acquisition and/or development of application software and hardware by end users. End-user computing began in the 1970s and exploded in the 1980s. The primary driving force behind the explosion of end-user computing in the 1980s was the personal computer. The PC, along with application development tools that decrease the technical computer knowledge necessary to develop an application, resulted in many applications that are developed directly by end users. There are vast opportunities in end-user computing, as well as significant management and control questions. But there is no doubt that end-user computing is an important wave of the future in information systems. Certainly, those who use an application have a great deal more knowledge about the requirements of the application. Thus, if end users have the capability to implement an application on the computer, firms are much more likely to get applications that are useful to them.

Security of Information Systems

Security of information systems has been a significant issue since the beginning of computers. However, with the dispersion of information systems resources, primarily because of the use of PCs, security questions have become much more important. Sensitive, confidential, and/or valuable information is being stored on dispersed PCs. Computer hackers have broken into computer systems on networks over great geographical distances. There have been many instances of computer fraud where large sums of money were embezzled and computer viruses have become a significant threat to all computer systems.

Outsourcing

Outsourcing is the purchase of information system services from a vendor outside the firm. Outsourcing can range from the purchase of application software such as an accounts receivable system all the way to complete purchase of the management, development, and maintenance of the firm's information system. Outsourcing became a significant trend in the late 1980s as many firms decided that they did not have the internal expertise to manage an information system efficiently and effectively.

All firms purchase some information systems services such as application software. The primary issue in outsourcing is not whether outsourcing will or will not occur, but the degree to which a firm should outsource. Outsourcing the complete information systems function could result in foregoing the opportunity to use information systems for competitive advantage. Any information system hardware, software, or service that can be purchased is also likely to be purchased by a firm's competitor. Thus, a competitive advantage may not materialize.

The above discussion is a small sample of contemporary information systems issues. (Application 1–4 covers a survey of critical issues in technology.) As you will see in this textbook there are many such issues and usually they don't have a black or white answer. Finding an answer is a matter of looking at the characteristics of an individual firm and making a decision on those issues that best fit that firm and its strategic objectives. However, the degree to which good decisions are made about these issues can have a significant impact on the success or failure of a business firm in today's competitive environment.

Why Study Information Systems?

There are likely to be two types of students taking this course. First there are those students who plan a career as information systems professionals. It is obvious why these students need a solid background in the under-

14

Survey Looks at Critical Issues in Technology

By Michael Alexander

When it comes to advanced technology, senior information systems managers are preoccupied with technologies that are more valuable to the IS organization than to the business at large.

Top 5 emerging technologies with the greatest level of interest

Percent of respondents (total: 394 IS executives)

1 **75.9%**
CASE and other software productivity tools

2 **40.8%**
Image systems and processing

3 **35.4%**
Expert systems

4 **22.1%**
LANs/Networking

5 **16.7%**
Database tools and management

That is one of the primary conclusions of a survey of 392 top IS executives conducted by Cambridge, Mass.-based Index Group, Inc. Fortunately, this tinkering with self-serving technology appears to be lessening slightly, Index Group reported in its fourth annual survey of IS issues called "Critical Issues of Information Systems Management for 1991."

Computer-aided software engineering, image processing, expert systems, local-area networks and database tools were cited as the top five emerging technologies in which IS executives had the greatest level of interest.

It is encouraging to see image processing and expert systems among the top five technologies because they play a more direct role in changing business processes than in changing internal IS work, said Robert Morison, vice president and director of the Prism research program at Index Group.

The remaining three technologies are not really all that new, but they are technologies that the executives feel most comfortable with, according to Morison.

"The average IS organization in a large company is populated with technophobes who would rather not introduce new technologies that are going to disturb the installed base."

The executives expressed only a passing interest in neural networks, voice recognition, supercomputing or handheld computers, all of which will probably have a profound impact on business processes in the next five years, Morison said.

Exactly half of the companies reported having a formal process for identifying and exploring new technologies. The IS executives said this process included advanced technology groups, task forces and steering committees, among other forms of technology-watching.

standing of information systems development and the administration and management of information systems. However, what about those students who do not plan careers in information systems, for example, students who plan careers as managers in functional areas such as accounting, finance, marketing, engineering, and other business disciplines?

The American Assembly of Collegiate Schools of Business (AACSB), which accredits colleges of business in the United States, requires that a person receiving an undergraduate or graduate business degree take a course in information systems. Why are information systems so important? It is because of the pervasive uses of computer-based information systems and their critical importance in the success of a business firm.

Information has always been important to business management. However, prior to the advent of computers and even during the 1960s and 1970s, management relied heavily on informal sources of information. Often these sources were haphazard and/or were costly byproducts of transaction processing systems. But in the '70s and especially in the '80s, the cost of information processing technology declined drastically.

Information applications for computers became widespread. In fact, today all white-collar professionals use computers in one way or another. The cost effectiveness of computer information systems and the opportunities for their use for competitive advantage exploded in the 1980s. Thus, information is always valuable to business management. And the hardware necessary to produce that information is inexpensive relative to twenty years ago. Thus, individuals who know how to apply this hardware to business problems and business information needs have extremely valuable skills.

Of course, the individuals who are most able to apply computers are those that know information systems technology and also the application area in which the computer is to be applied. To get the most out of information systems, not only should a firm's information systems professionals know the business to which they are applying the computer, but it is extremely important for the end users and managers of the firm to be information systems-literate. To gain the most advantage from a computer-based information system, the firm must plan an information architecture that encompasses the company's complete business. This requires significant participation by managers and executives at all levels within the firm.

An Overview of this Textbook

This is a book on information systems, not a book on computers. Business people who use computers successfully are not computer experts. They understand the basics of computers and how to use them for business purposes, but they are most concerned about their information needs and how to build computer-based information systems to meet those needs.

Accordingly, the first part of this book is designed to give you an overview of the conceptual foundations that underlie all information systems. In this part we will cover systems fundamentals that provide you with the tools to understand the components of any system. Chapters 3 and 4 cover information systems and their relationships to both individual human behavior and organizational behavior. Chapter 5 covers business strategy and the use of information systems for competitive advantage.

Part II of the text deals with information systems applications. These include information systems for the individual functions within a business, such as marketing information systems and accounting information systems. Chapters 7, 8, and 9 cover specific types of information systems including decision support, executive information systems, artificial intelligence, expert systems, and office automation.

Part III discusses the underlying technology of information systems. In the hardware area we cover the central processing unit, input and output devices, and data communication hardware. In the software area we cover system software and programming languages, data storage and processing, database management systems, and communications. Part IV covers some of the most important material in this text, how user applications are developed. We will focus on information resource planning, systems analysis, system design, implementation, application development by users, computer system evaluation and acquisition, and information systems control and security. The final part of the text covers the management of information systems resources, the relationship of information systems to society, and how information systems may affect you and your career.

Summary

- Information systems have become crucial to the functioning of modern organizations and businesses. Firms are using information systems technology to gain competitive advantages over their rivals. An information system is a formalized computer information system that can collect, store, process, and report data from various sources to provide the information necessary for management decision making.

- An information system can be broken down into six parts: inputs, processes, data files, outputs, personnel, and hardware.

- Prior to the 1980s, information systems were usually classified as data processing systems or management information systems. Data processing systems were oriented toward capturing, processing, and storing data whereas MIS is oriented toward using the data to produce management information.

- In the 1980s the term data processing system went out of style and was replaced with the term transaction processing system. The term MIS was given a more restricted meaning and the term information systems was used to refer to the complete computer-based information systems of a firm.

- The current types of information systems include transaction processing systems, office automation systems, executive information systems, expert systems, decision support systems, and management information systems.

- Transaction processing systems keep track of daily business events, such as purchase of raw materials and payment of an accounts payable.

- Office automation systems use the computer to automate many of the routine tasks that are performed in a typical office.

- Executive information systems provide for the communication of summary-level information to executives.

- An expert system is a computer program that enables a computer to make (or give advice concerning) an unstructured decision normally made by humans with special expertise.

- A decision support system is an integrated set of computer tools that allow a decision maker to interact directly with computers to create information useful in making semistructured and unstructured decisions.

- The term management information systems has undergone changes in meaning over the past twenty years. Today the term MIS is generally accepted to mean a system that provides recurring information about routine and anticipated business events. An MIS is also called a management reporting system.

- Information systems is a dynamic field. New types of systems are being created and older systems are being modified. Thus, the major types of information systems are likely to continue to change.

- Computer information systems have had major impacts on business. Among these impacts are increased competitive advantage, increased product quality, shorter product cycles, easier business growth, improved productivity, automation of decisions, and more and better information.

- Today's businesses, when they put together a strategic plan to map out their future, also consider how computer information systems can be used for competitive advantage to further the business's strategic objectives.

- Connectivity is the tying together of individual computers through communication networks.

- Computer information systems are necessary to the globalization of business. Computer information systems and communication advances now enable firms to perform a task when individuals who contribute to that task are located in many different countries or geographical locations.

- Expert systems promise to have profound effects through the augmentation of human judgment. They also have the potential of replacing some human judgment.

- Computer-aided software engineering automates the process of developing information systems.

- Some of the ethical issues in information systems are the copying and use of personal computer software without paying for it, the use of computers to monitor human beings, and the collection and storage of confidential data.

- Information resource management is an attempt to align information resources with the competitive strategy of the organization.

- End-user computing is the direct acquisition and/or development of application software and hardware by end users. There are significant management and control questions concerning end-user computing.

- The dispersion of information systems resources along with their connectivity has increased the concern over security of information systems.

- Outsourcing is the purchase of information system resources from a vendor outside the firm.

- The study of information systems is important because of the pervasive uses of computer-based information systems and their critical importance to the success of a business firm.

Key Terms

Information system

Data processing systems

Transaction processing system

Transaction

Office automation systems

Executive information systems

Expert system

Decision support system

Competitive advantage

Connectivity

Single system image

Artificial intelligence

Critical success factors

End users

End-user computing

Outsourcing

Review Questions

1. What is the definition of an information system?

2. List the six parts of an information system. Which of these parts is the most important?

3. How are the orientations of data processing systems and management information systems different?

4. Name the three basic objectives of transaction processing systems.

5. What are executive information systems used for?

6. Provide a definition of an expert system.

7. What is the basic idea underlying decision support systems?

8. Why can it be difficult to classify an individual system as an EIS, MIS, or DSS?

9. Why is information so vital to businesses?

10. What has caused an emphasis on quality of products and services and how can this quality be improved?

11. What advantage have information systems such as computer-aided design and manufacturing systems given firms in terms of developing products?

12. Define productivity. Have computers increased productivity in the workplace?

13. Are increased amounts of information always useful to managers?

14. What does connectivity mean?

15. How will the role of mainframes change as connectivity between personal computers increases?

16. What is the purpose of artificial intelligence?

17. State the primary objective of information resource management.

18. What is end-user computing?

19. Define outsourcing. What is the primary issue involved with outsourcing?

20. How can a firm gain the most advantage from a computer-based information system?

Discussion Questions and Cases

1. Some people argue that computers are capable of making intelligent decisions and that the work computers do is a form of intelligence. These people further argue that as time goes on, computers will make higher levels of intelligent decisions. Others argue that computers are simply dumb machines that execute programmed instructions and therefore will never possess true intelligence, as human beings do. Take one side of this argument and support your position.

2. If you are planning a career in the design and implementation of computer-based business systems, is it better to have an educational background in

computer science or in information systems (IS)? A typical computer science curriculum emphasizes the technological aspects of computing, whereas a typical IS curriculum emphasizes business and how computers are used in the business area. Select the best curriculum and explain why you chose it.

3. Some people argue that personal computers soon will be used in most households to perform many different types of tasks, such as assisting in balancing bank accounts. Others argue that many of the tasks that have been advocated as good applications for personal computers in a household can be done more efficiently manually. They say that home computers are a passing fad. For example, some say that using a personal computer to balance your bank account is like using a Rolls Royce to go to the mailbox daily to pick up your mail. Take one side of this argument and support your position.

4. Food Town is a medium-sized grocery chain located in the Eastern Seaboard states. John Wilson, the chief executive officer of Food Town, is very concerned with the information he is getting from his data processing system. A large amount of data is gathered and stored in company disk files. Most of the company's typical accounting systems—such as accounts payable, accounts receivable, and general ledger—are computerized. In addition, the company has computer-based inventory control systems, personnel systems, and sales and marketing systems. John explains his problem as follows: "With all these data being collected and stored, why can't I get better management information reports? My assistant should be able to sit down at a terminal and pull information from these various systems and integrate it in a way that is meaningful. Sure, I can get information from the personnel system or from the payroll system, but whenever I need information from two or more of these systems, it seems to be a major undertaking to provide it. More often than not, by the time I get the information, a decision has already been made and the information is not used. These computers just don't help me a great deal in my decision making." Does John have a valid point? Is it possible to provide the type of information he is requesting?

5. Western University is a large university with many departments that do a large amount of funded research. The manager of each research project is called a principal investigator (PI). In addition to ensuring that the research is done properly, the PI makes sure that the funds expended on a research project do not exceed the funds allotted for the project. When overexpenditures do occur, the funds to cover them come directly from the university budget. Therefore, before committing to additional expenditures on a project, the PI must be sure that there is enough remaining project budget to cover them.

   The university has a central accounting system that allows a PI to retrieve the current project budget balance through on-line computer terminals. Many academic departments in the university do not trust the central accounting system and maintain their own separate accounting systems. Other departments feel that the central system is adequate and therefore do not maintain their own systems. The major complaint of those who do not trust the central system is one of timeliness of data. All commitments to expend resources, such as purchase orders for equipment, are executed through manual forms. These forms are processed through several administrative departments before being entered into the central accounting system. Often it takes four to five days for these expenditure commitments to be reflected in the central accounting system files. The university's vice president of finance is considering a policy that would prohibit university departments maintaining their own accounting systems. Should departments be allowed to maintain their own accounting systems? Does the central system need improvements? If so, what would you suggest? Would a simple policy prohibiting departmental accounting systems be successful?

INFORMATION SYSTEMS STRATEGIES

Paths to Information Power

By Jack W. Simpson

The global marketplace is changing—and not just because of Europe 1992. During the past few months, we've seen dramatic examples of how quickly things can change. By the time you read the daily newspaper, the political winds can shift, leaders can fall, and new governments can be installed.

By now, most information systems managers know that staying competitive in the '90s will depend on keeping up with this new change of pace: Information travels faster; opportunities come and go.

Yet, a poll taken last year by Louis Harris & Associates of New York reported that two-thirds of chief executive officers said that their companies' computer and communications resources were not properly integrated into their business operations.

Why not? Why would a company give up the advantage of real-time decision-making by operating without a sophisticated infrastructure for integrating information? Perhaps it's hard to see the big picture as it gets lost in bits and bytes and budgets.

Smart managers—those who recognize the importance of their company's information systems—will see that the answer lies in merging a company's internal data with important external information.

Merging internal and external data and the design of an information infrastructure takes a master plan. Typically, companies go through four phases in building an information infrastructure: introduction, growth, integration and power. To be successful, companies need to quickly get to the power stage—the stage at which a company sees the maximum benefit from its technology investment.

At this stage, companies also gain a competitive advantage by using internal and external information to forge decision-making links—both with its management team and with its customers, suppliers and others important to it.

In the introduction stage, a company is most likely to invest in IS machines that automate payroll, inventory and word processing. This is where computing began. Goals in this stage, such as reducing paper and increasing clerical productivity, are easily realized. However, it's hard to see the return on investment. For example, some thought that word processing would result in fewer secretaries, but most of us would agree that we've kept the secretaries and just added more computers.

Growth stage

The growth stage is a step up, but computing and information needs remain fairly simple. At this stage, the company takes on new capabilities. The art department, for instance, may produce graphics and typesetting. The marketing department may coordinate with the sales force to manage a direct mail list. These departmental applications and databases, as well as electronic mail, filing, scheduling, voice messages and portable personal computers help flatten a company's organizational structure and make it faster and more efficient.

A risk in the growth stage is that upfront costs can sometimes outweigh the near-term benefits and expectations. If promises are made and not delivered, a credibility gap occurs and the firm may cut spending before technology has a fair chance to improve the bottom line.

At this level, the manager or IS executive is left walking a tightrope. He has to make sure the company buys what it needs for today while still establishing the infrastructure for tomorrow. He needs to relate his activities to the bottom line and deliver on promises to build credibility.

Many companies today are in the integration stage. The driving force at this point is getting mission-critical information—the information people need to do their jobs—to each sales representative, market planner, product developer, strategist, manager and professional.

In this integration effort, the use of external information has broadened from one department to many. The critical management issue here is maintaining the completeness and the integrity of data from all departments as it's shuttled around on a real-time basis.

At this stage of integrating the internal and external information, the company will see a solid return on its investment in technology and data management. The efficient use of internal and external information will help a salesperson clinch a deal because of something he learned that morning. Marketing will act faster on segments previously undetected, or perhaps ignored, by the competition. Manufacturing can hear about problems when they happen and act while the trail is hot, or be linked to suppliers to ensure just-in-time inventory control. In addition, the sales force can be linked to customers for efficient ordering and problem-solving.

Power stage

From the integration stage, the successful merger of external and internal information will lead the firm into the power stage, which demands full-scale capture and application of external information.

The power stage delivers the broadest possible range of mission-critical information to everyone in the organization as well as to everyone important to the firm, such as customers and suppliers. Finally, in the power stage, the investment made in an IS infrastructure and the full utilization of external information can give a company the ability to react in real time.

Instead of relying on copious files of newspaper clippings, the evening news, a researcher in a library or a Freedom of Information request in Washington, D.C., a company can have the pertinent data relating to mission-critical information electronically in seconds.

Marketing managers, for example, use on-line information services for access to trade journals, newspaper articles, surveys and census figures to track trends and demographics, to stay aware of the latest issues and to find new business opportunities. Sales representatives use access to news,

biography files, Standard & Poor's Register of Corporations and Securities and Exchange Commission documents to create a profile before they call a prospective client.

Information explosion

Today, research indicates that at least 80% of U.S. corporations have their information systems somewhere in the growth or integration stages. Moreover, nearly 20% of U.S. firms have fully integrated outside information services into their daily business—the power stage.

How to get from one stage to another isn't obvious or easy. It takes a chief information officer with creativity and vision and a CEO who wants the benefits of information technology and who will provide an environment for change.

In the early stages, the CIO no doubt will be walking a tightrope: Making sure the company buys the technology it needs for today, while establishing the infrastructure and architecture for tomorrow.

The best way to achieve that credibility is to have a solid plan in place, one that integrates technology into the day-to-day work flow of key decision makers and is connected to the long-term business strategy of the organization, i.e., using information to create a competitive advantage.

The CIO must chart the course and be prepared to navigate the firm through the choppy seas that lie ahead. Competition in the '90s will be fierce, stirred by the increasing speed and breadth of available information. It's up to the CIO to make sure his firm has all the data it needs to seize emerging opportunities.

Discussion:

1. A well-planned infrastructure is the key to wielding information for competitive advantage. What does a well-planned infrastructure mean? How does it contribute to competitive advantage?

2. How does real-time information contribute to better decisions?

Simpson is president of Mead Data Central, a Dayton, Ohio, information provider.

Reprinted with permission from *ComputerWorld* (August 13, 1990), pp. 73–74. Copyright 1990 by CW Publishing, Inc., Framingham, MA 01701.

One

Conceptual Foundations

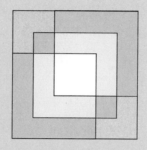

2

Systems Fundamentals

This chapter contains a general introduction to the concepts of systems. These concepts are often referred to collectively as **general systems theory**. Material of this type is very abstract and has broad potential application. The initial section of the chapter offers a rationale for studying this material. The second section defines systems and describes systems concepts. The remaining sections discuss system feedback, variety and control, the steps in information processing, and systems and information processing. Familiar examples are used to reinforce each concept.

Introduction

In education, economic savings can be realized if students master abstract material that has broad potential application. However, most students do not like to study abstract material. For example, students are usually required to study mathematics throughout the primary and secondary grades and in the early years of college. Math teachers are very familiar with the cry, "Where am I ever going to use this?" It is difficult for students to appreciate the time and effort they will save by learning these concepts early and having the math skills they may later need for the study of engineering, science, and business.

Why Study Systems?

Most colleges of business are organized along the functional lines of economics, finance, marketing, management, management science, information systems, and accounting. Such organizational structures result in specialization, and also condition student expectations. For example, business students often expect material in a business course to increase their ability to address specific business problems in one of these specialties. These students sometimes view abstract knowledge unfavorably because they fail to see its immediate application in their area of specialization. However, much of the abstract material they are asked to learn is also highly transferable; it can be used in any specialized business field.

Systems concepts are very abstract, and therefore not always appealing to students. But understanding systems can lead to the same benefits as understanding mathematics or understanding abstract business concepts.

Systems and **systems analysis** are, respectively, a philosophy and a methodology for viewing complex wholes at a manageable level of abstraction. It certainly should not be hard to convince someone that the information system of a multinational corporation is a complex entity. Where does one begin to analyze and understand such a system? One can be so overwhelmed with detail that one views the system as too complex to understand.

Systems analysis is a method for dealing with complex systems. It presents systems abstractly, using just enough detail to allow the analyst to identify and specify alternatives for the design and modification of a system. For example, examine the flow diagram in Figure 2–1. This diagram illustrates the decision process of a student electing to take a course in information systems.

Note that the diagram in Figure 2–1 does not include the detailed cognitive processes the student employs in making the decision. Even if it were possible to incorporate all that detail, it might require a diagram as large as this book. By identifying a reasonable level of abstraction, the diagram is a workable representation of the decision process. This ap-

FIGURE 2–1
Course Registration
Decision.

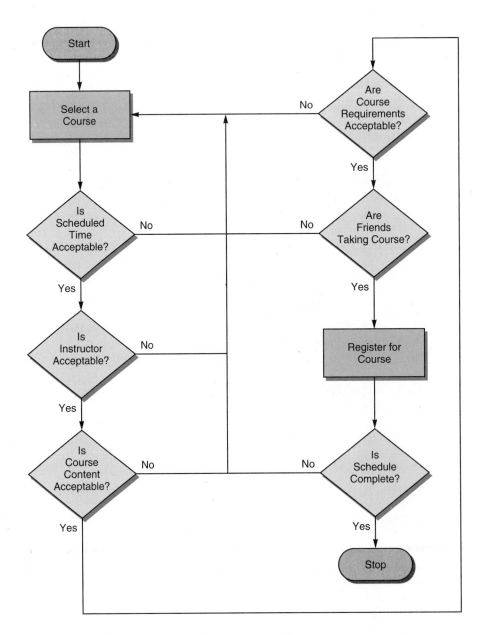

proach is the basis of systems analysis. It is educationally economical because the same method can be used to represent and analyze all types of
systems.

Another reason for studying systems is that many of their characteristics are similar, and the strategies for analyzing and improving them are
therefore similar. For instance, the systems approach is used to determine why an automobile is not operating properly. It can also be employed on an information system. In addition, when one begins to view
complex phenomena as systems, analogies can be drawn between systems that initially might seem unrelated. For example, airline reservation and university course registration systems have many common
characteristics.

Educational economy, transferability, simplification of complex concepts, and similar characteristics are only a few of the reasons for studying systems in an abstract form. Other reasons are discussed in this chapter as systems are defined and described.

Parts of a system and its environment include the system's components, boundaries, inputs, outputs, and interfaces. Systems are occasionally described using the black-box concept, and systems may be open or closed.

Systems

What Is a System?

In the abstract, a *system* is defined as a set of interacting components that operate within a boundary for some purpose. The boundary filters the types and flow rates of inputs and outputs between the system and its environment. The specification of the boundary defines both the system and the environment of the system.

Figure 2–2 provides an overview of a system. Essentially, a system accepts inputs from its environment and transforms them into outputs, which are discharged back into the environment. (Each item in this figure is discussed in more depth later in this chapter.)

Within the confines of this definition, it is possible to conceive of a system within a system. For example, a company can be viewed as a system and its particular industry as a **suprasystem**. Alternatively, the industry can be defined as a system and the company as a **subsystem**. To carry the example an additional step, the industry can be viewed as a subsystem within a national economy. Finally, the national economy can be viewed as a subsystem within the world economy.

An accounting information system also can be viewed in this manner. Payroll, accounts receivable, accounts payable, and inventory can be viewed as subsystems. This relationship is shown in Figure 2–3. Each of these subsystems can be considered a system, and the accounting system can be viewed as the suprasystem or it can be viewed as a subsystem of the

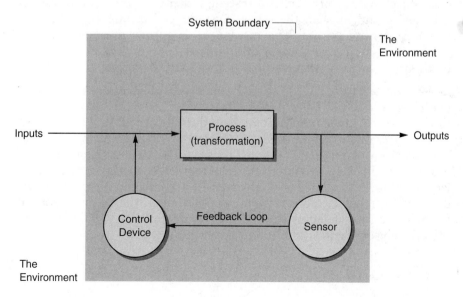

FIGURE 2–2
Overview of a System.

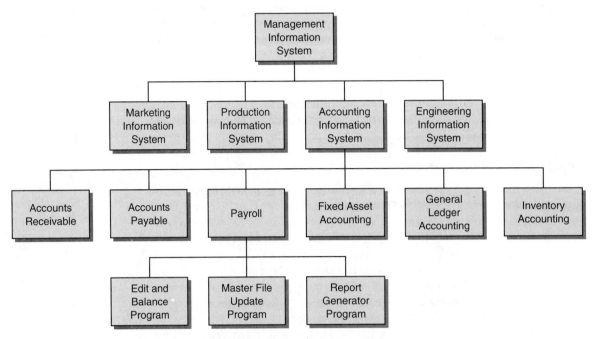

FIGURE 2–3
Relationships Within the Management Information System.

management information system. The ability to adjust the level of abstraction by altering the boundary is a major advantage of the systems approach.

Components

Components of a system are units (subsystems) acting in combination with other units to modify inputs in order to produce outputs. Components within a system do not have to be homogeneous. For example, a police officer directing traffic at a congested intersection is one component of a complex traffic control system. Other components include signals, signs, and lines in the street. Systems controlling air traffic and inventory control systems have many nonhomogeneous components.

Boundary

The **boundary** is the area separating one system from another. In information systems, the boundary is not physical in nature. It is a region through which inputs and outputs pass during exchanges with the system's environment. Defining the boundary of a system is an important step in systems analysis. C. West Churchman, a leading systems analyst, has suggested posing two questions in order to determine whether an object is within the boundary of a system.[1] First, can the systems analyst do anything about the object in question? Second, is the object important to the objectives of the system? If the answer to both questions is yes, then the object is within the boundary of the system.

---

[1] C. West Churchman, *The Systems Approach* (New York: Dell Publishing, 1968), 36.

The use of these questions to determine system boundaries is demonstrated in the following example. Assume that a university with a nationally ranked women's basketball team is located in a state with an extensive high school women's basketball program. The university's coach wishes to maintain her team's national ranking. She is considering whether to actively recruit qualified state high school players by offering them scholarships.

The object in question here is the high school women's basketball program. Does it lie within the boundaries of the university women's basketball program, or not? The answer to Churchman's second question is yes. Quality high school players (the object) are important to the objective (maintaining a national ranking) of the system (the university team). If the basketball coach decides not to recruit, the answer to the first question is no, and the state high school basketball program is part of the environment. The boundary of the university women's basketball program lies somewhere between the university and the high school program. If, on the other hand, the coach decides to recruit, then the high school program becomes part of the system to maintain an outstanding women's basketball program at the university. The boundary is then outside the high school program within the state.

In an accounts receivable system, if a firm's customer is defined as part of the environment, the firm has concluded that it cannot influence the time in which the customer pays a receivable. However, if the customer is defined as part of the system, the firm has determined that it can influence the timing of payment. Cash discounts, credit limits, interest charges, and other collection policies are actions the firm can take to influence the payment of receivables. A similar situation exists in an inventory control system. If a firm's supplier is considered part of the system, then the firm can influence delivery dates, quantities, and modes of transportation. If the supplier is defined as part of the environment, then the firm cannot influence the supplier's actions.

Environment

The **environment** of a system is defined as anything outside the boundary of the system that influences the operation of the system and cannot be controlled by the analyst. Weather is part of the environment of a vegetable garden. If a greenhouse with a climate control system is built over the garden, the boundary of the system changes. The environment of the system then includes systems that supply gas, water, and electricity to the greenhouse.

Inputs

Inputs are the energies taken into the system and are classified as either maintenance or signal. Maintenance inputs energize the system and make it ready to operate. Signal inputs are the energies processed to produce the outputs. Consider a coal-fired electrical generating plant. Maintenance inputs include the electricity that energizes the control systems, the lubricants for the machinery, and the human input that maintains the system. Signal inputs are the coal used to fire the system and the water that is transformed into steam to power the generators. Electricity and computer programs are the maintenance inputs into a computerized information system. Data are the raw materials, or signal inputs, processed to produce outputs from the system.

Outputs

Outputs are the energies discharged from the system into the suprasystem. They are generally classified as products useful to the suprasystem or as waste. The product from a generating station is electric power. Waste includes the steam, smoke, heat, and ash that are discharged into the environment. Modifying some of the waste output so that it goes into making a useful product is one means of improving a system's performance. For example, if a greenhouse is built next to the power plant, some of the discharged steam can be used to heat the greenhouse. Industry has used this approach to systems improvement extensively because of the recent emphasis on pollution control and energy conservation. Heat generated by computers and lights is now captured and used for heating some office buildings. CRT screens and reports are examples of the products of an information system.

Interface

Interface is a term frequently used in systems analysis. The **interface** is the region between the boundaries of systems and is also the medium for transporting the output from one system to the input of another system. It does not alter the output of one system that is input to another system.

For example, assume that an individual taxpayer and the Internal Revenue Service are systems. The U.S. Postal Service is the interface between the two systems. When two people are engaged in a conversation, air is the interface that transports the sound between them. The interface between two computer systems can be a telephone line or a microwave transmission system.

Black-Box Concept

It is often impossible to describe the way a system **process** transforms the inputs to produce outputs. In addition, it may not be economical to describe a complex system. In some cases, the structure of the transformation may be unknown. If the description of a complex system is too detailed, human beings may not be able to comprehend and manage it.

Under such circumstances, the analyst invokes the **black-box concept**. Rather than describe in detail the internal processes of a system, the analyst defines the system in terms of inputs and outputs. In other words, if the analyst knows the differences between a system's inputs and its outputs, then he or she knows what transformation occurs within the system, even though the exact steps that the system uses to effect the transformation may not be understood.

The black-box concept is based on two assumptions. First, the analyst assumes that the relationship between inputs and outputs will remain stable; in other words, that the internal operations of the black box will not change through time. Second, the analyst assumes that black boxes are independent. For example, if a subsystem is described as a black box and is linked to another black box, it should be possible to predict the output from the combination, given the input. The black-box concept makes it possible to enter a hierarchy of complex systems at any level.

The medical profession makes wide use of the black-box concept in diagnosis. Assume you visit a doctor complaining of stomach pain. First the doctor evaluates other outputs from the system by taking your temperature, blood pressure, pulse, and respiratory count. He or she then evaluates the appearance of the system by examining your eyes, ears, mouth, and skin color. Then the doctor questions you about your past medical history and about the inputs you have been placing into the system.

After completing the evaluation, the doctor suggests some changes in the inputs. A change in diet and some medication are prescribed. Outputs are then evaluated, especially pain. If the pain continues, the doctor alters the inputs again. When the combination of inputs that eliminates the output of pain is found, you are pronounced cured.

In this situation, the doctor assumes that your body is a black box. Only the inputs and outputs are considered in your treatment. The situation would have to be very serious before the doctor would consider entering the black box to observe its internal condition. Considerable risk is involved in opening the black box, because infection or other problems might result. It is also more economical to treat the system as a black box, since surgical investigation is expensive.

Now consider the information system of a large corporation. The system may be analyzed at a macro level by considering such subsystems as marketing, inventory control, and manufacturing to be black boxes. Another approach is to analyze each subsystem separately. For example, in the inventory control system, raw materials, work in process, finished goods, and supplies subsystems could be viewed as black boxes. At a micro level, the supplies inventory control system could be analyzed, and the subsystems for various types of supplies could be seen as black boxes. The analyst can move back and forth between macro and micro descriptions of the information system. In moving from macro to micro subsystems, a point is eventually reached where the black-box concept is invoked. Certainly, when considering an information system, one is not concerned with the molecular structure of the paper used in the system.

The black-box concept is used by systems analysts to obtain an understanding of complex information systems. Analysts begin by developing an understanding of the high-level processes of a system. They depict detailed processes as black boxes, which they later investigate and attempt to understand. Application 2–1 illustrates that the term black box can be used to indicate users' lack of understanding of a system. As discussed in the Application, data query software, such as DataNOW!, can be used to open up the black box to users.

Open and Closed Systems

Open systems accept inputs from the environment; **closed systems** are assumed not to interact with the environment. All systems are open to some degree, but it is often convenient to assume that a system is closed in order to simplify the analysis process.

Adding Value to Your Data

By Marion Guerin

UNICOM is the parent of several companies providing telephone service to rural Alaska. Their HP 3000 is used for customer billing and general accounting. Bob Shaw, system manager at UNICOM, says their data became more valuable after it became more accessible through DataNOW!. "In the past, some of our users viewed our system as a black box," says Mr. Shaw. "They fed data in, but couldn't always see what happened to it. These folks weren't computer professionals and the computer still had some degree of mystery attached to it. They would load the data required by the system, but they weren't really sure whether it was in there or not. There was some skepticism as to whether the computer really kept the data. When something went wrong, there was always the suspicion that 'the computer ate it.'"

"Now the users have the ability to query the database whenever they need to," he says. "When they are concerned about the accuracy of the input, they can immediately go into the database and verify that the data was entered correctly. As a result, their confidence in the system has gone up, and they are more eager to use the system to help them do their jobs. Not long ago, we were able to trace an error in our long-distance billing system because of the ability of our users to scan the database and look for suspicious data. Each month we process about 150,000 toll-call records which are loaded into the database from a tape supplied by another company. The records accumulate in an IMAGE dataset which holds three months' history - about 450,000 records."

Adapted with permission from *Super-Group Magazine* (May–June, 1991), p. 20(3). Copyright SuperGroup Magazine, 1991.

Open and closed systems differ in terms of entropy. **Entropy** is a measure of disorder within a system. In an open system, order is maintained by maintenance inputs. Depending on the quantity of the maintenance inputs, entropy can decrease, remain constant, or increase in an open system. In a closed system, entropy never decreases because maintenance inputs do not enter the system.

Consider a body in a sealed casket. It can be viewed as a closed system. The body slowly decomposes, and the matter that made up the body moves from a state of order to increasing disorder. Entropy within the system therefore increases.

A watch also can be viewed as a closed system. However, some watches must be wound periodically, and winding is an energy input. Some might believe that a self-winding watch is an example of a closed system. Battery-run watches can operate for several years before needing maintenance. However, at some point an input from the environment—a new battery—becomes necessary. This type of analysis leads to the conclusion that no system operates in isolation from its environment.

Now consider entropy in terms of a human organization viewed as a system. The Shakers were a religious group that did not believe in engaging in sexual relations. Therefore, new membership was limited to those born outside the church who elected to join. New members could not join the church as a result of being born into Shaker families, since birth was precluded by the beliefs of the church. This is an example of a system that is open, but only to a limited degree. Members die, and the church moves toward a state of disorder. Eventually it will cease to exist unless new members from outside the church can be found.

On the other hand, a bureaucracy is an example of a human organization that moves toward increasing order. The bureaucratic solution to any variation within the organization is to create rules and procedures for dealing with the new situation. This may explain in part why bureaucracies are frequently considered inefficient. As the system moves toward more order, part of its input is utilized to make the increasing order possible. As order increases, more input is employed to maintain the existing order within the system.

Assuming that a system is closed greatly simplifies the definition and analysis of that system. However, this assumption also limits analysis. Since all systems exist within a suprasystem, the outputs from a system must be acceptable inputs for some component of the suprasystem. Also, the inputs required by the system must be supplied by some component of the suprasystem. Therefore, when a system is viewed as being closed, there is a danger that the support relationship between the system and its suprasystem will not be considered.

The term *open systems* is widely used today in information systems. It refers to those systems that can interoperate directly with hardware and software from multiple vendors. *Closed systems* are those systems that can only use hardware and software from a single vendor. Open systems are more flexible; they can grow and adapt more readily than systems whose components are supplied by a single vendor. This use of the terms open and closed systems is derived from the meaning of these terms in general systems theory. As illustrated in Application 2–2, we are moving slowly but surely to this desirable goal of open systems.

Feedback

Systems survive and adapt to their environment through feedback. **Feedback** is a process by which the output of a system is measured against a standard. Any difference between the two is corrected by altering the input. Systems with and without feedback loops are shown in Figure 2–4.

Consider a traffic light that is operated by a timer. Every ninety seconds the light changes, and the direction of traffic through the intersection is altered. This signal often causes traffic jams because it stops traffic on a heavily traveled street when there are no vehicles on the cross street. This is an example of a system without feedback. The performance of this system could be improved by installing sensors in the surface of the street. The sensors would indicate when a vehicle was waiting at the intersection. This feedback loop would keep the signal from cycling when no vehicles were in the cross street.

Incorporating a memory into a feedback loop also improves system performance. For example, the traffic light's feedback loop could contain a memory that would operate the light at different sequences at various times of day.

Output from the feedback in an information system is used in decision making. If the output is not relevant to the decisions, then the system is of little use to management. Therefore, feedback loops are incorporated into a system to determine the relevance of output to the decision environment.

An example of a feedback loop in an information system is the inclusion of standard costs in a purchasing subsystem. Signal inputs into the system are the quantities purchased, specifications, identification codes,

APPLICATION 2–2

Mixing Products a First Step Toward an Opening

By Barbara Bochenski

"The definition of open systems seems to vary depending on the phase of the moon and the tide," said Arun Taneja, vice president of marketing for the Distributed Systems Division at Unisys Corp. in San Jose, Calif.

There are so many claims of openness that one cannot help but question how so many vendors could become so open, so fast. Certainly some systems are more open than others, but skeptics say the main thing some vendors are open to is criticism for their extravagant claims.

Why are open systems so important? Primarily so users can achieve interoperability along with vendor and platform independence. Users need different vendors' products, but they need them to interoperate. They also need systems that work on diverse platforms.

Openness and interoperability—traditionally associated with communications and networking—extend to the full range of software systems, including graphical user interfaces (GUIs), repositories, CASE tools, operating systems, distributed environments and architectures.

Experts suggest that users today should insist on as much interoperability as they can get, wherever and however they can get it—at least until the millennium of "open systems" arrives.

Interoperability today is achieved on a case-by-case implementation basis by individual vendors. In the future, the hope is that it will be achieved more easily through standard interchange formats, data content standards and data communications standards.

Most vendors are working hard to ensure that their client/server tools interoperate, because

interoperability is a key selling point. Customer sites have a wide variety of hardware platforms and an even wider variety of software tools. The more hardware platforms and software tools their products can interact with, the more customers vendors can target.

While the drive for interoperability is not new, the diverse mix of LANs and wide-area networks (WANs) within a large enterprise, and the need to interconnect client/server components across these heterogeneous environments, are combining to make the strongest demand for openness to date in data processing.

and actual purchase prices. Outputs from the system that serve as inputs to the inventory control system are the quantities purchased at the standard unit cost. In the feedback loop, the standard and actual costs for the purchased items are compared. This information is then forwarded to the purchasing manager, who takes the necessary steps to ensure that future purchase costs do not deviate significantly from standard costs.

In this example, if the standard costs are out of date, the feedback information cannot help identify inefficiencies in the purchasing operation. Therefore, maintenance inputs are needed to adjust standard costs in order to keep them current.

Variety and Control

Suppose a basketball team has such skill that its members never miss a shot, make a bad pass, or commit a foul. Given these attributes, it is impossible for this team to lose a game. It might be interesting to play against this team or watch it play once or twice. But interest would quickly decrease for spectators and opponents alike.

If all activities were similar to those of this hypothetical basketball team, life would be very boring. Indeed, we enjoy basketball and other contests because of the potential variety in their outcomes. Even the greatest basketball players miss shots, commit fouls, and throw bad passes.

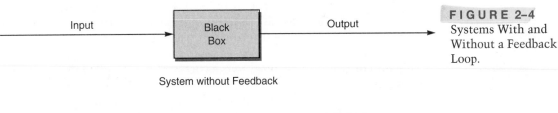

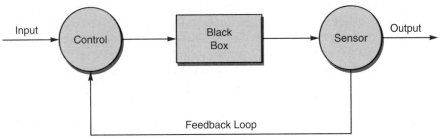

FIGURE 2-4
Systems With and
Without a Feedback
Loop.

Basketball is a game with a generally accepted set of rules that are enforced by officials. The rules state that for a player to advance the ball, it must be passed or dribbled. Body contact is limited, and a defensive player must follow certain rules when guarding an offensive player. For each violation of the rules, there is a penalty. When a player walks with the ball, his or her team loses possession. If one player blocks another, that player is charged with a foul. Under certain conditions, the fouled player can shoot a foul shot. Other circumstances may allow his or her team to gain possession of the ball. There is a limit to the number of fouls a player can be charged with before disqualification from the game.

For every variety of infraction of the basketball rules, the referees have a countermeasure. In this way they can control the game, ensuring that, in their judgment, it is played according to the rules. This is an example of a law developed by Ross Ashby that relates to the **variety and control** of systems. **Ashby's law of requisite variety** states that to control a system there must be available a number of countermeasures equal to the variety displayed by the output of the system.[2]

For example, if a basketball player commits a foul in getting the ball and there is no countermeasure (penalty) available to the referee to enforce the rule, the game is out of control. The player can continue to violate the rule indefinitely. With a countermeasure, the referee can penalize the offending player and control the game. In general, to control a system, the control mechanism must possess the same amount of variety as displayed by the system.

In the real world, we often develop countermeasures only for events that have a high probability of occurring. While reading this material, you probably do not have a countermeasure for the sudden collapse of your building's roof. And you probably will not count the words in this

[2] H. R. Ashby, *Introduction to Cybernetics* (New York: John Wiley, 1963).

chapter because you are quite sure your instructor will not ask how many it contains. Indeed, this is how individuals learn to control their environment. Without this filtering process, we could not cope with the variety in our environment.

To gain control of a system, two basic strategies are available: (1) decreasing the variety of outputs from the system or (2) increasing the number of countermeasures. When dealing with large systems that exhibit a great variety of outputs, Ashby's law gives the analyst a sense of proportion. For instance, it may not be feasible for the analyst to obtain the number of countermeasures needed to gain control over a system. In this situation, the analyst seeks countermeasures only for events that have a high probability of occurring or that will produce a large expected loss.

The business world contains many examples of how the variety of system output is controlled by various countermeasures. For instance, in an inventory control system, procedures accounting for gold used in a production process are different from those accounting for metal fasteners with a unit cost of one cent. Credit card companies use different procedures to evaluate your available credit when you purchase an appliance than they use when you purchase a sweater.

The Steps in the Processing of Data to Produce Information

As we have seen in this chapter, general systems theory concepts are applicable to all types of systems. Thus, they can also be used to describe the steps that occur in the processing of data to produce information. Prior to discussing these steps, let's first distinguish between the terms data and information.

Data are collected facts that are generally not useful for decision making without further processing. Conversely, **information** is directly useful in making decisions because it is based on processed data and is therefore the output of a data processing system. In practice, this distinction is often difficult to make. One individual's data may be another's information. For example, hours worked by individual employees are information to a front-line supervisor. However, when the decision maker is the president of a company, hours worked by individual employees are simply data that can be further processed and summarized. These summarized data may then be information to the president. Therefore, to determine whether a particular fact is data or information, one must keep in mind the particular decision to be made.

The primary steps that occur in the processing of data to produce information are input, process, store, and output. As we shall see in Chapter 10, input, process, store, and output are also the basic capabilities of computers. Several information processing operations occur in each of these four primary information processing steps, as shown in Figure 2–5. These are discussed in the next four sections.

Input

The **input** step begins the data processing operation. In this step, data are originated, classified, and edited.

Originate   Data often **originate** as a result of a business event or transaction. These data are then input to a data processing system. For example,

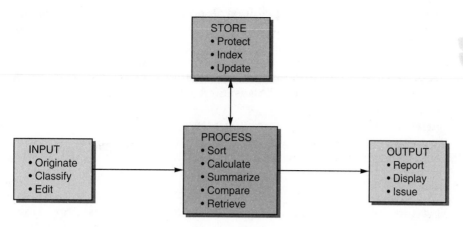

FIGURE 2-5
The Steps in Data
Processing.

the event of your purchase of an airline ticket causes the origination of data that are input to the airline's reservation system.

Classify   To **classify** input data is to identify those data with a certain category. For example, your airline reservation input data are classified when the reservation agent identifies your flight number and the category of seat you are reserving—either first class or coach. In this case, your reservation is classified on a certain flight and perhaps classified as first class.

Edit   Data are edited when they are input, to detect any errors that may exist in them. An **edit** may also occur during any of the other three basic steps of data processing to detect errors that may have occurred during these steps. However, most editing occurs upon input of the data. There are many different ways to edit data, and a well-designed data processing system edits data for all possible errors. Upon detection of an error, the individual who is performing the input is given the opportunity to correct the error.

Process

Several different data processing operations are performed within the **process** step. These include sorting, calculating, summarizing, comparing, and retrieving.

Sort   To **sort** is to place data in some order. Normally, sorting arranges a file of records according to keys, which are used to determine the sequence of the records. For example, sorting may be used to arrange the records of a personnel file into alphabetical sequence by using employee names as sort keys.

Calculate   The **calculate** operation includes all standard arithmetic operations, such as addition, subtraction, multiplication, and division.

Summarize   To **summarize** is to aggregate data into totals or condensations that are more meaningful than the unsummarized data. Summarization in a data processing context is normally the addition of arithmetic data into meaningful totals.

Compare   The **compare** operation is the process of examining two pieces of data to determine if they are equal, if they are not equal, or if one is greater than the other. This is often called logical comparison.

Retrieve   In the **retrieve** operation, data are moved from secondary storage to the central processing unit so that other data processing operations may be performed.

Store

The **store** step in data processing includes three operations: protecting, indexing, and updating. Some information systems professionals would place the retrieval operation (identified here as a process operation) under the store step, since a large part of the retrieve operation is performed by the storage unit in a computer system.

Protect   In the **protect** operation, stored data are safeguarded from unauthorized erasure, modification, or usage. Protection, or control, of data systems is being expanded since a large amount of sensitive and valuable information is now stored in computer systems.

Index   To **index** is to create and maintain addresses indicating the physical storage location of a particular piece of data. Therefore, indexes are often used to find the storage location of a piece of data in a retrieval process. These indexes are the equivalent of a card catalog in a library.

Update   The **update** operation is the adding, deleting, and changing of stored data to reflect new events. For example, when an employee wage rate is increased, the payroll file is updated to reflect the new pay rate.

As illustrated in Application 2–3, innovative devices to store data are continually being developed.

Output

The **output** step includes the operations of reporting, displaying, and issuing.

Report   To **report** is to print management information on a hard-copy medium, normally paper. A report is often a summary of detail data and is used to provide management with information needed to control business operations.

Display   A **display** contains information that is similar to or perhaps the same as that on a report. However, the information appears on a video display instead of on paper. Most individuals refer to the information appearing on a video display as a display rather than a report.

Issue   To **issue** is to prepare output documents (such as checks, purchase orders, or invoices) needed to originate or complete a transaction.

Credit-Card-Sized Storage for 100 Faxes

By Linda Rohrbough

Drexler Technology has developed a device for attachment to a computer and a standard fax machine that allows the storage and viewing of over 100 faxes, allowing control over storage, printing, and sending.

The device is named the Lasercard fax storage system, and Drexler says the device will interface directly with conventional facsimile machines and a computer. A 3-megabyte (MB), credit-card-sized Lasercard stores the images in digital format, each

card being capable of storing up to 100 average pages, including an index of the faxes. The cards can be removed and stored or carried in a shirt pocket, Drexler said. The text of the faxes on the card can be displayed on the computer monitor, printed, or sent out as a fax.

Incoming and outgoing faxes and local documents scanned by the fax are stored in a compressed format, Drexler said. Access to the index of images and information for the image index is keyed in on the computer's keyboard, the company added.

The card itself is written to by a laser and though the card can be updated, the information written to it is permanent. Updates are done transparently to the user by directing the Lasercard to the new information from the old. However, a listing of changes can be made available at any time, and the old information is always intact, Drexler said.

These documents are not the same as a report. For example, a weekly listing that contains the total amount of purchase orders issued to various vendors is a report, whereas the purchase orders themselves are transaction documents that are *issued* by the computer.

General systems theory, which is described in this chapter, is the theory underlying information systems. When systems analysis is covered in chapter 16, many of the concepts introduced in this chapter are used again. To deal with complex systems, analysts must break them down into manageable subsystems. This is the basic approach of both general systems theory and systems analysis.

An information system itself is a subsystem of a firm. It is the subsystem providing formal information for managing the firm from the highest to the lowest levels of decision making.

In analyzing and designing an information system, an analyst directly applies many of the concepts introduced in this chapter. The analyst draws the boundary around a proposed information system to help isolate the problem with which he or she is dealing. The black-box concept is useful in areas where it is not necessary for the analyst to understand the transformation process that is going on. Many information systems, especially accounting-type information systems, are essentially feedback systems for management. These systems produce reports summarizing results of the firm's operations. They also allow management to correct the firm's inputs to change future outputs. In designing an information system, an analyst must constantly keep in mind the concept of variety and control. There are many ways that information systems can get out of control and not function properly. An analyst must anticipate these problems and design countermeasures in the system to bring it back under control. For example, an erroneous material item number in a

Systems and Information Processing

manufacturing resources planning system could cause the wrong material to be ordered for manufacturing. The manufacturing assembly line would then be shut down for a period of time. The system should be designed to detect erroneous material item numbers and correct them before material is ordered.

In summary, it would be a mistake to conclude that general systems theory concepts are too abstract to be useful to an information systems practitioner. These concepts are the theoretical basis for many day-to-day actions taken by information systems professionals. The usefulness of general systems theory is also not limited to information systems. As stated earlier in this chapter, systems and systems analysis are a philosophy and a methodology of dealing with many different kinds of complex problems.

Summary

- In education, economic savings can be realized as students master abstract material that has broad potential application.

- Systems and systems analysis are a philosophy and a methodology for viewing complex wholes at a manageable level of abstraction.

- A system is defined as a set of interacting components that operate within a boundary for some purpose.

- The boundary is the area separating one system from another.

- The environment of a system is defined as anything outside the boundary of the system that influences the operation of the system and cannot be controlled by the analyst.

- Inputs are energies taken into the system.

- Outputs are energies discharged from the system into the suprasystem.

- An interface is the region between the boundaries of systems and is also the medium for transporting the output from one system to the input of another.

- Using the black-box concept, a system is defined in terms of inputs and outputs rather than in terms of the transformation that occurs.

- Open systems accept inputs from the environment.

- Closed systems are assumed not to interact with the environment.

- Entropy is a measure of disorder within a system.

- Feedback is a process by which the output of a system is measured against a standard. Any difference between the two is corrected by altering the input.

- Ashby's law of requisite variety states that to control a system there must be available a number of countermeasures equal to the variety displayed by the output of the system.

- Data are collected facts generally not useful for decision making without further processing. Information is based on processed data and is directly useful in making decisions.

- The four basic steps in data processing are input, process, store, and output.

- The input operations are originate, classify, and edit.

- The process operations are sort, calculate, summarize, compare, and retrieve.

- The store operations are protect, index, and update.

- The output operations are report, display, and issue.

- General systems theory is the theoretical basis for many day-to-day actions taken by information systems professionals.

Key Terms

General systems theory	Information
Systems	Input
Systems analysis	Originate
Suprasystem	Classify
Subsystem	Edit
Components	Process
Boundary	Sort
Environment	Calculate
Inputs	Summarize
Outputs	Compare
Interface	Retrieve
Process	Store
Black-box concept	Protect
Open systems	Index
Closed systems	Update
Entropy	Output
Feedback	Report
Variety and control	Display
Ashby's law of requisite variety	Issue
Data	

Review Questions

1. In the study of systems, what might a biologist, an economist, a psychologist, and an industrial engineer have in common?

2. Explain why marketing majors study finance and economics. Relate your answer to the study of systems.

3. A system consists of a set of interacting components (subsystems). For each of the following systems, identify some appropriate subsystems.
   a. Blood cell
   b. Human body
   c. County school system
   d. University
   e. Management information system

       f.   Industrial firm
       g. Legal system
       h. Basketball team

4.   Identify the objectives, inputs, outputs, and performance measures of your college or university. Make some recommendations for improving the performance of the system by analyzing the inputs and outputs.

5.   Explain why a system's boundary must be defined in systems analysis.

6.   Identify some of the maintenance and signal inputs received by a college student majoring in a business area.

7.   Identify and classify the inputs and outputs of a gasoline engine.

8.   Identify and classify the inputs and outputs of the U.S. income tax system.

9.   Is it possible to describe a system without invoking the black-box concept? Explain.

10.   Identify some examples in which an information systems analyst would employ the black-box concept.

11.   What are the advantages of viewing a system as open rather than closed? Under what circumstances might it be advantageous to view a system as closed?

12.   Describe the feedback mechanism in a budgeting control system.

13.   Describe some of the typical feedback mechanisms used in a collegiate educational system.

14.   Employing the concepts in Ashby's law of requisite variety, discuss your professor's guidance and control of your class.

15.   Assume you are watching five children, all under the age of four. Describe how you would use the two basic strategies from Ashby's law of requisite variety to control the situation.

16.   Arrange the following in a hierarchy from micro to macro systems.
       a.   Electron
       b.   Biological system
       c.   Organism
       d.   Tissue
       e.   Molecule
       f.   Universal system
       g.   Organ
       h.   Atom
       i.   Cell

17.   Indicate some of the countermeasures (requisite variety) that might be useful in the following systems that are considered out of control.
       a.   Murder in a social system
       b.   Overpopulation in a biological system
       c.   Missing cash in a cash receipts system
       d.   Theft of inventory in an inventory system

18.   Distinguish between data and information.

19.   What are the four basic steps in processing data to produce information?

20.   Identify the data processing operations that occur in each of the four basic steps in processing data to produce information.

Discussion Questions and Cases

1. Discuss the pros and cons of the following statement: General systems theory is abstract and rarely can be applied in the real world.

2. Most students using this text are pursuing a college degree. Discuss how the concepts of general systems theory can help you evaluate your pursuit of this degree.

3. The analysis and design of information systems is covered in depth in the next two chapters. Anticipate how general systems theory could be used in the analysis and design of information systems.

4. Sharon Smith is a new internal auditor for General Motors. During her recruitment she was told that General Motors has one of the most complex and effective cost accounting systems in the world. She knows that in her new job she will be expected to perform audits on this cost accounting system. She is very concerned about her capability to understand the cost accounting system. She feels that it is so large and complex that it will take years for her to master it. Do you think the black-box concept would be of any use to Sharon?

5. Ruth Kowalski is enrolled in an MBA program and she is also working as a manager of the product development department of the Southern Corporation. She is enrolled in an MIS course and has covered the concepts of variety and control. She was particularly interested in these concepts and thought they made a lot of sense. She feels she can apply them immediately to her job. She plans to look upon her job as the management of a system. In fact, she feels that she can anticipate most of the variety that will occur within her department. With predesigned controls she feels that she will be able to guide the department toward her objectives. Ruth is convinced that this will be her basic philosophical approach to management. Do you think that the concepts of variety and control can be the basic underlying theory upon which a manager builds his or her approach to management?

INFORMATION SYSTEMS STRATEGIES

Information Theater Could Overthrow Traditional Information Refinery

By David Coursey

The typical MIS [management information systems] organization's role is much like that of an oil refinery. Crude comes in and highly refined products go out, whether it is Texas Intermediate's crude product becoming super-unleaded or a database providing sales information for a business plan.

This is an easy analogy to make and an apt one, the stuff of which all the cliches about "turning data into information" are made. There are, however, limits to the ability to turn raw data into useful facts, and researchers at Xerox Corp.'s Palo Alto Research Center (PARC) are trying to overcome

these limits by the use of a new model, that of "Information Theater."

Information Theater refers to the presentation of related information from many sources in a manner that is meaningful to the user. This compares to a theatrical production in which the audience is presented with information from many different characters who, taken together, make up the story.

Xerox researcher Robert Bauer said the key to advanced data access in the future will be adding people to the loop. No longer, he said, will machines simply "chug away" at information and try to find sought-after facts: People will play a key role in choosing useful information at the time it is presented to them.

"Information refining is fine for transaction-based processing, but having access in the un-structured, document-based world that business operates in is much more complex," said Bauer, whose work at Xerox centers on groupware and other networked applications. One of his group's projects is developing user interfaces and searching tools for image-based systems containing the scanned images of thousands of documents.

Bauer said he does not believe the real need of business is to access reams of data in some central repository, such as the compilation of numerical reports. Instead, he believes managers need better access to the analysis performed by other people, which ultimately becomes understanding.

"You first acquire the information, but you then have to understand it. That understanding is an iterative, spiraling kind of process. There is lots of presentation of the data, and some people add their value to it. It's handed off to someone else as a memo or document, which then has to be accessed by someone who finally makes a judgment, perhaps getting more information from a database," Bauer said.

Analyzing information becomes a cooperative process between the individual doing the analysis and the system that contains it, so that the analysis is more a user interface problem than simply one of pulling documents off a hard disk.

Future data access methods will not be concerned with just the "correctness" of the response to a query, but also with whether the scope of the search was wide enough to catch all the information relating to the request. In some ways, these issues of precision versus accuracy work against one another, because widening the search will increase the amount of unneeded data that is presented. Widening, however, also increases the likelihood that the right unstructured information will be presented for the user to select from.

This is the reason a human being should be involved in the loop and should use an interface that provides the physical images of documents, as well as their contents. "The documents themselves convey the information, not just in the content they contain, but also in the form in which it exists," Bauer said.

"I might remember that, when I made progress, I was on the airplane and the document had a diagram on the third page. That's all I remember,"

Bauer said. This method also enables hand-written documents to be scanned into the system and searched at a later date.

Ultimately, Bauer said, users should be able to ask the system to present documents based upon their appearance and when they were created. A typical request might be for "documents with diagrams and annotations on page 3 stored in February."

Nothing in the request took into account what information the document contained, but it did address the way human beings tend to retrieve information from a huge system.

Bauer said systems designers need to recognize these issues as key differences between a document base and a traditional database. From this, they can develop an understanding that the user interface can be as important as the actual data content in providing the right information to the user.

The end products of Information Theater, then, are texts or fragments of text arranged in a way meaningful to the user. Accomplishing this goal will require a system that weaves the user interface, information presentation and search function in a "mutually reinforcing fashion," said Per-Kristian Halvorsen, another Xerox researcher.

PARC is developing a system that enables documents and information to be clustered by topics and groups of related topics, by whether the document is for or against a particular position and by which parts of the document are most emphasized either textually or graphically.

By retaining information not only about the content of the documents, but also about their form and the context in which they were created, additional information is associated with the document. This includes the name of the author and date of creation, the origin of the information contained in the document, and references within the document to other documents.

Discussion Questions

1. What contribution is provided by adding people to the loop?
2. What are the key differences between a document base and a traditional database?

Reprinted with permission from Fairchild Publications, *MIS Week* (June 25, 1990), p. 31.

3

Information Systems and Individual Human Behavior

Introduction

Managers see computers as tools for providing the information on which to base their decisions. People who are successful with computers know that when developing computer applications they should first focus on information needs rather than on hardware technology. What they need most is to know management's information requirements and how computers can be used to meet those requirements. This chapter and the next explore concepts of individual human behavior and organizational behavior and how these concepts affect information needs.

Organizations are made up of individuals. Thus, to understand the relationships between information systems and organizations, we first must look at individual human behavior. This chapter will first explore the roles of managers. Next, we will look at the relationships between objectives, decisions, and information, and explore decision making in more depth. Humans are also information processors. We will look at some of the strengths and weaknesses of humans as information processors. Next, the chapter covers the qualitative characteristics that information should have and then explores the types of reports that information systems can produce. Individuals differ in their approaches to thinking and decision making. We will explore these differences. Finally, we will discuss ethics and information systems.

What are the Roles of Managers?

Henry Mintzberg specifies ten different managerial roles. A role is a managerial behavior.[1] These ten managerial roles are grouped into three different categories: *interpersonal roles, informational roles,* and *decisional roles,* as illustrated in Figure 3–1.

Interpersonal Roles

A manager's **interpersonal roles** flow directly from his or her formal authority and status. In the manager's relationships with others, the *figurehead* role includes the handling of symbolic and ceremonial tasks for the organization. The *leadership* role involves directing and coordinating the task of subordinates. The *liaison* role involves the development and maintenance of information sources.[2]

Informational Roles

A network of contacts is built through interpersonal roles. These contacts allow the manager to gather large amounts of information, which is gathered and processed through three **informational roles**. In the *monitor* role the manager gathers information. As a monitor, a manager should be the best informed individual in the organization. Much of this information is gathered from feedback loops, as we discussed in Chapter 2, in general systems theory. In the *disseminator* role the manager distributes information to others in the organization. In the *spokesperson* role the

---

[1] H. Mintzberg. *The Nature of Managerial Work* (New York: Harper and Row, 1973), 54-100.

[2] D. Hellriegel, J. Slocum, and R. Woodman, *Organizational Behavior* 5th ed., (St. Paul: West Publishing, Co., 1989), 11-12.

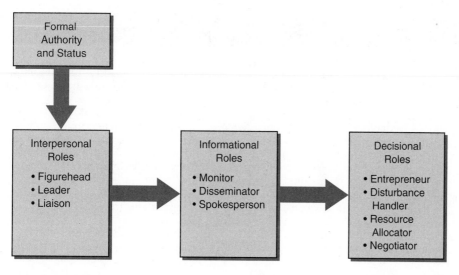

FIGURE 3-1
Managerial Roles.

Source: D. Hellriegel,
J. Slocum, and R. Woodman,
*Organizational Behavior 5th
ed.,* Copyright 1989 by West
Publishing Co. Used with
Permission of West
Publishing Co.

manager makes the official statements for the organization through speeches, reports, press releases, and so on.[3]

Decisional Roles

Information is used to make decisions. In a ***decision*** the manager commits the organization's resources to a course of action. **Decisional roles** include the ***entrepreneur*** role, in which the manager initiates new projects and makes changes in the organization. In the ***disturbance handler*** role managers settle conflicts between departments or subordinates. In the ***resource allocator*** role a manager decides which departments, subordinates, or projects receive resources and how much they will receive. This is often done through a budgeting process. Finally, in the ***negotiator*** role a manager represents the organization in the bargaining process with others.[4]

Information is truly the lifeblood of these managerial roles. Sources of information are often developed and maintained through interpersonal roles. The information is gathered and processed through informational roles, and then this information is used in decision roles. All of the types of information systems discussed in Chapter 1 are used to support the manager in gathering, processing, and using this information. In fact, it is the speed and efficiency with which this information can be gathered and processed with a computer-based information system that has led many organizations to use information systems for competitive advantages. Application 3–1 illustrates how K mart Corp. is using wireless, radio-based networks to speed the flow of inventory data and gain a competitive advantage.

---

[3] *Ibid.,* 12-13.
[4] *Ibid.,* 13-14.

APPLICATION 3–1

K Mart Chooses Cellular Network for Fast Updates

By Stephen Loudermilk

K mart Corp., one of the world's largest retailers, is tapping into radio airwaves with a cellular network system designed to keep its stores up to date on inventory and the latest pricing.

The mass merchandising chain, based in Troy, Mich., is installing a spread-spectrum radio-frequency network from Symbol Technologies, Inc. to automate merchandise ordering, inventorying and other in-store tasks that previously were done manually.

K mart in essence is installing "baby monitors and cordless telephones on an in-store wireless network," said John Kemp, director of product marketing at Symbol Technologies in Bohemia, N.Y.

Officials said that they hope to have the network, which is currently installed in more than 300 K mart stores, up and running in nearly 3,300 of the company's 4,000 stores by November 1992. K mart expects a full return on its $25 million investment in approximately two years.

The cellular network includes Symbol Technologies' Laser Radio Scanner (LRT 3800) and a portable laser diode scanner, as well as the Spectrum One Network, a spread-spectrum radio-frequency system that the company launched in January 1990.

Officials say that they are unable to determine the total cost of the system but estimate that a package for a single store—which includes an LRT 3800 scanner, a transceiver and a network con-troller card—could cost between $5,000 and $10,000.

K mart is employing the technology for bar-coded advance merchandise-ordering applications, including in-store shelf inventory; price verification; shipping and receiving; warehouse inventory control; and factory automation, according to David Carlson, senior vice president of corporate information systems at K mart.

The procedure itself is fairly simple, according to Fred Heiman, executive vice president and developer of spread-spectrum technology at Symbol Technologies.

"You scan an item on the shelf," Heiman explained. "It goes by radio back to the computers in the back room to check the pricing and description of the item, all over a Token-Ring network via 386 and 486 computers."

K mart employees use the 1.4- pound, 7.1-by-8.4-by-3.3-inch scanners to scan a product's bar code for pricing information or to enter inventory data on the scanner's integrated keyboard.

The discount chain will salvage valuable manpower hours lost to archaic data-collection methods once used by "thousands of people writing down little numbers in little boxes [manually]," said Carlson.

The system will speed transactions such as price checks by as much as 60 percent. By keeping up to date on merchandise needs, store managers can reduce their inventory by 20 percent to 30 percent, according to officials. K mart expects a full return on its $25 million investment in approximately two years.

For example, employees can now quickly determine how many items are in stock and order additional items using the scanner. The data is passed to a host computer via a transceiver at distances as great as 500 feet using the Spectrum One technology, officials said.

The cellular network transmits data at speeds as high as 60.6K bps over a radio frequency of 902MHz to 928MHz, said Heiman. K mart can now hold tent and parking lot sales without any interfering signals on the scanner, he said.

Each store, Heiman explained, has two central file servers—a DOS-based, 16-bit file server and a Unix-based 486 server. In the evening, a central server takes over and updates inventory needs for all the stores, he added.

"K mart set themselves up with real-time information both at the receiving dock and the central host computer to keep better track of information and to reduce inventory if need be," said George Goldberg, publisher and editor of the Scan Newsletter in Great Neck, N.Y.

The advent of spread-spectrum technology, said Symbol Technologies' Kemp, has "opened new doors in productivity and functionality in K mart stores."

Objectives, Decisions, and Information

How does one determine what information a manager needs? Information needs are determined by the decisions that must be made, which in turn are determined by objectives. This relationship between objectives, decisions, and information is illustrated in Figure 3–2.

For example, assume that a company has an objective of increasing its net profit by 50 percent. Decisions need to be made about which prod-

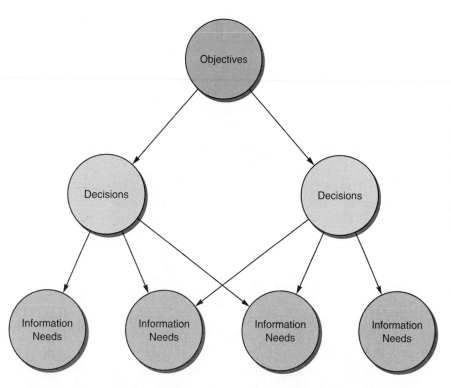

FIGURE 3–2
The Relationship between Objectives, Decisions, and Information Needs.

Sometimes it is tempting to think about information needs without first thinking about business objectives and decisions. Such an approach often results in information systems that do not meet business needs.

ucts should be emphasized in order to reach the desired 50 percent increase in profits. Choosing a certain product might require further decisions concerning expansion of plants, or a decision to purchase the product from outside. All of these decisions are based, in part, on information from the computer-based information system. As the company moves toward the 50 percent increase in net profit, reports showing how well each product is selling are crucial. These reports could indicate that a decision should be made to emphasize an alternative product that might be more profitable. This approach to determining the information needs of management is essential to the development of information systems. The systems analyst, who is responsible for developing the system, must always keep in mind the decisions and the objectives that the information system supports.

Decision Making

Decision making is a complex process involving many variables that we do not yet fully understand. However, many aspects of business decision making are clear. Business decisions are made at different levels within the organization. Individuals make two general types of decisions: programmable and nonprogrammable. And for all decisions, decision makers go through certain stages to reach a solution.

Levels of Decision Making

Decisions can be classified as (1) strategic, (2) tactical, and (3) operational. These levels of decision making correspond to management levels. Strategic decisions are made by top management; tactical decisions

F I G U R E 3–3
Levels of Decision
Making.
Transaction processing
supports these decisions
with data that can be
further processed to
produce information for
decision making.

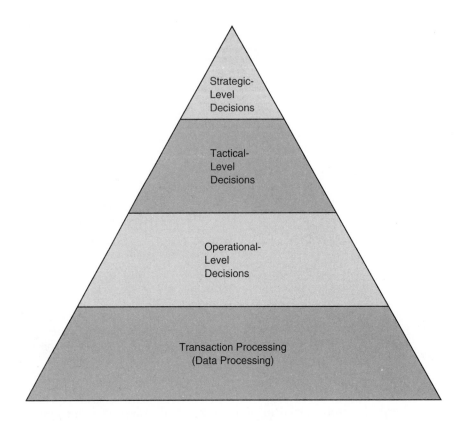

by middle management; and operational decisions by low-level management. As illustrated in Figure 3–3, all three of these levels of decision
making rely on data processing for portions of their information.

Table 3–1 summarizes the characteristics of the three levels of decision
making. Strategic decisions are made for the future and involve a great deal
of uncertainty. **Strategic decision making** involves establishing objectives
for the organization and outlining long-range plans for attaining those objectives. Decisions regarding the location of plants, about capital sources,
and about which products to produce are examples of strategic decisions.

T A B L E 3–1
Characteristics of the
Three Levels of
Decision Making

Characteristic	Level of Decision Making		
	Operational	Tactical	Strategic
Problem variety	Low	Moderate	High
Degree of structure	High	Moderate	Low
Degree of uncertainty	Low	Moderate	High
Degree of judgement	Low	Moderate	High
Time horizon	Days	Months	Years
Programmable decisions	Most	Some	None
Planning decisions	Few	About half	Most
Control decisions	Most	About half	Few

Tactical decision making is concerned with implementing the decisions made at the strategic level. This includes allocating the resources
needed to meet organizational objectives. Examples of tactical decision
making include plant layout, personnel concerns, budget allocation, and
production scheduling.

Operational decisions involve executing specific tasks to assure that they are carried out efficiently and effectively. These decisions are made primarily by lower-level supervisors. Guidelines against which performance is measured are usually preset for operational decisions. Managers and supervisors at this level are expected to make decisions that keep the operation in line with the predetermined standards. Examples of operational decision making include accepting or rejecting credit, determining inventory reorder times and quantities, and assigning jobs to individual workers.

The discussion of levels of decision making touched on some of the characteristics of the information required at each level of decision making. Table 3–2 summarizes those characteristics. Most of the entries in this table are self-explanatory. However, some are more complicated. For example, look closely at the use of real-time information. Real-time systems provide information about ongoing events that reflects the status of those events in a completely up-to-date manner. Operational decision making depends heavily on real-time information. For example, your school probably uses a real-time system for course registration. The operational decision to allow you to sign up for a particular class depends on the real-time information of whether the class is full or not. On the other hand, strategic decision making depends much less on real-time information. For instance, one type of information used at the strategic level is income statements. These statements identify the profitability of plants, products, and so on. Income statements are usually generated at the end of each month. Therefore, they are not real time. Strategic-level decision making also tends to rely heavily on financial information. Decision makers at this level deal with capital requirements and profitability in dollars. On the other hand, a front-line supervisor is more concerned about the hours worked on a job, the number of orders shipped, the number of defective units produced, and other information of this type.

Information Characteristic	Level of Decision Making		
	Operational	Tactical	Strategic
Dependence on computer information systems	High	Moderate	Low to moderate
Dependence on internal information	Very high	High	Moderate
Dependence on external information	Low	Moderate	Very high
Degree of information summarization	Very low	Moderate	High
Need for on-line information	Very high	High	Moderate
Need for computer graphics	Low	Moderate	High
Use of real-time information	Very high	High	Moderate
Use of predictive information	Low	High	Very high
Use of historical information	High	Moderate	Low
Use of what-if information	Low	High	Very high
Use of information stated in dollars	Low	Moderate	High

TABLE 3–2
Characteristics of Information Required at Each Level of Decision Making

Types of Decisions

Decisions may be categorized as being either programmed or nonprogrammed. In a **programmed decision**, the rules for making the decision are explicit. That is, given a certain set of conditions, a certain set of actions will be taken. Programmed decisions are often incorporated into transaction processing systems, and thus computer systems can make those decisions without human intervention. An example of such a decision is the inventory reorder decision. Based on economic order quantity and safety stock rules, a computer automatically reorders inventory items. In designing an information system it is very important to isolate decisions that can be programmed, thereby relieving human beings of the necessity of making those routine day-to-day decisions.

Nonprogrammed decisions deal with nonrepetitive and ill-defined problems, and require human decision making. Nonprogrammed decisions are made at all levels within an organization, including operational, technical, and strategic levels. However, as one moves to higher levels of decision making, a greater percentage of the decisions made are nonprogrammed. Examples of nonprogrammed decisions include plant location, product line expansion, merger, and employee hiring decisions.

Programmed decisions require timely, accurate, and reliable information, whereas nonprogrammed decisions require a great deal of flexibility on the part of the information system. The decision maker must interact with the information system to gain information to make a nonprogrammed decision. The methods covered in this text to build information systems are designed to produce flexible information systems.

Stages in Decision Making

Herbert A. Simon has identified three stages in decision making: (1) intelligence, (2) design, and (3) choice.[5] In the **intelligence stage**, a decision maker becomes aware that a problem exists. In this stage the decision maker also gathers information concerning the problem. In the **design stage**, the decision maker attempts to develop alternative solutions to the problem. This stage may require additional information concerning alternative solutions. The final stage, the **choice stage**, relies heavily upon the quality of the design stage, including the alternative solutions and the information concerning them. If stage 2, design, is done properly, stage 3, choosing a solution, is straightforward.

Information permeates the decision-making process. It is necessary for the identification of problems. It is also the basis of considering possible alternative solutions. Finally, it is used to evaluate alternative solutions. Much of this information can come from a firm's information system. However, nonprogrammed decision making relies heavily upon human beings as information processors. The next section of this chapter discusses characteristics of human beings as information processors in a decision-making context.

Human Information Processing and Information Systems

The primary advantages of **human information processing** over machine information processing are that humans have (1) the ability to use a complex, associative, long-term memory to focus on likely problem solutions; and (2) a facility for guiding the information search for problem solutions. Computer-based information systems can store large amounts of data for long periods of time, but computers lack the ability to associate related data quickly, as human beings can. Computers can, if instructed to, associate related data, but humans must provide the instructions.

---

[5] Herbert A. Simon, *The New Science of Management Decision* (New York: Harper & Row Publishers, 1960), 2.

There is no question that human beings are efficient information processors and decision makers. However, research shows that people have certain biases in the decision-making process. The remainder of this section discusses those biases and suggests some aids in counteracting them.

Generally, humans fail to consider a sufficient number of alternative solutions to problems, tending to rely on a small subset of the available information concerning solutions. Such behavior makes for an efficient information search. After all, large amounts of information may produce an overload, leading to confusion on the part of the decision maker. However, research has shown that almost every decision maker who at any time considered the correct solution to a problem selected this solution as his or her final choice.[6] These findings illustrate the critical nature of the search for possible solutions to a problem. If the correct solution is identified it is highly likely to be chosen. Narrowing the search for alternative solutions may produce an efficient information search, but it may also result in overlooking the correct solution.

In designing information systems, one should keep in mind the need to augment a human being's short-term memory. As indicated by the name, **short-term memory** is a capacity to store items for a short period—perhaps minutes, or at the most a few days. Humans cannot be expected to remember all possible solutions to problems even though they have been aware of those solutions in the past. Interactive menu-driven information systems are an example of systems that compensate for people's failures to consider a sufficient number of alternative solutions to a problem. On the screen, these systems provide a checklist of possible actions, thereby guiding a decision maker in the information search and assuring that possible solutions are not overlooked.

A second bias that human beings have in the decision-making process is a failure to search for evidence that contradicts an apparent solution to a problem, or neglecting such information once it has been gathered. Once a decision maker has used a particular solution in the past or is leaning toward a particular solution currently, he or she narrows the information search quickly. People tend to anchor on a particular solution and do not like contradictory evidence about that solution even if an alternative may be better. This bias commonly manifests itself when an information systems designer is told by a manager that a particular piece of information is important in making a decision. The systems designer knows that other types of information are more important and in fact would lead to a different decision than what the manager makes. A systems designer must realize that the manager is not likely to change his or her opinion quickly about what information is needed. A long and skillful educational process may be needed before the manager will use different information.

The final human information processing bias discussed here is the limited ability to integrate information from multiple sources into global judgments. This bias is related to the previous two. Human beings tend to use a narrow range of information in making decisions. They have difficulty assessing information from multiple sources and then integrating

---

[6] A. S. Elstein, L. Schulman, and S. A. Sprafka, *Medical Problem Solving: An Analysis of Clinical Reasoning* (Cambridge: Harvard University Press, 1978).

it into a decision. They are much better at selecting and gathering information than at integrating it. Solutions to this bias fall into two categories. First, the decision maker can be replaced with a decision-aiding model in at least a portion of the decision process, and second, the format in which the information is presented to human beings can be changed.

Decision-aiding models, such as expert systems, multiple regression, and linear programming, are used successfully in a number of business areas. However, the introduction of such models is often met with defensive reactions from decision makers. Their objections are usually along the lines of (1) there are technical problems with a model, (2) models dehumanize the decision process, and (3) models are an attack on the decision maker's prized judgment abilities. The adoption of models is not a straightforward and easy task. However, as managers see the additional profits to be had through the use of some models, they gradually adopt those models.

Changing the way information is presented can have a large impact on the ability of human beings to integrate multiple pieces of information. A. S. C. Ehrenberg suggests that a good report makes patterns and exceptions obvious when the probable exceptions and patterns are known beforehand.[7] He provides four basic guidelines for a good report:

1. Round to two significant digits.

2. Use row and column averages.

3. Present the main pattern of data in the columns.

4. Order the rows and columns by some measure of their size.

Rounding to two significant digits may seem severe, but it is necessary for mental arithmetic. Averages help one keep important relations, such as above or below average, in mind. Columnar presentation allows one to compare individual digits by running the eye up and down the column, and an ordering by size aids in interpreting the figure because one can see the general pattern of the surrounding figures.

Another way of changing information format is through the use of graphics. Currently available hardware and software make graphics presentation inexpensive. Graphics combining several variables in a multidimensional format can be particularly effective. One such technique is Chernoff schematic faces.[8] **Chernoff faces** are constructed by assigning each variable of interest to a different feature on a schematic face. Figure 3–4 illustrates Chernoff faces for the W. T. Grant Company from 1965 to 1974.[9] W. T. Grant declared bankruptcy in 1974. In Figure 3–4, thirteen

---

[7] A. S. C. Ehrenberg, "Some Rules of Data Presentation," *Statistical Reporter* 7 (1977), 305-10.

[8] H. Chernoff, "The Use of Faces to Represent Points in k-Dimensional Space Graphically," *Journal of the American Statistical Association* 68 (June 1973), 361–8.

[9] S. Moriarity and W. Roach, *Chernoff Faces as an Aid to Analytic Review*, unpublished paper presented to the committee on statistics in accounting, American Statistical Association annual meeting (August 1977).

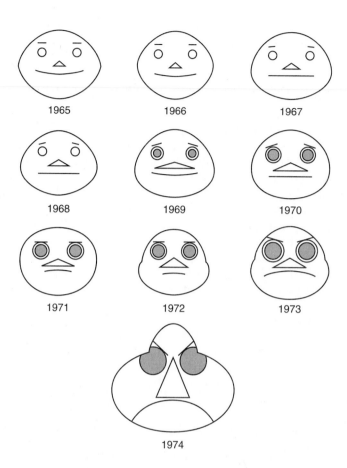

FIGURE 3–4
Chernoff Faces
Representing W. T.
Grant Data (Courtesy
of S. Moriarity and W.
Roach).

key financial ratios are represented by different features on the face. Even if you know little about key financial ratios, you can probably see that something was seriously wrong with W. T. Grant in 1974. In fact, you can see the trend starting in 1967 and getting progressively worse. This is one example of the possibilities for using multidimensional graphics in presenting information for decision making. Such approaches can be particularly useful for integrating several different pieces of information into one composite, thereby compensating for human beings' inability to integrate information from different sources.

Thus far the discussion has focused on biases that all human beings tend to exhibit in decision making and information processing. The next section looks at individual differences in decision making.

Individual Differences in Decision Making

Often the study of information systems is based on the assumption that human components in the system can be viewed as deterministic black boxes; that is, all humans act the same. However, a large set of outcomes is possible in decision making due to individual differences.

Individuals often conclude that their personal view of the world is correct and is shared by most other people. In a decision-making situation, human beings often assume that if everyone saw the facts as they see them, everyone would reach a similar decision. This position fails to consider the role of the personality in decision making. This section discusses a decision-making model that includes the variable of personality.[10]

Basic Personality Theory

Carl Jung is responsible for the theoretical and empirical research that supports the problem-solving model adopted in this section.[11] He employs an open system view of personality that results in two important concepts. One is that subsystems within the personality can interact with each other, and the other is that subsystems can change as a result of interactions with each other or with the environment. Jung identifies four basic psychological functions that serve as a basis for the model: (1) thinking, (2) feeling, (3) sensing, and (4) intuition.

Thinking and feeling are at extreme ends of a continuum. They are each a basis for dealing with external facts when making decisions. Sensation and intuition are paired opposites along another continuum that represents extremes in individual perception preferences. This perception, or information search process, is the means by which an individual becomes aware of events in the environment.

According to Jung's theory, only one of these four psychological functions is dominant in an individual, and it is backed up by only one of the other functions. In describing the model, each of the four psychological functions is considered. The two **perceptual orientations** (sensation and intuition) are then considered in combination with the two **decision-making orientations** (thinking and feeling).

Feeling-Thinking Decision-Making Orientations

People who are **feeling** types "[are] aware of other people and their feelings, like harmony, need occasional praise, dislike telling people unpleasant things, tend to be sympathetic, and relate well to most people."[12] These people are aware of the feelings of other people and enjoy pleasing them. They tend to avoid conflict and are likely to alter their position on an issue if they perceive that a new position will be more acceptable to other group members. Establishing and maintaining friendly relationships is of primary importance to a feeling type. In summary, an individual with a feeling decision-making orientation is likely to emphasize affection and personal processes in decision making for the purpose of obtaining approval from others.

At the other end of the continuum are the **thinking** types, who typically "[are] unemotional and uninterested in people's feelings, like analysis and putting things into logical order, are able to reprimand people or fire them when necessary, may seem hardhearted, and tend to relate well only to other thinking types."[13] Thinking types tend to be impersonal, and they employ standard procedures in decision making. They often

---

[10] This section is based on D. Hellriegel and J. Solcum, *Organizational Behavior*, (St. Paul: West Publishing, 2nd ed., 1979), 221–36.

[11] C. G. Jung, *Collected Works* (especially vols. 7, 8, and 9 of part I), edited by H. Read, M. Fordham, and G. Adler (Princeton: Princeton University Press, 1953), 110.

[12] *Ibid.*, 114.

[13] *Ibid.*, 110.

base decisions on external data and are frequently accused of neglecting humanistic considerations. Frequently, they neglect personal health, family, and finances for the sake of achieving some goal.

The intellectual processes of thinking types are often modeled on the scientific method. This rational, problem-solving approach is probably a result of contemporary educational practices. Thinking types tend to be productive because their style leads to the discovery of new concepts based on seemingly unrelated empirical data.

Sensation-Intuition Perceptual Orientations

Individuals with **sensation** perceptual (information-gathering) orientations "dislike new problems unless there are standard ways to solve them, like an established routine, must usually work all the way through to reach a conclusion, show patience with routine details, and tend to be good at precise work."[14] Sensation types find the uncertainty of unstructured problems and environments distasteful. They also dislike situations in which a great deal of discretion must be exercised. They prefer positions in well-structured bureaucracies with an environment dominated by rules and standard operating procedures. Because sensation types are oriented toward realism and external facts, they are not inclined toward personal reflection and they avoid making personal decisions in unstructured areas.

On the other hand, a person whose perceptual orientation is **intuition** "likes solving new problems, dislikes doing the same things over and over again, jumps to conclusions, is impatient with routine details, and dislikes taking time for precision."[15] Sensation types view the external environment in terms of details and parts; intuition types view the whole environment and look for relationships. When engaged in problem solving, intuition types tend to identify and evaluate alternatives rapidly. They also keep the overall problem in mind while considering means of redefining it at the same time. Intuition types dislike stable conditions and seek new situations in which they are intellectually challenged. When they are oriented toward people, they are capable of identifying the potential abilities of others.

A Composite Model

A model of individual decision-making styles based on the decision-making and perceptual orientations of individuals is presented in Figure 3–5. Although this model is simplified, it demonstrates the impact of personality on individual decision making.

Sensation-feeling individuals (type I) are primarily concerned with facts about people that they can collect and verify directly by their senses. Because of their feeling orientation in decision making, these people evaluate facts with a personal and human concern. They tend to be very organized and to give great attention to detail.

---

[14] *Ibid.*, 115.
[15] *Ibid.*, 116.

FIGURE 3–5
A Model of Individual
Problem-Solving
Styles.

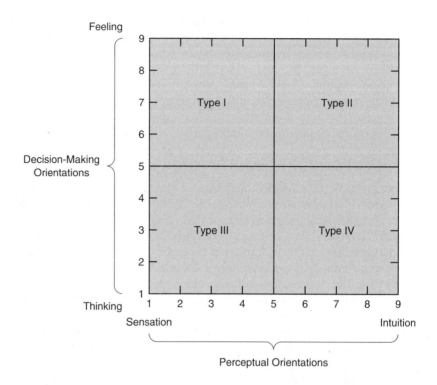

For a senstation-feeling type, an ideal organization consists of a well-defined hierarchy with a well-defined set of rules to specify relationships. Such types believe that an organization should satisfy the members' needs and should allow for open communication.

Intuition-feeling individuals (type II) rely primarily on intuition in their perception and on feelings when making decisions. They generally avoid specific details. They like to be involved with new projects, ideas, and concepts, and they prefer to focus on broad themes, such as serving humanity and satisfying human needs. In their view, the ideal organization is decentralized, has few rules and standard operating procedures, has no strong leaders, and has loosely defined lines of authority.

Sensation-thinking individuals (type III) tend to focus on external facts and to analyze problems logically. They focus on the specific details of a problem and are very practical in their problem solving. Their ideal organization is a classic bureaucracy. They prefer well-defined positions and extensive use of rules. They believe that an organization should contain a well-defined hierarchy and that people should be evaluated on the basis of their technical ability.

Intuition-thinking individuals (type IV) emphasize a theoretical or technical approach to problem solving, and favor situations that lack structure and require abstract skills. They prefer impersonal organizations that emphasize conceptual skills. They believe that the goals of an organization should be consistent with the environment and the needs of the members of the organization. Intuition-thinking types handle issues from an impersonal, abstract frame of reference.

The Implications for Information Systems

The model of individual styles of decision making shown in Figure 3–5 has several implications for people involved in information systems. First, in a problem situation, different personalities seek different types of information. Second, people interpret the same information differently because of variations in their perceptions. Third, personality influences the individual's perception of an ideal organization. Therefore, an organizational policy (or information system design) that seems quite reasonable to one individual might elicit a hostile reaction from another.

So, should different information systems be designed to fit each user's perceptual and decision-making styles? No, such an approach would not be economical. Rather, systems should be designed to be flexible, to be user friendly, and to provide a variety of user interfaces. Many fourth-generation computer languages are beginning to provide this variety of user interfaces. For example, FOCUS provides the user with electronic spreadsheet, database query language, menu-driven, and natural (English) language interfaces.

No amount of information processing equipment and standard operating procedures will ensure consistent communication, perception, and decision making by individuals within an organization. All people are different—and even with some understanding of information systems, designers are not capable of controlling human behavior. On the other hand, the human component is the only component in an information system that is capable of adapting the system to meet the ever-changing demands from the environment. Throughout the life cycle of any information system, it will be necessary to alter the goals of the system. Because humans alone possess the ability to adapt, they make the most significant contribution to the successful functioning of an information system.

Humans are also capable of both ethical and unethical behaviors. The next section will consider ethics and information systems.

Ethics and Information Systems

Ethics are accepted principles of right and wrong governing the conduct of a group, and are very important to the functioning of business in a capitalistic society. Ethical principles are different from laws. Laws are passed by governmental bodies and enforced by the courts. Laws attempt to prevent wrongs, empowering governmental authorities to arrest and punish those who commit these wrongs.

The establishment of laws and their enforcement is an expensive process. Ethical principles, on the other hand, govern those rules of good conduct that most of society can be expected to follow. Thus, rules of ethical conduct are a much more inexpensive way of ensuring good conduct than laws are. If sufficient numbers of people in a society break an ethical principle, either the government must step in and pass a law to enforce it or it may be found that the ethical principle was not necessary. For example, let's look at the copying of software. Software is covered by the copyright law and it is illegal to copy it. Yet software producers lose billions of dollars each year through unauthorized and illegal copying. Thus, governmental bodies incur substantial expense to enforce the copyright laws. However, if there were a strong ethical belief that software should not be copied, then both the losses to software firms and the expense of enforcing copyright laws would be reduced dramatically. It is obvious that the least expensive way for society to handle this problem is through having a widely held ethical belief that copying software is unethical.

Information systems have produced a wide range of ethical issues. Richard Mason has categorized these issues into four areas: issues of privacy, accuracy, property, and accessibility.[16] We will cover each of these areas in the next four sections of this text. Most of this discussion is based on Mason's article.

Privacy

Privacy is the right to keep to one's self, secluded from the intrusion of others. Privacy in relation to information systems concerns the extent to which an individual can keep information about one's self or one's associations from others. Assuming a crime has not been committed, how much can an individual be forced to reveal to others? Even in the case of a crime an individual cannot be forced to reveal incriminating evidence. Mason sees two information systems forces that threaten our privacy. One is the increasing power of information technology with its enhanced capabilities of surveillance, processing, storage, and reporting of information. The second force is the increased value of information in decision making and, thus, the incentive that decision makers have to gather and store more information.

Let's look at two examples. First, many companies are now using computer technology to monitor the work performance of employees. This has been applied in many areas, but one of the most widespread uses is to monitor individuals who key information into the computer. A great deal of information can be collected, for example, the number of mistakes made, the rate at which information is keyed in, and how long the employee is away from the keyboard on breaks, lunch hours, or trips to the restroom. Is this an invasion of privacy or is management simply exercising its right to monitor employee performance?

Another example is the collection and storage of medical data about individuals. When you apply for life insurance, disability, or health insurance, the information that you provide, including the results from medical tests, can be stored in a medical database. This is a nationwide database that is accessible by a wide range of companies. Let's assume that you apply for a life insurance policy in the amount of $200,000 and you are required to have a medical exam before the insurance is approved. Signing the release forms for the medical exam that the insurance company requires normally also allows the insurance company to place the results of the medical exam in the medical database. If, for example, your medical exams reveal that you have a serious illness that might manifest itself in the future, you might not get the life insurance. In addition, this information will be stored in the medical database, which is accessible to other insurance companies, and you might not be able to get health, life, or disability insurance in the future.

[16] Richard O. Mason, "Four Ethical Issues of the Information Age," *MIS Quarterly* (March 1986), 5–12.

This problem of privacy is likely to get worse. A current project called the Human Genome Project is working to determine the normal set of human genes. With this medical breakthrough you could have tests that would determine if you had a genetic disposition toward a certain disease such as some type of cancer. This information obviously has advantages to you. You could take steps to try to avoid contracting the cancer. But, at the same time, the information could be stored in a medical database, accessible to a wide range of individuals and companies, with disastrous consequences for you. For example, you might be turned down for a job simply because the company did not want to hire someone who had a predisposition to a certain type of cancer that tends to manifest itself by the age of forty.

Another threat to privacy is the ability to merge information from different databases to provide greater information than either of the two databases provide independently. Diverse and isolated files may provide relatively limited information about a single individual. But, when information is merged from many different files into one database, the collection of data may reveal the most intimate details about individuals. Your act of providing information to an individual database should not give someone else the right to collect this and other information from different databases and merge it into one. Application 3–2 provides further information about the threats to privacy that electronic databases present.

Accuracy

Accuracy is a quality held by that which is free of error. Inaccurate information stored about individuals can have adverse impact on their lives. For example, Equifax and other companies store credit information on individuals. If this information is inaccurate, perhaps showing that your credit history is not good, your access to credit and perhaps jobs may be curtailed. In the case of credit information you do have the right to review this information and challenge its accuracy. However, relatively few people avail themselves of this opportunity. In addition, individuals often are not aware that the data is being stored. Those who store information have a special ethical responsibility to be sure that the information is accurate.

Property

Information and programs both obviously have value. In the case of programs, there is currently a fairly widespread practice of copying personal computer programs. This is not only unethical, but it is also illegal. It is a violation of copyright laws. Most software licenses give you the right to use a package that you buy on one machine at one time. You cannot share it with others, which would imply using it on two machines simultaneously.

The taking or sharing of information that is someone else's **property** is also unethical and illegal. For example, in Virginia two employees of a large bank left and went to work for a smaller bank. When they left they took a printout of the list of customers of the large bank with the intention of using it to lure these customers to the smaller bank. The larger bank took the two former employees to court and won.

Lawmakers Begin to Heed Calls to Protect Privacy and Civil Liberties as Computer Usage Explodes

By Michael W. Miller

Is the computer explosion weakening civil rights and liberties?

Some computer entrepreneurs, public-interest groups, a rock-music lyricist and influential lawmakers think so. They are drawing up an ambitious battle plan to bring legal rights into the computer age.

Their agenda ranges from protecting privacy in an era of ballooning data bases of personal information to assuring public access to government records as they become electronic. Alarmed by recent police raids on electronic bulletin boards run by "hackers," they are also pressing for new curbs on searches and seizures of computers.

Some businesses and government officials worry that this new campaign will make computing less efficient and more expensive. The campaign is even stirring debate within the ranks of civil libertarians. The American Civil Liberties Union is leading the fight for privacy of computer data and pushing for expanded access to government computer files. But ACLU leaders are also struggling to make sure those two missions don't undermine each other.

Some media groups also fear that the emotional privacy issue will lead to new restrictions that could make it harder for reporters to expose bureaucratic malfeasance.

Still, the move toward a high-tech view of constitutional rights is gathering momentum in Washington.

"Our major information statutes were crafted in an era when records were maintained on paper almost exclusively," says Robert Veeder, the Office of Management and Budget's acting chief of information policy. Now, he says, they "need revision to bring them in line with the way we do business today."

Sensitive Data

Congressmen this year have introduced bills to keep the credit-reporting industry from selling its sensitive data to junk mailers and to protect telephone users from having their phone numbers flashed to everybody they call.

Another bill, by Rep. Robert Wise (D., W.Va.), would create a new federal "data-protection board" to oversee government and businesses as they gallop into new ways of using electronic information. Multinational companies are watching that bill closely, because a new European Community proposal would prohibit member nations from moving computer files into any nation that doesn't have "adequate" privacy protection.

Earlier this year, Rep. Andy Jacobs (D., Ind.) held hearings about the spreading use of Social Security numbers to link an individual's multiple files in far-flung computers.

And in the Senate, Patrick Leahy (D., Vt.) is preparing a bill to apply the Freedom of Information Act to electronic files as well as paper. Sen. Leahy also has set up a government and industry "privacy and technology task force" to study whether wiretap laws have been outdated by such new communications tools as cordless phones and electronic mail.

Earlier Technologies

All of these areas raise tangled questions that can't easily be answered by laws written for earlier technologies.

For instance: Exactly what free-speech rights apply in the flourishing world of computer bulletin boards, where thousands of hobbyists post public notes and send each other private messages?

"The government should not be able to seize [a computer running a bulletin board] any more easily than they can seize a printing press," says Mitch Kapor, who founded software maker Lotus Development Corp.

Mr. Kapor today helps run a new advocacy group called the Electronic Frontier Foundation, along with Apple Computer Inc. co-founder Steve Wozniak and John Perry Barlow, a computer hobbyist who wrote the words to "Hell in a Bucket" and several other Grateful Dead songs. The group recently proposed new guidelines for courts that issue search warrants, warning that seizing computers may violate the First Amendment by posing a "prior restraint" to speech.

Landmark Trial

Some law enforcers call this argument overly broad. "Not everything transmitted electronically is a publication," says Mark Rasch, the Department of Justice prosecutor in last year's computer-virus trial of Robert Morris. "You can't hand a bank teller a note saying, 'Give me all your money, I have a gun,' and then argue: 'That's a publication, I have the right to free speech.'"

The privacy debate is equally thorny. Virtually every big company and government agency today keeps electronic data bases of their customers and constituents, and many of them do a brisk business selling this information.

The U.S. has a patchwork of privacy laws protecting such

areas as video rentals and cable TV. But more-important subjects, such as medical and financial records, are still largely unregulated.

Fears about privacy are turning into a potent political issue. "The privacy movement is becoming more and more mainstream, and the average legislator is hearing about more privacy problems from constituents," says Rep. Charles Schumer (D., N.Y.). "You can't sit down and eat a meal at home without somebody calling you up from some list."

Mr. Schumer is one of four congressmen who introduced bills this year to reform the credit-reporting industry. It's currently regulated by a 20-year-old law, written long before computers let the industry send personal-credit files instantaneously to any desk with a PC.

But the privacy movement also faces some slippery debates about whether the movement itself threatens other important rights.

In 1986, privacy advocates successfully pushed for a law that made it illegal to eavesdrop on conversations sent through the airwaves by cellular phones. The law has drawn howls of protest from radio hobbyists, who argue that it should be legal to put up an antenna and pick up any signal that happens to be in the air. Confusingly, the 1986 law party accepted this logic by making it legal to eavesdrop on cordless phones.

Business groups argue that banning the sale of customer data violates their traditional property rights. "Businesses have constitutionally protected rights to protect their own assets, and customer lists are as traditional an asset as there is," says Ronald Plesser, a Washington lawyer who represents the Direct Marketing Association.

Harassment Calls

The debate over "Caller ID," the phone service that identifies callers' numbers, is especially subtle, pitting one kind of privacy advocate against another. Supporters of the service think that it could help them filter out telemarketers and harassment calls. But opponents think callers should be able to choose to remain anonymous.

Finally, some media advocates are nervous about a political push that could make government data bases less open to scrutiny by outsiders.

"In the zeal to protect personal privacy, we're creating one of the most marvelous opportunities for governments to enact sweeping confidentiality provisions - with the hearty support of the public," says Jane Kirtley, executive director of the Reporters Committee for Freedom of the Press, a Washington nonprofit group. "The underlying supposition is that somehow it's safe in the hands of the government, but it's not safe in the hands of the public."

The ACLU wound up in the unusual position of opposing the media group in a Supreme Court case involving freedom-of-information access to an FBI data base of police arrest records. The ACLU argued that the FBI's move to computerize and cross-reference nationwide police files raised troubling questions about suspects' rights.

"We think that both the First Amendment and privacy are fundamental," says Jerry Berman, director of the ACLU's information-technology project. "But there is tension at the edges when you're dealing with personal information that's not clearly private and not clearly public."

The basic problem here is that both information and programs can be extremely costly to produce. But with electronic technology the copying and sharing of this information is very inexpensive and, of course, it does not destroy the original copy. Thus, many individuals are tempted to copy programs and information that do not belong to them. From an ethical standpoint there is no difference in copying a program or information that belongs to someone else and stealing goods from a store or a person.

Access

There are two aspects to the ethical considerations about **access** to information and computing power. First, there is an ethical responsibility to protect information from unauthorized access. This concern is very much related to the privacy considerations discussed above. Particularly when information is stored about individuals the protection of that information from unauthorized access is extremely important. For example, many states now require doctors and other health professionals to report the fact that an individual has contracted the AIDS virus to public health authorities. The public health authorities use this information both to help the individual and to prevent further spread of the virus. These public health authorities are required by law, and also by ethical considerations, to protect this information from access by others who do not have an ethical or legal right to know whether or not an individual has contracted the AIDS virus.

The second concern is whether or not we are creating a large group of information-poor people who have no direct access to efficient computer technology and have little or no training in its use. There is no question but that use of computers and the information they store provides a competitive advantage to those who know how to use it. Is computer technology widening the gap between the economically well off in our society and those who are economically poor? A whole series of ethical questions surrounds this concern. For example, how can we use computer technology to improve the lives of the disadvantaged?

Code of Ethics

Several of the information systems professional societies, such as the Association for Computing Machinery and the Data Processing Management Association, have established formal codes of ethics. These codes provide general guidelines for the membership of these societies to follow. Figure 3–6 illustrates the code of ethics of the Association for Computing Machinery.

FIGURE 3–6
The Association for Computing Machinery Code of Professional Conduct.

Courtesy Association for Computing Machinery Inc.

ACM Code of Professional Conduct
PREAMBLE

Recognition of professional status by the public depends not only on skill and dedication but also on adherence to a recognized code of Professional Conduct. The following Code sets forth the general principles (Canons), professional ideals (Ethical Considerations), and mandatory rules (Disciplinary Rules) applicable to each ACM Member.

The verbs "shall" (imperative) and "should" (encouragement) are used purposefully in the Code. The Canons and Ethical Considerations are not, however, binding rules. Each Disciplinary Rule is binding on each individual Member of ACM. Failure to observe the Disciplinary Rules subjects the Member to admonition, suspension or expulsion from the Association as provided by the Procedures for the Enforcement of the ACM Code of Professional Conduct, which are specified in the ACM Policy and Procedures Guidelines. The term "member(s)" is used in the Code. The Disciplinary Rules of the Code apply, however, only to the classes of membership specified in Article 3, Section 5, of the Constitution of the ACM.

CANON 1

An ACM member shall act at all times with integrity.

Ethical Considerations

EC1.1. An ACM member shall properly qualify the member's expressed opinion outside the member's areas of competence. A member is encouraged to express an opinion on subjects within the member's area of competence.

EC1.2. An ACM member shall preface any partisan statements about information processing by indicating clearly on whose behalf they are made.

EC1.3. An ACM member shall act faithfully on behalf of the member's employers or clients.

Disciplinary Rules

DR1.1.1. An ACM member shall not intentionally misrepresent the member's qualifications or credentials to present or prospective employers or clients.

DR1.1.2. An ACM member shall not make deliberately false or deceptive statements as to the present or expected state of affairs in any aspect of the capability, delivery, or use of information processing systems.

DR1.2.1. An ACM member shall not intentionally conceal or misrepresent on whose behalf any partisan statements are made.

DR1.3.1. An ACM member acting or employed as a consultant shall, prior to accepting information from a prospective client, inform the client of all factors of which the member is aware which may affect the proper performance of the task.

DR1.3.2. An ACM member shall disclose any interest of which the member is aware which does or may conflict with the member's duty to a present or prospective employer or client.

DR1.3.3. An ACM member shall not use any confidential information from any employer or client, past or present, without prior permission.

CANON 2

An ACM member should strive to increase the member's competence and the competence and prestige of the profession.

Ethical Considerations

EC2.1. An ACM member is encouraged to extend public knowledge, understanding, and appreciation of information processing, and to oppose any false or deceptive statements relating to information processing of which the member is aware.

EC2.2. An ACM member shall not use the member's professional credentials to misrepresent the member's competence.

EC2.3. An ACM member shall undertake only those professional assignments and commitments for which the member is qualified.

EC2.4. An ACM member shall strive to design and develop systems that adequately perform the intended functions and that satisfy the member's employer's or client's operational needs.

EC2.5. An ACM member should maintain and increase the member's competence through a program of continuing education encompassing the techniques, technical standards, and practices in the member's fields of professional activity.

EC2.6. An ACM member should provide opportunity and encouragement for professional development and advancement of both professionals and those aspiring to become professionals.

Disciplinary Rules

DR2.2.1. An ACM member shall not use his professional credentials to misrepresent the member's competence.

DR2.3.1. An ACM member shall not undertake professional assignments without adequate preparation in the circumstances.

DR2.3.2. An ACM member shall not undertake professional assignments for which the member knows or should know the member is not competent or cannot become adequately competent without acquiring the assistance of a professional who is competent to perform the assignment.

DR2.4.1. An ACM member shall not represent that a product of the member's work will perform its function adequately and will meet the receiver's operational needs when the member knows or should know that the product is deficient.

CANON 3

An ACM member shall accept responsibility for the member's work.

Ethical Considerations

EC3.1. An ACM member shall accept only those assignments for which there is reasonable expectancy of meeting requirements or specifications, and shall perform his assignments in a professional manner.

Disciplinary Rules

DR3.1.1. An ACM member shall not neglect any professional assignment which has been accepted.

DR3.1.2. An ACM member shall keep the member's employer or client properly informed on the progress of his assignments.

DR3.1.3. An ACM member shall not attempt to exonerate himself from, or to limit his liability to clients for the member's personal malpractice.

DR3.1.4. An ACM member shall indicate to the member's employer or client the consequences to be expected if the member's professional judgement is overruled.

CANON 4

An ACM member shall act with professional responsibility.

Ethical Considerations

EC4.1. An ACM member shall not use the member's membership in ACM improperly for professional advantage or to misrepresent the authority of the member's statements.

EC4.2. An ACM member shall conduct professional activities on a high plane.

EC4.3. An ACM member is encouraged to uphold and improve the professional standards of the Association through participation in their formulation, establishment, and enforcement.

Disciplinary Rules

DR4.1.1. An ACM member shall not speak on behalf of the Association or any of its subgroups without proper authority.

DR4.1.2. An ACM member shall not knowingly misrepresent the policies and views of the Association or any of its sub-groups.

DR4.1.3. An ACM member shall preface partisan statements about information processing by indicating clearly on whose behalf they are made.

DR4.2.1. An ACM member shall not maliciously injure the professional reputation of any other person.

DR4.2.2. An ACM member shall not use the services of or membership in the Association to gain unfair advantage.

DR4.2.3. An ACM member shall take care that credit for work is given to whom credit is properly due.

CANON 5

An ACM member should use the member's special knowledge and skills for the advancement of human welfare.

Ethical Considerations

EC5.1. An ACM member should consider the health, privacy, and general welfare of the public in the performance of the member's work.

EC5.2. An ACM member, whenever dealing with data concerning individuals, shall always consider the principle of the individual's privacy and seek the following:
to minimize the data collected,
to limit authorized access to the data,
to provide proper security for the data,
to determine the required retention period of the data, and
to ensure proper disposal of the data.

Disciplinary Rules

DR5.2.1. An ACM member shall express the member's professional opinion to the member's employers or clients regarding any adverse consequences to the public which might result from work proposed to the member.

The Responsibilities of Management

Most research has shown that the ethical tone of a business is set by its management, especially its top management. If management is strong in its support of clearly enunciated ethical principles, the firm's employees will generally comply with those principles. Ethical conduct becomes a part of the culture of the firm and individuals feel a great deal of peer pressure to act ethically.

When we covered accuracy's relationship to ethics we briefly touched on the qualitative aspects of information. In the next section we will cover these in more depth.

Qualitative Characteristics of Information

Without quality, information loses its usefulness. A term often used in information processing to describe the lack of data quality is *garbage in–garbage out* (GIGO). This term means that if data does not meet qualitative characteristics upon input, the information output from the data processing system will be useless, or "garbage."

Information must meet four qualitative characteristics: relevance, timeliness, accuracy, and verifiability.

Relevance

Information has **relevance** when it is useful in making a decision. In other words, if information improves the decision, it is relevant. For instance, if an airline reservation agent is making a decision whether or not to grant a customer a reservation on a particular flight, the number of empty seats on that flight is relevant information. On the other hand, personal characteristics of the potential customer, such as occupation or sex, are not relevant information in this decision.

Timeliness

Information also has **timeliness**, or time value. In the context of most management information systems, as information becomes older its value decreases. Generally, lower-level decisions in an organization must have current and timely information; as you move up the ladder to higher-level decisions, the information can be somewhat older. For example, if you are making the routine and low-level decision of whether to ship a customer the 150 shirts that were ordered, you must know the number of shirts that are on hand at that particular moment. The number of shirts that were on hand five days or two weeks ago is completely useless information in making this decision, so that information is not timely. Conversely, a high-level decision concerning whether to expand your company's capacity for making shirts by building an additional plant would depend partially upon the historical sales trends of shirts. These types of decisions may be based on information that is several years old.

Accuracy

Accuracy refers to information's freedom from error. The amount of error tolerable in information is related to other factors, especially timeliness and the dollar value of the decision to be made. If a decision maker must make a decision quickly, a larger amount of potential error can be tolerated than if he or she has considerable time and resources available to reduce data error. For example, if you smell smoke in your home, you are likely to make a quick decision to call the fire department without taking the time to establish, without error, the location and actual existence of a fire. On the other hand, if you are reconciling your checkbook to a bank statement, you may want to decide to call the bank and accuse it of making an error only after you have information that is accurate to the nearest penny.

Verifiability

Verifiability refers to the ability to confirm the accuracy of information. Information may be verified by comparison with other information that has known accuracy. However, quite often accuracy is verified by tracing information to its original source. The term *audit trail* is often used to describe the means by which summarized information can be traced back to its original source or by which detailed input data can be traced forward to summarized information. Without an audit trail, the accuracy of information is usually impossible to determine. Consequently, the usefulness of the information is brought into question.

Types of Reports

Earlier in this chapter we covered management decision making and the need for information to support those decisions. But in what form is this information produced? Four types of computer reports (or displays) are issued by information systems: scheduled, demand, exception, and predictive. Figure 3–7 summarizes the characteristics of these types of reports.

Scheduled Reports

Scheduled reports are produced on a regularly scheduled basis such as daily, weekly, or monthly. These reports are widely distributed to users

FIGURE 3–7
Information Systems Reports Issued to Management.

Although many of these reports are now available on CRTs or VDTs, many managers still prefer reports to be printed out on paper, primarily because of the flexibility and portability of paper.

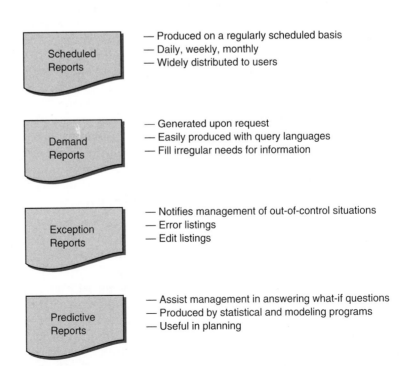

Scheduled Reports
— Produced on a regularly scheduled basis
— Daily, weekly, monthly
— Widely distributed to users

Demand Reports
— Generated upon request
— Easily produced with query languages
— Fill irregular needs for information

Exception Reports
— Notifies management of out-of-control situations
— Error listings
— Edit listings

Predictive Reports
— Assist management in answering what-if questions
— Produced by statistical and modeling programs
— Useful in planning

and often contain large amounts of information that are not used regularly. As the use of video display terminals (VDTs) and personal computers becomes more widespread, scheduled reports will diminish in importance. Managers will not feel compelled to ask for information on a scheduled listing just in case they may need it in the future—with a VDT the information can be retrieved on demand.

Demand Reports

Demand reports are generated on request. These reports fill irregular needs for information. In the earlier days of computing, the contents of a demand report had to be anticipated to avoid delays. It often took weeks or months to modify programs to produce information that filled unanticipated demands. Today, largely through the query languages of database management systems, unanticipated demands for information are fulfilled very quickly, often within minutes. This is possible because users and managers themselves can use the query languages to produce reports.

Exception Reports

One of the most efficient approaches to management is the management-by-exception approach. **Management-by-exception** means that managers spend their time dealing with exceptions, or situations that are out of control. Activities that are proceeding as planned are in control and, therefore, do not need the manager's attention. **Exception reports** notify management when an activity or a system is out of control so that corrective action can be taken. Listings that identify all customers with account balances that are overdue are examples of exception reports. Error reports are another type of exception report. **Error reports** identify input or processing errors occurring during the computer's execution of a particular application.

Predictive Reports

Predictive reports are useful in planning decisions. They often utilize statistical and modeling techniques such as regression, time series analysis, and simulation. These reports assist management in answering what-if questions. For example: What if sales increased by 10 percent? What impact would the increase have on net profit? The statistical and modeling techniques that produce predictive reports depend largely on historical data. Such data must be readily accessible by the information system in a form that can be used by the models; otherwise, those models will be of little use to management.

Summary

- Organizations are made up of individuals. Thus, to understand the relationships between information systems and organizations, we must look first at individual human behavior.

- There are ten different managerial roles, grouped into three different categories: interpersonal roles, informational roles, and decisional roles.

- A manager's interpersonal roles flow directly from his or her formal authority and status. In the manager's relationships with others the figurehead role includes serving as spokesperson and handling ceremonial tasks. The leadership role involves directing and coordinating the task of subordinates. The liaison role involves the development and maintenance of information sources.

- Information is gathered and processed through three informational roles. In the monitor role, the manager gathers information. In the disseminator role, the manager distributes information to others in the organization. In the spokesperson role, the manager makes the official statements for the organization through speeches, reports, press releases, and so on.

- Information is used in the decisional roles of a manager. In the entrepreneur role the manager initiates new projects and makes changes in the organization. In the disturbance handler role managers settle conflicts between departments or subordinates. In the resource allocator role a manager decides which departments, subordinates, or projects receive resources and how much they receive. Finally, in the negotiator role a manager represents the organization in the bargaining process with others.

- Information needs are determined by the decisions that must be made, which in turn are determined by objectives.

- Strategic decision making involves establishing objectives for an organization and outlining long-range plans for attaining those objectives.

- Tactical decision making is concerned with implementing the decisions made at the strategic level.

- Operational decisions involve executing specific tasks to ensure they are carried out efficiently and effectively.

- Programmable decisions are decisions for which policies, standards, or guidelines are already established.

- Nonprogrammable decisions deal with ill-defined and unstructured problems.

- The three stages in decision making are intelligence, design, and choice.

- The primary advantages that human beings have over machines in decision making are

  (1) the ability to use a complex, associative, long-term memory to focus on likely problem solutions; and

  (2) a facility for guiding the information search for problem solutions.

- Human beings fail to consider a sufficient number of alternative solutions to problems.

- Those who design information systems should keep in mind the need to augment a human being's short-term memory.

- Human beings often fail to search for evidence that contradicts the likely solution to a problem, or they neglect such information once it has been gathered.

- Human beings have a limited ability to integrate information from multiple sources into global judgments.

- Changing the way information is presented can have a large impact on the ability of human beings to integrate multiple pieces of information.

- Individuals differ in their approaches to decision making and information gathering.

- Decision-making approaches may be categorized along a feeling-thinking continuum.

- Perceptual (information-gathering) orientations may be categorized along a sensation-intuition continuum.

- Types of decision making among individuals are sensation-feeling, intuition-feeling, sensation-thinking, and intuition-thinking.

- In a problem situation, different personalities seek different types of information, people interpret the same information differently because of variations in perception, and personality influences individuals' perceptions of an ideal organization.

- Ethics are accepted principles of right and wrong governing the conduct of a group.

- Information systems ethical principles can be categorized into four areas: issues of privacy, accuracy, property, and accessibility.

- Privacy in relation to information systems concerns the extent to which an individual can keep information about one's self or one's associations from others.

- Accuracy is a quality held by that which is free of error. Inaccurate information stored about individuals can have adverse impact on their lives.

- The copying of programs and the taking or sharing of information that is someone else's property is unethical and illegal.

- There is an ethical responsibility to protect information from unauthorized access.

- There is an ethical concern of whether a large group of information-poor people have no direct access to efficient computer technology and have little or no training in its use.

- Most research has shown that the ethical tone of a business is set by its management, especially its top management.

- Information is relevant when it is useful in making a decision. If a piece of information improves the decision, it is relevant.

- Information has time value. In most management information systems, as information becomes older its value decreases.

- Accuracy refers to information's freedom from error. The amount of error that can be tolerated in information depends on timeliness and the dollar value of the decision to be made.

- Verifiability refers to the ability to confirm the accuracy of information.

- Scheduled reports are produced on a regularly scheduled basis such as daily, weekly, or monthly.

- A demand report is generated on request.

- Exception reports notify management when an activity or a system is out of control.

- Predictive reports assist management in answering what-if questions.

Key Terms

Interpersonal roles

Figurehead

Leadership

Liaison

Informational roles

Monitor

Disseminator

Spokesperson

Decision

Decisional roles

Entrepreneur

Disturbance handler

Resource allocator

Negotiator

Objectives

Strategic decision making

Tactical decision making

Operational decisions

Programmed decisions

Nonprogrammed decisions

Intelligence stage

Design stage

Choice stage

Human information
   processing

Short-term memory

Decision-aiding models

Chernoff faces

Perceptual orientations

Decision-making
   orientations

Feeling

Thinking

Sensation

Intuition

Sensation-feeling
   individuals

Intuition-feeling individuals

Sensation-thinking
   individuals

Intuition-thinking
   individuals

Ethics

Privacy

Accuracy

Property

Access

Relevance

Timeliness

Verifiability

Scheduled reports

Demand reports

Management-by-exception

Exception reports

Error reports

Predictive reports

Review Questions

1. What are the three major categories of roles that managers play?

2. What are interpersonal roles managers play?

3. What are the informational roles managers play?

4. What are the decisional roles managers play?

5. What is the relationship between objectives, decisions, and information?

6. Identify the three levels of decision making and discuss each one.

7. Differentiate between programmable decisions and nonprogrammable decisions.

8. Identify the characteristics of information required at each level of decision making.

9. What are the three stages in decision making?

10. How can information help in each stage of decision making?

11. In which stage is information most important?

12. Outline the basic weaknesses human beings have as information processors.

13. Research has shown that human beings have a limited ability to integrate information from multiple sources into global judgments. What are some potential solutions to this bias?

14. Define the two basic orientations in decision making.

15. Define the two basic orientations in perceptions.

16. Describe type I (sensation-feeling) individuals.

17. Describe type II (intuition-feeling) individuals.

18. Describe type III (sensation-thinking) individuals.

19. Describe type IV (intuition-thinking) individuals.

20. Explain why privacy, accuracy, property, and access are related to information systems ethics.

21. Identify and discuss the four qualitative characteristics of information.

22. Identify the types of reports that an information system can produce.

Discussion Questions and Cases

1. Listed here are several different decision situations. Which are programmed and which are nonprogrammed? Explain your rationale for each situation.
   a. Selecting a new plant site
   b. Ordering parts for an aircraft assembly line
   c. Assigning production personnel to individual jobs in a machine shop each day
   d. Selecting stocks for an investment portfolio
   e. Selecting the best location for a warehouse from which deliveries are to be made to customers
   f. Deciding whether to discontinue a product line

2. Think for a few minutes about the following questions.
   a. Do you like solving new problems, or do you prefer having a structured job situation that is more routine?
   b. Would you have any difficulty in firing an employee who works for you?
   c. Do you show patience with routine details and tend to be good at precise work?
   d. Do you like an organization that contains a well-defined hierarchy?
   e. Do you evaluate facts with a personal and human concern, or do you tend to handle issues from an impersonal, abstract frame of reference?

   Based on these questions, which of the four types of decision-making styles and perceptual orientations do you fall into?

3. John Gilmer is a senior systems analyst for Montgomery Furniture Company. John has been assigned the task of developing an information system master plan that would govern the future direction of information

system development for Montgomery Furniture. Bill Harmon is manager of the systems development office. John reports to Bill.

Early one morning, John and Bill are discussing the basic approach to developing the master plan. John feels that starting with objectives and deriving the decisions to reach those objectives is a waste of time. He believes that the best approach is to conduct interviews with company executives and ask them what information they need to perform their functions. He says to Bill, "Executives just don't think in terms of objectives and decisions. It would be very difficult to get them to think in those terms and to take the logical steps from objectives to decisions to information." Furthermore, he feels that he should not suggest various types of information to the executives. He states, "I want to find out what information they feel they need, and I don't want to contaminate their requirements with my own opinions." Evaluate John's positions.

4. Barbara Olds is the senior systems analyst on a project to analyze and design a new budgetary control and reporting system for the McGregor Company. In the initial stages of the project, she and her staff interviewed many different management personnel who make use of budgetary reports. The primary purpose of the interviews was to determine a consensus of reporting for the new system. However, the most striking feature concerning the interviews was a lack of consensus as to the type of reporting the managers want. For example, some managers like to see a great deal of detailed reporting on a very frequent basis. At the other extreme are managers who would rarely use reports produced by the existing system or the proposed system. Barbara is not sure how the new system will meet this wide variety of needs. Are there any behavioral characteristics of humans that would explain this lack of consensus? How would you advise Barbara to proceed?

5. Discuss your ethical concerns (if any) and what your actions would be if you were confronted with the following cases.

   a. Your friend has asked you to allow him to make a copy of your Lotus 1-2-3 spreadsheet software. Would your conclusions differ if he only asked to borrow your software?

   b. The company for which you work has asked you to copy its only purchased copy of Lotus 1-2-3 to use in your work. You must have an electronic spreadsheet to perform your duties.

   c. You are disabled and living on a monthly disability check from Social Security. You also have a government-guaranteed student loan that is not completely paid off (it is in default). You discover that the federal government plans to match its files of unpaid student loans with Social Security check recipients. It is likely that your disability checks will be reduced by the amount of your unpaid student loan.

   d. You are a computer input technician for Access Corporation. You learn that the company plans to start a computerized monitoring system that will monitor all your work.

   e. Your company, Target Marketing, Inc., has recently acquired a detailed marketing database that contains a vast amount of information about the buying habits and personal characteristics (such as income, age, and ethnicity) of households in your area. Target Marketing plans to use this information to market products and services to particular households that might buy them. For example, from the database they can determine households whose residents are elderly and might buy financial planning advice. Can you think of ways that this information can be used unethically and ways to use it that would be ethical?

The Ethics Gap

By Glenn Rifkin

For Alana Shoars, the ethics of electronic mail snooping are black and white. "You have to be able to look in the mirror," says Shoars, who was fired last year as E-mail administrator at Epson America, Inc. for questioning the company's alleged monitoring of employee messages. "Right is right, and wrong is wrong. There is no in-between."

In much of the computing and business world, however, opinions are quieter and much less definite—when there are any opinions at all.

Despite Shoars' much publicized dismissal and a related $75 million class-action suit against Epson now pending in a California court—as well as a similar lawsuit filed against Nissan Motor Co.—the topic of computing ethics remains largely the province of consultants and academicians and is largely ignored by information systems professionals.

Ironically, such indifference comes at a time when network monitoring technology and other computing tools raise a whole new series of complex ethical questions for IS [information systems], its organizations and the courts.

Much of what discussion there is focuses on E-mail monitoring, thanks to the medium's popularity, well-publicized lawsuits and high potential for snooping.

However, other important issues include personal, emotional and controversial questions about information access, monitoring and ownership, software copying and database privacy.

Despite the enormous personal, professional, corporate and legal importance of such questions, genuine debates and policies about ethics among computing professionals are still relatively rare, according to IS chiefs and academicians.

Michael Simmons, chief information officer at Bank of Boston Corp., says the subject of ethics doesn't often arise among IS professionals. If the topic was discussed, he says, "It would be a very short meeting."

Observers say the main reasons for this disinterest appear to be the nature of IS people and their tasks, fear of losing one's job and a widespread belief that an ethics policy is best handled by general management.

Many technology executives deny assertions that IS has ignored the issue.

"I've not seen ethics as an issue," says John Coman, manager of networks and information services at Atlantic Richfield Co. in Los Angeles. "In 28 years in this business, I could count on one hand the number of times I or somebody else had to point out ethical issues in IS."

However, that widely held view is at odds with what researchers in the field say. They note that corporate codes seldom address computing issues specifically and assert that IS has a professional responsibility to take a more active role in defining ethics for the information age.

"IS is falling short of meeting the [ethics] challenge," asserts Eugene Spafford, a computer science professor at Purdue University who teaches a graduate-level course in ethics for computer professionals.

"You teach somebody to drive a car, and there is a component on responsibility built in. But when it comes to computers, we don't do enough of that in universities or in corporate America," says Karen Forcht, associate professor of information and decision sciences at James Madison University in Virginia and author of a key study on student computing ethics. "Computer practitioners think they have their backsides covered, but they don't," she adds.

One obstacle, according to F. Warren McFarlan, a professor at Harvard Business School, is that for people whose math, science and engineering backgrounds can make the world precise and quantifiable, the social ambiguities of ethics discussions may be of very little interest. "This is a group that has not traditionally thought of these issues," McFarlan says.

Such lack of familiarity has led technologists to approach information resources a in unique way, notes Detmar Straub, assistant professor of MIS at the University of Minnesota.

"They say, 'If the system can do it, let's do it,' rather than, 'Should the system do it?'" Straub says. "I've talked to systems managers who say they wouldn't hire a programmer who couldn't break into any system."

Some confusion also stems from emerging laws regarding electronic communications. The federal

Electronic Communications Privacy Act of 1986 protects the privacy of electronic messages sent to public networks.

However, there are few guidelines for internal corporate E-mail networks. Worse, some 200 or so state statutes covering related issues further complicate matters.

Another factor is that IS departments have long been considered service organizations and have removed themselves from ethical debates by saying, "Don't shoot us, we're just the messengers," according to academicians.

Is IS Wimpy?

However, H. Jeffrey Smith, assistant professor at Georgetown University's school of business administration, says this stance is no longer acceptable.

"If we [IS professionals] are going to be leaders in bringing strategic advantage to a corporation, we have to be leaders in ethical issues as well," Smith says. "There is no evidence that the IS community is willing to stand up and do that."

While completing a doctoral thesis at Harvard Business School on IS concerns about information privacy, Smith says, he discovered that most computing professionals took a subservient role in dialogues about information use. "The attitude seemed to be: 'Providing the data is our job, but using the data is the responsibility of the users.' This is troubling coming from an IS person."

The attitude of one bank IS executive is typical: "Even though I have . . . concerns [about how information is used], it is not our role in the IS community to beat the business people over the head about this. It is our role to take their requirements and to implement them, not to bring our personal views in."

DuWayne Peterson, retired CIO of Merrill Lynch & Co., also notes that there are practical limitations on how much of a role IS can play in protecting information. He recalls back-and-forth discussions at the New York brokerage in which IS maintained that information protection was each supervisor's responsibility. At the same time, though, supervisors saw it as an IS function. "But IS can't possibly be everywhere," Peterson says.

To be fair, IS professionals differ little from other workers, who will generally defer to an executive or corporate decision before putting their jobs on the line.

Though no one questions the basic honesty and integrity of most computer professionals, there is an unstated belief that when push comes to shove, fearless honesty won't put bread on the table.

PCs Create New Issues

The spotlight has shifted to IS in recent years because of the proliferation of powerful personal computers and vast communications networks.

"In the past, you couldn't be a miscreant and get a job in data processing," Bank of Boston's Simmons says. Computer professionals "were weird guys with plastic pocket protectors, but they were straight arrows. But in 1981, when anyone could buy a computer and get on the network, that changed the world."

Suddenly, as keepers of the information resource, IS folks faced a laundry list of ethical dilemmas ranging from privacy, data integrity and hacking to personal use of technology by employees.

These developments begged the question: How much ethical responsibility does an IS professional have? A full decade after the PC revolution, opinions vary widely.

"IS people should be held to a higher level of ethics than the general population, just as doctors and lawyers are," asserts Donn B. Parker, a senior management consultant at SRI International in Menlo Park, Calif., who for 35 years has done extensive research and writing about ethics and information systems.

Unfortunately, even the noblest statements of values can run smack into the harsher realities of business. Few IS executives, for example, would have much sympathy for Shoars.

If anything, the monitoring of E-mail is growing, and many CIOs agree that E-mail is part of the business property and, therefore, employers have a legal right to see what it is being used for.

Simmons, for example, points to a previous job in which he discovered an employee using his computer to handicap horse races. Another worker ran his Amway business on his terminal at work, according to Simmons.

Both employees were fired on the spot, Simmons says. "The guy handicapping horses was using 600M bytes of memory," he adds.

Company Assets

For Simmons and many others, the answer is clear: "If the corporation owns the equipment and pays for the network, that asset belongs to the company, and they have a right to look and see if people are using it for purposes other than running the business."

This view is shared by many firms, including Federal Express Corp., American Airlines, Pacific Bell and United Parcel Service, Inc., whose E-mail system automatically informs employees that the company reserves the right to monitor E-mail messages.

Simmons does concede that employees must be informed from the day they start working what the rules are about E-mail and other computing resources. "If they are not told they are being monitored, that's not fair," Simmons says.

Others, such as Mike Godwin, general counsel for the Electronic Frontier Foundation, a nonprofit group, insist that monitoring E-mail or searching through electronic files is flat-out wrong. "It's inconceivable to think of a circumstance where you should look at anybody else's electronic mail," Godwin says.

"Even if a company does post notice, is that something they should do?" Purdue's Spafford asks. "The legal question is fine, but is it ethical? The company may say it is, but the employees say it isn't, and there's a conflict."

Shoars, now an E-mail administrator at Warner Brothers, Inc. in Burbank, Calif., also sees the case as clear-cut. "You don't read other people's mail, just like you don't listen to their phone conversations."

"Asking who owns the E-mail or the phone call is asking the wrong question," Godwin adds. "A better question is, 'What kind of environment do people work most happily and efficiently in?' If I worked in a place where they reserved the right to look at my E-mail, I'd be less happy." Others, including labor unions, have pointed out that employee monitoring can be demoralizing and counterproductive.

Issue Heating Up

Despite such controversies, it seems unlikely that most IS organizations will be taking the lead by articulating their own policies on ethics any time soon.

According to Simmons, such policies must be a compendium of "what others believe we are doing and should be doing." He suggests that IS leaders meet with corporate executive committees to form codes of ethics rather than attempting to dictate policy themselves.

Even so, there are recent indications that the issue is far from dead and will probably heat up in coming months. In August, The First National Conference on Computing and Values, held at Southern Connecticut State University, drew luminaries from IS, computer security, privacy law, academia and philosophy. Organizers called the conference a success and said they were planning another.

The Privacy for Consumers and Workers Act, which calls for the regulation of electronic monitoring, is working its way through the U.S. Senate and House of Representatives. Verdicts in the suits against Epson and Nissan will undoubtedly send lawyers and corporations scrambling.

Besides the Electronic Frontier Foundation, groups such as the Electronic Mail Association, Computer Professionals for Social Responsibility, the American Civil Liberties Union and others continue to lobby to raise public awareness.

An increasing number of colleges and universities have begun teaching computing ethics, and more articles and seminars on the topic are being published in trade and academic journals. Parker and two associates from SRI, Susan Swope and Bruce Baker, recently published a book on the subject.

In early October, the Electronic Mail Association released a detailed "tool kit" for companies interested in creating corporate privacy policies about E-mail.

Despite such activity, many say that major changes are unlikely to occur unless backed by corporate heads. "The only way to get people to stand and defend ethical positions is if they believe that people at the top are ethical," Peterson says. "IS is part of the culture."

Parker points out that unlike medicine or law, which have had centuries to evolve ethics, IS has been around for fewer than 40 years. Despite the field's relative youth, Parker says, a whole new set of ethics for computing is unnecessary. "We have all the ethics we need, and we know what they are," he says. "The Golden Rule still applies."

The big challenge, Parker says, is applying those values in a new environment, so that "when a person logs on to a computer or network, they don't automatically turn off their ethical values."

Arco's Coman says he agrees: "When it comes down to it, ethics are what your mom and dad taught you when you were a little boy or girl, and those things are still valid."

What Are IS Ethics, Anyway?

The ethical concerns that now confront information systems professionals fall into several categories, according to consultants, academicians and IS managers:

- **Privacy:** How is personal information collected, used and protected?
- **Integrity:** Who is responsible for data integrity, and how much effort is made to ensure that integrity?
- **Influence:** Reduced judgment in decisionmaking. How much does IS add to the automating of processes and decisionmaking, and what are the results in relation to human safety and well-being?

- **Impact:** What are the consequences of IS applications on the work force through up-and down-skilling of jobs? Also, what are the consequences on the work force due to surveillance, monitoring and measuring through computers?

Ethicists suggest that such a list could go on forever, with combinations of issues that encompass specific situations and work environments.

Eugene Spafford, a computer science professor at Purdue University, says technology has developed so rapidly that "the target is not well defined."

Right or Wrong?

What is ethical? Unethical? These were the questions behind a landmark study of computing ethics by SRI International in Menlo Park, Calif.

Some 27 business and information systems professionals, ethical philosophers and lawyers were asked to respond to two dozen scenarios and decide if they were ethical.

Their responses later formed the basis of a book titled *Ethical Conflicts: In Information and Computer Science, Technology and Business* (published by QUED Information Sciences, Inc., 1990).

Read the following scenes and decide if they are ethical or not. Responses from the SRI panel are listed below.

Situation 1: The Silent Manager

A programming department manager discovers that one of his programmers and another from the inventory control department are involved in a corporate plan to defraud company stockholders by inflating company assets.

The programs in question passed his quality assurance testing because they were identified as simulation and test files. Eventually, the fraud was discovered and the perpetrators were prosecuted. The programming manager—who is responsible for all applications programming throughout the company but who had no knowledge of the scheme—was identified as an unindicted conspirator.

Question: Was the manager unethical in not responding to evidence of wrongdoing?

Situation 2: The Bare-Bones System

A programming analyst at a large retailer is charged with project responsibility for building a customer billing and credit system. During the project, money runs out.

The programming analyst had continually warned management about impending problems but was told to keep going and finish the development of a bare-bones system as quickly and cheaply as possible.

To meet this directive, several key features—including safeguards, error detection and correction—had to be left out until later versions.

After a difficult and costly conversion to the new system, a great many unfixable problems arose, including wrong and unreadable billings and credit statements. Customers were outraged, fraud increased, company profits fell, and the project leader was blamed for it all.

Question: Was it unethical for the project leader to order the system into production prematurely?

Situation 3: The Nosy Security Manager

The information security manager at a large company also acted as administrator of a huge electronic mail network. During his regular monitoring of mail, the manager discovered personal messages about football bets, sexual encounters and other nonbusiness matters.

Printed listings of the messages were regularly given to the company's human resources director and corporate security director. In some cases, managers punished employees, using the messages as evidence.

Employees became angry, charging their privacy rights on E-mail were the same as the company's telephone or interoffice mail system.

Question: Was it ethical for the information security manager to monitor E-mail and inform management of personal use?

Situation 4: All Work, No Play

The manager of research at a computer company explicitly told workers that anyone found playing games on company computers would be subject to dismissal.

On a random inspection, a computer game was discovered in the files of a programmer, who was then punished.

Question: Was it ethical for the manager to prohibit the use of computer games in employee files?

Situation 5: It's Not Our Job

A software professional was charged with developing control software for part of a large system. The job looked straightforward and trouble-free. To work, the software required input from other units in the system.

The developer then read an article by a noted software specialist and was convinced that input from the other units could not be trusted. So he decided that neither the software he was designing nor the unit his company was providing would do the job they were supposed to.

He showed his supervisor the article and explained his concerns, but was told only to worry about his group's part of the project.

Question: Was it ethical for the developer to continue working on the project?

Responses

Situation 1: unethical: 23; not unethical: 1; no ethics issue: 0. **Situation 2:** unethical: 24; not unethical: 0; no ethics issue: 0. **Situation 3:** unethical: 22; not unethical: 2; no ethics issue: 0. **Situation 4:** unethical: 7; not unethical: 5; no ethics issue: 13. **Situation 5:** unethical: 12; not unethical: 7; no ethics issue: 1.

Guidelines for Action

Experts say certain guidelines can be helpful in solving ethical dilemmas. The first set of suggestions is from Donn B. Parker, a senior management consultant at SRI International:

- **Informed consent.** When in doubt about performing any particular action, inform those whom your action will affect of your intentions, and obtain their consent when applicable.
- **The higher ethic.** Take the action that achieves the greater good.
- **Most restrictive action.** Take the action, or avoid the action, by assuming the most severe loss that could happen.
- **Kantian universality rule.** If an act or failure to act is not right for everyone to commit, then it is not right for anyone to commit.
- **Descartes' change rule.** A sufficient change in degree produces a change in kind. Whereas many small losses may be acceptable individually, taken as a whole, they may result in unacceptable losses.
- **Owners' conservative rule.** Assume that others will treat your assets as belonging to the public domain. Explicitly declare the products of your efforts and your property to be either private or public in reasonably visible ways.
- **The users' conservative rule.** Assume that any tangible or intangible item belongs to somebody else unless an explicit declaration or convention identifies it as being in the public domain or authorized for your use.

The following guidelines are from Ouellette & Associates Consulting, Inc.:

1. Specify the **facts** of the situation.

2. Define the moral **dilemma**.

3. Identify the **constituencies** and their interests.

4. Clarify and prioritize the **values** and **principles** at stake.

5. Formulate your **options**.

6. Identify the potential **consequences**.

Discussion Questions:

1. Is ethical behavior a more important concern for the information systems function than for other business functions? Why or why not?

2. Some would argue that any business behavior that is not illegal is appropriate. Take either side of this argument and make a case for your position.

Rifkin is a free-lance writer and a former *Computerworld* features editor based in Sudbury, MA.
Reprinted from Computerworld (October 14, 1991), pp. 83-85, with permission of Glenn Rifkin.

4

Information Systems and Organizational Behavior

Information systems operate within organizations. The behaviors of organizations have significant impacts on information systems. Advanced information systems can also have impacts on organizations.

Organizations are persons or groups united for some purpose. Each person or group has specific responsibilities to carry out in meeting the organization's purpose. Organizations can also be described using systems theory. Under this definition, organizations consist of a process that accepts inputs from its environment and produces outputs consisting of goods or services. In this chapter we will first look at the four most common organizational forms and explore the ways information systems are designed to fit these organizational forms. We will next look at organizational culture and its impact on information systems. Finally, we will explore the concept of organizational change and how it relates to successful information systems.

Introduction

Since information systems operate within organizations they must be tailored to fit the form or the design of an organization. This section explores the four most common organizational forms and relates them to information systems.

Organizational Design and Information Systems

Functional Form

In the **functional organizational form** an organization's structure is aligned with basic managerial functions, such as marketing, personnel, manufacturing, engineering, finance, and accounting. Figure 4–1 illustrates the functional form of organization. This form allows clear assignment of responsibilities. It also increases the opportunity for mutual support of employees doing similar kinds of work. The primary disadvantage of the functional form of organization is that it may narrow an individual's viewpoint. He or she may concentrate on optimizing the function's performance and ignore the well-being of the organization as a whole.

FIGURE 4–1
Functional Form of Organization.

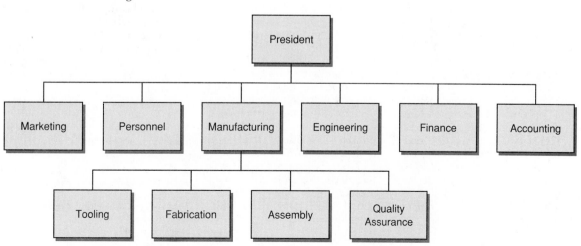

Information systems for functional forms of organizations are usually hierarchical in nature. The reporting task is subdivided by function, and data reported in low-level functions are hierarchically summed to provide reporting at the high-level functions.

In a functional organization, it is often difficult to produce summary information by product. This is because information systems for such organizations are generally set up to report by managerial function. If information systems designers recognize this possible shortcoming during the analysis and design phases of the system, they usually can provide for product reporting capabilities at that time.

Another problem is that information systems may be built that support only individual functions. It is difficult to integrate these systems to produce systems that span several functional areas. For example, in such a system it may be difficult to implement computer-integrated manufacturing, which supports several functional areas including engineering, manufacturing, accounting, and marketing.

Most organizational structures today are hierarchical. However, there is a trend toward flattening these structures by using more teams within organizations. Flattening organizations may be difficult, though, as illustrated in Application 4–1.

APPLICATION 4–1

Applying Behavioral Science to Information Systems

By Clinton Wilder

What do macaque monkeys in Bermuda and chimpanzees in Zaire have in common with your average information systems staff?

They both make excellent subjects for behavioral science observation.

Say what?

Okay, the analogy is a little bit exaggerated. But Cathy Walt, an anthropologist with a Ph.D. in behavioral science, applies her unusual training as an IS [information systems] management consultant. Companies interested in Walt's offbeat approach to IS management challenges include Merck & Co., Meridian Bancorp, Inc. and McNeil Pharmaceutical. For the past year, Walt has worked as an industry specialist with CSC Partners, the IS consulting subsidiary of Computer Sciences Corp.

"A lot of IS people thought it was hocus-pocus at first, but now I'm getting calls from major companies doing re-engineering," said Walt, who is based at CSC Partners' office in Wayne, Pa. "Anthropology is the study of cultures, and business is just another culture."

Among Walt's presumptions is that the success or failure of a systems development team or project depends more on the behavioral skills of the participants than their technical skills. And the success of re-engineering critical business functions depends first and foremost on changing behaviors.

"We talk about flattening organizations, but if you look at primate societies, that goes against the culture," she says. "A hierarchy is supposed to be established. Getting an IS group to understand that the hierarchical boundaries go away is a very difficult thing to do."

Overcoming Barriers

By matching employees' behavioral skill sets with others to form effective teams, Walt has helped knock down some of those boundaries. At Meridian, a $12 billion bank in Reading, Pa., Walt helped employees migrate to a distributed environment that allows users to send letter-of-credit applications directly from their workstations.

She has also been hired to help clients figure out what cultural barriers prevented a new technology from doing what it was supposed to do.

"Some people accuse me of overanalyzing them," Walt said, "but I just take note of things that other people don't."

Reprinted with permission from *Computerworld* (July 15, 1991), p. 51. Copyright 1991 by CW Publishing, Inc., Framingham, MA 01701.

Product Form

Figure 4–2 illustrates the **product organizational form**. In this organizational form activities are grouped together by outputs of the firm or by products. For example, in Figure 4–2, the organization of a large chemical firm is illustrated. The organization is subdivided by major product groups, such as paints and pigments, fibers, and fertilizers. Each of these product divisions is organized internally by managerial function, such as engineering, marketing, and manufacturing. The primary advantage of the product form of organization is that it allows individuals to build expertise and knowledge of particular product lines rather than spread their abilities over many different types of products.

However, personnel costs can be higher in the product form of organization than in the functional form, since each product division requires managers with expertise in functional areas such as engineering, manufacturing, and marketing. In addition, duplication of activities can easily occur in a product organization. For example, the paints and pigments division may develop a sales information system, while at the same time the fibers division may also develop such a system. Lack of coordination between the divisions may result in two separate sales information systems instead of one set of software that could be used by both.

Information systems personnel in the various product divisions must communicate freely with one another to avoid duplication of activities. Communication is often accomplished through a formal information steering committee that has representatives from all product divisions. As would be expected, reporting within a product form of organization tends to follow product lines. Consequently, the ability to report in summary form by managerial function, such as engineering, may be overlooked.

Bureaucratic Form

Max Weber, a German scholar of the early 1900s, described the **bureaucratic organizational form**. When people hear the term *bureaucracy*, they often envision an organization with unreasonable and complex rules that is also incompetent and full of red tape. Therefore, the term bureaucracy

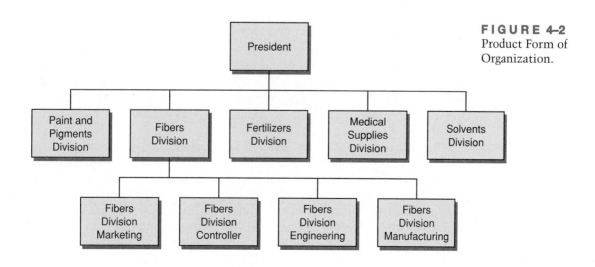

FIGURE 4–2
Product Form of
Organization.

has developed a negative connotation. In reality, the bureaucratic form of organization can be very efficient. This organizational form assumes that an individual employee cannot be trusted to perform his or her job satisfactorily without specific rules and procedural specifications.

A bureaucratic organization has six basic characteristics:

- A definite hierarchy of authority is defined.

- A division of labor based on functional specialization exists.

- A set of rules governs the actions and responsibilities of individuals holding specific positions.

- Procedural specifications provide a sequence of steps an employee must follow in performing tasks and dealing with problems.

- Employees as well as outsiders are treated in an impersonal manner. (The primary rationale for this characteristic is to prevent excessive personal favoritism on the part of those in power.)

- Technical competence is the primary measure used in selection, retention, or advancement of employees.

A bureaucratic organization is often mechanistic and impersonal. Type III (sensation-thinking) people usually prefer a bureaucratic form of organization.

Information systems in bureaucracies tend to reflect the bureaucratic approach; they are often very formal, have predetermined rules for actions, and may be inflexible. Because of these characteristics, bureaucratic information systems can easily become outdated. In fact, this has happened with several systems at the federal government level in the United States. For example, both the Internal Revenue Service tax processing system and the Social Security system have, at times, been on the verge of collapse as a result of outdated equipment and software.

Matrix Form

Figure 4–3 illustrates a **matrix organizational form** for a large aerospace firm. The primary feature of a matrix organization is duality of authority, information reporting relationships, and systems. A matrix organization is subdivided into functional departments. At the same time, each major program or product is assigned to a different program department. Usually these programs are headed by an individual at the vice-presidential level.

A matrix form of organization is a hybrid of the functional and product forms of organization. For example, individuals within the engineering department report both to functional executives and to program executives.

The matrix form of organization allows firms to adapt quickly to new products. Team members assigned to individual programs usually come from diverse functional backgrounds, therefore bringing a broad and rich level of expertise to an individual program. The primary disadvantage of the matrix form of organization is the ambiguous nature of authority. Individuals who expect a hierarchical, one-superior approach to management are often frustrated in a matrix organization. They do not like

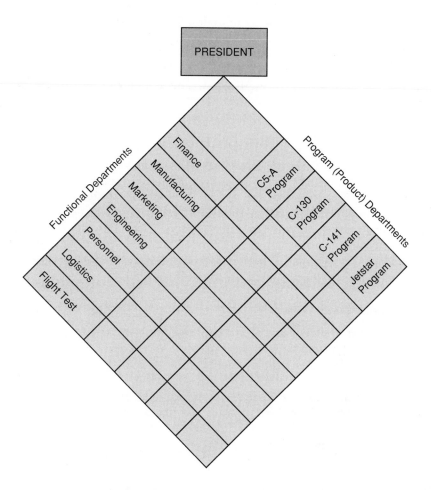

FIGURE 4–3
Matrix Form of
Organization.

reporting to two different command hierarchies, both functional and program. The problem of split loyalties is very difficult for some individuals.

The information system for a matrix form of organization is more
complex than for the other types of organizations. Such a system must be
able to report from both the functional and the program viewpoints.

**Business Func-
tions and Infor-
mation Systems**

Although, as discussed above, the functional form of an organization is
only one of the four common organizational designs, all businesses must
perform the functions upon which the functional form is based. These
functions include finance, production, accounting, and engineering.
Thus, computer information systems tend to be designed around these
functions. In fact, a computer information system can be described as a
federation of **functional information systems**. This concept is illustrated
in Figure 4–4. Specialists in each of the functional areas such as finance,
marketing, production, or accounting are much more familiar with the
information requirements of that function than anyone else in the firm.
These specialists can design systems to produce the information required
to manage their functions. The functional information systems interact
with one another and often share the same data. As discussed in Chapter
13, database management systems greatly enhance the ability of these

functional systems to share the same data. The important point to remember is that these integrated functional information systems form the overall computer information system.

Each of the functional information systems is in turn made up of application systems as shown in Figure 4–4. The accounting information system includes several applications. Each application system is also made up of one or more programs.

Information systems have evolved as federations of functional information systems. However, today there is a move toward viewing the information system of a firm as a whole rather than as individual functional systems. If an information system is going to be used for competitive advantage it is very important that the system be planned and designed from a top-down standpoint. That is, the functional information systems must articulate with one another and use common data. Thus, information systems professionals are involved in a balancing act to build systems that meet the needs of individual functions but at the same time share common data and meet the needs of the organization as a whole.

Organizational Culture and Information Systems

What is Organizational Culture?

The **culture of an organization** is a complex pattern of shared philosophies, ideologies, values, beliefs, assumptions, expectations, attitudes, and norms.[1] Organizational culture includes the following:

1. *Observed behavioral regularities* when people interact, such as organizational rituals and ceremonies and the language commonly used.

2. The *norms* shared by working groups throughout the organization, such as "a fair day's work for a fair day's pay."

3. The *dominant values* held by the organization, such as "product quality" or "price leadership."

4. The *philosophy* that guides an organization's policy toward employees and customers.

5. The *rules* of the game for getting along in the organization or the ropes that a newcomer must learn in order to become an accepted member.

6. The *feeling or climate* conveyed in an organization by the physical layout and the way in which its members interact with customers or other outsiders.[2]

---

[1] R. H. Kilmann, M. J. Saxton, and R. Serpa, "Introduction: Five Key Issues in Understanding and Changing Culture." In R. H. Kilmann, M. J. Saxton, R. Serpa, and Associates (eds.), *Gaining Control of the Corporate Culture* (San Francisco: Jossey-Bass, 1985), 5., cited by D. Hellriegel, J. W. Slocum, Jr., and R. W. Woodman, Organizational Behavior, 5th ed. (St. Paul: West Publishing Company, 1989), 302.

[2] E. H. Schein, *Organizational Culture and Leadership* (San Francisco: Jossey-Bass, 1985), 6., cited by D. Hellriegel, J. W. Slocum, Jr., and R. W. Woodman, *Organizational Behavior*, 5th ed. (St. Paul: West Publishing Company, 1989), 302.

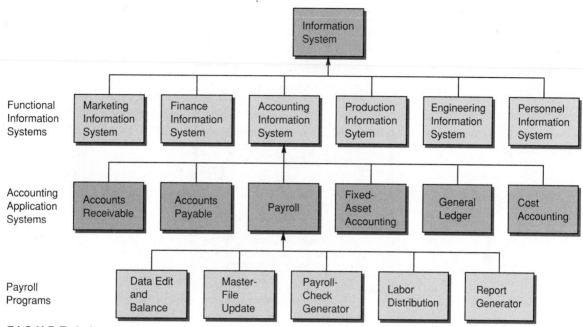

FIGURE 4–4

The Information System as a Federation of Functional Information Systems.

Any information system can be broken down this way into its constituent parts. This hierarchical decomposition of a system is an important tool in understanding complex systems, as discussed in Chapter 16.

As Figure 4–5 illustrates, the content of organizational culture generates manifestations of that culture in terms of goods and services, verbal expressions, behaviors, and emotions. These manifestations are perceived by employees and interpreted by them to form the meaning of organizational culture. The behaviors of individuals within organizations are generally influenced strongly by organizational culture.

Figure 4–6 illustrates the methods that organizations use to maintain their culture. Organizations tend to hire members who fit in with the culture and they also tend to remove or fire members who deviate from the culture. However, other factors often maintain and reinforce the culture. These factors include what managers pay attention to, managers' reactions to organizational crises, managerial role modeling and teaching, criteria used to distribute organizational awards, criteria for selection of personnel and promotion, and organizational ceremonies and rituals.

The Relationships Between Organizational Culture and Information Systems

In general, organizational culture has effects in four key ways. First, culture provides employees with an understanding of the firm's history and current approach. This understanding provides guidance about expected behaviors. Second, organizational culture serves to establish commitment to corporate philosophy and values, thus providing employees with

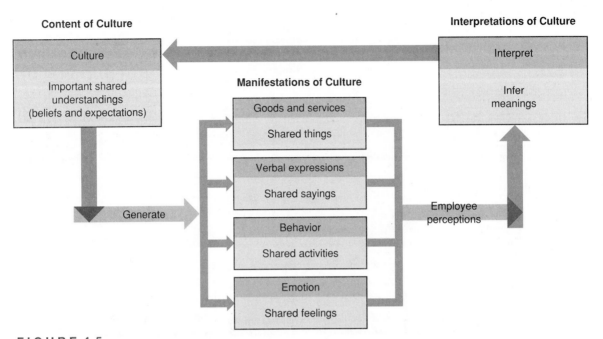

FIGURE 4–5

Cultural Relationships.

Source: D. Hellriegel, J.W. Slocum, Jr., and R.W. Woodman, *Organizational Behavior*, 5th ed. (St. Paul: West Publishing Co., 1989), 312 as adapted from V. Sathe, "Implications of Corporate Culture: A Manager's Guide to Action," *Organizational Dynamics* (Autumn 1983), 8.

shared feelings of working toward goals they believe in. Third, organizational culture provides a control mechanism to channel employee behaviors toward what is desired and away from what is undesired. Finally, there is some evidence that certain organizational cultures are related to greater effectiveness and productivity than others.[3]

Based on our brief review of organizational culture you can see that organizational culture is a powerful influence on the behavior of individuals and the organization as a whole. Since the information system is a major component of organizations, the information system can be influenced substantially by the culture of the organization. For example, the culture of the organization may not reward substantial risk taking. Since the implementation of advanced information systems involves taking substantial risk, an organization that does not reward risk taking might have difficulty with or perhaps might never try to implement a state-of-the-art information system. It is very important to consider the organizational culture when designing a new computer-based information system for an organization. Many information systems have failed simply because they do not fit the organizational culture for which the system was designed.

---

[3] J. Martin and C. Siehl, "Organizational Culture and Counterculture: An Uneasy Symbiosis," *Organizational Dynamics* (Autumn, 1983), 52-64., cited by D. Hellriegel, J. W. Slocum, Jr., and R. W. Woodman, *Organizational Behavior*, 5th ed. (St. Paul: West Publishing Company, 1989), 311–312.

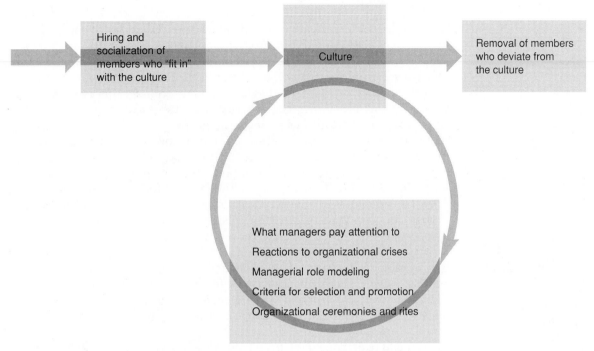

Hiring and socialization of members who "fit in" with the culture

Culture

Removal of members who deviate from the culture

What managers pay attention to

Reactions to organizational crises

Managerial role modeling

Criteria for selection and promotion

Organizational ceremonies and rites

FIGURE 4–6
Methods of Maintaining Organizational Culture.
Source: D. Hellriegel, J.W. Slocum, Jr., and R.W. Woodman, *Organizational Behavior*, 5th ed. (St. Paul: West Publishing Co., 1989), 312 as. adapted from V. Sathe, "How to Decipher and Change Corporate Culture." In R. H. Kilmann, M. J. Saxton, and R. Serpa, *Gaining Control of the Corporate Culture* (San Francisco: Jossey-Bass, 1985), 245.

There is evidence that firms having participative cultures and well-organized workplaces have better performance records than firms not having these characteristics.[4] This evidence is related in two ways to information systems. First, information systems professionals have long known that the success of an information system is closely related to the participation of users in the development of the system. In fact, participative management of information systems development is a crucial practice. Many information systems are developed by teams whose members include individuals from the systems development organization and users from many different functions of the organization.

The second culture–performance relationship to information systems is that a well-organized workplace is both required for successful information systems and is often a result of the development of an information system. In the development of an information system a thorough study must be made of the tasks and information flows that occur within an organization. Then the tasks, the information flows, and the stored information are organized in such a way that a major part can be controlled by a computer. This obviously results in a move toward a more organized workplace.

---

[4] D. Hellriegel, J. W. Slocum, Jr., and R. W. Woodman, *Organizational Behavior*, 5th ed. (St. Paul: West Publishing Company, 1989), 312.

Another impact of organizational culture is its effect on ethics. In the previous chapter we discussed information systems ethics and the fact that employees' ethics are often modeled after the ethics of top management. An organizational culture that emphasizes ethical norms provides support not only for lower-level employees but also for middle- and upper-level employees to behave in an ethical manner. Thus, the presence or absence of ethical behavior in managerial actions is both influenced by the prevailing organizational culture and in turn partially determines the culture's view of ethical issues.[5]

Finally, organizational culture can be a powerful force that resists change. As mentioned above, the culture may not reward risk taking. Certainly, computer-based information systems are very much involved with change. For a company to use the latest information technology, it must be continuously involved with rapid change. Thus, organizational change concepts have significant relationships to information systems. These concepts will be covered in the next section.

Organizational Change and Information Systems

Information technology is one of the largest sources of change in organizations today. Successful use of this technology requires understanding the basic concepts of **organizational change**. In fact, as illustrated in Application 4–2, organizational change is necessary to gain the full benefits from information technology. In this section we will first look at the pressure for and resistance to change, then present a systems model of change, and finally discuss some topics concerning the management of change.

Pressure for and Resistance to Change

Figure 4–7 illustrates the major sources of pressure for change and resistance to change. Of the five items listed under pressure for change, the first three, changing technology, knowledge explosion, and rapid product obsolescence are very much related to information systems. The most dramatic source for changing technology in organizations is information systems technology. This technology is having a dramatic impact on how organizations are formed, how they operate, what their strategies are, and how managers and employees do their work. The knowledge explosion is making the use of information technology to manage this explosion imperative. Finally, most information technology becomes obsolete approximately five years after it was introduced, requiring organizations to change to new technology.

Resistance to change comes from both individuals and organizations. Through selective attention individuals may ignore the need for change. Habits and old ways of doing things are difficult to break. We are all dependent on others to some extent. Thus, we may look to others for endorsement of change before we accept it ourselves. Employees who are highly dependent on their boss for feedback on their performance may not accept change until the boss endorses it. There is a natural tendency among individuals to fear the unknown future. We also tend to resist any change that may lower our income. And finally, many individuals seek the security of the current way of doing things and in some cases regress to previous ways of doing things because they were comfortable.[6]

---

[5] Ibid., 314.
[6] Ibid., 543–545.

APPLICATION 4–2

Business Transformation Is Route to Competitive Advantage

By John Mahnke

While many business strategists will seek to cast information technology in a starring role over the next decade, high returns on investment will be achieved only by those executives also willing to transform virtually all aspects of their businesses.

Adding new technology to old structures, processes and staff operations is likely to yield only incremental gains, and small returns on investment, not the radical improvements that spell sustained competitive advantage.

Business transformation requires top management to establish a clear vision of where a company is headed, users and consultants said.

Then, to harvest information technology's potential to realize that vision, MIS [management information systems] and senior management must work together to implement simultaneously flexible new organizational structures, to redesign business processes and to empower knowledge workers.

Courtaulds Textiles, London, a division of Courtaulds PLC, put these principles to work and as a result cut clothing design cycles from six weeks to three days, said Michael Fisher, head of information technology.

The company also is able to identify more quickly which clothing lines are succeeding and

which are failing, a process which gives it more flexibility in reacting to the market and, in one business unit, has increased return on investment by 214 percent.

Perhaps, however, the most significant mark of Courtaulds' success in transforming its business is that, in the shrinking British textile market, it has survived in a period during which one month saw three competitors go out of business.

As recently as five years ago, senior managers had no involvement in information technology planning and, in fact, half the company's business units were without information technology support, Fisher said.

One of Courtaulds' primary customers is Marks & Spencer PLC, Britain's most popular department store chain. The chain maintains a competitive, multi-supplier policy, however, and Courtauld's senior management, which was pressured by competition from imports, more fashion lines per season, the fickleness of consumers, and low margins in an established industry, realized a radical new approach to this customer, and others, was required.

The chairman and the board responded by transforming the company's strategy into one in which information technology became part of the formal business plan. End-user-operated computer-aided design tools were

put into place; they cut product development time and improved the quality of processes. And a pioneering use of electronic data interchange improved management control over production and suppliers and differentiated Courtaulds from its competitors, Fisher said.

A key initiative in Courtaulds' business transformation was to empower its field executives at the profit-center level with systems that enabled them to make informed, strategic decisions quickly. Business analysts designed the systems. The business units retain responsibility for running and maintaining the systems.

"We're embarking on a different form of competition," global in nature, for which many companies prepared during the 1980s by restructuring to become "lean and mean," added Stewart Richards, [director of Nolan, Norton & Co.'s business architecture practice].

Now, however, noted Charles Feld, chief information officer at Frito-Lay, Inc., the task for companies is to become "big and mean," to build a company combining the coordination and economic clout of a big company with the responsiveness and flexibility to handle niche markets that decentralization provides.

Adapted with permission from *MIS Week* (March 12, 1990), p. 29. Copyright Fairchild Publications, 1990.

Organizations and groups also resist change. Groups within the organization may perceive change as a threat to their power and influence. The organizational structure itself is often an impediment to change. After all, a structure of an organization implies some rigidity and stability. Organizations generally don't perform well when rapid change is occurring, thus some stability is necessary.

Some organizations may want to implement change but simply do not have the resources to do so. In fact, in the area of information systems it is very easy to underestimate the resources required to implement a new

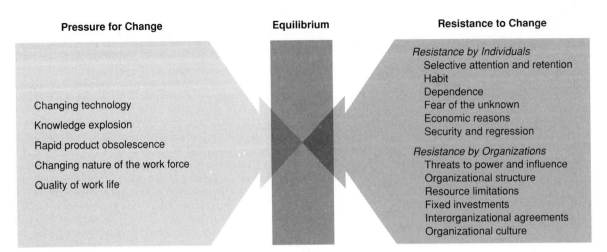

FIGURE 4–7
Pressure for and Resistance to Change in Organizations.
Adapted with permission from D. Hellriegel, J. W. Slocum, Jr., and R. W. Woodman, *Organizational Behavior*, 5th ed. (St. Paul: West Publishing Company, 1989), 550.

system, which comprise much more than the cost of the hardware and software. There is also the cost of training employees and the cost of lost productivity during the initial training.

Investments that have already been made can hamper change. For example, a firm may have spent substantial amounts for new hardware and software that doesn't perform as well as they would like. This firm may prefer a different system, but cannot afford one because of the fixed investment in the current system that performs at a suboptimal level.

Agreements with other organizations can delay change. For example, labor agreements that specify certain work rules may slow down a change to new systems. Finally, as we discussed previously in this chapter, organizational culture has a powerful influence on the organization and its members. It can either impede or facilitate change.[7]

A Systems Model of Change

The **systems model of change** presented in Figure 4–8 depicts the organization as five interacting components: people, task, strategy, structure, and technology. These components can serve as a focus for planned change. The people, of course, are the individuals working in the organization. The tasks are the jobs that are to be done in the organization. The strategy is the overall approach the organization uses to achieve its goals. The structure component is the communication, authority, and responsibility systems within the organization. And finally, technology is the techniques and problem-solving methods, including information systems, used in the organization. These five components are highly interdependent. Changing one component generally affects or changes

---

[7] Ibid., 545–548.

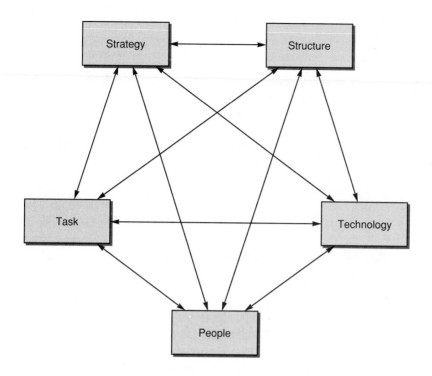

FIGURE 4-8
A Systems Model of
Change.
Reprinted with permission
from D. Hellriegel, J. W.
Slocum, Jr., and R. W.
Woodman, *Organizational
Behavior*, 5th ed. (St. Paul:
West Publishing Company,
1989), 553.

another component. Thus, a system approach to change requires a thorough understanding of all five variables before changing any of them. This understanding is crucial in the implementation of a new information system.[8]

Approaches to Organizational Change

Many approaches have been proposed and used to produce organizational change. In this section we will explore two of these approaches that are closely related to information systems. These approaches, which focus on tasks and technology, are job design and high performance–high commitment work systems.[9]

Job design is a deliberate change in the way work is performed in order to increase employee motivation, involvement, and efficiency. Some of the approaches used in job design are job enlargement, job enrichment, redesign of tasks, and job rotation. In the design of a new information system, the systems analyst is deeply involved in job design. The analyst not only designs the tasks to be performed on the computer, but also designs the tasks that are performed by humans within the system. This job redesign produces change in the organization.

---

[8] Ibid., 552–553.
[9] The concepts covered in this section are based upon D. Hellriegel, J. W. Slocum, Jr. and R. W. Woodman, *Organizational Behavior*, 5th ed. (St. Paul: West Publishing Company, 1989), 572–576.

As the analyst designs the system, she must design the manual tasks so that they fit the individuals who are to perform them. Thus, the tasks have to be interesting. Sometimes systems fail because the tasks left for humans to perform are of low interest. However, in most cases computers perform the mundane and routine portions of the job, leaving the more interesting tasks for humans to perform.

Another approach to organizational change that is highly related to information systems is **high performance–high commitment work systems**. In these work systems a highly participative management structure and work culture is created to engender a sense of ownership in the work force. Employees work in teams and are responsible for their own performance appraisals, devising solutions to many problems, some scheduling, and so on. High performance–high commitment work systems are designed to foster a work culture having the following characteristics:

1. *Delegation.* People who have the most relevant and timely information and the appropriate skills are given responsibility for decisions.

2. *Teamwork across boundaries.* All employees are focused on servicing the product and the customer rather than focusing on their own function or department.

3. *Empowerment.* All employees are expected to accept and exercise the responsibility necessary to do their jobs and to help others accomplish their jobs.

4. *Integration of people and technology.* The people are in charge of the technology instead of the technology being in charge of the people.

5. *A shared sense of purpose.* People share a vision of the organization's purposes and the methods for accomplishing these purposes.

Many firms are finding that a high performance–high commitment work system is essential to obtaining the best results from high technology information systems. For example, the Shenandoah Life Insurance Company in Roanoke, Virginia recently introduced a new state-of-the-art, computer-based information system. They introduced the system into the old type of work system, which was highly structured. Each individual was responsible for certain tasks. Shenandoah found that not only did the output of the organization fail to increase, it actually decreased. They changed their work culture to a high performance–high commitment work system with teams of employees who were cross-trained to do most of the tasks that were required to process life insurance policies with the new system. This change resulted in a dramatic increase in productivity with a reduced work force.

In summary, information systems and organizational change are highly intertwined. Information systems are one of the largest pressures for organizational change. At the same time, analysts who attempt to implement changes in information systems must take an overall approach that considers all the factors involved in organizational change. Implementing an information system is not just an isolated act that does not have impacts on other components of the organization. Also, organizations now realize that to benefit from high technology information systems they must often change the work culture of the organization.

Summary

- Information systems operate within organizations. The behaviors of organizations have significant impacts on information systems.

- Since information systems operate within organizations they must be tailored to fit the form or the design of an organization.

- A functional form of organization is based on major managerial functions, such as engineering, marketing, and finance.

- A product form of organization organizes the firm by major product or product groups.

- A bureaucratic form of organization assumes that employees need specific rules and procedural specifications to perform their job satisfactorily.

- A matrix form of organization is a hybrid between the product and functional forms. Its major characteristic is a duality of reporting to both functional executives and program or product executives.

- A computer information system can be described as a federation of functional information systems.

- The culture of an organization is a complex pattern of shared philosophies, ideologies, values, beliefs, assumptions, expectations, attitudes, and norms.

- The behaviors of individuals within organizations are generally strongly influenced by organizational culture.

- Organizational culture provides employees with an understanding of the firm's history and current approach.

- Organizational culture serves to establish commitment to corporate philosophies and values.

- Organizational culture provides a control mechanism to channel employee behaviors toward desired and away from undesired behaviors.

- Certain organizational cultures are related to greater effectiveness and productivity than others.

- The information system, being a major component of organizations, can be influenced substantially by the culture of an organization.

- Participative management of information systems development is a crucial practice.

- Information systems and well-organized workplaces go hand in hand.

- An organizational culture that emphasizes ethical norms provides support to employees for behaving in an ethical manner.

- Information technology is one of the largest sources of change in organizations today.

- Resistance to change comes from both individuals and organizations.
- The systems model of change depicts the organization as five interacting components: people, tasks, strategy, structure, and technology.
- Two approaches to organizational change are job design and high performance–high commitment work systems.
- Job design is a deliberate change in the way work is performed in order to increase employee motivation, involvement, and efficiency.
- Many firms are finding that a high performance–high commitment work system is essential to obtain the best results from high technology information systems.

Key Terms

Functional organizational form

Product organizational form

Bureaucratic organizational form

Matrix organizational form

Functional information systems

Culture of an organization

Organizational change

Systems model of change

Job design

High performance–high commitment work systems

Review Questions

1. What is the functional form of organization?
2. What is the product form of organization?
3. Certain aspects of information systems may be overlooked in functional and product forms of organization. What are these aspects?
4. What is meant by a federation of functional information systems?
5. What are the six components of organizational culture?
6. What are the methods that organizations use to maintain their culture?
7. What are the relationships between organizational culture and information systems?
8. How are organizational change and information systems related?
9. What are the sources of pressure for and resistance to change?
10. Why is a systems model of change important to the implementation of information systems?
11. Discuss how two approaches to organizational change are related to information systems.
12. What are the characteristics of a high performance–high commitment work system?

Discussion Questions and Cases

1. How would the information systems department fit within the different forms of organizational structure?

2. Would a matrix form of organization be useful in an information systems development effort? Explain your answer.

3. What impacts do you think that advanced information systems will have on organizational structure in the future?

4. The McGregor Company has recently implemented a new state-of-the-art information system. They had hoped to process customer orders in a much more expeditious manner with less cost. However, they are finding that their costs have increased while the time it takes to process a customer order is the same. Discuss some of the reasons why this failure may have occurred.

5. Sam Oliver is the new vice president of information systems for the Atlantic Corporation. Sam likes information systems technology very much and is convinced that the way to develop better information systems for the corporation is solely through the application of technology. Has Sam ignored any of the other components of an organization? Is he likely to have difficulty in implementing his new information systems? Support your answers.

6. The Champion Corporation is experiencing a severe shortage of space in its administrative offices. One proposal to alleviate this space shortage is to encourage workers whose jobs are closely tied to working with computers to work at home. Those advocating the work-at-home plan argue that individuals like programmers will be much more productive at home and perhaps would enjoy their work more since they would not have to commute every day of the week. In addition, employees with small children could be with their children while they were working. Some of the strong supporters of this idea feel that there will be basic changes in organizations in the future as more and more administrative tasks are performed at the computer. Would you advocate a company adopting this approach? What are its advantages and disadvantages?

INFORMATION SYSTEMS STRATEGIES

Playing Integration Politics

By Alan J. Ryan

Soft-soled shoes and kid gloves may become standard attire in the 1990s for organizations carrying out integration projects. After all, when toes must be stepped on and egos crushed, it should be done as gently as possible.

Experienced information systems managers and consultants say that technology is often the least difficult aspect of integration projects. Managing politics and user fears can be a bigger challenge, they say.

People problems are likely "whenever you start to move toward common and shared data," says Dudley Cooke, president of The Executive Insight Group in Bryn Mawr, Pa. "If the people in the division have the attitude that 'this is my data; I own it,' you'll have a war from the start."

When a company decides to share information—whether across business units or interdepartmentally—business managers and other information "owners" often feel backed into a corner. Some may even react by trying to sabotage the project.

What's IS [information systems] to do? Experts say that building strong working relationships before any changes take place is key. SO is a willingness to provide detailed information on the integration process. Both approaches can help stanch the inevitable fears and internal politics that arise as businesses are transformed and workers change the way they go about their jobs.

And problems do arise. Just ask Larry Potter, director of IS at American Industries, Inc., a steel service center company in Portland, Ore. He's seen the best laid plans of management and IS put into slow motion.

When Potter joined the company's American Steel subsidiary, the firm had plans to redesign its business systems so that information could be shared across independent business units. Potter's department was called in to help, and users were suspicious, he says.

"They were afraid DP would come in and say, 'This is how you will have to run your businesses,'" Potter says. The five profit centers that make up American Steel feared changes they thought might hurt their bottom line.

An Old Tale

Potter's story is not unusual. Kathleen Lennon, director of corporate systems at fuel conglomerate Coastal Corp. in Houston, says integration always involves political problems.

However, she believes the primary role of IS is not problem solving but acting as a discussion facilitator: "The data belongs to the individual organization, and we need to work that out. It is not our data."

In the worst cases, IS executives say, politics can indefinitely delay or scuttle an integration project.

At one Massachusetts-based life insurance company, for example, the biggest barrier to integration is the remnants of a former chief executive officer's philosophy of product line autonomy.

Today, a new CEO is pushing for greater information sharing, but the IS vice president there, who requested anonymity, says the transition has been slow and difficult. "There is a lot of parochialism, with people saying, 'This is my division data, my client base, and I don't want anyone else fooling around with it,'" he says.

Unfortunately, the roots of many of the political problems surrounding integration can be traced back to how organizations automated various functions.

In many companies, the passing of strict centralized computing induced individual departments and functions to computerize independently. But smoothing out the resulting technological patchwork can be very difficult, says Mike Natan, senior vice president of Philadelphia-based Cigna Systems, the information subsidiary of insurance giant Cigna Corp.

Natan approached integration by conducting a re-engineering study that zeroes in on Cigna's business strategy. The effort involves interviews with users to help focus the business strategy.

Once the strategy is clear, the IS staff examines the systems and "takes the approach of 'How do we meet that strategy, unconstrained by the systems that exist today?'" Natan says. That way, there is no question that IS is only acting to support the business plans.

Another built-in tension arises when user departments think of information as their own, Cooke says.

"Nobody owns the data," he says. "People have stewardship responsibility for the data to protect it and have an obligation to share it with the people who have the need to know."

Another way companies can overcome fear and avoid squabbles is to get users to buy into the project early, Cooke says.

"If you have the right kind of working and partner relationships to begin with, that provides you with a springboard to move forward with less difficulties," Cooke says. IS managers who lack these relationships may be in trouble, he adds.

Natan agrees, saying integration champions should spend time with middle managers to help them understand the roles they play in the process. "You can't just ignore them," he says.

When the integration takes place, it may cause jobs to be eliminated or changed, and workers may resist retraining. One way some companies smooth over the issue is by relocating jobs to other locations or by totally restructuring departments, according to M. Victor Janulaitis, CEO of Positive Support Review, Inc., a change management consultancy in Los Angeles.

"You have got to shake the tree in order for people to do their jobs differently," Janulaitis adds.

Flooding the opponents of such a project with information is also important.

"The No. 1 enemy of internal politics is facts," says Art Schneiderman, vice president of quality and productivity improvement at Analog Devices, Inc. in Norwood, Mass.

At Analog, Schneiderman says, an integration philosophy has been in place for years. "When you start to limit accessibility to information, then you create a barrier against cross-functional problem solving and cross-functional understanding," he says.

Historically, each Analog manufacturing division maintained its own information systems for nonfinancial data. If a customer wanted information on the product reliability of another division's product, for example, "We had to find out the product and the division and then go to them to see their information on reliability," Schneiderman says.

Moreover, he says, many divisions had different methodologies for measuring reliability, which often left customers confused.

Today, Analog is working to correct problems by standardizing measurement processes and following the Japanese technique of quality function deployment, Schneiderman says, which is the ability to design products rapidly that meet customer needs while ensuring the soundness of the manufacturing process.

However, IS managers and consultants say that information dissemination won't work in companies where middle management's fears make whole departments reluctant to participate in integration projects.

Cooke says that high-level managers as a rule tend to take a more global view of how integration can help the company. In contrast, midlevel managers tend to take a bit narrower view of their jobs, he says, and are likely to be fearful of and resistant to the process. They often will try to slow or sabotage a project by saying that it won't work, that it is too expensive or that it is wrong, Cooke says.

"What they are really saying," he explains, "is 'Don't fiddle with my turf.'"

At the middle management level, Natan adds, "You are now dealing with people who feel changes are not in their control and are going to affect them. The threat is higher to the middle manager, and therefore resistance is higher."

Beyond Fear

To get beyond the fear of integration at American Steel, Potter gathered users from each profit center and asked what kinds of information they would not be willing to share with other profit centers. They were told, "If there is data that you don't want other folks to see, we will lock it up and not let them see it," Potter says.

In 1984 a shared inventory database was up and running, giving American Steel's five subsidiaries the ability to search one another's stock lists for the best price on steel for customers. The units realized that the more information they had about each other, the better off they would be, Potter recalls: "They would say, 'Gee, it would be helpful if I could see your data. I'll trade you my data for your data.'"

This kind of sharing has helped the company's bottom line. "In 1982, we were an $80 million company and marginally profitable," Potter says. "In 1989, we were a $115 million company and very profitable."

During that period, American also increased its market share while trimming the number of employees from 500 to 300, Potter says. Moreover, 1989 inventory levels dropped to $25 million, down from $40 million in 1982, he adds.

Discussion Questions

1.   Who "owns" the data in a firm? Who should have stewardship responsibility over the data, the users or the information systems organization?

2.   What approach would you use to help avoid the political problems associated with data integration?

Ryan is a *Computerworld* senior writer.

Reprinted with permission from *Computerworld* (April 2, 1990), pp. 65, 78. Copyright 1990 by CW Publishing, Inc. Framingham, MA 01701.

CHAPTER

5

Business Strategy and the Use of Information Systems for Competitive Advantage

In the mid-1980s many business firms began to view information systems as tools to gain advantages over their competitors. These systems are often called **strategic information systems**. The use of information systems to support management planning and control has always been directed at making business operations more effective and efficient, but this emphasis on using information systems to gain competitive advantage is new. Several major firms have gained significant competitive advantages through the strategic use of information technology. For example, American Airlines Sabre System and United Airlines Apollo System are used by reservation agents to book flights on all airlines. Each system was originally designed to show the owners' (American's or United's) flights first on the computer screen when agents checked for available flights. Thus, agents were more likely to book passengers on an American or a United Flight. These systems gave such a competitive advantage to their owners that competing airlines successfully appealed to both the courts and the government to change the order in which flights appear on these systems' screens.

Another example of a firm that has used information technology competitively is American Hospital Supply. This firm was the first to install on-line order entry computer terminals in hospitals, thus making it extremely convenient and fast to order hospital supplies from American Hospital Supply. American Hospital Supply initially gained a competitive advantage. But, because of their failure to continue to innovate, the company fell behind competitors who imitated and surpassed them. American Hospital Supply was purchased by Baxter-Travenol and after a massive effort they were able to catch up with their competitors. American Hospital Supply's experience illustrates the importance of continual innovation if a firm is to maintain a competitive advantage.

For a firm to use information systems for competitive advantage, the strategy should be a part of the firm's overall business strategy. Thus, in this chapter we will first discuss developing a business strategy. Then we will look at the difference between competitive advantage and competitive necessity. Next, we will explore ways that firms can develop a competitive information systems strategy. And finally we will look at some of the risks in the use of information systems for a competitive advantage.

Introduction

An organization's **business strategy** is its plan of moves and approaches, devised by management, to produce successful organizational performance. A strategy is in effect management's game plan for success.[1] A business strategy has five interrelated tasks,[2] illustrated in Figure 5–1. First, management must develop a concept of the business and form a vision of where the organization is going, thus establishing a mission. Information systems can be a major part of that mission. For example, an oil company operating in California has decided that its mission is not only to provide petroleum products to trucking firms, but also to provide

Developing a Business Strategy

---

[1] A. A. Thompson, Jr. and A. J. Strickland, III, *Strategic Management Concepts and Cases* (Homewood, IL: Richard D. Irwin, 1990), 3.
[2] Ibid., 4–13.

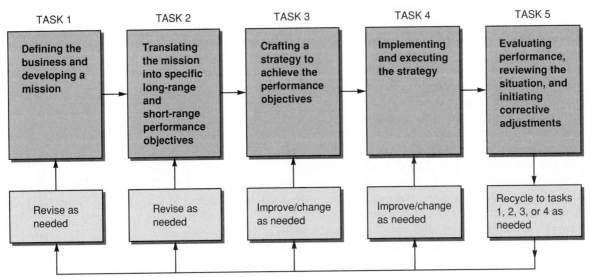

F I G U R E   5–1

The Five Tasks of Strategic Management.

Reprinted with permission from A. A. Thompson, Jr. and A. J. Stickland, III, *Strategic Management Concepts and Cases*, (Homewood, IL: 1992), Richard D. Irwin, 4.

them information about the operation of their trucks. Operating statistics on the trucks that refill at one of the oil company's stations are entered into the oil company's computer system, statistics such as the mileage on the truck, the date and time of refill, the driver's identification, the destination, and the cargo. These statistics and others calculated from the input data are provided to the trucking firm at no cost. Thus, trucking firms have a powerful incentive to buy diesel and other services from this oil company. The oil company has changed its mission through the use of information systems. This system obviously provides a competitive advantage over other oil companies.

The next task in the strategic management process is a translation of the mission into specific long-range and short-range performance objectives. These objectives must be concrete, measurable performance targets that specify what the organization will do to meet the overall objectives. Each organizational unit within the firm should have written objectives that support their overall objectives.

A third task is the crafting of a strategy to achieve the targeted performance. In this step the details of the strategic plan are delineated. Crafting a strategy has a strong entrepreneurial character. Managers must make decisions about committing resources and taking risks for new ventures. Of course, all of the strategy is not based on new ventures. Much of the strategy should be based on approaches that have been used in the past and are still working well. In this step the use of information systems to gain a competitive advantage should be looked at closely. For example, development of an information system that makes ordering products from the firm easier than from the firm's competitor may get the firm significant competitive advantage.

The next task in strategic management is the effective and efficient implementation and execution of the chosen strategy. This step is the most complicated and time-consuming part of strategic management. Developing a strategic plan is relatively straightforward. As we discussed in the previous chapter, implementing a new information system is a process of organizational change. Certain approaches to the development of information systems are more successful than others. These will be covered in more depth in Part IV of this text.

The final task in the strategic management process is evaluating performance, reviewing the situation, and initiating corrective action that may change any or all of the above four tasks. Information systems play a crucial role in this task because they provide a substantial portion of the feedback information that is necessary to evaluate the organization's performance.

In summary, a business strategy is necessary for any firm's success. Increasingly, information systems are becoming a major component of business strategies. Firms such as Federal Express (see Application 5–1) see information technology as absolutely key to their operations. Managements realize that if they are to gain the advantages that information technology offers, they must incorporate the plans for using this technology in their overall business strategy. Information systems can become a major product or service of the organization or they can become a major factor in support of a firm's service to customers.

Competitive Advantage Versus Competitive Necessity

Before looking at the strategies that may bring a firm competitive advantage, we should first distinguish between competitive advantage and competitive necessity. Strategic **competitive advantage** from information systems refers to the application of innovative information technology for the purpose of getting ahead of competitors. For example, a system that allows a company to increase its market share gives that company a competitive advantage. On the other hand, the use of an information system for **competitive necessity** refers to the application of information technology for the purpose of keeping up with competitors. For example, most banks now have automatic teller machines (ATMs). Therefore, a bank currently deciding to invest in ATMs is doing so because of competitive necessity and not competitive advantage.

The distinction between competitive advantage and competitive necessity is important. The difference between the two approaches lies primarily in the amount of risk a particular firm wishes to take. Applying information systems to gain competitive advantage may entail significant risks since the information system may not be successful. However, a firm that is attempting to gain competitive advantage can expect much higher returns if the system is successful. On the other hand, implementing an information system for competitive necessity means that the firm is, in effect, copying a system that another firm has developed in order to keep up with the competing firm. This approach obviously has lower risks of failure, but the firm may lose significant business returns while it is trying to catch up by installing information technology similar to that of the competitor. Both approaches are valid. In fact, most firms would use a combination of competitive advantage and competitive necessity approaches with more aggressive and risk-taking firms going more toward the competitive advantage end of the spectrum.

Being the Best in Business

By Joseph Maglitta

Federal Express Corp. Chief Executive Officer Frederick W. Smith doesn't have a personal computer on his desk. "I never have liked to type," admits the amiable founder of the world's largest express transportation company.

But don't be fooled. Smith's Memphis office is among the few corners of the $8 billion company that doesn't boast the latest computer and telecommunications technology.

It's no surprise that Smith, 46, credits the effective use of technology with Fedex's having won the 1990 Malcom Baldrige National Quality Award. Technology, Smith says, "is absolutely the key to our operations."

To keep abreast of new developments, Smith, a Yale graduate and former U.S. Marine Corps officer, reads voraciously, consuming computer and defense trade newspapers, Wall Street analyses and business publications. He has strong opinions on technology and how it should be used.

On the Role of Information Technology in Quality

Smith says the quality goals that technology must support at Fedex are as simple as they are awesome: "100% on-time deliveries, 100% accurate information on every shipment to every location in the world and 100% customer satisfaction."

The task is enormous. Fedex delivers 1.5 million packages every workday to 127 countries around the world with the help of its 420 aircraft, 94,000 employees and 30,000 computer- and radio-equipped delivery vehicles.

The entire quality process depends on statistical quantification, according to Smith, which in turn depends on state-of-the-

art technology. "That measurement system is the key link in our overall quality effort. Without it, there would be no quality, no Cosmos or Cosmos 2 or Cosmos^2," Smith says, referring to the company's various package tracking systems.

"We had to come up with a system that actually measured our performance on every transaction–regardless of the fact that we're talking about hundreds of thousands of transactions," Smith explains.

"[You must have] the ability to manage information on a real-time basis and be able to slice and dice it to really understand what's happening in the operation. Whether it's the number of rejects per 10,000 units of widgets or measuring the SQI indicator at Fedex, if you don't have the ability to measure that and improve on it, then you're not going to be effective. And, in most cases, that has to be produced by the application of information and telecommunications technology."

Smith can barely contain his enthusiasm about the systems–or technology in general. "It's amazing," he says. "You go into [Cosmos] and ask where that shipment is, and 99.99% of the time it's going to tell you within a very short period of time exactly where that thing is. In fact, it's generally limited by the time it takes the systems to dial up and get into the computer."

On Measuring Service Quality

"We used what we call SQI pronounced sky) service quality indicators. We have 12 things that we know disappoint our customers, and we measure them every single day–how many packages were delivered on the wrong day, how many were delivered on the right day, how many packages were

delivered late, how many we damaged, how many billing corrections we had to make and things like that.

"These 12 indicators are weighted in terms of the way they are viewed by the customer. If we lose a package, it's rated 10 times more than if something is a little bit late."

On Fedex's Philosophy of Information Technology

"Our approach has always been more pedestrian than a lot of people. I have always felt . . . that the application of information and telecom technology has to be very incremental and very user-friendly. Its main goal must be to improve quality one way or another, whether it's the quality of the employee's work life or the quality of the information to the customer. [We don't do] what a lot of people have tried to do—use technology to save labor or to be Big Brother to employees."

On Technology Spending

"We certainly are pouring the coals, trying to exploit information and telecommunications advantages. We do a lot of justifying; we don't want to just spend money for the hell of it. We think we understand where the high leverage points are, and when we put the money in there we can get a good return on it."

On Tracking Technology's Success

"We monitor the rollout of all our strategic projects, many of which are information- and telecommunications-based. Presentations are made monthly to the entire senior management group of 12 people, which includes the chief operating officer and the chief information officer."

On Organizing Information Systems

"We consider our information technology division a line organization; it's an operating unit that is absolutely involved in the day to day operation of the company. We measure its performance. I'm just as close to the information technology division as to our sales division—and the salespeople are the ones who bring in all the bacon."

On IS Project Failure

"[Unsuccessful projects] are usually run by people who have unrealistic expectations of human nature on the one side and funded by corporate executives who have a very poor knowledge of what the technology can do on the other side. I think that people who follow that model in the future are going to be competitively annihilated."

Federal Express uses a team approach that gives IS [information systems] a degree of participation unmatched in most organizations. Smith depends heavily on COO James L. Barksdale, a former IBM executive who previously ran Fedex's Informa-tion and Telecommunications Division, and CIO Ron J. Ponder.

Because of his appreciation of technology, Smith keeps his IS staff hopping. "I keep asking for the moon, and they keep saying they can only provide a small satellite," he says. Judging by Fedex's recent technological accomplishments, that may be enough.

Adapted with permission from *Computerworld* (February 25, 1991), pp. 61, 64. Copyright 1991 by C. W. Publishing, Inc., Framingham, MA 01701.

Competitive Advantage Strategies

In this section of the chapter we will first discuss how to look for competitive advantages and then cover an example of one firm's planning process for a competitive advantage.

How to Look for a Competitive Advantage

Bakos and Treacy argue that competitive advantage stems from two factors: **comparative efficiency**, meaning that a firm can produce goods and services at lower cost than its competitors; and **bargaining power**, which allows a firm to settle bagaining situations with its customers and suppliers to its own advantage. As shown in Figure 5–2 each of these factors are in turn influenced by even more fundamental factors: bargaining power by search-related costs, unique product features, and switching costs; and comparative efficiency by internal efficiency and interorganizational efficiency. **Search-related costs** refer to the firm's, supplier's, or customer's cost of shopping for the best prices. **Unique product features** are the features of products or services that make them different from those of a competitor. **Switching costs** refers to the costs that either customers or suppliers must incur if they cease doing business with a firm. **Internal efficiency** refers to the level of costs that a firm incurs inside the firm. **Interorganizational efficiency** refers to the cost that firms incur in its dealings with external organizations.[3] Application 5–2 illustrates how global networks are being used to decrease the costs of both inter- and intraorganizational communications.

Figure 5–3 provides examples of ways that competitive advantage can be obtained for each of the factors displayed in Figure 5–2. As can be seen from the examples in Figure 5–3, there is a wide variety of possible strategies that have the potential to produce competitive advantage. However, remember that to gain competitive advantage a firm must do these things before its competitors, otherwise the firm would be using these strategies because of competitive necessity. In the next section we will examine how one firm approaches the planning process for competitive advantage.

---

[3] J. Y. Bakos and M. E. Treacy, "Information Technology and Corporate Strategy: A Research Perspective," *MIS Quarterly* (June 1986), 107–119.

FIGURE 5–2

The Factors that Influence Competitive Advantage.

Reprinted with special permission from J. Y. Bakos and M. E. Treacy, "Information Technology and Corporate Strategy: A Research Perspective," *MIS Quarterly* (June 1986), 114. Copyright (1986) by the Society for Information Management and The Management Systems Research Center at the University of Minnesota.

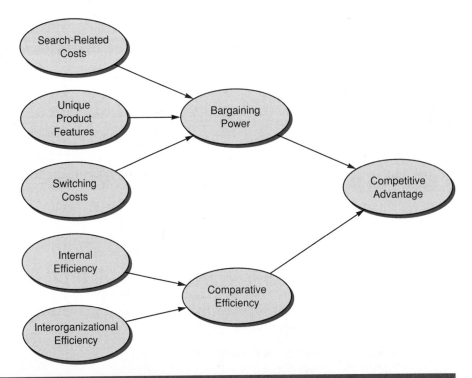

  APPLICATION 5–2

Globalization: Key to Corporate Competition

By Elisabeth Horwitt

The use of global networking to gain competitive advantage is just taking off among the more savvy international firms, according to a recently completed study by KPMG Peat Marwick. However, most of the 50 firms profiled in the study use their international networks to support basic operations and justify the high-speed backbones on the basis of cost, said William Synnott, a director at Peat Marwick subsidiary Nolan Norton & Co.

The one-year study "focused on how networks are used in support of corporate globalization," as well as emerging trends within "the regulatory, political and market structure in which global networks operate," Synnott said.

A number of companies interviewed by Nolan Norton had indeed found inventive ways to use their global networks to outmaneuver their rivals. One set of strategic applications ran on delivery networks, which are used to bring the company closer to the customer, supplier or other business partner. Such applications include electronic data interchange, automated teller machine networks and airline reservation systems.

Firms that wrung the most advantage from delivery networks used them for much more than simple provision of customer services. For example, American Express Travel Related Services has made digitized images, rather than copies, of customers' statements so that they can be electronically transmitted not only to the customer, but also to different parts of the credit card firm.

The data is then used in strategic applications such as "micro marketing on the basis of consumers' buying habits," Synnott said.

Even more strategic potential is to be found in the information type of network, which is "used to leverage total staff and resources, bringing a totality of ideas, skills and experiences together," Synnott said. This is important in a firm where such resources are scattered around the world, he added.

At Digital Equipment Corp., for example, an engineer "puts a problem on the network of 50,000 terminals and VAXs around the world, goes to bed and the next morning finds half a dozen solutions," Synnott said.

International clothing retailer Benetton uses its network to collect daily sales data from its outlets so that it can "track what's hot and what's not moving" for planning purposes, Synnott said.

Bargaining Power

Search-Related Costs

—Lower cost of "shopping" via links to suppliers; control, observe, or profit from shopping via links to customers
—Improve customers' ability to shop for a third-party product that generates fee income or additional sales of primary product
—Suggest alternative product specifications that reduce customers' costs or improve customers' performance
—Get the best available prices on purchased commodity materials
—Alert customers to opportunities to obtain volume discounts by altering order patterns slightly

Unique Product Features

—Make product easier or less expensive to select, order, handle, use, or account for
—Enhance product image as state-of-the-art
—Improve customer service by identifying and reporting problems more quickly, allowing more accurate diagnosis and faster response
—Provide immediate feedback on product availability and price
—Lower required inventory levels

Raising Switching Costs

—Raise users' need to retrain personnel, to modify operating procedures, or to invest in new or additional hardware or software if they change to a different system
—Threaten change in status of personnel if automated system is replaced by nonautomated system

Comparative Efficiency

Internal Efficiency

—Lower inventory costs by allowing "just-in-time" delivery
—Encourage standardization of data representation, making data easier to manipulate and analyze internally
—Capture data more quickly, leading to faster analysis and shorter response time

Interorganizational Efficiency

—"Export work" by getting customers or suppliers to do data entry and editing
—Allow customers to "shop" and check order status electronically, without tying up customer service representatives
—Provide benefits of vertical integration (more control, coordination, lower costs) without requiring actual ownership of other organizations
—Facilitate cross-selling of additional or higher margin products
—Permit inexpensive, rapid electronic transmission of sales and service messages
—Increase sales of company products, due to ease and efficiency of ordering and to favorable display on order-entry screens
—Remove a level of the distribution chain by going direct to customer or user rather than through an intermediary
—Capture more precise, timely usage data, allowing production scheduling according to use rather than according to sale or shipment
—Evaluate quickly and economically the effects of advertising, rebates, and other marketing programs
—Extend market reach to customers who could not be economically served by conventional field sales calls
—Relate sales message, including price and other terms, to buyer's previous experience with seller and with product
—Ship in more economical lots and be prepared to receive incoming goods by communicating with transportation companies
—Deliver products or services (e.g., software or financial advice) electronically, monitor compliance with policies related to customers, dealers, etc.
—Observe ordering pattern for, and usage of, competitors' products

FIGURE 5–3
How Competitive Advantage Can Be Obtained.
Adapted with special permission from H. R. Johnston, and M. R. Vitale, "Creating Competitive Advantage with Interorganizational Information Systems," MIS Quarterly (June 1988), 157–158. Copyright (1988) by the Society for Information Management and The Management Information Systems Research Center at the University of Minnesota.

A Planning Process for Strategic Information Systems

Risks in the Use of Information Systems for Competitive Advantage

GTE is a diversified international telecommunications and electronics company with 185,000 employees and revenues of over $14 billion.[4] GTE's information management (IM) staff saw the planning process as twofold:

1. Introduce management to the new perspective of the use of information systems for a strategic competitive advantage and secure management support.

2. Create a mechanism for generating and evaluating strategic information systems (SIS) proposals.

To accomplish these tasks they designed a five-phase strategic information systems planning process as displayed in Figure 5–4. Phases A through C dealt only with the management of the information management function while in phases D and E the planning process was expanded to all the corporate executives. The strategy was to introduce the strategic information systems concept and refine the idea-generation methodology within the information management staff before going on to the corporation as a whole in phases D and E. The idea-generation meetings that occurred in phases B, C, and E consisted of seven individual steps as displayed in Figure 5–5.

FIGURE 5–4
Strategic Information Systems (SIS) Planning Process.

Reprinted with special permission from N. Rackoff, C. Wiseman and W. A. Ullrich, "Information Systems for Competitive Advantage, Implementation of a Planning Process," *MIS Quarterly* (December 1985), 285. Copyright (1985) by the Society for Information Management and The Management Information Systems Research Center at the University of Minnesota.

Phase	Activity	Content	Purpose
A	Introduce IM chief executive to SIS concepts	Overview of SIS concepts; cases of SIS applications in other companies	Gain approval to proceed with SIS idea-generation meeting for IM group
B	Conduct SIS idea-generation meeting for IM middle management	Execute SIS idea-generation methodology; evaluate SIS ideas	Test SIS idea-generation methodology; identify significant SIS ideas for executive consideration
C	Conduct SIS idea-generation meeting for IM executives	Execute SIS idea-generation methodology; evaluate SIS ideas	Identify SIS ideas and evaluate these together with ideas from previous meeting
D	Introduce top business executive to SIS concept	Overview of SIS concept and some candidate SIS ideas for the business	Gain approval to proceed with SIS idea-generation meeting for business planners
E	Conduct SIS idea-generation meeting for corp. business planners	Execute SIS idea-generation methodology; evaluate SIS ideas	Identify SIS ideas and evaluate these together with ideas from previous meetings

[4] The planning process discussed in this section is adapted with permission from N. Rackoff, C. Wiseman, and W. A. Ullrich, "Information Systems for Competitive Advantage, Implementation of a Planning Process," *MIS Quarterly* (December 1985), 288–292.

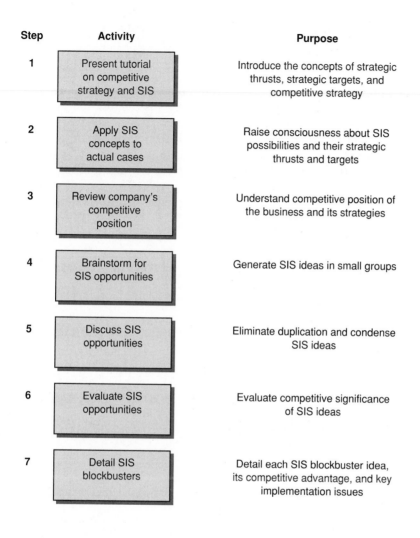

F I G U R E   5–5
Strategic Information
Systems (SIS Idea-
Generation Meeting
Steps.

Reprinted with special
permission from N. Rackoff,
C. Wiseman and W. A.
Ullrich, "Information
Systems for Competitive
Advantage, Implementation
of a Planning Process," MIS
Quarterly (December 1985)
290. Copyright (1985) by the
Society for Information
Management and The
Management Information
Systems Research Center at
the University of Minnesota.

The brainstorming step was done in separate groups of five to eight participants. Each session generated over a hundred strategic information systems ideas. In each group about ten were considered real winners. Because of overlapping ideas between the groups, eleven ideas were eventually classified as being worthy of implementation and management made an immediate allocation of resources to implement the three best blockbuster ideas.

This planning process convinced top management of the value of strategic information systems opportunities. They now believe that information systems can play a critical role in shaping the company's business strategy. Because of this, top management elevated the information management function within the corporate hierarchy. They created senior information systems positions at corporate headquarters and at the telephone operating companies. These senior positions report directly to the chief operating officer of the unit instead of to the chief financial officer as they did in the past.

Risks in the Use of Information Systems for Competitive Advantage

Although many companies have successfully implemented strategic information systems, others have failed. For example, in the mid-1980s Federal Express instituted a service called Zapmail. This service had the capability of taking a customer's letter and sending it electronically to the recipient. Zapmail service was expected to be grossing over $1 billion by the early 1990s. However, after Federal Express lost approximately $350 million on Zapmail it discontinued the project. Strategic information systems can fail and successful SISs can be copied quickly by competitors. Sustaining a competitive advantage is often difficult. A firm must continue to innovate in the SIS area or it will be overtaken by competitors.

Kemerer and Sosa have identified several potential pitfalls that management must face when they work with strategic information systems. These pitfalls are outlined in Figure 5–6.

FIGURE 5–6
Strategic Information Systems Pitfalls.

Reprinted with permission from C. F. Kemerer, and G. L. Sosa, "Systems Development Risks in Strategic Information Systems," *Information and Software Technology,* (April, 1991), 212–223.

A. **Feasible opportunities identification is difficult.**
   1. Conception of ideas for SISs requires teamwork.
   2. Current technical infeasibility can limit innovation.
   3. SISs are expensive.
   4. External SISs still require customers. There may not be a market for the SIS.

B. **SISs are complex to develop.**
   1. Telecommunications can dramatically increase system complexity in today's environment.
   2. SISs that require a vendor to deliver the technology can be extremely risky. Most developers rely on outside vendors for parts of the system.
   3. Interorganizational systems require interorganizational cooperation.
   4. The "leading edge" may be the "bleeding edge."

C. **Maintaining and adapting SISs requires constant management.**
   1. Competitors may copy the system quickly.
   2. Systems may be so successful that an unanticipated demand overwhelms the system.
   3. The expense of maintaining and enhancing installed SISs can be very costly.
   4. Firms may invest so much in an SIS that exiting from the system may be prohibitive. They must continue in order to recoup at least some of their investment. For example, the failure of Zapmail has forced Federal Express to market networking services at extremely low rates.

As outlined in Figure 5–6, there are many potential pitfalls in the pursuit of strategic information systems. However, managers are in the business of taking risks. Thus, managers' tasks are to be aware of the risks and evaluate them in relation to the capabilities of the firm and the potential rewards to be gained from an SIS. Kemerer and Sosa advocate that managers should assess their firm's relative position along each of the following dimensions:

1. *Monetary resources.* Does the firm have access to the capital that will be required to embark upon and successfully complete an SIS project?

2. *Technological sophistication.* Relative to the competition, is the firm a technological innovator or a late adopter of innovations?

3. *Organizational flexibility.* Is the firm one that can adapt quickly and easily to change or is it one whose organizational culture makes it relatively inflexible?[5]

Application 5–3 illustrates what can happen when organizational change is not managed properly in the implementation of a strategic information system.

In summary, strategic information systems require managers to innovate, evaluate the risks and rewards, and successfully implement and maintain SISs that are deemed to be potentially profitable. In reality, these steps are no different than managers' responsibilities for non–information systems types of innovations. A competitive advantage gained by an SIS may not be sustainable over the long run, but neither are many non-IS innovations that a firm implements. Constant and continual innovation is the strength of free-market economies. Many firms are now finding that strategic information systems can be valuable in their continual competitive advantage quest.

APPLICATION 5–3

A Case Study of Systems Failure

A firm neared the completion of the development of a huge, new computer-based information system that was to retrieve data from its large database via computer terminals on the desks of its employees. When these employees first began to test the system, the developers discovered that the response time (that is, the delay between typing a command and receiving a reply) for simple queries was several minutes—much too long for the workers. The computer technicians attributed the problem to "database design" errors and made many attempts to reduce the response time. Ultimately, they gave up. Hundreds of thousands of dollars had been sunk into the project and were lost. A cursory examination of the events suggested that a technical failure had taken place.

However, a closer examination revealed something very different. Months earlier, the computer technicians had attempted to learn about the users' application in great detail. However, they had failed. Perhaps the users had not been sufficiently committed to the new system and had not provided enough time to make clear explanations. Or maybe the computer technicians had conflicting priorities and had not given sufficient effort. Regardless of the party at fault, the communication between the two groups had been egregious.

Hence when the computer experts organized the users' data onto databases on computer disks, they did so erroneously because they did not understand the users' application and did not know how the users would eventually access the data. As the technicians began to test the new system, they learned much more about the application. At that time they rearranged the data repeatedly to more appropriately fit the users' needs. The slow response time, apparently due to the convoluted arrangement and repeated rearrangement of data, was in fact due to the initial communication failure between computer technicians and users.

The apparent technical failure was not a technical failure at all. Instead, it was a failure to manage organizational change.

Reprinted with permission from A. L. Lederer, and R. Nath, "Managing Organizational Issues in Information Systems Development," *Journal of Systems Management* (November, 1991), p. 27, Cleveland, Ohio.

[5] C. F. Kemerer, and G. L. Sosa, "Systems Development Risks in Strategic Information Systems," *Information and Software Technology*, (April, 1991), 212–223.

Summary

- Many business firms view information systems as tools to gain advantages over their competitors. These systems are often called strategic information systems.

- An organization's business strategy is its plan of moves and approaches devised by management to produce successful organizational performance.

- A business strategy has five interrelated tasks: to define the business and develop a mission; to translate the mission into specific long-range and short-range performance objectives; to craft a strategy to achieve the performance objectives; to implement and execute the strategy; and to evaluate performance, review the situation, and initiate corrective adjustments.

- A strategic competitive advantage from information systems refers to the application of innovative information technology for the purpose of getting ahead of competitors.

- Competitive necessity as related to information systems refers to the application of information technology for the purpose of keeping up with competitors.

- Competitive advantage stems from two factors: comparative efficiency, meaning that a firm can produce goods and services at lower cost than its competitors; and bargaining power, which allows a firm to settle bargaining situations with its customers and suppliers to its own advantage.

- Search-related costs refer to the firm's, suppliers', or customers' cost of shopping for the best prices.

- Unique product features refer to the features of products or services that make them different from those of a competitor.

- Switching costs refer to the costs that either customers or suppliers have to incur if they cease doing business with a firm.

- Internal efficiency refers to the level of costs that a firm incurs inside the firm.

- Interorganizational efficiency refers to the costs that a firm incurs in its dealings with external organizations.

- The primary pitfalls of strategic information systems are: there is a lack of feasible opportunities; the identification of opportunities is difficult; SISs are complex to develop; and maintaining and adapting SIS requires constant management.

Key Terms

Strategic information systems

Business strategy

Competitive advantage

Competitive necessity

Comparative efficiency

Bargaining power

Search-related costs

Unique product features

Switching costs

Internal efficiency

Interorganizational efficiency

1. What are strategic information systems? Give examples of firms that have successfully implemented strategic information systems.

2. What is an organization's business strategy?

3. What are the five interrelated tasks that must be done in developing a business strategy and carrying it out?

4. What are the differences between using information systems for competitive advantage and using information systems for competitive necessity?

5. What are the two major ways for a firm to gain competitive advantage?

6. Discuss the ways that bargaining power may be enhanced.

7. What are the two components of comparative efficiency?

8. Outline the basic steps in the planning process for strategic information systems.

9. What are the major pitfalls in the use of information systems for competitive advantage?

10. If a firm is considering developing a strategic information system, what are the three primary areas in which the firm's managers should assess the firm's relative position?

Discussion Questions and Cases

1. You are the new vice president for information systems at the Smith Corporation. The firm's chief executive officer has invited you to discuss with her whether or not the Smith Corporation should use information systems for competitive advantage or develop information systems when they become a competitive necessity. Take a position on this question and support your position.

2. All colleges and universities are in competition with one another to attract the best students. Outline and discuss how information systems could be used to give a college or university a competitive advantage in the attraction of the best students.

3. Some individuals argue that the risks of developing a strategic information system are too great for the potential rewards. Do you think this is true? Why or why not?

4. Denver Airport is a hub for both American Airlines and Continental Airlines. The competition between these two airlines is intense. However, American Airlines has an advantage, the Sabre System. American has used the data in the Sabre System to locate the names of those Continental passengers who have a long layover in the airport waiting for a departing Continental flight. If these Continental passengers are booked on a departing Continental flight that leaves later than an American flight to the same destination, American accesses the airport's public address system and asks these Continental passengers to come to an American counter. At the counter American personnel offer the Continental passengers a chance to switch their Continental flight to the earlier American flight. Thus, American

has used its Sabre System to try to capture Continental passengers. Is this an ethical use of the Sabre System? Why or why not?

5. Can companies located in developing countries use information systems to gain competitive advantages over those companies located in the developed world? Why or why not?

INFORMATION SYSTEMS STRATEGIES

An Illuminating CEO-CIO Alliance

By Connie Winkler

A long-running tango at Lithonia Lighting between the CEO (chief executive officer) and CIO (chief information officer) has forged award-winning, strategic information systems that have made the Georgia-based company a market leader.

Jim H. McClung has a standing $100 bet that he won't ever have a personal computer in his office. So far, Charles J. Darnell, the senior vice president for Information Management Services (IMS) at Lithonia Lighting, is still waiting to collect that $100 from his CEO boss.

Being the shrewd businessman that he is, McClung just this year had a PC installed, albeit in the executive conference room adjacent to his office. Of course there's an explanation. Says McClung, "We're trying to formulate and evaluate alternative ways of pricing on a total product basis. We found it advantageous to put a good bit of the data on PCs. And we put the PC in the executive conference room so anyone could go in and run [it]."

McClung's tactic notwithstanding, Darnell is not forgiving the $100. In fact, as far as Darnell's concerned, he's won the bet.

At recent meetings with Lithonia's other five senior vice presidents, McClung commented about the company's inconsistent pricing over the years. "He wouldn't know that if the machine hadn't been in place," reports Darnell, noting that his staff loaded the IBM Personal System/2 model 55Z with 10 years of historical data.

Not that Darnell actually has spotted the CEO-president at the keyboard, but he has other telltale evidence: Lithonia's two microcomputer spreadsheet experts have logged calls from McClung's office.

The PS/2 in the boardroom of the Conyers, Ga., company is the latest development in the enormously effective partnership between Lithonia's CEO and CIO. "It's like shortstop and a second baseman who have been playing ball together a

long time," says Darnell in describing his relationship with McClung. "You know who's going to cover second and who's going to go after the ground balls . . ."

Since 1970, when McClung became head of manufacturing, the two executives have been working closely together to integrate information processing with other operations at Lithonia. "Our basic thrust is to effectively serve the marketplace and, to the extent information technology helps do that, it's a very important part," McClung says. "The most important thing is knowing what kind of business you are in—what markets you are seeking to serve–and understanding what you need to do and do well to more effectively serve those marketplaces. We have grappled with the task of applying this [philosophy] to information technology."

In addition to IMS, Darnell has product line responsibility for three division—lighting controls, emergency lighting and wiring. All of the products Darnell controls have electronic components, which are being used increasingly in lighting products.

To McClung, adding product responsibilities to Darnell's job description was an opportunity to expand Darnell's management talents. "He had an interest in learning more about various aspects of the lighting business and a desire to manage some product operations. He wanted to be involved, and we had the need," says McClung about Darnell's promotion in the mid-1980s.

The result of their efforts is Light*Link, the dial-up communications network that links Lithonia's independent agents, distributors and contractors to its internal systems for order entry, manufacturing, inventory control and distribution. Light*Link makes it easy to do business with Lithonia because a contractor, architect or engineer can verify the size, specifications and price of a lighting fixture. With Light*Link, an agent can make sure a fixture is in stock before placing an order.

Thus, Light*Link has the same competitive lockout effect as, for a common example, American Airlines' SemiAutomated Business Reservation Environment (SABRE). In 1988, McClung and Darnell's shared vision and success was recognized by the Society for Information Management's (SIM) "Partners in Leadership" award.

Award-winning Light*Link and its four related systems were created in the late 1970s and early 1980s when the lighting industry suddenly grew complex. New competitors were appearing from around the world, and new technologies, such as sodium vapor lighting, were being introduced. Lithonia wanted to beef up its earnings/profit growth, but quickly realized it had a serious bottleneck in the middle of the distribution chain: its 70-odd agent representatives couldn't handle the increased workload and paperwork to meet Lithonia's growth projections.

"Our agents were our customers, and it was intuitively obvious they weren't going to be able to handle the increased volume," says Darnell. "They were going to have to have a partner." Luckily, Lithonia realized that the strong internal information systems it had built, which its competition lacked, could be shared with the agents. Thus began Lithonia's aggressive and comprehensive effort to sell the Light*Link approach and train the agents' employees to use it . . .

Planning, Planning, More Planning

Perpetuating the company's efficacy in the market should not prove too difficult, since McClung and Darnell's technology vision has radiated to every top Lithonia executive. Foremost, Darnell says, the alliance between the executives is one of peers. McClung also believes in strict strategic planning and subsequent control of proposed projects.

Unlike organizations that are madly decentralizing or experimenting with matrix or other types of management styles, Lithonia sticks with a traditional pyramid-style organization chart. Five people report to Darnell: the vice president of IMS, who is responsible for day-to-day operations; vice presidents of each of the three product divisions; and an administrative assistant. Six senior vice presidents report to McClung. In addition to Darnell are SVPs of sales and marketing and division chiefs of the three remaining product divisions . . .

Because McClung is so intent on maintaining the company's long-term direction, he and the team of SVPs don't make short-term decisions based solely on financial criteria, even in a slower economy. Still, much of the planning revolves around profit projections. Lithonia has an annual financial planning cycle for a fiscal year that begins in September. In late spring and early summer, the six senior vice presidents present their financial projections and plans. Out of the many discussions, the six SVPs develop project plans, typically for a period of six months.

"The project management activities come out of the basic business plan, which is a subpart of the company's broader strategic plan," says McClung. "It's those things we really need to do to improve not only IS [information systems] but all the product divisions."

McClung keeps the vice presidents' feet in the fire with regular control checks on the new projects. Because of his vigilance, it's hard for any project, once agreed upon, to slip through the cracks into oblivion. "We review at the end of the six months. And during the course of the six months we will carry on whatever reviews and conversations are needed," he explains.

For technology projects that affect the company's strategic direction or that would have a major financial impact, Darnell first submits a written proposal to McClung and his fellow "seniors," as he describes them. As the VPs hammer out the proposals, Darnell provides revisions until the group agrees on a final version. Darnell then shepherds the project to completion.

In today's quirky economy, Lithonia, like many other companies, is caught between ever-growing demands on IS and spending limits. When tough technology choices are on the table, Darnell often relies on analogies to get his points across. Instead of presenting new technology initiatives strictly in terms of dollars, Darnell asks, for example, "If you don't want to pay for steak every night, what do you want to eat? Do you want to eat steak on Tuesday and Thursday and SPAM and hash the rest of the week?"

What Darnell frequently hears in response is that not only do the SVPs want steak all week, they want a new dessert, too. Yet, he keeps asking those choice questions, following Lithonia's policy of regularly examining the costs and appropriateness of a technology. "It's a written policy that we will [always] examine our computer and information systems to make sure we can afford them and that they're appropriate."

Darnell frequently briefs McClung on technology plans and developments. McClung is a "simplitician," says Darnell, "He requires that you talk to him in everyday, elementary, down-to-earth terms." McClung also monitors what other organizations are doing with technology, but forget suggesting he attend a vendor's presentation. "I've tried, and he won't go," Darnell admits.

Mutual Admiration Society

Both men say a big part of their successful technology partnership is their long-running friendship. "I think, first of all, we're good friends," says Darnell. "We mutually respect what the other knows and his goals and directions." Both executives, Darnell says, want to work with their fellow associates, helping them to grow as individuals and develop in their careers.

"You have to go back to the individual," continues McClung about Darnell. "He's hardworking and aggressive and really wants to improve his overall effectiveness as a business manager and leader. He didn't want to be restricted to functional responsibility . . . His [business management] skills were very transferable" . . .

Dos and Don'ts in the IS Two-Step

It takes two to tango, and nowhere is that more true than in using information technology to leverage a business. Here are some basic steps used by the two key partners at Lithonia Lighting.

Tips for CEOs

1. Keep your eyes on the business, especially when dealing with complex and at times far-out technical decisions.

2. Know your customers and keep them, rather than the organization, in mind when setting up large internal information systems.

3. Plan, plan, plan. And follow through with your senior staff on the results of the planning process.

4. Manage, manage, manage.

5. Groom your IS staff for added responsibilities.

6. Pay attention to new technologies. Your company could invent the equivalent of the SABRE reservations system in your industry.

7. Use a personal computer. It's an experience you can no longer avoid—even if you can't type.

8. Ask dumb questions–especially about technology. The point is to get your IS experts to explain their plans in business terms.

9. Take your CIO to lunch. Informality makes it much easier to grope through all the ramifications of technology decisions.

10. Respect your CIO. There's no partnership if the two players can't join hands.

Tips for CIOS

1. No surprises. What CEOs hate most is being blindsided by a problem or development. Keep the CEO apprised of all tornadoes on the horizon—even just big breezes.

2. Just say no to being the chief computer nerd in your company. This is an easy road for longtime, data-processing managers to follow, but in 1990 it's a dead end. This may require asking for additional responsibility to demonstrate business management skills.

3. Plan, plan, plan. This old standby procedure is critical for complex technology projects, which can run over several years and cost untold millions.

4. Manage, manage, manage. Too often, because of complexity or frenzy, technical projects disappear or certainly slip through deadlines.

5. Groom your staff for added responsibilities.

6. Use simple analogies to work up to explaining the full complexity of technical decisions.

7. Look beyond what your vendor says. (And, most probably, protect your CEO from your vendor.)

8. Go to lunch with your CEO. If you don't get asked, speak up.

9. Respect your CEO. Just because your CEO can't boot up Lotus 1-2-3 doesn't mean he or she is a bad person.

Discussion Questions

1. Why is a good relationship between the CEO and the CIO essential to firms today?

2. Of the tips for CEOs, which one do you think is most important?

3. Of the tips for CIOs, which one do you think is most important?

Reprinted with permission from *Datamation* (August 15, 1990), p. 79(3), Copyright 1990 Cahners Publishing Company.

TWO

Information Systems Applications

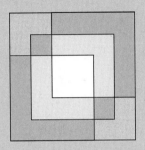

6

Functional Information Systems

As we saw in Chapter 4, an information system can be viewed as a federation of functional information systems. For example, marketing personnel tend to view their part of the information system as a marketing information system. Personnel in each function (accounting, production, and engineering, for example) engage in activities that support the objectives of the business. In this chapter, we first look at the activities within the business cycle. We then explore the typical information systems applications that support these activities.

Introduction

Figure 6–1 illustrates the **business cycle**, which is a process of converting cash into goods and services for sale and then selling these goods and services in order to convert resources back into cash. A successful business, of course, takes in more cash from selling goods and services than it spends for materials, goods, and/or services. Any business, regardless of whether it sells goods or services, has a business cycle. **Manufacturing firms** produce goods, whereas **merchandising firms** simply purchase goods for resale. An increasingly important business is the service firm. **Service firms** sell the services of their employees to clients. Examples include advertising agencies and accounting firms.

The Business Cycle

First, a business must raise cash through its **finance activity**. Normally, cash comes from investors, such as stockholders, or the firm's creditors (those who loan money to the business), such as banks. This cash is spent in the **spending activity** in order to acquire the services of employees through the payment of wages and to purchase materials, goods, and services from outside suppliers.

These purchased materials, goods, and services are converted into other goods or services through the **conversion activity**. In a manufacturing firm the conversion activity is called production. In a merchandising firm, the conversion activity may consist of receiving goods and placing them in a warehouse so they are ready to be shipped when orders are received.

The **revenue activity** consists of selling the goods or services to customers and collecting from the customers either cash or accounts receivable. The financial activity is responsible for collecting the accounts receivables from customers and paying the accounts payable to the firm's employees and suppliers. During the financial activity, idle cash is invested in short-term securities, such as U.S. Treasury bonds, until the cash is needed in the spending activity. At this point the business cycle begins anew, with the spending of cash for additional purchased materials, goods, and services. In fact, this flow in the business cycle occurs continuously.

Each of the firm's traditional functions, such as accounting/finance, production, and marketing, is involved in these activities. Sometimes a function is involved in more than one activity. For example, accounting/finance is involved in the financial, spending, and revenue activities, whereas production is involved in the spending and conversion activities. Marketing, however, is involved primarily in the revenue activity.

To illustrate typical business information systems applications, we will use a manufacturing firm. Most manufacturing firms have, as a minimum, the systems and applications shown in Figure 6–2. As we shall see in the following section on computer-integrated manufacturing, production systems can be much more pervasive.

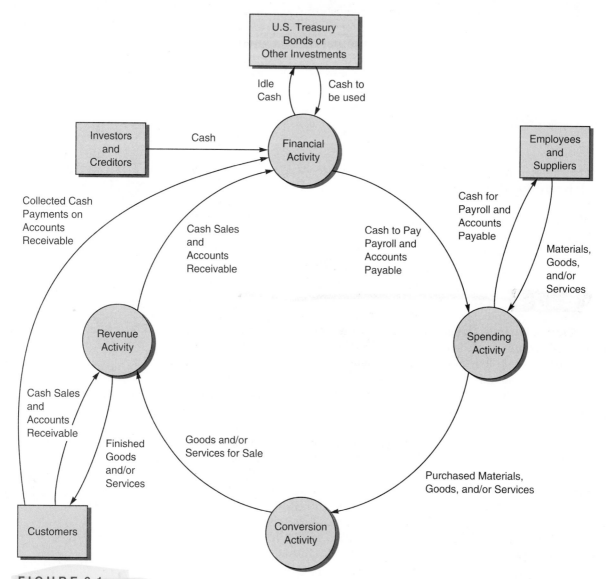

FIGURE 6–1

The Business Cycle.

Note that the four activities—financial, spending, conversion, and revenue—form a cycle that converts cash into goods and/or services which are sold and converted back into cash.

Data needed for the multiple applications shown in Figure 6–2 are shared among relevant applications. In most businesses today, these systems are all on-line; that is, inputs and outputs are processed through computer terminals. Both queries and reports shown in later figures in this chapter can be viewed by management through a terminal (although a significant number of managers still prefer to see reports on paper). Many of these computer systems are also real time, in that their files are updated as soon as real-world events (business transactions) occur. The remainder of this chapter discusses these and other information systems applications.

WORK-in-PROGRESS   Prod nosed

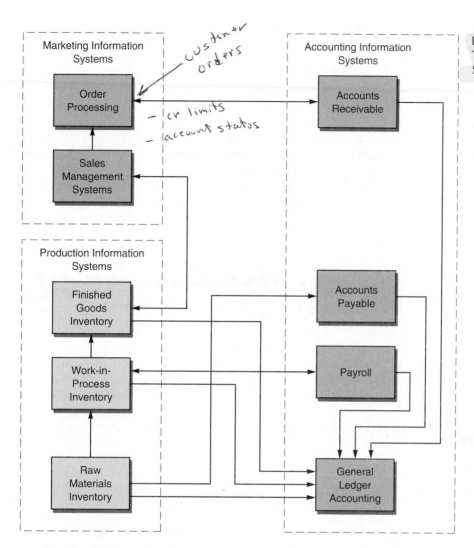

FIGURE 6–2
Typical Information
Systems Applications.

Marketing Information Systems — Order Processing — Sales Management Systems

customer orders

– cr limits
– account status

Accounting Information Systems — Accounts Receivable

Production Information Systems — Finished Goods Inventory — Work-in-Process Inventory — Raw Materials Inventory

Accounts Payable — Payroll — General Ledger Accounting

Inventories

A manufacturing firm has three types of inventory: **raw materials**, **work-in-process**, and **finished goods**. A merchandising firm has only one type of inventory: **finished goods**, or **merchandise inventory**. Since a service firm sells services rather than goods, it does not maintain an inventory system. Regardless of the type of inventory, an **inventory system** has two primary objectives: (1) to minimize costs due to out-of-stock situations, and (2) to minimize inventory carrying costs. The two objectives often conflict.

At the finished goods level, out-of-stock situations can result in loss of sales; at the raw materials level, out-of-stock conditions can result in the unnecessary idling of production employees and facilities. However, a company cannot keep large quantities of inventory on hand in order to avoid out-of-stock situations. Such an approach would increase inventory carrying costs beyond acceptable levels. Inventory carrying costs include such things as interest, insurance costs, and warehousing costs. As

**Production Infor-
mation Systems**

the amount of inventory increases, carrying costs also increase. Companies could minimize inventory carrying costs by not carrying any inventory; however, out-of-stock costs (loss of sales) might then be unacceptable.

Inventory must be closely monitored to minimize both out-of-stock and inventory costs. Computer-based inventory systems are useful in providing this close monitor. Computers can be programmed to automatically make inventory reorder decisions that minimize these two costs.

Techniques that minimize both out-of-stock and inventory costs are sometimes called **just-in-time inventory systems**. The goal of these systems is to deliver inventory to the firm just in time for use. Thus, the inventory on hand is minimal, yet out-of-stock situations are also minimal. With just-in-time inventory systems, a firm shares production information with suppliers through computer links, enabling the suppliers to deliver materials just in time.

The work-in-process inventory system monitors goods while they are being produced. It has two objectives in addition to the ones discussed earlier: (1) to provide scheduling control over individual production jobs so that an accurate prediction of their completion dates can be made; and (2) to accumulate the unit costs of individual products. In large companies, these objectives are often met by two separate applications: a scheduling system and a cost accounting system.

There are many similarities among the three types of inventory systems. The merchandise (or finished goods) inventory system shown in Figure 6–3 illustrates how all three systems operate. This figure provides

FIGURE 6–3
A Merchandise Inventory System.

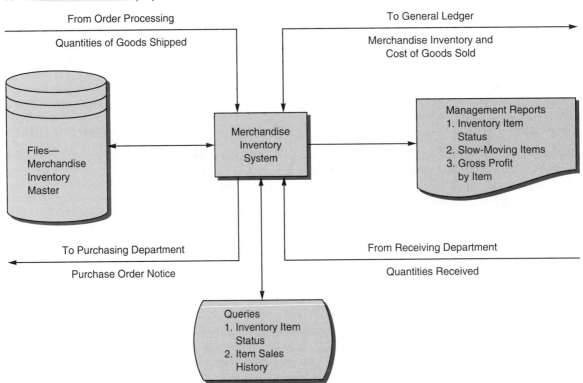

Inventory Item Number
Item Description
Location in Warehouse
Current Quantity on Hand
Current Quantity on Order
Quantity Sold—Year-to-Date
Quantity Back-ordered
Standard Cost

FIGURE 6-4
Typical Fields in a
Merchandise
Inventory Master File
Record.

an overview of the system, which maintains a merchandise inventory master file. Some of the data fields contained in each record in this file are listed in Figure 6–4. At any time, the master file should accurately reflect the quantities stored in the fields indicated in Figure 6–4.

The two primary inputs that update the merchandise inventory master file are quantities of goods shipped (input from the order processing system) and quantities of goods received (input by the receiving department).

The merchandise inventory system produces outputs updating the general ledger system in the areas of current inventory on hand and cost of goods sold. The system also provides the purchasing department with a purchase order notice. This notice identifies the items whose quantities are at or below the reorder level. Many merchandise inventory systems produce a purchase order instead of a purchase order notice. This purchase order, which may be in hard copy or electronic form, is sent to the purchasing department for approval before being sent to a vendor. Figure 6–5 illustrates three typical kinds of inventory management reports. These reports may be printed on paper or displayed on a monitor screen.

Computer-Integrated Manufacturing

The inventory system described above are the minimum systems that a manufacturer uses. Many firms now go much further. Manufacturing is an information-intensive activity. For example, the engineering design of a product must be communicated to manufacturing before the raw materials and parts can be ordered for making the product. Purchase orders must be sent to suppliers. The availability of raw materials in inventory must be known before production can start. Scheduling of materials and labor must be performed. Costs must be accumulated. Often, the same pieces of information flow throughout the production process from engineering to shipment of the final product to customers. Thus, manufacturing firms are viewing the manufacturing process as an information-intensive process that can be managed with an integrated database. The database is used in the entire manufacturing process, from engineering, to scheduling, to cost accounting, to marketing of the product, with all the intermediate steps driven by the same database. This approach is called **computer-integrated manufacturing (CIM)**.

F I G U R E 6–5
Typical Inventory Management Reports.

```
                                                         PAGE 1
                        GROSS PROFIT BY ITEM
                              REPORT
                        MONTH ENDING 10-31-9X
```

					QTY
ITEM	ITEM		QTY	GROSS	SOLD
NO	DESCRIPTION	SALES	SOLD	PROFIT	YTD
1003	PAPER,3H,LOOSE LEAF	187.50	250	40.00	3520
1004	PAPER,TYPING,BOND	7187.50	1250	1000.00	7500
1005	PAPER,MIMEO,8.5X11	2835.00	750	885.00	6000
7085	PEN,BALLPOINT	3185.00	3500	385.00	24500
4106	PENCIL,DRAWING 3H	1425.00	475	209.00	1900
8165	STAPLER REMOVER	675.00	1500	90.00	16500

```
                                                         PAGE 1
                        SLOW MOVING ITEMS
                              REPORT
                          AS OF 10-31-9X
```

		STD	DAY OF		QTY
ITEM	ITEM	UNIT	LAST	QTY ON	SOLD
NO	DESCRIPTION	COST	SALE	HAND	YTD
6405	BOOKCASE,37,5X55X5	133.03	04159X	1000	250
6408	CHAIR,SWIVEL,ARMS	138.29	06109X	75	20
8082	CUSHION,15X16	5.74	08239X	60	15
3015	FAN,WINDOW	38.28	05309X	25	10
6440	TABLE,MULTI-PURPOSE	121.68	07259X	30	7
6017	TRANSPARENCY,8.5X11	20.93	07239X	550	325

```
                                                         PAGE 1
                        INVENTORY ITEM
                        STATUS REPORT
                        AS OF 10-31-9X
```

			QTY	QTY	QTY	QTY		STD
ITEM	ITEM	WAREHOUSE	ON	ON	BACK	SOLD.		UNIT
NO	DESCRIPTION	LOCATION	HAND	ORDER	ORDER	YTD	UNIT	COST
6045	BOOKCASE,37.5X55X5	7340	1000	500	0	350	EA	133.03
3403	CABINET FILE,8"	7340	400	0	0	150	EA	162.15
8002	CALENDAR,PAD,#SD 170	7428	75	60	0	25	EA	.98
3403	CLOCK,WALL,8",ELECT	7428	20	50	30	35	EA	27.88
9005	FOLDER,MANILA,LETTER	7419	50	750	250	950	BOX	3.78

Figure 6–6 illustrates the concept of computer-integrated manufacturing. Engineering personnel use computer-aided design (CAD) software and very high resolution graphics workstations to design a new product and its component parts. As shown in Figure 6–7, these workstations are capable of displaying a realistic model of the product. Thus, design errors

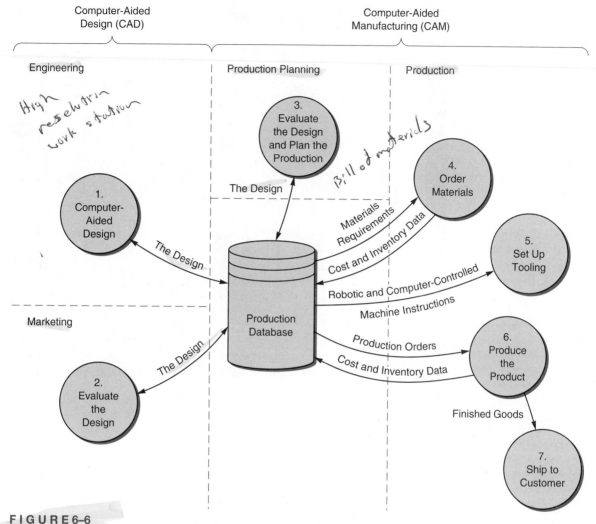

FIGURE 6–6

Computer-Integrated Manufacturing (CIM).

CIM systems may also include electronic ties to outside suppliers and customers, enabling suppliers and customers to review designs, schedules, and other production data.

are substantially reduced because the user can see and experiment with this realistic model. Marketing and production-planning personnel as well as the customer can view the design, and any changes they make can be quickly incorporated.

A part of the product design is the bill of materials. The **bill of materials** contains quantities and specifications for all the materials necessary to produce one unit of the product. Thus, the bill of materials can be used for ordering materials. Once the product design is complete, the production planning is finalized and materials are ordered.

In factories today, many production machines and tooling processes are automated. Robots perform fabrication, assembly, and finishing tasks. These automated machines are computer controlled, and the computer instructions for specific products are provided by the production database.

FIGURE 6–7
Computer-Aided
Design (CAD).

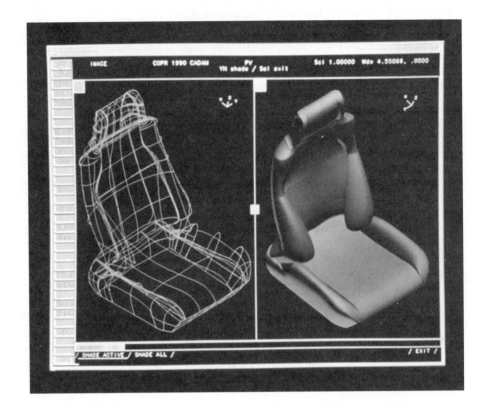

In fact, some factories are completely automated. After computer-aided design is complete, the computer orders the materials and feeds the instructions to the automated production machines. Then the product is produced by these computer-controlled machines and robots. Even the warehousing of the finished product, prior to shipment, is automated.

Here are some of the many advantages of CIM:

1. The labor costs of production are reduced.

2. The time from product conception to product delivery is reduced. This is a major advantage, because beating a competitor to the marketplace almost always results in higher sales.

3. Small quantities of a particular product become economical to produce. Such products would not have been produced in the past. The demand was not sufficient to make a profit. This leads to a greater variety of products for the consumer. Thus, small (niche) markets can be exploited.

4. The ability to quickly manipulate and change the product design results in products that have a better design.

CIM is likely to become a must as firms attempt to maintain their competitive advantages. However, implementing CIM is a large undertaking. Most firms buy the necessary software rather than develop it themselves.

Electronic Data Interchange

Marketing Information Systems

Electronic data interchange (EDI) is the computer-to-computer transmission of transaction data between business trading partners. EDI systems can transmit all the necessary data to complete a purchase transaction from the initial order to the payment for the goods with direct electronic deposit of the funds to the supplier's bank account. Thus, the transaction can be completed without paper documents flowing between the trading partners. EDI networks are currently being widely used between trading partners in the United States and worldwide. Department stores such as Wal-Mart and J. C. Penney use EDI extensively. EDI is very popular among clothing manufacturers. Even small businesses can obtain EDI software that executes on personal computers.

Among the several advantages of EDI are the following:

1. The expense and errors associated with multiple manual entry of the data are avoided.

2. The elapsed time between the initial order to the receipt of the goods and payment for them is greatly reduced. This saving of time helps make just-in-time inventory systems possible. It also means that the supplier receives payment for the goods quicker, thus reducing financing costs.

3. The costs of processing and storing paper documents associated with transactions between trading partners are eliminated.

There are some pitfalls in the implementation of EDI. These include the following:

1. The costs of implementing EDI can be substantial. In a large firm they can be well over $1 million.

2. Customers or suppliers may not have the capability of implementing EDI, thus preventing a firm from using EDI until its trading partners reach EDI capability.

3. The electronic interchange of data between firms requires standard protocols that govern the interchange. Within the United States, Western Europe, and Japan such standards have been established. Thus, EDI between firms located in one of these three areas is relatively easy. However, incompatibilities between hardware and/or software can still occur. EDI between international trading partners is more difficult, primarily because of the different interchange standards that are used in the United States, Western Europe, and Japan. But recent attempts to establish a global standard for EDI promises to solve this problem. This international standard is called EDIFACT (EDI for Administration, Commerce, and Transportation).

We have discussed EDI under marketing systems because a transaction between trading partners starts in the marketing function with entry of the order. However, an EDI system has an impact on other functional information systems, particularly production and accounting. EDI is a prime example of how contemporary information systems cut across many functions of a business. We must remember that for systems to provide a competitive advantage they must automate information flows across functional lines. When planning an information system, users must have a broad vision of a business in addition to their awareness of their own functional area.

Order Processing

The **order-processing** system (see Figure 6–8) is the place of entry for customer orders, and it initiates the shipping of orders (see Figure 6–9). The system is often called an order entry system. The primary objectives of an order-processing system are (1) to initiate shipping orders, (2) to maintain a record of **back-ordered** items (items that are out of stock and will be shipped later), and (3) to produce sales analysis reports. Application 6–1 illustrates how Champion Products, Inc. uses automated order-processing systems.

A shipping order is illustrated in Figure 6–9. The shipping order is issued in triplicate-a copy is sent to the warehouse to tell employees which goods to ship, a copy is put inside the shipping box, and a copy is kept as a record. Some companies use a fourth copy, which serves as a customer acknowledgment and is sent to the customer when the shipping order is issued.

FIGURE 6–8
An Order-Processing System.

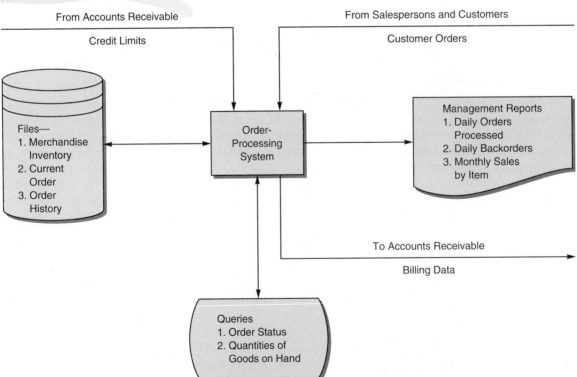

APPLICATION 6–1

T-Shirt Company Champions Automated Ordering Process

By Richard Pastore

If someone gave you the wrong-size Three Stooges sweatshirt as a gift, you have probably already returned it. You are satisfied, but the T-shirt company is stuck with a slightly used Moe.

The losses get serious when customers such as Notre Dame's Fighting Irish football team return mismatched jersey orders. Champion Products, Inc., a manufacturer of silk-screened T-shirts, jerseys and Champion- emblemed sweatshirts, is hoping to trim costly order mistakes by equipping its field sales representatives with laptop personal computers and an automated order-entry system.

The number of variables in jersey specifications makes ordering as complicated as a trip to a tailor shop. "It's very easy to make mistakes," especially when the representatives were doing everything manually, said Peter Youngman, director of major projects at Rochester, N.Y.-based Champion.

The homegrown menu system eliminates the need for representatives to write or type any of the complicated style, size and color codes for the 42,000 retail shirt designs. "They don't type 003 for a code or b-l-a-c-k for a color," Youngman said. "All you have to know is where the enter key is and the arrow keys . . ."

Faster with Less Mistakes

The total reduction in order errors among both field sales groups will pay for the system in just under three years, said Michael Moore, vice president of MIS [management information systems].

The representatives access headquarters and upload orders via a 24-hour, toll-free, 2,400 bit/sec. line. The orders are updated nightly to Champion's Unisys Corp. A17 mainframe. From there, mainframe-based applications process the order fulfillment.

The laptops provide inquiry access to the mainframe as well. A salesperson can check order status and current and projected inventories over the same dial-up lines.

"If a customer says he needs a shipment Aug. 15, you can look at what's available in inventory for Aug. 15 and make your promises from there," Youngman said. Field representatives previously had to rely on paper inventory updates that were two weeks old by the time they arrived in the mail.

The mainframe, which holds the customer and master product databases, can download data such as design changes, customer address changes and the locations of new customers to the laptops. Champion is establishing a CC:Mail, Inc.-based electronic-

mail service that will alert sales representatives to updates.

The laptops also save time in up-front order processing. "Prior to the laptops, they had to handwrite orders and mail them into a central office, or as we called it, 'the black hole,'" Youngman said. The orders would then languish on office desks for up to three weeks before data entry personnel could retype them into the mainframe.

With lead time reduced to 24 hours, Champion's internal reaction time is more immediate. "We have a hold on customer demand that much quicker," which leads to better inventory planning, Youngman said.

All Hands in the Pie

The system design and implementation were a team effort, Moore said. A task force of sales representatives was assigned the job of shaping the parameters. Because the resulting system was not an information systems design, the sales staff was told to direct any complaints to fellow sales representatives who helped set the parameters.

Before producing a shipping order, most order-processing systems access the merchandise inventory file to determine whether particular goods are on hand. If given items are not on hand, they are placed on back order. The inventory master file is updated to reflect the number of goods shipped. Back orders remain on file so that when the goods are available the order-processing system can initiate a shipping order.

In addition to maintaining an inventory file, the order-processing system maintains a current order file and an order history file. These two files are identical in format. The typical fields in a record of these two files contain the same information that is displayed on the shipping order in Figure 6–9.

FIGURE 6–9
Typical Shipping Order.

```
                                                           PAGE 1
                        SHIPPING ORDER
                      ORDER DATE 10-31-9X

         SHIP TO:
             NAME:  PERDUE PROCESSORS
          ADDRESS:  104 LANDSDOWNE LANE
                    BLACKSBURG, VA 24060
      PACKAGE NO:   764290
   SHIPMENT NO:     1721

   ITEM  ITEM                    QTY      QTY            UNIT
   NO    DESCRIPTION           ORDERED  SHIPPED  UNIT   PRICE

   1003  PAPER,3H,LOOSELEAF      100      100     PKG    .75
   1004  PAPER,TYPING,BOND       500      500     PKG   5.75
   1005  PAPER,MIMEO,8.5x11       30       30     RM    3.65
   9090  PAD,SCRATCH,4x6          12       12     DOZ   1.69
   8039  RUBBER BANDS,1=8x3       10       10     BOX    .79
   1035  STENCIL,8.5x14           12       12     DOZ   3.10
```

After a short period of time (for example, three months), records are deleted from the current order file and placed in the order history file. This procedure prevents the current order file from growing too large. The records in the order history file are usually maintained for at least a year to support sales analysis reports that the system produces.

Figure 6–10 illustrates typical order-processing reports. The daily orders processed report is primarily a control report providing daily information about orders processed. Management can use the totals on this report to monitor trends and the number of orders processed. The daily back-order report is also a control report, enabling management to monitor the level of back orders. If the quantity of back orders becomes excessive, customer relations may suffer. The monthly sales-by-item report is an example of the many types of sales analysis reports that can be produced. This particular report enables management to monitor sales trends by following the numbers of individual items sold.

Sales Management Systems

As discussed above, a few sales analysis reports can be produced from the order-entry system. A complete marketing information system goes far beyond the scope of these reports and includes many sales management tools. In addition to providing information about past sales, the systems can assist in estimating future sales and managing the marketing activities, and even help in optimizing marketing strategy for certain products through a market research approach.

Sales management systems can be used to support account management, direct marketing, lead tracking, mapping, sales forecasting, sales presentations, and telemarketing. Examples of the functions that these systems provide are listed below:

Account Management: Maintains information about customers such as notes, contacts, and sales histories. Produces form letters.

Direct Marketing: Provides mailing list management, finds duplicates, sorts by zip code, produces list analysis and reports.

Lead Tracking: Provides sales lead tracking, autodialing, sales scripts, form letters, and labels.

Mapping: Analyzes address, demographic, and spending habits information and provides color graphics maps pinpointing sales information.

Sales Forecasting: Uses various mathematical techniques to forecast seasonally adjusted sales.

Sales Presentations: Provides visual graphics for use in sales presentations, prepares quotes and formal proposals, and provides training for sales closings.

Telemarketing: Receives calls, plays back prerecorded messages, performs autodialing, and transfers to a human telemarketer if there is an answer.

Accounting Information Systems

Accounting systems have traditionally been at the center of the information system of a firm. They gather much of the data that arises from the transactions of the firm. However, accounting data in the past has had one major disadvantage: It is financial data, such as the costs of producing a product. Increasingly, managements realize that they need nonfinancial data to manage a business, such as the average time it takes to process an order and the number of customer complaints. This nonfinancial data is normally gathered by other functional information systems, such as marketing. Thus, accounting systems should be closely integrated with other functional information systems so that complete data can be provided to management. The major accounting systems are accounts receivable, accounts payable, payroll, and the general ledger.

Accounts Receivable

The objectives of an **accounts receivable** system are (1) to bill customers for orders shipped, (2) to maintain records of the amounts customers owe and pay, and (3) to provide information to assist in the collection of past-due accounts. The billing function is the sending of the initial invoice to the customer. This function can be performed by the order-processing system, by a separate billing system, or by the accounts receivable system.

F I G U R E 6–10
Typical Order-Processing Reports.

PAGE 1

```
                    DAILY ORDERS PROCESSED
                          REPORT
                        FOR 10-31-9X
```

ORDER NO	CUSTOMER NO	CUSTOMER NAME	ITEM NO	SHIPMENT NO	SHIPPING DATE
764290	25190	PERDUE PROCESSORS	1004	1721	12-31-9X
764290	25190	PERDUE PROCESSORS	1005	1721	12-31-9X
764290	25190	PERDUE PROCESSORS	9090	1721	12-31-9X
889233	27300	KINKO'S	1005	2930	12-31-9X
889233	27300	KINKO'S	1750	2930	12-31-9X
931240	31790	POLYSCIENTIFIC	9005	3501	12-31-9X

PAGE 1

```
              DAILY BACK-ORDER REPORT
                    FOR 10-31-9X
```

ITEM NO	ITEM DESCRIPTION	QTY ORDERED	QTY BACK ORDERED	UNIT	UNIT PRICE
3403	CLOCK, WALL,8",ELECT	50	30	EA	27.88
9005	FOLDER, MANILA, LETTER	750	250	BOX	3.78
6412	LETTER TRAY, LEGAL	50	20	EA	6.88
9090	PAD, SCRATCH, 4X6	625	300	DOZ	1.04
4106	PENCIL, DRAWING 3H	200	150	DOZ	2.56

PAGE 1

```
                   SALES-BY-ITEM
                       REPORT
                 MONTH ENDING 10-31-9X
```

ITEM NO	ITEM DESCRIPTION	QUANTITY	CURRENT MONTHLY SALES	SALES YTD
1003	PAPER, 3H, LOOSE LEAF	250	187.50	2640.00
1004	PAPER, TYPING, BOND	1250	7187.50	43125.00
1005	PAPER, MIMEO, 8.5x11	750	2835.00	22680.00
7085	PEN, BALLPOINT	3500	3185.00	22295.00
4106	PENCIL, DRAWING 3H	475	1425.00	4864.00
8165	STAPLER REMOVER	1500	675.00	6435.00

Figure 6–11 shows an accounts receivable system. The accounts receivable system maintains one file—the accounts receivable master file. Typical fields contained in a record in this file are illustrated in Figure 6–12. This file is updated with billing data from order processing. All other data in the file are input from the accounts receivable department.

Queries to the accounts receivable system are shown on a monitor screen and include information such as account status and payment his-

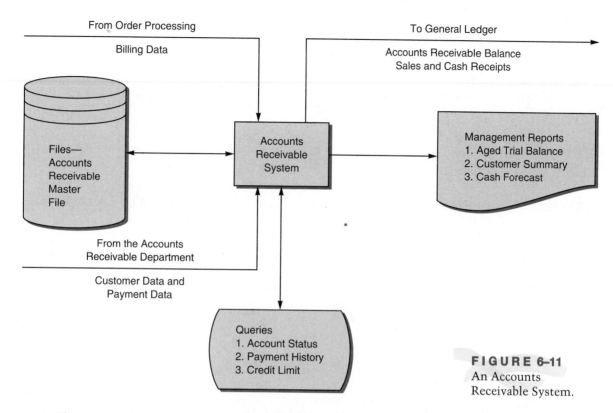

FIGURE 6–11
An Accounts
Receivable System.

tory. The account status screen displays unpaid purchases and recent payments; the payment history screen provides detailed information about the payment habits of a particular customer.

Figure 6–13 displays three typical management reports in the accounts receivable system. The aged trial balance is a valuable report for collection purposes, since it indicates the accounts that are past due and how far they are past due—one to thirty days, thirty-one to sixty days, or over sixty days. The customer status report provides detailed information about a specific customer. This information can be valuable to the salesperson assigned a given customer.

Since the accounts receivable system is the primary cash receipt system, it can provide useful cash forecasts. Information in a cash forecast

Customer Number
Customer Name
Customer Address
Credit Rating
Average Days Late
Credit Limit
Purchase Date
Purchase Reference
Purchase Amounts
Payment Date
Payment Reference
Payment Amounts
Current Balance

FIGURE 6–12
Typical Fields in an
Accounts Receivable
Master File Record.

report is usually based on statistics concerning a customer's payment habits, such as the average number of days the customer is late in making payments.

FIGURE 6-13
Typical Accounts Receivable Management Reports.

AGED TRIAL BALANCE
REPORT
AS OF 10-31-9X

CUSTOMER NO	CUSTOMER NAME	AMOUNT NOT DUE	AMOUNT 1-30 DAYS OVERDUE	AMOUNT 31-60 OVERDUE	AMOUNT >60 DAYS OVERDUE	TOTAL BALANCE DUE
25190	PERDUE PROCESSORS	1000.00	195.00	.00	.00	1195.00
27300	KINKO'S	550.00	25.00	.00	.00	575.00
31790	POLYSCIENTIFIC	1500.00	200.00	90.00	.00	1790.00
51230	BANDY, MW	.00	350.00	400.00	.00	750.00
61359	DORN, HC	195.00	55.00	.00	.00	250.00
73401	JONES, LT	.00	25.00	75.00	.00	100.00

PAGE 1

ACCOUNTS RECEIVABLE
CUSTOMER STATUS
REPORT
AS OF 10-31-9X

CUST NO	CUST NAME	CREDIT RATING	CREDIT LIMIT	AMNT DUE	AMNT REC'D	BALANCE
25190	PERDUE PROCESSORS	9	5000.00	2695.50	1500.00	1195.50
27300	KINKO'S	7	3500.00	1325.00	750.00	575.00
31790	POLYSCIENTIFIC	10	7500.00	5290.00	3900.00	1790.00
51230	BANDY, MW	0	.00	750.00	.00	750.00
61359	DORN, HC	6	1000.00	625.00	375.00	250.00
73401	JONES, LT	0	.00	100.00	.00	100.00

PAGE 1

CASH FORECAST
REPORT
AS OF 10-31-9X

PROBABLE PYMT DATE	DUE DATE	INVOICE NO	CUSTOMER NAME	PYMT TERMS	DISC AMT	AMOUNT DUE	PYMT
0109X	01159X	23910	PERDUE PROCESSORS	2/10,N/30	10.00	490.00	490.00
01159X	01319X	24920	PERDUE PROCESSORS	2/10,N/30	9.00	441.00	441.00
01319X	02059X	39011	KINKO'S	3/10,N/30	7.50	242.50	242.50
01319X	02159X	39015	KINKO'S	3/10,N/30	2.25	47.75	47.75
01319X	02159X	31920	KINKO'S	3/10,N/30	1.50	38.50	38.50
02059X	02159X	45270	DORN, NH	********	.00	125.00	75.00

TOTAL CASH FORECASTED $1334.75

Accounts Payable

Whereas the accounts receivable system keeps records of the amounts owed to the firm, the **accounts payable** system keeps records of amounts owed to suppliers of the firm. The objectives of the accounts payable system are (1) to provide control over payments to vendors of goods and suppliers of services, (2) to issue checks to vendors and suppliers, and (3) to provide information for effective cash management.

Figure 6–14 shows an accounts payable system. Typical fields contained in an accounts payable master file record are illustrated in Figure 6–15. The accounts payable department provides the input to the accounts payable system. The primary types of input are data concerning vendors, such as vendor name and address, and data from new invoices received from vendors and suppliers.

Typical accounts payable management reports are illustrated in Figure 6–16. The cash requirement report is based on amounts owed and the dates those amounts are due. The discounts lost report is a type of cash management report. Many vendors offer customers a discount on payments—say, 2 percent off the invoice, if payments are made within ten days. The discounts lost report identifies payables for which discounts were not taken. Such cases are usually deviations from management policy and therefore require investigation.

FIGURE 6–14
An Accounts Payable System.

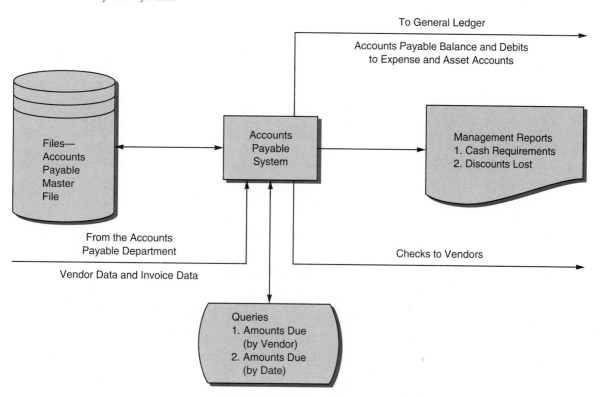

FIGURE 6–15
Typical Fields in an
Accounts Payable
Master File.

Vendor Number
Vendor Name
Vendor Address
Payment Terms
Amounts Owed by Invoice
Payments—Year-to-Date
Discounts Taken—Year-
    to-date
Discounts Lost—Year-to-Date

FIGURE 6–16
Typical Accounts Payable Management Reports.

```
                                                              PAGE 1
                        CASH REQUIREMENT
                            REPORT
                        AS OF 10-31-9X
```

DUE DATE	VENDOR NO	VENDOR NAME	PYMT TERMS	INVOICE NO	AMOUNT DUE	DISC AMOUNT	BALANCE DUE	PYMT
01319X	25190	INTERNATIONAL PAPER	2/10,N/30	07519	450.00	9.00	441.00	441.00
02109X	31723	LLOYD'S MANUFACTURIN	*****	21340	652.00	.00	652.00	200.00
02159X	45310	ABDICK	2/10,N/30	17001	107.50	2.15	105.40	105.00
02159X	51377	IBM	3/10,N/30	00910	963.00	28.89	934.11	934.11
02289X	63784	PENTEL	*****	50003	93.00	.00	93.00	50.00
03019X	72111	XEROX	1/10,N/30	43000	70.00	7.00	63.00	63.00

```
                     TOTAL CASH REQUIREMENTS 10-31-9x  $1793.51
```

```
                                                              PAGE 1
                        DISCOUNTS LOST
                            REPORT
                        AS OF 10-31-9X
```

VOUCHER NO	VENDOR NO	VENDOR NAME	INVOICE AMOUNT	AMOUNT LOST	EFF APR	DAYS LATE
15270	25190	INTERNATIONAL PAPER	7500.00	150.00	24%	10
29563	31723	LLOYD'S MANUFACTURIN	1350.00	13.50	13%	5
14021	45310	ABDICK	1080.00	21.60	13%	4
83910	51377	IBM	2532.00	75.96	25%	9
85674	63784	PENTEL	950.00	9.50	15%	4
93201	72111	XEROX	1500.00	30.00	22%	6

The accounts payable system also produces checks, which are sent to vendors after review by the accounts payable department. Queries to the system usually involve amounts due to be paid. Management may need to know the amount due a particular vendor or the amount due by a certain date. Application 6–2 illustrates how Bechtel Group, Inc. uses an all-electronic system to pay its bills.

APPLICATION 6–2

Bechtel Loses the Paper, Wins the Prize

By Mitch Betts

It is easy to see why many companies have created sophisticated systems for accounts receivable. Every business wants to efficiently capture income. But San Francisco-based Bechtel Group, Inc. has developed an all-electronic system that makes it easier to pay the bills.

The manual processes involved in paying a corporation's bills are very expensive. So in 1989, Bechtel created what is believed to be the first full service electronic disbursements system.

Converting from paper to electronic funds transfer reduced the cost of making those payments by 80%, according to Bechtel. In recognition of such dramatic cost savings, the National Automated Clearing House Association se-

lected Bechtel's vice president and controller V. Paul Unruh last month to receive the 1991 Payment Systems Excellence Award.

Bechtel's system, developed along with First National Bank of Chicago, allows the company to pay bills using any one of four formats: electronic data interchange, automated clearinghouse, Fedwire or check.

Cash Advantage

One big financial advantage is that the information system gives Bechtel's treasury a clearer idea of how much cash will be needed to pay the bills each day so it can keep the rest of the company's cash in money-earning investment accounts. Furthermore, the direct-deposit system makes it possible for Bechtel to take advantage of any vendor cash discounts.

As for paperwork, the electronic disbursement system eliminates about 120,000 forms and 200,000 computer printout pages per year. It also eliminates company-produced checks by nearly 100% and reduces costs of issuing remaining checks by 50%.

"Bechtel's payment system approach . . . provides a model for corporations to remove themselves from the burdens of operating an assortment of electronic and paper disbursement systems," said David P. Smay, assistant treasurer at Chevron Corp., in his letter nominating Unruh for the award.

———

Reprinted with permission from *Computerworld* (March 4, 1991), p. 51. Copyright 1991 by CW Publishing, Inc., Framingham, MA 01701.

Payroll

Payroll is often the first system a company converts to computer processing because it is a relatively simple operation that does not interface with many other application systems. The primary objectives of the **payroll** system are (1) to pay both hourly and salaried employees on a timely basis, (2) to maintain records of payments to employees and of taxes withheld, and (3) to provide management with the reports needed to manage the payroll function.

Figure 6–17 shows a payroll system. This system maintains a payroll master file. The contents of a typical payroll master file record are shown in Figure 6–18. The payroll department provides most of the payroll system input in the form of personal employee data, such as name, address, pay rate, and hours worked during a pay period. In some cases the sales department provides data for commission payments to salespeople. Output from the payroll system includes required government forms, such as the W-2 form used for reporting wages to the Internal Revenue Service. The system also produces paychecks for employees.

Management reports include the deductions-not-taken report and the payroll register (see Figure 6–19). The payroll register is a record of wages paid and amounts withheld for each employee. The deductions-not-taken report lists employees whose deductions were not taken on schedule due to insufficient pay. Queries to the payroll system generally are for information concerning individual employees, such as personal data or earnings.

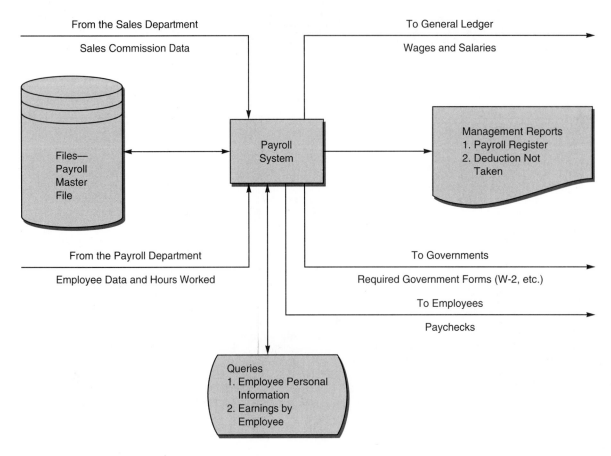

FIGURE 6–17
A Payroll System.

FIGURE 6–18
Contents of a Typical
Payroll Master File
Record.

Employee Number
Employee Name
Employee Address
Department
Occupation
Pay Rate
Vacation Time
Sick Leave Time
Gross Pay Year-to-Date
Federal Income Tax Withheld
State Income Tax Withheld
FICA Tax Withheld
Health Insurance Withheld
Credit Union Savings
   Withheld
Bank Code

FIGURE 6–19
Typical Payroll Management Reports.

DEDUCTIONS NOT TAKEN
REPORT
AS OF 10-31-9X

EMP NO	EMP NAME	DEDUCTION DESC	AMOUNT TAKEN	AMOUNT NOT TAKEN	NOT TAKEN BALANCE
00001	TURNBALL, JW	UNITED FUND	.00	25.00	25.00
00001	TURNBALL, JW	CREDIT UNION	40.00	.00	57.00
00002	CLARK, TC	HOSPITALIZATION	26.00	.00	5.00
00003	JONES, FL	PENSION	45.00	.00	40.00
00003	JONES, FL	BONDS	.00	65.00	70.00
00005	JAMES, CL	CREDIT UNION	40.00	.00	40.00

PAYROLL REGISTER
REPORT
AS OF 10-31-9X

EMP NO	EMP NAME	RATE	REG HOURS	OT HOURS	TOTAL EARNINGS	FEDERAL TAX	FICA TAX	STATE TAX	EARNINGS YTD
00001	TURNBALL, JW	4.51	40	10	248.05	32.20	25.41	13.04	7840.21
00002	CLARK, TC	5.37	40	0	214.80	16.81	12.10	6.75	8250.00
00003	JONES, FL	3.35	21	0	70.35	6.91	4.21	2.10	2615.00
00004	SMITH, AJ	3.35	30	0	100.50	9.22	6.90	4.12	3700.12
00005	JAMES, CL	5.37	40	5	255.08	41.90	31.76	15.02	9215.91
00006	FREDERICKSON, JR	4.51	40	0	180.40	12.13	10.91	5.33	7651.00

General Ledger

The **general ledger**, a common computer application, maintains the financial accounts of a business. This system is responsible for producing financial statements, such as the income statement, the statement of financial position, and the statement of changes in financial position. This application maintains a record of a firm's assets, liabilities, owner equities, revenues, and expenses.

Most ledger systems can also maintain a budget, especially for revenues and expenses. Reports can be prepared that compare actual revenues and expenses to budgeted amounts. Such reports help maintain control of a business organization.

Human Resource Information Systems

Another application many firms use is a **human resource information system**. This system maintains data about a firm's employees. Typical data are name, address, birthdate, salary, skills, foreign language proficiency, and training courses completed. The information from the human resource information system is typically used by the personnel department for benefits administration, compensation administration, personnel planning, employee relations, government regulation compliance, and employee profile information. Substantial data are shared between this system and the payroll system. Application 6–3 illustrates how Colonial Williamsburg uses a human resource information system.

The personnel function of the firm is responsible for implementing and managing the human resource information system. Since the early 1980s two major forces have increased the importance of human resource information systems for firms. First, increased competition from both international and domestic sources has increased the importance of utilizing employees in the most productive manner. Second, increased government regulation, such as the Occupational Safety and Health Act (OSHA) and Equal Employment and Affirmative Action programs, have greatly increased the importance of maintaining accurate data concerning personnel actions.

APPLICATION 6–3

A Modern Slant on Colonial Times

By Frank Irving

Amid last year's Fourth of July celebration in the restored 18th century city of Colonial Williamsburg—complete with its parade of fife and drums, fireworks spectacular, strolling balladeers and jugglers, and gambols in the taverns—it was difficult to imagine midrange technology whirring away behind the scenes. Anachronistic as it might seem, however, such was the case.

Under the organizational umbrella of Colonial Williamsburg, hotel operations subsidize a not-for-profit foundation. An independent child care center also is affiliated with the organization. In all, Colonial Williamsburg employs nearly 4,000 people.

Bonnie Devine, director of IS [information systems] for human resources at Colonial Williamsburg in Virginia, tells MIDRANGE Systems that within the past year, the organization purchased an AS/400, which handles hotel reservations, a donor system, and materials planning. Devine's department, charged with providing record-keeping services for the organization, uses a System/38 running human resources software from Hyannis, Mass.-based Software 2000.

"If I wanted to be historically cute, I'd say we've gone from the quill pen to the modern days in human resources," remarks Devine. "But it would be more accurate to say we've gone from the Bic pen to the present." Before going live with the Software 2000 package in July 1985, all human resource records except payroll were on paper and manually administered. "In 1985, no one in human resources had ever used a computer before—just pens and typewriters."

Now, Colonial Williamsburg is on the current release of the human resources software and has found upgrading from one release to the next to be a routine task. The organization has automated dependent care, unreimbursed medical and 401K administration as well as processing for five health plans on the S/38. Devine notes that IS has proposed purchasing another AS/400 to allow for continuing expansion of services.

Devine adds that the system has adapted well to the special circumstances of 18th century life: "The position files handle hundreds of positions, from coopers and shepherdesses to domestic services such as spinners, weavers and candlemakers, to archaeologists and researchers. Even the children who sit at someone's knee have a defined position."

Since employees work in expensive costumes, it doesn't make sense to hire extra people for secondary positions, according to Devine. For instance, as in colonial times, many of the city's shopkeepers also assemble for militia musters. One ambitious employee held 14 different positions.

In addition, Devine says the system has become invaluable in tracking employee training records. "If we've got a special group coming in and need to find an employee who has been trained in 18th century gardening and also speaks Japanese, we can look up the requirements in the system."

And so it goes in Williamsburg, a colonial city quietly closing in on the 21st century.

Finally, it is important to recognize that information systems are becoming increasingly integrated across functions within firms. For example, computer integrated manufacturing systems touch engineering, marketing, manufacturing, human resources and accounting. Because of this trend it is somewhat arbitrary even today to classify systems by functions as we have done in this chapter. However, such classifications do help you understand the systems and to identify which function has primary responsibility for the system.

Summary

- The business cycle consists of finance, spending, conversion, and revenue activities.

- The two primary objectives of an inventory system are (1) to minimize costs due to out-of-stock situations, and (2) to minimize inventory carrying costs. The two objectives often conflict.

- Computer-integrated manufacturing (CIM) systems provide information to manage manufacturing from a single, integrated database.

- Electronic data interchange (EDI) is the computer-to-computer transmission of transaction data between business trading partners.

- The primary objectives of an order-processing system are (1) to initiate shipping orders, (2) to maintain a record of back-ordered items, and (3) to produce sales analysis reports.

- The sales management system is used to support account management, direct marketing, lead tracking, mapping, sales forecasting, sales presentations, and telemarketing.

- The objectives of an accounts receivable system are (1) to bill customers for orders shipped, (2) to maintain records of the amounts customers owe and pay, and (3) to provide information to assist in the collection of past-due accounts.

- The objectives of an accounts payable system are (1) to provide control over payments to vendors of goods and suppliers of services, (2) to issue checks to vendors and suppliers, and (3) to provide information for effective cash management.

- The objectives of the payroll system are (1) to pay both hourly and salaried employees on a timely basis, (2) to maintain records of payments to employees and of taxes withheld, and (3) to provide management with the reports needed to manage the payroll function.

- The general ledger maintains the financial accounts of the business and produces financial statements. Other typical applications include marketing information systems, human resource information systems, and specialized applications such as reservations systems.

- The human resource system maintains and reports information concerning a firm's employees.

Key Terms

Business cycle

Manufacturing firms

Merchandising firms

Service firms

Finance activity

Spending activity

Conversion activity

Revenue activity

Production information
  systems

Raw materials

Work-in-process

Finished goods

Merchandise inventory

Inventory system

Just-in-time inventory systems

Computer-integrated
  manufacturing (CIM)

Bill of materials

Marketing information system

Electronic data interchange
  (EDI)

Order processing

Sales management system

Accounting information
  system

Back order

Accounts receivable

Accounts payable

Payroll

General ledger

Human resource information
  system

Review Questions

1. What is the business cycle?

2. How do merchandising, service, and manufacturing firms differ? Can the basic activities of these three types of firms be depicted by the business cycle?

3. How are the traditional business functions of accounting, production, and marketing related to the business cycle activities?

4. What are the primary objectives of an inventory system?

5. For the merchandise inventory system, identify the following: primary inputs, typical data maintained on the master file, and some examples of output.

6. What is a computer-integrated manufacturing system?

7. What are the advantages of electronic data interchange?

8. What are the primary objectives of the order-processing system?

9. For the order-processing system, identify the following: primary inputs, typical data maintained on the master file, and some examples of output.

10. What are some of the applications of a sales management system?

11. What are the primary objectives of the accounts receivable system?

12. For the accounts receivable system, identify the following: primary inputs, typical data maintained on the master file, and some examples of output.

13. What are the primary objectives of the accounts payable system?

14. For the accounts payable system, identify the following: primary inputs, typical data maintained on the master file, and some examples of output.

15. What are the primary objectives of the payroll system?

16. For the payroll system, identify the following: primary inputs, typical data maintained on the master file, and some examples of output.

17. What is a general ledger system?

18. What is a human resource information system?

Discussion Questions and Cases

1. Of the applications covered in this chapter, which do you think could justify the use of real-time master files? Support your position.

2. A company is installing a computer for the first time. The company plans to eventually computerize all the applications discussed in this chapter. However, its managers think it is impossible to implement all these applications simultaneously and that some applications must have priority over others. Rank the applications in the order you would implement them.

3. Roanoke Power Company, an electrical utility, has a batch accounts receivable system. The system is updated daily on the night shift. On line terminals allow users to inquire about the status of accounts. Because of the batch update, an account could be out of date as much as a full day. The company is considering installing a real-time accounts receivable system. If you were a consultant to Roanoke Power, what would you say were the advantages and disadvantages of a real-time accounts receivable system? Would you advise the company to install such a system?

4. James River Supply is a medium-sized hardware wholesaler. At any one point, it has approximately nine hundred retail hardware stores as customers. The vice president of marketing is dissatisfied with the marketing information produced by his staff and computer-based systems. He has initiated a systems development study to figure out the major characteristics of an ideal marketing information system. Outline the characteristics of three or four reports or computer terminal screens that would be most useful in a marketing information system. Where would the data come from to support these reports or screens?

INFORMATION SYSTEMS STRATEGIES

Douglas Brings Costs Back to Earth

By Janet Mason

Back in 1983, Douglas Aircraft Co. decided that to make any money, it needed to either throttle back on climbing operating costs or risk falling from the sky.

Despite sales of $1.9 billion and a stream of new commercial and military aircraft orders, the Long Beach, Calif.-based subsidiary of McDonnell Douglas had operating losses of $52 million. Overworks and reworks were common, and assignments were made at random. Chillingly, company officials say, workers often ignored plans and built from memory. Worst of all, nobody knew where the high costs were coming from.

Not surprisingly, the few information systems supporting final assembly and test flight operations were slow and nearly useless. Often, status reports arrived a full 24 hours after the events they tracked, says Larry Selby, Douglas' manager of production systems operations control. "We found that what systems did exist were tailored to provide reports to the folks in the offices rather than for the workers actually building the planes," Selby says.

Problems only worsened as production increased and more assembly workers were hired. Hoping to turn things around, Douglas executives began a huge internal shake-up. Management was flattened from eight layers to four, manufacturing information systems were rethought, and assembly line workers were given a much wider charge.

New Culture, New System

Today, Douglas is no longer a dollar-eating giant. In 1988, the company raked in profits of $127 million on sales exceeding $4 billion. While Wall Street analysts continue to voice concerns about Douglas, they say the company appears to have hit clearer skies. Douglas officials credit at least part of the turnaround to a new integrated Assembly Tracking and Management System (ATMS) that reflects the firm's new, sleeker, worker-oriented culture.

"We wanted to design a computer system to address the line workers first and then, as a by-product, to provide information to the administrative people," Selby explains.

The $3.5 million ATMS system integrates six Douglas manufacturing locations around the country. Its goal is to improve work flow and quality assurance by giving line workers immediate access to on-line information.

Using ATMS, assembly workers can stay informed about the current status of each assembly operation on every commercial and military airplane being built at Douglas plants in Palmdale, Calif., Columbus, Ohio, Salt Lake City, Macon, Ga., and Long Beach.

ATMS lets workers track the assembly process, including each aircraft's status, project delays, work assignments and the availability and skill levels of employees. It also enables supervisors to schedule tasks more efficiently, assist quality assurance inspectors and provide management with reports.

The ATMS system is written in Mapper, a fourth-generation language (4GL) program from Unisys, explains Richard Brundridge, group leader of ATMS.

What's remarkable, Selby notes, is that every one of more than 275 different programs was written by analysts without any help from programmers. The end result? "Design, development and maintenance was done with about one-tenth the resources previously required," he says.

Such dramatic savings are possible, Selby says, because the 4GL lets analysts develop prototypes and programs literally overnight. The result is savings of thousands of dollars and hours in development and maintenance costs and time. Instead of being patched, old programs are simply discarded and rewritten.

The payoff: Defects that needed rework were reduced by 25% using the system, according to Selby. What's more, he adds, line workers now have more of a role in deciding how to assemble aircraft, rather than having "the boss telling them what to do."

Piece by Piece

Prototyping for ATMS took place late in 1983. A prototype of 10 programs was developed by one analyst in just three days. Over the course of the next six months, two analysts worked on the initial set of production programs. Most of the time was spent coordinating organizational definition and work flow. In all, Brundridge estimates that ATMS took 4,000 man-hours to develop.

The initial implementation took place early in 1985 on the MD-80 line, formerly known as the DC-9, in Long Beach. "We started in one department and followed the airplane down the assembly line, starting with the nose, wings and fuselage and going to the flight ramp," Brundridge recalls.

During implementation, another issue emerged: How do you bring a Unisys-based system into a traditionally all-IBM shop?

"It was difficult," Brundridge recalls. "We encountered some resistance, but we were able to convince people that in labor savings alone, it was worth it."

Because of previous bad experiences with service from the former Sperry Corp. (now part of Unisys) more than a decade ago, some people were hesitant about Unisys, he says. To assuage IS [information systems] and general management's fears, the production systems team had the Unisys ATMS application up and running within six months.

The C-17 military cargo units came on-line in 1988. Installation on the MD-11 line is about halfway completed, officials say, with work expected to be done by the end of the year.

Along with providing line workers with the information they need, Douglas officials say that ATMS also benefits other employees.

Time Saver

"Prior to using ATMS, the first-line supervisor spent two to six hours making work schedules, using paper and pencil and organizing employees for a day's activity," Brundridge says. Now, because all the information is in one place, the same work can be scheduled in 10 minutes, he says.

Another benefit is that managers and planners can "see into the shop through the terminal on their desks," Brundridge explains. "They can check attendance, analyze recurring problems and enter the data into graphics packages to create reports" for senior management and the U.S. Air Force.

The reports contain information on how many airplanes are produced per assembly line in a given time period and whether the production team is meeting its schedule. The system accurately records what time was spent on each task instead of estimating it.

Employees can also check the system for information on the assembly line in front of or behind them, Brundridge says. "If they wanted to, they could check information on other [plane model] assembly lines," he says.

Officials say ATMS has also helped with troubleshooting. Now, when an assembly line employee comes across a problem that hinders production, a "job delay" comment is entered on the record. The work team then concentrates on resolving the glitch.

When the assembly job has been completed, quality assurance inspectors are notified by the system's electronic bulletin board.

According to Brundridge, "The system brings work teams together." The teams—consisting of line workers (mechanics), planners, management and staff members in the tool department—use the computer as a communications vehicle.

"If the mechanic can't complete the job because something was planned incorrectly," Brundridge says, "the group finds out immediately [through the computer system] and meets as a team to solve the problem."

Because the system instantly shows whether there are any delays or needed parts, the line workers do not have to wait for the quality assurance inspectors to catch the problems later.

Only a Start

Despite such successes, Douglas can hardly afford to rest on its laurels, says Martin Bollinger, an aerospace industry analyst at Booz, Allen & Hamilton, Inc. in New York.

"Douglas Aircraft has had trouble shipping aircraft, and its financial performance has been poor in the last five years," Bollinger says.

Military aircraft sales are down, he notes, and Douglas is not meeting the demand as well as it could. "These are good times for the commercial aircraft business, but Douglas hasn't been able to meet the demand that is out there," Bollinger says.

Wayne Brewster, a Unisys sales manager in Los Angeles, notes that participative management and shop-floor information systems have helped make Douglas more competitive.

"The days of cost overruns are over," he says. "Both commercial and military operations have to become more efficient."

Discussion Questions

1. How does a system like ATMS improve quality?

2. ATMS was developed by analysts without the help of programmers. Is it realistic to think that most systems can be developed this way?

7

Decision Support and Executive Information Systems

Bob Lexington is the chief executive officer of Phillips Products Incorporated. In a recent meeting with his vice president, Bob said that computer information systems are very valuable for transaction processing and for support of operational-level decision making. He feels, however, that computer information systems are a long way from providing significant support for tactical- and strategic-level decision making, especially for unstructured and unanticipated decisions. He stated, "For the type of decisions I make, most of the data and information comes from informal and often outside sources. Of course, our computer information systems can provide me with background information. But this is a relatively small percentage of the information I need to make most decisions. The idea of a decision support system for tactical- and strategic-level decisions is just too new. I think we should wait several years before investing our resources in this untried concept." Do you agree with Bob?

Computer information systems follow a natural evolution in organizations. Most organizations start with data processing systems that support transaction processing, and evolve to management information systems to support tactical- and strategic-level decision making. In the past few years a new type of system called a decision support system has gained popularity in the information systems field. This text views decision support systems as an evolutionary extension of a management information system.

This chapter defines a decision support system, describes its software, and identifies its functions. It also explores the need for such a system, examines some of the organizations in which a decision support system is likely to be successful, and covers the steps in building a decision support system. Finally, the chapter covers executive information systems, which hold great potential for application in business situations.

Introduction

In Chapter 3 we explored the relationship between objectives, decisions, and information. We stressed that the purpose of information systems is to provide information for decision making. Management information systems in the past have been successful in providing information for routine, *structured*, and anticipated types of decisions. (In structured decisions, the methods and rules for making the decision are well defined and known. Examples are when to reorder inventory, and whether or not to grant credit to a customer.) In addition, MIS systems have succeeded in acquiring and storing large quantities of detailed data concerning transaction processing. They have been less successful in providing information for semistructured or unstructured decisions, particularly those that were not anticipated when the computer information system was designed.

A **decision support system (DSS)** is an integrated set of computer tools that allow a decision maker to interact directly with computers to create information useful in making unanticipated semistructured and unstructured decisions. For example, a DSS is useful in making decisions involving mergers and acquisitions, plant expansion, new products, stock portfolio management, and marketing.

A distinction must be made between a decision support system and the software and hardware tools that make it possible. Electronic spread-

What Is a Decision Support System?

sheets, such as Lotus 1-2-3 and Excel, are DSS software tools (often called DSS generators). A particular decision support system is an application of DSS tools, not the tools themselves.

A DSS must be inherently flexible to respond to unanticipated needs for information. This type of flexibility requires that decision makers be directly involved in designing a DSS. Thus, building and using a DSS is a form of application development by users. In fact, many of the hardware and software tools (such as personal computers, electronic spreadsheets, and financial modeling software) used for application development by users are also used in decision support systems. Application 7–1 illustrates how Lotus 1-2-3 was used to build a decision support system to assist in billion-dollar deals.

APPLICATION 7–1

Dealmaking at Equico

By Sylvia Helm

Two weeks after Cleveland Christophe joined the TLC Group L.P. in 1987, the New York-based leveraged-buyout firm asked him to evaluate the possible purchase of Beatrice International Food Company from Kohlberg Kravis Roberts & Company. Christophe eyeballed the deal overnight, priced it at $950 million, and said, "Let's do it."

He made the determination—and subsequently structured the entire financing—on his own Symphony-based decision support model. The deal eventually totaled $985 million.

Today Christophe and his model sift through potential deals for Equico Capital Corporation, a wholly owned subsidiary of the Equitable Life Assurance Company. In February Christophe became a vice president at the firm, which has financed more than 72 small businesses since its formation in 1971.

Christophe's 1.2-megabyte model now runs in 1-2-3 Release 3, boasts 5,000 lines of macros, and offers six custom menus. It generates a full set of financial statements, including cash flow

and debt analysis, and calculates the rate of return for seven levels of investors. "Without this tool," says Christophe, "there's no way I could do the in-depth analysis, testing, and planning in time." He asserts that the model lets him do in about five hours what used to take a week.

"The model substantially enhances our ability to respond to investment proposals," agrees Duane Hill, president and CEO of Equico. With sufficient data, Hill says, Equico can make its decisions in 24 to 48 hours and still get "a much more intelligent and informed view than we had in the past."

Christophe's model offered a significant improvement in speed and flexibility over Equico's existing 1-2-3 templates. Equico has already used the model to evaluate a variety of deals, including acquiring a couple of banks and a $40 million purchase of a national service company that acquired a new subsidiary midway through the analysis. Equico must look at more than 100 possible deals to find three that are worth pursuing.

To identify deals worth pursuing, Christophe's model concen-

trates on the optimal ratio between debt and equity. Unfortunately, the factors that influence this ratio affect one another in a circular fashion. In a given period, a company's interest expense depends on its debt level. The debt level depends on the amount of cash flow the company can generate to pay down its debt. Cash flow depends—at least in part—on what the company must pay in interest expenses. The model has to juggle multiple calculations to converge on the value that solves all the equations.

Christophe's model has more than proved its worth. While the pressure of crushing debt loads on many leveraged buyouts has led to a collapse in the junk-bond market, Christophe's 1-2-3-based financing of Beatrice Food hasn't stumbled. "It's doing OK," he says. "It's not one of the ones you read about." That's something you can't say about a lot of other such deals.

Adapted with permission of Sylvia Helm from *Lotus* (Dec., 1990), p. 68(3). Copyright Sylvia Helm, 1990.

The earlier concepts of a DSS focused on its capability to be tools for individuals to use in decision making. In the late 1980s substantial research and development began on group decision support systems. A **group decision support system (GDSS)** is designed to support more than one individual in a joint decision-making task where the decisions are unstructured. Groups make decisions in many different settings, ranging from boardrooms to conferences to teleconferences where individuals are not assembled together in one room but speak to one another over telephones. Table 7–1 illustrates GDSS elements and types. The elements are listed at the left of the table and the major types are listed across the top. The first two elements identify the hardware and software used in each type of GDSS. The third element, organizationware, identifies how the group meeting is organized and conducted. The final element identified is the people who participate in the group. Across the bottom of the table are specific examples of each type of GDSSs.

As can be seen from Table 7–1, there is a wide variety of GDSS types. However, all of these systems attempt to provide participants in the decision-making process with computer-based support that includes data, management, retrieval, graphical displays of data, decision analysis capability, modeling, and so on.

The hardware element in Table 7–1 shows that five of the six types of group decision support systems specify a conference room as the location of the hardware and the decision-making process. Figure 7–1 provides an illustration of the PLEXSYS conference room.

Group decision support systems have a promising future. For instance, one type is the group decision support system that allows participating individuals to be in different locations. These systems have the potential to significantly reduce the travel costs of business managers and executives.

Group Decision Support Systems

The software components for decision support systems are illustrated in Figure 7–2. The major components include a **language system**, which enables the user to interact with the decision support system; a **problem processing system**, which is made up of several components that perform various processing tasks; and a **knowledge system**, which provides data and artificial intelligence capabilities to the decision support system.

The language system may have both procedural and nonprocedural language capabilities. A **procedural language** requires that the user provide the logical steps or procedures to be used in solving a particular problem. Examples of procedural languages are FORTRAN, COBOL, and BASIC. Most decision makers do not use procedural languages; these languages are generally used by professional programmers. However, a DSS may process specific problems that a nonprocedural language cannot address; therefore, a procedural language could be useful.

With a **nonprocedural language,** the user simply specifies the characteristics of a problem or information query and lets the DSS determine the logical steps necessary to provide the information. An example of a nonprocedural command is "Retrieve sales for last year for all stores in the state of New York." This nonprocedural query is very English-like. Nonprocedural languages can be English-like or they can be in many other forms that are user friendly.

Decision Support System Software

TABLE 7–1

Major Group Decision Support Systems Elements and Types

Reprinted with permission from K. L. Kraemer, and L. K. King, "Computer-Based Systems for Cooperative Work and Group Decision Making," *ACM Computing Surveys*, Vol. 20, No. 2, June 1988, pp. 120–121. Copyright 1988 Association for Computing Machinery, Inc.

Element	Electronic Boardroom	Teleconference Facility	Group Network
Hardware Software Organizationware People Examples	Conference room; audiovisuals; graphic displays; computer Interactive graphics Audiovisuals; corporate reports; standard meeting protocols Participants; audiovisual technician These are custom tailored for each site although some "modular" audiovisual rooms exist	Conference room; audiovisuals; audio, computer or video telecommunication controller Communications Audiovisuals; teleconference protocols Participants (in two or more locations); teleconference facilitator Picturephone Meeting Service	Offices; file server and computer work stations; telephone; computer network Interactive/asynchronous computer conferencing; terminal linking; real-time meeting scheduling; shared bit-map display Conference chair conducts meetings Participants (in two or more *local* places), group leader MIT Lab for Computer Science RTCAL and MBlink EIES, NOTEPAD, PARTICIPATE CONFER II

Information Center	Decision Conference	Collaboration Laboratory
Conference room; large-screen video projector; computer; display terminals Database management software; statistical packages; retrieval, graphics, and text-processing software Corporate and other databases; standard meeting protocols; standard meetings (e.g., annual report, market forecast) Participants; computer specialists; modeling specialists HOBO System: SYSTEM W; EIS, EXPRESS, XSIM	Conference room; large-screen video projector; display terminals; voting terminals Decision analysis software; modeling software; voting tally and display software Democratic decision-making protocols (e.g., one person one vote; all major interests represented; majority opinion rules) Participants; decision analysts; group process facilitators Group Decision Aid; Decision Conferences of DDI; Decision Tectronics, SUNY, Albany; Planning Lab, University of Arizona; GDSS Lab, University of Minnesota	Conference room; electronic chalkboard microcomputer workstations, electern Multiuser interface; Wysiwis; outlining (COGNOTER); evaluating (Argnoter) Standard meeting protocols Participants Colab Project, Xerox PARC; Project NICK, MCC

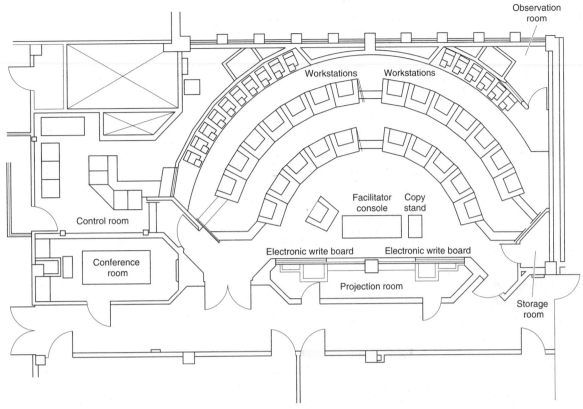

F I G U R E 7-1

The PLEXSYS Decision Room.

PLEXSYS is a group decision support system that has been operational at the University of Arizona since 1985 and has been installed in industrial sites.

Reprinted with special permission from A. R. Dennis, J. F. George, L. M. Jessup, J. F. Nunamaker and D. L. Vogel, "Information Technology to Support Electronic Meetings," *MIS Quarterly*, December 1988, p. 624. Copyright (1988) by the Society for Information Management and the Management Information Systems Research Center at the University of Minnesota.

The problem processing system is the heart of the decision support system. It should contain several capabilities, including the ability to collect information from databases through database management systems. It should make available a wide variety of management science models, such as regression, time-series analysis, and goal programming.

F I G U R E 7-2

Components of a Decision Support System.

A DSS typically has several tools. Each tool provides one or more of the components illustrated here. Not all DSSs have, or need, all the components listed here.

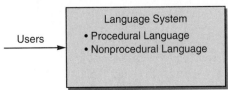

It also should have a graphics capability and an electronic spreadsheet feature similar to those offered by packages such as Lotus 1-2-3 and SuperCalc. Many decision support systems are being built with an electronic spreadsheet as the main focus. Most decision support systems include standard financial functions such as return on investment and net present value.

The knowledge system is made up of the database management system and the associated files stored and managed by the DBMS. These files contain detailed data that have been collected through transaction processing and from other sources. Another type of knowledge that is beginning to be useful in decision support systems is an expert system (also called **artificial intelligence**). It acts much like a human expert consultant, providing advice and explaining the advice when necessary. Expert systems are beginning to be applied successfully in several areas, including medicine and prospecting for minerals. The next chapter in this text covers expert systems in more depth.

Functions of a Decision Support System

Warren G. Briggs has provided a summary of several functions and features that DSS applications should contain.[1]

Model Building

The building of a model of the decision-making problem is a central purpose of most decision support systems. This model is often in the form of a two- (or more) dimensional table, such as the electronic spreadsheet. The first two dimensions of the table might contain an income statement, a third dimension could represent various products, and a fourth dimension could represent multiple retail outlets. Developing this model involves specifying in mathematical terms the relationships among the various sales and expense variables. For example, one may assume that sales is a function of advertising expense. In mathematical terms this function might be stated as Sales = 20 x Advertising Expense. This function indicates that for each dollar spent on advertising, sales will increase by twenty dollars.

Procedural and Nonprocedural Languages

As discussed earlier, these languages allow the user to communicate with the DSS. Most users find nonprocedural languages more convenient to use.

What-If Analysis

The ability to show the impact of changes in data and assumptions is perhaps the most useful feature of a DSS. For example, a DSS could show the impact on profit if sales grew at a rate of 7 to 10 percent instead of 5 percent. Most DSS applications can show instantaneously on the CRT the impact of such changes in assumptions. Electronic spreadsheets are especially good for **what-if analysis.**

---

[1] Warren G. Briggs, "An Evaluation of DSS Packages," *Computerworld*, Vol. XVI, No. 9 (1982), 31.

Goal Seeking

A DSS shows what value a particular independent variable (such as advertising expense) would have to be in order to produce a certain target value for the dependent variable (such as sales). Thus, the DSS can answer questions such as: "If my goal is $20 million in sales, what must the advertising expense be?" Most electronic spreadsheets for personal computers do not have this capability. However, mainframe financial modeling tools that now run on personal computers, such as the Integrated Financial Planning System, perform **goal seeking**.

Risk Analysis

A useful piece of information for a decision maker is a probability distribution, which is obtained through a **risk analysis**. The probability distribution provides the probabilities that a particular critical measure, such as profit, will reach a certain level. For example, it would be useful to know the probability that the profit growth rate will be zero, the probability it will be 5 percent, and the probability it will be 10 percent. Such information can be generated using management science techniques, provided that certain data are available. The necessary data are the probability distributions of the underlying independent variables, such as sales and expenses.

Statistical Analysis and Management Science Models

A good DSS is able to provide several useful **management science models** such as regression and time-series analysis. These two models may be used to project historical data, such as sales, into the future.

Financial Functions

Preprogrammed **financial functions** for commonly used calculations are usually included in DSS packages. These may include corporate tax rates, depreciation methods, and return-on-investment functions.

Graphics

An extremely important feature in a decision support system is a graphics generator. The system should be able to depict any of the data contained in the system in various graphic forms, such as line or pie graphs.

Hardware Capabilities

Decision support systems in one form or another can be implemented on machines as small as personal computers and as large as mainframes. When a DSS is installed on a PC, the PC should have large amounts of primary and secondary data storage. Mainframes usually have large data storage and processing capacity, so more complex models can be implemented on them. A current trend (which is expected to continue) is the use of PCs in combination with mainframes for decision support systems. The PC is linked to the mainframe to retrieve data for subsequent processing on the PC, if the data volume and processing volumes are relatively small. If, on the other hand, large amounts of data and processing are required, some parts of the DSS may be performed on the mainframe. Many of the DSS software tools, such as IFPS and FOCUS, can run on both PCs and mainframes.

Databases and External Files

A DSS must be able to access data stored in the organization as files. Much of the knowledge-producing data that a DSS uses are stored in these files. File access can be done either through the database management system's capabilities or through the DSS's own capability to access external files. In addition, most DSS tools have the capability of maintaining their own internal files once the data are retrieved from other sources. Application 7–2 illustrates how Sanyo Securities' decision support system is used to monitor immense amounts of data.

APPLICATION 7–2

Volume Trading

By Paul Gillin

The first sound a visitor makes as he steps from the elevator on the fourth floor of Sanyo Securities is usually a gasp.

Sanyo Securities, though little known outside the Japanese market, boasts the world's largest trading room. In fact, Sanyo claims that the airline hangar-size structure, situated about 20 minutes from downtown Tokyo, is the largest continuous open work space in the world.

Just as striking as its 40,000 sq.-ft. expanse is the amount of information on display within the trading center. Four giant flat-panel displays flash tables and graphs at one end of the room. Exchange figures flicker across tote boards on two side walls. And each of the 750 trader posts on the floor faces three video screens and one dedicated computer terminal.

Sanyo Securities views technology as its edge against top players. "We cannot win by competing on the same basis as the big four" Japanese securities firms, says

Shojiro Ono, general manager of the systems planning department. "We are using our computers as a competitive weapon."

Two major new thrusts are Sanyo Investment Research New Information System (Sirnis), an integrated sales support system, and Personal Computer Analysis System for Your Portfolio (Pasport), a home computer-based customer investment support and order system.

Sirnis is a PC-based system with a built-in link to one of Sanyo's three IBM Model 3090 mainframes. Salespeople can use it to make timely and well-grounded recommendations to customers, using current quotes, a built-in real-time news ticker and the latest reports from Sanyo's stock analysts. Sales representatives can pull up historical information on individual stocks, look at detailed price information for the last several days and graphically display stock performance over time. Recommended buy and sell points from Sanyo analysts are built into the displays, giving sales representatives

the benefit of expert advice in one neat package.

Similar information is also available to individual clients through Pasport, a home portfolio analysis and ordering system that runs on more than 70 brands of PCs as well as on Japan's ubiquitous Nintendo systems.

Investors with more than 3 million yen (about $20,000) in a Sanyo Securities account can call a local number from their PC and tap into investment information on Sanyo mainframes.

Among other services, they can get real-time quotes, news wire information and stock data for graphical display on the PC; electronic mail to their sales representatives; and access to a Sanyo bulletin board of information about the market. These users can also buy and sell stocks and bonds electronically.

A need for the types of information that a DSS produces has always existed. Decision support systems themselves have become popular primarily because of developments concerning the hardware and software tools that make them possible. First, the declining cost of computer hardware has made computer processing and computer storage relatively inexpensive. Second, the advent of database management systems in the 1970s provided means for storage and management of large amounts of detailed data. These data are now relatively easy to retrieve for use in a decision support system. Third, the number of software packages that incorporate the functions of a DSS has greatly increased. These packages can be used directly to implement DSS applications. And finally, many college graduates trained in analytic techniques are now reaching the middle and upper levels of management where most semistructured and unstructured decisions are made. These individuals know how to use the tools that decision support systems provide.

Why Do Managers Need Decision Support Systems?

Organizations that have been successful in implementing decision support systems share several characteristics. First, they have well-controlled and well-structured data processing systems. Second, they have the extra dollars and personnel to maintain a research and development focus. This focus is needed because establishing a DSS is a development effort. Therefore, an organization must be willing to commit dollars and personnel to a project for which the benefits may be unknown. Third, the line departments of the organizations have established open communication with the central computer groups. Fourth, the line departments have sufficient confidence to initiate and manage system projects, and they are continually looking for new ways to use computer-based systems. Fifth, the computer groups act primarily as consultants to assist line departments in implementing systems. Sixth, the computer groups have several people on their staffs who either came from line departments or have substantial background in disciplines such as manufacturing, finance, accounting, or marketing. And finally, these organizations use education and training to build understanding between their line departments and computer groups.

Many of these characteristics are similar to those of organizations that have adopted application development by users. As mentioned earlier, the subject of application development by users is closely related to DSS. (The techniques discussed in Chapter 18 can be applied to decision support systems.)

Organization Environment for a Successful Decision Support System

Chapter 16 presents the structured systems development life cycle (SDLC) which includes the major processes involved in developing either a data processing or a management information system. Briefly, these processes can be summarized as system analysis, system design, implementation, and evaluation. The SDLC processes tend to be performed in a sequential manner. Building a DSS is quite different from the systems development life cycle. Analysis, design, implementation, and evaluation of decision support systems tend to be done at the same time. These processes are evolutionary in that upon initial implementation, a decision support system is likely to be incomplete. Owing to the semistruc-

Building a Decision Support System

tured and unstructured nature of problems addressed by a DSS, managers change their perceived needs for information, and therefore the DSS must also change. There may be no precise end to implementation. Since decision support systems are likely to be in a constant state of change, it is most important that users be directly involved in initiating and managing this change.

Peter G. W. Keen and Michael S. Scott Morton have outlined the major processes involved in building a decision support system: predesign, design, implementation, and evaluation.[2] Figure 7–3 is a summary of these processes.

FIGURE 7–3

Steps in Building a Decision Support System.

Building a DSS is a highly iterative process, with many of these steps going on simultaneously and being repeated. In essence, a DSS is continually being refined.

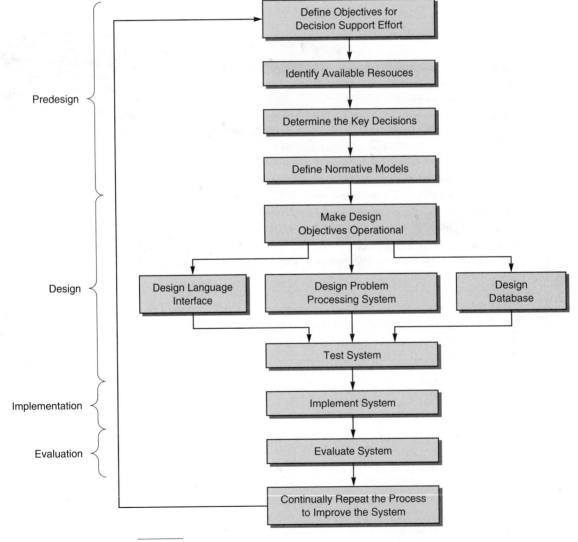

---

[2] Peter G. W. Keen and Michael S. Scott Morton, *Decision Support Systems: An Organizational Perspective* (Reading, Mass.: Addison-Wesley Publishing, 1978), 167–225.

Predesign

The first step in the predesign process is to define the objectives for the decision support effort, which involves laying out the overall goals of the project.

The second step is to identify the available resources that can be applied to the project. Often a firm already has hardware and software, such as a database management system, that can be used in a DSS.

Perhaps the most crucial step in the project is to determine the **key decisions** in the problem area. For example, in a stock portfolio management system the key decision might be to select the correct stocks for a particular customer's needs. You may conclude that it would be difficult for a DSS to provide information that would tell a portfolio manager which stocks to select because of the many factors involved, such as varying customer needs. Some customers might be very conservative and therefore would want their money invested in safe stocks. Others might prefer high-risk situations because of their potential high gains. Two points address this concern: (1) The decision support system is only a tool that provides information to the portfolio manager. The portfolio manager makes the final decision as to what stock to select. (2) Even though it may be difficult for a DSS to provide relevant information for a decision, it is still crucial to identify the key decision. Providing relevant information for the wrong decision is nonproductive. Providing marginally helpful information for the key decision is a useful contribution.

The next step is to define the normative models. A **normative model** is a highly rational approach to providing useful information to the manager making key decisions. The word *normative* means a standard, or what should be. Normative models are likely to be highly idealistic and theoretical. For example, in a stock portfolio DSS, ideal information would be the price of stocks at some future date, which is impossible to obtain.

It is unlikely that the level of a normative model will be attained in the actual implementation of a DSS. A normative model represents a goal that a firm attempts to implement in a real-world situation. For example, although a DSS would not be able to provide actual future stock prices to a stock portfolio manager, it could furnish information to improve the manager's forecast of future stock prices. It may not be practicable or advisable to implement a normative model, but it is necessary to keep the normative model in mind when designing the actual DSS. Normative models become a major part of the design objectives.

Design

The first step in the design process is to make the design objectives operational. In this step, systems designers decide what can be done in a real-world implementation of the DSS. The next step is to design the language interface. Ideally, this language interface is a nonprocedural language, since most users find it easier to communicate a problem to a DSS than to tell the DSS the procedural steps necessary to solve the problem. Designing the problem solving system is largely a matter of selecting the management science models (such as regression) and the computer software (such as graphics and electronic spreadsheet) that can be applied to the DSS application. These models and software must be combined in a way that allows the user to readily select and use them in operating the DSS.

Portions of the knowledge system may already be in place. Most companies that implement a DSS already have a great deal of basic data stored in database management systems. The final step in design is to thoroughly test the system before its implementation.

Implementation

In the implementation step, the user is asked to change from something he or she is doing now and to accept a new system. The organization or individual must feel a need for the new DSS. This need can be created in several ways. If a manager tells employees that they must use the new DSS, the manager is creating a need. However, in the long run this tactic may be counterproductive. Perhaps one of the most effective ways to develop user confidence in and need for a system is to involve the user as much as possible in the development process. As mentioned previously, the ideal situation would be to have the user initiate and manage this process, with a computer system specialist acting as a consultant. If this occurs the user will see a system as his or her own and therefore will be more likely to support and use the DSS.

Evaluation

To evaluate the contributions of a DSS, there must be criteria for evaluation. It is particularly difficult to establish such criteria for a DSS since the system is evolutionary in nature and therefore does not have a neatly defined completion date. It is unlikely that a DSS will be justified through reductions in clerical costs. Usually the justification is the provision of more timely and better information. This is a very general benefit and difficult to evaluate. However, it should be possible to measure the impact of this information on better decisions and, therefore, better ultimate results. For example, in a portfolio management system used by an investment firm, the ultimate result should be more satisfied customers and, in turn, greater revenue for the firm.

The evaluation process has three key steps. First, definitions of "improvements," or criteria for evaluation, are established very early in the building process. Second, a means of monitoring the progress toward these improvements is defined. And finally, a formal review process that periodically measures performance against the definitions of improvements is established.

Executive Information Systems

An **executive information system (EIS)** is a computer-based system that accesses data concerning the critical success factors of an organization and allows high-level executives to display this information on demand. Executive information systems are often called executive support systems, and are sometimes confused with decision support systems. Although executive information systems can be viewed as a type of decision support system, they are also closely related to management information systems. An executive information system can be viewed as the method by which executives access, on demand, the information stored in management information systems. Figure 7–4 illustrates this concept. As can be seen from Figure 7–4, the domain of an executive in-

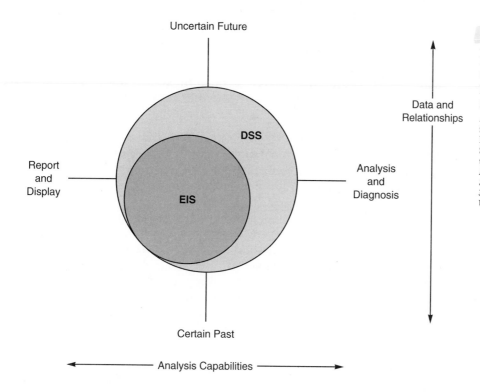

Uncertain Future

Report and Display

Analysis and Diagnosis

Certain Past

Data and Relationships

Analysis Capabilities

DSS

EIS

FIGURE 7–4

An Executive Information System Compared with a Decision Support System. Adapted with permission from Gary Anderson, "The ESS Revolution: Decision Support Software Reaches the Board Room," *Industrial Management and Data Systems*, No. 7, 1989, pp. 3–8. Published by MCB University Press Ltd.

formation system lies more in the reporting and displaying of past information and data, whereas a DSS covers these areas and future projections, and also leans more towards analysis and diagnosis rather than reporting and displaying.

The essence of an EIS is to provide quick, user-friendly access to information by nontechnical, high-level executives. The data can come from internal and/or external databases. Executive information systems should entice executives to interact directly with the computer. Many executives who do not use a computer are increasingly learning to use computers due to the popularity of executive information systems.

The characteristics of a good executive information system are as follows:

- Simple user interfaces are crucial. Good systems provide a wide variety of user interfaces such as a mouse, a touch screen, or a keyboard and allows the executive to choose whichever he or she is comfortable with.

- An EIS should be secure because the data that is contained and/or accessed by an EIS is obviously important and often proprietary information. Otherwise, the executive wouldn't be using it.

- An EIS should support what-if analysis and ad hoc queries. Thus, an EIS should contain some of the modeling capabilities of a DSS.

- An EIS should have the capability of allowing the executives to drill down into the data. Executives prefer summarized information, but they also like the capability of looking into the details if they wish. This capability is called drill down.

need not know this info. !

- Very quick response times are necessary.

- Color graphics capabilities are important for displaying information.

- The data used in an executive information system may reside in many different locations. Therefore, network connections between the executive's computer and the computers on which the data resides is desirable.

- While reviewing information, executives often like to send pieces of the information along with comments to others in the organization. Thus, cut and paste, simple word processing, and electronic mail capabilities are desirable for executive information systems.

Executive information systems may be developed in-house, but many firms purchase an off-the-shelf package and adapt it to their needs. There are several such packages on the market. Three of the most popular are Pilot's Command Center, Comshare's Commander, and Execucom's Executive Edge. These and other packages were recently reviewed in *Computerworld*. The results of this comparison for these three packages are illustrated in Table 7–2.

Executive information systems are likely to have several impacts on the organization. First, they may change the organizational structure.

TABLE 7–2
An Evaluation of Three Leading Executive Information Systems

User Requirements	Pilot's Command Center	Comshare's Commander	Execucom's Executive Edge
Data Access			
Integrating data from different sources	7.9	7.8	7.9
Efficient data extraction from existing databases	6.4	7.5	7.4
Efficient access to external databases	6.3	7.5	7.3
Multilevel ad hoc query capability	7.2	7.3	7.4
Well-integrated DSS	6.2	7.7	8.2
Application Development			
Ease of screen design and maintenance	8.8	7.5	8.8
Ease of customization	7.9	7.5	8.3
Support for rapid prototyping	8.1	8.1	8.2
Effective support for multiple user interfaces	7.4	7.4	7.3
Good security for data, screens, and systems	6.8	7.6	6.4
Varied application skills	7.7	7.0	7.9
User Features			
Well-presented graphics, text, tables, on screens	8.5	8.6	8.3
Quality of service and technical support	7.4	7.3	8.5
Effective interfaces to support such as Profs and Lotus	7.5	7.0	6.4
Pricing of installations and maintenance	6.7	5.7	7.5
Easy to create hard copy output	7.2	6.4	7.3
Useful on-line help screens	6.3	6.1	7.7

Adapted with permission from Michael L. Sullivan-Trainor, "Command Center Slips Past Commander (Barely)," *Computerworld*, July 16, 1990, pp. 88–93, Copyright 1990 by CW Publishing, Inc., Framingham, MA 01701.

Middle management often acts as a conduit of information from the lower levels to executive levels. If executives can get part of their information through executive information systems, fewer middle managers may be needed. Thus, an EIS could produce a flatter organization.

In practice, firms are finding that lower level managers use executive information systems as well as executives. These managers use the systems to obtain a day-to-day picture of what's going on within and outside the organization. Thus, managers at all levels are better informed when they make decisions because of the use of executive information systems. Application 7–3 illustrates how an EIS can help steer managers toward better use of their time.

APPLICATION 7–3

EIS Can Help Steer Managers Toward Better Use of PC Time

By Dennis Eskow

Increasing use of PCs and decreasing support staffs are conspiring to rob middle managers of management time, a Georgia Institute of Technology economist's analysis indicates.

Peter Sassone, an economist at Georgia Tech's Ivan Allen College of Management in Atlanta, analyzed 17 studies conducted over the past five years of managers' use of time. He said the unpublished report, compiled at the request of a client, suggests that corporations may have to redefine specialties to get the most out of managers.

"We found an increasing number of senior managers doing the work of junior professionals and even support staff," Sassone said. "It isn't just the time wasted in typing letters that should have been handled by a support person. It's the time spent in doing such non-management tasks as scheduling meetings and following up memos. This is work that can be done by junior-level people."

But the study notes that staff levels are being reduced as businesses struggle to cope with an increasingly difficult economy.

Sassone said there is a point at which the money saved by removing junior or support staffers is eaten up by the loss of management efficiency.

"Good PC planning strives to avoid forcing the manager into nonmanagement tasks," said Darryl Stewart, senior systems consultant at Macmillan Publishing Co. in New York. "But that in itself can be difficult to control. You put the PC in the hands of the manager, and you are counting on him or her to protect their own schedules" by not getting overwhelmed with nonmanagement chores.

But Sassone's study found that managers don't always protect their own time. Sassone said that a study of 184 managers' workdays revealed that, on average, they spent less than 27 percent of their time attending to management-level responsibilities.

Stewart said, "In the future, the best way to control the manager's use of PC time is going to be through the Executive Information System [EIS].

"By placing the PC in the manager's office and telling him or her to use the EIS, you are providing strong guidance. You are saying, 'This is a management tool.' If the EIS is the main reason for a manager to have a PC, they will be less likely to wander off into non-management areas."

Sassone agreed that keeping managers from doing nonmanagement tasks has to be stressed by upper management. "It really boils down to corporate culture," Sassone said. "If the corporation gives a manager a computer and pulls out support staff, it is saying one thing. If it maintains support staff levels, then middle managers can delegate responsibility."

If given a choice, Sassone said, middle managers will generally allow themselves to slip into other roles, losing effectiveness as managers.

Warren Winter, systems coordinator for Pfizer Hospital Products Group Inc. in New York, said, "We have talked about what managers should be doing with computers, and we have concluded that in our company they don't give up much management time to perform clerical duties."

Sassone said, "There are a lot of progressive companies where the management role is clearly defined and managers create business plans, do personnel functions—hiring and firing—and they represent the company outside.

"But the majority of corporations today are letting the senior manager do work that an entry-level manager can do, or letting a middle manager stand in line for the photocopier or having the manager set up a meeting.

"In the future," he said, "somebody is going to have to define positions that handle the nonmanagement functions. You don't want to settle for managers who manage 30 percent of the time."

Reprinted with permission from *PC Week* (October 29, 1990), pp. 185, 187. Copyright Ziff-Davis Publishing Co. 1990.

Summary

- A decision support system is an integrated set of computer tools that allow a decision maker to interact directly with computers to create information useful in making semistructured and unstructured decisions.

- A group decision support system is designed to support more than one individual in a joint decision-making task where the decisions are unstructured.

- The major components of a decision support system include the language system, problem processing system, and knowledge system.

- Organizations that have been successful in implementing decision support systems share several characteristics:

  A well-controlled and well-structured data processing system

  A willingness to commit dollars and personnel to the project

  Good communication between line departments and central computer groups

  Line departments with sufficient confidence to initiate and manage system projects

  Central computer groups that act primarily as consultants

  Central computer groups that have several people on their staffs with expertise in the user disciplines

  Education and training that are used to build understanding between line departments and the computer groups

- The development and implementation of a decision support system have no precise end. The major steps in building a DSS are predesign, design, implementation, and evaluation.

- An executive information system is a computer-based system that accesses data concerning the critical success factors of an organization and allows high-level executives to display this information on demand.

- The essence of an EIS is to provide quick, user-friendly access to information by nontechnical, high-level executives. The data can come from internal and/or external databases.

- Some of the features of a good EIS are quick response, ad hoc query capability, color graphics, simple user interfaces, and drill-down capability.

Key Terms

Decision support system (DSS)

Group decision support system (GDSS)

Language system

Problem processing system

Knowledge system

Procedural language

Nonprocedural language

Artificial intelligence

What-if analysis

Goal seeking

Risk analysis

Management science models

Financial functions

Key decisions

Normative model

Executive information system
(EIS)

Review Questions

1. What is a decision support system?

2. What is a group decision support system?

3. What are some of the major types of GDSS?

4. What are the major components of a decision support system?

5. Distinguish a procedural language from a nonprocedural language.

6. What is an electronic spreadsheet?

7. What are the components of a knowledge system in a decision support system?

8. What are the major functions of a decision support system?

9. What type of hardware capabilities should a decision support system have?

10. Why is a database management system important to a decision support system?

11. What are the characteristics of organizations that have had success in implementing DSS?

12. How does building a decision support system differ from following the structured systems life cycle used in other data processing or management information systems?

13. What activities occur in the predesign step of building a DSS?

14. What is meant by the phrase "operationalize the design objectives"?

15. What is the essence of the implementation process?

16. Define the key components of the evaluation process.

17. What is an executive information system?

18. What are the characteristics of a good executive information system?

Discussion Questions and Cases

1. Some people have argued that a decision support system is no different than a good management information system. They would argue that conceptually there is nothing new in the decision support system idea. Take one side of this argument and support your position.

2. Discuss how the functions of what-if and incremental analysis are related to risk analysis. Why are these areas so important to decision support systems?

3. Some people argue that decision support systems, especially those having artificial intelligence components, will evolve until they supplant human decision makers. Others argue that machines will never have the ability to think (when thinking is defined as the process of understanding why a particular decision is made). Take one side of this argument and support your position.

4. The Morton Manufacturing Company has recently installed a complete management information system on its mainframe. The next item in Morton's strategic plan for computing is to install a decision support system. Several analysts have already been assigned to a project team to evaluate decision support software. Their first task is to interview various user managers to determine what type of decisions the managers make from the data that are already in the new management information system. Next, the analysts must document their findings and evaluate vendor literature on decision support software. In addition to being able to answer the questions posed by the user managers, what are some specific features that should be in a good decision support package?

5. Wythe Industries is a fast-growing clothing manufacturer located in the Southeast. Most of Wythe's data processing applications are computer based. However, none of them are installed on a database management system. Each application stands alone, although some applications are linked. Traditionally, central data processing and its systems development staff have done all of the applications development within the company. Most staff members have a computer background, with very little experience in user areas. The management at Wythe is considering a decision support system. Would you advise Wythe to invest resources in a decision support system at this time? Support your answer.

6. You are the chief information officer (CIO) for the Carolina Companies, owner of a large number of Hardee's restaurants. The CEO of the Carolina Companies has recently learned about the capabilities of executive information systems from a friend who is the CEO of another firm. He has asked you to meet with him to outline and discuss the types of information that should be available on an EIS for the Carolina Companies. As CIO, are you the appropriate person to outline and decide what information will be available through the EIS? Regardless of your answer to the previous question, what broad types of information do you think should be available through the EIS? Outline a plan for specifying this information.

INFORMATION SYSTEMS STRATEGIES

Striking Oil in Decision Support

By Joseph Williams and James A. Nelson

Well-designed decision support system (DSS) can guide decision makers by providing detailed information tailored specifically to their needs. Whether it be a Wall Street foreign exchange broker whose DSS automatically loads currency rates each morning into a model that calculates what is best to buy or a retailer who logs onto a DSS to get the latest financial statistics about competitors, the potential for these systems seems unlimited.

To date, however, the body of knowledge about designing high-quality DSSs has scarcely emerged above generalized prescriptions for system functions and isolated case studies. With an eye toward bridging this DSS information gap, we selected the uncertain and volatile petroleum industry as fertile soil for the development and widespread use of DSSs and as an ideal survey subject.

Drilling an oil well is a complex, costly endeavor. The major variables in deciding when and where to drill derive from geologic and economic factors, although legal and environmental considerations can also be critical. The three types of geologic factors involve the presence, quantity and recoverability of hydrocarbons, otherwise known as oil or gas. The oil company must account for the costs of drilling and production, the profits on the sale of the petroleum and the timing of those receipts. Each of these elements, of course, varies from prospect to prospect. This study of DSSs in the petroleum industry can provide wider lessons about the development and use of decision support systems in other markets.

In extensive field studies and a survey of several hundred oil companies, we collected data on the design and use of DSSs in petroleum drilling. The data yielded three conclusions. First, none of the decision makers using a DSS had been involved in the design or implementation of the system. Second, companies use DSSs to control the behavior of decision makers. Although this can help meet organizational needs, it can also be detrimental to decision makers. Third, user control of decision variable values is critical to user satisfaction with and optimum performance of DSSs.

None of these conclusions should invalidate the conventional wisdom regarding DSS design and use. Instead, this article serves to illuminate areas for IS [information systems] managers to monitor carefully in setting up their own decision support applications.

Sensible Design

It is often assumed that decision support systems should be designed specifically for the executive user. We can see little basis for this assumption. It is founded on the supposition that the decision maker is a nontransient being who will remain in place during the design, implementation and use phases of the DSS. In our field studies, no one, among the six sets of DSS users, had been involved in the system design or implementation; they had all inherited their systems. We suspect that job turnover, promotion and the like would quickly render obsolete any system tailored to a particular decision maker's cognitive style.

Many information systems management scholars dispute the notion that user involvement in DSS design is necessary to ensure use of the system. T. P. Liang, in "Critical Success Factors of Decision Support Systems: An Experimental Study," *Data Base* (Winter 1986, pp. 3–15), showed that the quality of DSS design, rather than the designer, is the most critical factor in successful implementation. Other studies have argued persuasively that DSS design is best handled by DSS professionals, not by executive users.

Consequently, we must conclude that a DSS should be built around the information required for a decision rather than around the personality of the user. An excellent drilling decision support systems is likely to last a lot longer than the executive who ordered it.

Unquestionably, DSSs are powerful tools that can aid decision makers. But our studies showed that they are also used to control the behavior of decision makers. Although such control can be useful for meeting organizational needs, it can be detrimental to those making decisions.

One way oil companies use DSSs to control the behavior of decision makers is by requiring them to justify their decisions made vis-a-vis the recommendation of the DSS. Some decision makers said they were free to ignore the results of the drilling DSS, but they were held accountable if the decision [unsupported by the system] proved to be a bad one. The decision maker's primary function was to reconcile the recommendations of the staff, the DSS and his or her own intuition. In this way, the oil companies use their DSS to establish and maintain uniform standards of analyses for drilling decisions.

Organizational performance may indeed be enhanced by placing restrictions on the decision maker, and these restrictions can be enforced through a DSS, according to Miami-based Florida International University's Daniel Robey in "Cognitive Style and DSS Design: A Comment on Huber's Paper," *Management Science* (May 1983, pp. 580–582). This conclusion was borne out in the field studies, where organizational performance was clearly identified as a reason for both decision accountability and variable control.

Control through DSS accountability can have a detrimental impact on executive decision making, however. In a couple of studies, management expert Chris Argyris of Harvard Business School in Cambridge, Mass., observed that executives feel they have fewer options available to them when their decisions have to compete with the results of any information system. They are likely to feel just as powerless when their decisions must compete with the requests of a DSS, particularly if the cognitive model in the DSS is of their own design.

Controlling Decision Makers

Competing with a DSS is even more frustrating if the variable values in the DSS model have been predetermined by someone else in the organization. This type of system, called an input-distributed DSS, is a second means that companies use to control decision makers' behavior. For instance, all the major oil companies in the field studies set the DSS' variable values for the selling prices of the oil and gas; despite the unpredictability of these prices, in no case was the decision maker permitted to substitute his or her own estimation of future prices for that of the firm's forecast.

Argyris has argued that executives may feel powerless to overrule a system embodying standards and variables set by others, and, ultimately, may feel they have been reduced to custodians of the DSS. Indeed, decision makers using DSSs universally expressed dissatisfaction with their lack of control over the decision variable values. Many thought that a DSS recommendation was binding, even if they disagreed with it, because the variable values reflected the expectations of the corporate headquarters.

In fact, in almost 90% of the DSS models surveyed, one or more critical decision variables were set by someone other than the decision maker. In nearly all cases, financial variables were primarily set by headquarters personnel who were independent of the drilling decision maker. Similarly, geology variables were set by staff geologists at the district or division level. In fact, the decision maker rarely had control over any of the critical model inputs.

Expecting any decision maker to determine all of the DSS model's variable values may be impractical. Unless the decision maker were a geologist, it would be unrealistic to expect him or her to perform the complex geologic analyses necessary to decide on a drilling prospect's potential success.

Administrative Isolation

The substantial percentage of DSS users who do not exercise control over the values assigned to their models' variables merely confirms previous findings that the decision makers are administratively isolated from all aspects of preparing drilling prospects.

Obviously, the most critical risk is conceding authority over variable values is the resulting quality of the DSS' output—and, by extension, the quality of the decision maker's ultimate decision. A lack of reliability, accuracy and timeliness are but a few factors that can negatively affect the integrity and usefulness of an input-distributed DDS.

A badly conceived and poorly managed input-distributed DDS can have devastating results. For example, the largest company in the field study forecasted prices for oil and gas at its world headquarters. Every subsidiary was required to use these forecasted prices in all revenue and investment analyses. Unfortunately, in 1984, the prices forecast by the company were unrealistically high ($50 per barrel for 1987), despite the softening of oil prices at the time. The executives we interviewed were appalled by the prices they were forced to use in the DSS models; thus, some ignored the DSS results. But several confided that, although they personally felt the forecasted prices were overly optimistic, they nonetheless approved projects that were probably of marginal profitability because they didn't think they could successfully challenge the DSS' pricing assumptions. A solution to an executive user's frustration may be to make the variables flexible so they can be overridden when the user believes such action necessary.

DSS users from other industries can use the conclusions from our study on the design and use of decision support systems. First, in designing a DSS, IS should structure it according to the informational and decision-making process involved, rather than the target executive user. Second, if a DSS is to be used to control a decision maker's behavior in the interest of enhancing organizational performance, management must address the potential negative impact on executive users. Such impact could be mitigated by allowing the executive user to override variable values set by someone else. IS managers who address these potential weak spots in DSS design and use should be more assured of creating systems that are sound and reliable.

Discussion Questions

1.   What are some likely consequences if decision makers are held responsible for bad decisions that differ from the recommendations of a DSS? Are these consequences good or bad?

2.   If the decision maker has no control over the design or the major input values to a DSS and feels compelled to follow its recommendations, is the DSS of any value? To what extent do you think that the decision maker's drilling decision should be controlled by the DSS?

8

Artificial Intelligence and Expert Systems

Introduction

At Pepboys Automotive Service Center in Norcross, Georgia the resident mechanic provides a detailed analysis of each customer's automobile from engine ignition to exhaust and never takes a coffee break or a lunch hour. This diagnostic mechanic is an expert system running on a personal computer. The application of computers to tasks that normally require human intelligence is called artificial intelligence. Since the field's beginnings in the 1960s, it has had ups and downs. "Smart machines" did not always live up to the great expectations. However, today businesses are increasingly applying artificial intelligence techniques to real-world problems and succeeding. In this chapter we will first look at the definition of artificial intelligence and the various types of artificial intelligence. Next, we will cover the most successful business application of artificial intelligence, expert systems. In our coverage of expert systems we will look at what an expert system is, how they differ from conventional information processing systems, examples of expert systems, the components of expert systems, the advantages of expert systems, their limitations, how to pick a good application for an expert system, and finally, how to develop an expert system. In the last section of this chapter we will explore how computers are being used to mimic some of the activities of the human brain with neural networks.

Artificial Intelligence

Artificial intelligence is the use of computers to perform tasks that normally require high-level human intelligence. An example of such a task is the diagnosis of a specific illness and the prescription of a course of treatment by a physician. There are artificial intelligence programs called expert systems that will perform limited diagnosis of illness with an accuracy rate greater than that of physicians.

Human intelligence consists of three basic attributes: learning, reasoning, and the manipulation of symbols. Various types of artificial intelligence attempt to duplicate a part of and in some cases all of these three attributes. Computers have been most successful in attempts to manipulate symbols. In reality all computer-based information systems, at their most basic level, only manipulate symbols. In addition to manipulation of symbols, humans have highly developed abilities to acquire and input data to their brains. Our sources of input are our five senses: vision, hearing, smell, taste, and touch. Likewise, for computers to duplicate human intelligence they must also have a way of mimicking one or more of these five human sensing capabilities. A large amount of work has been done in the computer vision and speech recognition (hearing) areas, as we will see below. The two areas in which we have had less success in applying the computer are learning and reasoning.

Expert systems attempt to reach the same conclusions about a problem as the best human experts would. Thus, expert systems do, in a sense, mimic human reasoning. However, they do not reason the same way that humans do, they simply manipulate symbols and rules. Expert systems do not have to mimic human reasoning to perform as well as or better than humans in judgment tasks.

The area of human intelligence that probably will be the most difficult for computers to master is learning. Today computers certainly cannot learn on their own as humans do, but knowledge can be captured and input as rules by an expert system and these rules can be continually updated by humans. Ideally, we would like to have machines that would learn through experience as humans do. The first steps toward this capability are being made today with neural networks. But a computer learning capability on the level of humans is likely to be several decades away.

The primary areas of artificial intelligence research and applications today are robotics, computer vision, speech recognition, natural language processing, expert systems, and neural networks.

Robotics

Robotics is the application of computers to tasks that normally require human intelligence and physical manipulations. Examples include robots that perform welding tasks, assembly of parts, or movement of goods in a warehouse. Robots have had widespread use since the early 1980s in business tasks, particularly in manufacturing. Robotic devices are often designed to be general purpose, particularly those that are used on manufacturing assembly lines. Because they are general purpose, the tasks that an individual robot performs can be easily changed by simply changing the computer program that controls the robot. Such robots have dramatically decreased the labor costs of manufactured products. But perhaps the most important advantage of robots in the manufacturing process is that a much wider variety of products can be produced at a lower price. Training all the employees on a production line to make a different product can be expensive. With robots the complete production line can be changed with the change of a program. Thus, much smaller production runs can be produced economically.

Computer Vision

Another form of artificial intelligence that is closely related to robotics is computer vision. It is sometimes called image processing. **Computer vision** is the acquisition and processing of sets of visual signals in order to recognize and interpret high-level patterns and to make these patterns meaningful. Thus, computer vision is much more than the simple input of images to a computer, which is a very easy thing to do. Computer vision is the interpretation and derivation of meaning from images. In some ways computer vision could be much more capable than human vision. Human vision is limited to a certain part of the total spectrum of light. Computers can accept infrared light as input and make interpretations based on the infrared light. Computers can also see and interpret images at a much faster rate than humans can.

One of the biggest applications for computer vision is on the assembly line where products are visually inspected by computers and defective products automatically removed from production. Much of the research on computer vision is funded by the Defense Department. There are very important applications for the military. For example, smart weapons that can determine the difference between an enemy tank and a friendly tank have obvious applications.

Speech Recognition

Another form of computer acquisition and interpretation of input is speech recognition. **Speech recognition** attempts to capture human speech and convert it to the language being spoken, for example, English words. (The domain of speech recognition ends at the recognition of a spoken word. The ability to interpret the meaning of words placed together in a sentence is the domain of natural language processing, which we will discuss below.) In many applications it is only necessary for the computer to be able to recognize individual spoken words. Examples include dictation to produce typed output and a production line where the human's hands are busy and thus cannot input data directly to the computer. In this hands-busy environment, speech recognition systems can pick up spoken words that may consist of such things as the destination of a package in a Federal Express sorting room.

Speech recognition systems have been in use by business since the mid 1980s. Where the vocabulary to be recognized by the computer is rather limited, say a hundred different words, speech recognition systems can be highly accurate. They also can be very accurate over large vocabularies (up to 30,000 words) where the system is trained to recognize the voice of a single human being. For example, telephone companies now have the technology to monitor all the voices coming through a particular telephone switching network and pick out the speech of a single person. This capability has been used by law enforcement agencies to capture the conversations of individuals who are being investigated for crimes. Thus, it is no longer necessary to tap a specific telephone to pick up a person's conversation. We will cover other aspects of speech recognition in the next chapter under office automation.

Natural Language Processing

Natural language processing takes speech recognition a step further and in fact natural language processing does not necessarily have to be tied with speech recognition. The sentences input can be typed through a keyboard. **Natural language processing** refers to parsing a sentence and using a set of rules and conventions for that particular language to derive the meaning of the sentence. Natural language processing is a difficult task, since all languages have subtle ambiguities in their structure and meaning. For example, a simple question like "What is the firm's income for the year?" can have many different meanings. Is it the firm's revenues for the year? Is it the firm's net income for the year? Is it the firm's net income before taxes for the year? Is it the firm's net income after taxes for the year? Many other interpretations could be made.

Despite these difficulties natural language processing is being used today, quite often when giving commands to a computer system. One example is the use of English commands to query a database system. A typical dialog might be as follows:

Human: What were the firm's sales of shoes last year in the southwest?

Computer: I don't understand sales. Do you have a synonym for sales? Some possibilities are revenue and cash received. Please input a synonym for sales. Thank you.

Human: Revenue.

Computer: I understand the word revenue. I do not understand the word southwest. Southwest may refer to a geographic area, if so input the specific states you are referring to.

Human: California, Arizona, New Mexico, Texas.

Computer: Thank you. The revenue from last year in the states of California, Arizona, New Mexico, and Texas from shoes was $315,000.

A great deal of work is being done on natural language processing. This is an important area because the normal way that human beings communicate with one another is through language. Perhaps the ideal way for humans to communicate with computers would be through natural language processing. There will be a huge market for the firm that perfects natural language processing.

Expert systems and neural networks are two types of artificial intelligence that hold great promise for applications in business. Because of their importance for decision making, we will cover these areas in more depth in the next two sections of this text.

Expert Systems

Expert systems have a wide variety of potential applications in business. The application of expert systems to business decisions began to grow in the 1980s. This section defines expert systems, provides examples of expert systems, explains the components of expert systems, discusses the advantages and limitations of expert systems, explains how to pick the correct problem for such systems, and describes the steps in the development of an expert system.

What is an Expert System?

An **expert system** is a computer program that enables a computer to make (or give advice concerning) an unstructured or semistructured decision that is normally made by a human with special expertise. Expert systems usually operate as consulting experts to give humans advice in certain specialized areas. Examples of decisions that have been made or supported by expert systems are the diagnosis of bacteriological diseases in patients, the diagnosis of malfunctions in diesel electric locomotives, and the configuration of computer systems based on a customer's anticipated application workload. Application 8–1 illustrates how the Campbell Soup Co. uses an expert system to control the quality of its products.

Components of Expert Systems

There are two basic types of expert systems: rule-based and frame-based. We will cover rule-based systems in this chapter. This is the most widely used type of expert system. Figure 8–1 provides an overview of the components of a rule-based system.

A rule-based system consists of processing and storage facilities, often referred to respectively as an **inference engine** and a **knowledge base**. A knowledge base is illustrated in the top right part of Figure 8–1. The knowledge base stores facts and rules in the form IF (condition) THEN (action). For example, a rule in a personal injury expert system might state:

IF the plantiff did receive a back injury and the injury did require
   surgery and the recovery from the injury was almost complete,

THEN increase the injury trauma claim by $50,000.

The rules specify the actions that the system should take when the conditions are present that satisfy the conditions of a rule. When facts

APPLICATION 8–1

Simon Says Soup Is Good Food

By Johanna Ambrosio

How does Campbell Soup Co. ensure that its soup is "mm-mm good"? An expert system, chosen and implemented by an end-user department, helps the company determine when something goes wrong with the processing of the soup and what to do about it.

The expert system, dubbed Simon, was installed two years ago and became fully operational a year later. "We tested it for a year to make sure it's right," said Michael S. Mignogna, corporate process authority at Campbell. "We wanted to make sure that when it decided something, it was the same as if one of our people had made the decision." Thus far, the system has saved Campbell's about $5 million. Simon was written using Aion Corp.'s Aion Development System shell.

Mignogna's department, thermal process development, sets the standards for how soup should be cooked to ensure sterility and to avoid conditions such as botulism. It also makes the calls about what to do if something goes wrong.

For instance, a batch of cream of mushroom needs to be cooked for 50 minutes at 250 degrees, and halfway through the cooking, the plant loses steam pressure or the conveyor belt slows down. Mignogna's group has to decide whether to OK that batch for sale or destroy it. The goal is to destroy as few items as possible while guaranteeing quality. "It's that one can of soup that we worry about," he said.

With the old PC system, whenever there was a problem the plant would notify Mignogna's people and send data about all the conditions. Thermal process would look at the data and use the PC program to do mathematical simulations to decide whether the product was safe. This process took up to eight weeks, and the product in question needed to be held in a warehouse until a decision was made. With Simon, however, that decision-making process is cut to about three minutes, and most of the decisions are made by Simon with little human intervention . .

Simon makes the decisions about 90% of the time, Mignogna said. In the other 10%, all the data may not be immediately available. Nor does Simon contain rules for all the possible combinations—such as container defects, for instance. "These are the sorts of things that are not toxic and won't kill anyone," Mignogna said.

Because the expert system can separate the business rules from the mathematical calculations, Mignogna said, either can be changed without affecting the other. This can come in handy when Campbell adds new products or changes the recipes for old ones. When the company introduced its low-salt soups, for example, Simon needed to be changed to accommodate. "Salt is a preservative, so when you take it out, there's some impact," Mignogna said.

Besides the cost savings, benefits include improved efficiency of the decision-making process and improved morale at the plants, Mignogna said. Plant employees feel more in control of things because they no longer have to wait for his group to make a decision.

arise in the working memory that satisfy the conditions of a particular rule in the knowledge base, that rule is selected (triggered) and interpreted by the rule interpreter. The combination of selecting and interpreting rules is known as the **firing of rules**. The working memory of an expert system stores facts that apply to the particular case to which the expert system is being applied. The knowledge base, in contrast to the working memory, contains rules and facts that are long-term and that are applied to any case that the expert system is used for. For example, if an expert system were being used to diagnose the illness of a patient, the working memory would contain data about that particular patient, like the patient's temperature, blood pressure, pulse, and laboratory test results.

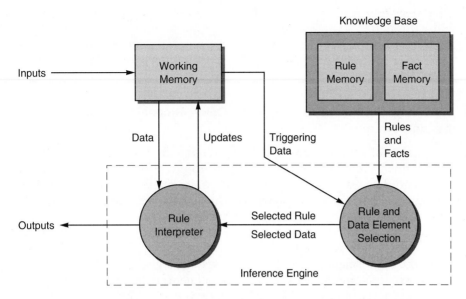

FIGURE 8–1
The Components of a
Rule-Based Expert
System.
Reprinted with permission
from "Rule-based Systems,"
*Communications of the
ACM* (September 1985), 924.
Copyright by Association for
Computing Machinery.

A simple RBS (rule-based system) consists of storage and processing elements, which are often referred to respectively as the knowledge base and the inference engine. An expert system's storage includes components for long-term static data (knowledge base) and short-term dynamic data (working memory). The long-term storage, which is the knowledge base, contains rules and facts. Rules specify actions the system should initiate when certain triggering conditions occur. These conditions correspond to patterns of data that can arise in the working memory. The working memory contains data that apply to the specific case, for example, data that apply to a particular patient in an expert medical diagnostic system. During the basic cycle of an RBS the processing element, the inference engine, selects or triggers rules for which there is data that satisfy the condition in the rule. The rule interpreter interprets the selected rule to draw inferences. These inferences become new facts concerning the case being examined by the system. These facts are then used to update the system's working memory, which may in turn cause additional rules in the knowledge base to fire. In contrast to conventional data processing systems, most rule-based systems distribute their logic over numerous independent condition action rules, monitor dynamic results stored in the working memory for triggering patterns of data, determine their sequential behavior by selecting their next activity from a set of candidate-triggered rules, and store their intermediate results exclusively in a global working memory.

The output of the rule interpreter can be a request for new inputs from the user or it can be inferences that are new facts to the system. For example, the following rule might be contained in a medical diagnostic expert system:

IF the patient's temperature exceeds 100 degrees Fahrenheit,

THEN the patient has a fever.

If this rule is fired, we have an inference or a fact that the patient has a fever. This inference could be output to the user and would be used to update the working memory's store of facts. Note that new facts or inferences change this expert system's knowledge of the conditions that apply to the case that the system is being used for, which can in turn cause different rules to be selected and new inferences to be generated. Thus, facts can come from the knowledge base, the inputs, and they can be derived by the system from the firing of rules. An expert system continues cycling through this process of asking for input, firing rules based on conditions or facts that arise in the working memory, generating new facts, asking for more input, and so on until a final decision or recommendation is reached.

How Do Expert Systems Differ From Conventional Information Processing Systems?

Conventional information processing systems are organized in a sequential manner. Programs are executed from top to bottom and their logic is built into the system through individual statements that are executed sequentially. Expert systems distribute their logic over numerous independent condition-action rules. Expert systems cycle through this rule-based knowledge and monitor intermediate results looking for triggering patterns of data that would fire a rule. As rules are fired the expert systems store their intermediate results exclusively in a global working memory. Thus, expert systems determine their sequential behavior by selecting their next activity from a set of potentially triggered rules. This compares with a conventional information processing system where the next activity is determined by the next step in the computer program. In an expert system the next step is totally dependent on which rule has been triggered.

Examples of Expert Systems

According to a recent report in *Electronic Engineering Times*, more than 4,000 expert systems are now in place and some ten times more are being developed. Expert systems are used in a wide range of industries. According to Paul Harmon, editor of the San Francisco–based newsletter *Expert Systems Strategies*, approximately 34 percent of the existing systems are found in manufacturing, 24 percent in defense and other government agencies, 18 percent in finance, 8 percent in education, 5 percent in corporate research and development, and 11 percent in other industries such as transportation and communications.[1]

Perhaps the most successful expert system is Digital Equipment Corporation's Expert Configurer (XCON). XCON is used to configure computer systems ordered by customers to assure that they contain consistent elements that work well together. XCON began to be used in 1979 and it is fully integrated with other DEC in-house systems. As soon as a customer order comes in, XCON analyzes and processes it. XCON and other knowledge-base systems at DEC save the company $200 million by eliminating labor-intensive processes such as final assembly and testing.

Another example of a successful expert system can be found at Xerox. A knowledge-base system called the Remote Interactive Communication (RIC) system identifies potential problems in copying machines and dispatches service personnel before breakdowns occur. "We knew that sensors on our copiers provided substantial information about the machines' operating status," says Xerox's . . . Maletz. "So we leverage the

---

[1] E. F. Roth, "AI Comes of Age," *World*, No. 3 (1990), 9–10.

knowledge of the product designers and problem solvers to predict machine failures based on sensor data. A diagnostic system in each copier interacts with a more sophisticated centrally located expert diagnostic system. If the copier system suspects a problem, a modem in the copier calls a central host computer and feeds the copier's memory to the central computer at night. The host computer, the smartest component of this knowledge-base system, analyzes the data, diagnoses the problem, and then alerts the service force to perform a service call. With RIC Xerox has translated what would have been customer complaints into exceptionally timely service visits while more efficiently allocating its service resources."[2]

The RIC and XCON systems are prime examples of using information systems for competitive advantage. In both cases, the systems are used to directly improve service to customers.

Advantages of Expert Systems

Businesses are interested in applying expert systems for a variety of reasons, the most important being to gain a competitive advantage. Specifically, expert systems are expected to have the following advantages:

1. They reduce the need for highly paid experts or at least make these experts more productive.

2. Expert systems are a way of preserving, replicating, and distributing expert knowledge.

3. They improve the consistency and accuracy of decisions in their specific area of application, often called a domain. Some expert systems have proven that they produce more accurate decisions than do the average employee assigned to the task. Digital Equipment Corporation's XCON is such an expert system.

4. They produce better documentation of the rationale for a decision than many human experts do. One essential feature of expert systems is that they be able to explain the rationale by which they reached a decision. Humans will not accept advice or a decision from a computer unless the rationale behind it can be explained. Thus, good expert systems have the capability of documenting all the facts and inferences that surround and affect a decision. This capability is particularly valuable if a decision may be challenged in a future lawsuit. Lawsuits are increasingly common where professional decisions are perceived as being incorrect, especially in medical and financial auditing decisions.

5. They provide insight into the decision-making process. The development of a knowledge-base expert system requires a detailed step-by-step procedure that elicits the knowledge of a human expert and encodes this knowledge into the rules of an expert system's knowledge base. This process can be extremely valuable in understanding how decisions are made.

---

[2] *Ibid.*, 10.

6. They can be used as training tools for novices. This advantage comes from an expert system's capability to explain the rationale behind its advice. As novice employees use an expert system, they can learn from the system's explanations of the rationale for a specific advice. In time, novice employees may learn enough from the expert system to become experts themselves.

Limitations of Expert Systems

Since the field of expert systems is in its infancy, expert systems currently have many limitations. Among them are the following:

1. Expert systems are overrated. There has been a great deal of hype about the capabilities of expert systems and, thus, many individuals' expectations for expert systems are not justified.

2. Expert systems can be very expensive to develop and maintain. For example, DEC spends over $2 million per year to maintain its XCON system. Another expert system, Prospector, which is designed to help locate deposits of valuable minerals, took sixteen staff years to develop.

3. It is difficult to elicit the knowledge of experts. Sometimes experts cannot specify exactly how they make a decision. Converting expertise to IF-THEN rules is not an easy task.

4. There may be disagreement and conflict among the experts on the best solution to a given problem.

5. The area of application may change rapidly, thus requiring rapid changes in the expert system. Examples of fields that change rapidly include medicine, tax, and information systems.

6. Expert systems lack common sense. Common sense is the intelligence that we acquire over our lifetimes and thus is immense and cannot be reduced to IF-THEN rules for an expert system. Experts often use common sense in making a decision.

7. Currently, expert systems cannot learn. Thus, humans must constantly maintain them for changing conditions. However, as we will see below when we discuss neural networks, work is being done on artificial intelligence systems that have the potential to learn.

8. Expert systems have very narrow domains of application. When problems that must be solved occur on the boundaries of the expert system's domain of application it does not say, for example, "I don't know, but if I had to guess . . . ." Humans can often rely on their breadth of knowledge to solve problems that are on the boundaries of their knowledge.

9. The rigid interaction format between an expert system and a human does not permit vague or unusual questions and answers. Communication between two humans can be vague, and information can be gleaned by the human expert from these vague

answers and questions. Also, humans often communicate through body language. Thus, the communication between humans is much richer than between an expert system and a human.

10. The validation of an expert system can be difficult. How can we be sure it works unless it is presented with all the possible cases that could be presented to it in the future? This, of course, is an impossible task. We can only be sure that it gives valid answers in a rather narrow domain of tested applications.

11. In the long run, as humans use expert systems, humans may lose their capability of dealing with real-world problem solving. The basic assumption is that unless you manually work through a problem to reach a solution you eventually lose your ability to work such a problem. There is disagreement about whether this is a long-run problem for humans. It can be argued that humans shouldn't be spending their time solving problems that computers can solve at a much cheaper cost.

Despite these limitations, there are many successful implementations of expert systems. Application 8–2 illustrates how Alamo Rent A Car, Inc. uses an expert system to set prices.

Picking The Right Problem For An Expert System

Expert systems are best applied to certain types of problems. The characteristics of suitable problems are as follows:

1. Recognized experts work in the problem's field and they are committed to the idea of developing an expert system. These experts are provably better than amateurs at making decisions in their domain of expertise.

2. The task is routinely taught to novices. Thus, the process by which a decision is reached can be explained and encoded in an expert system's knowledge base.

3. The problem takes a human expert a few minutes to several hours to perform. This characteristic is desirable because the development of an expert system usually requires a high investment of time and resources. Thus, the problem's application must have a high potential payoff.

4. No common sense is required to solve the problem. Instead the problem requires facts for its solution. No one has developed a way to give expert systems common sense, but computers are good at sifting through large volumes of facts.

5. The domain of the problem's application is limited. Expert systems technology has not yet evolved to the point at which it can be applied to wide areas of expertise.

6. An important criteria is that the expert system must address a fundamental business need. A good example of such a system is XCON, which efficiently assembles customer's computer systems.

APPLICATION 8–2

Expert System Drives Rental Rates

By John Pallatto

Some businesses can manage their price list on the back of an old envelope. But at Alamo Rent A Car, Inc. of Fort Lauderdale, Fla., price setting is a superhuman effort. That's why the company turned to expert-system technology to maintain more than 4 million different rental rates on a fleet of 110,000 vehicles, because at least 5,000 of the rates must be changed every day.

The expert system can analyze the enormous number of rental rates faster and far more efficiently than a battalion of market analysts, said Tom Loane, director of information systems for Alamo.

Alamo used IBM's The Integrated Reasoning Shell (TIRS) to develop an OS/2-based expert-system application running on IBM PS/2 Model 70s that evaluates thousands of rental rates for hundreds of car models, Loane said. "There are a tremendous number of ways to rent cars," he said. "Think of all the variables we have to keep track of, all the different locations, the different

models. There is a different price for every one of them, with specials and discounts."

As the fifth-largest car-rental agency in the country, Alamo has to keep rates competitive with its rivals everywhere. The company selected TIRS, Loane said, because it could be embedded in a larger business system, and it proved to be one of the faster systems available.

The TIRS application is built into more complex C language programs that comprise Alamo's rate-management system, he said. The system uses rental-fee data that has been downloaded from the company's IBM mainframe Customer Information Control System database application.

Alamo's use of an embedded expert system has become the norm in industry as the most effective way to apply the technology, according to computer scientists.

"The days of the stand-alone expert system are long gone," said Tod Loofbourrow, CEO of Foundation Technologies, Inc., an expert-system programming con-

sulting firm in Cambridge, Mass. "To be successful, the expert system has to completely disappear within the host application, so the users don't ever confront the system—they only see the screen or the form they are used to dealing with."

Most of the widely used expert-system development packages, including TIRS, Nexpert Object from Neuron Data Inc. and 1KBMS from AICorp., use this approach, Loofbourrow said.

The analysts who work with Alamo's expert system aren't fussy about the look and feel, according to Loane. "We could have embellished the expert system with a lot of pretty charts and graphs," he said. "But we are dealing with people who are intensely numerically oriented, and they wouldn't pay attention to the graphs anyway."

7. Expert systems that are well integrated with a firm's information system have the highest likelihood of success. In the 1980s many expert systems failed because developers focused on the expert system's technology rather than on meeting a fundamental requirement in the current information system. For example, DEC's XCON system is fully integrated with its in-house order entry system. Expert systems embedded in existing information systems that address a fundamental business need are most likely to be successful.

Developing an Expert System

Developing an expert system can be a major project. Most useful expert systems have taken at least five employee years to develop. Certainly one should select the right kind of problem for an expert system based on the criteria discussed earlier. But even after selecting the right problem, difficulties can arise.

Typically an expert works with a **knowledge engineer** (a person who develops expert systems) to encode into IF-THEN rules the steps a human would use in reaching a decision. But experts often have difficulty explaining the mental steps they go through in making a decision. Thus, a major difficulty in developing expert systems is the transfer of knowledge from the human expert to the expert system.

There are two basic approaches to the development of an expert system. One is to develop it from scratch using one of the two programming languages that are most widely used for writing expert systems, PROLOG or LISP. Of the two, LISP is more widely used in the United States. If the system is written from scratch, the knowledge engineer writes all modules of the system including the inference engine and the knowledge base. The development approach that is used for almost all business expert systems is to use a purchased expert system shell. An **expert system shell** already has the inference engine or processing part of the system created. It also has the necessary processing and storage capability to input and maintain a knowledge base. With an addition of a knowledge base for the particular application the expert system shell becomes a full-fledged expert system. Thus, the knowledge engineer can concentrate on developing rules and facts for the knowledge base. Of course, the same expert system shell can be used to develop many different individual expert systems.

Figure 8–2 illustrates the steps that are typically performed in the development of an expert system. As with any system, the identification of the application is crucial.

It has been found that building a prototype is the best method for developing an expert system. At this stage the goal should be to develop a prototype that is sufficiently complete so that it can be used in a test mode in the real application. Of course, the human expert continues making the decisions and giving advice while the prototype is being tested. As the prototype fails to perform correctly it is modified. This process of modifying and testing the prototype continues until a sufficiently sophisticated system is developed. Experience has shown that the completed system is substantially different from the original prototype.

The next step is to formally test and evaluate the completed system with a wide range of inputs. Once the system has been validated, it is implemented. Maintaining an expert system is an ongoing process. This is particularly true in a dynamic field where the rules change often. Even though the system has been formally implemented, in effect it is still a prototype over its whole life span with continual modifications being made.

Despite their limitations, expert systems are a valuable tool for business information systems. Certainly as we gain more experience with expert systems many of their current limitations will be overcome.

Neural Networks

One of the major limitations of expert systems is the fact that they cannot learn on their own. Neural networks are an attempt to overcome this limitation. **Neural networks** are composed of elements that perform in a manner analogous to the most elementary functions of the biological

F I G U R E 8–2
The Expert System
Development Life
Cycle.

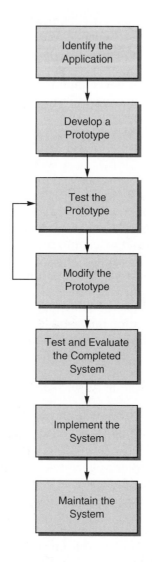

neuron in animal brains. These elements are organized in a way that may or may not be related to the anatomy of the brain.[3]

The human brain contains over 100 billion computing elements called **neurons**. A neuron and its components are illustrated in Figure 8–3. All of human thought, reasoning, feelings, and so on arise from a network of biological neurons. Although we don't know exactly how the human brain works, we do know enough to say that the neuron is its fundamental building block. Neurons are cells. As shown in Figure 8–3, they consist of three sections: the cell body, the dendrites, and the axon, each with separate but complementary functions. The dendrites receive signals from other cells at connection points called synapses. Synapses are capable of determining the strength of the signal that is passed to the succeeding cell body. This capability is called the synaptic strength.

---

[3] P. D. Wasserman, *Neural Computing Theory and Practice* (New York: Van Nostrand Reinhold, 1989), 1.

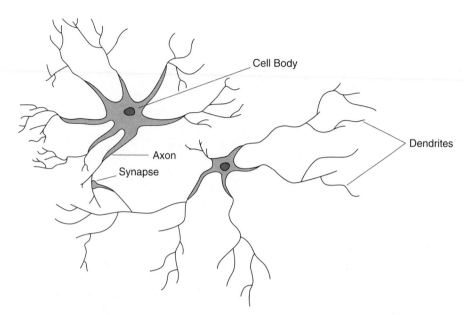

F I G U R E 8–3
A Biological Neuron
Reprinted with permission
from P. D. Wasserman,
*Neural Computing Theory
and Practice* (New York: Van
Nostrand Reinhold, 1989),
13.

Synaptic strength weights the incoming signal based on the signal's importance. Many such signals may be coming into a single cell body from its connections with other cell bodies. Some of these signals tend to excite the cell body to fire, others tend to inhibit the cell body from firing. In effect, all the incoming signals are averaged and at some point the average of these signals reaches a sufficiently large threshold to cause the cell body to fire. The firing cell body in turn passes a pulse down its axon that is passed on across synapses to the dendrites of succeeding cells. Eventually, a pattern of neuron firings occurs that produces a thought or a bodily action. It is these patterns of neuron firings that underlie all human (and animal) brain activities. We know that this simple computational function underlies most of the known activity of the brain.[4]

Artificial neural networks that are built with computers attempt to mimic these biological neural networks by tying patterns of artificial neuron firings to the action or advice desired from the neural networks. Neural networks are trained to fire certain patterns of neurons when certain input conditions exist, thus producing a certain output (action or advice).

At the level of an individual neuron, a set of inputs are applied to the neuron, each representing an input value or the output of another artificial neuron. Each input is multiplied by a corresponding weight analogous to brain's synaptic strength and all the weighted inputs are then summed to determine the activation level of the artificial neuron.[5] Figure 8–4 illustrates this concept. Networks of these artificial neurons form a neural network that is somewhat analogous to a biological brain. However, the artificial neural networks today are extremely primitive compared to the processing capability of the human brain, which can process about ten million billion interconnections between neurons per second. Nothing in the computer world comes anywhere close to this capability.

---

[4] *Ibid.*, 190–192.
[5] *Ibid.*, 13.

FIGURE 8–4

An Artificial Neuron.

Reprinted with permission from P. D. Wasserman, *Neural Computing Theory and Practice* (New York: Van Nostrand Reinhold, 1989) 15.

In this figure the Xs are the input signals and the Ws are weights. The inputs are multiplied by the weights and then summed to produce the Net signal. Then the activation function determines if the Net signal is sufficiently strong to fire the neuron and produce an Out signal.

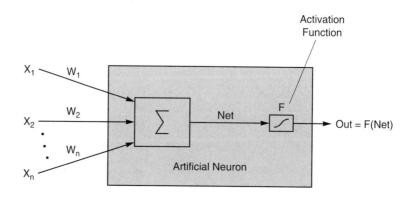

As mentioned above, the primary advantage of neural networks is their potential to learn. This learning capability arises from the system's ability to adjust the input weights and the activation functions' thresholds either up or down to allow an individual artificial neuron to fire and thus pass a signal to succeeding or interconnected neurons. In essence what occurs during the training of a neural network is that many cases of the decision to be made, including the value of various input variables and the desired decision, are input to the artificial neural network. Each time an incorrect decision is made various weight and threshold levels are adjusted. This training process continues until the neural network produces the correct decision for an acceptable majority of the cases.

To illustrate this training process, let's assume we are training a neural network to make decisions about whether to grant credit to customers. Our training cases would include many past histories of credit being granted to customers. In this data would be various pieces of information that are used by humans to make a credit decision. These might include family income, existing monthly payments, a measure of previous credit paying history, the amount of the purchase, and so on. Also, of course, would be whether or not this particular past case resulted in the customer paying off the loan. Obviously, we want the neural network to turn down those customers who defaulted in the past. We would input many of these cases to the network and train it until it began making the correct decision at an acceptable level.

This training of neural networks has been incredibly successful in some applications. For example, at Eastman Kodak management wanted to free workers from the tiring tasks of reading tiny fuzzy numbers at the edge of rolls of film to catch manufacturing defects. These numbers are .09 inches high and .085 inches wide, so small that a person must be less than 8 inches from the film to read the numbers. Using an experimental neural network chip from INTEL, Kodak has devised a laboratory machine to read these numbers. After 10,000 training tests, the neural network reads the numbers accurately 99.8 percent of the time with the film flying by at 1,000 feet a minute, obviously much faster than a human can read the film.[6] Another use for neural networks is illustrated in Application 8–3.

---

[6] "Machines Learn to Read Tiny Numbers on Film," *The Wall Street Journal*, May 22, 1991, B1.

Bank Enlists Neural Net to Fight Fraud

By Kim S. Nash

The holiday rush will soon be but a fond memory for shoppers, but Mellon Bank Corp. will be dealing with the repercussions well into 1992. The bank's Mastercard and Visa cardholders rang up about 3 million transactions in November and December.

Those may be the two busiest months of the year for cardholders, but credit-card crime knows no season.

To fight back, Mellon Bank is testing a mainframe-based neural network designed to flash warning signs when it finds potentially fraudulent transactions. This year, the bank expects to swallow a bitter $3 million fraud-related pill when it closes the books on 1991 financials, according to Philip Samson, vice president and portfolio performance manager. The 18th largest bank in the U.S.,

based here, wants to curtail fraud losses in the coming years.

"We want to better protect our cardholders and ourselves," Samson said.

System Too Simplistic

Right now, credit purchases are monitored with an in-house-developed, rules-based system. The system triggers a request for positive customer identification if activity on the card is unusually high or if a purchase exceeds a preset dollar amount.

However, this method is too simplistic, according to Samson. "Fraud changes all the time. Criminals constantly try to outdo the banks," he said.

As Mellon Bank's resident expert on neural networks, Samson is overseeing a pilot of the Fraud Detection System (FDS), an application from Providence, R.I.-based Nestor Corp. FDS will "learn" to

recognize irregular charge-card patterns, then rate the situation on a fraud possibility scale.

For example, the fictitious Joe Charger typically uses his Visa card twice a month, once at a restaurant and once at a local department store. Suddenly, Joe apparently starts running up four or five purchases over a week's time.

The next time Joe's card is passed over a shopkeeper's counter or his number is presented to an order taker over the phone, FDS will match current buying patterns against Joe's charging history and spit back either a flat denial or a prompt to ask for positive identification.

"The neural network can see patterns of activity a busy human can't," Samson explained.

How Do Neural Networks and Expert Systems Differ?

Neural networks do not use IF-THEN condition-action rules. Although humans tend to think in terms of IF-THEN rules, underlying these rules are a network of neurons. Thus, in a sense neural networks are an attempt to mimic the more basic capabilities of the brain than expert systems are. The primary difference between a neural network and an expert system is the capability that a neural network has to learn from experience. In effect, as we train a neural network we are providing it with case histories of past experience. Once it reaches an acceptable level of performance, we start using the neural network. Of course, the learning does not stop at the point when we start using the neural network. Each time it makes a decision the neural network ultimately receives feedback as to whether it made a correct decision or not and thus learns from experience. In contrast, an expert system's knowledge base has to be modified by humans who learn from experience. Thus, a neural network does not claim to solve any particular problem or have knowledge about any particular problem. It simply has the capability to learn how to make a correct decision in a problem area.

In summary, artificial intelligence is beginning to provide tools that augment the reasoning and decision-making capabilities of humans. As these systems are developed and implemented we are likely to see profound changes in human tasks and organization.

"In a most fundamental sense organizations will increasingly be regarded as joint human-computer knowledge-processing systems. Human participation in these systems, from the most highly skilled to the least skilled positions, can be regarded as knowledge workers. Collectively, they will work with many types of knowledge, in a variety of ways, and with various objectives. Their knowledge management efforts will be aided and supported by computers. Not only will these computer coworkers relieve us of the menial, routine and repetitive, they will also actively recognize needs, stimulate insights, and offer advice. They will highly leverage an organization's unique human skills of intuition, creative imagination, value judgment, the cultivation of effective interpersonal relationships, and so forth."[7]

Summary

- Artificial intelligence is the use of computers to perform tasks that normally require high-level human intelligence.

- Human intelligence consists of three basic attributes: learning, reasoning, and the manipulation of symbols.

- Artificial intelligence research and applications are being studied in robotics, computer vision, speech recognition, natural language processing, expert systems, and neural networks.

- Robotics is the application of computers to tasks that normally require human intelligence and physical manipulations.

- The most important advantage of robots in the manufacturing process is that a much wider variety of products can be produced at a lower price.

- Computer vision is the acquisition and processing of sets of visual signals in order to recognize and interpret high-level patterns and make these patterns meaningful.

- Speech recognition attempts to capture human speech and convert it to the language being spoken, for example, English words.

- Natural language processing uses a set of rules and conventions for a particular language to derive the meaning of sentences.

- An expert system is a computer program that enables a computer to make (or give advice concerning) an unstructured decision that is normally made by a human with special expertise.

- There are two basic types of expert systems: rule-based and frame-based.

- A rule-based expert system consists of processing and storage facilities. These are often referred to respectively as an inference engine and a knowledge base.

- The knowledge base stores facts and rules.

---

[7] C. W. Holsapple and A. B. Whinston, *Business Expert Systems* (Homewood, IL: Irwin, 1987), 301.

- When facts arise in the working memory that satisfy the conditions of a particular rule in the knowledge base, that rule is selected (triggered) and interpreted by the rule interpreter. The combination of selecting and interpreting rules is known as the firing of rules.

- An expert system continues cycling through this process of asking for input, firing rules based on conditions or facts that arise in the working memory, generating new facts, asking for more input, and so on until a final decision or recommendation is reached.

- Expert systems determine their sequential behavior by selecting their next activity from a set of potentially triggered rules. This compares with a conventional information processing system where the next activity is determined by the next step in the computer program.

- Expert systems have the following advantages:

  1. They reduce the need for highly paid experts.
  2. They are a way of preserving, replicating, and distributing expert knowledge.
  3. They improve the consistency and accuracy of decisions.
  4. They provide better documentation of the rationale for a decision than do many human experts.
  5. They provide insight into the decision-making process.
  6. They can be used as training tools for novices.

- The limitations of expert systems include:

  1. Expert systems are sometimes overrated.
  2. Expert systems can be expensive to develop and maintain.
  3. It is difficult to elicit the knowledge of experts.
  4. Rapidly changing areas of application require constant maintenance of the expert system.
  5. Expert systems lack common sense.
  6. Expert systems cannot learn.
  7. The rigid interaction format between an expert and a human does not allow for vague or unusual questions and answers.
  8. The validation of expert systems can be difficult.

- Suitable problems for an expert system have the following characteristics:

  1. Recognized experts' work in the problem's field.
  2. The steps in solving the problem are routinely taught to novices.
  3. The problem takes a human expert a few minutes to several hours to solve.
  4. The problem requires facts rather than common sense for its solution.
  5. The domain of the problem is limited.

- A major difficulty in developing expert systems is the transfer of knowledge from the human expert to the expert system.

- The development approach that is used for almost all business expert system is the use of a purchased expert system shell.

- An expert system shell already has the inference engine or processing part of the system created.

- It has been found that building a prototype is the best method for developing an expert system.

- One of the major limitations of expert systems is the fact that they cannot learn on their own. Neural networks are an attempt to overcome this limitation. Neural networks are composed of elements that perform in a manner analogous to the most elementary functions of the biological neuron in animal brains.

- Neural networks are trained to fire certain patterns of neurons when certain input conditions exist, thus producing a certain output (action or advice).

- The primary advantage of neural networks is their potential to learn.

- The training of neural networks has been very successful in some applications.

- Neural networks do not use IF-THEN condition-action rules. In a sense neural networks are an attempt to mimic the more basic capabilities of the brain than expert systems are.

- Organizations will increasingly be regarded as joint human-computer, knowledge-processing systems.

Key Terms

Artificial intelligence

Robotics

Computer vision

Speech recognition

Natural language processing

Expert system

Inference engine

Knowledge base

Firing of rules

Knowledge engineer

Expert system shell

Neural networks

Neurons

Review Questions

1. What is artificial intelligence?

2. What are the three basic capabilities of human intelligence?

3. What is robotics and how is it used in business?

4. What is computer vision? Discuss some of its applications.

5. What is speech recognition and why is it an important capability for computers?

6. How does natural language processing differ from speech recognition?

7. What is an expert system?

8. What are some reasons why firms are interested in applying expert systems?

9. What are the major limitations of expert systems?

10. What types of problems are good candidates for an expert system?

11. What are the major components of expert systems?

12. How does an expert system differ from conventional information processing systems?

13. What are the two basic types of expert systems?

14. How does a rule-based expert system work?

15. What is a knowledge engineer?

16. How does an expert system shell help in developing an expert system?

17. What is the best approach to developing an expert system? Why?

18. What is a neuron?

19. What is a neural network?

20. How is a neural network trained?

21. How do neural networks and expert systems differ?

Discussion Questions and Cases

1. To be successful, must computer-based artificial intelligence systems duplicate the ways that humans exhibit intelligence?

2. Which capability is more important for a computer application: speech recognition or natural language processing?

3. Can a machine think?

4. If you were ill, which would you rather have to diagnose your illness and prescribe a course of treatment: an expert system, a doctor using an expert system, or a doctor not using an expert system? Why?

5. Some people argue that expert systems are a mirage. They say that experts can always make better decisions than expert systems because experts have common sense. They further argue that it is highly unlikely that we will be able to develop computer systems that have common sense. What do you think?

6. Are expert systems likely to have an impact on the content of education and the methods by which you learn?

7. The following quotes are from *The Age of Intelligent Machines* by Raymond Kurzweil (Cambridge, MA: MIT Press, 1990, pp. 427–428): "Most factories built today employ substantially fewer workers than the factories they replace. Even if robotic technology is not employed the computerization of material handling and work flow has substantially reduced the direct labor content of most products. There is little question that this trend will continue and intensify over the next two decades. By

early in the next century a relatively small number of technicians and other professionals will be sufficient to operate the entire production sector of society . . . . As employment in the factory dwindles employment in the office will be stable or increase. However, what we do in offices will substantially change. Clerical work will largely disappear. Completing a trend already underway, by early in the next century, computers will type our letters and reports, intelligently maintain our files and records, and help to organize our work. The areas likely to continue to require significant human involvement, particularly during the first half of the next century, will be communication, teaching, learning, selling, strategic decision making, and innovation. The office worker of the next century will have sustained contact with both human and machine intelligence . . . . A constructive change in our concept of work will be to think of the process of learning as part of work rather than just as a prerequisite for work. The worker of the future may spend as much as half of his time learning rather than just doing." Do you agree with these statements? Why or why not?

INFORMATION SYSTEMS STRATEGIES

Choices Abound in Expert-System Shells

By Mark L. Van Name and Bill Catchings

Perhaps one of the most natural applications of expert-system technology is in decision support. An expert system can automate many of the decisions inherent in complex tasks such as medical diagnoses, insurance-claim payments and quality control in manufacturing.

In choosing an expert-system shell, buyers must balance the programming expertise that different shells require against the available staff.

An expert-system shell is basically an expert system awaiting a knowledge base—a body of information about the topic, or domain. Knowledge bases typically contain two basic kinds of information: assertions and rules.

In essence, an assertion is a fact about the domain. Most expert systems represent assertions as text strings. Some assertions are permanent parts of the knowledge base, such as "The normal body temperature is 98.6 degrees Fahrenheit." Users can enter others, such as "The machine that winds the fiber-optic cable is making a loud screeching noise," as they use the expert system to make a decision.

Rules are typically "If . . . then" statements that guide the expert system in the decision-making process. Many rules contain a single "If" clause, but can also have many clauses.

These rules are not, however, the same as the If . . . then statements of traditional programming languages. Standard If . . . then statements appear at fixed points in a program's flow, and they must list all the conditions that the programmer wishes to check at those precise points.

In contrast, users can enter expert-system shell If . . . then rules in any order, and those rules can contain either one or a few conditions. It is up to the shell to figure out when to use the rules and in what order to use them.

Structuring the Knowledge Base

There are many different ways to store or structure information in an expert-system knowledge base, but most use one or both of two common approaches.

The more common method is to store rules and assertions much as users enter them, as sets of If . . . then rules.

This sort of discrete-rule structure works best in applications that have many assertions and rules that may appear almost unrelated.

Despited their popularity, however, rule-oriented structures have several short-comings. A major drawback is the search time required: The shell must scan the knowledge base looking for candidate rules to try. As the number of rules and input assertions grow, the search time can quickly get out of hand.

The other major method is to store knowledge in frames. In contrast with the individual statements of rules and assertions, frames are basically structures that contain a set of data attributes, or slots, and usually some rules related to those slots.

Each of these slots can contain a piece of information (or a rule) about whatever the frame describes, so a single frame can hold a great deal of information. Frames are very similar in structure to the objects of object-oriented programming. Frames typically fall into classes, or groups, and a frame can inherit traits from their classes.

Structural Issues

The biggest advantage of frames is that they can represent knowledge about real-world things simply and easily. Their inheritance abilities also make frames the best choice for applications in which the domain knowledge is naturally hierarchial or depends heavily on context, such as simulation or natural-language translation.

On the downside, however, expert-system shells that use frames generally require more powerful inference engines than those that use discrete rules to organize their information.

This is perhaps the main reason that most PC expert-system shells structure their knowledge as rules.

Whether an expert system shell uses rules or frames, buyers should make sure the shell offers good tools for maintaining the knowledge base. Crucial features include the ability to comment on rules or frames and the ability to examine and edit all or part of the knowledge base at any time.

Expert-system shells combine a knowledge base with a set of user-entered input assertions (the problem description) to try to find a solution (the goal). The part of the shell that handles this task is known as the inference engine. While every expert-system shell's inference engine uses different problem-solving algorithms, most shells employ one or both of two basic methods.

The more common strategy is known as backward chaining. In general, a backward-chaining shell starts with an answer and tries to work backward to reach the input assertions. It chooses rules to try (or "fire," in expert-system parlance) based on their conclusions, starting first with one goal and firing all the rules that have that goal as their conclusion. The shell repeats this process until either the starting goal leads to the input assertions or until it cannot find any more rules to fire, in which case it moves on to the next possible goal.

Forward chaining is, as its name implies, the procedural opposite of backward chaining. A forward-chaining shell starts with the input assertions and fires every rule that those assertions can possibly trigger. The shell then checks to see if any of those rules led to a goal. If not, it repeats the process, this time firing every rule that the results of the previous tries made possible. The shell keeps up this iterative process until it reaches a goal.

Inference-Engine Issues

Forward chaining is best for those applications in which the user knows initially everything that the shell will need to make a decision and those in which input assertions typically outnumber the possible answers. Applications that commonly produce Yes/No answers, such as insurance-claim systems, are good candidates for forward chaining.

Backward chaining is best for applications in which the user can supply a good starting guess. In addition, it is often better than forward chaining for applications in which there are many possible answers and fewer input assertions.

The more powerful expert-system shells often offer both types of inference-engine search strategies.

A final and crucial issue regarding any inference engine is speed. Unfortunately, a shell's speed can be extremely difficult to gauge. There are no established benchmarks, because the performance of a shell often depends heavily on how closely an application matches the shell's strengths.

One performance aid that buyers can consider is the ability to tune the way the shell searches its rules: Can developers prioritize rules, or does the shell search the rules in a predefined order? Finer control over the shell's search strategies offers the promise of better performance—but only for developers who are willing to take the time to study and experiment with the tuning options.

Determining a Shell's Personality

A powerful inference engine and good knowledge-representation facilities are only part of the story. Equally important is the set of tools that the shell provides developers.

The most obvious tool is the development interface itself. Most expert-system shells are highly interactive, largely nonprocedural programs that let users define the knowledge base and, in some cases, the inference strategies for their applications. Some shells also provide procedural languages.

Every shell has a distinctive development method that it encourages. As with most products, potential buyers should try to get some hands-on time with each shell to see if its preferred development method matches their needs.

One issue here is ease of use. If users define rules and otherwise control the shell with commands, buyers should examine whether the command language is reasonably intuitive and consistent. If the shell is menu-driven, the question to ask is whether the menu options are clear and easy to find.

Another important consideration is the degree to which developers can customize the expert systems they build. Buyers should decide whether they want users to be aware that they are in the shell, or whether they prefer the development team to produce turnkey applications.

Buyers must also address how developers must deliver their applications. Expert-system shells typically either generate code for a stand-alone expert system or require that users own a run-time version to execute the final system. Buyers should note whether a run-time version is necessary and, if so, what it costs.

Maintenance Facilities

Another concern that is easy to overlook initially is maintenance. As with most software, the first version of an expert system is usually much more a beginning than an end.

Developers will need to refine the system over time, and a shell can provide tools to simplify that task.

One important tool for both maintenance and regular use is an explanation facility, which provides a way for users and developers alike to discover how the shell reached its decision. Sometimes, as in insurance-claim adjudication, such an explanation can be a vital part of the application or might even be required by law.

The shell should be able to produce a clear, readable display or printed explanation of the rules that it followed in making its decision. Ideally, the shell should also be able to show its progress at any point in the decision process, so that developers can see how it is doing and spot areas that they should improve.

Another key area is the shell's support for maintaining the knowledge base. Central maintenance issues to consider include whether the developers read the knowledge base a rule or a frame at a time, and whether the shell produces an overall—

ideally, graphical—display. Buyers should also determine whether a shell can spot and flag redundant and inconsistent rules, or if developers must handle those tasks.

A final major topic that buyers must consider is the shell's ability to work with the external world of the target application: target machines, external data and other programs.

At first, the issue of target machines might seem almost trivial. But making sure the shell runs on the target system—say, an MS-DOS PC—can prove more complicated than it seems. Developers might want to work on a more powerful system—perhaps a mainframe or a workstation—and then port the resulting application to a PC. Thus, the buyer must determine whether the shell runs in both worlds, as must the resulting expert systems.

A similar issue is access to external data. If the target expert-system application is to work with any of that data, the shell's ability to deal with other data formats is crucial.

On PCs, this usually means support for at least the Ashton-Tate dBASE and Lotus Development Corp. Lotus 1-2-3 file formats. Buyers should also decide whether they need only read existing data, or read and write it. If data vital to the expert system is in the format of another database system, then the shell must either be able to work with that database system or allow developers to add programs that can.

The ability to write programs that communicate with the shell is the last external-world concern. Some expert-system applications, such as process monitoring, can require the shell to communicate with physical devices, while others may demand only that an enveloping menu system be able to call the shell.

Discussion Questions

1. Why can expert systems rules be in no particular order in the knowledge base?

2. Why is it important for an expert system to be able to display the logic it used to reach a particular recommendation?

Reprinted with permission from PC Week (March 5, 1990), pp. 77–79. Copyright Ziff-Davis Publishing Co., 1990.

9

Office Automation

Introduction

As information processing equipment continues to move out of the information systems department and into users' offices, office workers depend more and more on the computer to do their jobs. Some of the most significant effects of this distribution of computer processing have been in the area of office automation. Computers are being applied to most routine office tasks. These applications include both written and oral communications, the processing and storage of data, and the processing and storage of documents. In this chapter we will define office automation and then explore the primary ways that computers are used to automate offices, including word processing, desktop publishing, electronic mail, voice processing, computer and video conferencing, electronic calendaring, facsimile transmission, image processing, forms processing, personal support systems, and integrated office automation tools. We will end the chapter by discussing some of the issues surrounding office automation.

What Is Office Automation?

The activities that occur in an office include managing documents, managing schedules for individuals and groups, managing projects, communicating with individuals and groups, managing data, and making decisions. The management of data is done through traditional information systems (covered in previous chapters) and the making of decisions is supported with various decision support systems (also covered in a previous chapter). The other activities of an office can be reduced to one basic activity, and that is communicating. Essentially, communications are used to support almost all activities within an organization and communications are the essence of activities that occur within offices. As Figure 9–1 illustrates, communications can be created, modified, maintained, stored, retrieved, sent, and received. These communications are in three basic types: voice communication, text communication, and image communication. All office automation support tools are designed to assist in one or more of the three basic types of communication. **Voice communication** is human voices or computer-generated simulations of human voices. **Text communication** includes both handwritten and typed text material. Text communication may be processed by a computer in character form, where each character is individually processed by the computer, or in image form, where, in effect, a picture of a whole page of text is processed by the computer. **Image communication** include graphs, pictures, drawings, and moving video images.

    Office automation is the application of computer technology to the information communication functions of an office. Today office automation tools primarily support the communications function in offices. In the future as expert systems and perhaps decision support technology is integrated with some of the office automation tools, these tools may also directly assist in the making of decisions in some of the higher level management functions.

Word Processing

Just as computers can process numerical data, they can also process words. Textual materials such as letters, reports, and books can be stored on the same storage media as numerical data. In fact, the most widely

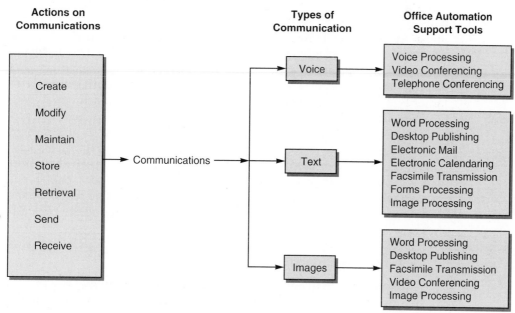

FIGURE 9–1
How Office Automation Tools Support Communications.

used application on personal computers today is word processing. Many good word processing packages are available at inexpensive prices.

Figure 9–2 illustrates the capabilities of a **word processing** system. Inputs may be made from a variety of input devices. Processing can be performed on any size of computer although most word processing is done on personal computers. The processing power necessary to do word processing is very small compared to other applications, such as decision support systems and electronic spreadsheets. The most widely used storage media for word processing systems are disks and the output can be printed on paper, stored on a disk, communicated over networks to other computers, or sent by fax to a remote fax machine. The printed output

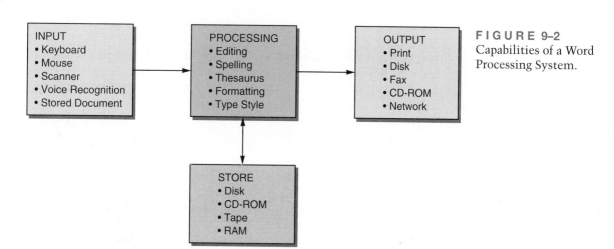

FIGURE 9–2
Capabilities of a Word Processing System.

from a word processing system can be done on a dot matrix printer if only draft quality is needed. For high-quality output laser printers are most widely used. However, high-quality output can also be obtained from ink jet printers at about half the cost of laser printers. The disadvantage of ink jet printers is that they are slower than laser printers. Fax boards may be placed in PCs that allow PCs to fax material directly to other PCs that contain a fax board or to stand-alone fax machines.

The advantages of word processing are based on the fact that the system stores textual data on a disk and retrieves, modifies, or prints them on command. A report, for example, can be initially typed through a keyboard, then stored on disk, and finally printed. Corrections to the report can be made directly through the keyboard. Words, sentences, paragraphs or even whole pages can be inserted, deleted, or moved. The report can be corrected and polished before a final copy is printed. Among the capabilities of word processing are the following:

- Detection and correction of spelling errors
- Automatic changing of margin widths without retyping of the material; the operator simply tells the system the new margins, and the system automatically sets them
- Deletion, insertion, or modification of any textual material
- Automatic centering
- Automatic underlining
- Automatic hyphenation of words
- Automatic page numbering
- Choice of multiple fonts for printing

The advantages of word processing include:

- Reduced typing time (some say up to 50 percent of the typing and retyping time is saved with a word processor)
- Reduced proofreading time
- Cleaner, more professional-looking final copies.

Most individuals who are not skilled typists find that typing on a word processor is easier than on a typewriter since corrections can be made readily. The fear of making an error and having to correct it with an eraser or correction fluid is eliminated. If the material is dictated, the typist enters the material on a word processor. Then the originator of the text calls it up on his or her computer, reviews it, makes final corrections, and prints the final copy.

Integrated Word Processing/Data Processing

Often businesses need to combine the output of their information processing systems with textual material to create a final document. If data processing and word processing are performed on separate systems, it was necessary in the past to retype some of the information in order to obtain the final printout. **Integrated word processing/data processing (WP/DP)** systems can save this extra labor by processing the data and then using the results as input to a word processing operation. These systems are used to generate customer correspondence and reports, and they are available for personal computers.

Customer Correspondence

Data from accounting or marketing records can be combined with text to create high-quality correspondence material. For instance, a hospital computer can search patient records to find people who have not been in for a checkup in over a year. After checking the current appointments file, the system can automatically produce letters to remind patients to come in for their annual visits. Figure 9–3 shows how the system would print a high-quality letter by merging data files with precomposed text.

Reports

Managers frequently prepare reports that include both data and descriptive text. For example, a report from a regional sales manager may include detailed sales data as well as a subjective evaluation of the future market. Figure 9–4 illustrates how an integrated WP/DP system would produce a tabular report combined with the manager's remarks. In addition, systems are now available that can insert graphics output in a report, along with the data and text.

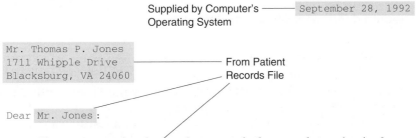

Supplied by Computer's ——— September 28, 1992
Operating System

Mr. Thomas P. Jones
1711 Whipple Drive ——————— From Patient
Blacksburg, VA 24060   Records File

Dear Mr. Jones :

According to our records you have not had a complete physical checkup since August 1991 . As part of our Community Preventive Medicine Program, we strongly recommend that all residents of this area take an annual medical examination.

We urge you to arrange for an examination at your earliest convenience. Appointments may be made by calling our business office (753-2531), weekdays between 9 a.m. and 5 p.m. If you have already made an appointment, kindly disregard this letter.

We look forward to hearing from you soon.

Sincerely,

Mark J. Williams, CHA
Chief Administrator
Blacksburg City Hospital
1600 Main Street East
Blacksburg, VA 24060

Precomposed Text

FIGURE 9–3
A Personalized Letter Produced by Integrated Word Processing/Data Processing.

FIGURE 9–4
Sales Report Including
Both Data and Text.

The report-generating
capability is very useful
to most businesses.
Executives like to have
data reports analyzed and
explained through text
comments, as shown
here.

Green Forest Products, Inc.
Quarterly Sales Summary ($000)
Southwest Region
2nd Quarter 199X

Data {

Product	% Change	April	% Change	May	% Change	June
White Paper	+ 1.40%	162	+ 0.62%	163	− 7.89%	150
Hardboard	+ 0.85%	85	+ 2.35%	87	+ 5.75%	92
Plywood	+ 1.43%	123	+ 4.88%	129	+ 6.20%	137
Wallpaper	+ 3.15%	55	− 23.64%	42	+ 21.43%	51

Comments

Text {

1) White paper sales dropped in June,
mainly owing to school and office
vacations.
2) Hardboard and plywood sales were up
sharply because of a seasonal rise in
construction activity.
3) Wallpaper sales fell drastically during
May. The major reason was the low
introductory prices of a new competitor,
Frisco Paper Company. However, we were
able to regain our market share in June,
because of aggressive marketing and an
increase in Frisco's prices.

Integrated Personal Computer Software

Personal computer spreadsheet, database, and word processing software
allow for the transfer of both data and text between each type of software
to facilitate the rapid integration of data and/or text. In addition, graphical user interfaces, such as Microsoft Windows and Presentation Manager in OS/2, allow users to cut and paste (transfer) data and text between
applications. Also, both Windows and OS/2 have a feature called dynamic data exchange. *Dynamic data exchange* (DDE) allows two or more applications to exchange data. To illustrate how DDE can be used, let's
assume we have the same piece of data stored in both spreadsheet and
database files and also plotted in a graph. With DDE, if this data is
changed in the database it will automatically be changed in the spreadsheet and graph also.

Desktop Publishing

Because word processing packages could not produce output having the
same layout and print quality of typeset documents, desktop publishing
was developed in the early 1980s. **Desktop publishing (DTP) systems** provide the capability of writing, assembling, designing, and printing high-
quality documents. However, the quality is not yet as good as
professional typesetting.

The hardware of a DTP system includes a personal computer, a high-
resolution monitor, a mouse, and a laser printer. General-purpose DTP
software is at the heart of desktop publishing. These programs offer page

layout, text, and graphics features. Images and graphics are easily incorporated into DTP documents. Figure 9–5 shows a document produced by a DTP system.

The advantages of DTP include lower cost, reduced lead time for producing final output, and easier and faster modifications. Also, many companies are using DTP to improve the attractiveness of their internal communications, which in the past were printed by regular word-processing systems.

Desktop publishing does have some disadvantages. First, the programs are complex, and it takes a while to learn to use them. Perhaps the biggest disadvantage is that designing high-quality documents is an art. Simply buying a desktop publishing package and learning how to use it will not give the user the ability to design attractive and professional

FIGURE 9–5
A Document Produced by a Desktop Publishing System.

WEST'S FEDERAL TAXATION

Newsletter   by C. Douglass Izard, CPA, Ph.D   Volume 6, Spring 1992

In This Issue

- President Bush's Tax Proposals in his State of the Union Address 1

- Middle Income Tax Relief 1

- Future Meetings 3

- Teacher's Thought 4

- Update on Changes Effective for Tax Returns Filed in Spring 1992 5

- Increase in 1992 Social Security Taxable Wage Base Announced 6

- Call For Submissions 7

Middle Income Tax Relief

The Staff of the Joint Committee on Taxation has prepared a description of proposals relating to middle income tax relief and economic growth that were scheduled for hearings before the House Committee on Ways and Means in late December, 1991. These proposals represent bills that will be considered by Congress in 1992. A summary of key elements of the proposals is provided below:

(Continued on page 2)

President Bush's Tax Proposals in his State of the Union Address

President Bush, in his budget plan submitted to Congress January 29, proposed reducing the capital gains rate to 15.4%, tax credits targeted to home buyers and middle income Americans, and changes in income tax withholding rates. President Bush asked Congress to pass an economic growth package that would pull the country out of the recession.

The President said that his package would not require increased federal spending or an increase in tax rates. However, he did say that he would be willing to partially renegotiate the budget agreement to use defense spending reductions to offset his proposed $500 increase in the personal tax exemption for children.

The President said that administratively he would accelerate spending for programs already authorized, reduce income tax withholdingrates, and issue a 90-day moratorium on proposed new federal regulations. Some of the key points of the President's message were:

1. Reduce the capital gains rate to 15.4% from the current 28% (he had previously called for a 19.6% rate).

2. Provide a temporary tax credit for first-time home buyers of up to 10% of the price of a home, (limited to $5,000) over two years, and penalty-free withdrawal

from individual retirement accounts for first-time home purchases.

3. For taxable years ending on or after December 31, 1992, a taxpayer who materially participates in real estate development would not have to treat income and loss from such activity as "passive." Real estate development activity would be treated as a single activity and would be defined as the construction, renovation, and management operations in which the taxpayer actively participates, the lease-up and sale of real property in which the taxpayer has at least a 10% ownership interest, and rental operations if the rented property was developed by the taxpayer.

4. For businesses, a 15% investment tax allowance designed to stimulate investment through additional depreciation, a permanent change to the alternative minimum tax rules, and a permanent research and development credit. The President also called for repeal of the 10% luxury excise tax on boats and airplanes (but not cars).

5. Increased funding for public and government-assisted housing; passage of his enterprise zone initiative; and an extension of the low-income housing credit.

6. The personal exemption for children be raised by $500, above the current level of $2,150, and indexing the exemptions for inflation.

The change would be effective October 1.

7. Families also should be allowed to deduct the interest they pay on student loans.

8. Funds in individual retirement accounts could be withdrawn without penalty for "qualifying medical and educational expenses.

9. To encourage increased personal savings, a new form of individual retirement account, a flexible individual retirement account (FIRA), would allow taxpayers to contribute up to $2,500 a year, with a limit of two accounts per family. Unlike a traditional IRA, however, the contributions would not be deductible. Instead, earnings on amounts contributed would be excluded from income while in the account and would be permanently excluded if the contribution to which they relate remains in the account for more than seven years. FIRAs would not be available to single individuals with income in excess of $60,000 or to families with income exceeding $120,000. Amounts in existing IRAs could be rolled over into a FIRA between Feb 1 and Dec. 31 of this year and would be included in income ratably over a four year period.

10. A 90-day moratorium on new federal regulations, stating that a constant stream of regulations can hinder growth. ■

printed documents. Unless a company produces a large volume of high-quality documents, it may be better off contracting with someone outside to do the desktop publishing. Many graphic arts and printing firms offer desktop publishing at a reasonable price.

Electronic Mail

Many companies with networked information-processing systems are expanding them into an **electronic mail** (E-mail) network (see Figure 9–6). Since the textual material is stored in electronic form in the word processing system, it can be transmitted easily over long distances through regular commercial channels such as microwave and telephone lines. Many companies, such as Amoco Oil and Citicorp, have extensive electronic mail capabilities.

When an executive receives electronic mail on his or her local workstation, the message can be read from the screen. Also, a printed copy is readily available if needed. These systems have several advantages:

1. The time between creation of information and its receipt by interested parties is minimized.

2. By relying on typed messages rather than voice communications, managers do not have to waste time dialing the phone, only to hear a busy signal.

3. Messages and documents do not need to be physically copied in order to be routed to many people on a distribution list.

4. Electronic mail may be filed by the recipient or dispatched to an "electronic wastebasket." The wastebasket retains messages for a period of time before destroying them.

Electronic mail can also raise significant privacy issues, as shown in Application 9–1.

Voice Processing

The human voice and all other sounds can be digitized, stored, and transmitted by computers. **Voice processing** combines the power of the computer with the telephone to process and transmit human voices. There are five major areas of voice processing:

FIGURE 9–6
Electronic Mail.
Electronic mail is becoming widespread within large firms. It is used much less between firms.

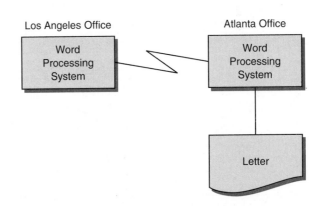

APPLICATION 9–1

Who Can Open E-Mail?

By Jim Nash and Maura J. Harrington

Blistering "Dear John" notes, embarrassing wisecracks and even sexual fantasies are showing up on corporate electronic-mail systems with greater frequency. And in some cases, they are finding their way into personnel folders and even to court.

Last week, two information systems employees filed a suit in California Superior Court against Nissan Motor Corp. in U.S.A. claiming the company violated their privacy by intercepting their electronic messages. The E-mail notes allegedly led to the firing of one and the forced resignation of the other, the employees said.

It is the second such E-mail privacy suit to be filed in California in the past year, although the first suit was thrown out of court last week in a ruling that rejected any right to privacy on employer-owned systems.

Bonita Bourke and Rhonda Hall, former Nissan employees, claimed last week they were each shown a stack of their E-mail last year and told to stop their non-work-related E-mail.

Days after filing grievances with Nissan's human resources department, Hall said she was fired and Bourke said she was offered the opportunity to resign. Hall and Bourke admitted to using E-mail for personal communication. Bourke said the messages Nissan collected included interdepartmental "business correspondence, messages people sent me [and] some wisecracks about the company."

Hall said management had told employees that confidential passwords protected their messages from any interception.

Last week, however, a Los Angeles County Superior Court judge dismissed a class-action lawsuit brought against Epson America, Inc. for allegedly violating its employees' privacy by intercepting their E-mail.

A spokesman for Epson in Torrance, Calif., said Judge Barnet Cooperman found on Jan. 7 that the company did not violate a state penal code prohibiting electronic eavesdropping on private communications. "In essence, the judge said companies have the right to manage their E-mail systems." Epson has maintained that it randomly intercepts messages in the process of maintaining its systems. . . .

E-mail is widely credited with enticing technophobes onto computers by humanizing the devices. But if recent events are any indication, E-mail may be doing its job too well.

At Belmont, Calif.-based Oracle Systems Corp., an employee reportedly used E-mail to bare her feelings in a scathing message to her boyfriend, also an Oracle employee.

"Boy, did she let him have it," said one of the inadvertent recipients of the message. When the woman had finished her letter, she hit the wrong transmit key and broadcast the message to every computer user in the firm.

According to University of Washington at Seattle professor Mark Haselkorn, "People who use E-mail open up so much sometimes that it's too much." Haselkorn was part of a national congressional study on the effects of E-mail within the government and organizations.

While some firms take the position that personal use of E-mail is a waste of time and property, others seem willing to tolerate judicious use of the software for anonymous or open forums.

Adapted with permission from *Computerworld* (January 14, 1991), pp. 1, 88, Copyright 1991 by CW Publishing, Inc., Framingham, MA 01701.

1. **Voice mail** provides users with the capability of recording, storing, forwarding, and broadcasting voice messages through touch-tone phones.

2. **Automatic call distribution** routes telephone calls based on the caller's responses to questions through touch-tone phones. When a call is received the caller is given several options to route the call. After listening to the options spoken by a computer-generated voice, the caller is asked to touch the number on the phone keypad that corresponds to the choice he or she wishes to make. These systems can save companies a substantial amount because no operator is needed to answer and route the call.

3. **Voice response systems** provide callers with prerecorded cues. Based on these cues callers can instruct a computer to complete a transaction or recite information by pushing the correct key on a touch-tone phone. Fidelity Investments uses these systems to provide customers with automated access to mutual fund prices.

4. **Audio text systems** provide recorded entertainment and information over the phone. These systems are often combined with 900 phone numbers that charge customers by the minute for connect time while accessing the information.

5. **Speech recognition systems** enable computers to "understand" and respond to the human voice.

Of these five voice-processing capabilities, voice mail and speech recognition are the two that have the widest potential application and are of the most interest. We will discuss these in more depth below.

Voice mail is often installed as a part of digital networks (often called digital switches), which are computer-based telephone networks where voice, image, text, and data are transmitted and stored. This digital network is in effect a computer network. Thus, when you talk over such a phone system you are really talking over a computer system. On such a system a voice message may be sent to another phone, stored, or routed to many phones on a distribution list.

Voice mail has all the advantages of electronic mail plus some extra ones. Voice mail's major advantage over electronic mail is that voice mail is easier to use because typing skills are not necessary and it is faster to talk than it is to type a message. These systems provide other capabilities such as "camping on" a person's phone. Camping on is useful when you are trying to reach someone by phone, but the line is busy. With camping on, the telephone digital switch rings both the caller and receiver's phone simultaneously when the receiver's phone becomes free. Another new capability is caller identification. With caller identification the calling party's phone number is provided to the receiving party. This can be used to screen incoming calls. Mail order companies use caller identification to input the caller's number automatically to the order-entry system. Thus, if the caller is a previous customer, his or her records are immediately available to the order taker. In the future most telephone systems will be digitally based so these voice mail capabilities will be available to everyone.

Speech recognition is the ability of computers to recognize or to interpret human speech and convert it to the characters that make up each spoken word. Currently there are speech recognition systems that will recognize speech almost without error if the vocabulary is very limited. These systems are being used primarily in hands-busy applications. Such an application is the sorting of mail. The U.S. Postal Service uses speech recognition to allow mail sorters to read zip codes for bundles of mail and speak these zip codes into a microphone while they use their hands to sort packages. These systems have allowed mail sorters to sort four times as much mail as before, when they had to key in the zip code with one hand while sorting with the other hand.

The ultimate in speech recognition is to build a system that will process continuous human speech at its normal pace and convert this speech into its characters in the computer. This type of speech recognition is not easy. Figure 9–7 illustrates some of the difficulties in continuous speech recognition.

However, systems are currently available that can recognize up to 30,000 words of speech. Thirty thousand words are far beyond the vocabulary of almost all humans. Thus, these systems can convert to text almost anything you might say. Such a system is Dragon Dictate, which currently sells for $9,000. However, as you talk to this system you must pause unnaturally between each word. Because of the pause this system can only process up to 40 words per minute. A proficient typist can type, on the average, 80 words

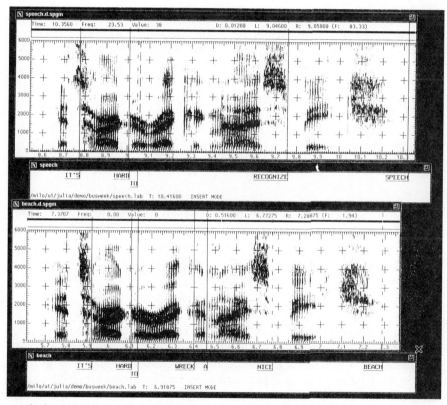

FIGURE 9–7
The Difficulties of Speech Recognition or "How to Wreck a Nice Beach."

Reprinted with special permission from "A Computer That Recognizes Its Master's Voice," *Business Week*, June 3, 1991, p. 131, Copyright © 1991 by McGraw-Hill, Inc.

The human voice can be represented as a pattern of changing audio frequencies (above). Speech recognition systems compare human voices with patterns of known sounds of syllables and words stored in a computer. The computer makes comparisons—sometimes thousands of them—until it finds the pattern that most closely matches.

But this method has limitations. For example, the word "wreck" closely matches the first syllable in "recognize." When patterns are this close, the computer must make a best guess. And, as is the case with human hearing, the correct choice usually depends on the context of the sentence or phrase. That's where advances in linguistical methods help. Those involve statistical models to guess how likely it is that a person will say "recognize" as opposed to "wreck a nice."

The final choice often depends on the application. For instance, if a computer is trained for making hotel reservations, it would understand a customer who says, "I want to check in" But, if it were programmed to take fast food orders, it might take that as "I want two chicken."

per minute. Currently, Dragon Dictate is used in making computers accessible to handicapped people who cannot use keyboards (such as paraplegics), in situations where people need to input data while their hands are otherwise occupied, and as an alternative for those who cannot or will not type.

In the future speech recognition promises to revolutionize the way humans interact with computers. In the past, computer systems have forced humans to adapt to unnatural means of interfacing with the computers. The most natural means by which humans interface with others is through speech.

Voice processing capabilities are here today. They can greatly increase the efficiency with which we work. For an example of how various voice processing technology is being used today take a look at Figure 9–8.

Computer and Video Conferencing

Computer conferencing is a type of electronic mail. A number of individuals can exchange information, data, and comments interactively over a computer network, thus removing the necessity for long-distance travel to a conference. These conferences may occur over a specified short period of time, or they may last for days or even weeks.

Another form of long-distance conferencing is **video conferencing**, where two-way TV systems are set up among all sites of the conference. Thus, individuals can interact both verbally and visually with the other participants. Many firms have their own video conferencing facilities. Others rent them from hotels and telephone companies.

Electronic Calendaring

Office automation systems also provide **electronic calendaring** capabilities. The appointment calendars of employees and resources, such as conference rooms, are kept on the computer so that they can be accessed by people throughout the organization. Through workstations, personnel can reserve conference rooms and schedule employees to attend meetings.

Facsimile Transmission

Facsimile transmission (usually called **fax**) has been in existence since the 1960s. In the late 1970s and 1980s it became more popular as the capabilities of fax machines increased and their costs decreased. These machines, costing as little as $500, scan a document bit by bit and transmit a complete image of the document (including photos, graphics, and text) to remote locations over standard telephone networks. At the receiving end, the facsimile machine creates an exact copy of the document transmitted. Typical transmission rates are one page per minute, but these are increasing. Facsimile machines are as easy to operate as a copying machine and enable the transmission of documents anywhere in the world that has telephone lines and a receiving fax machine. Personal computers can also transmit text and images directly to a receiving fax machine or another PC. Application 9–2 illustrates how one chief executive uses a PC with faxing capability.

Fax machines have been a factor in increasing the number of people who work at home. With a fax machine, a personal computer, and a copier, many people can perform their office work at home.

The Complete Fax/Portable Drives
Cincinnati Auto Dealership

By Sara Humphry

Like other company chiefs, Bill Woeste must deal with the conflicting needs of traveling as well as keeping daily tabs on office matters. As owner of Beechmont Motors Inc., an auto dealership in Cincinnati, Woeste originally bought a Compaq Computer Corp. 286 LTE laptop for his trips. Soon, he realized the need for portable fax capabilities and chose The Complete Fax/Portable from The Complete PC of San Jose, Calif. "I liked it because it was portable, and it looked to me to be simple to use," he said.

Recently, Woeste moved to an IBM PS/2 Model 70 portable. "I thought about getting the internal fax card with it, but I decided to stay with The Complete Fax/Portable because when I'm in Microsoft Works, I can fax my letters via a hot key right out of [that integrated program]," he said.

In The Complete Fax/Portable, a hot key activates a window that pops up, requesting the name of the file to be faxed, the recipient, and the recipient's company and fax number. A two-line memo section allows the user to add a message to the cover letter. The fax software then automatically converts the file to a CCITT Group III fax format and faxes the information at 9,600 bps.

Woeste also said that the PC-based portable fax device is not only used when he's traveling. "While I'm in my office, I plug it into the same line as my [stand-alone] fax machine so I can use it as a backup fax machine if the stand-alone machine should run out of paper," he said. "In our business, receiving a fax can mean a big difference."

To Woeste, one of the biggest benefits to PC-based faxing is the amount of money he saves on telephone bills. "The time actually spent on the phone with The Complete Fax/Portable is considerably less—I'd say it's got to be half as long as the time it takes

the [stand-alone] fax machine to connect, send and then finish the process," he said. "The computer isn't reading the letter. It's immediately sending it.

"Based on phone savings alone, I've saved money. But from the time standpoint, for recreating documents, it's definitely a time saver," he said, explaining that he orders office supplies for his dealership by fax. "I can call up the last memo I sent to the supplier by entering the company name, and then I just edit the memo and send it out," he said. Next to its portability, Woeste said the product's most important feature is that it remembers the faxes that he sends to other people.

Reprinted with permission from *PC Week* (July 22, 1991), p. 105(1). Copyright Ziff-Davis Publishing Co., 1991.

One of the most difficult problems in an office is storage of paper documents. Paper files can get very voluminuous, and the time necessary to retrieve and refile documents can be substantial. Copies of paper documents are often called images. Companies have long used microfiche and microfilm images to reduce the volume of paper storage. However, retrieving and reading microfiche and microfilm can be slow and expensive. Microfiche systems are being combined with computer retrieval of microfiche images to decrease the time and expense of image retrieval and refiling.

In addition, systems are now available that will scan documents and convert them to digital code (digitize them) so that their images can be stored on regular computer disks rather than on microfiche. These documents can be quickly retrieved and displayed on high-resolution graphics terminals. This digital image storage and retrieval of documents is certainly the direction of the future in this area. Eventually, very few paper documents will be stored.

Image Processing

Before leaving for her job as sales manager for Bio Logic Tech Corp., Nancy dials into the computer that runs her company's voice-mail system. There's a message from one of her sales reps saying that Genechip Co. plans to choose a supplier for a major order of bio-electronic chips by noon today

Nancy decides to head straight for Genechip's facility. To avoid highway congestion, she calls a computer that has up-to-the-minute traffic information. The computer sends a map to her home facsimile machine showing the best route to skirt a current traffic jam

Arriving at Genechip, Nancy dials into her voice mailbox again and discovers that there's an electronic mail message from her sales rep. But she can't receive it because she left her laptop computer at home. So she orders the computer to convert the e-mail into a facsimile and send the fax to a nearby machine

Bob, Genechip's CEO keeps Nancy cooling her heels. But she makes good use of the time by phoning a computer that stores audiotex information. She finds out that Genetronix Industries, which uses her company's biochips, has won a big order. This is a morsel of information that should impress Bob, who competes with Genetronix

Bob likes the description of the chips, but he's worried about service. What if there's a sudden snafu? No problem: Nancy gives him a 24-hour, toll-free number. By using his phone's touchtone pad, he can order spare parts from a computer and get next-day delivery

The deal clinched, Nancy heads for lunch. Enroute to the restaurant, she calls her office from the car phone. Rather than take her hands off the wheel, she just says "boss"—and a voice-recognition chip automatically dials Bio Logic's CEO. "Well, we've nailed down another big order," she reports cheerfully

FIGURE 9–8
What Voice Processing Is Doing Today.

Reprinted with special permission from "Your New Computer: The Telephone: Voice Processing Puts a Powerful Tool at Everyone's Fingertips," *Business Week*, June 3, 1991, pp. 126–127, Copyright © 1991 by McGraw-Hill, Inc.

Forms Processing

Companies have traditionally used forms for a great deal of their internal transmission of data from one person to another. Thus, employees feel very comfortable filling out forms. In recent years, **forms processing** software has become available that automates filling out forms as well as the transmission and storage processes. Forms that look very much like paper forms can be created on computer workstations, and employees can fill them out.

Forms processing systems can be front ends to database management systems, where the input data are captured and processed by database management systems in a traditional way, or the forms can be transmitted and stored as if they were paper forms.

Forms processing systems are an example of a concept known as direct manipulation of objects of interest. Under this concept, computers allow personnel to directly manipulate objects in a fashion similar to the way they did these tasks prior to computers. Thus, forms processing systems allow personnel to directly manipulate forms or directly use forms on the computer. Human/computer interfaces are moving toward this concept of direct manipulation of objects of interest. Application 9–3 illustrates how Southern California Edison uses forms processing software in other ways.

APPLICATION 9–3

Power Company Automates Tasks Using Forms Software

By Caroline A. Duffy

The convenience of filling in forms on-screen and curbing the proliferation of paper forms initially drew Greg Friedman, of Southern California Edison Co., to forms processing software. However, Friedman, who manages the public utility's transition to Windows, said JetForm Corp.'s products have taken him several steps beyond that goal.

JetForm Designer 2.21, Jet-Form Merge/DDE and JetForm servers for OS/2 and DOS have simplified and expedited a number of forms-related applications for the Rosemead, Calif., utility company.

"When you start thinking about forms, you tend to think of filling them in on your screen," Friedman said. "What I'm saying is, that's nice, but there are better ways of using electronic forms."

For example, JetForm has hastened the utility company's facility-repair process. Previously, when a facility was damaged, a claims adjuster went to the site, assessed the damage and drafted a report. A secretary would then type the report and send it to corporate headquarters. About three weeks later, the repair work would be done. Now the headquarters personnel access the adjuster's report from a mainframe. The report is downloaded to a PC and printed on a JetForm form.

"That form essentially gets stored in a file, and every night these forms get printed out right at departmental headquarters," Friedman said. "So it takes [about] one to two weeks out of the process." In another application, the JetForm server facilitates the compilation of proposals for capital budget expenditures, Friedman said. Accounting information from several databases gets consolidated on a mainframe. That information is downloaded to the JetForm server, which generates the report.

JetForm has also been used to redesign a monthly engineering and construction report traditionally generated using a database. "The [report] had a lot of information, a lot of formatting," Friedman said. "Even in a tool like [Borland's] Paradox, this thing was difficult to do. The department essentially designed a form in a sort of report format. So all the formatting is done by Jet-Form, and all they have to do is essentially pass the summarized numbers to JetForm, and it prints."

JetForm has also made the report more readable. "It was a difficult report to read because there was so much information jammed on the form," he said. "Now there's still a lot of infor-mation, but because of [JetForm's] formatting capabilities, it's just a pleasure to read, and the information is much more useful in that sense."

Friedman said he measures JetForm's impact on productivity qualitatively rather than quantitatively. "It's not so much doing things faster," he said. "The important piece is like that report I described. This report is much more readable, much more usable. You can't put that into dollars and cents, but management can look at this information and grasp it much faster, and, ultimately, much better."

Friedman said he views the financial advantages in much the same way. "The cost benefits are definitely there. It's just that they are more intangible, not as easily identifiable," he said. "We are trying to limit budget increases, trying to do things better. Jet-Form is one tool we're using to do that."

Friedman said he hopes to see more features added to the Jet-Form products, such as dynamic forms, in which additional fields or boxes appear in response to information the user fills in.

Personal Support Systems

Much of the work that individuals do in an office does not require the full power of professional word processing, desktop publishing, and database management systems. **Personal support systems** offer basic but very flexible capabilities for electronic calendaring, database management, and word processing to individuals. These systems are often centered around an electronic calendar. They are also often tailored toward individual industries, such as real estate, financial planning, and other industries that require a great deal of contact with clients. Personal support system calendars display an individual's appointments for the day. The user can point to a particular appointment with, for example, John

Smith, click a button on a mouse and the system will pull up from its database a large amount of detailed information about John Smith. This information might include his name, nickname, telephone number, notes about the client, and even his children's and spouse's names and birthdays. Practically any type of information one would want to keep about a client can be included. Since these systems are often tailored toward a specific industry, they can store industry-specific data such as the financial holdings of a client in the case of financial planning systems.

The word processing portion of the personal information or personal support system provides the user with basic word processing capabilities for writing correspondence, simple reports, and so on. One capability is to automatically send birthday congratulations to each person in the client database on his or her birthday.

Integrated Office Automation Tools

Increasingly, office automation tools will be integrated. That is, the various tools that we have discussed in this chapter will work with one another. One of the underlying technologies that will make this possible is the ability to digitize all media including voice, data, text, moving images, and still images. Converting these forms of communication to digital form (i.e., converting them to the 0s and 1s of binary digits) allows us to store and process them in a computer system. Some of this integration is beginning to occur already. For example, systems such as IBM's PROFS support both electronic calendaring and electronic mail. Fax boards can be inserted into PCs, allowing text and images stored on a PC to be sent to a fax machine or vice versa. Both images and voice communications can be stored and retrieved with a text document. Currently, most laser printers only serve as printers. In the near future a single machine will be a laser printer, a copier, a scanner, and a fax machine.

Underlying all office automation capabilities are the technologies of computers and communications. Currently, the cost of these technologies is not sufficiently low to allow for some of the integration. For example, high-resolution scanning of images, their storage, and particularly the storage of moving videos takes a great deal of computer power. In the 1990s, though, computer and communications capabilities will be inexpensive enough to combine the input, processing, storage and communication of all media into an **integrated office automation system**.

Some Office Automation Issues

Is the Paperless Office a Mirage?

In the late '70s and early '80s there was quite a bit of speculation that office automation technology would produce a **paperless office**. Paperless offices certainly haven't occurred yet, for several reasons. The technology is not available at an acceptable price. A second reason is that humans are conditioned by experience to use paper. Paper is very convenient. It is easy to carry around and it is easy to read. You can mark and make notes on paper. You can produce additional copies of it cheaply.

However, office automation technology is continually progressing toward a paperless office. Electronic mail and image processing are two of the primary reasons why less paper is necessary for office functions. If we didn't have computer-based information systems and office automation, certainly businesses would be swamped with paper. It may be some time before paperless offices are a reality, but we are steadily making progress toward that goal. Image processing systems where documents are scanned and stored in digital form are a huge step in the direction of a paperless office.

Office Decentralization and Productivity

A major incentive for office automation is improved productivity. Information-processing technology serves the cause of productivity in two ways. First, computers perform many of the routine tasks that people used to perform manually. This not only speeds up the work, but also reduces errors in the results. Second, information-processing equipment lets people produce output in greater quantities and of better quality.

Using distributed data processing, many firms are now decentralizing their office operations. Marketing professionals use portable terminals to enter data from remote places. Executives save on travel time by employing "teleconferencing." Technical experts improve their productivity by staying home and working with personal computers and fax machines. This not only saves people much commuting time, but also helps them avoid the distractions of the office. In short, office automation reduces the need for direct person-to-person contact and accelerates the throughput of work.

Unfortunately, this increased productivity is not an unmixed blessing. Many workers do not like to work in isolation. The opportunity to socialize in the work environment is of significant value to them. To take it away would have a negative impact on their morale. The business itself may suffer if employees do not interact on a personal basis. Many new ideas and strategies develop during informal communication between employees. Excessive decentralization of the office would be detrimental to such brainstorming.

Human Factors

Just as the "scientific management" techniques of the early twentieth century caused concern among factory workers, "office automation" is a disturbing phenomenon for many office personnel today. Since the technology is still evolving, there is great uncertainty about its ultimate impact on office life.

Many white-collar workers fear losing their jobs to a machine. These fears are not justified. Although computers do automate many manual functions, they also tend to create new jobs that are more interesting and challenging. What is really needed is a retraining of existing personnel to take over the newly created jobs. Most information systems installations arrange seminars and hands-on training courses for user department personnel. Many private firms and software vendors provide similar services on a commercial basis.

People often prefer reading printed text rather than text displayed on computer screens. Also, electronic mail suffers from lax pickup—that is, people often do not read their electronic mail promptly.

As more experience is being gained with office machines, the design of computer equipment is being more closely tailored to human needs and comfort. Design engineers are making keyboards and video display screens to fit the human physique better. These improvements favorably affect the work environment of clerical personnel, who have to use computer terminals for long periods of time.

Some executives are reluctant to use computer terminals because they don't like to type. Light pens, mice, and touch-sensitive screens can help them overcome this "terminal phobia." Letter-quality printing and graphic output are other means of winning over skeptical top managers.

One major obstacle to users' acceptance of a system is poorly designed software. Sometimes, a program is written without much regard for whether users can interact with it easily. A good system designer must always keep in mind the technical competence and knowledge level of the end user. Although actual system design depends on the unique requirements of the business, the following guidelines should be considered in order to make the software "user-friendly" or ideally, "user-seductive."

1. Screen messages should be clear and concise so that a nonprogrammer can understand them. Unnecessary abbreviations must be avoided.

2. Whenever possible, provide complete error messages on-line instead of listing error numbers. The user probably has more important things to do than to search through heavy manuals to find out what error number "X953-E22$G" stands for.

3. Provide on-line help facilities. If a user does not know what to do at any point in the program, the system should display the available options.

4. User menu-driven systems that allow the user to choose among several options as a way of providing instructions to a computer. A menu-driven system is easier to use than a system that requires users to type in commands.

5. Design input and output formats to coincide with the user's conceptual view of documents.

6. Supply easy-to-use but comprehensive user manuals written in plain language, not programmer jargon. For instance, a record may simply be called a line or a row, and an attribute, a column. The purpose is to aid the user in operating the system, not to write a formal technical document. A friendly, easy-to-use system is much more likely to be accepted by office personnel than an exacting and intolerant program that does not allow any human error.

Summary

- The activities that occur in an office include managing documents, managing schedules for individuals and groups, managing projects, communicating with individuals and groups, managing data, and making decisions.

- Most of the activities of an office can be reduced to one basic activity, communications.

- Office communications are in three basic types: voice communication, text communication, and image communication.

- Voice communication refers to human voices or computer-generated simulations of human voices.

- Text communication includes both handwritten and typed text material.

- Image communication includes graphs, pictures, drawings, and moving video images.

- Office automation is the application of computer technology to the information communication functions of an office.

- Word processing greatly improves the ability of typists and professionals to produce typed materials.

- Desktop publishing systems provide the capability of writing, assembling, designing, and printing high-quality documents.

- Electronic mail enables personnel to communicate quickly and effectively through electronically transmitted text messages.

- Voice processing combines the power of the computer with the telephone to process and transmit human voices.

- There are five major areas of voice processing.

  1. Voice mail provides users with the capability of recording, storing, forwarding, and broadcasting voice messages through touch-tone phones.

  2. Automatic call distribution routes telephone calls based on caller's responses to questions through touch-tone phones.

  3. Voice response systems provides callers with prerecorded cues. Based on these cues, callers can instruct a computer to perform certain actions.

  4. Audio text systems provide information over the phone.

  5. Speech recognition systems enable computers to understand and respond to the human voice.

- Computer conferencing enables a number of individuals to exchange information, data, and comments interactively over a computer network.

- Video conferencing allows meetings to occur through the media of closed circuit television.

- Electronic calendaring allows individuals to keep an appointment calendar on the computer.

- Facsimile transmission (fax) can scan and transmit documents over standard telephone networks to receiving fax machines or personal computers.

- Image processing systems scan, store, retrieve, and display documents in digital form.

- Forms processing systems allow employees to enter data into a database management system through forms that appear on the computer screen and look much like paper forms.

- Personal support systems offer basic but very flexible capabilities for electronic calendaring, database management, and word processing to individuals.

- Increasingly office automation tools will integrate the processing of voice, data, text, moving, and still images.

- Paperless offices have not occurred yet, but we are steadily making progress toward this goal.

- Office automation has allowed offices to become decentralized and has begun to improve the productivity of employees.

- As more experience is being gained with office automation the design of computer equipment is being more closely tailored to human needs and comfort.

Key Terms

Voice communication

Text communication

Image communication

Office automation

Word processing

Integrated word processing/data processing (WP/DP)

Desktop publishing (DTP) systems

Electronic mail

Voice processing

Voice mail

Automatic call distribution

Voice response systems

Audio text systems

Speech recognition systems

Computer conferencing

Video conferencing

Electronic calendaring

Facsimile transmission (fax)

Image processing

Forms processing

Personal support systems

Integrated office automation tools

Paperless office

Human factors

Review Questions

1. What is office automation?

2. What are the three basic types of office communications?

3. Describe the major capabilities of a word processing system.

4. What are some applications for integrated word processing/data processing?

5. What is desktop publishing?

6. What are the advantages of electronic mail?

7. Describe the five major areas in voice processing.

8. How does voice mail differ from electronic mail?

9.   What are some of the applications for speech recognition?

10.   How do computer conferencing and video conferencing differ?

11.   What are the advantages of electronic calendaring?

12.   What is facsimile transmission?

13.   How does image processing store documents on a computer?

14.   What is forms processing?

15.   Describe some of the capabilities of personal support systems.

16.   What is meant by the integration of office automation tools?

17.   Is the paperless office a mirage?

18.   What effect has office automation had on productivity?

19.   What are human factors and what is their importance to computer-based information systems?

Discussion Questions and Cases

1.   Which office automation technologies do you think have been most productively applied?

2.   Productivity statistics show that while blue collar productivity has increased through the 1970s and 1980s, white collar productivity has not increased. One would think that with the application of computers to office work during the 1980s, white collar productivity would have increased substantially. Why do you think that the productivity numbers for white collar work hasn't shown a significant increase? Do you expect increases in white collar productivity to occur in the future?

3.   Video conferencing has the potential to drastically reduce business travel costs, yet many business persons still prefer to travel for a meeting rather than conducting the meeting through video conferencing. Why do you think that video conferencing has been slow to catch on?

4.   Randy Brown uses his personal computer for many functions including word processing and electronic mail. However, he has yet to use the computer for electronic calendaring. He continues to use a paper calendar book which he carries around in his coat pocket. Randy does not see the advantages of electronic calendaring. What are the likely reasons why Randy has not adopted electronic calendaring? What arguments would you use to convince Randy that electronic calendaring is the approach to use?

5.   Do you think that computer manufacturers and software designers have ignored human factors? What are some of the ways that computers are becoming easier to use?

6.   Do you think that the concept of direct manipulation of objects of interest is an appropriate basis on which to design the human-computer interface?

7.   Managers at the Real-Time Orange Juice Company are concerned about the growing amount of paperwork inundating the corporate headquarters. A computer is being considered as a way of eliminating some paperwork. One manager suggested using the value-added concept of transaction processing for the purchasing department. A manager in a department

would complete a purchase requisition on a computer terminal and would authorize it with a password and a user identification number. The requisition would be sent electronically to purchasing for approval. Each purchasing agent would have an electronic "in basket," or computer file, in which requisitions would be stored until approved. The purchasing agent would "add value" to each item in the computer file by attaching his or her identification number to the item. This "electronic signature" would serve as the approval to purchase the item. The document would then be sent through the proper channels until the items had been ordered and the invoice paid. The computerized document would be stored on a magnetic-tape history file. What would be some considerations in implementing this type of paperless purchasing system?

INFORMATION SYSTEMS STRATEGIES

Northwest Productivity Takes Off with Imaging

By Ellis Booker

To be successful, a document imaging application must do more than store paper records in electronic form. It must change the quantity and caliber of the data available to a business, altering the way people and processes work.

Northwest Airlines is a prime example of an imaging user that planned for this change and is now reaping the benefits. One year ago, Northwest—the nation's fourth-largest carrier—began deploying a massive, 450-user imaging system to capture and process the ticket stubs printed by Northwest gate agents and independent travel agents and carried by Northwest passengers.

"We can now do everything on a timely basis, with a slightly smaller staff and a larger airline," said Scott Grengs, project analyst of distributed services and one of the people closest to the passenger revenue accounting (PRA) system.

On-Time Processing

Although Northwest has not yet tallied the hard dollar savings that have accrued from the imaging system, Grengs said, one notable benefit has been to bring the processing load up to date. "When I started here four years ago," Grengs said, "we were, at times, as much as six months behind [in processing the ticket stubs]." Today, the system produces revenue or audit reports "accurately and on time," Grengs said.

Under the 20-year-old manual system, the revenue and marketing departments could only extrapolate their numbers, manually conducting a 5% audit of all the tickets. The problem was the volume of these ticket coupons: In peak months, Northwest processes 270,000 daily.

The 5% audit, while adequate for billing and revenue projections, fell far short of the needs of Northwest's marketing department, which wanted more timely and detailed information to monitor the effectiveness of its marketing campaigns.

"Marketing needs to know a lot more about what's happening, where and when people fly and which products they're using," said Mike Shields, project manager of the marketing analysis system at Northwest's Information Services Group.

"Now we capture 100%," said Shields, adding that several benefits have flowed from this change. For example, Northwest can now accurately monitor the fares and commissions charged by independent travel agents. An even greater value, he said, will be a not-yet-operational subsystem to track incentive and promotional programs. For example, this will let Northwest monitor, for the first time, the effectiveness of short-term flight discounts or promotional tie-ins with hotel chains.

Shields emphasized that the data coming from the PRA system is being integrated with other sources, such as Northwest's flight schedules. "We're working now on bringing these data sources together so that they can be accessed by marketing and applications development," Shields said.

Shields said mainframe-based DB2 databases will continue to handle the marketing department's needs for the foreseeable future. "But as we move down road," he added, "we may look at distributed databases and take more advantage of intelligent workstations."

Late last year, Northwest, which employed Chicago-based Andersen Consulting as the systems integrator on the project, added the last 100 users to its PRA system.

The 442 users, working on Sun Microsystems, Inc. SLC diskless workstations, are connected over a Sun local-area network, which is attached to a Filenet Corp. image server and image library. The libraries contain as many as 408 optical discs for a total on-line capacity of 40 million documents.

Discussion Questions

1.   Document imaging systems only store an image (a picture) of ticket stubs. Thus, the individu- al data items on the stub cannot be processed separately. Discuss some possible ways to inte- grate these images with character and numeric data contained in Northwest's other systems.

2.   Why is real-time data so important to mar- keting professionals in the airline industry?

Reprinted with permission from *Computerworld* (March 11, 1991), p. 31, Copyright 1991 by CW Publishing, Inc., Framing- ham, MA 01701.

Three

Information Systems Technology

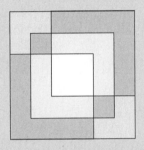

10

Information Processing Technology

Ann Martin is thinking about buying a computer to help her manage her small construction business. The choices she has to make concerning primary memory and secondary storage confuse her. Terminology such as CPU, RAM, and ROM is unfamiliar to her. And there are floppy disk drives, hard disk drives, and laser-optical disk drives to consider. She would like to know what these devices are and to have a good understanding of the advantages and disadvantages of each.

    This chapter first explores the capabilities and characteristics of a computer and presents a brief overview of a computer system. We then look at the primary components of a CPU and explore the differences between supercomputers, mainframes, minicomputers, and microcomputers. We explore how computers can be used in parallel processing to vastly increase their power. In the latter parts of the chapter we look at how data is stored, how it is entered, and how information is output from the computer.

Introduction

Definition

A **computer** can be defined as an information processor that is able to perform substantial computation, including numerous arithmetic or logical operations, without intervention by a human operator. The term *substantial* in this definition is open to wide interpretation. Is a pocket calculator that performs a series of statistical computations without human intervention a computer? It may or may not be. In recent years, the distinction between calculators—particularly programmable calculators—and computers has become blurred.

What Is A Computer?

Characteristics and Capabilities

A computer has the following characteristics and capabilities (see Figure 10–1):

- *Is electronic.* A computer operates by the movement of electronic pulses through circuits rather than by the mechanical movement of parts. This characteristic is essential to the speed of modern computers. Electronic pulses flow through the circuits of today's computers at roughly half the speed of light (about 6 inches in a billionth of a second). This is incredibly fast compared with mechanical movement.

- *Can perform arithmetic operations.* A computer is able to add, subtract, multiply, and divide.

- *Can compare.* The ability to compare one piece of information with another (to determine whether they are equal, whether one is less than the other, and so on) is essential to the operation of a computer. Comparison operations are also called logical operations.

- *Has internal storage and retrieval of data.* Today's computers have vast capabilities for storage and retrieval of data. Some computers can store several million characters of data in their central processing unit.

- *Can execute a stored program.* A computer can internally store (or hold) the instructions for operations to be performed on data. This set of instructions for a particular computer run is called a **program**.

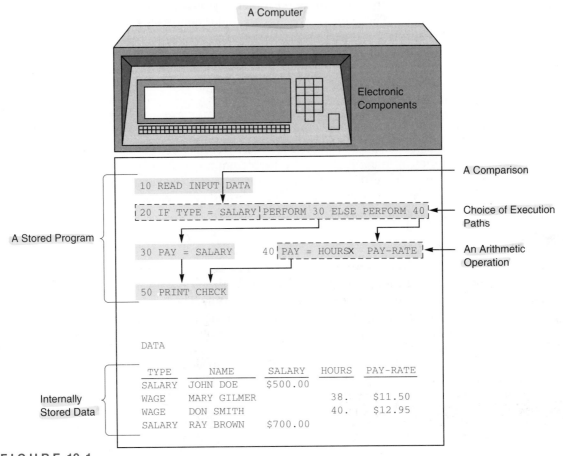

F I G U R E   10–1

Capabilities of a Computer.

Both the program and data are stored internally within the machine. The program is executed in order by statement number, starting with statement 10, until a branching statement is encountered. Statement 20 is a branching IF statement. If the type is equal to salary, then statement 30 is performed. If the type is not equal to salary, then statement 40 is performed.

- *Has choice of alternative execution paths* within a program. A computer can choose (or branch) among different sets of program instructions based on the values of the input data. For example, in a payroll program, one series of instructions is executed if the employee is paid according to hours worked. A different series is executed if the employee is paid a fixed salary.

Although all these items are important, the two most crucial are that computers are electronic and that they can execute stored programs. Before the computer there were machines, such as the mechanical calculator, that performed arithmetic operations, and there were many ways to store and retrieve information, including filing it in cabinets. However, the electronic basis for the computer gives the computer incredible speed and accuracy while the stored program enables this speed and accuracy to occur without human intervention.

Stored Programs

A stored program gives the computer three advantages: (1) it enables the computer to operate at electronic speeds, (2) it provides tremendous reliability, and (3) it makes the computer general-purpose. The electronic speed of the computer would be of little value if not for the stored program. For example, suppose a computer had no stored program. Then an operator would have to sit at the computer and manually enter an instruction for each step to be performed, such as an addition, a subtraction, or a comparison. Such a machine would be of little more use than a basic pocket calculator. The speed of the machine would be limited by the speed of the person operating it. Furthermore, with a person deciding what sequence of operations is executed next, the accuracy and reliability of the machine would be decreased because of the potential for human error.

Once a computer program has been written to perform a task and has been thoroughly checked so that all errors have been removed, the computer will execute the task with extreme accuracy and reliability—producing results with essentially no errors. Many experts would argue that this ability to capture human decision-making and processing capabilities in a computer program is by far the most significant contribution of computers. Society no longer has to train people to perform that task, and humans are free to perform tasks of which computers are not capable. This is indeed revolutionary. We have long had machines and animals—such as tractors, horses, automobiles, and lawnmowers—that lighten the burden of manual labor. However, the computer is the first machine that assists us in the intellectual burden of storing, processing, and retrieving data and of making decisions based on those data.

The stored program capability makes the computer general-purpose in that the stored program can be changed. Thus, a single computer can be used for many different tasks. These tasks may be as varied as data processing; editing, formatting, and typing the contents of this book; and controlling robots that weld the parts of an automobile body.

Overview of a Computer System

Figure 10–2 shows an overview of a computer system. All computer systems have four categories of devices: input, processing, storage, and output. These devices are illustrated with the personal computer system shown in Figure 10–3.

Input Devices

There are many types of input devices, the most widely used being a keyboard with an attached monitor (sometimes called CRT terminals). Optical scanners, speech recognition devices, and various devices that read magnetically coded tape or disk are other examples. Many of these devices overlap into two or more of the four categories; for example, CRT terminals are both input and output devices.

Central Processing Unit

The processing role in a computer system is performed by the **central processing unit (CPU)**. The CPU is the centerpiece of a computer system;

FIGURE 10–2
Overview of a
Computer System.

Data and programs are moved back and forth between primary storage (within the central processing unit) and secondary storage as they are needed for program execution.

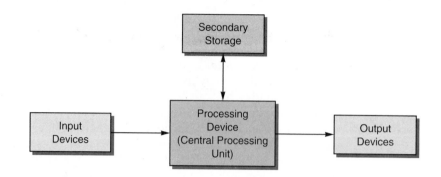

strictly speaking, it is the computer. Its function is to interpret and execute the instructions of the program. Thus, the CPU controls the complete computer system. As shown in Figure 10–4, the CPU has two primary components: the main processing and primary storage units. The main processing unit is a semiconductor chip containing millions of circuit elements. In a personal computer this main processing unit is called a microprocessor. It contains a control unit and an arithmetic-logic unit. The **control unit** decodes program instructions and directs other components of the computer to perform the tasks specified in the

FIGURE 10–3
A Personal Computer System.
Although the monitor is sometimes called a cathode-ray tube (CRT), technically the CRT is only a part of the monitor. In fact, monitors on portable PCs use light-emitting diodes (LEDs) or gas plasma rather than CRTs.

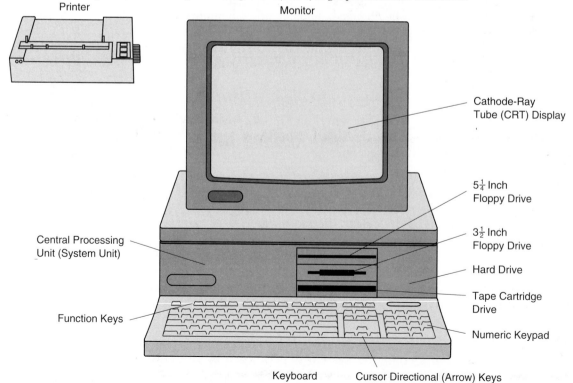

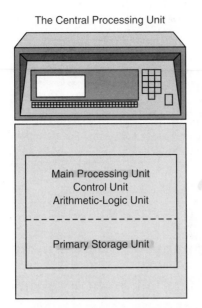

The Central Processing Unit

Main Processing Unit
Control Unit
Arithmetic-Logic Unit

- - - - - - - - - - - - - - - - - - -

Primary Storage Unit

2 components

F I G U R E 10–4
The Central
Processing Unit.
The main processing unit
in a personal computer is
a microprocessor.

program instructions. Arithmetic operations such as multiplication, division, subtraction, and addition are performed by the **arithmetic-logic unit**. This unit also performs logical operations such as comparing the relative magnitude of two pieces of data. Primary storage stores the program instructions that are currently being executed and also stores data while they are being processed by the CPU.

The concept of a central processing unit directly applies to supercomputers, mainframes, and minis since these computers contain a separate unit called the central processing unit that contains only those components illustrated in Figure 10–4. However, with the advent of the personal computer the concept of a single central processing unit containing only a main processing unit and primary storage has been modified. Figure 10–5 illustrates the main circuit board of a personal computer. As can be seen from the figure, this main circuit board (often called a motherboard) contains the microprocessor and random-access memory (RAM), which is the primary storage. However, the board also contains several other components, such as slots for expansion boards. These expansion boards may contain circuits that control input/output devices, a modem, or additional random-access memory. In a personal computer, the complete box containing the motherboard and various storage drives such as hard and floppy disks is called the system unit. Thus, strictly speaking, in the personal computer world there is no single device called the central processing unit, but the motherboard of a personal computer does contain all the devices of the central processing unit along with other components.

Secondary Storage

Secondary storage is used for relatively long-term storage of data. The most widely used secondary storage media are magnetic disks, such as the floppy and hard disks used in personal computers, and magnetic

F I G U R E 10–5

Main Circuit Board of a Personal Computer.

The major elements of the main circuit board of a personal computer are identified here. A large number of silicon chips carrying integrated circuits are attached to the main circuit board; each chip is about a quarter of an inch square and is encased in a rectangular plastic package fitted with electrodes. The chips and elements, such as resistors and capacitors, are interconnected by conductors printed on the board. "System programs" are stored permanently in the read-only memory (ROM); random-access memory (RAM) stores programs and data that change from time to time.

From Hoo-min D. Toong and Amar Gupta, "Personal Computers," *Scientific American*, December 1982. Copyright 1982 by Scientific American, Inc., all rights reserved.

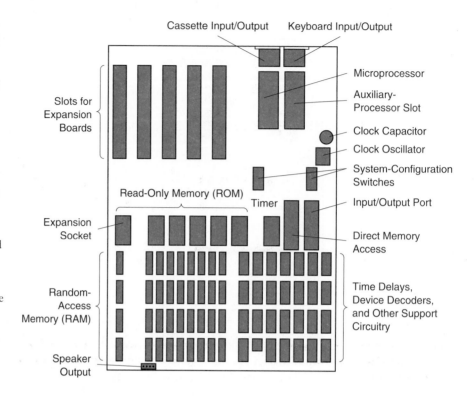

tapes. The bulk of information used by a computer application is stored in secondary storage but must be transferred to primary storage before it can be processed by the CPU. Therefore, information is continually being read into and written out of primary storage during the execution of a program. The data not being used by the CPU are stored in secondary storage. The main differences between primary and secondary storage are that primary storage is a part of the CPU, allows very fast access to data, is more expensive than secondary storage, and is volatile. (Memory that is volatile loses whatever is stored in it when the power is turned off.)

Output Devices

Output devices record data either in forms humans can read, such as printouts, or in machine-readable forms such as on magnetic disks and tapes. Output devices include a wide variety of printers that use different technologies—such as impact, ink jets, and laser imaging—to produce print. Other examples are voice synthesizers and plotters, which display information directly in graphic form, such as in bar charts and line graphs. Many of the types of input and secondary storage already discussed (magnetic tape, disk, and CRT terminals) also serve as output devices or media. Figure 10–6 illustrates the input, processing, secondary storage, and output devices typically used in a medium-to-large computer system.

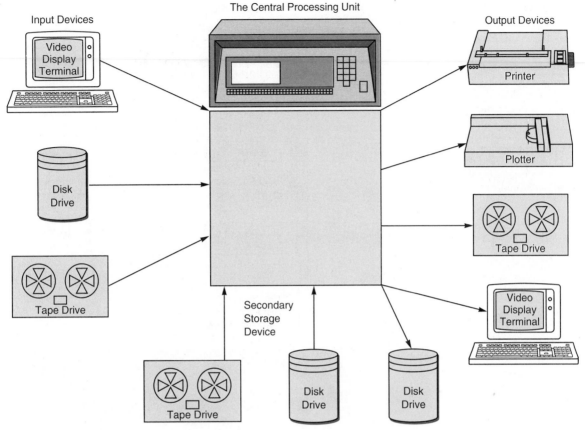

FIGURE 10–6
A Medium-to-Large Computer System.
There is a large variety of input and output devices for computers. Only the most common ones are shown here.

As illustrated in Figure 10–4, the central processing unit contains primary storage and a main processing unit that holds the arithmetic-logic unit and the control unit. We will discuss each of these below.

The Central Processing Unit

Primary Storage

Primary storage has three functions:

1. It stores operating system programs that assist in managing the operation of the computer.

2. It stores the program being executed.

3. It stores data being processed by the CPU.

The bulk of data used by a computer application is stored in secondary storage devices, but data must be stored in primary storage whenever the CPU is using them in processing. Therefore, data are continually being moved into and out of primary storage during the execution of a program (see Figure 10–7). For example, a complete customer record—that is, all the

F I G U R E 10–7
The Movement of
Data Between Primary
and Secondary Storage.
Some programs, such as
electronic spreadsheets,
move a complete file into
primary storage rather
than part of it at a time.
Others, such as database
management systems,
move only a few records
from a file into primary
storage at a time.

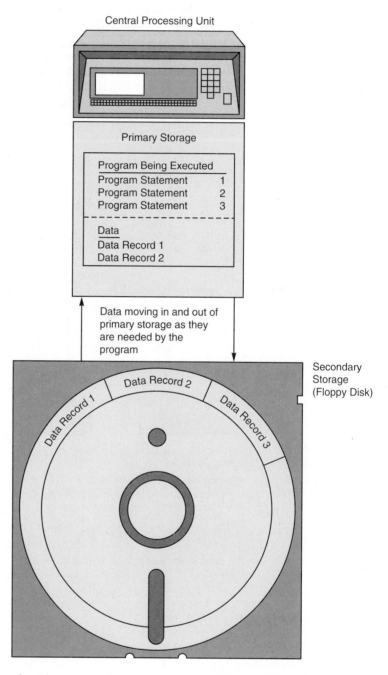

data associated with a particular customer—would most likely be stored in
primary storage while the CPU was processing that customer's record.

Compared with secondary storage, primary storage allows faster access. Fast-access primary storage is necessary because the other components of the CPU, the control unit and the arithmetic-logic unit, operate
at electronic speeds. If the CPU had to depend on mechanical movement
to retrieve specific pieces of data, as is the case with disk- or magnetic-
tape storage, the primary storage access speed would become a major bottleneck for the CPU. Ideally, the CPU should have a lot of very

fast-access primary storage; however, fast-access memory is more expensive than slower-access memory. Today, large computer systems may contain 5 to 500 megabytes of primary storage. Even personal computers have 640 kilobytes to 16 megabytes of primary storage.

The primary memory used in today's computers is made of very large-scale integrated (VLSI) semiconductor chips. **Semiconductor chips** contain electronic circuits that can be reproduced photographically in a miniaturized form on silicon chips. These chips are often referred to as large-scale integrated (LSI) circuits or, in the case of advanced semiconductor technology, VLSI circuits.

The control unit and arithmetic-logic unit of the main processing unit can be placed on a single semiconductor chip. The processors on a chip are often called **microprocessors** (see Figure 10–8). In fact, a CPU with much more computing power than the ENIAC computer of the 1940s can be placed on a chip approximately a quarter-inch square, whereas the ENIAC required a large room.

Note that microprocessors contain only the control unit and the arithmetic-logic unit. Primary storage is contained on separate (semiconductor) memory chips.

There are two advantages of using the semiconductor chip in computer hardware. First, it can be reproduced in great quantities by automated means and is therefore inexpensive. Second, the miniaturization of circuits has greatly enhanced the speed of the computer. The speed at which a CPU operates is limited by two factors—the speed at which electrical currents flow (about one-half the speed of light) and the distance over which they must flow.

Semiconductors used in primary storage represent a bit of data by means of an individual circuit that either conducts or does not conduct electricity. From this fact arises the primary disadvantage of using semiconductors for primary storage. When the electrical supply to semiconductor storage is interrupted, none of the circuits conducts electricity. Therefore, the computer loses the data contained in primary storage, including any programs located there. Semiconductor storage is **volatile**, that is, the storage loses its data representation when electrical power is interrupted. This can be overcome with an uninterruptible power source (provided by backup batteries and generators). Table 10–1 illustrates the storage capacities of some typical memory chips.

There are three basic types of semiconductor memory: **random-access memory (RAM)**, **read-only memory (ROM)** and **flash memory**. The term RAM comes from the fact that access to a particular area of the memory can be performed on a random basis. The CPU can perform read or write

Chip Size	Capacity in Bits	Capacity in Bytes (Characters)	Capacity in Double-Spaced Typed Pages
64K-bit chip	65,536	8,192 or 8K bytes	5
265K-bit chip	262,144	82,768 or 32K bytes	19
1-megabit chip	1,048,576	131,072 or 128K bytes	75
4-megabit chip	4,194,304	524,288 or 512K bytes	300
16-megabit chip	16,777,216	2,097,152 or 2048K bytes	1200

TABLE 10–1
Storage Capacities of Semiconductor Memory Chips

FIGURE 10–8

A VLSI Microprocessor.

This is a 32-bit microprocessor, meaning that when it performs operations on data it moves 32 bits at a time (the equivalent of four characters).

operations at any memory position of random-access memory at any point in time. RAM and the term primary storage as we have been using it are synonymous. RAM is volatile memory.

Read-only memory can be read from but not written to. ROM comes from the manufacturer with programs already stored on it, so the computer user cannot modify it. Because the storage is permanent, ROM is nonvolatile memory. ROM is used to store programs that are frequently used by many computer applications. For example, some personal computers store a BASIC interpreter in ROM. They also store part of the PC-DOS operating system, the basic input/output system (BIOS), in ROM. This technique of placing software or programs in hardware (the ROM semiconductor chip) is often termed **microcoding** (also called **microprogramming** or **firmware**).

Flash memory is a new type of semiconductor memory. Like RAM, it is random access and can be written to many times, but it is nonvolatile. Flash memory has several advantages and disadvantages compared to other types of primary and secondary storage. Compared to RAM, its access speed is not as fast and it is much more expensive, but it is nonvolatile. Since volatility of primary memory is not a major problem, flash memory is not likely to replace RAM as the primary storage media in computers. Compared to ROM, the major advantage of flash memory is that it can be updated by having new programs or data written to it from a floppy disk. To change the programs in ROM you would have to physically remove the ROM chips and replace them with new ROM chips containing the new programs. Thus, flash memory is likely to replace ROM. Compared to hard disks, flash memory has an extremely fast access speed, about 120,000 times faster. In fact, this is where the term "flash memory" comes from. It can be accessed in a flash compared with hard disk. Flash memory is also much more compact and lighter than hard disks. However, the cost of flash memory is too great for it to completely replace hard disks. In the next few years it is likely to be used in portable computers to replace hard disks. In the longer term, it has the potential to replace many more hard disks.

Arithmetic-Logic Unit

The **arithmetic-logic unit** performs arithmetic operations such as multiplication, division, subtraction, and addition. It also performs logic operations such as comparing the relative magnitude of two pieces of information. Arithmetic-logic operations are performed serially (that is, one at a time), based on instructions from the control unit.

Control Unit

The **control unit** decodes program instructions and directs other parts of the CPU to perform the tasks specified. The program instructions are in machine language. They consist of an **operation code** to be performed, such as add, subtract, move, or compare, and the **operands**, which are the entities to which the operation is applied, such as data and input/output units.

Two cycles are performed for each program instruction—the instruction cycle and the execution cycle. The process of executing an individual program instruction begins with the control unit moving the instruction from primary memory into the control unit for decoding. The operation code and the operands are examined and decoded. This process of decoding the instruction is called the **instruction cycle**. The **execution cycle** begins when the control unit causes the appropriate unit to perform the operation called for in the instruction. This unit may be the arithmetic-logic unit or an input/output unit.

Microcomputers

The smallest and least expensive computer system is called a personal computer or **microcomputer** (see Figure 10–9). Since the system is often used by one person, the term personal computer has become popular. Microcomputer systems typically have between 640K and 16 megabytes of primary storage. They can handle peripheral devices such as terminals, relatively slow-speed printers, cassette tapes, floppy disks, and Winchester hard disks. Because of their low cost, microcomputer systems are used by even the smallest of businesses. Microcomputers come in three basic sizes: desktop, laptop, and notebook computers. Desktop computers are not portable, while laptop and notebook-size computers are very portable.

Minicomputers

Minis or **minicomputers** are medium-sized systems that typically have from one to several megabytes of primary storage (see Figure 10–10). Today, minicomputers are often also called midrange computers. They have greater processing power than micros but less than mainframes. Minicomputers were first developed for use in process-control, scientific, and engineering applications. They were used, for example, to monitor automated manufacturing processes such as steel rolling and to adjust the equipment automatically in order to keep the output within specified tolerances. However, it was soon discovered that these computers had tremendous potential in data processing, especially for smaller companies.

Micros, Minis, Mainframes, and Supercomputers

F I G U R E 10–9
Microcomputer
System.

These computers are the
IBM Personal System 2
Model 50. They are
currently the most
popular model of the
PS/2 line. Many
corporations are using
them as personal
workstations in
computer network

F I G U R E 10–10
A Minicomputer
System.

This Unisys U 5000/35
minicomputer is
compatible with a wide
variety of operating
systems and will
communicate with other
manufacturers'
computers.

Minicomputer systems can be equipped with most of the input/output devices and secondary storage devices that the large mainframe systems can handle, such as terminals and hard disks. They are also used in **distributed data-processing** systems. Instead of a company having one large mainframe computer, it can distribute its data processing with a minicomputer at each of its remote locations, and connect them to each other through telecommunication links.

Mainframe Computers

Mainframes are large systems having 5 to 500 megabytes of primary storage and the input/output units associated with a large computer system (see Figure 10–11). They can support several hundred on-line terminals. For on-line secondary storage they use high-capacity magnetic disk drives capable of storing up to 7.5 **gigabytes** of data in each disk-drive unit. Each computer can access several of these 7.5-gigabyte disk-drive units. Mainframe computers typically use high-capacity magnetic tape for off-line storage of data. Most medium-sized to large companies have one or more mainframe computers, which perform the bulk of their information processing. Applications that run on mainframes tend to be large and complex, and the data and information are shared by many users throughout the organization. However, as discussed in Application 10–1, many firms are moving applications from mainframes to personal computers. Today, information systems professionals have a great deal of choice as to the size of computer to use.

Minis overlap mainframes, and micros overlap minis. As minis become more powerful, they tend to perform with equal efficiency the jobs that were done by mainframes. Some companies are even using networks of personal computers to replace their mainframe and minicomputer systems. The boundary lines of the three types of computer systems are constantly changing.

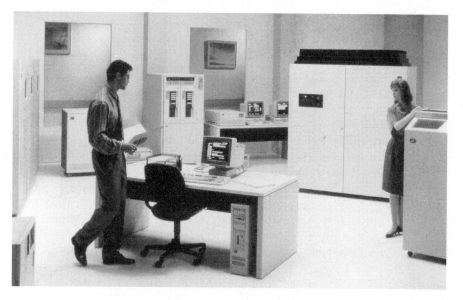

FIGURE 10–11
Mainframe Computer.
The IBM ES 9000, shown here, is one of IBM's largest mainframes. It is widely used by large businesses.

APPLICATION 10–1

IS Survey Uncovers Cost-Saving Methods

By Nell Margolis

Confronted two years ago with the universal information systems question of how to deliver more and better technology-based aid to the company at a justifiable cost, Sidney Diamond resorted to an age-old information-gathering tactic: Ask around.

In fact, the vice president of IS [information systems] at Black & Decker Corp. talked with approximately 75 IS directors at multinational companies, including the likes of Pepsico, Inc., Nynex Corp., Pan Am Corp. and Cadbury-Schweppes PLC. He asked which low-cost computing strategies worked—or bombed—for them.

"One answer that came back repeatedly was 'De-emphasize the mainframe,'" Diamond said.

Virtually every one of the IS directors who participated in the survey reported large-scale, ongoing efforts to offload as much computing work as is practical to less-expensive personal computers and workstations.

Increasingly, IS directors are de-emphasizing not only mainframes but hardware altogether, according to many respondents.

"Hardware is a commodity; software is where it's at," said Gad J. Selig, vice president of IS at New York-based Nynex. "And one of the cost-saving principles we have consistently preached is, 'Buy it, don't build it.'"

The risks of pushing out computing power and responsibility—lessened security, for instance—are outweighed by patent rewards, said another of the surveyed IS directors, who works at a Fortune 500 company and asked not to be identified.

Not all surveyed executives see giving control to users as a path to IS savings. Centralized processing wherever practical also ranked high on the list of suggested strategies.

Using common systems minimizes duplication and saves money, said Joseph Nash, IS vice president at Stamford, Conn.-based Cadbury Beverages, Inc. "It also has a valuable side benefit: It makes acquisitions and divestitures much easier," he said.

Ironically, Diamond noted some IS departments can save money by resisting the temptation to dive headlong into a common systems initiative. "The global systems concept has tremendous payoff—but only if the system can actually be implemented," he pointed out.

As with outsourcing—another popular, if controversial, IS cost-saving alternative—many IS leaders are finding that the most cost-efficient way to go initially is to implement discrete functions or applications on a centralized, global basis while allowing others to remain dispersed, Diamond said.

Buying commercial software is a well-acknowledged money saver; buying it in bulk, the anonymous IS director added, saves still more. However, while "standardizing on a software platform worldwide can save you millions," it also ups the ante on scoping out the most reliable vendors.

The one magic answer that clearly emerged from his research, according to Diamond, "is that there's no magic answer."

Supercomputers

In terms of processing power, **supercomputers** are even larger than mainframes (see Figure 10–12). They are rarely used for business information systems. Their primary use is in scientific applications, especially where large simulation models are needed. In **simulation**, mathematical models of real-world physical systems are coded into software that is executed on a computer. The execution of the computer software then models the real-world system. For example, the National Oceanic and Atmospheric Administration uses supercomputers to model the world's weather system; such models improve weather predictions. Simulation models are often large and complex. For these models to execute in a reasonable length of time, a supercomputer is necessary. This fact points to the primary difference between a supercomputer and a mainframe—most supercomputers have a processing speed that is four to ten times faster than mainframe computers.

FIGURE 10–12
A Supercomputer.
This computer is capable of performing one billion combined arithmetic-logic operations per second! Its central processing unit is cooled with a liquid refrigerant to increase its speed.

Almost all CPUs in today's computers execute programs and process data in a serial fashion; that is, they process one piece of data at a time. With the advent of inexpensive microprocessors on a chip, computer designers have produced CPUs that contain several of these microprocessors (some contain as many as 2,000). These computers are designed so that all the microprocessors work simultaneously on the same application. Computers that use multiple processors to execute a single application are known as **parallel processors**. Applications are divided into tasks that can be processed simultaneously by the various processors. This method greatly reduces the amount of time necessary to complete a given application. However, the difficulty in finding methods to divide applications into tasks that can be processed simultaneously is holding back the use of parallel processors. Current computers and programs are designed to process applications sequentially.

Parallel Processing

Although parallel processing was developed for scientific and military applications, it is now being used in business. For example, consider an application where the same process must be performed on a large number of records, such as calculating net pay for each employee on a company's payroll. If parallel processing were used, many payroll records could be processed simultaneously, instead of one at a time, as would be the case in a single processing system. Obviously, the processing time would be greatly reduced by parallel processing.

An elementary form of parallel processing has been in use by personal computers since the early 1980s. The IBM PC standard computers can contain a math co-processor chip that takes over the mathematical computations from the computer's main processor and thus greatly speeds up math computations.

Parallel processing is a quickly growing field in the computer industry; it is expanding at a rate of 35 percent a year. As parallel processing develops, it will no doubt become more important in the business world.

Secondary Storage

Primary versus Secondary Storage

Earlier in this chapter, we covered primary storage and its characteristics. As illustrated in Figure 10–4, primary storage is part of the CPU, and it must allow very fast access in order to increase the speed at which the CPU can operate. **Secondary storage**, on the other hand, is physically separate from the CPU. Why are there two types of storage? Why isn't the CPU designed with large amounts of primary storage so that all of the data can be randomly accessible at electronic speeds, with no mechanical movement? The answer is cost.

Primary storage is more expensive than secondary storage. Furthermore, the most widely used primary storage, semiconductor chips, is volatile. Secondary storage must be nonvolatile; that is, it must be able to retain the data stored in it even when the electrical current is off. All widely used secondary storage media require mechanical movement for accessing data. Therefore, secondary storage is relatively slow.

Magnetic Tape

Magnetic tape has long been an important medium for secondary storage. Today, it is used almost exclusively for backup purposes. For mainframes it is supplied on reels up to 2,400 feet long; the tape is usually one-half-inch wide and, except for being larger, is similar in appearance to that used with tape recorders. Figure 10–13 illustrates data encoded on magnetic tape. Nine-track magnetic tape is by far the most common, although seven-, eight-, and ten-track tapes are available. They use different coding schemes for each character. Figure 10–14 illustrates typical magnetic tape drives.

Magnetic tape cartridges with a storage capacity of 10 to 300 million characters are now being widely used to **back up** data stored on microcomputer hard disks (see Figure 10–15). As with all storage media, hard disks are subject to failure. Periodic copying of the data onto tape cartridges insures against loss of data and programs stored on hard disks.

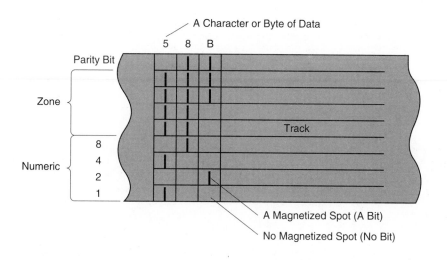

FIGURE 10–13
Data Stored on a
Magnetic Tape.
A character is recorded
across the tape. The
parity bit is used for
checking purposes. Zone
bits are needed only for
encoding alphabetic and
special characters, since
only the four lower
numeric bits are
necessary to encode
numeric data. In fact,
when all the data to be
stored are numeric, two
numeric characters can
be stored in one eight-bit
byte. One of them is
stored in the four zone
bits. This type of storage
is known as packed
decimal

The advantages of magnetic tape are as follows:

1. The cost of tape is low compared with other forms of secondary storage.

2. Computer systems can use several tape drives simultaneously.

3. The rate at which data may be transferred to and from tape is very high for sequentially organized files.

4. As a storage medium, magnetic tape is very compact and portable.

5. Magnetic tape is ideal as backup storage of data.

6. Magnetic tape devices have several self-checking features; therefore, the recording and reading of data on magnetic tape are highly reliable.

7. Record lengths on magnetic tape can be very large, as long as they are within the limits of the individual computer system.

8. We can use magnetic tape over and over for storage of different data simply by writing the new data over the old. We can also correct mistakes by writing over the old data.

Disadvantages of magnetic tape including the following:

1. Magnetic tape is a sequential storage medium. Therefore, if a user wants to find an individual record stored on magnetic tape, the tape must be read up to the location of the desired record. This is very time consuming.

2. Damage to magnetic tape can result in the complete loss of data stored on the section of tape that is near the damage: therefore, critical data should be stored on a backup tape or another storage medium.

3. Magnetic tape is sensitive to dust, humidity, and temperature changes; consequently, the environment in which it is stored must be controlled.

Hard Disks

Magnetic disks are the most popular form of secondary storage. There are two basic types of disks: hard and floppy. Hard disks are widely used with all sizes of computers. They range in capacity from the 20-megabyte disk drives used with microcomputers to very high-capacity disk drives such as IBM's 3380 Model K, which can store 7.5 gigabytes of data.

Hard disks are aluminum or magnesium rigid platters with an iron-oxide (rust) coating. Data are stored as magnetic patterns in the coating. Figure 10–16 illustrates one type of hard disk used with mainframes. It has eleven individual platters, each with two surfaces, top and bottom. Since this is a *removable disk* pack, data are not stored on the top surface of the top platter or the bottom surface of the bottom platter because of potential for damage to those surfaces. Therefore, there are twenty sur-

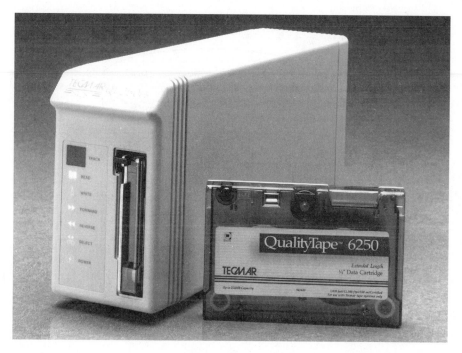

FIGURE 10–15
A Cartridge Drive and Tape.

Cartridge tapes are widely used to back up data stored on fixed hard disks in personal computers. Copying data onto tape is much faster than copying data onto floppy disks. Data is copied onto tape at the rate of five megabytes per minute. One cartridge tape can store from 125 to 500 megabytes of data.

faces in the disk pack on which data can be stored. Within each surface, data are stored on **concentric tracks**. The same amount of data is stored on the outside tracks as on the center tracks, even though the circumferences of these tracks differ substantially. This is so because the time it takes for the disk to complete one revolution is the same for any track on the disk.

If the disk in Figure 10–16 has two hundred tracks on each surface, then the access arms can move horizontally and position themselves in two hundred different track positions. When an access arm is positioned over one of these tracks, data can be read or written onto one track on each recording surface without the access arm moving. The twenty tracks located at one position of the read/write access arms make up a **cylinder**. When data are stored sequentially on a disk, they are stored by cylinder; that is, all the tracks in one cylinder are filled before any tracks in the adjacent cylinder are filled. The cylinder approach improves read and write access speeds to the disk. The speed of access to data on a disk is a function of the rotational speed of the disk, the speed with which the access arms move, and the relative position of the desired record to the read/write head once the correct track is located. Using the cylinder approach minimizes or eliminates the need for moving the access arms.

Microcomputers use a type of hard disk known as a **Winchester disk**. A Winchester disk unit contains a small (usually 5¼-inch) hard disk with multiple platters, and it typically stores twenty to five hundred megabytes of data. It can be in the form of a removable cartridge or *fixed disk*. A removable cartridge usually stores ten to twenty megabytes, whereas a fixed disk can store several hundred megabytes.

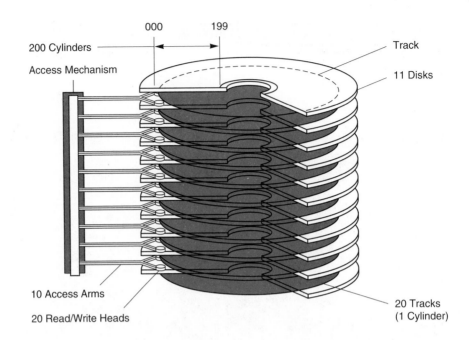

FIGURE 10–16
A Hard Disk.
The access mechanism can position itself to access data from each of the two hundred cylinders. A cylinder is a set of all tracks with the same distance from the axis about which the disk pack rotates. In this example, there are twenty tracks in each cylinder.

Floppy Disks

Floppy disks (often called cassette disks, diskettes, or minidiskettes) are flat 3½- or 5¼-inch disks of polyester film with an iron-oxide magnetic coating. As shown in Figure 10–17, the disk is covered with a protective jacket, and reading/writing from or to the disk is performed through the head access slot. A floppy disk has a capacity of 360K to 2.88 megabytes.

Floppy disks were developed by IBM in the early 1970s for use as secondary storage on minicomputers. However, they have become a widely used medium for secondary storage on microcomputers. Also, they are an important medium for *batch* data input to mainframe computers.

Users of PCs are switching from 5¼-inch disks to 3½-inch disks. The primary advantage of the 3½-inch disk is its higher storage capacity, even though it is smaller. The 3½-inch disk owes this storage advantage to its rigid protective cover. This cover protects the storage medium and thus data can be stored more concisely and at a higher density. In addition, the rigid structure allows faster rotation of the disk. The primary advantages of floppy disks are their relatively low cost, large capacity, and small size.

The advantages of magnetic disks (both hard and floppy) include the following:

1. The magnetic disk is a **direct-access storage** medium; therefore, the user can retrieve individual records without searching through the entire file.

2. Although disks are more expensive than magnetic tape, their cost has steadily declined over the years.

3. For on-line systems where direct access is required, disks are currently the only practical means of file storage.

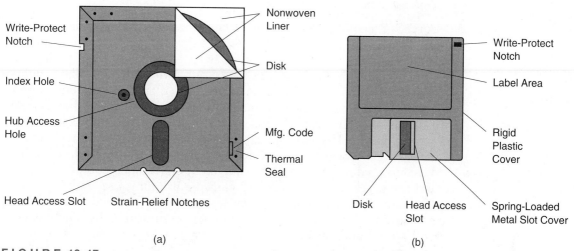

FIGURE 10–17
5¼-Inch and 3½-Inch Floppy Disks.
The 5¼-inch diskette is often called a minidiskette because the first floppy disk produced was an 8-inch diskette. It was introduced in the 1970s for use with minicomputers. The 3½-inch disk was first used in the Apple Macintosh and was later used by IBM on the PS/2 series.

4. Users can easily update records by writing new information over the area where old information was stored.

5. With removable disk cartridges, a single disk drive can access a large number of disk cartridges. This method is especially economical with batch-processing applications that do not require frequent switching between disk cartridges. Because the same disk drive can be used to access more than one disk cartridge, the cost of the disk drive can be spread out over a larger volume of stored data.

6. Interrelated files stored on magnetic disk allow a single transaction to be processed against all of these files simultaneously. In addition, data can be retrieved from interrelated files simultaneously. This capability makes relational database systems possible.

The disadvantages of magnetic disks are as follows:

1. Compared with magnetic tape, hard disks are expensive.

2. Updating a master file stored on disk often destroys the old information. Therefore, disks may not provide an automatic **audit trail** and backup the way magnetic tape does. Subsequent to updating a master file stored on magnetic tape, there exist the old master file, the new master file, and the transaction file, on three separate reels of tape. When a disk is used, equivalent backup and audit trail require that each old master file record be copied to another storage area prior to update.

3. For periodic batch-type systems where there is no need for between-run data retrieval from the files, magnetic tape serves just as well as disks for file storage purposes—at substantially less cost.

Optical Disks

A type of secondary storage that is becoming increasingly popular is **optical disks** (see Figure 10–18). One type of these disks shares the same technology as the digital compact disk (CD) players used with stereo systems. Thus, they are often called CD-ROMs. Originally, data could be written on them only one time; however, there are now erasable versions. These disks are called magneto-optical disks, since they combine features of both magnetic and optical disks. The primary advantage of optical disks is large storage capacity at low cost; some of them cost less than ten dollars and hold 200 to 1,000 megabytes (one gigabyte) of data. Five hundred megabytes is the equivalent of 300,000 double-spaced typewritten pages, or the entire Encyclopedia Britannica several times over! For mainframes, jukeboxlike devices are being designed that will store and automatically retrieve large numbers of optical disks. These devices will store hundreds of gigabytes of data or text. Optical disk drives for microcomputers cost about $500.

The write-once optical disks are known by the acronym WORM, (write once, read many). They are often used for backup of hard disks. Once they are full, they can be discarded since they are inexpensive. WORM disks also are often used for storage of text and data that are infrequently updated, such as dictionaries, encyclopedias, full text copies of magazine and journal articles, and other reference works.

The primary disadvantage of these disks is their slow access time compared with hard disks. Accessing data on optical disks is approximately ten times slower than on hard magnetic disks.

Optical disks are used for storing large volumes of data that are not accessed or changed often. They are likely to replace magnetic tape for

FIGURE 10–18
Optical Disks.

These optical storage disks can hold as much data as can be stored on fifty or more reels of magnetic tape.

backup purposes. Optical disks can also provide microcomputer users with large data banks and reference material such as financial data on companies, historical stock market prices, journal articles, and encyclopedias. One of the most promising uses for these disks is in libraries—card catalogs, microfilm holdings, and Library of Congress collections are being put on optical disks. Application 10–2 illustrates how Gateway Bank uses optical disks for backup.

APPLICATION 10–2

Gateway Puts Pennies in Its Bank

By Michael Alexander

The vendors and value-added resellers who trooped through Martin Brennan's office in 1987 pitching document imaging systems simply did not get the picture.

"I kept asking them, 'What are we saving?'" recalls the senior vice president of operations at Norwalk, Conn.-based Gateway Bank.

What Brennan needed was not a way to store documents but a substitute for microfiche. Gateway, a medium-sized bank with $1.3 billion in assets, was spending $130,000 per year to have tapes from the bank's IBM 4341 copied to microfiche.

None of those who came to pitch their document storage solutions were interested in solving the bank's microfiche problem, Brennan says. "In 1987, they told me that it couldn't be done, and that didn't make sense to me," says the veteran of more than 25 years in bank information systems management.

That was the prelude to Brennan convincing Gateway to spend $12,000 for then-unproven personal computer-based optical-disc technology. That is not a lot of money for many businesses, but banks have a cautious attitude toward capital expenditures, says David DiVincenzo, president of Integrated Financial Systems, Inc. (IFS), the value-added reseller in New Haven, Conn., that developed the system.

"This is a case where [Gateway] went out on the edge a little bit and realized a benefit starting in 1988, while everyone else sat on the sidelines," DiVincenzo says.

Brennan says he had to get approval from the bank's chairman for the $12,000 needed to attempt the project. "He said, 'Go ahead and try it,'" Brennan recalls. "At worst, we would have bought a PC."

The initial system, installed at the operations division in Newtown, Conn., included a no-frills IBM Personal Computer AT, a 5¼-in. write-once read-many (WORM) optical disc drive, a tape station and a printer. All of the equipment was from IBM.

"This is an all-IBM shop, and they wanted to be able to get the equipment fixed easily if there was a problem," DiVincenzo says.

IFS developed the software needed to archive and retrieve the reports easily once they had been stored on optical discs.

"In the first month, we saved $2,000 on microfiche," Brennan says. "From there, it got to be a snowball."

Following its early success, the bank shifted all of its applications to optical disc, completing the job in 1988. Now there are 14 banking applications stored on discs. They include customer and commercial checking and savings accounts, installment loans and mortgages—all of the banking reports that the bank generates. . . .

Unlike in days past, few of the reports are ever printed on paper.

When the auditors want to look at the general ledger, for example, they no longer have to leaf through a 900-page report on computer paper. They merely pop a pocket-size disc into a drive and enter a few simple keystrokes to retrieve data. . . .

Brennan is now more receptive to image documenting systems than he was three years ago. He is currently researching what it would take to move images of checks on rolls of photographic film onto optical discs.

The current system records only the information on the magnetic ink character recognition line at the bottom of checks. When a complete image of the actual check is required, the bank's clerks must retrieve it from film and have it processed into hard copy, which is time consuming.

"Ninety percent of the lookups are for checks," Brennan explains. What Brennan needs now is a document imaging system for checks, but he says he cannot get what he wants just yet.

"IBM, Unisys Corp. and NCR Corp. are catering to the large banks," he says. "Five years from now, they may have it for guys like us."

If the past is any indication, Brennan may not wait that long.

Adapted with permission from *Computerworld* (February 11, 1991), pp. 51, 52. Copyright 1991 by CW Publishing, Inc., Framingham, MA 01701.

Cache Memory

A **cache** is a reserved area of memory used to improve execution speed of a computer. There are two types of cache, disk cache and memory cache. In this chapter, we learned that primary storage is fast-access memory. Its storage capacity is limited because it is relatively expensive. On the other hand, secondary storage is nonvolatile, has a large storage capacity, and is relatively inexpensive. Secondary storage access time is always slower than primary storage. Often, a computer's CPU must wait idly while data or programs are being read from or written to the relatively slow secondary storage. A disk cache helps in solving this problem of an idle CPU. **Disk cache** is semiconductor memory (RAM) that has been set aside to store data temporarily while they are in transit (in either direction) between primary and secondary memory. Thus, a disk cache serves as a buffer between the access speeds of primary and secondary memory. The CPU deals primarily with the fast-access disk cache and can continue processing while data are in transit to and from the disk cache and the slower secondary storage.

As the speed of microprocessors improved, a problem developed. The microprocessors were so fast that they sat idle while waiting for program instructions and data to be retrieved from RAM. Memory cache was developed to solve this problem. **Memory cache** acts as a buffer between the microprocessor unit and RAM memory. Thus, in concept it is very similar to disk cache. The primary difference between the two is that memory cache is very high speed memory, faster than RAM, and more expensive. Many microprocessors have memory cache built into them. A typical size of memory cache is 64 Kbytes. Most computers today use disk and memory cache to speed up processing.

Certainly, new forms of primary and secondary storage will be developed. However, magnetic disks, semiconductors, and optical disks will probably continue to be the major storage types of the 1990s and perhaps even longer, simply because improvements in these technologies continue to significantly reduce their cost.

Data Entry

Data-entry and **information-response** devices provide a link between the central processing unit (CPU) and the people who use it. Data-entry devices are used to provide input to the CPU. Information-response devices provide output from the CPU. Advances are continually being made in the human/computer interface, making it easier and more natural for us to communicate with the computer. The term *peripheral device* often refers to any hardware device that is not the CPU. Thus, data-entry, storage, and output devices are also called **peripheral devices**. As we examine data-entry devices, note that often the same media (such as magnetic disks) are used for data entry and secondary storage.

A distinction is usually made between the media and devices used for data entry, storage, and output. The **medium** (such as a magnetic disk) is the material on which the data are recorded, whereas the **device** (such as a disk drive) is the complete unit that reads or writes on the medium. Similarly, a printer is an output device, and paper is an output medium.

Off-line versus On-line Data Entry

In off-line data entry, data are entered through devices that are not connected (they are not on-line) to the CPU or to the disk master files that are to be updated. Thus, after being keyed in, data are transmitted to the processing CPU either electronically or by someone taking the storage medium (floppy disk or magnetic tape) to the processing CPU for input. Key-to-diskette and key-to-disk data entry (discussed below) are both off-line data-entry methods.

With on-line data entry, the input device is connected electronically to the processing CPU and the data are usually processed immediately after being entered. Interactive data entry is a type of on-line data entry, whereas source-data automation can be off-line or on-line. Both interactive data entry and source-data automation will be discussed below.

Key-to-Diskette Data Entry

Key-to-diskette data entry is a form of off-line data entry where data are keyed in through a keyboard and then stored on a floppy disk. Devices were designed to be used exclusively for this type of data entry in the early 1970s. However, with inexpensive microcomputers now available, key-to-diskette data entry is performed using general-purpose microcomputers. The primary advantages of key-to-diskette data entry are the same as those for key-to-disk, which will be covered in the next section. However, key-to-diskette data entry does have the additional advantage that the equipment required is very inexpensive and well suited for small operations.

Key-to-Disk Data Entry

Many medium- and large-sized companies use **key-to-disk** data input, as shown in Figure 10–19. With this approach, a minicomputer (or sometimes a network of microcomputers) performs the data-entry function. This minicomputer supports a number of terminals that are on-line to it. Also on-line to the minicomputer is a hard disk unit that stores the data that have been keyed into the system. The typical procedure for using a key-to-disk input system is to key the data initially from the **source document** onto the disk from a keyboard. As the data are keyed in, the minicomputer can execute programs to screen the data for errors. Errors, such as alphabetic data in numeric fields, can be detected without reference to the files to which the input data pertain.

Once the data have been stored on the disk, **key verification** can be performed through a program executed by the minicomputer. Essentially, the data are keyed in a second time, and the key verification program compares the data on the storage disk with the data that are keyed in the second time. After the data have been verified, the minicomputer produces **control totals** for balancing purposes. When the balancing phase has been completed and any necessary corrections to the data have been made, the data are transferred to the mainframe CPU for processing. This transmission is usually performed through electronic communication lines between the minicomputer and mainframe CPU; however, it can be done by other means, such as magnetic tape.

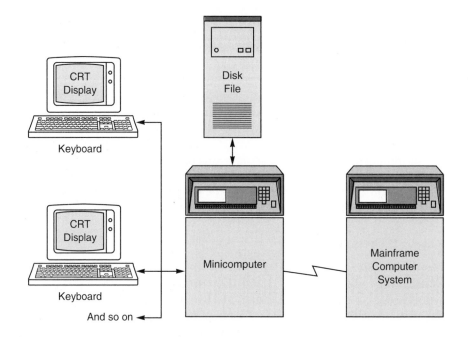

The advantages of a key-to-disk input system are as follows:

1. A large percentage of the editing and control-total balancing can be
    performed at the time of data entry. Keying errors are often detected
    as they occur; therefore, the operator has a much better chance of
    correcting them.

2. Key verification is easily performed on a key-to-disk system where a
    mini or microcomputer is dedicated to the data-entry system.

3. The minicomputer can execute various programs that provide
    instructions, prompts, or **input masks** to assist the operator in
    entering data.

4. The minicomputer can compile and report various statistics
    concerning the data-input operation, including operator productivity
    statistics and error rates. These statistics can be very valuable in
    helping a company determine which operators need additional
    instruction.

5. A key-to-disk system relieves the mainframe of much input
    processing and allows the mainframe to do the jobs for which it is
    best suited.

The primary disadvantages of key-to-disk data entry are as follows:

1. The initial cost of a separate computer system dedicated to data
    input may be prohibitive to small firms. However, the cost of
    computer hardware continues to decline.

2. A separate computer data-entry system may not be necessary when a company's mainframe computer system has excess capacity. In this case, the data can be entered directly to the mainframe system and processed immediately, or stored in batches for later processing in a batch system.

Interactive Data Entry

With **interactive data entry**, data are input directly to the production CPU through a data-entry terminal (see Figure 10–20), for either immediate processing against the master file or storage in batches on magnetic disks for later processing. A **production CPU** is the CPU that processes the application to which the input data pertain. If the system is a batch-processing application, this type of data input is very similar to key-to-disk, except that the production CPU handles the tasks that the minicomputer would handle. For a real-time application such as an airline reservation system, interactive data entry is the only practical type of input since the master file must be updated when an event occurs in order for it to reflect the current status of an activity.

Interactive input has all the advantages of a key-to-disk system, since the production computer can perform the same functions as a minicomputer. Other advantages are as follows:

1. Additional **data editing**, which is not possible with a minicomputer data-entry system, can be performed if the master files to which the transaction data pertain are on-line. Many edit checks depend on data stored in the master file. For example, if all valid employees have a master file record, the input of weekly time data for an employee can be checked against the master file so the user can see whether the Social Security number being input exists on the master file.

2. If excess capacity exists, the data-entry function can use production-CPU time that otherwise would not be used.

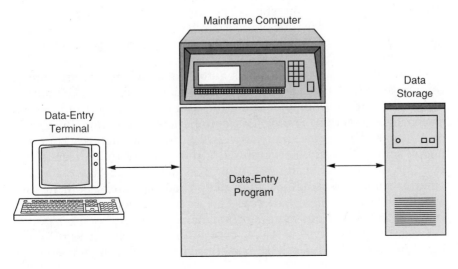

Mainframe Computer

Data-Entry Terminal

Data Storage

Data-Entry Program

F I G U R E 10–20
Interactive Data Entry.
Interactive data entry is necessary for systems that maintain real-time files. Some companies may use interactive data entry for batch systems when they have excess capacity on the mainframe computer.

Disadvantages of interactive input are as follows:

1. The production CPU may not have enough excess capacity to perform the data-entry operation without increasing turnaround time on other jobs.

2. Unless master files are on-line and can be used for editing input data, a mini- or microcomputer can perform data-entry operations for batch-type systems more efficiently than a mainframe CPU.

3. The production CPU may be located far from where data are being entered, requiring the use of expensive communication lines.

Source-Data Automation

Source-data automation is the capture of data in computer-readable form at the location and time of an event. This type of data capture is sometimes called **point-of-origin data capture**. Often the capture of data is a by-product of some other operation. A good example is the capture of data by a computer-connected cash register upon the sale of merchandise.

Figure 10–21 illustrates traditional data entry through keying from source documents. As you can see, data entry, editing, and update of the computer files involve many steps. Errors always occur in data entry, whether keying from source documents or source-data automation is used. However, keying from source documents has disadvantages in terms of correcting errors. As shown in Figure 10–21, if step 5 uncovers significant errors, corrections are keyed and key verified (as in steps 2 and 3) and then combined with the original data-entry records, and steps 4 and 5 are repeated. This process continues until no significant errors exist. The file update can then be done.

Also, correcting errors is more difficult with keying from source documents than with source-data automation. Since the process depicted in Figure 10–21 is usually separated both in time and distance from the original event, we often must go back to the people involved in the event in order to correct the data input. For example, if the event were customer payments on an account, the payment and the completion of the source document may have occurred several days ago and in another office, perhaps in a distant state. The individuals who completed the source document at the time of the event have the information needed to correct errors. It is preferable to detect and correct errors at the place and time of the event, since the particulars are at hand.

Figure 10–22 depicts source-data automation. When data are entered through a device located at the site of the event, the data can be immediately edited by the computer and errors can be sent back to the device screen for correction. Source-data automation that allows immediate data entry and error correction has very significant advantages. However, not all source-data automation involves immediate error correction. For example, the **optical scan (opscan)** process depicted in Figure 10–22 is often a batch-processing operation performed separately, both in time and distance, from the event. Therefore, it has many of the same disadvantages as keying from source documents.

Regardless of the type of source-data automation, it reduces the number of times the data have to be transcribed from one medium to another,

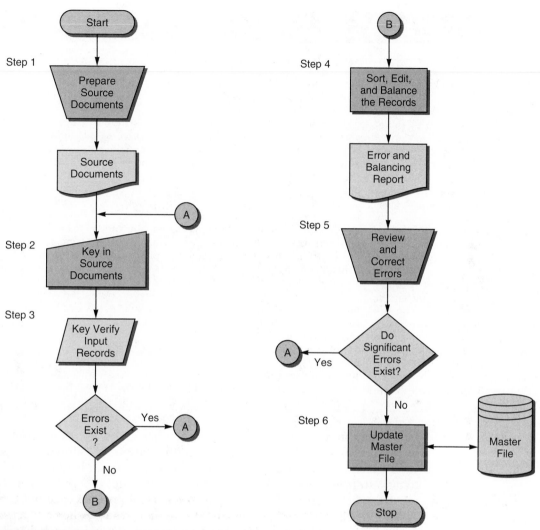

FIGURE 10–21
Keying from Source Documents.
When batch data are keyed, they are usually keyed to a disk, then key verified. The steps are the same in key-to-disk and key-to-diskette data entry.

and therefore significantly reduces chances for error. Furthermore, all source-data automation reduces the amount of human labor needed for data entry.

Source-data automation is sometimes called distributed data entry. Essentially, what we are doing is changing from a centralized data-entry function to a situation in which data entry is distributed to the locations where significant business events occur. In this way, we can capture data about those events directly and immediately with on-the-spot error correction. This is the way most data entry will be performed in the future. Application 10–3 illustrates how the San Jose police use pen-based computers to automate data entry at the source.

APPLICATION 10–3

San Jose Police First to Use Gridpad

By James Daly

An amber dusk creeps over Northern California as a blue-suited San Jose police officer preparing for duty runs through a checklist of the tools needed for another 10-hour shift. Shield? In place. Service revolver? Tucked in the holster. Nightstick? Dangling loosely. Gridpad? Huh?

During the next week, the latest crimefighting feature of the largest police force in the Silicon Valley will be in place as the San Jose Police Department becomes the first major law enforcement agency to use Grid Systems Corp.'s Gridpad [a pen-based, hand-held computer]. . . .

Although the machine will not batter down the doors of drug czars or fell fleeing robbery suspects, the Gridpad will battle what is frequently regarded as an officer's most tiring enemy: paperwork. The 4½-pound Gridpad—which is about the same size as the clipboards the officers already carry—will be used to enter information directly into the computer at the crime or accident scene.

Unlike many portable computers, the Gridpad does not use a keyboard or mouse to enter data. Instead, information is handwritten into the computer using a pen and pad. Therein lies its potential for success.

"The processing of reports is quite a lengthy procedure," systems liaison officer Tony Weir said. A submitted report typically travels through a series of coding and quality-control steps. Inspectors may scrutinize the document to make sure the correct forms are attached or to see if any suspects immediately spring to mind. But such vigilance has its price: It often takes anywhere from three to five days from the time an officer signs his name on the report until it reaches an investigator.

With the Gridpad, a disk is popped out at the end of a shift and uploaded to the department's main record management system. Processing time is reduced to only a few hours. "With nearly 1,000 officers filing more than 100,000 reports per year, the time savings is going to be enormous," Weir said.

Adapted with permission from *Computerworld* (January 21, 1991), p. 37. Copyright 1991 by CW Publishing, Inc., Framingham, MA 01701.

POS Data Entry   Source-data automation has given rise to **point-of-sale (POS)** equipment. In a typical POS configuration, as shown in Figure 10–23, cash registers are on-line to a minicomputer that is in turn on-line to disk storage files containing such data as product descriptions, selling prices, and collected sales statistics. A **universal product code (UPC)** appears on each item sold (see Figure 10–24). It is read by the cash register with either a reader embedded in the checkout counter or a light wand reader (see Figure 10–25). The UPC is transmitted to the minicomputer, which retrieves a description and selling price for the item and transmits them back to the cash register. Simultaneously, sales statistics are collected and used to update cash receipts and inventory master files. For small businesses, UPC readers can be attached directly to microcomputers, and the same functions can be performed as with larger minicomputers.

POS equipment is used most extensively by the grocery industry, although it can be applied to any merchandising operation. There are also other applications for POS equipment. For example, some libraries place UPC stickers on books and library cards. When books are checked out, the patron's identification number on the card and the code of each book are read by a light wand. Similarly, when books are returned, their code is also read with a light wand. Master files maintained by minicomputers contain book codes and the corresponding Library of Congress identification, titles, authors, and other information. Other files contain patron identification numbers, names, addresses, and information on checked out books.

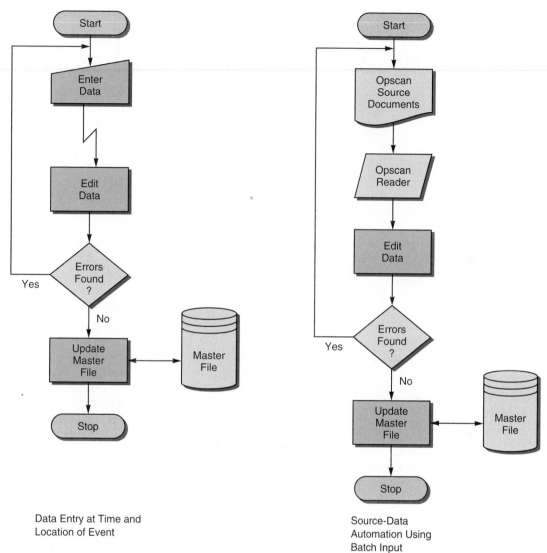

Data Entry at Time and
Location of Event

Source-Data
Automation Using
Batch Input

FIGURE 10–22
Source-Data Automation.

If possible, the input of data to a system should be done through source-data automation. Its advantages of reducing errors in data and reducing the human labor in data input are very significant.

Magnetic-Ink Character Recognition   **Magnetic-ink character recognition (MICR)** was developed by the banking industry for use on checks. MICR equipment reads data according to the shape of each individual character printed with magnetic ink. Preprinted checks contain the bank's identification number and the depositor's checking account number in MICR code at the bottom of the check, as shown in Figure 10–26. When a check is processed, the amount is printed in MICR code in the lower right corner. MICR codes are used for sorting and routing checks to banks and for updating the depositor's account. The use of MICR is limited mostly to the processing of checks and credit card transactions.

F I G U R E 10–23
Point-of-Sale Data
Entry.

Have you ever examined
your grocery receipt to
see whether the
computer made a
mistake? It is extremely
rare to find such errors
because of the error-
checking capabilities
built into POS
equipment. However, you
may discover that the
price stored in the
computer is different
from that marked on the
shelf.

F I G U R E 10–24
Universal Product
Code (UPC).

Some railroad companies
use a larger bar code
(similar to this) on the
side of railroad cars.
Reading stations identify
the cars as they pass by.
In this way the railroad
company can keep track
of the progress of its rail
shipments.

Optical-Character Recognition and Optical-Mark Recognition   **Optical-character recognition (OCR)** devices read printed characters optically. Figure 10–27 illustrates an OCR document. OCR devices can read almost all fonts, although their error rate increases with certain fonts. This equipment is very useful in word processing applications. Essentially, it provides automated input of text that has been previously typed in a wide variety of fonts, including standard typewriter fonts.

Optical-mark recognition (OMR) equipment can detect marks on a specially prepared form. Figure 10–28 illustrates an OMR form. OMR is widely used in academic testing and is sometimes used on **turn-around documents** where the recipient marks data to be read subsequently by OMR equipment.

Other Input Media and Devices   In **speech recognition**, a computer recognizes the patterns of an individual's (or several individuals') speech. Essentially, a person speaks into a microphone that converts the speech into analog electrical signals. These signals are recognized by the computer and converted into the digital signals of a digital computer system to represent individual word patterns.

Telephone touch-tone devices are increasingly being used to enter small amounts of data directly over telephone systems into computer systems. Many variations of these devices exist.

Other data-entry devices becoming increasingly popular are portable (laptop and notebook) personal computers. Data can be entered, stored, and subsequently transmitted at high speed to the central computer. One application for these portable computers has been designed for traveling salespeople. In a customer's office the salesperson can connect the terminal over a regular telephone line or cellular phones (perhaps using a toll-free number) to the company's computer. The salesperson can inquire about the availability of goods that the customer wishes to order and can immediately enter the customer's order into the computer. This can reduce the delivery time of the goods by several days.

FIGURE 10–25
Light Wand Reader
Being Used in the
Counting of Inventory.
The UPC identification
code is read from the tag.
Then the inventory is
counted and the count is
keyed into the reader.

Visual Display Terminals

**Information
Response**

The most widely used output device is the **visual** (or video) **display terminal (VDT)**. This terminal consists of a monitor with a cathode ray tube (CRT) and an attached keyboard. Visual display terminals are also often called CRTs. The CRT is very similar to the picture tube in a television. VDTs have several advantages: they are inexpensive (less than $500) and they produce output without making noise as most printers do. But perhaps their most important advantage is the speed with which they produce output. This speed is determined largely by the speed of the communication line between the VDT and the computer. Typical speeds range from 1,920 to 5,600 characters per second. The primary disadvantage of VDTs is that data must be read from a screen; many people prefer reading data from printed copy. Some people develop eyestrain from reading data on CRTs. Manufacturers are taking these complaints into consideration and are improving the readability of CRT screens.

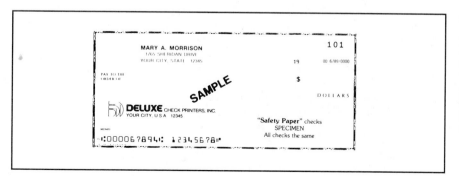

FIGURE 10–26
MICR Coded Check.
Banks process huge
numbers of checks.
Without the automated
processing made possible
by MICR, banking would
be considerably more
expensive for customers.

FIGURE 10–27
Optical-Character
Recognition
Document and Input
Device.
OCR can be used to read
identification tags on
merchandise. It is also
often used on bills that
are turn-around
documents, where a
portion of the bill is sent
back by the customer
with payment and OCR
equipment reads the bill.

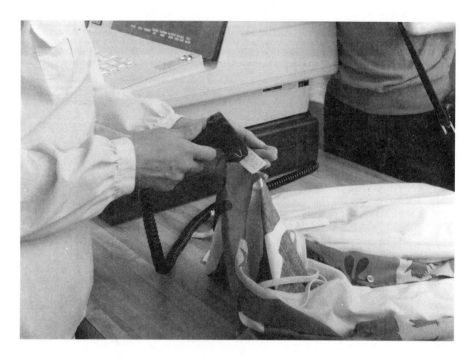

FIGURE 10–28
Optical-Mark
Recognition Form.
OMR is most often used
in academic testing.
Many universities also
use it for student
registration.

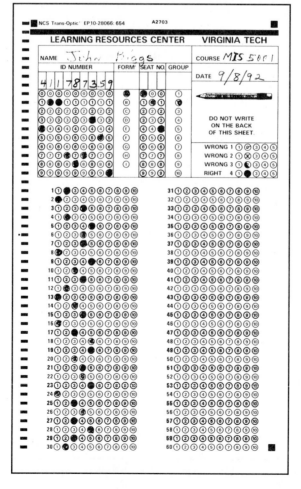

Most companies are replacing VDTs with personal computers. The personal computer can act as a terminal connected to a host minicomputer or mainframe. For a few hundred dollars more than what a VDT costs, a firm can have the equivalent of both a VDT and a personal computer in one device called a **personal workstation**. It can act as a display terminal as well as a data-entry terminal, it can upload and download information from the host computer, and it can act as a stand-alone personal computer.

A disadvantage of the CRT display is its bulkiness. The tubes are long, therefore causing the monitor to have a substantial depth. In some applications, such as laptop portable computers, it is advantageous to have a very thin display (less than an inch).

An increasingly important type of VDT is the **flat-panel display**. There are several types of flat-panel displays, the most common being **liquid crystal diode (LCD) display**. LCD technology is the same as that used in digital watch displays. LCD displays available in the mid-1980s were difficult to read. However, substantial improvements have been made in LCD technology. Today's LCD displays use back lighting that makes them bright and very easy to read. They are also available in full color.

Printers

Printers produce printed copy of information output. Printed copy is often called **hard copy**. A wide variety of printers are available; they may be categorized as character, line, and page printers.

Character printers print one character at a time, similar to typewriters. The technology used for producing the print is usually **dot matrix**. Dot-matrix printers usually give lower-quality output. Therefore, when high-quality output is needed, such as in word processing, laser printers are often used.

Line printers print a complete line in one operation. Their speeds are as high as 2,000 lines per minute, and they are generally used for high-volume printed output. Line printers use print drums, print bands, or print chains to do the printing.

Page printers print a complete page at a time. An example is a **laser printer**, which is a nonimpact printer. Thus far, we have described **impact printers**, which print characters and lines by having the type font strike the paper through an inked ribbon. **Nonimpact printers** do not use physical impact to transfer characters to paper. Examples are **laser** and **ink-jet printers**.

Some page printers (such as ink-jet and laser) can produce very high-quality, letter-perfect printing. For example, laser printers are capable of producing a wide range of type fonts and print quality better than the best typewriters. Laser printers are also very fast, producing output at speeds of up to 21,000 lines per minute. Laser printers for personal computers cost about $1,000 to $2,500 and produce output at 250 to 450 lines per minute. Laser printer technology is very similar to that of copying machines. Ink-jet printers spray ink onto paper and produce print quality better than dot-matrix and not quite as good as laser printers. For PCs, they cost about $500, making them a good alternative to dot-matrix printers.

Other advantages of nonimpact printers over impact printers are that they are usually much faster and require less physical movement for printing; therefore, they are more reliable and quieter. A very significant

advantage of laser, dot-matrix, and ink-jet printers is the ability to produce graphic output interspersed with text on the same page. Some printers can also produce color output, which is especially important for
graphics applications. Over the long run, nonimpact technologies such as
laser and ink-jet will, to a great extent, replace impact printers. Table
10–2 provides a comparison of the speed and quality characteristics of
various printing devices.

T A B L E 10–2
Comparative
Characteristics of
Printing Devices

Device	Category	Speed	Quality of Printout
High-Speed Line Printer	Impact Line Printer	High	Low/Medium
Dot-Matrix Printer	Impact Character Printer	Low/Medium	Low/Medium/High
Laser Printer	Nonimpact Page Printer	Medium/High	Very High
Ink-Jet Printer	Nonimpact Charac- ter Printer	Medium	Very High

Most ink-jet printers can print in color. They can even print color onto transparencies used in overhead
presentations.

Optical Disks

Optical disks have become important output media. Their primary advantage is that they can store very large amounts of data—up to one billion bytes. In fact, they have made computer-output microfiche obsolete.
Computer-output microfiche (COM) is a microfilm-based method for
storing large amounts of printed computer data.

Graphics

The ability to display computer-based data directly in graphic form is an
important business tool. Generally, the significance of data can be grasped
much more easily by studying bar charts and line graphs than by examining
the numerical data directly. Two types of graphics-output equipment are
available: the **plotter**, which draws graphs directly on paper and the **graphics
terminal**. Plotters and graphics terminals can produce both black-and-white
and color output. Depending on the computer that supports the terminals
and the communication lines available, graphics terminals can almost instantaneously display a complete graph on their screens. Therefore, management can quickly examine sales trends, profit trends, and other
information. The newer personal computers, such as the PS/2 and the Macintosh, have very good graphic capabilities for typical business uses. Thus,
they have decreased the need for specially designed graphics terminals.

Other Output Media

Many input and secondary storage media, such as magnetic tape and
disk, serve as output media as well. **Audio-response output** devices are
also being used. For example, some railroads use audio-response devices
for customer inquiries. Through a touch-tone telephone, customers can
access the railroad's computer system, key in a shipment code, and receive an audio response indicating where their shipment is and when it
is likely to arrive at their door.

Summary

- The central processing unit of a computer is its single most important component.

- The primary storage unit stores the program being executed and the data records being processed.

- Primary storage must be a fast-access device in order for the CPU to be able to function at electronic speeds.

- Random-access memory (RAM) allows the CPU to read any particular data or program statement on a random basis.

- Read-only memory (ROM) can be read from but not written to. It is used to store programs that are frequently used by many computer applications and that do not need to be modified.

- The arithmetic-logic unit performs arithmetic operations and logic comparisons on data.

- The control unit interprets program instructions and arranges for their execution. Typically it calls on other units to execute the instructions.

- Computers are classified into four groups: microcomputers, minicomputers, mainframes, and supercomputers.

- Parallel processors use multiple processors to simultaneously execute multiple tasks in a single computer application.

- Secondary storage is an essential part of a computer system. It stores the bulk of data and programs not in use. Secondary storage devices usually use some mechanical movement to access data, thereby making it a relatively slow process.

- Magnetic reel tape and cartridge tape are widely used secondary storage media.

- Magnetic tapes have the advantages of being inexpensive, compact, fast, accurate, portable, and reusable. However, it is necessary to handle them carefully and protect them from dirt and humidity.

- Magnetic disk is the most popular form of secondary storage. Its major advantage is its random-access capability. Any piece of information on the disk can be accessed quickly with very little mechanical movement.

- The cost of disk storage is steadily declining. It is a very useful direct-access medium for on-line systems. Its major disadvantage is that it does not provide an automatic audit trail or backup facility.

- Optical disks with large storage capacities (one gigabyte per disk) are becoming a very important form of secondary storage. They are used for storing large volumes of data that are not accessed or updated often.

- Cache memory acts as a buffer between the fast access speed of primary memory and the slow access speed of secondary storage.

- Data-entry and information-response devices provide a link between the central processing unit and the people who use it.

- In a key-to-diskette data-entry system, data are transferred from the keyboard to a floppy disk. Floppy disks are low-cost, reusable storage devices.

- A key-to-disk data-entry system allows some editing and verification of data upon entry. A mini or microcomputer is used to perform the editing and verification functions. It may also provide other data-input assistance, such as instructions, prompts, control totals, and error rates.

- Interactive data entry allows the input of data directly to the production CPU. This kind of data entry is essential for real-time systems where the master file must be updated immediately. Since data are entered directly to the master file, it is possible to execute a large variety of edit checks, including comparisons with existing data.

- Source-data automation permits the capture of data as a by-product of a business event. Some source-data automation techniques are point-of-sale data entry, magnetic-ink character recognition, optical-character recognition, optical-mark recognition, voice recognition, and portable terminals.

- Visual display terminals are the most widely used method of displaying output for reading by humans.

- Printers are output devices that provide information response in the form of hard copy. Printers may be categorized as line, character, or page printers, or as impact versus nonimpact printers.

- A line printer prints a complete line at a time, whereas a character printer prints a character at a time, just like a typewriter. A page printer prints a page at a time.

- The type font of an impact printer actually strikes the paper to create character images. Nonimpact printers use techniques such as laser beams and ink jets to transfer information to paper.

- Plotters and graphics terminals are popular information-response devices. They help summarize business data by presenting them in an easy-to-understand pictorial format.

Key Terms

Computer	Microprogramming
Program	Firmware
Central processing unit (CPU)	Operation code
Control unit	Operands
Arithmetic-logic unit	Instruction cycle
Secondary storage	Execution cycle
Output devices	Microcomputer
Semiconductor chips	Minicomputers
Microprocessors	Distributed data processing
Volatile	Mainframes
Random-access memory (RAM)	Gigabytes
Read-only memory (ROM)	Supercomputers
Flash memory	Simulation
Microcoding	Parallel processors
	Magnetic tape

Back up

Magnetic disks

Hard disks

Concentric tracks

Cylinder

Winchester disk

Floppy disks

Direct-access storage

Audit trail

Optical disks

Cache

  Disk cache

  Memory cache

Data entry

Information response

Peripheral devices

Medium

Device

Key-to-diskette

Key-to-disk

Source document

Key verification

Control totals

Input masks

Interactive data entry

Production CPU

Data editing

Source-data automation

Point-of-origin data capture

Optical scan (opscan)

Point-of-sale (POS)

Universal product code (UPC)

Magnetic-ink character
  recognition (MICR)

Optical-character recognition
  (OCR)

Fonts

Optical-mark recognition
  (OMR)

Turn-around documents

Speech recognition

Visual display terminal (VDT)

Personal workstation

Flat-panel display

Liquid crystal diode (LCD)
  display

Hard copy

Character printers

Dot matrix

Line printers

Page printers

Laser printer

Impact printers

Nonimpact printers

Ink-jet printers

Plotter

Graphics terminal

Audio-response output

Review Questions

1. What is the most important piece of equipment in a computer system?

2. List the three components of a central processing unit.

3. What are the major functions of the primary storage unit?

4. Why does primary storage have to be faster than secondary storage?

5. Describe the advantages of semiconductor memory.

6. Why is nonvolatile memory more desirable than volatile memory?

7. Describe random-access memory and explain its advantages.

8. Why is the arithmetic-logic unit crucial to a computer's operation?

9. Describe the two cycles performed by the control unit.

10. How can you differentiate between mainframes, minis, and micros?

11. How does parallel processing increase the amount of work that a CPU can perform?

12. Why is a computer's memory divided into primary and secondary storage?

13. List four advantages of using magnetic tape for secondary storage.

14. Describe the concept of a cylinder in connection with magnetic disks.

15. What is the advantage of a direct-access storage device?

16. What is cache memory and how does it increase the amount of work that a CPU can perform?

17. Distinguish between data-storage and data-entry devices.

18. What is the difference between a data-input medium and a data-input device?

19. What are the major advantages of key-to-diskette data entry?

20. What are the major functions of the computer in a key-to-disk data entry configuration?

21. Explain the advantages of interactive data entry.

22. What is source-data automation?

23. What is the advantage of entering data at the time and place the actual business event occurs?

24. What do the initials UPC stand for?

25. Why are personal computers replacing visual display terminals?

26. What are the three ways to categorize printers?

27. What is the advantage of using graphics information response in business data processing?

28. What types of printers are most widely used with personal computers?

29. What are the major advantages of laser printers?

30. What are the major advantages and disadvantages of optical disk?

Discussion Questions and Cases

1. A large primary storage unit enables the computer to retrieve and store programs and data quickly, and thus operate at a high speed. However, primary storage is more expensive then secondary storage. What factors need to be considered when deciding on the amount of primary storage to purchase? Give one example of a business application that would require large primary storage and one that would require small primary storage.

2. Mary Delafore is a freshman in an introductory information systems class. She is an aspiring accounting major and hopes to become an auditor with a large accounting firm. The first topics in the course are the internal design of the computer and the differences in various sizes of computers

including supercomputers, mainframes, minicomputers, and microcomputers. She feels this study of hardware is a waste of time because it does not have anything to do with accounting and auditing. Can you think of any situations in which Mary will need to know about computer hardware and processing in her career as an auditor?

3. Lowes Incorporated is a medium-sized regional department store. The company has a medium-sized IBM mainframe at its central headquarters. Accounts receivable is run on this mainframe, and terminals have been placed in the various stores so that inquiries can be made concerning customer accounts. Some store managers think accounts receivable should be kept locally at each store. They argue that a microcomputer such as the IBM PS/2 Model 70 could be used to keep up with the accounts receivable at each store. People in the central data-processing department argue that the volume of customers is too great for micros to handle accounts receivable. The managers counter this with the argument that two or more micros can be networked together to provide the necessary capacity, and that the micros in the various stores can be networked together. Which direction do you think Lowes should go? Should the firm maintain accounts receivable on the mainframe, as it is doing now, or should it convert the system to microcomputers?

4. Hunter Martin is the proprietor of a small but rapidly growing business. He is still using a manual record-keeping system, which is becoming large and very complex. Mr. Martin has decided that a personal computer with the adequate software would help him run his business better. How should Mr. Martin go about choosing the right personal computer for his business? What features offered by the personal computer might interest him?

5. Anthony Wilson has just been given a proposal to add optical (CD-ROM) disk storage systems to the company's computer systems to replace three magnetic-tape systems that are currently used for backup purposes. Mr. Wilson does not involve himself in the use of computers, and he is not very familiar with computer technology. He does know that optical disk storage is a new technology likely to be used widely in the future. How would you explain optical disks to Mr. Wilson? What effect would this system have on the secondary storage capabilities of the company? Would the benefits gained outweigh the costs of optical disk storage? Where would you advise Mr. Wilson to go to get additional information on which to base his decision?

6. Data-entry costs can be a significant portion of a business firm's total data-processing costs. If you had to choose between an on-line interactive and an off-line key-to-disk data-entry system, what decision criteria would you use?

7. Interactive real-time data entry provides for up-to-date data files and powerful data-editing facilities. Unfortunately, processing costs for real-time data entry tend to be high. Batched data entry (such as key-to-disk) is much cheaper, but it involves a time lag between data entry and master-file updating. Which kind of data entry should a bank use for its deposits and withdrawals? Justify your answer by comparing the pros and cons of the suggested system.

8. While futurist writers predict paperless, computerized offices, high-speed printers continue to print tons of paper every hour. If businesses want to control the quantity of paper they use, what are some suitable alternatives to printed output? Is it possible to continue using paper, but in a more economical and efficient manner? How?

9. The Smith Company is a manufacturer of envelopes and paper products. When employees need to purchase supplies or equipment, they fill out a form and send it to the purchasing department for processing. Several managers complain that the paper handling slows down the purchasing process by as much as two to three days. They recommend that a purchase request be initiated through on-line computer terminals. Under this proposal, the purchasing department would retrieve the purchase requisition on its own computer terminal, verify the information, and assign the purchase to a vendor.

   Some people at Smith, including the internal auditors, argue that with paper forms, an individual authorized to make the purchase writes his or her signature on the purchase requisition. Thus the purchasing department has assurance that each purchase is authorized. They further argue that this vital control would be lost if an on-line terminal were used, since the purchasing department could not be assured that the individual inputting the purchase requisition was actually authorized to do so. Those advocating on-line terminals say that the person entering the purchase requisition would first have to enter a password that only he or she knows. The other group argues that passwords are easily misplaced and are often discovered by those who are not authorized to make a purchase. They argue that a signature is unique to an individual and cannot be easily copied by someone else. Which side of this argument would you support? State your reasons.

10. Lincoln Incorporated is developing a new budget-control system. This system will produce information on a weekly and monthly basis and will keep the managers informed of their spending in relation to their budget. Preliminary plans are to produce output only on personal computer workstations. Many managers already have workstations in their offices. When the new system is implemented, each manager will have a workstation and therefore will be able to call up budget information at any time.

    John Decker is manager of manufacturing operations at Lincoln. John likes to play the role of a good old country boy, but in fact he is a very sharp and astute manager and very valuable to the company. In a recent meeting, system development presented the preliminary design of the system to the company's managers. When the plan to produce output only on workstations was discussed, John made this comment: "It seems that today, the only thing anyone ever mentions as far as computer output is concerned is workstations." He held up a piece of paper, and in his drawl said: "One of these days somebody is going to discover paper and say, 'Isn't this the best thing that has come down the pike? I can read it, I can write on it, I can put it in my briefcase, I can even take it to the bathroom with me.'" After the laughter died down, several managers joined John in insisting that output be available in traditional paper form. System development countered with the following arguments: many companies have almost been choked to death by paper; the trend is toward a paperless business environment through the use of sophisticated computer technology; and the sooner the company gets used to this environment the more competitive it will be. Which side of the argument would you support? Why?

11. Susan Harris and Jane Howard were discussing their company's current high demand for high-quality documents. The company has been experiencing increased costs owing to the fact they have to go outside for such documents. Their discussion led to a possible need for laser

printers, better word processing software, and even desktop publishing software. They were not terribly concerned about the cost of the software packages, which are reasonably priced. They were more concerned with the expense of buying laser printers when there are already a number of dot-matrix printers in the company. With the demand for high-quality documents so great, would a laser printer be worth the cost? Does the laser printer significantly increase the capability of producing high-quality documents? Are there other alternatives?

12. Jonathan Smythe is the president of a large company, and he has decided to upgrade the company's computer system. Jennifer Jones, his MIS vice president, has given him a report on the alternatives available. The first choice is to update the current mainframe system and add terminals to additional offices that need them. The next alternative is to update the system by providing microcomputers to all users and then linking them to the mainframe, giving each employee that uses the computer system a personal workstation. What advantages would the second alternative have over the first in the long run, if any? What disadvantages would it have?

INFORMATION SYSTEMS STRATEGIES

Restaurant Chain Cooks Up Time-Saving IS Strategy

By James Connolly

The premise seems simple. If you have a chain of restaurants captained by a team of carefully chosen managers, you want them making decisions that lead to profits rather than spending their time filling out forms.

The basic idea is behind a personal computer-based systems strategy through which Au Bon Pain—a 100-site chain of cafes and express food stands—is reducing the time managers spend on daily reports and administrative tasks.

The company recently completed a three-month, 50-site rollout of store management and point-of-sale systems. The information gathered by this system may also provide a foundation for the growing 10-year-old chain's first efforts to implement a companywide IS [information systems] strategy.

"We want to have the managers spending less time calculating and more time analyzing results," said Mark Factor, director of MIS [management information systems] at Au Bon Pain.

When the former Coopers & Lybrand consultant joined Au Bon Pain two years ago, he discovered that store managers had at most only a few hours per week to study their results, plan staffing and production and identify cost problems. "We hired good managers and then buried them in paperwork," he said.

The heart of Au Bon Pain's business is its cafes, which serve croissants, sandwiches and muffins baked on the premises using dough that is prepared and frozen at headquarters.

Until recently, managers at those sites did their planning and cost analysis the way fast-food chains have done for two decades: by taking raw numbers from cash registers and plugging them into paper forms. Even at headquarters, there were only a handful of PCs and an NCR Corp. Tower-based accounting system. In most cases, information moved from one location or department to another on paper.

Factor drew on the IS strategies of other chains, including Mrs. Fields Cookies, in designing the Au Bon Pain system—called Amigo, for Assisting Managers in Getting Out.

Running on Intel Corp. 80386SX-based NCR PCs, the core back office management software was provided by Management Information Support, Inc. in Lakewood, Colo. Those PCs gather sales information from the six to 15 NCR cash registers in each store.

A store PC acts as the manager's system and uploads data to headquarters when polled by a 80386-based PC each day. The host also manages downloading of software, troubleshooting and communications with nine laptop computers used by district managers.

Factor reported that Au Bon Pain has selected an architecture for a headquarters system that will be put in place during the course of a year. That system, drawing information originating at the stores and supporting all management and operational needs, will be based on a relational database management system and either an Intel I486 or 80386 server.

Amigo lets the manager react to sales by increasing or decreasing staff and food preparation. The latter can be crucial because it takes two hours for raw goods to become finished products. Cooking too many eats up profits. Cooking too few means lost business.

To help achieve a balance, Amigo automates what previously was a rough, manual system. Drawing on information such as sales patterns for previous months and even the day's weather, the system suggests what is likely to be sold throughout the day.

Alan Camuso, manager of one of Au Bon Pain's Boston cafes, has been using the system since it was in beta testing in June 1990. He said the production planning aspects have saved him $50 to $60 per day in the cost of leftovers.

In addition to projecting sales, Amigo helps to identify areas of waste by, in effect, assigning dollar values to ingredients and tying those figures to Au Bon Pain's recipes. This helps a manager to determine, for example, whether a sandwich preparer is regularly applying a few cheese slices too many.

An expert system-based labor scheduler that examines sales figures and suggests staffing levels is now being phased in. Au Bon Pain has eliminated some data entry and saved wage expenses by replacing time cards with automated employee punch-in through Amigo. Not only do employee time records go electronically to a payroll service, but the system prevents an employee from punching in too early. "If you cut even five minutes per shift by eliminating early punch-ins, that can mean $200,000 on the company's bottom line," Factor said.

The time stamps on the automated system provide a more precise audit trail as managers handle cash throughout the day.

However, Amigo is giving managers the most relief by reducing paperwork. "I was doing eight hours of paperwork every day. That's now four hours, and I can do other things," Camuso said. "Now, when I get my weekend numbers, I can sit down and look at them. In the past, by the time you were done with the paperwork, all you wanted to do was go home."

Discussion Questions

1. Would Au Bon Pain's system have been possible prior to the advent of low-cost, powerful personal computers?

2. Describe other applications that could be placed on Au Bon Pain's current hardware.

11

System Software
and Programming Languages

Introduction

The computer is a valuable part of most organizations. Among its resources are processing time, storage space, printers, and input devices. The management of these resources is performed largely by a type of system software called an operating system. When users interact with a computer much of this interaction is with the system software. System software directly affects the ease with which users interact with the computer. Furthermore, system software is a significant determinant of whether a particular computer's resource are used optimally. For these reasons it is important that computer users have a basic knowledge of system software.

Software for large, complex, and/or unique applications is usually written by an application programmer to fulfill a particular user or application requirement. A program is a set of instructions executed by the computer. The instructions cause the computer to perform a desired task. The selection of a language depends primarily on the nature of the problem or application as well as the programmer's choice, the standard language used by the company, and the hardware capabilities. In this chapter we will distinguish between system software and application software. Then we will explore the functions, components, and types of operating systems. Next, we will see how operating systems make possible multitasking, virtual storage, time-sharing, and multiprocessing computer systems. Finally, we will explore the types of programming languages and the criteria to be used in selecting a language.

System Software Versus Application Software

There are two broad categories of software: system software and application software. **System software** is a set of programs that manage the resources of a computer system (processing time, storage space, and so on) so that they are used in an optimal fashion. These programs also provide routine services, such as copying data from one file to another, and assist in the development of application programs. System software consists of general programs that assist the computer in the efficient execution of application programs. **Application software**, on the other hand, performs specific tasks for the computer user. Figure 11–1 illustrates the different types of system and application software.

System Software

System software began to be used extensively with the second-generation computers in the early 1960s. Before this, the operation of a computer was controlled primarily by humans. Operators monitored the processing of each job. Typically, when a job ended, a bell rang or a light flashed to indicate that another job should be input to the computer and started by the operator. If a job ended while the operator was having a coffee break, the computer might sit idle for five or ten minutes or longer. In addition, the operator had to activate each peripheral device when that device was needed by the computer. This type of human intervention wasted large amounts of computer time and human resources. To automate these functions, companies developed programs called operating systems.

An **operating system** is a set of integrated programs that controls the execution of computer programs and manages the storage and processing

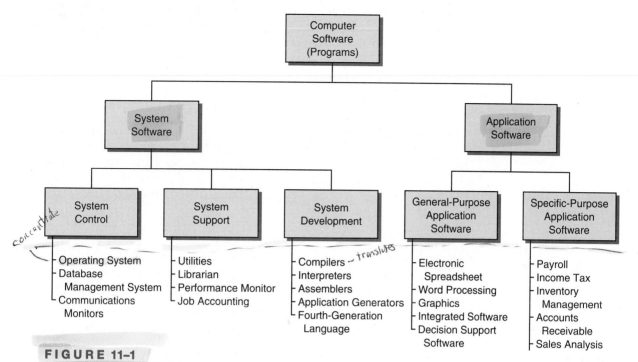

FIGURE 11–1

Types of System and Application Software.

Application software performs tasks for the computer user. System software assists in the control, support, and development of application software.

resources of a computer system. These programs are stored partly in primary storage and partly in direct-access secondary storage so the computer can access them immediately when they are needed. With operating systems, a **queue** of jobs that are awaiting execution is read onto a disk. The operating system starts each job when system resources are available for its execution. Since human intervention is eliminated, idle computer time is significantly reduced.

There are three types of system software:

- **System control programs** control the execution of programs, manage the storage and processing resources of the computer, and perform other management and monitoring functions. The most important of these programs is the operating system—all computers must have an operating system. Other examples are database management systems and communication monitors.

- **System support programs** provide routine service functions to other computer programs and to computer users. Examples are utilities, librarians, performance monitors, and job accounting.

- **System development programs** assist in the creation of application programs. Examples are language compilers such as COBOL and fourth-generation languages such as FOCUS.

System programs are developed and sold by both computer companies and specialized software firms. **Systems programmers** write system software. Most large firms have their own staff of systems programmers who are capable of modifying an operating system to meet the unique requirements of the firm.

Application Software

An **application program** is a program written for or by a user to perform a particular job. **General-purpose application software**, such as an electronic spreadsheet, has a wide variety of applications. **Specific-purpose application software**, such as payroll and sales analysis, is used only for the application for which it is designed. **Application programmers** write these programs.

Generally, computer users interact with application software as shown in Figure 11–2. The system software controls the execution of the application software and provides other support functions, such as data storage. For example, when you use an electronic spreadsheet on a personal computer, the storage of the worksheet files on disk is handled by MS-DOS, the computer's operating system.

Types of System Software

As stated earlier, there are three types of system software: system control, system support, and system development.

System Control Software

A very important part of the system control software is the operating system, which performs many functions. Two of its most critical tasks are starting the computer (performing the **initial program load**, or **bootstrap**) and initiating the processing of each job. To understand these functions, let's examine the Microsoft Disk Operating System used on personal computers. The components of MS-DOS are illustrated in Figure 11–3. Figure 11–4 shows the steps that MS-DOS goes through in bootstrapping the computer and loading an application program written in BASIC.

Operating systems on minis and mainframes also perform **job scheduling** functions by examining the priority of each job awaiting execution. Jobs with high priorities are executed first. **Access security** is also

FIGURE 11–2
The Interaction between Users, Application Software, System Software, and Computer Hardware.
Application and system software act as interfaces between users and computer hardware. If this software did not exist, very few people would use computer hardware. As application and system software become more capable, people find computers easier to use.

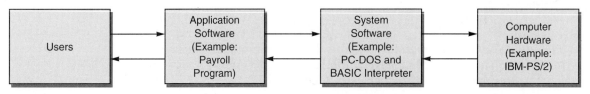

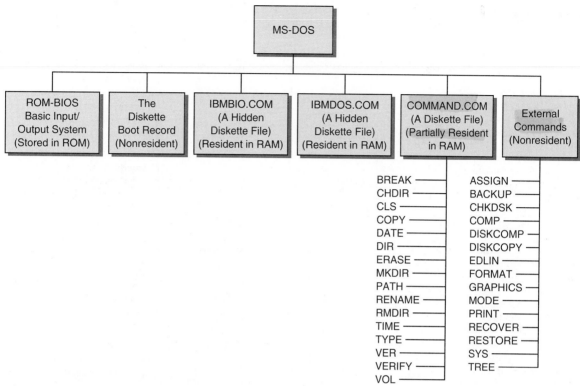

FIGURE 11–3

Microsoft Disk Operating System Used on Personal Computers.

ROM-BIOS provides fundamental services needed by the computer, such as a self-test of memory, start-up (boot) of the computer, and input/output services between the central processing unit and peripheral devices such as printers and disks. It is stored permanently in ROM. The diskette boot record is a very short and simple program stored at the beginning of the DOS diskette. Its purpose is to begin the process of loading the operating system when the PC is first turned on. Nonresident means that it is not stored in RAM while the PC is operating. Both IBMBIO.COM and IBMDOS.COM are extensions of ROM-BIOS. They provide additional input/output interfaces with peripheral devices. They are stored on the DOS diskette, but they are hidden files. Hidden files are not displayed when a DIR (directory) of the diskette is produced. They are resident in RAM while the PC is operating. The primary job of COMMAND.COM is to process and interpret the commands that you type into DOS. It also contains the programs that execute several DOS commands. These programs are resident in RAM. The final part of DOS, the external commands, is not resident in RAM; these commands are moved from the DOS diskette to RAM whenever they are needed.

a function of the operating system. This function is carried out through various password schemes that identify valid users and determine which data files they may access.

Figure 11–5 illustrates the storage of a mainframe operating system. The **system residence device** stores the complete operating system. Today this device is usually a disk unit. As portions of the operating system are needed for execution, they can be readily loaded into primary storage.

There are generally four types of operating system programs: the **initial program loader (IPL)**, the **supervisor**, the **job control program**, and the **input/output control program**. In mainframe computers, the bootstrap program is known as the initial program loader. Its purpose is to start operations. It performs this function by reading the resident portion of the

FIGURE 11–4

Loading an Application Program on a Personal Computer.

Functions of the operating system are illustrated by the successive events required to load an application program. (1) Switching the computer on actuates a bootstrap program that loads the operating system into primary memory. The operating system transfers a file directory from disk memory to primary memory; in the file directory is listed the address, or position, of every program and data file recorded on the disk. In response to the next instruction, (2) the operating system finds the BASIC interpreter on the disk and, after making certain there is enough space for it, loads it into primary memory; the user is notified that the interpreter is ready. (Some personal computers perform step 2 automatically as part of the switching-on sequence.) The operating system is called on to load the application program itself. (3) Now, with the interpreter again in control, the application program can be run. Output will be a new data file in primary memory, which can be transferred to disk storage.

From Hoo-min D. Toong and Amar Gupta, "Personal Computers," *Scientific American*, December 1982. Copyright 1982 by Scientific American, Inc., all rights reserved.

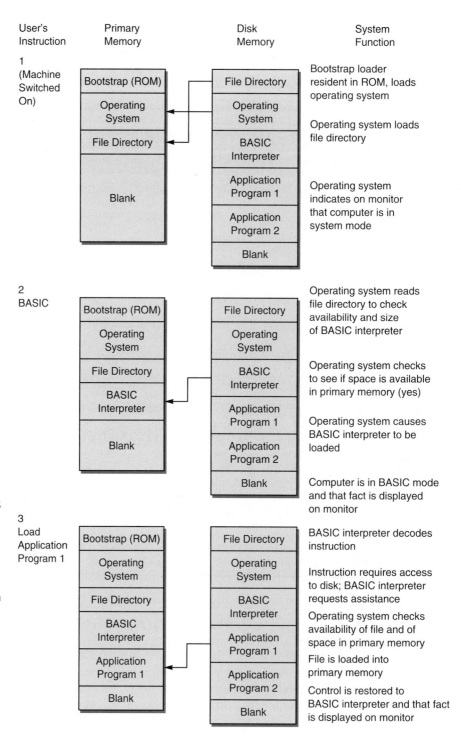

supervisor from secondary storage and loading it into primary storage. Since the operating system is constantly supervising and monitoring the computer, a frequently used portion of the operating system, called the

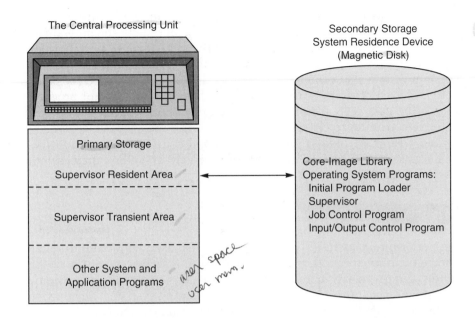

The Central Processing Unit

Primary Storage

Supervisor Resident Area

Supervisor Transient Area

Other System and Application Programs

Secondary Storage
System Residence Device
(Magnetic Disk)

Core-Image Library
Operating System Programs:
Initial Program Loader
Supervisor
Job Control Program
Input/Output Control Program

FIGURE 11–5
Storage of a Mainframe Operating System.

A core-image library means that the programs stored on the disks can be moved directly into primary storage without modification. This improves the speed with which parts of the operating system can be moved into the supervisor transient area as needed.

resident supervisor, is stored in primary storage while the computer is operating. Other parts of the supervisor are used less frequently. They are stored only temporarily in the supervisor transient area of primary storage when they are in use (refer to Figure 11–5).

Once the resident portion of the supervisor is loaded into primary storage, control is passed to the supervisor and the operation of the computer begins. The supervisor programs (often called **monitor** or **executive programs** are the principal managers in an operating system. They organize and control the flow of work by initiating and controlling the execution of other computer programs.

As operating system software replaced human operators in the control of mainframe computers, new languages were developed to enable users and programmers to communicate with the operating system. A **job control language (JCL)** requires that the user include several job control statements along with a program. The statements identify the job and its steps, and specify the system resources to be used (for example, expected run-time, input/output device to be used, and memory space required). Job control language also describes the data sets or files that are to be used in the various job steps. Job control languages are used primarily with the large multiuser computer systems. JCL is not used with personal computers since they are usually single-user systems. The information provided through JCL can be furnished to a personal computer interactively or by defaulting to standard assumptions for the information.

The supervisor and job control programs acting together issue many instructions to the human operator. Examples include instructions to mount or dismount a tape or to load or unload a disk pack. If special forms are needed for printing the output, the programmer specifies these forms through the JCL statements. When the job is ready to be printed, the computer sends a message to the operator to mount the special forms on the printer. A large percentage of the work a computer operator performs is in response to instructions from the operating system. These instructions originate from the JCL that the programmer includes with the program.

Input/output control programs manage the movement of data between primary storage and peripheral devices such as disk and tape drives. These programs also can check for errors. For example, if an error is detected while a program is reading from a disk, the I/O control program rereads the data several times in an attempt to obtain error-free data. If the error continues to occur, an appropriate error message is displayed or printed. (Database management systems and communication monitors are discussed in Chapters 13 and 14, respectively; therefore, they are not described here.)

System Support Software

Most computer systems have support software called **utility programs** that perform routine tasks. These programs sort data, copy data from one storage medium to another, output data from a storage medium to the printer, and perform other tasks. Utility programs are usually supplied by the computer manufacturer as part of the operating system. They may be called by any application program and used by that program.

Another common type of support software is a librarian. The primary function of the **librarian** is to maintain a catalog of the locations and usage of all program and data files. Librarians often execute password controls.

Performance monitors such as IBM's system management facilities (SMF) are part of most system software. **Performance monitors** collect and record selected activities that occur within a computer system. For example, they collect data about CPU idle time, which operations are using the system (and how long they use it and what hardware they employ), whether each job is successfully executed, and how much primary storage is employed by each job. This information can be used in charging departments within the firm for use of the computer facility. Most firms feel that charging users for computer services is part of the task of controlling computer resources.

Monitors also collect information about which files are used in performing a job. This information provides an audit trail concerning data and file usage. It makes it possible to determine, for example, which files were used when a particular program was run. It also identifies who the user was when the file access was made, plus the date and time of the access.

System Development Software

System development programs assist a programmer or user in developing and using an application program. Examples of these programs are language translators, linkage editors, and application generators.

A **language translator** is a computer program that converts a program written in a procedural language, such as BASIC, into machine language that can be directly executed by the computer (see Figure 11–6). Many different language translators exist; in fact, there is one for each programming language. They are categorized as compilers, interpreters, or assemblers. (Programming languages and language translators are discussed in more detail later in this chapter.)

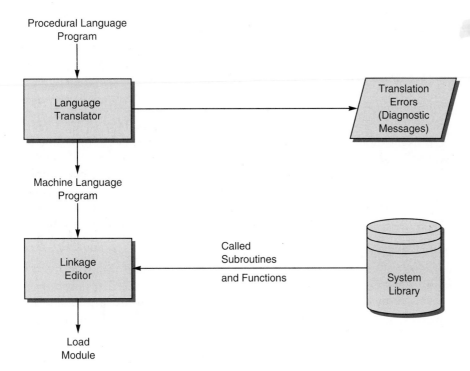

FIGURE 11–6
Language Translation.
Computers can execute only machine language programs. Programs written in any older language must be translated into a machine language load module which is suitable for loading directly into primary storage.

Quite often in writing a program, a programmer calls prewritten subroutines (or subprograms), which are stored on the system residence device, to perform a specific standard function. For example, if a program requires the calculation of a square root, the programmer does not write a special program. He or she simply calls a square root subroutine to be used in the program. The **linkage editor** gathers these called subroutines and places them into the application program. The output from the linkage editor is called a load module. (The term *module* is often used synonymously with the term *program*.) A **load module** is a program that is suitable for loading directly into primary storage for execution.

Application generators and fourth-generation languages are programming productivity tools that partially automate the programming process. For example, one type of application generator, the report generator, allows a programmer or user to simply describe the contents of a report rather than write the report in a procedural language such as COBOL. Some report generators (or query languages) even allow report requests to be made in conversational English. For example, a query language called Intellect will process the following query:

```
Report the Base Salary, Commissions and Years of Service
Broken Down by State and City for Sales Clerks in New
Jersey and Virginia.
```

Fourth-generation languages, such as FOCUS and ORACLE, are often employed by end users as well as programmers. These languages require many fewer statements to accomplish a task than typical third-generation languages such as BASIC and COBOL.

Open Systems

Since the beginning of computers, the inability of different hardware, systems software, and application software to interoperate has been a problem for information systems. Now a movement called open systems promises to increase the interoperability of computer systems. **Open systems** are those systems that can interoperate with hardware and software from multiple vendors. Operating systems are central to the move toward open systems, since they must be designed to work on multiple types of hardware and to execute applications designed for other operating systems. Some personal computer operating systems are now able to execute applications designed for a variety of operating systems. For example, the personal computer operating system OS/2 will execute applications deigned for DOS and for Windows, as well as those designed for OS/2. IBM has traditionally had difficulty in getting its various size computers—mainframes, midrange, and personal computers—to interoperate. OS/2 is central to IBM's move to produce interoperability between its computers. OS/2 has embedded communication capabilities that enable communication between different computers. In addition, OS/2's graphical user interface will become IBM's user interface that is common to all its computers. However, the term open systems encompasses more than just operating systems and there continues to be some confusion about what the term means, as discussed in Application 11–1.

Types of Operating Systems

There are basically two types of operating systems: batch and interactive.

Batch Systems

A **batch operating system** accepts jobs and places them in a queue to await execution. As execution time becomes available, the operating sys-

---

APPLICATION 11–1

Open Book on Open Systems

A big part of the confusion in open systems revolves around defining the term. Virtually everyone, it seems, has his own take on what an open system is.

Still, some agreement is being reached. Based on interviews with more than 40 users, consultants, vendors and consortium representatives, the following definition is pretty much agreed on:

An open system has three basic criteria: interoperability, scalability and portability. That is, it communicates with other systems, both open and proprietary; it allows a choice of anything from a desktop computer to a mainframe; and it allows software to be run across the board without being recompiled for various hardware systems.

Also, an open system is precisely that—a system. It encompasses a wide range of hardware and software, from operating systems to databases and applications, all of which meet the three criteria above. . . .

The arguments begin when a fourth item is added to the definition. Some users insisted that a truly open system is based on vendor-neutral standards achieved by consensus, such as the International Organization for Standardization's Open Systems Interconnect model for commu- nications. Furthermore, proponents said, these open standards must be controlled by consortia, not by any one vendor.

However, some insisted that the industry cannot wait for formal standards to be developed because that takes too long. What is needed in the interim are products that adhere to some generally agreed upon ways of doing things, even if they are not yet based on written standards.

Adapted with permission from *Computerworld* (June 24, 1991), p. 123. Copyright 1991 by CW Publishing, Inc., Framingham, MA 01701.

tem selects jobs based on priorities from this job queue. Batch jobs may be executed on a serial basis (one job at a time) or on a multitasking basis (multiple jobs concurrently). Most operating systems in personal computers work on a batch-serial basis without using spooling. (Serial versus multitasking execution is discussed in more detail later in this chapter.)

Interactive Systems

An **interactive operating system** allows users to interact directly with a computer from a terminal. With an interactive system, the user can interrupt a low-priority batch job and cause the computer to perform his or her high-priority work. An **interrupt** suspends the execution of a computer program in such a way that the program's execution can later be resumed. Interrupts are caused by events external to the program, such as requests for data or inputs of data from an interactive terminal.

Interactive operating systems must be multitasking systems. In addition, real-time systems must be interactive since real-time files must be updated immediately after real-world events occur.

In the next few sections of this chapter we will explore in more depth batch versus interactive operating systems and their relationships to multitasking, virtual storage, time-sharing and interactive computing, and multiprocessing. These systems are the predominant mainframe operating systems today. Personal computer operating systems are moving toward many of these capabilities, such as multitasking and virtual storage.

Multitasking (sometimes called multiprogramming) is the capability of a CPU to execute two or more programs concurrently. Multitasking capability is accomplished through the operating system. Two or more programs are stored concurrently in primary storage and the CPU moves from one program to another, executing part of each program in turn. Early computer systems and many personal computers execute programs on a batch-serial basis; that is, they execute each program in the order in which it is read into the system, and they execute only one program at a time. Newer PC operating systems, such as OS/2, support multitasking. Even Microsoft Windows, which is not a true operating system, allows PC users to multitask.

Multitasking

Advantages of Multitasking

Multitasking has four primary advantages: increased throughput, shorter response time, ability to assign priority to jobs, and improved primary storage allocation.

Increased Throughput   One disadvantage of the batch-serial approach to program execution is that it does not maximize throughput. **Throughput** is a measure of the total amount of processing that a computer system can complete over a fixed period of time. The disadvantage is due to the relative speeds of computer system components. The CPU operates without mechanical movement, depending only on the flow of electronic pulses, which travel at about half the speed of light. Therefore, it is very fast compared to input/output devices, which depend on mechanical movements or humans to operate them.

Figure 11–7 depicts the elapsed times necessary to execute one job under batch-serial and three jobs under multitasking. Total throughput is significantly increased in multitasking, because the CPU does not wait for input/output for the program it is executing. It simply rotates to another program and begins executing.

Shorter Response Time   Another disadvantage of the batch-serial approach is its longer turnaround time or response time. **Turnaround time** refers to the elapsed time between the submission of a batch job and the availability of the output. **Response time** refers to the elapsed time between submission of a command to an on-line system and the completion of that command as evidenced by a message on the terminal screen or printer.

Turnaround on small jobs usually takes longer in a batch-serial environment than it does in a multitasking environment. For example, refer to Figure 11–7. Assume that jobs 1 and 2 are long, requiring 1.5 and 0.75 hours of CPU time, respectively, and job 3 is short, requiring 1 minute of CPU time. Under the batch-serial approach, the turnaround time for job 3 would be 2.25 hours, plus execution time of about 1 minute. Under multitasking, the turnaround time for job 3 would be approximately 3 to 4 minutes, plus output printing time. Job 3 executes completely in a short elapsed time by utilizing the time in which the CPU would otherwise be waiting for I/O for jobs 1 and 2.

FIGURE 11–7
Elapsed Time under Batch-Serial and Multitasking Systems.

In this illustration, three jobs are executed in four minutes under multitasking, whereas only one job is executed in four minutes with a batch-serial operating system. The reason for the difference is that the multitasking operating system allows the CPU to execute other jobs while it is waiting for input/output to occur.

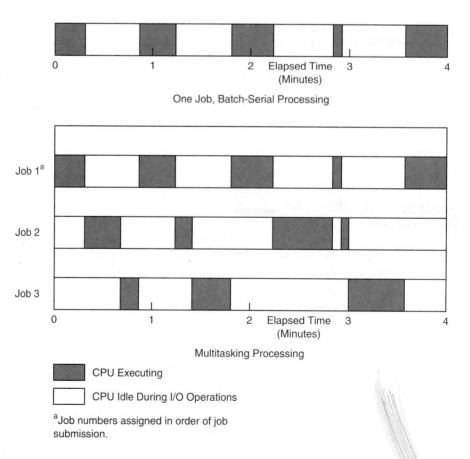

Turnaround time for short jobs can be greatly improved under multi-tasking, but turnaround time for long jobs is usually lengthened since the CPU devotes part of its time to short jobs. This is not a disadvantage, however, because long batch jobs usually have a lower priority than short jobs. Multitasking systems usually have priority schemes whereby any job, including a long one, can be executed under a high priority, if necessary.

Ability to Assign Priorities to Jobs   Most multitasking systems have schemes for setting priorities for rotating programs. They specify when the CPU will rotate to another program and which program it will rotate to. The user, through JCL or other control software, can specify the priority under which a job will execute.

Multitasking with priority schemes improves **system availability**; that is, it increases the speed with which the system can respond to high-priority, unanticipated requests on its resources. System availability under the batch-serial mode can be very poor when long jobs are executing. Under multitasking, high-priority jobs can be executed almost immediately.

On-line, real-time, and time-sharing systems would not be practical without multitasking. The response time at the terminals would be intolerable if all instructions from the terminals and the batch jobs were executed on a batch-serial basis. Instructions from terminals must be executed under high priority.

Improved Primary Storage Allocation   In early multitasking systems, the programs being executed all had to reside in primary storage until their execution was complete. A constraining factor on the throughput of a multitasking system is the number of jobs that can reside in primary storage at a given time. If only two large programs will fit in main memory, the CPU may be idle a large percentage of the time while waiting for I/O. The greater the number of programs that primary storage can hold, the greater the probability that the CPU will be able to execute at least one program while waiting for I/O for the others. This line of reasoning led to the approach of writing out to secondary storage the programs that were waiting for I/O. They were written back into primary storage when the I/O operation was completed and they were ready for additional execution. In the vacated primary storage space, a program that was ready and waiting for execution was written in. This approach cleared main storage of all programs waiting for I/O. Therefore, in principle, all the programs residing in primary storage were either running or awaiting execution. This technique led to the concept of virtual storage, which is discussed later in the chapter.

Disadvantages of Multitasking

Multitasking does have its disadvantages, but they are minor. One problem is that multitasking is implemented through an operating system, which is a program that requires space in primary storage since it is executed by the CPU. The operating system overhead (its primary storage requirements and CPU execution time requirements) is greater with multitasking than with batch-serial.

Another potential problem with multitasking systems is **interprogram interference**, either intentional or accidental. While executing, a program can theoretically write to any area of primary storage. Under multitasking other areas of primary storage contain other programs or their data. Therefore, a program can accidentally or intentionally interfere with another program while both are concurrently executing. To prevent these interferences, operating systems assign each program its own unique password while it is executing. In order to write to or read from, for example, program A's assigned area of primary storage, the writing or reading program must present the proper password. This password is known only to program A. Therefore, only program A has access to its area of primary storage and it is protected area from interference by other programs. Thus, the term **protected mode** is often used to refer to this capability.

Multitasking with Personal Computers

Most of us only execute one program at a time on a personal computer. Why would we want a multitasking capability in a PC operating system? (Current versions of MS-DOS do not support multitasking). As mentioned above, OS/2 and Windows support multitasking and MS-DOS 5.0 allows several programs to be resident in memory simultaneously. This allows users to quickly switch between these memory-resident programs. There are several reasons why multitasking is desirable for PCs:

1. Some PCs are set up in a multiuser configuration, with several simultaneous users connected to the same large PC. Thus, all the advantages of multitasking in a mini or mainframe environment apply here.

2. The resources of single large PCs (servers) are shared in a network. As networks of PCs increasingly replace minis and mainframes, multitasking will be required for PCs.

3. Even for stand-alone users of PCs it is convenient to be able to execute several applications simultaneously. Such capability allows a user to quickly move back and forth between applications without waiting for programs to load. Data and text can be moved easily between these simultaneously executing applications. Or you could have a continually executing program that monitors the stock market while you go about your daily work. Such a program could alert you to investment opportunities.

4. The essence of multitasking is the sharing of computer resources. Multitasking will help us share the power of PCs.

Virtual Storage

Virtual storage is primary storage that does not actually exist. It gives the programmer the illusion of a primary storage that is, for all practical purposes, unlimited. The computer system itself maintains this illusion through a combination of hardware and software techniques.

Before a program can be executed, each of its instructions must be resident in the real primary storage, but not all instructions of a program have to be resident at the same time. With virtual storage, only the instructions of the program that are currently executing are stored in primary storage; the remainder are stored on less expensive secondary storage, such as disks. Figure 11–8 illustrates virtual storage.

A virtual storage system divides every program into pages, each of which has a specified size (for example, 4K). The operating system rolls pages of programs into primary memory as they are needed for execution. Only the page of the program that is currently executing is stored in primary storage. All other program pages are stored on a peripheral disk unit until required for execution. The operating system also maintains tables that tell the CPU where in primary storage each page of a program is located. Figure 11–9 illustrates **paging**.

Advantages of Virtual Storage

Virtual storage has two major advantages. One advantage is that it fully utilizes the CPU. Pages of many different programs can reside in main storage simultaneously since only one page of each program is resident in primary storage at any time. Thus primary storage can contain pages of many different programs before encountering size constraints.

The second advantage is that programmers do not need to concern themselves about primary storage size constraints when writing programs for systems that use virtual storage. When the complete program has to reside in primary storage, an individual program's primary storage requirements cannot exceed the primary storage remaining after the operating system's requirements have been met. Under virtual storage, there is no practical limit on a program's primary storage requirements.

As mentioned before, personal computer operating systems are moving toward virtual storage capabilities. This allows them to execute larger programs. For example, the size of most electronic spreadsheets is constrained by primary memory size. Virtual storage capabilities will accommodate much larger spreadsheets.

Current developments in the virtual storage concept are tending toward a single-level storage concept. Single-level storage treats all storage, primary and secondary, as a single unit or level. Therefore, the real difference between primary and secondary storage is transparent to the user or programmer; in other words, a user or programmer can ignore the difference when using the system.

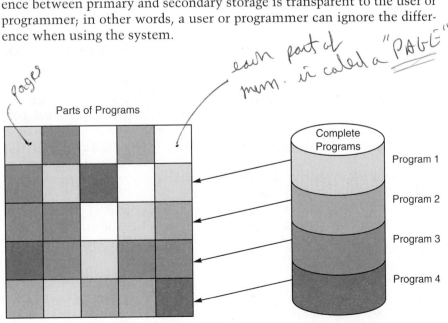

Parts of Programs

Primary Storage

Complete Programs

Program 1

Program 2

Program 3

Program 4

Secondary Storage

FIGURE 11–8
Overview of Virtual Storage.

Virtual storage allows the computer to execute a program even though only part of the program is in primary storage. The parts of a program are called pages. They are moved into and out of primary storage as they are needed for execution.

FIGURE 11–9
Paging in a Virtual Storage System.

Notice that to store all three of the illustrated programs would require 48K. However, because of the virtual storage capability, the CPU can execute all three of these programs concurrently even though only 16K of primary storage are available. For execution of a program to occur, only one page of the program must be in primary storage.

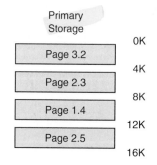

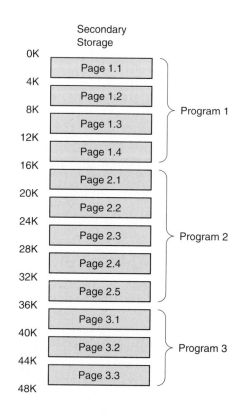

Disadvantages of Virtual Storage

As one might expect, there are disadvantages to virtual storage. Overhead costs are high. CPU and disk time is required to page (read/write) all those pages into and out of main storage. Additional primary storage is required to hold the tables that keep track of the pages, and to hold a virtual storage operating system.

Time-Sharing

A **time-sharing** system allows access to a CPU and data files through many remote terminals or workstations. The central computer system is often owned by the company whose employees use it, but there are also public time-sharing systems owned by time-sharing vendors which require users to pay for their services. The cost is based on a fixed charge plus a usage charge. The services that you can access with your personal computer to retrieve data or order products (such as the Source and the Dow Jones News Retrieval) execute on public time-sharing systems.

From the viewpoint of the user, the computer system appears to be dedicated exclusively to the user's terminal because of the fast response of the CPU to commands from the terminal. In reality, the CPU is servicing many terminals and perhaps several batch jobs. Multitasking is the method of implementing time-shared operations, since fast response to terminal commands is necessary.

Multiprocessing

As explained earlier in the chapter, a multitasking system executes two or more programs concurrently on a single CPU. In contrast, under **multiprocessing**, a single program is processed by two or more CPUs. The most typical type of multiprocessing occurs in systems that support both a batch mode and many remote terminals (see Figure 11–10). When a system has only a few remote terminals to support, the main CPU can handle all the terminal interrupts and trivial jobs, such as editing. However, the processing requirements of a large number of remote terminals can overload the main CPU. In this case, terminal interrupts and trivial jobs can be handled by a minicomputer, which in the configuration shown in Figure 11–10 is called a **front-end processor**. The main CPU processes batch jobs and executes interactive programs that the front-end processor cannot handle.

Personal computers often use multiprocessing. For example, many PCs use a math co-processor that handles mathematical processing at speeds up to 80 times faster than the PC's microprocessor.

Multiprocessing systems substantially increase the throughput capabilities of a system with an overloaded CPU. Another advantage of multiprocessing is the backup CPU capability provided by two or more CPUs, which are, in some cases, identical.

F I G U R E 11–10
A Multiprocessing System.

Multiprocessing is widely used with large computers. Some mainframe systems have several communications processors attached to them.

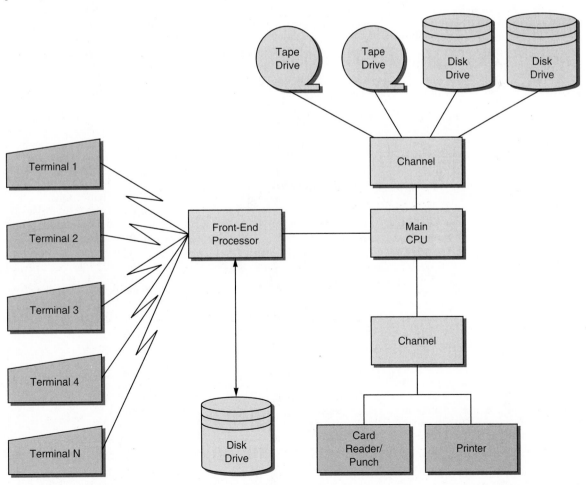

In recent years a new term, cooperative processing, has been used to signify a certain type of multiprocessing. Application 11–2 defines and provides an example of cooperative processing.

Types of Programming Languages

Software for large, complex, or unique applications is usually written by an application programmer to fulfill a particular user or application requirement. The development of application software should be performed using structured methodology, as discussed in Chapters 16 and 17. Before any coding (programming) is done, the application must be analyzed and a structured physical design must be developed. (The design is the programmer's blueprint for coding the application.) From the structured design specification, a suitable language is used to code each **program** (set of instructions executed by the computer.) The instructions cause the computer to perform a desired task.

APPLICATION 11–2

IS Takes Its First Steps into New Land

By David Gabel

Information systems managers discussing cooperative processing can be likened to the three blind men who described an elephant after respectively feeling its trunk, leg and tail. Cooperative processing means different things to different people.

Some IS [information systems] professionals who have developed cooperative processing to varying degrees, however, agree that the efforts have delivered payoffs at little cost and that the technology is poised to grow.

In a nutshell, cooperative processing refers to a system in which two or more computers, typically a host and workstations, share the processing of an application, with each handling the functions it does best while addressing the same database and communicating at the application level. . . .

Sony Corporation of America in Park Ridge, N.J., has encountered technical and managerial stumbling blocks in developing cooperative processing systems, but Robert Trenchard, senior vice president of MIS [management information systems], said the technology is the wave of the future.

Across the Board

With help from SQL, Information Builders, Inc. Focus and other products, Sony has employed cooperative processing in a variety of applications, including computer-aided software engineering, decision-support tools and systems for configuring complex products such as broadcast studio equipment. With a configuration system, users take orders on a PC, check them against information on the mainframe and then configure and price the orders using the mainframe.

"You're processing at different levels of your architecture," Trenchard said. "The PC is capturing, consolidating and concentrating, editing, validating and then transferring data to the mainframe."

Cooperative processing can cut the costs of running such systems, Trenchard said. Enabling PCs to handle the presentation work reduces communication between terminals and the host. That increases system throughput and response time, boosting the transactions that can be processed in a given period of time.

Among the obstacles Trenchard has encountered, however,

is the inability of PCs and their communications links to handle the transaction volumes Sony requires from some of the systems. Improvements in those products and modifications made to them by Sony have partially relieved such bottlenecks, he said.

Of greater concern, however, have been people problems. Even though Sony's move to cooperative processing is driven by top management in Japan, Trenchard found that some user managers are reluctant to yield control over their PC systems by having them linked with mainframe applications.

In such situations, it is better to try to introduce cooperative processing by "negotiating from above," Trenchard said. "If you can't get cooperation from the people, then don't try to use cooperative processing. It will fail every time. A large part of being in data processing is being a salesman."

Adapted with permission from *Computerworld* (January 31, 1989), pp. 23, 27. Copyright 1989 by CW Publishing, Inc., Framingham, MA 01701.

All computers understand only binary machine language, a string of 1s and 0s. However, programmers have developed complex programming languages that can instruct computers. Some are easy to learn, others are not. Some are better for business applications, others are better for scientific applications. Some languages are even like English.

The evolution of software is characterized by four stages, or generations. These begin with machine language and evolve through symbolic and procedural languages to the present-day fourth-generation languages.

Machine Language

Machine language, as the name implies, is a machine-oriented language. Programmers using such a language must be extremely familiar with the design, operation, and peripherals of a particular computer.

A machine language program is a set of instructions that have a one-to-one correspondence to every operation that must be performed by the computer. It is the only language that a computer can understand. All programs written in other languages must be compiled or translated into machine language for execution. A machine language program is also known as **object code** since its production is the *objective* of compilation or translation. Object code is machine-readable and requires no translation process before execution. This feature allows for extremely fast processing time and efficient use of primary storage.

However, programming in machine code is very tedious because the programmer is concerned not only with problem definition but also with clerical tasks such as manually assigning primary storage locations in which to store the data and program. The probability that the programmer may inadvertently write data or instructions into primary storage locations that contain other data or instructions, and thereby destroy them, is very high. Changes in instructions are extremely difficult to make because the programmer must reassign all references to storage locations manually, making the program inflexible. Because of the difficulties of programming in machine language, it is not used today. Instead, symbolic, procedural, or fourth-generation languages are used.

Symbolic Languages

As the evolution of software continued, second-generation **symbolic languages** were developed. The IBM **assembly language**, which uses **mnemonics** or symbols for each machine language instruction, is an example. Assembly language allows the programmer to specify constants and storage locations symbolically. This feature takes some of the tediousness out of programming in machine language and gives the responsibility to a program called an **assembler**. The assembler translates the assembly language program into machine code and then references and assigns all addresses and storage locations.

Like machine language, an assembly language is designed for a specific machine. Therefore, the program makes efficient use of the time and resources of the CPU. In general, it maintains a one-to-one correspondence between instructions and actual computer operations. Each symbol corresponds to one machine operation and is descriptive of that particular operation.

An assembly or higher-level language program is known as **source code**. It is written by an application programmer and must be translated or compiled into object code (machine language code) before it is executed.

Since machine language code and assembly languages are difficult to comprehend, a simple example is used to illustrate the nature and complexity of programming in these languages. Figure 11–11 illustrates a simple program that adds two variables, X and Y, and then places the result in a third variable, SUM. In **pseudocode**, the program is expressed as follows:

```
program ADD;
  declare X      real initial (1),
          Y      real initial (2),
          SUM    real;
  SUM = X + Y;
end ADD;
```

Today, application programmers seldom write in assembly language, though some use it to write programs that are executed many times (such as arithmetic functions and specialized input/output programs). Assembler is also used to provide access to operating system resources that may not be available in high-level languages, such as graphics and physical input and output. Because assembly language programs are efficient in terms of processing time and primary storage utilization, assembly language is generally used by systems programmers who write operating system programs. For these programs, execution time is a primary consideration.

Procedural Languages   *3rd generation*

The third generation of software evolution brought about the development of procedure-oriented, high-level languages (FORTRAN, COBOL, and PL/1). A **procedural language** is a language in which the programmer gives step-by-step instructions to the computer. A **compiler** for the procedural language generates the necessary machine language instructions for the computer. These languages help bridge the semantic gap between problem definition and the language.

With these machine-independent languages, the programmer needs to know very little about the machine on which the program is executed. Programming is simplified because a buffer, the compiler, handles all cross-referencing and storage allocation. However, processing speed and efficient use of computer memory are sacrificed for the advantage of simplified programming.

The procedural language program must go through three processes before it is ready to be executed:

1. **Translation** (compilation)—The translator (compiler) program translates the source code into object code (machine language code).

2. **Linking**—The linkage editor combines with the program any called instructions or library routines.

3. **Loading**—The loader program loads the object code and its appended library functions and instructions into main memory for execution.

Machine Code					Assembly Language			Explanation
MEMORY					STMT	SOURCE	STATEMENT	
LOCATION	OBJECT	CODE	ADDR1	ADDR2	1 ADD	CSECT		;IDENTIFIES BEGINNING/NAME OF PGM
0000000					2	USING	*,15	;IDENTIFIES R15 AS BASE REGISTER
				00000	3	L	2,X	;LOAD '1' INTO R2
000000	5820	F010	00010		4	A	2,Y	;ADD '2' TO CONTENTS OF R2
000004	5A20	F014	00014		5	ST	2,SUM	;STORE CONTENTS OF R2 IN SUM
000008	5020	F018	00018		6	BR	14	;RETURN CONTROL TO CALLER PGM
00000C	07FE							
00000E	0000				7 X	DC	F`1'	;RESERVE MEMORY LOCATION FOR X, INIT TO '1'
000010	00000001				8 Y	DC	F`2'	;RESERVE MEMORY LOCATION FOR Y, INIT TO '2'
000014	00000002				9 SUM	DS	F	;RESERVE MEMORY LOCATION FOR SUM
000018					10	END		

FIGURE 11–11

A Program Coded in Machine and Assembly Language.

These two programs merely add X to Y and place the result in SUM. What an incredible amount of detail to perform such a simple operation! It is no wonder that procedural languages for computers were developed.

Figure 11–12 illustrates these processes. They are performed for most high-level programming languages.

In the following discussion we will illustrate selected languages with an example that calculates and prints a payroll report called the payroll register. A description of the program is as follows:

1. Print the header for the payroll register.

2. For each employee, read in a record containing the job code that identifies the type of job the employee holds, the employee's Social Security number, the number of hours worked, and the current hourly wage.

   a. If the job code is equal to 1111 then the employee works part-time and no deductions are taken except for federal and state income taxes.

   b. If the job code is equal to 1120 then the employee works full time and all deductions are taken except for credit union dues.

   c. If the job code is equal to 1122 then the employee works full time and all deductions are taken.

3. Calculate the payroll for each employee with a valid job code, or print an error message.

4. Finally, when the end of the input file is reached, print the totals for the payroll register.

This program is designed to process any number of employees and print the total net earnings. A sample of the output, the payroll register, is illustrated in Figure 11–13.

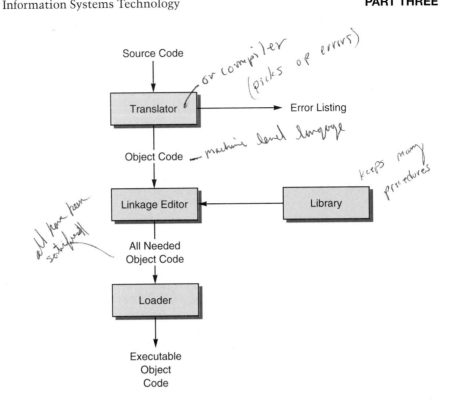

or compiler (picks of errors)

machine level language

keeps many procedures

all have been satisfied

	Payroll Register									
Job Code	Employee Number	Hours Worked	Hourly Wage	Gross Pay	Social Security Tax	Federal Income Tax	State Income Tax	Credit Union	Retirement	Net Pay
1111	400941648	33.00	4.51	148.83	0.00	1.04	1.19	0.00	0.00	146.60
1122	224949460	40.00	5.10	204.00	13.67	23.05	6.12	10.20	10.20	140.76
1120	900221792	44.00	4.51	207.46	13.90	23.44	6.22	0.00	10.37	153.52
1122	224885493	45.00	7.25	344.38	23.07	38.91	10.33	17.22	17.22	237.62
1111	900120001	25.00	3.25	81.25	0.00	0.57	0.65	0.00	0.00	80.03

FIGURE 11–13
Payroll Register.
The term *register* is often used for computer reports, especially those used for accounting applications.

COBOL   COBOL (Common Business-Oriented Language) is one of the leading and most widely used business-oriented programming languages today. Thus, we have selected COBOL to illustrate procedural languages. This language is considered to be the industry standard for business-oriented languages. COBOL was first conceived in 1959 by a group of users, programmers, and manufacturers from the government and business sectors, referred to as the CODASYL Committee (Conference On DAta SYstems Languages). The goal of this committee was to design and implement an English-like common business language. In December, 1959, the initial specifications for COBOL had been drafted with the basic objectives of being highly machine independent and enough like English to be self-documenting.

The first version of COBOL, known as COBOL–60, was published in 1960. The second version was released in 1961, and it included many changes in the procedure division. An extended version of COBOL–61 became available in 1963, which included sorting and report writing routines. The different versions of COBOL led to a **portability** (transferability) problem: there were too many dialects in the language to allow programs to be transferred from one machine to another. In September 1962, the American National Standards Institute formed a committee to standardize COBOL. This committee finally used COBOL–68 as a basis for COBOL standardization. The standardization process was a very strict one, thereby solving the portability problem. This makes COBOL a truly common language. The CODASYL Committee, in an effort to update the language, meets on a regular basis every year.

Because COBOL is English-like, the language is easy to read and code. COBOL can be loosely compared to an English composition that consists of headings, sections, paragraphs, and sentences. Various aspects of the COBOL language are shown in Figure 11–14.

The COBOL program is divided into four major parts called **divisions**. Each division and its function is listed here in the order that it must appear within a program.

1. The *identification division* identifies the name and various documentary entries of the program.

2. The *environment division* identifies the input/output hardware needed to support the program.

3. The *data division* identifies the storage record layout for the input, the output, and the intermediate results (working storage).

4. The *procedure division* contains the instructions that tell the computer what operations to perform. This division is most like programs written in other languages.

All divisions except the identification division are further divided into **sections**. The procedure division has a structure different from the other divisions. It consists only of **sentences**, which are combinations of **statements**. For example, look at statement 64 in Figure 11–14:

```
MOVE 0.067 TO WS-FCRATE.
```

This is an imperative sentence that tells the computer to assign the value 0.067 to the variable WS-FCRATE.

Next look at statements 54 through 56:

```
IF I-JOBCODE IS EQUAL 1122
    THEN
        PERFORM JOBCODE-1120-PARA
        PERFORM JOBCODE-1122-PARA.
```

This is a conditional sentence in which
```
        PERFORM JOBCODE-1120-PARA.
```

is a statement beginning with the verb PERFORM.

FIGURE 11–14
Payroll Program
Written in COBOL.
Notice how long this
program is compared to
the payroll register
program written in
FOCUS in Figure 11–17.
No wonder COBOL is
considered wordy! This
wordiness supposedly
improves COBOL's
readability. Examine the
procedure division
starting at statement 33
and determine whether
you think COBOL is
more understandable
than the FOCUS
program.

```
     IDENTIFICATION DIVISION.
     PROGRAM-ID.
         PAYROLL.
     ENVIRONMENT DIVISION.
     CONFIGURATION SECTION.
     SPECIAL-NAMES.
         C01 IS TOP-OF-PAGE.
     INPUT-OUTPUT SECTION.
     FILE-CONTROL.
         SELECT CARD-IN-FILE ASSIGN TO UT-S-SYSIN.
         SELECT LINE-OUT-FILE ASSIGN TO UT-S-SYSOUT.
     DATA DIVISION.
     FILE SECTION.
     FD CARD-IN-FILE
         LABEL RECORDS ARE OMITTED.
     01 CARD-IN-RECORD.
         05 I-JOBCODE      PICTURE X(4).
         05 I-EMPNO        PICTURE X(9).
         05 I-HOURS        PICTURE 999V99.
         05 I-RATE         PICTURE 99V99.
         05 FILLER         PICTURE X(58).
     FD LINE-OUT-FILE
         LABEL RECORDS ARE OMITTED.
     01 LINE-OUT-RECORD  PICTURE X(133).
     WORKING-STORAGE SECTION.
         77 WS-EXTRA       PICTURE 999V99.
         77 WS-OTIME       PICTURE 999V99.
   1     77 WS-TOTAL       PICTURE 999V99 VALUE ZEROES.
         77 WS-FCRATE      PICTURE 9V999.
         77 WS-FTRATE      PICTURE 9V999.
         77 WS-STRATE      PICTURE 9V999.
         77 WS-RTRATE      PICTURE 9V999.
         77 WS-CURATE      PICTURE 9V999.
         77 WS-WHRS        PICTURE 999V99.
         77 WS-GROSS       PICTURE 9999V99.
         77 WS-FICA        PICTURE 999V99.
         77 WS-FIT         PICTURE 999V99.
         77 WS-SIT         PICTURE 999V99.
         77 WS-CUNION      PICTURE 999V99.
         77 WS-RETIRE      PICTURE 999V99.
         77 WS-NET         PICTURE 9999V99.
   2     01 OUT-OF-CARDS-FLAG PICTURE X VALUE 'N'.
         88 OUT-OF-CARDS                 VALUE 'Y'.
   3     01 FLAG             PICTURE X VALUE 'N'.
         01 WS-DETAIL-LINE.
   4        05 FILLER         PICTURE XXX VALUE SPACES.
            05 JOBCODE        PICTURE X(4).
   5        05 FILLER         PICTURE X(5) VALUE SPACES.
            05 EMPNO          PICTURE X(9).
```

```
6       05 FILLER            PICTURE X(4) VALUE SPACES.
        05 HOURS             PICTURE ZZ9V99.
7       05 FILLER            PICTURE X(4) VALUE SPACES.
        05 RATE              PICTURE ZZ9V99.
8       05 FILLER            PICTURE X(4) VALUE SPACES.
        05 GROSS             PICTURE ZZZ9V99.
9       05 FILLER            PICTURE X(5) VALUE SPACES.
        05 FICA              PICTURE ZZ9V99.
10      05 FILLER            PICTURE X(6) VALUE SPACES.
        05 FIT               PICTURE ZZ9V99.
11      05 FILLER            PICTURE X(4) VALUE SPACES.
        05 SIT               PICTURE ZZ9V99.
12      05 FILLER            PICTURE X(4) VALUE SPACES.
        05 CUNION            PICTURE ZZ9V99.
13      05 FILLER            PICTURE X(6) VALUE SPACES.
        05 RETIRE            PICTURE ZZ9V99.
14      05 FILLER            PICTURE X(6) VALUE SPACES.
        05 NET               PICTURE ZZZ9V99.
15      05 FILLER            PICTURE X(14) VALUE SPACES.
    01 WS-HEADER-LINE.
16      05 FILLER            PICTURE X(51) VALUE SPACES.
        05 FILLER            PICTURE X(16)
17         VALUE "Payroll Register'.
18      05 FILLER            PICTURE X(66) VALUE SPACES.
    01 WS-COL-LINE-1.
19      05 FILLER            PICTURE X(57) VALUE SPACES.
        05 FILLER            PICTURE X(28)
20         VALUE 'Social Federal State'.
21      05 FILLER            PICTURE X(58) VALUE SPACES.
    01 WS-COL-LINE-2.
22      05 FILLER            PICTURE XX VALUE SPACES.
        05 FILLER            PICTURE X(118)
23      VALUE 'Job       Employee    Hours     Hourly      Gross
    -   '           Security   Income    Income    Credit
    -   '                       Net'.
24      05 FILLER            PICTURE X(16) VALUE SPACES.
    01 WS-COL-LINE-3.
25      05 FILLER            PICTURE XXX VALUE SPACES.
        05 FILLER            PICTURE X(117)
26         VALUE 'Code    Number    Worked    Wage      Pay
    -              '   Tax       Tax        Tax      Union    Reti
    -              'rement Pay'.
    -              'rement Pay'.
27      05 FILLER            PICTURE X(16) VALUE SPACES.
    01 WS-FOOTER-LINE.
28      05 FILLER            PICTURE X(96) VALUE SPACES.
        05 FILLER            PICTURE X(16)
29         VALUE 'Total Earnings: '.
        05 TOTAL-EARNINGS PICTURE ZZZZ9.99
30      05 FILLER            PICTURE X(14) VALUE SPACES.
```

```
31  01 EMPTY-LINE        PICTURE X(133) VALUE SPACES.
    01 ERROR-MSG         PICTURE X(21)
32      VALUE 'Invalid job code'.
33      PROCEDURE DIVISION.
        MAIN-LINE-ROUTINE.
34          OPEN INPUT CARD-IN-FILE
                    OUTPUT LINE-OUT-FILE
35          PERFORM HEADER-PARAGRAPH.
36          READ CARD-IN-FILE
37              AT END MOVE 'Y' TO OUT-OF-CARDS-FLAG.
38          PERFORM PROCESS-PAYROLL
                    UNTIL OUT-OF-CARDS.
39          PERFORM FOOTER-PARAGRAPH.
40          CLOSE CARD-IN-FILE
                    LINE-OUT-FILE.
        MAIN-LINE-ROUTINE-EXIT.
41          STOP RUN.
        HEADER-PARAGRAPH.
42          WRITE LINE-OUT-RECORD FROM WS-HEADER-LINE
                AFTER ADVANCING TOP-OF-PAGE.
43          WRITE LINE-OUT-RECORD FROM WS-COL-LINE-1
                AFTER ADVANCING 2 LINES.
44          WRITE LINE-OUT-RECORD FROM WS-COL-LINE-2
                AFTER ADVANCING 1 LINES.
45          WRITE LINE-OUT-RECORD FROM WS-COL-LINE-3
                AFTER ADVANCING 1 LINES.
46          WRITE LINE-OUT-RECORD FROM EMPTY-LINE
                AFTER ADVANCING 1 LINES.
        PROCESS-PAYROLL.
47          MOVE 'Y' TO FLAG.
48          MOVE ZEROS TO WS-OTIME, WS-FCRATE, WS-FTRATE,
                          WS-STRATE, WS-RTRATE, WS-CURATE
49          MOVE 1-HOURS TO WS-WHRS.
50          IF 1-JOBCODE IS EQUAL 1111
                THEN
51                  PERFORM JOBCODE-1111-PARA
                ELSE
52          IF I-JOBCODE IS EQUAL 1120
                THEN
53                  PERFORM JOBCODE-1120-PARA
                ELSE
54          IF I-JOBCODE IS EQUAL 1122
                THEN
55                  PERFORM JOBCODE-1120-PARA
56                  PERFORM JOBCODE-1122-PARA.
57          PERFORM COMPUTE-PAYROLL-PARAGRAPH.
58          PERFORM WRITE-LINE-PARAGRAPH.
59          READ CARD-IN-FILE
60              AT END MOVE 'Y' TO OUT-OF-CARDS-FLAG.
        JOBCODE-1111-PARA.
61              MOVE 0.007 TO WS-FTRATE.
62              MOVE 0.008 TO WS-STRATE.
```

```
63                MOVE 'N' TO FLAG.
         JOBCODE-1120-PARA.
64           MOVE 0.067 TO WS-FCRATE.
65           MOVE 0.113 TO WS-FTRATE.
66           MOVE 0.03 TO WS-STRATE.
67           MOVE 0.05 TO WS-RTRATE.
68           IF I-HOURS IS GREATER THAN 40.0
                  THEN
69                   SUBTRACT 40.0 FROM I-HOURS GIVING WS-EXTRA
70                   COMPUTE WS-OTIME ROUNDED =
                           WS-EXTRA * I-RATE * 1.5
71                   MOVE 40.0 TO WS-WHRS.
72           MOVE 'N' TO FLAG.
         JOBCODE-1122-PARA.
73           MOVE 0.05 TO WS-CURATE.
74           MOVE 'N' TO FLAG.
         COMPUTE-PAYROLL-PARAGRAPH.
75           COMPUTE WS-GROSS ROUNDED = (WS-WHRS * I-RATE) + WS-OTIME.
76           MULTIPLY WS-GROSS BY WS-FCRATE GIVING WS-FICA ROUNDED.
77           MULTIPLY WS-GROSS BY WS-FTRATE GIVING WS-FIT ROUNDED.
78           MULTIPLY WS-GROSS BY WS-STRATE GIVING WS-SIT ROUNDED.
79           MULTIPLY WS-GROSS BY WS-RTRATE GIVING WS-RETIRE ROUNDED.
80           MULTIPLY WS-GROSS BY WS-CURATE GIVING WS-CUNION ROUNDED.
81           COMPUTE WS-NET = WS-GROSS -
                     (WS-FICA + WS-FIT + WS-SIT + WS-RETIRE + WS-CUNION)
82           ADD WS-NET TO WS-TOTAL.
         WRITE-LINE-PARAGRAPH.
83           IF FLAG = 'N'
                  THEN
84                   MOVE I-JOBCODE TO JOBCODE
85                   MOVE I-EMPNO TO EMPNO
86                   MOVE I-HOURS TO HOURS
87                   MOVE I-RATE TO RATE
88                   MOVE WS-GROSS TO GROSS
89                   MOVE WS-FICA TO FICA
90                   MOVE WS-FIT TO FIT
91                   MOVE WS-SIT TO SIT
92                   MOVE WS-CUNION TO CUNION
93                   MOVE WS-RETIRE TO RETIRE
94                   MOVE WS-NET TO NET
95                   WRITE LINE-OUT-RECORD FROM WS-DETAIL-LINE
                        AFTER ADVANCING 1 LINES
                  ELSE
96                   WRITE LINE-OUT-RECORD FROM ERROR-MSG
                        AFTER ADVANCING 1 LINES.
         FOOTER-PARAGRAPH.
97           MOVE WS-TOTAL TO TOTAL-EARNINGS.
98           WRITE LINE-OUT-RECORD FROM WS-FOOTER-LINE
                  AFTER ADVANCING 2 LINES.
99           WRITE LINE-OUT-RECORD FROM EMPTY-LINE
                  AFTER ADVANCING TOP-OF-PAGE.
```

A statement is a combination of **words**, symbols, and phrases beginning with a COBOL verb. COBOL words are of three types:

- **Reserved words** have special meaning to the compiler. The COBOL verbs COMPUTE, ADD, and SUBTRACT are examples.

- **User-defined words** are created by the programmer. Examples in Figure 11–14 are CARD-IN-FILE, LINE-OUT-FILE, and MAIN-LINE-ROUTINE.

- **System names** are supplied by the manufacturer of the hardware to allow certain elements in the program to correspond with various hardware devices. Examples are UT-S-SYSIN specifying the card reader and UT-S-SYSOUT specifying the line printer in the input/output section of the environment division in Figure 11–14.

COBOL is a very standardized language and therefore can be easily used by different kinds of computers. The advantage of COBOL is that it was conceived especially for data processing. It can manipulate many different types of data files, and it is much more readable and self-documenting than most languages. However, users sacrifice efficient coding and execution because of its wordiness. Also, because of the nature of the syntax of COBOL, **semantic errors** can occur that are difficult to detect. For report generation, COBOL can be an extremely useful tool because of its report writer facility. COBOL has limited facilities for mathematical notation, but excellent capabilities for character and file processing. COBOL compilers are available for microcomputers.

Fourth-Generation Languages

A **fourth-generation language (4GL)** is a flexible development tool that enables users and programmers to develop applications by describing to the computer what they want rather than by writing a procedural program. A procedural program specifies the detail steps that a program must execute. Because 4GLs do not specify the detail steps, they are often called **nonprocedural languages**. Examples of fourth-generation languages include electronic spreadsheets, query languages, and application generators.

Many different fourth-generation languages are available, and they execute on all sizes of computers. Fourth-generation languages are one of the primary reasons that application development by users is possible. This section examines FOCUS and dBASE, which are representative of 4GLs.

FOCUS   FOCUS was developed in the mid-1970s by Information Builders. Initially it would execute only on IBM mainframes. However, today it will execute on a wide variety of mainframes, minis, and personal computers, and it is the most widely used 4GL of its type. FOCUS is best classified as an application development tool that is suitable for use by both programmers and end users.

FOCUS has data storage, data maintenance, and data analysis capabilities. In data storage it has a complete database facility that stores data in hierarchical, relational, or a combination of hierarchical and relational forms. A master file description is used in FOCUS to establish a database. Figure 11–15 illustrates a master file description of an employee file. This file is hierarchical, with segments on two levels, as illustrated in Figure 11–16. FOCUS also has an interactive facility called FILETALK, which creates a master file description for the user. This facility interactively asks the user for the information required in a master file description and simultaneously creates the description at the bottom of the display screen. FOCUS also accesses data stored in a wide variety of non-FOCUS databases and files, such as IBM's Information Management System (IMS) and DB2 database management systems.

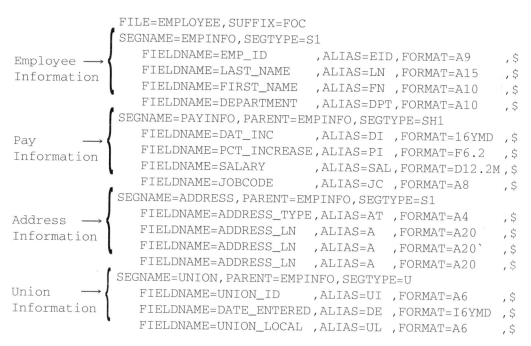

```
                        FILE=EMPLOYEE,SUFFIX=FOC
                        SEGNAME=EMPINFO,SEGTYPE=S1
Employee  ──┐              FIELDNAME=EMP_ID           ,ALIAS=EID,FORMAT=A9      ,$
Information ┤              FIELDNAME=LAST_NAME        ,ALIAS=LN ,FORMAT=A15     ,$
           ┤              FIELDNAME=FIRST_NAME       ,ALIAS=FN ,FORMAT=A10     ,$
           ┘              FIELDNAME=DEPARTMENT       ,ALIAS=DPT,FORMAT=A10     ,$
                        SEGNAME=PAYINFO,PARENT=EMPINFO,SEGTYPE=SH1
Pay       ──┐              FIELDNAME=DAT_INC          ,ALIAS=DI ,FORMAT=16YMD   ,$
Information ┤              FIELDNAME=PCT_INCREASE     ,ALIAS=PI ,FORMAT=F6.2    ,$
           ┤              FIELDNAME=SALARY           ,ALIAS=SAL,FORMAT=D12.2M  ,$
           ┘              FIELDNAME=JOBCODE          ,ALIAS=JC ,FORMAT=A8      ,$
                        SEGNAME=ADDRESS,PARENT=EMPINFO,SEGTYPE=S1
Address   ──┐              FIELDNAME=ADDRESS_TYPE     ,ALIAS=AT ,FORMAT=A4      ,$
Information ┤              FIELDNAME=ADDRESS_LN       ,ALIAS=A  ,FORMAT=A20     ,$
           ┤              FIELDNAME=ADDRESS_LN       ,ALIAS=A  ,FORMAT=A20`     ,$
           ┘              FIELDNAME=ADDRESS_LN       ,ALIAS=A  ,FORMAT=A20     ,$
                        SEGNAME=UNION,PARENT=EMPINFO,SEGTYPE=U
Union     ──┐              FIELDNAME=UNION_ID         ,ALIAS=UI ,FORMAT=A6      ,$
Information ┤              FIELDNAME=DATE_ENTERED     ,ALIAS=DE ,FORMAT=I6YMD   ,$
           ┘              FIELDNAME=UNION_LOCAL      ,ALIAS=UL ,FORMAT=A6      ,$
```

FIGURE 11–15
FOCUS Master File Description of an Employee File.

In the data maintenance area FOCUS has complete transaction processing facilities. Input data may be validated and logged before files are updated. Transaction data may originate from disk, tape, or on-line terminals. FIDEL (FOCUS Interactive Data Entry Language) enables the user to easily develop formatted screens for on-line data entry and display.

The data analysis and reporting facilities of FOCUS allow reports, queries, monochrome and color graphics, statistical analysis, and financial modeling. FOCUS also has its own electronic spreadsheet called FOCCALC.

Reports are produced in FOCUS through the TABLE command. Figure 11–17 illustrates a FOCUS procedure that produces the same payroll register produced by the COBOL program in this chapter. First, notice how short this procedure is compared to COBOL. FOCUS automatically handles many of the details that COBOL and other languages require a programmer to specify at great length.

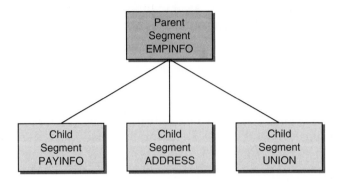

In the first part of the procedure, the programmer used the DEFINE FILE PAYFILE ADD command to create temporary files that would hold the appropriate rates for the taxes, retirement, and union dues rates. These rates vary depending on the employee's job code. FOCUS allows the IF-THEN-ELSE selection logic for the rates to be coded directly in the arithmetic assignment statements, as illustrated.

FIGURE 11–17
Payroll Program
Written in FOCUS.

Notice how concise this
program is compared to
the third-generation
programs. They all
produce the same payroll
register.

```
                 DEFINE FILE PAYFILE ADD
   FCRATE/D4.3 = IF JOBCODE EQ 1120 OR 1122 THEN .067
                 ELSE 0.0;
   FTRATE/D4.3 = IF JOBCODE EQ 1111 THEN .007
                 ELSE IF JOBCODE EQ 1120 OR 1122 THEN .113
                 ELSE 0.0;
   STRATE/D4.3 = IF JOBCODE EQ 1111 THEN .008
                 ELSE IF JOBCODE EQ 1120 OR 1122 THEN .03
                 ELSE 0.0;
   RTRATE/D4.3 = IF JOBCODE EQ 1120 OR 1122 THEN .05
                 ELSE 0.0;
   CURATE/D4.3 = IF JOBCODE EQ 1122 THEN .05
                 ELSE 0.0;
TABLE FILE PAYFILE
  HEADING CENTER
    "PAYROLL REGISTER"
  PRINT JOBCODE AND EMPNO AND HOURS AND RATE AND COMPUTE
    GROSS AS 'Gross,Pay' =
      IF HOURS LE 40.0 THEN WHRS*RATE
      ELSE (40.0*RATE)+((HOURS-40.0)*RATE*1.5);
    FICA AS 'Social,Security,Tax'=GROSS*FCRATE;
    FIT AS 'Federal,Income,Tax'=GROSS*FTRATE;
    SIT AS 'State,Income,Tax'=GROSS*STRATE;
    CUNION AS 'Credit,Union'=GROSS*CURATE;
    RETIRE AS 'Retirement'=GROSS*RTRATE;
    NET AS 'Net,Pay'=GROSS-(FICA+FIT+SIT+RETIRE+CUNION);
  SUM NET AND COLUMN-TOTAL
END
```

The command TABLE FILE PAYFILE produces the payroll register. First the user prints the report heading. Then the user tells FOCUS which data fields to print in each column of the report. Notice that most of the fields are computed in the PRINT command with the COMPUTE verb. The column headings for EMPNO, HOURS, and RATE are picked up from headings entered in the master file description. Column headings for the computed fields are entered in the COMPUTE statement with the AS phrase. Finally, the user tells FOCUS to sum the net field and to print it as a total at the bottom of the column.

FOCUS has an interactive reporting facility called TABLETALK, which works with reports as FILETALK does with master file descriptions. TABLETALK interactively queries the user for the specifications necessary to produce a report while simultaneously creating the TABLE FILE procedure at the bottom of the screen.

Fourth-generation languages like FOCUS will be used widely in the future. They have many advantages. Applications can be developed up to ten times faster with 4GLs than with third-generation languages. In addition, 4GLs allow end users to develop many of their own applications.

Unfortunately, FOCUS and other fourth-generation languages do have disadvantages. Generally, they do not perform well in a high-volume, on-line, transaction processing application in which a large number of terminals update files simultaneously. With such a system, they produce terminal response times that are much too slow. For example, recently a motor vehicles system was built for the state of New Jersey using a 4GL language. The system was supposed to handle 1,000 terminals. But with only 220 terminals on-line, it bogged down and frequently produced response times of one to two minutes. The transaction processing parts of the system had to be rewritten in COBOL to solve the response time problem. It should be noted, though, that the high-volume transaction processing capabilities of 4GLs are gradually being improved. Also, as computers become more powerful, they will execute the 4GLs faster.

dBASE   dBASE II, dBASE III plus, and most recently dBASE IV are different versions of **dBASE**, a relational database management system for personal computers marketed by Ashton-Tate. While many people use only dBASE's interactive query language, the package also comes with the ability to create program files that access and manipulate database files (see Figure 11–18). These program files are made up of the commands available in the interactive query language and of certain program control commands (for example, DO WHILE, IF-ELSE) that can be used only within a program or command file.

Users of dBASE create command files for a number of reasons. They may routinely issue a set of commands to input or extract certain information from a database. It takes less time to link these commands together in a command file than to type them in each time they are used. Longer, more complicated programs are written by many dBASE users to create a user interface of menus, screens, and reports that guide the user through a set of tasks.

dBASE is used almost exclusively for business applications. It is considered by most to be a fourth-generation programming language. It does have a number of advantages over procedural languages. First, since dBASE is part of a database management system, easy-to-use but very powerful file management commands are available to the user. Consider the payroll application that has been used as an example in this chapter. A dBASE program that accesses that same payroll file and prints the employee number and the hours worked for all employees who worked more than forty hours could be written in one line:

```
LIST EMPNO, HOURS FOR HOURS>40 TO PRINT
```

A program to do the same thing in a third-generation procedural language would require a number of lines set into and around a loop that sequentially accesses the file. The dBASE program states *what* it wants, not *how* to do it. Languages of this sort are called nonprocedural because they state only the result of a procedure and not the steps in the procedure itself.

```
PROCEDURE MAIN
SET MARGIN TO 5
SET TALK OFF
SET PRINT ON
? "                                          SOCIAL    FEDERAL
  STATE"
? " JOB        EMPLOYEE HOURS HOURLY  GROSS  SECURITY  INCOME
INCOME CREDIT             NET"
? "CODE         NUMBER  WORKED WAGE   PAY    TAX       TAX
 TAX  UNION  RETIREMENT  PAY"
?
SET PRINT OFF
USE PAYFILE
DO WHILE.NOT.EOF( )
   STORE 0 TO FTRATE
   STORE 0 TO STRATE
   STORE 0 TO FCRATE
   STORE 0 TO RTRATE
   STORE 0 TO CURATE
   IF JOBCODE=1111
      STORE 0.007 TO FTRATE
      STORE 0.008 TO STRATE
      DO CALC
   ELSE
     IF JOBCODE=1120.OR.JOBCODE=1122
        STORE 0.067 TO FCRATE
        STORE 0.113 TO FTRATE
        STORE 0.03 TO STRATE
        STORE 0.05 TO RTRATE
        IF JOBCODE=1122
           STORE 0.05 TO CURATE
        ENDIF
        DO CALC
     ELSE
        DO ERROR
```

```
      ENDIF
   ENDIF
   SKIP
ENDDO
SUM NET TO RAMNETPAY
SET MARGIN TO 62
SET PRINT ON
?
? "TOTAL NET EARNINGS ARE:",RAMNETPAY
?
SET PRINT OFF
SET MARGIN TO 0
CLOSE DATABASES
RETURN
PROCEDURE CALC
STORE 0 TO OTIME
IF HOURS>40
   STORE (HOURS-40)*RATE*1.5 TO OTIME
   REPLACE GROSS WITH (40*RATE)+OTIME
ELSE
   REPLACE GROSS WITH (HOURS*RATE)
ENDIF
REPLACE FICA WITH GROSS*FCRATE
REPLACE FIT WITH GROSS*FTRATE
REPLACE SIT WITH GROSS*STRATE
REPLACE RETIRE WITH GROSS*RTRATE
REPLACE CUNION WITH GROSS*CURATE
REPLACE NET WITH GROSS-(FICA+FIT+SIT+RETIRE+CUNION)
SET PRINT ON
? JOBCODE,EMPNO,HOURS,RATE,GROSS,FICA,FIT,SIT,CUNION,RETIRE,NET
SET PRINT OFF
RETURN
PROCEDURE ERROR
SET PRINT ON
? JOBCODE,EMPNO,HOURS,RATE," **** ERROR: INVALID JOBCODE ****"
SET PRINT OFF
RETURN
```

dBASE also provides tools for screen, report, and even program generation. A screen generator is a tool by which a user can quickly design a screen on which data are input or read. The dBASE report generator is a form filling tool by which a person can format a report that is generated from one or more files without ever writing a single line of program code. In fact, the payroll program illustrated in this chapter could be quickly and easily generated in this manner. An application or program generator uses screen and menu definitions, file structures, report forms from the report generator, and so on to generate actual program code for an application. The combination of ease of use and power that dBASE provides makes it an extremely popular personal computer programming language.

Object-Oriented Programming

Programming has been and continues to be a labor-intensive process. If we are to realize the full potential of computer information systems we must find ways to reduce the costs of producing programs. Traditionally, programmers have started from scratch in building a program. This is true even though many of the tasks that must be done are very similar to those in other programs. Why can't programming code developed for one program be used in others? Why can't we turn programmers into "quilters" instead of "weavers"? For example, every payroll program in the United States must compute federal withholding taxes. The steps to compute federal withholding taxes are the same regardless of the payroll program. Programmers should be able to pull a module (object) off the shelf that computes federal withholding tax and "sew" it into their program just as quilters sew pieces of fabric together to produce a quilt rather than weaving each individual piece. In the case of federal tax withholding, commercially available modules can be purchased and incorporated into payroll programs. However, there are many similar tasks for which no modules are available.

Object-oriented programming is a programming methodology whose objective is to produce program modules that can be reused in other programs. Reusability is the essence of object-oriented programming. With object-oriented programming each module (object) in a program is a self-contained object having within itself all the data and instructions that operate on the data. Thus, when a programmer requires the computation of federal withholding tax, the federal withholding tax module knows where the necessary data is and also contains the instructions to compute the tax. It's like a manager asking an employee to prepare a sales report. The employee knows where to get the data and how to prepare the sales report. Thus, the manager can be confident that each time she asks for a sales report, she will get a particular sales report containing certain data and formatted in a certain way.

The first object-oriented language was Smalltalk, developed by Xerox. Today several programming languages allow programs to be developed with an object orientation. One that is very popular is C++. Some of the dBASE clone languages also provide object-oriented capabilities; one such package is Clipper 5.0. Object-oriented programming systems (sometimes called OOPS) are becoming an important methodology for increasing the reusability of programming code and thus decreasing the cost of developing applications.

Language Selection

This section does not attempt to compare the languages just discussed. Rather, it explains the factors that influence language selection. Selecting a language for a particular programming application is a very important and sometimes difficult task. The first consideration is the relevance of the language to the application for which it is to be used. Many languages are designed to be used for a particular application and are subordinate choices in other applications. For example, COBOL was designed for business data processing and does not have the facilities to support complex numerical computations characteristic of scientific applications.

A second consideration is, Can the language be efficiently implemented on the existing system? Efficiency is measured in terms of compilation time, execution time, primary storage requirements, and the labor required to use the language. For example, Pascal and BASIC are excellent languages for microcomputers, because these languages require very little primary storage for compilation and execution.

Organizational aspects must also be considered. Staff requirements should be determined, and the cost of training the staff should be weighed against the cost of acquiring new talent. The language can play a big role in determining the amount of time and cost required for orientation. The language should also be versatile and flexible enough to meet the changing needs of the organization. The selector must consider all the objectives and try to make an optimal decision. No language will satisfy all objectives; the selector must allow for trade-offs among desired objectives.

Keeping in mind these factors, the discussion now turns to the various features of a programming language. The following is a brief outline of essential features determining a language's effectiveness:

- Readability and overall writing features
  Modularity
  Structural clarity
  Compactness
  Simplicity

- Application-oriented features
  Functional support
  Flexibility
  Versatility

- Standardization and portability features

- Software development features
  Editing/debugging facilities

- Efficiency features
  Compilation
  Execution
  Primary storage requirements
  Labor efficiency

These features should be viewed with varying degrees of importance depending on how and in what environment the language will be used. For example, in an interactive on-line system, execution time is critical. That is not necessarily the case in a batch processing environment in which jobs can be run overnight.

Desirable qualities of a language are ease of overall writing and readability. These can directly affect the personnel costs associated with learning and acquiring proficiency in the language. Modularity and structural clarity is essential in enhancing readability and coding; it should be possible to break down the program into visible, logical units. These features also aid in the development and continual maintenance and modification of structured software throughout its life cycle. An example of a modular language with structural clarity is Pascal.

Other features desirable for ease of overall writing are compactness and simplicity. Compactness refers to the ability to write a program with a minimum number of keywords and symbols. These features also aid in the maintenance of the language. Examples of a compact language are Pascal, BASIC, FOCUS, and dBASE. COBOL is not a compact language because its goal of being English-like requires the use of words instead of symbols when coding.

Once again, relevance of a language to a given application is very important. When selecting a language, evaluate the language's functional support facilities. Does the language support facilities that enhance its performance within a given application, thereby making less work for the programmer? For example, FORTRAN has several built-in functions for evaluating complex numerical equations, and COBOL supports a built-in report writer and sorting routine. Flexibility is essential in meeting the changing needs of the organization. Application software that can be quickly and accurately altered to specification is desirable. Versatility is another feature that enhances a language's performance. FOCUS is a versatile and flexible language.

For most business information systems, another consideration is the ability to run a program on different computers. This capability is known as portability, as discussed earlier. It is convenient to be able to upgrade to new hardware without having to modify programs. The standardization of languages contributes greatly to portability. Standardization is a continuing challenge to the profession. The most prominent organization to produce standardization is the American National Standards Institute.

Software development aids are a feature that cannot be overlooked. The selector should evaluate the implementation's editing and debugging facilities—are the compile time and execution time diagnostics adequate? The WATFIV version of FORTRAN is an example of an implementation with superior debugging facilities (that is, descriptive diagnostics that aid in debugging).

Finally, efficiency of a programming language is measured by compilation time, execution time, and primary storage requirements. Machine and assembly languages utilize these resources very efficiently, at the expense of portability, flexibility, and programmer time. COBOL has a large compiler and therefore uses a lot of primary storage and takes a long time to compile, whereas Pascal uses very little primary storage. The machine efficiency of programming languages is becoming less important as hardware costs decline. Much more important is the human labor required to use the language.

Summary

- System software is a set of programs that manage the resources of a computer system, provide routine services such as copying data from one file to another, and assist in the development of application programs.

- Application programs are written to perform specific jobs for computer users.

- System control programs control the execution of programs, manage the storage and processing resources of the computer, and perform other management and monitoring functions. The most important of these programs is the operating system. Other examples are database management systems and communication monitors.

- System support programs provide routine service functions to other computer programs and to computer users. Examples are utilities, librarians, performance monitors, and job accounting.

- System development programs assist in the creation of application programs. Examples are language translators, such as a BASIC interpreter, and fourth-generation languages, such as FOCUS.

- The major functions of an operating system are to control the execution of computer programs and to manage the storage and processing resources of a computer system.

- The programs in an operating system start the computer, schedule the execution of various user programs, supervise the allocation of resources to these programs, and facilitate interaction between the CPU and I/O devices like disks and printers.

- Batch-type operating systems line up jobs as they are received and then process them when time is available. In contrast, interactive systems start executing a job as soon as it is received, so that the user does not have to wait at the terminal.

- The major advantages of multitasking are increased throughput, slower response time, ability to assign priorities to jobs, and improved primary storage allocation. These advantages are achieved primarily through the use of job rotation and priority schemes.

- The concept of virtual storage refers to storing only the active segments or pages of a program in primary storage. The rest of the program is stored in secondary storage and parts of it are called in when required.

- A time-sharing system allows many interactive users to use the CPU concurrently. This system is made possible through the use of multitasking operating systems. CPU processing time is distributed among users by a sophisticated job rotation and priority allocation system.

- Multiprocessing systems allow the same job to be run on two or more CPUs. This approach improves system throughput by letting the different CPUs specialize in the functions they perform best.

- Software may be purchased or developed in-house. If it is internally developed, a suitable programming language must be selected.

- Machine language, which is written in binary representation, is the only language the computer understands. Programs written in other languages must be translated into machine language with the help of a compiler or translator.

- Assembly language is similar to machine language in that every machine operation must be individually described. But in assembly language operations and variables are represented by mnemonics instead of by binary numbers. This makes assembly language programs easier to read.

- A procedural language is much easier for people to write and understand than a machine language. With procedural languages, the compiler automatically generates most of the routine machine instructions.

- COBOL is an English-like language designed for business applications. A COBOL program contains paragraphs, sentences, and clauses. The major advantages of this language are high portability and self-documentation.

- Fourth-generation languages, the latest generation, provide facilities that allow users to develop many of their own applications.

- FOCUS is a popular fourth-generation language that runs on personal computers, minicomputers, and mainframes. It has many facilities that both programmers and users can employ to develop applications.

- dBASE is a personal computer database management system. Since program (command) files may be created in dBASE, many business applications can be programmed in dBASE. It is the most widely used personal computer database management system.

- The objective of object-oriented programming is to produce program modules (objects) that are reusable in other programs.

- When evaluating a computer language, the selector should consider the following characteristics:
  Readability and overall writing features
  Application-oriented features
  Standardization and portability features
  Software development features
  Efficiency features

Key Terms

System software	Job scheduling
Application software	Access security
Operating system	System residence device
Queue	Initial program loader (IPL)
System control programs	Supervisor
System support programs	Job control program
System development programs	Input/Output control program
Systems programmers	Resident supervisor
Application program	Monitor or executive programs
General-purpose application software	Job control language (JCL)
Specific-purpose application software	Utility programs
Application programmers	Librarian
Initial program load, or bootstrap	Performance monitors
	Language translator
	Linkage editor

Load module

Application generators

Batch operating system

Open systems

Interactive operating system

Interrupt

Multitasking

Throughput

Turnaround time

Response time

System availability

Interprogram interference

Protected mode

Virtual storage

Paging

Time-sharing

Multiprocessing

Front-end processor

Machine language

Object code

Symbolic languages

Assembly language

Mnemonics

Assembler

Source code

Pseudocode

Procedural language

Compiler

Translation

Linking

Loading

COBOL

Portability

Divisions

Sections

Sentences

Statements

Words

Reserved words

User-defined words

System names

Semantic errors

Fourth-generation language
  (4GL)

Nonprocedural languages

FOCUS

dBASE

Object-oriented
  programming

Review Questions

1. What is system software? How is it different from application software?

2. Describe the major functions of an operating system.

3. What are the functions of the three types of system software?

4. What is a JCL? What functions does it perform for an application program?

5. For what kind of job would you use a utility program?

6. Briefly describe the two types of operating systems.

7. Why is an interrupt handling capacity necessary for an interactive operating system?

8. What are the disadvantages of the batch-serial approach to computer job execution?

9. How does multitasking overcome the disadvantages of the batch-serial approach to computer job execution?

10. Explain the concept of job rotation in a multitasking system.

11. What is paging?

12. What are the advantages of virtual storage?

13. How are time-sharing, interactive computing, and multitasking related?

14. What is the importance of multitasking to personal computers?

15. Give an example of a multiprocessing system.

16. What is machine language? How does it differ from assembly language?

17. In what ways do procedural languages aid the programming process?

18. Describe the three processes that a procedural language program must go through before it is executed.

19. What were the objectives in developing COBOL?

20. Discuss the functions of the four major divisions in a COBOL program.

21. Explain the difference between procedural and nonprocedural language.

22. What are some of the facilities of a fourth-generation language like FOCUS?

23. What is the objective of object-oriented programming?

24. What essential features would you consider when determining the effectiveness of a language?

Discussion Questions and Cases

1. Assignment of processing priorities to different users can often be difficult. Operating-level personnel may desire a higher priority because they need a short turnaround time to keep the production process moving. Middle managers might feel that precious executive time is wasted waiting for computer output because the operating-level people overload the CPU with long routine jobs. How would you approach the problem of assigning user priorities in a large business firm? Is it feasible to allow the same user to use different priorities depending on the importance of the job? How would you control the abuse of such a system?

2. The First Federal Savings and Loan Association is a small local firm. Its record keeping is done through time-sharing with a computer service bureau. The association is satisfied with the time-sharing service. However, several software firms have recently presented the firm with a complete package (including software and personal computers) that could perform the association's information processing needs locally. The software companies claim that their systems are flexible and can produce a wide variety of information for management needs. They also maintain that processing customer records locally would improve the confidentiality of the association's records. They argue that there have been instances of customer data being divulged to unauthorized persons at service bureaus. Do you think the savings and loan association should continue using the time-sharing service, or install its own system?

3. Tieko, Incorporated is trying to decide which of two personal computers to choose as the company's standard. The computer selected will be used throughout the company. One of the machines has available a multitasking

operating system that allows the personal computer to execute two or more programs concurrently. The other machine does not have a multitasking operating system, but otherwise it is somewhat superior to the first machine. Those in the organization who favor the machine without the multitasking operating system argue that a personal computer can have only one user at a time, therefore there is no need for a multitasking operating system. How would you respond to this position?

4. Your firm, Hokies International, plans to install a new computerized order processing system. Fast-Code Inc., a software firm, has offered to sell you its package FAST-SELL. It is a complete order processing program written in COBOL, and Fast-Code agrees to maintain it for three years. The chief programmer at Hokies International believes that she can write a more efficient program. This is estimated to cost only two-thirds of what Fast-Code charges for its package. Which alternative would you choose, and why?

5. Some people believe that the existence of many different programming languages is undesirable. Some of the disadvantages of multiple languages are as follows:

    It is difficult to transport programs between installations.

    Training programmers in more than one language is costly and redundant.

    It is difficult to integrate programs written in different languages.

    In spite of these arguments, computer languages continue to proliferate. What are the possible reasons for this? Should the number of languages be controlled?

6. FOCUS is a useful language for writing a quick, informal program. COBOL is suitable for writing formal, well-documented programs. For each of the, following applications, decide which of these two languages is preferable.

    a. A one-time, strategic report for top management.

    b. A program occasionally used by middle managers to compare actual sales with budgeted sales.

    c. A statistical computation used by the factory engineer to schedule machine maintenance checks.

    d. An accounts receivable system that processes about eight hundred transactions daily.

7. Jill Johnson is designing a personnel tracking system for King William County. She was at home writing some of the computer programs in the COBOL language on her personal computer when her friend Susan Cox, a consultant for a CPA firm stopped by. Susan asked Jill why she was programming in COBOL. Jill said that COBOL was the only language she knew and that it was an excellent choice for implementing the system. Susan replied that there were many relational database management system packages such as dBASE IV on the market, and that dBASE would be more efficient; it would reduce programming time because of its database capabilities. Jill was adamant about not changing the language because she had already done quite a bit of programming. Do you think that Jill should continue writing in COBOL or should she try an alternative?

8. The Hercules Company recruits a large number of business graduates with majors in management, marketing, finance, management science, and

accounting. Ramon Noegel is director of personnel. Several operational managers in the company have suggested that he require all new-hires to have taken at least one programming course in their college career. They argue that a person must understand programming in order to use computers effectively and to really understand what the computer is doing. Ramon maintains that programming is becoming an obsolete skill. He states that business personnel can certainly utilize the computer in many effective ways without knowing how to program. He cites the fact that there are many user-friendly packages available for microcomputers, such as electronic worksheets, report generators, database management systems, and graphics, which can be used without programming. Do you think that learning at least one programming language is useful to a business student?

INFORMATION SYSTEMS STRATEGIES

OOP: More Smarts, Less Code

By David Coursey

Object-oriented programming, which to date has had a largely academic following, is sweeping from the classroom into the mainstream and promises to replace the structured programming techniques familiar to most programmers.

Language developers such as Microsoft Corp. and Borland International Inc. are adding object features to new releases of Pascal, while AT&T is planning an update to C-plus-plus, an object version of the C language.

These developments reflect a need for a more robust development environment, which is required for the graphics-oriented programs many expect to replace today's character-based applications. Developing these next-generation applications will be easier in an object-oriented environment because it allows programmers to write "smarter" applications with less code than do traditional means.

"Object-oriented programming is the future," said Peter Francis, managing editor of the "Seybold Outlook on Professional Computing," a Santa Clara, Calif.-based newsletter. "Most programmers are still writing structured code the way they learned in the 1970s. They are also not writing it very well. While objects are different in some ways, even very different, it (the programming) still allows non-programmers much better access to the nuts and bolts of how applications work or can be changed to work better."

Object-oriented languages are different from traditional languages in a very fundamental way. While traditional languages separate code from data, object-oriented languages bring the two together in a single, self-contained object, a concept Stewart Chapin, a group product manager in Microsoft's language group, called "more smarts in one place."

With each object is a set of methods (code) that is appropriate for it, and objects that share common methods are called a "class." This is a major benefit for developers because it allows them to create new portions of an application by using subclasses to specify only what is different from the existing code.

Although object-oriented programming is a new concept for many, objects themselves are not. In graphical user environments, such as those employed by the Apple Computer Inc. Macintosh and Microsoft Windows and Presentation Manager, users already treat files and disk drives as objects.

In the future, dragging a file to the modem or network icon might start a file transfer or initiate a host session. Further, files will come with operations or methods attached to them.

Clicking on a file would cause the computer to display all the operations or methods that are available for that file. Examples might include "copy," "delete," "compile," "edit," "print," etc. The object is selected first, followed by the file name.

Another type of object, in addition to those used in programming and the user interface, is objects created from data files and applications.

This is where the object concept becomes applicable to the system as a whole. Chapin said a spreadsheet data file, for example, could be treated as a system object, and the application considered a set of methods to deal with the object.

Just a Theory

In the future, object-oriented programming is expected to lead to object-oriented systems upon which entire corporate systems architectures will be based, although it is only at the theoretical stage today.

"The process of moving to object-oriented programming has barely begun and can be expected to be the most significant programming trend of the 1990. It's unlikely we will outgrow it anytime soon," said Francis.

A top Microsoft executive said users are at the beginning of a transition "from object-oriented stuff being a buzzword to being able to do something with it."

"Object-oriented programming is probably going to be to the 1990s what structured programming was to the 1970s, with both the pluses and minuses that go with that," said Chapin.

OOP, which unhappy users are almost certain to rename OOPS, will change the way software is built and should lead to greater developer productivity and reduced maintenance costs. But, like structured programming, it will almost certainly take longer to implement than most hope or expect.

"It's deceptively simple. The syntax of object-oriented programming is not that different. If you look at QuickPascal, there are only four new words. It's very easy to pick up the syntax, but down the road it requires a change in the way you think about designing software," Chapin said.

He said that first-time users often write, test and debug an application only to throw the work out and start over, based upon a new understanding of objects. "It really does require you to think in a different order."

One of Microsoft's goals for QuickPascal, released last month, is enabling programmers to develop an object-oriented mind-set with a minimum of frustration, by using a language with which they are already familiar.

Discussion Questions

1.   What are objects and how are they used in a graphical user interface like Windows? How do these objects relate to object-oriented programming?

2.   Identify and discuss the major advantages and disadvantages of OOP.

Reprinted with permission from Fairchild Publications, *MIS Week* (June 12, 1989), p. 53.

Data Storage and Processing

Dianna Davis is in the rare plant business, with mail-order customers from all parts of the United States. She has a mailing list of about ten thousand customers on her personal computer. When she makes a computer run that must access each record in the customer list, it takes the computer about fifteen minutes. Yet when she accesses a single record, the computer retrieves the record in a fraction of a second. Doesn't the computer have to search through all the records in a file to find a single record? How does it retrieve the record so fast?

In this chapter we will first look at how data is stored on a computer system. Then we will examine the basic record access methods used to retrieve that data. Next, we will explore four file organization approaches that support different types of record access. After understanding file organization we can examine which file organizations are suitable for different types of information processing modes. Finally, we will cover on-line direct-access systems and real-time systems.

Introduction

Data are represented by computers in various structures. These data structures are related to each other in a hierarchical way. There are also several different methods for organizing data in files. File organizations differ, primarily, in the ways that they allow data to be accessed.

Basic Data Storage

The Data Hierarchy

In ascending order of complexity, the structures of the information system data hierarchy are as follows:

1. Bit

2. Byte

3. Field, or item

4. Record

5. File, or data set

6. Database

This is called a data hierarchy because databases are composed of files, files are composed of records, and so on. Figure 12–1 illustrates the relationships among these structures of the information system data hierarchy.

Bit   The term **bit** is short for binary digit. It can assume either of two possible states and therefore can be represented by either 1 or 0. Typically a bit represents data through the positive or negative polarity of an electrical charge on a magnetic recording medium such as a tape or disk. In the case of semiconductor storage, a bit is represented by an electrical circuit that is either conducting or not conducting electricity.

Byte   The ability to represent only binary information in a computer system is not sufficient for business information processing. Numeric, alphabetic, and a wide variety of special characters such as dollar signs, question marks, and quotation marks must be stored in this type of sys-

FIGURE 12–1

The Data Hierarchy.

Databases contain files, files contain records, records contain fields, fields contain bytes, and bytes contain individual binary digits, or bits. Ultimately all data are represented through bits that have a value of either 1 or 0.

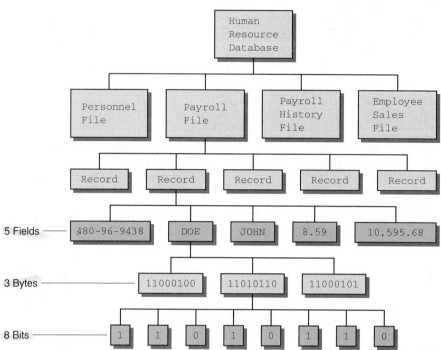

5 Fields

3 Bytes

8 Bits

1/2 bit = nimble

tem. In a computer system, a character of information is called a **byte**. A byte of information is stored by using several bits in specified combinations. One widely used coding scheme is IBM's Extended Binary Coded Decimal Interchange Code (EBCDIC), an eight-bit code illustrated in Table 12–1. Each 1 or 0 in the table corresponds to a single bit.

When data are stored using EBCDIC or any other coding scheme, an extra **parity** (or check) **bit** is added to the scheme for checking purposes. In an even parity machine, the computer expects the number of bits turned on in a byte always to be even. Refer to Figure 12–2, which illustrates how data are stored in EBCDIC on magnetic tape. Each bit within a byte is stored in a separate track on the tape. Note that the parity bit is turned on whenever necessary to produce an even number of on bits in a byte. Parity bits are a control feature built into most computer hardware. With a parity bit, EBCDIC becomes a nine-bit code. Therefore, a nine-track tape is used whenever EBCDIC-encoded data is written onto magnetic tape. Each track contains one bit of data.

Another commonly used code for storing bytes of data is the American Standard Code for Information Interchange–8 (ASCII–8) of the American National Standards Institute (see Table 12–1). This is also an eight-bit code. It is used widely in the area of data transmission and with microcomputers.

Field, or Item   The next level in the data hierarchy is a field, or item, of data. A **field**, or **item**, of data is one or more bytes that contain data about an attribute of an entity in the information system. For example, an entity in a payroll system is an individual employee. Attributes are the employee's name, hourly rate, and so on. The hourly rate is a field, or item, of data. Figure 12–3 shows a payroll record with typical fields of data.

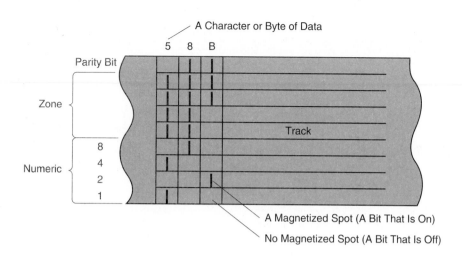

A Character or Byte of Data

FIGURE 12–2
Data Coded in
EBCDIC on Magnetic
Tape.

The number of on bits in
each byte is always even
in this example. Thus,
the data are recorded
with even parity.

Character	EBCDIC	ASCII–8
A	1100 0001	1010 0001
B	1100 0010	1010 0010
C	1100 0011	1010 0011
D	1100 0100	1010 0100
E	1100 0101	1010 0101
F	1100 0110	1010 0110
G	1100 0111	1010 0111

TABLE 12–1
A Portion of the
EBCDIC and ASCII–8
Coding Schemes

Record   A **record** is a collection of fields relating to a specific entity. For example, the payroll record shown in Figure 12–3 contains fields of data relating to a specific employee. An analogy can be made between a computer-based record and an individual folder in a manual file, as shown in Figure 12–4. A folder in a manual employee file may contain much the same information as a record in a computer-based payroll file. The field that uniquely identifies a record from all other records in a file is the record key. For example, the record key in a payroll record is normally the employee's Social Security number.

File   A **file** is a collection of related records. For example, all the payroll records for all of a company's employees are a payroll master file. There are seven basic types of files: master files, transaction files, table files, index files, summary files, program files, and backup files.

  Master files contain relatively permanent data. Examples include payroll, material inventory, finished goods, work-in-process, accounts receivable, and accounts payable. A typical payroll master file record might contain the fields shown in Figure 12–3. A registrar's file containing student information such as name, address, courses taken, and grades is another example of a master file record. Business data processing revolves around master files, which are an organization's central files. They contain the information necessary for the organization to operate. All other types of files are auxiliary to and support the maintenance of master files or facilitate the retrieval and reporting of information from them.

FIGURE 12–3

An Example of Data Fields Contained in a Payroll Master File Record.

The term *master file* often refers to the file that stores relatively permanent data. This payroll master file would be updated whenever employee paychecks are produced.

Payroll Master File Record
First Name, Middle Initial
Last Name
Street Address
City/State
Zip Code
Social Security Number
Sick Leave Eligibility Date
Effective Date of Salary Increase
Date of Birth
Department Number
Hourly Rate
Sick Hours
Overtime Earnings
Regular Earnings
Federal Tax Year-to-Date
Marital Status
Number of Dependents
Total Voluntary Deductions Year-to-Date
FICA Year-to-Date
State Tax Year-to-Date
City Tax Year-to-Date
Net Earnings Year-to-Date

Transaction files contain records used to change (update) master files. Any change to a master file is termed a transaction even if it is not a transaction under the traditional accounting definition—that is, an exchange by the company with an outside party. For example, a change in an employee's address is a transaction to the payroll master file. However, many transactions occur between the organization and external parties—for example, orders and payments on account. The data for these transaction records are taken from invoices, receiving reports, employee hiring and termination records, and the like.

Technically, transaction files are used only with batch systems. For example, a transaction file for a batch payroll system contains all the transactions that have accumulated between individual runs or updates of the system. These files usually contain several different record formats, since any system has several different types of transactions. For example, a payroll system can have the following types of transactions: the addition of a new employee, the deletion of an old employee, a change in pay rate, a change in address, and weekly hours worked. Codes in each record identify the record format. This enables the system to locate the data fields in each record format.

Although technically not a transaction file, the transaction log of an on-line real-time system operates as a transaction file. The transaction log of an on-line real-time system is created to provide a backup and an audit trail, whereas the transaction file in a batch system is created primarily to update the master file. However, the transaction file in the batch system also serves as a backup and an audit trail.

Table files contain relatively permanent information that is used to facilitate processing. An example is the freight rate table used to assign freight charges to customer invoices.

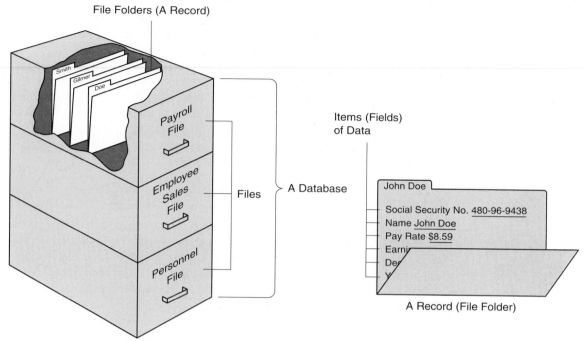

FIGURE 12-4

Files, Records, and Fields in a Manual File.

A computer file is analogous to a manual file drawer. Computer records are analogous to individual file folders within a drawer. Computer items of data are analogous to the data items contained in a file folder. Thinking of data storage in this manner may help you remember the way information is stored in a computer system.

Index files are used to indicate the addresses of records stored on secondary storage devices. They are analogous to a card catalog in a library, allowing computer systems to locate individual records without searching the entire file.

Summary files contain data extracted and summarized from other files. Examples include temporary work files used by the computer in processing and report files that contain the information needed for specific management reports.

Program files (sometimes called program libraries) are files containing the production copies of programs used in the day-to-day execution of information processing jobs. Program files contain both source and object copies of production programs. Object files eliminate the need to recompile a frequently executed program each time the program is run. Therefore, production program libraries actually used to execute jobs are kept in object form. When a production program is changed, the source copy of the program is changed, tested, and recompiled. The compilation also produces an object module, which is then stored in the production program library.

Backup files are either copies of current files or the only copy of noncurrent files used to reconstruct current files in case they are partially or totally destroyed. Backup files should be kept for all the different types of files. In addition, they are sometimes kept for long periods of time to serve as archive files. Archive files contain information that is not on current files but which may be useful in the future for long-term studies or for support documentation, as in the case of income tax returns.

Database   A **database** is all the files of an organization that are structured and integrated to facilitate information retrieval and update. The term *database* is used loosely by the information systems profession. Technically, a database consists of the files that are part of a database management system. However, the term database also designates all the files of an organization. (Database management systems are discussed in Chapter 13.)

Record Access Methods

Primary and Secondary Keys   In business information systems, records store the information that pertains to subjects in which we are interested, such as products, sales, employees, customers, and so on. Thus, we are primarily interested in retrieving the information stored in records. A major concern of business information systems is the way we access individual records in files.

To access an individual record, we must be able to uniquely identify it. We do this through a **primary key**, which is a field that uniquely identifies the record and thus separates it from all other records in the file. A student record is illustrated in Figure 12–5. The primary key of the record is the Social Security number, since an individual's Social Security number is different from all other Social Security numbers in the file. Normally, users or programs access individual records by supplying the primary key. Primary keys are also used when we change data within a record or delete a record. In performing these operations, we must uniquely identify the record on which the delete or change is being made.

Records may also be accessed through **secondary keys**. Any field in a record can be a secondary key. Secondary keys do not have to be unique. For example, in a student records file, as illustrated in Figure 12–5, there would be many freshmen. We might make class a secondary key, since we may often need to retrieve all the records of freshmen. Since secondary keys allow us to retrieve information based on any field in the record, they are very valuable.

Sequential Access   In sequential access, we process every record in the file. Starting at the front of the file, we process the records in a record-by-record order. Sequential access is efficient only in terms of time, when the file-activity ratio is high. The file-activity ratio is a percentage of file records used in a given processing run. For example, most payroll systems would use sequential access when producing paychecks since most if not all employees of a company receive a paycheck in each payroll period. A very large percentage of the payroll file records would be used during such a run. In much routine, high-volume business information processing, there is a high file-activity ratio; thus, sequential access is an efficient approach.

Random Access   Often we need to retrieve only one record from a file. Thus, the percentage of records we use in the file is extremely low. The

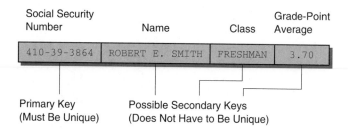

Social Security Number	Name	Class	Grade-Point Average
410-39-3864	ROBERT E. SMITH	FRESHMAN	3.70

Primary Key
(Must Be Unique)

Possible Secondary Keys
(Does Not Have to Be Unique)

FIGURE 12–5
Primary and Secondary Keys
Since the primary key must be unique, there can be only one record with a Social Security number of 410–39–3864. Since name, class, and grade-point average are used only as secondary keys, there could be multiple Robert E. Smiths, multiple freshmen, and multiple 3.70 grade-point averages.

need for these individual records usually occurs *randomly*. For example, when a grocery clerk uses a universal product code scanner, the grocery items are passed over the scanner in a random order. The computer must be able to immediately retrieve individual records from the pricing file in order to price each item. It obviously could not access these price records sequentially, since there would be thousands of individual records—one for each item in the grocery store. Keep in mind there may be fifteen to twenty checkout machines going simultaneously, all serviced by the same computer. File organization methods must be used that will allow quick, direct access to these randomly occurring requests for pricing data. Just as there is a need to process records sequentially, there is also a very large need in business information systems today to access individual records randomly. Many applications, like airline reservations, must have random access because information needs to be processed immediately.

As illustrated in Application 12–1, random access is also often referred to as direct access. To save money on the purchase of direct access storage devices (DASD), such as hard disk units, firms like Navistar use statistical models to detect the access patterns of particular files. If files are not accessed often they can be stored on inexpensive magnetic tape storage, a sequential access storage media.

APPLICATION 12–1

Smart Money Managers Can Avoid Cost of DASDs

By Johanna Ambrosio

When the going gets tough, the tough turn to systems software to help avoid costly hardware add-ons. Users report that with some software tools and upper management's increased willingness to give them personnel and money devoted to the job, they can get more out of existing systems, particularly during troubled economic times.

Navistar International Corp. in Chicago has managed to avoid adding direct-access storage devices (DASD) to its arsenal for the past three years because of an aggressive management program started in 1985. The original idea was to apply Deming's Statistical Process Control theories to the data center, said Mike Watson, manager of productivity and quality improvement.

Over the past few years, Watson said, Navistar has saved millions of dollars with a combination of off-the-shelf and in-house developed software. The company uses Legent Corp.'s MCS software and IBM's Hierarchical Storage Management (HSM) scheme with its own models.

"We have models to evaluate the costs based on the age and size of the data set, the number of times it has been accessed and the statistical probability of its being accessed again after a certain number of days," Watson said. "We can set the parameters that are most cost-effective for us, we can balance things out, and we can economically defend our decisions."

Adapted with permission from *Computerworld* (February 18, 1991), p. 29. Copyright 1991 by CW Publishing, Inc., Framingham, MA 01701.

FIGURE 12–6
Relative and Physical
Addresses.

A physical address is
equivalent to your street
address. A relative
address is equivalent to
your saying, "I live in the
fourth house on the left
from the street
intersection."

Physical Address

Relative Address	
1	Data Record
2	Data Record
3	Data Record
4	Data Record
5	Data Record

Cylinder	Track	Sector	
9	3	1	Data Record
9	3	1	Data Record
9	3	2	Data Record
9	3	2	Data Record
9	3	2	Data Record

File Organization

A few special terms are used in discussing **file organization**. The term *address* identifies the location in which the record is stored. Note the difference between an address and a primary key. A primary key uniquely identifies a record, but an address identifies where the record is stored on the storage medium, which is usually magnetic disk. For example, your name uniquely identifies you but it does not identify where you live—your address identifies where you live.

There are two types of addresses: physical and relative (see Figure 12–6). A **physical address** deals with the physical characteristics of the storage medium. For example, on magnetic disk the physical address is composed of a **cylinder**, a **track**, and a **sector** (see Figure 12–7). To find an individual record on a magnetic disk, a computer ultimately must know its physical address. Some file organizations, such as indexed sequential access, produce physical addresses for records. However, the more widely used file organizations today use the concept of **relative address** (refer again to Figure 12–6). In relative addressing an individual record's address depends on its relative position from the beginning of the file. If it is the third record in the file, then it has a relative address of 3. As mentioned earlier, a relative address must ultimately be converted to a physical address in order for the computer to find a record. However, the methods by which this is done are not important here.

Individual data records may contain the relative addresses of other data records. They are used to link together similar records. A file containing pointers of this type is called a **linked list**. In the linked list in Figure 12–8 the records that contain the same class are linked; all the freshman records are linked together. The first freshman record has a pointer to the relative address of the second freshman record, and it has a pointer to the third freshman record which is in relative address 5, and so on. Another example of a linked list appears in the discussion of direct file organization.

The last term defined before discussing file organization is directory. A **directory** is a list of the file names contained on a particular storage medium such as a magnetic disk pack. Figure 12–9 illustrates a PC file directory. It lists all the files stored on one floppy disk.

Figure 12–10 is an overview of the file organizations covered in this section. There are three basic types: sequential, direct, and indexed.

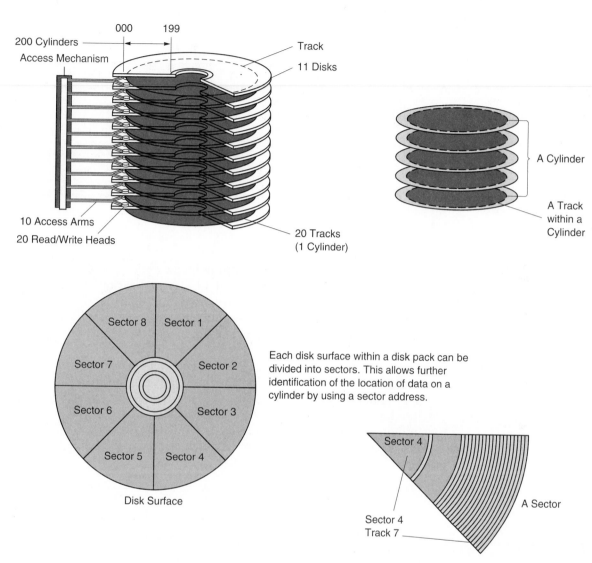

FIGURE 12–7
Cylinder, Track, and Sector Addresses.
The set of all tracks with the same distance from the center of the disk forms a cylinder. The number of cylinders on a disk pack is equal to the number of tracks across a disk surface. The number of tracks within a cylinder is equal to the number of disk surfaces on which data are stored.

Sequential File Organization

With **sequential file organization**, records are stored either in the order they are entered into the file or in ascending order by primary key. For example, in a sequential student records file the records are stored in ascending order by the students' Social Security numbers. For an individual record to be found, a sequential search beginning at the first record on the file must be performed. Each record must be examined until the required one is located. There is no index to the file.

FIGURE 12–8
A Linked List.

After reading the first nonfreshman record, the user can directly read each additional freshman record without reading freshman records. Record 1 points to record 4, record 4 points to record 5, record 5 points to record 7, and record 7 indicates (with a 0 in the pointer field) the end of that linked list.

Relative Address		Class	Pointer (to a Relative Address)
1	Other Data	Freshman	4
2	Other Data	Sophomore	3
3	Other Data	Sophomore	6
4	Other Data	Freshman	5
5	Other Data	Freshman	7
6	Other Data	Sophomore	8
7	Other Data	Freshman	0
8	Other Data	Sophomore	0
9	Other Data	Junior	0

Such a search can be time-consuming when a file is large. Therefore, sequential organization is impractical for an application that requires immediate access to individual records. On the other hand, sequential organization is good for a payroll system that produces paychecks every week, since almost every record on the file must be accessed during each paycheck run.

Certain storage media, like magnetic tape, allow only sequential file organization. To locate a record on a reel of magnetic tape, the tape must be read sequentially, beginning with the first record. It is physically impossible for a tape drive to locate individual records directly because of the amount of winding and rewinding that must be performed. However, a direct-access storage device (DASD), such as a disk, allows sequential, direct, and indexed file organization.

FIGURE 12–9
A Personal Computer File Directory.

This floppy disk has very little stored on it. There are 312,320 bytes of space that are unused.

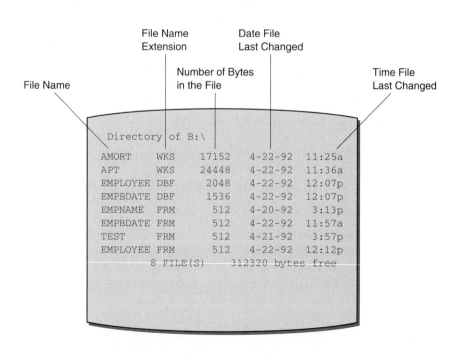

```
Directory of B:\

AMORT     WKS    17152    4-22-92    11:25a
APT       WKS    24448    4-22-92    11:36a
EMPLOYEE  DBF     2048    4-22-92    12:07p
EMPBDATE  DBF     1536    4-22-92    12:07p
EMPNAME   FRM      512    4-20-92     3:13p
EMPBDATE  FRM      512    4-22-92    11:57a
TEST      FRM      512    4-21-92     3:57p
EMPLOYEE  FRM      512    4-22-92    12:12p
        8 FILE(S)     312320 bytes free
```

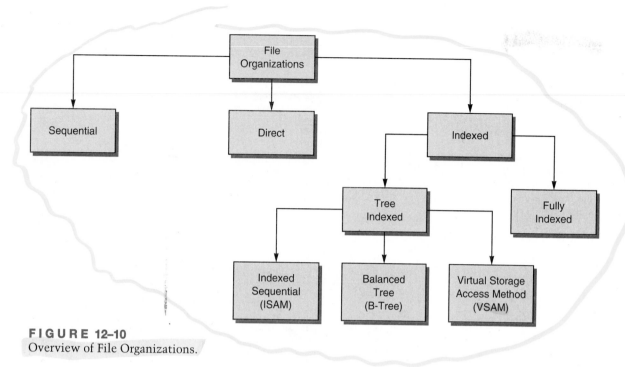

FIGURE 12–10
Overview of File Organizations.

Direct File Organization

A **direct file organization** allows immediate, direct access to individual records on the file. The organization scheme must allow retrieval of the individual record with little or no searching among the records on file. A direct file organization is usually used when there is a high volume of random requests for individual records and there is relatively little need to print out the complete file in sequential order by record key. An example of such an application is a grocery store checkout. Grocery items are processed at several checkout lanes in a random order. The price file has to be accessed very quickly so the checkout process is not slowed.

The essence of direct addressing is being able to quickly produce a relative address from a record's primary key. Figure 12–11 shows how this is done. The record key for a Social Security number is input to a hashing program which computes a relative address from the Social Security number. This relative address is a random number. (In fact, the word **hash** is a synonym for the word *randomize*.) The records in the file are

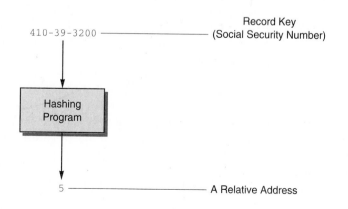

FIGURE 12–11
Overview of Direct Addressing.

One method by which a hashing program can derive a relative address is illustrated in Figure 12–12.

FIGURE 12–12
Computation of Direct
Addresses by the
Division/Remainder
Method.

Try dividing some of the
Social Security numbers
in the file by 999 to see
whether your result
matches the relative
address shown. Divide
your own Social Security
number by 999 to see at
what address your record
would be placed.

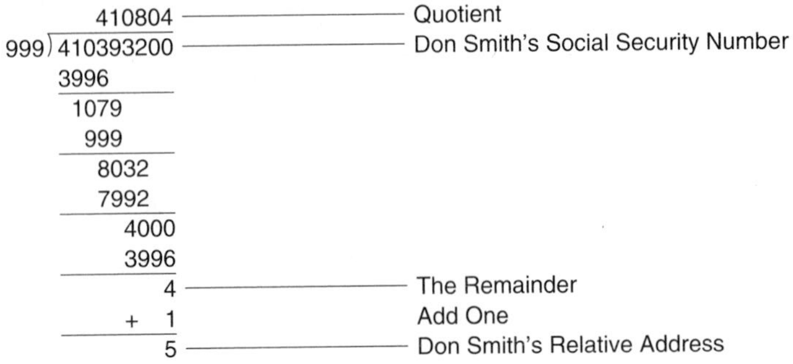

```
      410804 ─────────────── Quotient
999)410393200 ─────────────── Don Smith's Social Security Number
      3996
      1079
       999
      8032
      7992
      4000
      3996
         4 ─────────────── The Remainder
       + 1 ─────────────── Add One
         5 ─────────────── Don Smith's Relative Address
```

Relative Address	Social Security Number	Name	Class	Grade Point Average
1	780476742	Ray Jefferies	Sophomore	2.80
2	240653107	Susan Gilmer	Freshman	3.10
3	035237729	Mary Woods	Senior	3.28
4	480393129	Jane Randolph	Sophomore	2.50
5	410393200	Don Smith	Freshman	3.32
⋮				
999	029838131	Sam Akers	Junior	2.95

Notice that the Social Security number
is in random order

stored in order by relative address. However, they are stored randomly in
reference to the record key.

One of several hashing methods for computing direct addresses is the
division/remainder method, shown in Figure 12–12. At the bottom of the
figure is a file with student information stored. Assume you want to
store approximately 950 students in this file. You set aside space for 999
records on a magnetic disk. There are 999 record storage locations, each
with a relative address that shows the record's position within the file.

The division/remainder method divides the record key, in this case
the Social Security number, by a number very near the number of storage
locations set aside in the file. In this example, the Social Security number is divided by the number 999. The remainder of this division process
is added to the number 1 and the result is used as the relative address. In
this example, the remainder will always be between 0 and 998. When 1 is
added to the remainder, a Social Security number is very quickly converted into a random number between 1 and 999, which is used as a
record's relative address. After placing the record in its relative address
location, you can retrieve it by simply supplying the Social Security
number (which is the primary key); the hashing program will quickly
compute the relative address.

The primary advantage of direct file organization is that it can be used to
access an individual record in a very small fraction of a second, even if the

file has millions of records. Imagine how long it would take to find an individual record in a sequential file if the file contained ten million records.

The primary disadvantage of a direct file organization is that the records are actually stored in a random order. As shown in Figure 12–12, the records are not in sequential order by Social Security number. What if you needed to produce a report of these records in sequential order by Social Security number? If the need for this report was only occasional and the file was not too large, you could simply sort a copy of the file in order by Social Security number. You could also maintain a linked list similar to the one shown in Figure 12–8, except in this case you would link the records in order by Social Security number. Each pointer would point to the relative address of the next Social Security number, in ascending sequence. However, it takes computer time to maintain linked lists, since they must be changed when records are added or deleted. Also, space must be set aside in the record to store the pointer. Generally, when records in a file must be produced in some sequence on a frequent basis and accessed directly, an indexed file organization is used.

Indexed File Organization

In an **indexed file organization**, a separate file is used to indicate the address of the records stored in the primary file. The file that stores these addresses is called an index file. It is similar to a card catalog in a library. A library card catalog is an index to the actual books stored in the library. Similarly, an index file is an index to the records stored in the primary file. Two basic types of index files are discussed here: fully indexed and tree indexed.

Fully Indexed Files   A full index is illustrated in Figure 12–13. A **fully indexed file** has an entry in the index for each record in the primary file. Figure 12–13 shows a full index on the Social Security number primary key of the same file used in Figure 12–12. A full index may be constructed on any field in a file.

As files get large, a lot of time could be spent searching for the relative address of an individual record in the index. However, a full index can be searched rapidly if it is stored in RAM and if it is searched with a binary search. A **binary search** splits the index file in half and then determines in which half the desired key is stored. That half is then split in half again to determine in which quarter the key is stored, and so on until the required key is found. A binary search is considerably more efficient than a sequential search of the index file.

Tree-Indexed Files   Tree-indexed files include files with an indexed sequential file organization, a B-tree index, or a virtual storage access method.

Indexed Sequential File Organization   The **indexed sequential file organization**, or indexed sequential access method (ISAM; pronounced *isam*), is a cross between sequential and indexed file organizations. The records in the file are stored sequentially, but random access to individual records is possible through an index. Thus, records may be accessed either sequentially or randomly.

FIGURE 12–13

A Full Index.

In a full index, the relative address of each record in a file is stored. Although this may seem to be the best way to derive relative addresses, the process is time-consuming because the full index itself must be both maintained and searched.

Primary Key

Social Security Number	Relative Address
029838131	999
035237729	3
240653107	2
410393200	5
480393129	4
780476742	1
	⋮
998396732	128

Figure 12–14 illustrates a cylinder and track index for an ISAM file. Notice that this index has a treelike structure. (Actually, it resembles an upside-down tree.) For a record to be found, the cylinder index is searched to locate the cylinder address, and then the track index for the cylinder is searched to locate the track address of the record. Using Figure 12–14 to illustrate, suppose the required record has a primary key value of 225. The cylinder address is 2, since 225 is greater than 84 but less than 250. The program searches the track index for cylinder 2 and finds that since 225 is greater than 175 and equal to 225, the track address is 4. With the cylinder address and the track address known, the disk control unit can then search through the records on track 4 in cylinder 2 to retrieve the record. As this example shows, the ISAM provides a physical address (cylinder and track) rather than a relative address.

The ISAM is useful when records must be retrieved randomly and when they must also be processed in sequential order by the primary key. In checking accounts, the ISAM is used to allow customers to randomly access their accounts through automated teller machines. It also allows the bank to process checks on a batch basis once per day. The check processing run has a high file-activity ratio, and thus accesses the file sequentially.

B-Tree Index   An indexing technique that is very widely used is the **B-tree index** (balanced-tree index), illustrated in Figure 12–15. This index is called a balanced-tree index because all the leaves are on the same level of the tree. The B-tree index in Figure 12–15(*b*) is an index to the primary file shown in Figure 12–15(*a*). A search of the B-tree index begins at the root. Assume that you need to know the address of a record whose primary key value is 72. First look at 54 in the root and decide that 72 is greater than 54, and then branch to the right. (If the primary key you were looking for was less than 54, you would branch to the left.) Then examine the primary keys in the next lowest level index. Seventy-two is greater than 63 but less than 85; therefore, you go to the primary keys that branch between 63 and 85. At this point you are at the leaves of the tree that contain the relative address of each record. You find that 72 is in relative

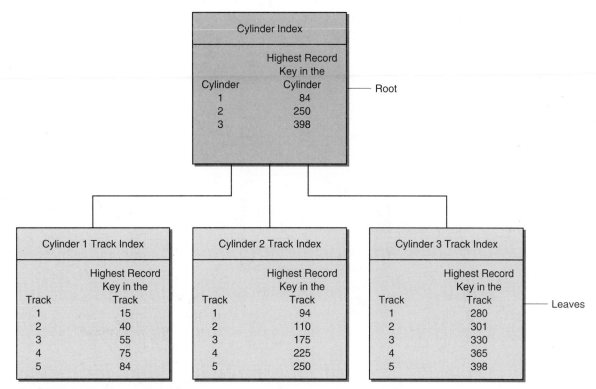

FIGURE 12–14
ISAM Cylinder and Track Index.
Notice the tree nature of an ISAM index.

address 6. With three accesses (at the root, at the intermediate level, and at the leaves), you have found one address out of eleven records.

B-tree indexes are very efficient in search time because a large number of primary keys can be placed in each of the nodes. For example, what if you put a hundred primary keys in each of the nodes in Figure 12–15? You would have a hundred primary keys in the root node, ten thousand primary keys in the intermediate nodes, and one million primary keys in the leaf nodes. With such a B-tree index, you could find the address of one in one million records with just three disk accesses! Of course, you would have to do some searching within the hundred primary keys in each root node, but this would be done in primary memory at very fast speeds. The slow part of searching for records is in reading data or indexes from magnetic disks. The B-tree index of one million records would require only three disk accesses to find the address of an individual record.

Most database management systems that run on all sizes of computers use B-tree indexes. They can be used whether the file is physically in sequential order by a primary key or is physically in random order. B-tree indexes can be created on any field within a file. They are very good at servicing ad hoc queries such as the following: "Provide a list of all students who are seniors and have a grade-point average greater than 3.2 and who have taken a Spanish course." If the file from which this information is to be retrieved has a B-tree index on class, grade-point average, and

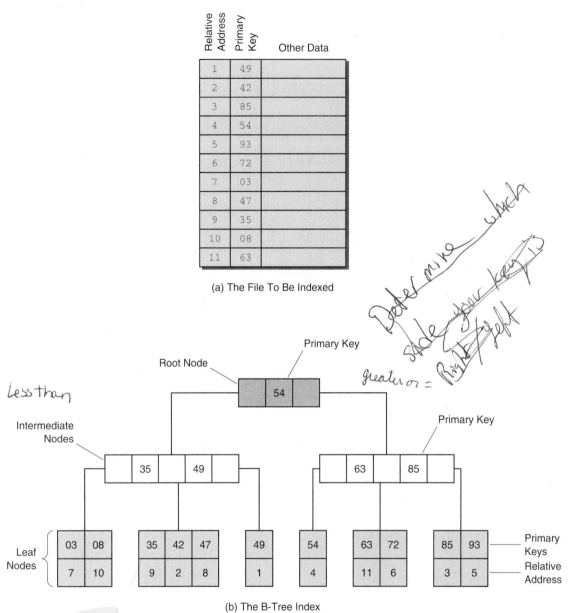

(a) The File To Be Indexed

(b) The B-Tree Index

F I G U R E 12–15
A B-Tree Index.
Most indexes used on personal computers are B-tree.

courses taken, the request can be met without having to search the complete file. The primary disadvantage of a B-tree index is that it must be kept up-to-date.

Virtual Storage Access Method   The **virtual storage access method (VSAM)** is used on IBM mainframes. VSAM uses a B-tree–type index to retrieve records from a file. The word *virtual* is used in VSAM because VSAM is independent of hardware; that is, it does not store and retrieve data by cylinders and tracks.

Selecting a File Organization

Several factors must be considered in determining the best file organization for a particular application: file activity, file volatility, file size, and file query requirements. **File activity** was defined earlier as the percentage of file records that are actually used or accessed in a given processing run. At one extreme (with a low file activity) is an airline reservations application, in which each transaction is processed immediately and only one file record is accessed. Since this file is rarely processed sequentially, the direct-access method is used. In between is the bank checking account application, in which records must be accessed both randomly and sequentially. This file is best organized with one of the indexing approaches. At the other extreme is the payroll master file, from which almost every record is accessed when the weekly payroll is processed. In this case, a sequential file organization is most efficient.

File volatility refers to the number of additions and deletions to a file in a given period of time. The payroll file for a construction company with an employee roster that is constantly changing is a highly volatile file. An indexed file is not a good choice in this situation, since many additions and deletions would necessitate frequent changes in the indexes. A sequential file organization is appropriate if there are no query requirements.

File query refers to the retrieval of information from a file. Table 12–2 provides a summary of file access methods. If the access to individual records must be fast to support a real-time operation such as airline reservations, then some kind of direct organization is required. If, on the other hand, requirements for data can be delayed, then all the individual requests for information can be batched and run in a single processing run with a sequential file organization.

Large files that require many individual references to records with immediate response must be organized under some type of random-access method. On the other hand, with small files it may be more efficient to search the entire file sequentially to find an individual record than to maintain complex indexes or direct-access schemes.

File Organization	Record Access Method Sequential	Random
Sequential	Yes	No
Direct	Usually no	Yes
Indexed-sequential	Yes	Yes
Balanced-tree	Yes	Yes
Virtual storage	Yes	Yes
Fully indexed	Yes	Yes

TABLE 12–2 Summary of File Access Methods.

A direct file organization allows sequential record access if the records are chained together in sequential order with a linked list.

This section has discussed only the primary factors in determining the best file organization. "Best" is a relative term; the final answer depends on the individual application. Other factors that most companies would consider are ease of implementing and maintaining a particular file organization, cost of the file organization, and whether software is readily available to implement the file organization.

Information Processing Modes

The preceding sections discussed two basic types of file organization and record access methods: those that allow sequential access to records and those that allow direct access to individual records on a random basis. There are also two ways to process data—batch and immediate. This section first examines batch and immediate processing. Then it further explains information processing modes by examining how the two types of record access methods are combined with the two ways to process data to form three information processing modes: batch-sequential, batch-direct, and immediate-direct. Immediate-sequential processing is impractical since records cannot be retrieved randomly from sequential files that are not indexed.

Batch Processing

Under **batch processing**, changes to and queries of the file are stored for a period of time, and then processing runs are made periodically to update the file and to obtain the information required by the queries and scheduled reports. The batch runs may be made on a scheduled periodic basis, such as daily, weekly, or monthly, or they may be made on an as-required basis.

Figure 12–16 illustrates batch processing with a sequential file stored on magnetic tape. As shown in the figure, a new master file on a separate volume of tape is produced whenever the file storage medium is magnetic tape. If the storage medium is direct access, then the updating is in-place updating, and the new master file records reside physically in the same area of the direct-access storage device as the old records. In-place updating, sometimes referred to as destructive updating, simply writes the new data over the physical area that the old data occupied on the DASD.

Application 12–2 illustrates how Nestle Foods uses batch processing to run noncritical and long-running jobs. They use an automated job scheduler to run these jobs without human intervention from a remote site.

Immediate Processing

Under **immediate processing**, transactions are processed to update the file immediately or shortly after a real-world event occurs. Usually these real-world events occur in a random order. Immediate processing is illustrated in Figure 12–17.

Batch-Sequential

The **batch-sequential mode** is illustrated in Figure 12–16. With this type of processing, changes and queries to the file are batched and processed periodically on a sequential-access basis. In a practical sense, the only way to process a sequential-access file is on a batch basis since there is no random direct access to individual records. Earlier data processing applications were always batch-sequential, but the mode is declining in popularity because of the decreasing costs of direct-access storage devices.

Batch-Direct

The **batch-direct mode** is used when random direct-access files are updated on a batch basis. For example, weekly payroll data are usually batched and processed on a batch basis even if the file is stored according to a ran-

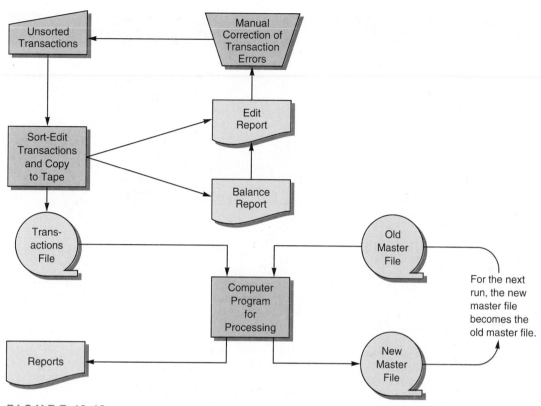

FIGURE 12–16
Batch-Sequential Processing with Tape Files.
If the files were stored on disks, the only difference in this figure would be that there would be no old and new master files since each record in the master file would be updated and then written back to its original location on the disk.

dom-access file organization. Batch-direct processing is sometimes done even though it is inefficient in a payroll run because the file activity ratio is high. The batch-direct mode is most efficient when the activity ratio is less than 50 percent. Batch-direct processing is illustrated in Figure 12–18.

Immediate-Direct

Immediate processing of random direct-access files is the predominant information processing approach today. The **immediate-direct mode** is essential for real-time files, which are required in many information systems. For example, an airline reservations system could not function without real-time files. Other examples of information systems that require real-time files are finished-goods inventory files in which order entry is computerized, and student record files for course registration systems.

Many other applications use immediate-direct processing because if transactions are captured near the point of the event, errors can usually be corrected easily. A properly designed immediate-direct processing system can potentially control input much better than a batch processing system. All the edit checks that are performed on batch input can also be

Nestle Foods Processes a New Batch

By Charlie Simpson

Automating its batch processing has been an issue cooking in Purchase, N.Y.-based Nestle Foods IS [information systems] ovens for a long time. Even during its System/38 days, Nestle had trouble controlling long-running batch jobs at remote sites, because the remote staff, mostly clerical, did not have the time to monitor and run the remote site jobs, and Nestle no longer wanted to spend overtime dollars to have personnel come in to start the jobs during off hours.

To ease the strain on its AS/400 network processing, Nestle combined Schaumburg, Ill.-based Advanced Systems Concepts' automated job scheduler called Pilot with its own front-end control code. Nestle

has implemented the package at 30 locations throughout the United States on AS/400s ranging from B20s to the new D60. Pilot allows Nestle to control data processing by shifting the execution of noncritical and long-running jobs to times when the machines are least likely to be in use.

Nestle gave its sites a week to install the software, and within that time, all 30 locations were fully operational. Nestle then wrote code that lets it access and maintain Pilot at each remote office or warehouse from one location. Joanne Hartley, technical analyst for Nestle's IS department, says the reason for the front-end code is to simultaneously control all sites from one location without having to sign on to each computer. This was especially needed during initial system setup. Al-

though each site installed the software, the central control site configured the systems.

The software uses a straightforward technique that lets Nestle control communications parameters, network status, and schedule object transfers. In fact, Hartley says, "Once the initial setup is complete, we never have to enter Pilot except to add jobs."

Hartley maintains that Pilot has automated its systems, saving Nestle man hours and dollars by eliminating overtime and part-time personnel needed to implement system backups and long, late night jobs.

Reprinted with permission from *Midrange Systems* (Nov. 12, 1991), p. 24(1). Copyright Professional Press, Inc., 1991.

performed on immediate input. In addition, under an immediate-direct system, errors are communicated immediately to the data entry operator, who is thus better able to correct them. Also, the computer can provide the operator with instructions and aids through the terminal. Figure 12–19 illustrates immediate-direct processing.

On-Line Direct-Access Systems

In the term *on-line direct-access systems*, **on-line** refers to any computer system, peripheral device, or file, such as a terminal or disk pack, that the CPU can control without direct human intervention. For example, a reel of magnetic tape in the library cannot be processed by the CPU without human intervention and therefore is not on-line. In contrast, a disk pack mounted on a disk drive that is accessible to the CPU is on-line. Peripheral devices or files not in direct communication with the CPU are **off-line**. **Direct access** refers to a file organization in which records can be retrieved by the CPU without much searching. Direct and indexed file organizations allow direct access.

Thus, an **on-line direct-access system** is one with several terminals in direct communication with the CPU, which in turn can retrieve data from one or more files directly for immediate processing without human intervention. Figure 12–20 shows a typical on-line direct-access system.

On-line terminals without on-line direct-access capability would be impractical. The turnaround time and processing costs would be intoler-

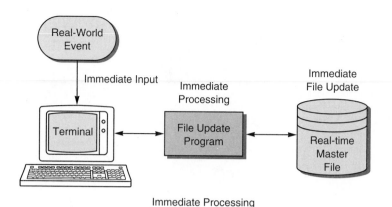

FIGURE 12–17
Immediate Processing.
Immediate processing is likely to be the predominant method of processing business transactions in the future.

able if an operator had to mount each file asked for and the record search were performed sequentially.

Random direct-access files are usually associated with on-line terminals. One primary reason for random direct-access files is to allow for immediate processing of inquiries and updates to the file from on-line terminals scattered throughout the user organization. Therefore, the terms *on-line* and *direct-access* are usually used together when referring to a complete computer system.

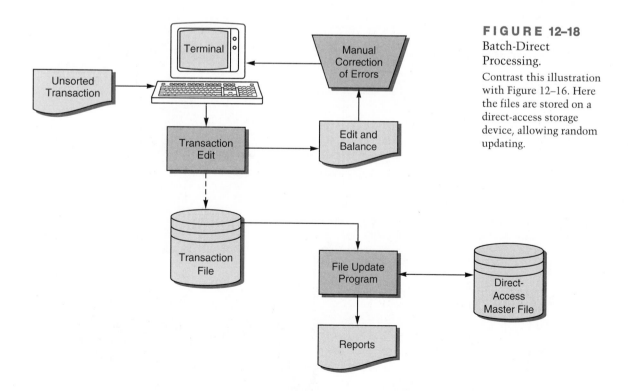

FIGURE 12–18
Batch-Direct Processing.

Contrast this illustration with Figure 12–16. Here the files are stored on a direct-access storage device, allowing random updating.

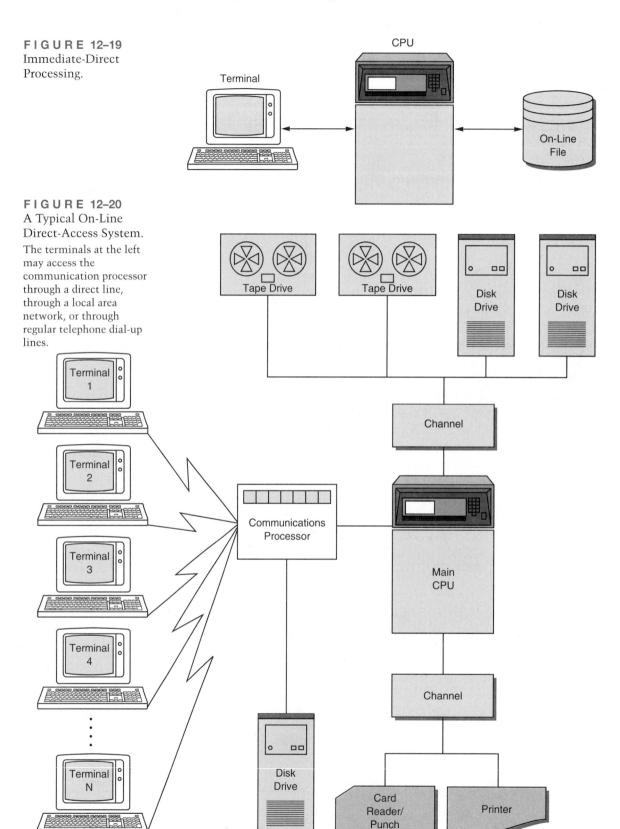

FIGURE 12–19
Immediate-Direct
Processing.

FIGURE 12–20
A Typical On-Line
Direct-Access System.
The terminals at the left
may access the
communication processor
through a direct line,
through a local area
network, or through
regular telephone dial-up
lines.

A final observation is that on-line direct-access systems are not necessarily real-time systems. These two terms are often erroneously used interchangeably. The distinction between them is discussed in the next section.

A **real-time information system** can immediately capture data about on-going events or processes and provide the information necessary to manage them. Examples of real-time systems are manufacturing process control and airline reservations systems. An essential component of a real-time system is real-time master files, which are updated immediately after a real-world event occurs. Consequently, at any point in time, the data in real-time master files should accurately reflect the status of the real-world properties they represent. For example, when a customer reserves a seat on an airline flight, the reservations agent keys in the customer's reservation and the inventory of nonreserved seats on that flight is immediately updated to reflect one fewer available seat. An immediate processing system is necessary to respond to customer inquiries about available seats. A batch system would be inadequate because the data on the master file would not be up-to-date.

Many colleges and universities use real-time systems to register students for classes. The students request classes through a computer terminal. They can be notified immediately about whether their schedules are confirmed because the inventory of unfilled class seats is on a real-time file. Figure 12–21 illustrates a real-time system.

Real-time systems are most useful at the transaction processing and operational decision levels, for example in order processing systems that depend on real-time inventory master files. Management decisions at the tactical and strategic levels generally do not require real-time information. Information that is a day, a week, or even a month old, such as profit and loss statements, can be just as valuable as real-time data for tactical or strategic decision making. However, as the costs of storage and processing decline, more real-time systems are being implemented for transaction processing. More of the data used in tactical and strategic decisions are becoming available on a real-time basis. For example, tactical sales analysis data can be retrieved from real-time point-of-sale systems, even though in some cases it is not necessary for such data to be real-time.

Certain transaction processing applications do not require real-time updating. For example, updating the payroll master file on a real-time basis for hours worked by each employee is unnecessary. If payroll checks are produced weekly, the information can be updated every week using the batch processing method.

The computer configuration to support a real-time system must allow on-line direct access to data. The files must be structured to allow random access, since fast response to inquiries is required, and update transactions are processed as they occur, rather than on a delayed, batch basis.

Real-time systems have the primary advantage of providing timely information. Certain computer applications can function only on a real-time basis. Others are most cost-effective using a batch mode. The primary disadvantages of real-time systems are that their hardware and communication costs are greater and the operating system and applications software necessary to support them are more complex.

Real-Time Systems

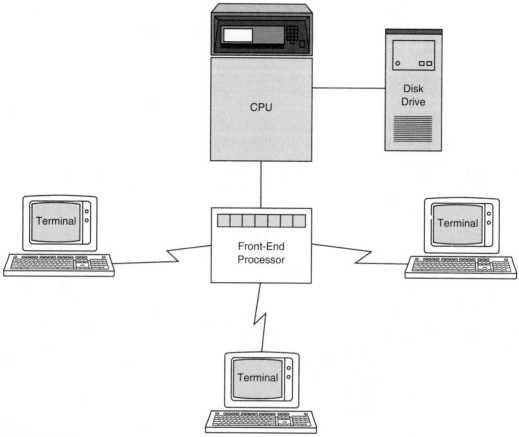

FIGURE 12–21
A Real-Time System.
In a real-time system, the terminals as well as the files must be on-line to the CPU.

Summary

- The components of the information system data hierarchy, in ascending order of complexity, are as follows:

    1. Bit

    2. Byte

    3. Field, or item

    4. Record

    5. File

    6. Database

- A bit is a binary digit.

- A byte is a character of data.

- A field is one or more bytes that contain data about an attribute of an entity.

- A record is a collection of fields related to a specific entity.

- A file is a collection of related records.

- A database is all the files of an organization that are structured and integrated to facilitate information retrieval and update.

- A primary key uniquely identifies an individual record.

- Secondary keys are used to access records based on the contents of fields within the record other than the primary key field.

- There are two types of access to records stored in files: sequential and random.

- Data records stored in a sequential file are ordered by the order in which they were entered or by record key. Sequential files are usually used for batch-type processes in which most of the records have to be accessed every time the program is run.

- Direct file organization allows rapid access to any individual record by converting its primary key directly to an address. This is usually done through the division remainder approach.

- Indexed files are associated with another file called an index, which is used to locate information records in the indexed file on a random-access basis.

- The indexed sequential access method (ISAM) uses an index to determine the cylinder and track location of a record, and then that track is searched sequentially for the desired record.

- B-tree indexes are widely used because they allow fast access to very large files and they can be used on any field in a file.

- To select the best file organization for an application, it is necessary to consider many factors, including file volatility, file activity, file size, and file query requirements.

- In a batch processing system, queries and updates to the system are accumulated for some time and are then executed all in one run. With immediate processing, on the other hand, transactions are individually entered into the files soon after the real-world event occurs.

- Three modes of information processing are used: batch-sequential, batch-direct, and immediate-direct. Most applications are now being designed for the immediate-direct mode.

- An on-line direct-access system consists of several terminals connected to the CPU, which in turn are connected to several random-access files.

- A real-time information system is a special kind of on-line direct-access system. It captures data immediately after the occurrence of an event, processes them right away, and returns information that is used to manage ongoing events.

Key Terms

Bit

Byte

Field or item

Record

File

Master files

Transaction files

Table files

Index files

Summary files

Program files

Backup files

Database

Primary key

Secondary keys

Sequential access

Random access

File organization

Physical address

Cylinder

Track

Sector

Relative address

Linked list

Directory

Sequential file organization

Direct file organization

Hash

Division/remainder method

Indexed file organization

Fully indexed file

Binary search

Indexed sequential file organization

B-tree index

Virtual storage access method (VSAM)

File activity

File volatility

File query

Batch processing

Immediate processing

Batch-sequential mode

Batch-direct mode

Immediate-direct mode

On-line

Off-line

Direct access

On-line direct-access system

Real-time information system

Review Questions

1. Explain the relationship among the elements in the data hierarchy.

2. What are the differences between a primary and secondary key?

3. What are the three record access methods?

4. How is a parity bit used to ensure data accuracy?

5. What are the three basic types of file organization?

6. Briefly explain how the direct addressing technique of data retrieval is performed.

7. Explain the differences between the three types of indexed file organization.

8. List the criteria used in selecting a file organization method.

9. Explain the difference between batch processing and immediate processing.

10. Is it possible to process direct-access files in a batch mode?

11. List the benefits of the immediate-direct approach to data processing.

12. What makes a system on-line?

13. Why is direct-access storage necessary for an on-line system?

14. What makes an on-line direct-access system a real-time system?

Discussion Questions and Cases

1. What type of file organization would be best suited for each of the following files?

   a. A payroll master file from which paychecks are issued biweekly

   b. An accounts receivable master file in a large retail department store

   c. A batch transaction file for a material inventory system in which the master file has an ISAM organization

   d. The master file for a work-in-process job order system used by management for operational control of production

   e. An on-line class registration master file used by a university for student registration from on-line terminals

2. Sequential file organization is conceptually simple and requires a minimum of storage space. Direct file organization, on the other hand, requires complex access methods and extra storage space for indexes. Discuss some business reasons for the predominance of direct-access systems. What technological developments have aided in this process?

3. A large bank with branches in several different cities in a single state is reevaluating its demand deposit accounting (DDA) system. It feels that there are three basic approaches to DDA:

   a. A centralized batch DDA system updated for changes on a daily basis. CD-ROM output would be produced daily containing the complete account history for each depositor. Each branch would receive a CD-ROM disk (through a courier service by 8:00 A.M.) containing the above information for all depositors. The daily cutoff for the DDA system would be 2:00 P.M. Therefore, the CD-ROM would reflect any transactions that have cleared by 2:00 P.M. the previous day. This CD-ROM would be used for depositors' inquiries concerning their accounts.

   b. A centralized batch DDA system similar to the system in part a above, but no CD-ROM would be produced. Instead, video display terminals (connected on-line through leased lines with the central CPU) would be used by each branch for processing depositors' inquiries concerning their accounts.

c. A real-time DDA system in which both transactions and inquiries are processed immediately through branch video display terminals through leased communication lines.

What are the advantages and disadvantages of the three alternatives? How would the necessity of using dial-up lines affect your choice of alternative c?

4. Basic Hardware is a medium-sized chain of hardware stores located primarily in the southeastern states. The company is considering some type of point-of-sale capture of sales data through cash registers for input to sales analysis and inventory reordering systems. The choices are a true real-time system and a batch system that is updated daily. With a real-time system, each cash register would be on-line to the central computer through regular telephone lines during business hours. Under the batch system, each cash register would have the capability of storing one day's worth of sales data. At the end of the day the data would be transmitted to the central computer. Although the real-time option has the advantage of providing real-time information, it also is more expensive primarily because it would tie up long-distance telephone lines during business hours. With the batch approach, a line would be in use for approximately fifteen minutes at the end of each day. Do you think real-time information in this situation would justify the additional communication costs?

5. The Lowery Engineering Consulting Company employs about seventy-five engineers who work with clients in product design for farm equipment. Leroy Jones, a computer consultant, was recently hired to design a new computerized timekeeping system in order for the firm to keep track of consultant hours charged to various projects. The new design requires that each engineer complete a time sheet every week for the number of hours charged to specific projects. The time sheets would be batched and would update the system on weekends. Leroy envisions three computer files: an employee master file, a project file, and a file of hours charged to projects per employee. Leroy still needs to determine the best file organization. Can you help him?

INFORMATION SYSTEMS STRATEGIES

Wendy's Chain Sells Fast Food Through Windows

By Ben Myers

From ordering hamburger buns to counting change for $20 bills, a Windows 3.0 application will soon automate record keeping for the Wendy's International, Inc. fast-food chain.

Described as "a bulletproof application for computer novices" by its developer, the new system was ready in record time—less than six months after development work began.

Compris Technology of Atlanta, a business partner of IBM, designed and developed from the ground up a Windows application that is slated to go into acceptance testing this month in many Wendy's hamburger outlets throughout the country.

The system keeps track of information such as cash sales, labor, speed of service, inventory levels and wasted materials, said Mike Dempsey, a senior analyst at Compris.

The PS/2 Windows 3.0 software maintains historical data and provides statistics for forecasting trends, from hourly peaks to busy days during the year, he added.

"If one chicken sandwich is wasted at each cooking point every day, and our system reduces that loss to zero, then the system pays for itself within a year," said Dempsey.

Most noteworthy about the software is the very short development cycle for the application: Compris started working on it in September.

The hub of the system is an IBM PS/2, to which specially designed IBM point-of-sale (POS) PCs with LCD VGA touch-screens are connected. The PS/2, typically installed in the store manager's office, collects data from the POS PCs, then analyzes and reports key business information to the manager.

The system also displays customer orders in real time on monitors at each station where food is cooked.

If sales in a store begin flagging, both the store manager and corporate decision-makers share the same facts and can agree more quickly about what needs to be done, Dempsey said. With accurate data about sales, a store manager can order more food and add people to a shift, confident that impending business demands will be met.

"As soon as inventories fall below a given safety level, the computer automatically prompts the manager to order more stock, so Wendy's won't run out of food," said Dempsey.

"Today, the store manager must interrupt work flow at each register to count cash. With our system, the cash balance of a store is always current and available at the touch of a key," he added.

Dempsey said that the system will shortly undergo acceptance testing at Wendy's headquarters in Dublin, Ohio. After the system is accepted, Wendy's plans to install it across the country in its company-owned stores. It will also be available to Wendy's franchisees.

Talking to the Boss

Future plans at Wendy's call for electronic links to corporate headquarters, where it will be possible to see up-to-date information about the performance of each outlet on a daily basis.

Dempsey said the Windows interface was built with ProtoView, a development package from ProtoView Development Corp. of Dayton, N.J. The software also uses a dynamic link library (DLL) for the Btrieve database and indexed sequential file-management software from Novell, Inc.

Dempsey evaluated several different development packages for Windows. "All of them generated the code to manage menus, dialog boxes and combo boxes," he said, "but only ProtoView provided the tight data editing that we needed to develop [this application].

"ProtoView does this through a DLL, and one of the great strengths of Windows is the seamlessness with which various DLLs from different vendors integrate together," he added.

Typically, development of the Windows graphical user interface consumes 70 percent to 80 percent of the time needed to create a Windows application. Dempsey estimated that without ProtoView, the development of the application would have taken three years instead of five months.

"It took one of our programmers just two days to design and generate 20 menus with ProtoView" during a carefully measured test, Dempsey said.

Discussion Questions

1. What types of file organization and access methods do you think are used in this system?

2. How does this real-time system contribute to the processing of individual customer orders? How does it contribute to the daily management of the restaurant?

13

Database Management Systems

The Atlantic Life and Casualty Insurance Company is a large firm located in an eastern city. It has millions of customers on whom it keeps data. Many applications, such as customer service, accounts receivable, accounts payable, and salesperson commission reports, use the data about customers and their insurance coverage. How do all these applications use the same data? What keeps track of where these data are stored and who may use or change them? Does a user have to know where the information is physically stored before using it?

Perhaps the most important challenge facing information systems is to provide users with timely and versatile access to data stored in computer files. In a dynamic business environment there are many unanticipated needs for information. Often the data that can satisfy these information needs are contained in computer files but cannot be accessed and output in a suitable format on a timely basis. Database management systems are meeting this challenge.

This chapter first contrasts the traditional and the database approaches to information systems. Then it looks at some of the logical ways users view data stored in a database. Next, it explores the advantages and disadvantages of database management systems. And finally, the chapter looks at some of the future trends in database management systems.

Introduction

The traditional approach to information systems is file oriented. Before the advent of database management systems, each application maintained its own master file and generally had its own set of transaction files. Figure 13–1 illustrates this traditional approach. Files are custom designed for each application, and generally there is little sharing of data among the various applications. Programs are dependent on the files and vice versa; that is, when the physical format of the file is changed, the program also has to be changed. The traditional approach is file oriented because the primary purpose of many applications is to maintain, on the master file, the data required to produce management information. Therefore, the master file is the centerpiece of each application.

The Traditional Approach to Information Processing

Although the traditional, file-oriented approach to information systems is still widely used, it does have disadvantages. Among them are the following.

Disadvantages of the Traditional Approach

Data Redundancy

Often identical data are stored in two or more files. Notice that in Figure 13–2 each employee's Social Security number, name, and department are stored in both the payroll and personnel files. Such **data redundancy** increases data editing, maintenance, and storage costs. In addition, data stored on two master files (which should in theory be identical) are often different for good reason; but such differences inevitably create confusion.

Lack of Data Integration

Data on different master files may be related, as in the case of payroll and personnel master files. For example, in Figure 13–2, management may

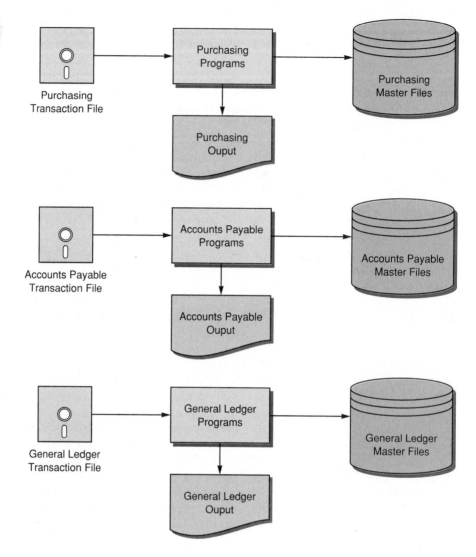

FIGURE 13-1
Traditional Approach to Information Processing.
Notice that each application has its own master file.

want a report displaying employee name, department, pay rate, and occupation. However, the application approach does not have the mechanisms for associating these data in a logical way to make them useful for management's needs. This lack of **data integration** leads to inefficient use of stored data.

Program/Data Dependence

Under the traditional, file-oriented approach, **program/data dependence** exists; this means that programs are tied to files and vice versa. Changes in the physical format of a file, such as the addition of a data field, require changes in all programs that access the file. Consequently, for each of the application programs that a programmer writes or maintains, he or she must be concerned with data management. There is no centralized execution of the data management function; data management is scattered among all the application programs. Think of the thousands of

Payroll File Social Security Number	Employee Name	Pay Rate	Year-to-Date Earnings	Department
385686293	Joseph Hawkins	$12.50	4005.50	380
390328453	Samuel Smith	$13.25	5100.60	390
410686392	Theodore Thatcher	$ 5.50	2495.60	312
425786495	Robert Benson	$25.80	8135.50	312
510933492	Thomas Benson	$12.50	4005.50	095
511945893	Jane Benson	$30.50	9617.55	100

unnecessary duplication

Personnel File Social Security Number	Employee Name	Department	Age	Date Hired	Occupation *fields*
385686293	Joe Hawkins	380	25	03 JAN 83	Wife's Brother
390328453	Sam Smith	390	55	05 SEP 65	Goof Off
410686392	Ted Thatcher	312	28	15 JUN 81	Golfer
425786495	Bob Benson	312	45	20 JUL 64	Superstar
510933492	Tom Benson	095	38	31 DEC 68	My Brother
511945893	Jane Benson	100	43	20 JUL 64	The Boss

FIGURE 13–2
Data Redundancy and Lack of Integration among Files.
A payroll file stores data concerning employees' wages and salaries. A personnel file contains data about employees' work and education histories as well as occupational skills. Many large firms have separate payroll and personnel departments. A database management system would allow the two departments to share data.

computer programs that had to be altered when the U.S. Postal Service changed from a five-digit to a nine-digit zip code. A centralized DBMS could have minimized the number of places this change had to be made.

Lack of Flexibility

The information retrieval capabilities of most traditional systems are limited to predetermined requests for data. Therefore, the system produces information in the form of scheduled reports and queries which it has been previously programmed to handle. If management needs unanticipated data, the information can perhaps be provided if it is in the files of the system. However, extensive programming is often required to retrieve and compile the information. By the time the programming is completed, the information may no longer be required or useful. This problem has long plagued information systems. Management knows that a particular piece of information can be produced on a one-time basis, but the expense and time involved are sometimes prohibitive. Ideally, information systems should be able to mix related data elements from several different files and produce information with a fast turnaround to service unanticipated requests for information. Flexible databases are necessary to provide the flexible information that large firms like Frito-Lay need to compete, as illustrated in Application 13–1.

Frito-Lay Dips into Flexibility

By Clinton Wilder

For companies trying to grapple with the transition from "big and slow" to "lean and mean," Frito-Lay, Inc. suggests a better alternative: big and mean. The key to that, according to Vice-President of Management Services Charles S. Feld, is a flexible information structure.

Frito-Lay found that it needed *decentralized* decision-making to respond to a rapidly changing market, but *centralized* controls to hold down expenses and leverage economies of scale. That meant designing the supporting relational database to be more flexible than the Frito-Lay organization itself, Feld told attendees at the annual Nolan, Norton & Co. symposium.

"In this environment, you can't be run on paper," he said. "You must have the kind of environment that allows the network to do the work. We had to disconnect the transaction base from the organizational form."

The centerpiece of that transaction base is known in Feld's unit as The Cube—IBM's DB2 database configured to track snack food sales by a variety of parameters. Within the U.S., the database tracks Frito-Lay's 32 geographic regions, four retail distribution channels and six to eight product categories—giving The Cube several hundred different "cells."

Each cell contains sales data, forecasts, trends and competitive information within its organizational parameters. For example, a cell may include sales of potato chip products through convenience stores in Chicago, or of tortilla chip lines sold in supermarkets in Atlanta. The sales plan for each cell is revised every 16 weeks.

"Within each cell, we plan our business as if we're a small business," Feld said. "In the past, we could have an annual plan to sell $1 billion worth of Doritos and tell our sales force to go work it out. Now we have to be short-term and flexible, and the system must respond. We can't have a national sales meeting every 16 weeks."

Less Salt in the Southwest

That flexibility may mean distributing specialized products to suit regional tastes, such as crispier Cape Code-style potato chips in New England or less salty restaurant-style tortilla chips in the Southwest. Or, pushing more low-calorie foods in stores that sell more diet sodas. Or, doing regional promotions, such as printing the 49ers logo on bags sold in San Francisco and the Browns logo on bags sold in Cleveland.

"In the past, we had national pricing and national promotions for Memorial Day and Labor Day weekends, and that was about it," according to Feld. "The business cycle was well-ordered and long."

However, that was before the proliferation of convenience stores, gas station minimarts as well as hundreds of smaller munchie makers springing up on the competitive horizon.

Now, 40 of Frito-Lay's senior executives have access to "slicing" The Cube in different ways to analyze sales trends and competitive factors. While the individual cells stay responsive on the micro-market level, the numbers can be combined for the macro overview by region, product and/or channel.

"The people at the local level know what's happening, and the centralized executives can look at that data and know what it means," Feld said.

The Database Approach to Information Processing

A **database management system** is a set of programs that serve as an interface between application programs and a set of coordinated and integrated *physical files* called a database. (A physical file is the actual storage of data on storage media.) A DBMS provides the capabilities for creating, maintaining, and changing a database. A **database** is a collection of data. The physical files of the database are analogous to the master files of the application programs. However, with DBMS, the data among the physical files are related with various **pointers** and keys, which not only reduce data redundancy but also enable the unanticipated retrieval of related information. Figure 13–3 illustrates the DBMS approach.

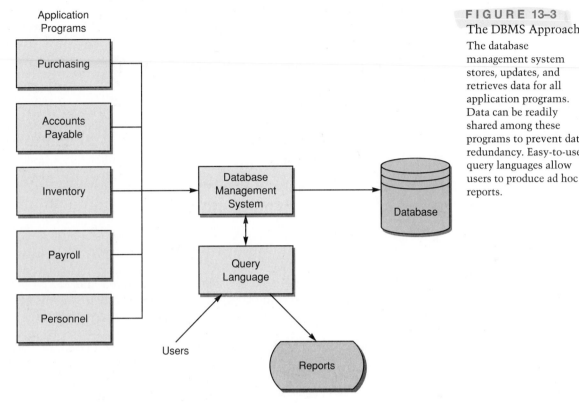

FIGURE 13–3
The DBMS Approach.
The database management system stores, updates, and retrieves data for all application programs. Data can be readily shared among these programs to prevent data redundancy. Easy-to-use query languages allow users to produce ad hoc reports.

Logical versus Physical Views of Data Storage

With most traditional data storage techniques, the programmer needs to be aware of the physical layout of data records on storage devices and thus needs to understand the technical characteristics of many kinds of hardware. The problem gets even more complex in a multi-application environment in which one programmer may have to use data files designed to another programmer. Often a lot of time is wasted just trying to figure out what a particular data field is supposed to represent.

A DBMS overcomes this problem by providing two views of data: physical and logical. The **physical view** of data is similar to traditional file systems. It deals with the actual locations of bits and bytes on memory devices. Some information systems personnel need this information to be able to make efficient use of storage and processing resources. However, knowledge of all these details serves no useful purpose for the application programmer who is interested only in using the information, no matter how it is stored.

The **logical view** represents data in a format that is meaningful to the user and the application programmer. It organizes data fields and records such that they represent actual business activities. For instance, a marketing executive's logical view of sales data may resemble Table 13–1. In this format the data can easily be used to generate reports needed in decision making. The database approach allows the user to maintain this kind of conceptual (logical) view of data.

TABLE 13–1
Logical View of Sales Data.

| Salesperson | | | Year-to-Date Sales | | |
ID #	Name	Region	Product A	Product B	Product C
223	Smith	S.W.	6,395	4,328	5,875
227	O'Neill	S.W.	4,326	898	1,587
241	Maxwell	S.W.	12,331	8,976	7,215
256	Ware	East	8,232	6,554	7,321
257	Charles	East	2,111	4,573	5,321
258	Scholar	Midwest	5,221	6,632	6,331
276	Williams	Midwest	11,213	10,709	9,318
283	Mufti	Midwest	2,124	5,335	6,326
285	Cadd	Midwest	7,224	5,019	2,020
300	Harris	N.E.	3,423	3,302	8,824
307	Bentley	N.E.	8,635	5,661	3,624
310	Curtis	N.E.	10,728	7,187	8,721
322	May	N.E.	7,853	5,354	6,332

This is only one logical view of sales data. Manufacturing managers might be interested in sales data by product, instead of data on salespersons and regions as shown here.

In a DBMS the data might be physically disaggregated and stored on magnetic disk according to some complex addressing mechanism; but the DBMS assumes the responsibility of aggregating the data into a neat, logical format whenever the application program needs it. This frees application programmers from having to worry about tracks and cylinders, and lets them concentrate on the business aspects of the problem to be solved.

Figure 13–4 shows how the DBMS insulates the user from physical storage details. The user or application programmer can refer to data items by using meaningful names, such as CUSTOMER-NAME and TOTAL-PURCHASE. He or she no longer has to worry about specifying things like the number of bytes in a field.

Components of the Database Approach

The database environment has four components: the users, the DBMS software, the database administrator, and the database. Figure 13–5 illustrates the interaction of these components.

The Users   Users consist of both the traditional users (such as management) and application programmers, who are not typically considered to be users. Users interact with the DBMS indirectly through application programs or directly through a simple **query language**. The user's interactions with the DBMS also include defining the logical relationships in the database (the logical view), and inputting, altering, deleting, and manipulating data.

The Database Management System   The database management system is a complex software package that enables the user to communicate with the database. The DBMS interprets user commands so that the computer system can perform the task required. For example, it might translate a command such as GET CUSTNO, AMOUNT, INVNO into "retrieve record 458 from disk 09."

A database management system uses two languages—a **data definition language (DDL)** and a **data manipulation language (DML)**. The DDL is the

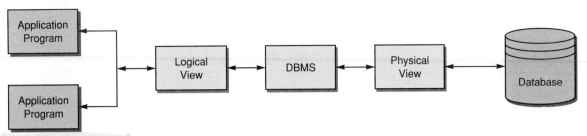

FIGURE 13–4
Logical versus Physical Views of Data.
The ability to establish different logical views of the same data while insulating the user from concerns about how the data are physically stored has been a major contribution to the user friendliness of information systems.

link between the logical and physical views of the database. As discussed earlier, *logical* refers to the way the user views data; *physical* refers to the way the data are physically stored. The logical structure of a database is sometimes called a **schema**. A **subschema** is the way a particular application views the data from the database. Many users and many application programs may utilize the same database; therefore, many different subschemas can exist. Each user or application program uses a set of DDL statements to construct a subschema that includes only data elements of interest. Figure 13–6 shows statements from a data definition language.

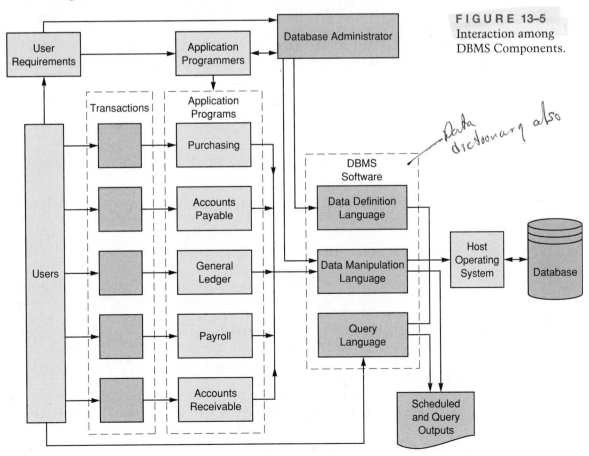

FIGURE 13–5
Interaction among DBMS Components.

FIGURE 13–6
Statements from a
Data Definition
Language.

This DDL describes the
physical characteristics of
the data, such as the data
type and the length of
each field.

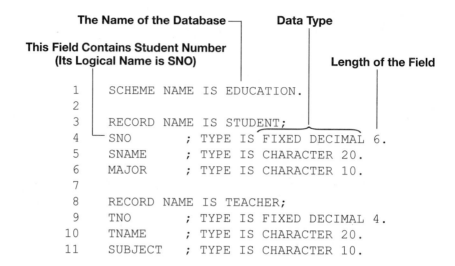

```
             The Name of the Database ─┐        Data Type

This Field Contains Student Number
(Its Logical Name is SNO)                                Length of the Field

    1 │  SCHEME NAME IS EDUCATION.│
    2 │
    3 │  RECORD NAME IS STUDENT;
    4 └─ SNO       ; TYPE IS FIXED DECIMAL 6.
    5    SNAME     ; TYPE IS CHARACTER 20.
    6    MAJOR     ; TYPE IS CHARACTER 10.
    7
    8    RECORD NAME IS TEACHER;
    9    TNO       ; TYPE IS FIXED DECIMAL 4.
   10    TNAME     ; TYPE IS CHARACTER 20.
   11    SUBJECT   ; TYPE IS CHARACTER 10.
```

The DDL is used to define the physical characteristics of each record: the fields within the record, and each field's logical name, data type, and length. The logical name (such as SNAME for the student name field) is used by both application programs and users to refer to a field for the purpose of retrieving or updating the data in it. The DDL is also used to specify relationships among the records. The primary functions of the DDL are to:

- describe the schema and subschemas

- describe the fields in each record and the record's logical name

- describe the data type and name of each field

- indicate the keys of the record

- provide for data security restrictions

- provide for logical and physical data independence

- provide a means of associating related data

The data manipulation language provides the techniques for processing the database, such as retrieving, sorting, displaying, and deleting data or records. The DML should include a variety of manipulation verbs and *operands* for each verb. (An operand is an entity to which an operation is applied; that which is operated upon.) Table 13–2 contains some of these verbs and corresponding operands. Figure 13–7 shows typical DML statements.

Most data manipulation languages interface with high-level programming languages such as COBOL or PL/1. These languages enable a programmer to perform unique data processing that the DBMS's data manipulation language cannot perform.

A key feature of a DML is that it uses logical names (such as CUSTNO for customer number) instead of physical storage locations when referring to data. This capability is possible since the data definition language provides the link between the logical view of data and their physical storage. The functions of a DML are to:

- provide the techniques for data manipulation such as the deletion, replacement, retrieval, sorting, or insertion of data or records

- enable the user and application programs to process data by using logically meaningful data names rather than physical storage locations

- provide interfaces with programming languages, including several high-level languages such as COBOL, PL/1, and FORTRAN

- allow the user and application programs to be independent of physical data storage and database maintenance

- provide for the use of logical relationships among data items

Verbs	Operands
DELETE	Record key, field name, record name, or file name
SORT	Field name
INSERT	Record key, field name, record name, or file name
DISPLAY	Record key, field name, record name, or file name
ADD	Field name

The verbs in this table are combined with operands to manipulate data. For example, a command might be DELETE CUSTNO 5.

TABLE 13–2
An Evaluation of Three Leading Executive Information Systems
Adapted with permission from Michael L. Sullivan-Trainor, "Command Center Slips Past Commander (Barely)," *Computerworld*, July 16, 1990, pp. 88–93.

```
1. Database Task Group (DBTG) DML defined for COBOL

   PERFORM UNTIL FLAG = 'RED'
      FIND NEXT OVERDUE WITHIN ACCOUNTS
      IF EOF NOT = 'YES'
         IF OVERDUE = 'YES'
            MOVE 'RED' TO FLAG
         END-IF
      END-IF
   END-PERFORM
2. Information Management System (IMS) DML (DL/1)

      GU ACCOUNTS (OVERDUE = 'YES'
   VA GN ACCOUNTS (OVERDUE = 'RED'
      go to VA
3. Structured English Query Language (SEQUEL)

   SELECT ACCTNO FROM ACCOUNTS
      WHERE OVERDUE = 'YES'
```

FIGURE 13–7
Statements from Three Data Manipulation Languages.
The verbs in data manipulation languages differ widely. For example, the verbs (such as FIND, MOVE, and SELECT) used in these three languages all differ from the verbs shown in Table 13–2.

The Database Administrator The database is managed by a **database administrator (DBA)**. The database administrator and his or her staff perform the following functions:

- Maintain a data dictionary. The data dictionary defines the meaning of each data item stored in the data base and describes interrelations between data items. Since the database is shared by many users, it is necessary to have clear and commonly agreed upon meanings for the stored items. Part of a data dictionary is shown in Figure 13–8. The trend in DBMS is to combine the functions of the data definition language and data dictionary into an **active data dictionary**. It is called "active" because the DBMS continuously refers to it for all the physical data definitions (field lengths, data types, and so on) that a DDL would provide.

- Determine and maintain the physical structure of the database.

- Provide for updating and changing the database, including the deletion of inactive records.

- Create and maintain edit controls regarding changes and additions to the database.

- Develop retrieval methods to meet the needs of the users.

- Implement security and disaster recovery procedures.

- Maintain configuration control of the database. **Configuration control** means that changes requested by one user must be approved by the other users of the database. One person cannot indiscriminately change the database to the detriment of other users.

- Assign user access codes in order to prevent unauthorized use of data.

A database administrator works very closely with users to create, maintain, and safeguard the database. In effect, the DBA is the liaison between the database and its users, and therefore must be familiar with users' information requirements. The administrator must also be technically competent in the areas of DBMS and data storage and processing. Database administration is becoming an attractive career option to individuals with programming, systems, and business backgrounds. Figure 13–9 indicates the position of the DBA in a business organization.

The Database The database is the physical collection of data. In a DBMS, the data must be stored on direct-access devices like magnetic disks. However, well-managed installations create backup copies of the database on off-line storage media such as magnetic tape. These security measures are extremely important in a database environment, since many departments and application programs may be dependent on a single, centralized database.

Database management systems are designed to optimize the use of physical storage and CPU processing time. The logical view may contain redundant data items in order to make them more understandable to users. But the physical implementation of the DBMS attempts to make the physical storage nonredundant. This not only saves space, but also precludes the possibility of different values existing for the same data item at one time. The DBMS also uses other techniques to optimize resource utilization. Data records that are seldom used may be placed on inexpensive, slow memory devices, whereas frequently used data may be put on faster but more expensive media.

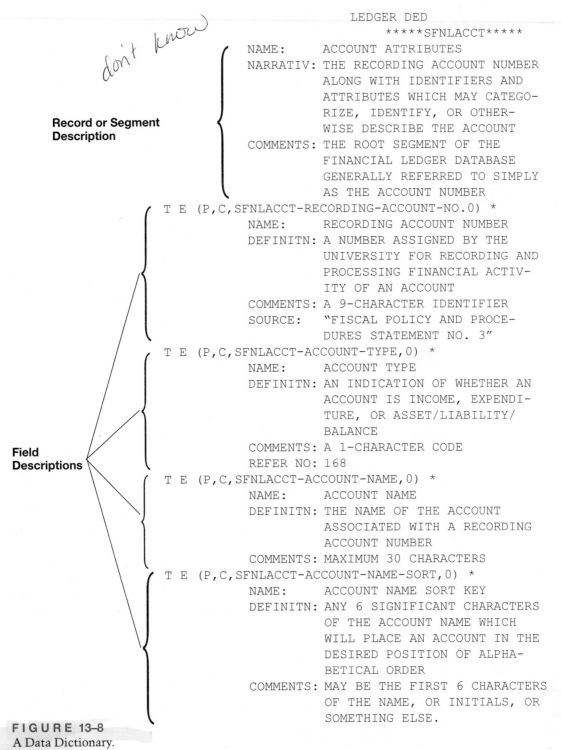

```
                                    LEDGER DED
                                  *****SFNLACCT*****
                     NAME:      ACCOUNT ATTRIBUTES
                     NARRATIV:  THE RECORDING ACCOUNT NUMBER
                                ALONG WITH IDENTIFIERS AND
                                ATTRIBUTES WHICH MAY CATEGO-
                                RIZE, IDENTIFY, OR OTHER-
                                WISE DESCRIBE THE ACCOUNT
                     COMMENTS:  THE ROOT SEGMENT OF THE
                                FINANCIAL LEDGER DATABASE
                                GENERALLY REFERRED TO SIMPLY
                                AS THE ACCOUNT NUMBER
     T E (P,C,SFNLACCT-RECORDING-ACCOUNT-NO.0) *
                     NAME:      RECORDING ACCOUNT NUMBER
                     DEFINITN:  A NUMBER ASSIGNED BY THE
                                UNIVERSITY FOR RECORDING AND
                                PROCESSING FINANCIAL ACTIV-
                                ITY OF AN ACCOUNT
                     COMMENTS:  A 9-CHARACTER IDENTIFIER
                     SOURCE:    "FISCAL POLICY AND PROCE-
                                DURES STATEMENT NO. 3"
     T E (P,C,SFNLACCT-ACCOUNT-TYPE,0) *
                     NAME:      ACCOUNT TYPE
                     DEFINITN:  AN INDICATION OF WHETHER AN
                                ACCOUNT IS INCOME, EXPENDI-
                                TURE, OR ASSET/LIABILITY/
                                BALANCE
                     COMMENTS:  A 1-CHARACTER CODE
                     REFER NO: 168
     T E (P,C,SFNLACCT-ACCOUNT-NAME,0) *
                     NAME:      ACCOUNT NAME
                     DEFINITN:  THE NAME OF THE ACCOUNT
                                ASSOCIATED WITH A RECORDING
                                ACCOUNT NUMBER
                     COMMENTS:  MAXIMUM 30 CHARACTERS
     T E (P,C,SFNLACCT-ACCOUNT-NAME-SORT,0) *
                     NAME:      ACCOUNT NAME SORT KEY
                     DEFINITN:  ANY 6 SIGNIFICANT CHARACTERS
                                OF THE ACCOUNT NAME WHICH
                                WILL PLACE AN ACCOUNT IN THE
                                DESIRED POSITION OF ALPHA-
                                BETICAL ORDER
                     COMMENTS:  MAY BE THE FIRST 6 CHARACTERS
                                OF THE NAME, OR INITIALS, OR
                                SOMETHING ELSE.
```

Record or Segment Description

Field Descriptions

FIGURE 13–8
A Data Dictionary.
This is a portion of the data dictionary entry that describes data concerning an account in a general ledger accounting system.

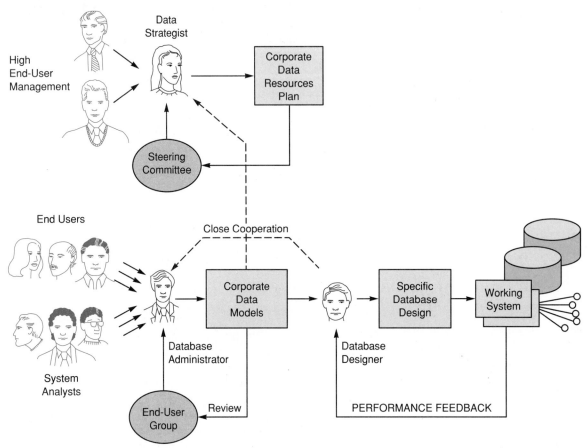

FIGURE 13–9

The Database Administrator.

Some companies have three people involved in the database administrator's job: a data strategist, a database administrator, and a database designer. The data strategist helps the end-user management define its logical data needs. The database designer handles the physical aspects of data storage.

Database systems are rapidly gaining popularity among business users. Since database operations tend to be high-volume processes, they often consume a large portion of the time and memory resources of the computer. Some vendors have developed computers that are dedicated entirely to database operations. These computers, frequently referred to as database machines, are special-purpose units. Certain capabilities are built into the hardware that make retrieval, sorting, updating, and other operations more efficient than with software programs.

Logical Database Structures

Two key features of a DBMS are the ability to reduce data redundancy and the ability to associate related data elements such as related fields and records. These functions are accomplished through the use of keys, embedded pointers, and linked lists. An **embedded pointer** is a field within a record containing the physical or relative address of a related record in another part of the database. The record referred to may also contain an embedded pointer that points to a third record, and so on. The series of records tied together by embedded pointers is a **linked list**.

Three basic types of logical structures are used by a DBMS: tree, network, and relational structures. These structures are models on which the user can build logical views of data. Some real-world database management systems allow users to model and implement data on a tree, network, or relational basis; others allow only one model, such as relational. Tree- and network-structured DBMSs usually tie related data together through linked lists. Relational DBMSs relate data through information contained in the data, as explained later in this chapter.

Tree Structures

Figure 13–10 illustrates student data in a tree (hierarchical) structure. The lower part of Figure 13–10 shows the data fields in each record. A **tree structure** consists of records (often called segments) that are linked to related records in a one-to-many relationship. The distinguishing feature of a tree structure is that each record may have only one parent, but an unlimited number of children. The top record is called the root. As shown in Figure 13–10, each student can attend many semesters and take many courses in each semester. However, each course is tied to a single semester, and the data in each semester record are in turn tied to a single student.

An important point to understand concerning tree structures (as well as network structures) is that they are logical representations of data. The physical storage of the data in Figure 13–10 might be quite different from that shown in the figure. Physically, the records could be stored one after another (sequentially) on a disk. The related records would be linked together by addresses or embedded pointers within each record. With a tree structure, each record must have a minimum of two embedded pointer fields. One field contains the address of the first child of the record; the other holds the address of the record's twin. In Figure 13–10, for example, the fall semester record contains the address of course CIS 3330 (the first child) as well as the address of the spring semester (the twin of the fall semester). Tree structures can represent many different types of data and are widely used in database management systems. For example, IBM's Information Management System (IMS), a mainframe DBMS, uses tree structures for modeling data.

Network Structures

A **network structure** allows a many-to-many relationship among the **nodes** in the structure. A node in a database structure is the point at which subordinate records or segments originate. Figure 13–11 illustrates a network structure between courses and students. Each student can enroll in several classes; each class has many students.

The physical storage, as well as data linkage in a network structure, involve embedded pointers in each record, as in a tree structure. There are several schemes for using pointers with network structures. One is similar to the scheme discussed for tree structures, in which each course record (for example, course 1) contains the address of the first student in the course and then the first student record, in turn, contains the address of the second student in the course, and so on, thereby forming a linked list.

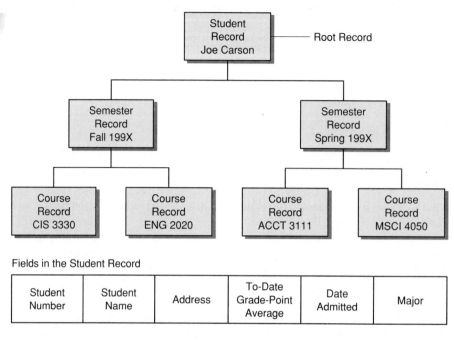

Fields in the Student Record

Student Number	Student Name	Address	To-Date Grade-Point Average	Date Admitted	Major

Fields in the Semester Record

Semester	Semester Fees	Fees Paid	Semester Grade-Point Average

Fields in the Course Record

Course Number	Course Grade

Data represented by a network structure can also be represented by a tree structure through the introduction of redundancy, as illustrated in Figure 13–12. The tree structure requires that the student information be stored two or more times, depending on the number of classes in which a student is enrolled. Tree structures are inefficient if there is substantial redundancy. The avoidance of redundancy is an advantage of network structures when many-to-many relationships exist in the data.

Relational Structures

Most business data have traditionally been organized in the form of simple tables with only columns and rows. In a relational DBMS these tables are called relations (see Table 13–3). This data structure is known as the **relational model**, since it is based on the mathematical theory of relations. One of the greatest advantages of the relational model is its simplicity. The relational, or tabular, model of data is used in a large variety of applications, ranging from your weekly shopping list to the annual report of the world's largest corporation.

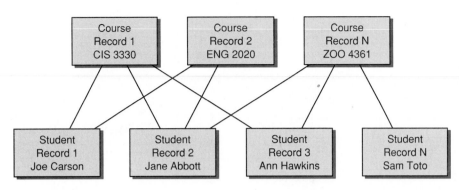

FIGURE 13–11
A Network Data
Structure.

With a network data
structure, the course
records are stored only
once. Contrast this with
the tree structure shown
in Figure 13–10, in which
the course record must be
stored for each student
who takes a particular
course.

Most people are familiar with the relational model as a table. But the
relational model does use some unfamiliar terminology. What is known
as a file in other structures is called either a **table** or a relation in the relational structure. Each row in the table is called a **tuple** (rhymes with *couple*). A tuple is the same as a record in regular file terminology. The
columns of the table are known as **attributes**; they are equivalent to
fields within records. Instead of using the formal relational terminology
of relations, tuples, and attributes, however, this text uses the familiar
terms of files, records, and fields, as do most real-world relational
database systems.

Table 13–4 shows how a college registrar may perceive some of the
data to be stored when using a relational DBMS. A relational DBMS allows a conceptually simple view of data, but also provides a set of powerful data manipulation capabilities. For example, if the registrar wants a
report listing student number, student name, course number, and grades
of students enrolled in CIS 3330, it could easily be derived from the files
shown in Table 13–4. But how will the information needed for the report
be related? It is in two different files and there are no linked lists or
pointers! This leads to the second major advantage of a relational DBMS:
The relationships among data are carried in the data themselves. As long
as two or more files contain the same field, a relational DBMS can relate
the files. In Table 13–4 both the student file and the registration file contain the student number; therefore, the relational DBMS can relate (tech-

FIGURE 13–12
Tree Representation of the Network Data Shown in Figure 13–11.

Some database management systems do not allow data to be stored in a network structure. As shown here, however, if
the DBMS does allow a tree structure, network data can be stored by introducing redundancy.

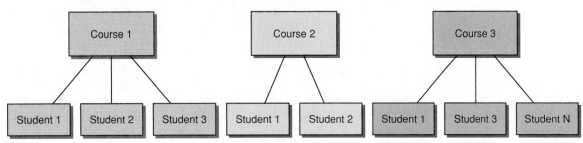

TABLE 13–3

Terminology of a Relational DBMS.

The correct (formal) terms for a relational DBMS are relation, tuples, and attributes. However, the terminology shown in parentheses in this table is often used.

Student Relation (Table or File)

Student Number	Student Name	Grade-Point Average GPA	Major
124693298	Joe Smith	2.58	ACCT
138942824	Chris Todd	3.62	CIS
362982353	Ray Gilmer	3.23	MSCI
468329312	Ann Sneed	2.95	MGT
560782392	Angela Brown	3.01	ECON

Tuples (Rows or Records)

Attributes (Columns or Fields)

nically, the word is *join*) the two files. In addition, both the registration file and the course file contain the course number. Thus, a user can join together all three of these files, producing any imaginable combination of information. The join is an extremely powerful capability!

Now examine how to produce the registrar's report. Using a simple DML statement such as the one shown in Figure 13–13(a), the registrar gets the report shown in Figure 13–13(b). With a traditional, file-oriented system it would have been necessary to write a complex computer program to perform this kind of data manipulation. A tree- or network-structured database would have allowed this manipulation, but only if it had been anticipated at design time and the necessary pointers had been embedded in the records. Since the relational approach does not suffer from either of these restrictions, it is a very effective tool for quickly generating such unanticipated reports for management. Relational databases are being implemented at a rapid pace, and they are the dominant database today.

Advantages of the Database Approach

A DBMS offers many advantages for management, including the elimination of redundancy, program/data independence, and increased security. In addition, its ability to associate related data in processing unanticipated requests for data and its improved interface between users and the system are indispensable tools in an information system.

Eliminates Data Redundancy

Under a DBMS, data that are normally stored at two or more places are stored in one location. This reduces both storage costs and the confusion that may occur when data are stored at two or more locations.

Associates Related Data

The ability to associate related data not only reduces data redundancy but also provides the ability to process unanticipated requests for data. This capability is best met by a relational DBMS.

Student
File

T A B L E 13–4
Student Database
Relations.

Student Number	Student Name	Grade-Point Average (GPA)	Major *Fields*
124693298	Joe Smith	2.58	ACCT
138942824	Chris Todd	3.62	CIS
362982353	Ray Gilmer	3.23	MSCI
468329312	Ann Sneed	2.95	MGT
560782392	Angela Brown	3.01	ECON

Registration File

Student Table is related to the course file through the Registration table.

Student Number	Course Number	Grade
124693298	CIS 3330	B
124693298	ACCT 3111	B
138942824	CIS 3330	A
362982353	MSCI 4050	A
468329312	CIS 3330	C
468329312	MGT 3010	A
560782392	ECON 2111	C

Records

Course File *3 Table*

Course Number	Course Title	Instructor
ACCT 3111	Principles of Accounting	Paton
CIS 3330	Information Systems	Hicks
ECON 2111	Principles of Economics	Samuelson
MGT 3010	Management Principles	Taylor
MSCI 4050	Applied Simulation	Forrestor

Notice that these files are subject-oriented. The student file contains information about students, the registration file contains information about student registration for particular courses, and the course file contains information about courses. The subjects of these three files are students, registration, and courses. One of the approaches to designing files for a relational DBMS is to concentrate on the subjects.

Allows Program/Data Independence

With a DBMS, programs can be changed without the data storage being changed, and data storage can be changed without the programs being changed. The DBMS serves as an interface between the programs and the data so that the programs are concerned only with the logical symbolic names of the data, not with physical storage. This advantage frees the programmer from the detailed and complex task of keeping up with the physical structure of the data.

Improves the Interface Between the User and the System

A DBMS provides simple query languages through which the user, or the user assisted by an application programmer, can retrieve information quickly to fill unanticipated needs for information. In addition, these languages enable users to write their own programs to retrieve information on an ad hoc basis.

FIGURE 13–13
A Relational
Database Query.

If the registrar wants the
report in ascending order
by grade, a line reading
ORDER BY GRADE is
added to the DML
statement.

(a) Simple DML Statement

The DML Statement — Identifies the Fields to Be Listed
Identifies the Files to Be Joined

```
     SELECT STUDENT NUMBER, STUDENT NAME, COURSE
NUMBER, GRADE
        FROM STUDENT.REGISTRATION
        WHERE STUDENT.STUDENT NUMBER=REGISTRA-
TION.STUDENT NUMBER
            AND COURSE NUMBER = CIS 1010
```

(b) Resulting Report   Identifies the Fields to Match in the Join

```
The Report                                      Date 02 MAY 8X
STUDENT NUMBER       STUDENT NAME     COURSE NUMBER      GRADE
   124693298          JOE SMITH        CIS 1010            B
   138942824          CHRIS TODD       CIS 1010            A
   468329312          ANN SNEED        CIS 1010            C
```

Increases Security and Integration of Data

Data contained in a database are likely to be more secure and better integrated than data in traditional files because the DBMS has a database administrator whose primary function is to provide for the integration, physical storage, and security of the data. Under the traditional approach, several individuals handle this job.

Disadvantages of the Database Approach

The disadvantages of database management systems are few, and in the long run are outweighed by the advantages. One disadvantage is that DBMS software is complex; the concepts used are often new to users. Therefore, a DBMS requires sophisticated data processing personnel and sometimes the reeducation of users. The current trend is to produce database management systems that are easier for users to understand.

Another disadvantage is that DBMS software creates additional overhead because it requires computer time to execute, disk space for software storage, and so on. However, as discussed in Chapter 11, this is a disadvantage of all system software. It is not likely to be a major problem in the future as the cost of computer hardware declines.

Future Trends in Database Management Systems

Object-Oriented Database Management Systems

Currently, many firms that develop database management systems software are adding object orientation to their existing systems or developing completely new object-oriented database management systems. These object-oriented database management systems will be widely used in the future. Object-oriented programming was covered in Chapter 11 of this text. As you recall from Chapter 11, the primary advantage of object orientation is reusability of code. Object orientation is not a new logical database structure. The object-oriented database management systems have as their underlying logical database structure the relational structure. Thus, object orientation is an extension of relational databases.

An **object-oriented database** allows the storage of objects (data, graphs, pictures, voice, text, or video). These objects have functions, attributes, and relationships, which are stored as an integral part of the object. This allows the functions, attributes, and relationships of an object to be reused and replicated. In object-oriented terminology this reuse is called **inheritance**. The storage of the functions, attributes, and relationships with the object is called **encapsulation**.

To illustrate the concepts of encapsulation and inheritance let's consider an object with which we are all familiar, an apple. Let's assume we are building a database for a company that grows and sells apples and apple products. In the database an apple is an object. Apples have functions, attributes, and relationships. We would like to encapsulate, or store information, about apples' functions, attributes, and relationships in the database. Some of the functions of apples might be to make apple pie, to make apple juice, and so on. Apples' attributes could be their color, their texture, their size, and their cooking qualities. And apples have relationships; for example, they are fruits and they are obviously related to apple pies and other objects. In this object-oriented database, the apple object would be capable of providing a recipe for making apples into apple pies. This is possible because the functions, attributes, and relationships are encapsulated with the apple object.

As the apple object can tell us how to make apple pie, in a business database an hours-worked object in a payroll database could tell us how to convert hours worked into a particular analysis called payroll analysis. Encapsulation of functions, attributes, and relationships allows the major advantage of object orientation, which is inheritance. Since all varieties of apples share certain functions, attributes, and relationships (in fact, they differ only slightly), when we describe a different variety of apple in our database we can inherit the functions, attributes, and relationships of previously described apples. Thus, we greatly reduce the time necessary to store and process different data in our database. In the payroll example, we might want to produce another report called overtime hours analysis. This report is likely to be very similar to the previous report called regular hours worked analysis. For example, the dimensions of the report, the layout of the data, and many items would be identical. Essentially, all that would change is that we are now dealing with overtime hours rather than regular hours. Thus, our new report would inherit the characteristics of the other report and save a great deal of time in producing that report. Object-oriented databases can increase the user-friendliness of databases by telling end users how to use the data stored in them, just as the apple object could tell a user how to make apple pie.

Another example of the use of inheritance in an object-oriented database could be a database in which a limited number of business procedures are encapsulated with each data type in a database. These business procedures could include edit checks and other control procedures. Thus, when a user attempts to update or modify the database, the transaction must conform to these business procedures or it will be rejected.

This capability shortens the development cycle for new data to be stored in the database since integrity, logic, and business rules no longer need to be programmed into each application.[1]

To summarize, you can see that one major advantage of object-oriented database management systems is that the functions, attributes, and relationships of objects can be reused and replicated through inheritance of these characteristics. The functions, attributes, and relationships of an object are stored with the object in the database management system through a process called encapsulation. The other major advantage of object-oriented database management systems is that most are designed to integrate a variety of real-world data types such as business procedures, policies, graphs, graphics, pictures, video, voice, annotated text, and traditional data. Most relational databases currently can only handle data expressed as numbers or text.[2]

Databases and Expert Systems

As databases grow larger in size and complexity, one of the difficulties that users have is in understanding the database and its contents sufficiently to use the data it contains. This is especially true with casual users who query the database for unanticipated, nonroutine types of decisions. To become really proficient in the use of data in a particular database you must use it regularly, otherwise you may lose your understanding of its contents. As discussed above, object-oriented DBMSs will help in this area. Also, expert systems can be used to assist users in retrieving data from a database. For example, several database services such as Compuserve provide a news clipping service. This news clipping service constantly monitors data entering the database and selects news items that may be of particular interest to an individual subscriber. In this way expert systems can be used to scan and monitor databases to search for items of interest. They can also be used to provide help for users as they attempt to query a database.

Expert systems will increasingly be used in conjunction with databases. The scope and complexity of many databases is too broad for one human to understand these databases completely. Application 13–2 illustrates how Du Pont used an expert system to reorganize the physical design of a database. The goal was to maximize the efficiency of storing and retrieving data.

Main Memory Databases

A query or a change to a database is called a transaction. Databases are shared. Thus, many users may be processing transactions against a database simultaneously. One of the primary concerns in designing a database is the number of transactions per second that a database can process. If the database design and the hardware that runs it do not have sufficient capacity to process the transaction demand, response times deteriorate. Any response time over a few seconds is annoying to users.

---

[1] Ted Rybeck, "DBMS Next Wave Could Be an Easier Ride," *Computerworld*, March 5, 1990, p. 68.
[2] *Ibid.*, p. 67.

APPLICATION 13–2

Du Pont Employs Expert Help to Increase Database Benefits

By Maryfran Johnson

Faced with the job of restructuring an enormous database for Du Pont Co., software engineer Greg Ballance called in some expert help and ended up with 20% better performance.

His helpmate was a bit unusual, however. In a field in which tedious, people-intensive work is required to tune and optimize a complex database, this assistant was a software tool: RDB Expert from Digital Equipment Corp.

The physical database design tool is equipped with its own expert system and is targeted at database administrators and developers working with VAX RDB/VMS and VAX database management system databases.

RDB Expert tunes and optimizes performance by analyzing the logical design, transaction work load, data volume and system environment of a database. Then it generates executable procedures for creating a new design or restructuring an old one.

Using the product in field test for the past six months, Ballance was able to tune the quality control applications that were straining Du Pont's systems. The company plans to extend its use of RDB Expert as a performance tool, tuning the quality management applications at individual plant sites, the engineer noted.

The debut of RDB Expert marks the first time DEC has made use of expert system technology in a high-volume product, said Vicki Farrell, a marketing manager for DEC's database systems group.

In one customer benchmark, Farrell said, three DEC consul-tants spent 20 weeks tuning and tweaking the design of the customer's database. Once they finished, they set RDB Expert to the same task. Five days later, the tool produced its own suggested design.

"It was not quite as good as what the experts came up with, but it took one expert only another week to tune it to where the three had gotten to in 20 weeks," Farrell said. "RDB Expert got about 7/8 of the job done."

Adapted with permission from *Computerworld* (February 18, 1991), p. 30. Copyright 1991 by CW Publishing, Inc., Framingham, MA 01701.

Some databases, such as those used by airline reservation systems where thousands of terminals are on-line to the database from reservation agents in airports and travel agent offices throughout the world, must be able to process approximately one thousand transactions per second.

Obviously, the speed with which transactions can be processed is related to how fast the data can be retrieved from storage. Almost all databases today are stored on secondary storage such as magnetic or optical disks. The access time to these secondary storage media is very slow compared to access time to data stored in main (or primary) memory. As the price of main memory declines, it will be possible to store very large databases in main memory, vastly improving the access time to the data. Thus, **main memory database management systems** where the complete database is stored in primary memory will be used in the future. One of the primary problems of main memory database management systems is the volatility of semiconductor primary storage. When the electricity is turned off, the complete storage is lost. Thus, these types of systems will have to have reliable power sources to keep the data from being lost through electrical power disturbances. This can be done through uninterruptible power supplies. Of course, backup copies of the database and all changes to it will be stored on nonvolatile secondary storage.

Summary

- Traditional information processing is file oriented, and each application has its own separate data storage. This approach has several disadvantages:

  - Redundant data may be stored.

  - It is difficult to integrate data from various sources.

  - Data storage is tied to specific application programs.

  - It is difficult to respond to unanticipated information requests.

- The database approach integrates the data into one large storage structure that may be used by many different users and application programs.

- The physical view of data defines the layout of data records on actual physical devices such as disk packs.

- The logical view represents data in a way that is meaningful to users and application programmers.

- The database may be accessed by users either directly or through an application program.

- A database management system is a complex program that manages a firm's data resources. It uses a data definition language to link the logical view with actual physical storage.

- A data manipulation language allows the user to input, access, modify, and retrieve data in a database. It is often used in conjunction with a regular programming language to process data in ways the DBMS by itself cannot.

- The database administrator is a key person in a database environment.

- The DBA is responsible for:

  - maintaining a data dictionary

  - ensuring physical security of the data

  - controlling changes in the logical and physical structures of the database

- The database is usually stored on direct-access devices. The DBMS tries to arrange data storage in a way that minimizes storage and processing costs.

- A nonrelational DBMS uses embedded pointers and linked lists to reduce data redundancy and to establish logical relationships among data elements.

- A tree structure is a logical data model that arranges data according to some natural hierarchy on a one-to-many basis.

- A network structure allows logical relationships among entities on a many-to-many basis.

- A relational structure organizes data in the form of two-dimensional tables. The data in these tables may be manipulated in many ways. Because of its conceptual simplicity and its ability to relate data, this data model is rapidly becoming popular.

- The database system has these major advantages:
  - Eliminates data redundancy
  - Integrates related data
  - Provides data independence
  - Provides an interface between users and data through query languages
- The disadvantages of a DBMS are that it can be complex and that it can require substantial computer resources to execute.
- An object-oriented database stores an object along with its functions, attributes, and relationships.
- Expert systems can improve the useability of a database.
- Main memory databases store the complete database in primary memory to improve the speed of access.

Key Terms

Data redundancy

Data integration

Program/data dependence

Database management system

Database

Pointers

Physical view

Logical view

Users

Query language

Data definition language (DDL)

Data manipulation language (DML)

Schema

Subschema

Database administrator (DBA)

Active data dictionary

Configuration control

Embedded pointer

Linked list

Tree structure

Network structure

Nodes

Relational model

Table

Tuple

Attributes

Object-oriented database

Inheritance

Encapsulation

Main memory database management systems

Review Questions

1. What is the relationship between a traditional file and an application program?
2. Explain the concept of data redundancy.
3. Why is program/data dependence undesirable?
4. Distinguish between a data file and a database.

5. What is the difference between a logical and a physical view of data? Which view is most relevant for the application programmer?

6. What are the four components of a database environment?

7. How does a database management system use its data definition language? Its data manipulation language?

8. Describe the major tasks performed by a database administrator.

9. What is the difference between a database and a database management system?

10. What kind of logical relationship may be expressed with a tree structure?

11. Describe the major characteristics of a network structure.

12. What is the conceptual advantage in using a relational structure? What other advantages does the relational model offer?

13. Why are indexes used by a DBMS?

14. What is the difference between the logical and the physical views of data?

15. How does a DBMS improve data independence?

16. What are object-oriented databases?

17. In object-oriented databases, what do the terms inheritance and encapsulation mean?

18. How can expert systems be used to improve DBMSs?

19. What is a main memory database management system?

Discussion Questions and Cases

1. Clemento Corporation has a large information processing facility that uses separate tape and disk files for different applications like production, sales, distribution, and payroll. You have been appointed to the newly created post of database administrator. It is your job to design a database for the corporation. You are also expected to convince the line and staff managers that it is to their advantage to switch from files to database usage. Outline the plan of action you will use to achieve these goals.

2. Many database users prefer one logical model over others. Proponents of the tree structure present a number of strong arguments in favor of that model:

   a. The tree structure is an excellent way to represent many hierarchical relationships that exist in the business world.

   b. Hierarchical data structures are efficient from the point of view of optimizing storage space and data-access time.

   c. IBM's Information Management System (IMS), one of the most widely used DBMSs, is based on the tree concept.

   Enthusiasts of the relational model hold that the relational model seems more natural to business users since they have used it for centuries; provides much easier data manipulation since one does not need to use pointers and chains; and is reasonably efficient because with decreasing hardware costs, machine efficiency is not as important a consideration as it once was.
       Evaluate the merits and demerits of each model. Which model would you select for your firm?

3.   If you are designing an inventory database for a grocery store, for which attributes would you provide indexes? Remember, an index is a tool for quick retrieval of data. It is useful to set up indexes only for attributes frequently used as a basis for retrieving records.

4.   During the last five years, Bohlin Incorporated has been converting its existing applications to IBM's Information Management System. The company has also developed most new applications on the IMS. The initial expectation was that the IMS database management system software would assist in producing highly integrated application systems. This would allow managers to easily associate related data within the database management system. However, this expectation has not been fulfilled. Personnel manager Chuck Bloss is very disappointed that the system does not integrate the personnel and payroll systems. When he retrieves data from the personnel system and attempts to retrieve related data from the payroll system, he finds no link between the two systems. In numerous other cases, integration of the systems is lacking on the DBMS. How do you think this situation occurred? Are all database management systems designed to produce integrated systems that can associate related data automatically?

5.   The Lord Delaware High School recently purchased IBM personal computers for both students and teachers. Cheryl Haymes, a math teacher, was put in charge of acquiring software. She has been trying to decide whether to buy a database management system, but she is confused by many of the software ads for database packages. Cheryl knows that relational database structures are the current technology, and many software vendors claim that their packages are true relational databases for a personal computer. What uses would a high school have for a PC database management system? What capabilities of a relational DBMS should Cheryl look for in choosing a package?

6.   The Town & Country Realty firm is considering developing a real estate listing management system. John Fitzpatrick, the director of information systems for the firm, is considering purchasing an object-oriented relational database management system as the software that will be used to develop the new real estate listing management system. How could an object-oriented relational DBMS be advantageous as the platform for a real estate listing management system?

INFORMATION SYSTEMS STRATEGIES

A Step Beyond a Database

By Gary H. Anthes

An interdisciplinary team at Johns Hopkins University has developed a new way to create and codify knowledge, one that combines the attributes of databases, electronic mail and books while blurring the distinction between creators and users of information.

The university's Laboratory for Applied Research in Academic Information has put together a linked pair of networked databases of human genetic information. One is On-line Mendelian Inheritance in Man (OMIM), a catalog of more than 5,000 inherited disorders and traits.

Logically tied to OMIM is the Genome Data Base (GDB), which was developed to support the international human genome initiative, whose goal is to completely describe the human genetic structure. GDB now holds 2,000 "mapped" genes showing the precise locations of genes on their respective chromosomes and information on 5,000 DNA segments. The GDB, which is based on Sybase, Inc. products, went on-line in September.

More than 3,200 users, mostly medical researchers and practitioners, access the two databases via Telenet or Internet.

More Than Simple Data

The databases are not just repositories of raw genetic data; they also capture and reflect the on-going wisdom of their creators and users. The GDB contains pointers to other databases and a bibliography of approximately 20,000 sources. Some are standard literature references, but increasingly, the sources are personal communications from researchers and users from the 75 to 100 scientific editors around the world who have authority to update GDB.

GDB draws data from the literature but also accepts unvalidated data directly from users for later submission to an on-line peer review process by globally distributed experts. "The database is both a product and a process," said Richard E. Lucier, the laboratory's director.

"Editors correspond with other experts; they have dialogs within the database," Lucier said. The dialogs are codified by an annotation and messaging system developed by Lucier's staff using C and Sybase's development tools.

A Credible Source

Because the resulting data is based on considerable give and take, the gene maps are known as "consensus maps." The consensus concept gives the GDB a very high degree of credibility among scientists, Lucier said.

Lucier calls the policies, procedures and technologies employed "knowledge management," which goes well beyond the traditional concepts of data storage and retrieval and whose goal is to integrate the library more fully into the scholarly communication process.

"People thought we wanted to build on-line books," Lucier said. "Electronic libraries just take existing information and digitize it. But GDB and OMIM are much more dynamic. Knowledge management forms partnerships with people creating information."

Because libraries focus on use of published data, their first worry is always access, Lucier said. However, the knowledge management approach worries first about collaboration between creators and editors, next about building a knowledge base and last about access. "We're not pushing the frontiers of technology; we are pushing useful applications of technology in everyday working environments," he said.

Lucier said the genome project could go forward without the database but in a slower, more disorganized way. "Results would be scattered throughout literature, there wouldn't be a dynamic gene map, and there wouldn't be the broad consensus of the scientific community."

Lucier said the knowledge management techniques developed at the laboratory are transferable to other disciplines besides medicine. "The primary problem is not technical; it's sociological, political and financial," he said.

Development of GDB and its associated software took one year, cost between $1 million and $2 million and was funded by the Howard Hughes Medical Institute. Although it is up and running, Lucier said, development will never be finished.

"Organization of the database will be good for about five years, then scientists will want to organize it differently, and that will require a whole new database," he said. Lucier added the successor to the relational database is likely to be a more flexible, object-oriented database.

Read-only copies of GDB are maintained in the UK and Germany, but all updates are networked to the database at Johns Hopkins. Both databases reside on a pair of Sun Microsystems, Inc. Sun-4/490 servers, which are attached to a campus-area network with gateways to Telenet and Internet.

One GDB editor is Phyllis McAlpine, a professor of human genetics at the University of Manitoba in Winnipeg. She has the final say on how each of the estimated 50,000 to 100,000 genes is to be named, and she said she may make 800 to 1,000 database entries per year, each of which is based on suggestions from around the world coming in by telephone, facsimile, mail or the database.

"It's a really neat concept," McAlpine said. "The contribution of the database to the field is invaluable. It's the one and only official record of every gene and piece of DNA that's mapped in the world."

Discussion Questions

1. How could a system such as this medical research database be applied to a business application? Describe such a business application.

2. This system facilitates the interaction between individuals who are geographically dispersed and working on the same project. What is the future for these types of systems?

Adapted with permission from *Computerworld* (March 4, 1991), p. 28. Copyright 1991 by CW Publishing, Inc., Framingham, MA 01701.

14

Communications and Distributed Processing

Introduction

Daily, huge quantities of information are moved between computers over communication channels. This information varies from detailed numerical data to written correspondence and images. Much of the high-volume data communication is between large mainframes or minicomputers, but personal computers also communicate with each other. PC users can readily access mainframes and capture information as diverse as stock market quotes, product prices, and sports results. PCs are also tied together through networks. How does this communication work? What are your alternatives when selecting a communication system?

Modern data communication is one of the primary factors that makes distributed processing possible. In the early days of electronic data processing the computer was a highly centralized company resource. High equipment costs and difficult-to-operate software systems prevented the spread of EDP resources to end-user departments. During the 1980s, however, this situation changed dramatically. The cost of hardware decreased sharply and software became easier to use. As a result, many people can now use the computer without the help of information systems specialists. By carefully dispersing computer resources throughout the organization a business can significantly reduce paperwork costs and improve turnaround time on applications. The management of dispersed information systems facilities is generally known as **distributed data processing (DDP)**. Communications, because it connects these dispersed information systems facilities, is often called **connectivity**. Near the end of this chapter, under Management Implications, we will cover some of the ways that processing can be distributed.

Another important and growing use of communications is electronic data interchange (EDI). EDI allows trading partners to transmit, electronically, all the data necessary to purchase and sell goods. Application 14–1 illustrates how Benetton uses EDI to maintain a competitive advantage in the international marketplace.

This chapter first covers the types of communication. Then it looks at the characteristics of communication channels. Next, it covers how the actual transmission process occurs. Then the chapter provides a broad overview of the concepts inherent in networks of computers. It explores electronic data interchange, which is a widely used application of networks. The chapter concludes with a discussion of the management implications of communications and distributed processing.

Types of Communication

There are two basic types of communications: computer to peripheral device and computer to computer.

Computer to Peripheral Device

Computer to peripheral device communications involves the transfer of data, text, or images between a CPU and a peripheral device, such as a terminal, a storage device, or a printer. The peripheral device is completely under the control of the CPU. It is customary to call this kind of communication a **master-slave relationship**. The master (the CPU) determines when and how data are to be transferred to and from the slave (the peripheral device). This type of communication can occur over relatively slow transmission channels, such as transmission between a PC and a

The United Systems of Benetton

By Lory Zottola

It's been 25 years since Giuliana and Luciano Benetton sold their first sweater on a street in Northern Italy. Since then, the siblings' clothing franchise company has become a global organization whose retail reach has expanded to more than 5,000 shops in 80 countries and whose fashions have graced the likes of Princess Diana and Princess Caroline of Monaco.

While many in the retail industry are struggling, Benetton Group S.p.A.—with the help of networking and electronic data interchange (EDI) technology—has translated its colorful sweaters, shirts and jeans into $1.2 billion in sales.

Integrating a company of such international scope has taken the efforts of a 100-member information systems staff and networks that let retail clients worldwide exchange information with Benetton as if they were located on the next *strada*.

"The company had an idea for a product that was new, stylish, cheap and aggressively marketed, and that idea helped it succeed," says Lorenzo Colucci, a Benetton watcher at London-based Smith New Court Securities. "But I don't know whether the company would have succeeded in the same way without its computer network. Idea and technology had to go together."

The IS [information systems] heart of Benetton is located in Ponzano Veneto, a small Italian town just outside of Venice. It is from here that Bruno Zuccaro, the company's 49-year-old IS director, has overseen the organization's IS operations since 1985.

Zuccaro and his team work with a budget of $12.8 million, which is approximately 1% of revenue, and centrally control the IS functions considered most important to the company.

Benetton's international EDI network is one of these key operations, supplied by General Electric Information Services (GEIS).

The GEIS network is at the core of Benetton's ordering cycle, which is initiated by "agents"—Benetton's term for the independent business clients in 73 worldwide locations who act as intermediaries between the Benetton Group and retailers. Working on commission, these agents set up franchises, show twice-yearly collections to retailers and place orders for merchandise with Benetton through the GEIS network.

Interaction between the human and technology networks keeps the highly decentralized Benetton structure together. As a franchiser, Benetton Group has little direct communication with the retail stores, owning only 1% of them. Although the independently owned shops must follow strict marketing, pricing and brand exclusivity guidelines, Benetton cannot legally mandate computer systems use at the retail level, and the majority of shops have no in-store information systems, Zuccaro says.

As a result, Zuccaro relies on agents using the network to bridge the gap between the franchiser's need for information and the franchisee's desire for autonomy.

To order merchandise for his retail clients, an agent dials up the GEIS network from a DOS- or Unix-based workstation and places his order using software developed by Benetton. The order handling system collects the orders and routes them to the appropriate factory. It then updates the agent's order portfolio and price lists, Zuccaro says. The system also handles electronic interchange of mail, reports and files between the corporation and agents and among the agents themselves.

"In the past, we used to have to send handwritten orders, which were at the mercy of time and human error," says Francesca Bertelli, the marketing and sales manager for Manhattan-area stores and assistant to that area's agent. She says the efficiency and fast turnaround of the network are crucial to getting orders right and to the retailers on time.

The data generated in the ordering process enables the Benetton Group to forecast the total number of orders early in the production cycle, Zuccaro says, so it can make faster purchasing decisions on raw materials and set up a production schedule.

More importantly, this system allows Benetton to keep inventory low and manufacture only what the franchises are paying for, he explains.

"Benetton has taken away the risk and cost of carrying excess stock," Colucci explains.

Furthermore, database access to Benetton's corporate IBM 3090 mainframe through the network enables agents to track orders by customer and item as well as to find out what is in production, in the warehouse or being distributed. Agents can also track customer credit, which allows them to restrict deliveries to those outlets that have exceeded their credit limits, Zuccaro says.

By analyzing data from point-of-sale (POS) systems installed in a number of Benetton-owned shops in Italy, the company knows what's hot and what's not, Zuccaro says. These shops, located mostly in upscale resort towns, receive merchandise earlier than the rest of Benetton's stores and keep tabs on bar-coded merchandise bought by their fashion-conscious customers . . .

The realities of the highly competitive retail market are not lost on Benetton, according to Zuccaro. "For us to do well, we must expand continually," he printer, to very high speed transmission that occurs between a CPU and a disk drive. CPU to disk drive transmission in a PC is done over the computer's internal bus to the disk drive controller card and then by cable to the disk drive. A PC's internal bus is the channel that the CPU uses to communicate internally with the peripheral controller cards within the system unit.

Computer to Computer

Data are often transferred directly from one computer to another. For instance, some grocery store chains link their computers to the computers of their major suppliers through communication lines. When an item needs to be reordered, the computer automatically places the order over the communication line. The supplier's computer can then process the order immediately. This procedure not only eliminates the possibility of human error, but also permits better inventory management by speeding up the reordering process.

Communication between two computers may be a master-slave connection. An example is the relationship between a mainframe computer and a special-purpose minicomputer. The minicomputer typically performs in an auxiliary function for the mainframe, such as editing input data. Since the minicomputer is in the position of a slave, it cannot initiate communication with the mainframe unless the mainframe allows it to do so.

On the other hand, a communication link may be a connection between equals. As in the grocery store example, two mainframe CPUs may interact. This type of communication is often called **peer-to-peer communication**. Either computer has the ability to initiate a communication session at its discretion. Almost all communication between personal computers on PC networks is peer-to-peer communication.

Communication Channel Characteristics

The **communication channel** is the physical line over which communication is accomplished. Since the communication channel is the hardware or is a major portion of the hardware involved in communications, this section deals primarily with hardware-oriented topics.

Analog versus Digital Communication

Computers operate through manipulation of digital signals. At the most basic level computers store, manipulate, and communicate either a zero or a one. A zero or a one, which is a bit of data, is represented by various means such as the presence or absence of a magnetic spot or, in communications, the presence or absence of an electrical or optical signal. Communication in computer systems to disk units and printers is digital communication.

In the past, all communications over public telephone lines were analog. These lines were meant to carry voice messages and they operate only in an analog wave form. Thus, before data can be transmitted over telephone lines the digital data signals must be converted into analog form (see Figure 14–1). The conversion from digital to analog signals is called **modulation**. At the receiving end, the analog signals are converted back to digital form through a **demodulation** process. A device called a **modem** (short for modulator-demodulator) is used for this purpose. PC modems typically operate at 1200 to 9600 bits per second and transmit data in an asynchronous mode (explained below under Transmission Mode).

Data communications are moving away from analog transmission with modems. Many of the networks discussed later in this chapter use digital transmission. Furthermore, most long-distance voice communication is now transmitted and stored by digital means. By the year 2000 most local telephone systems will be converted to digital transmission. Already many firms use digital phone systems. On a digital phone system, in effect, when you talk you are talking over a computer system. Your voice is converted to digital signals and processed just as if it were data by computers. The technological breakthrough that has caused the move to digital communications is fiber optics (discussed in more detail later in this chapter). Fiber optics transmit signals by either the presence or absence of a beam of light. Thus, they are ideal for representing digital signals, zeros and ones.

FIGURE 14–1

Conversion of Digital Signals to and from Analog Form.

Modems are designed to either send or receive data over analog telephone lines. Thus the same modem can perform both modulation and demodulation depending on the direction in which the data are flowing.

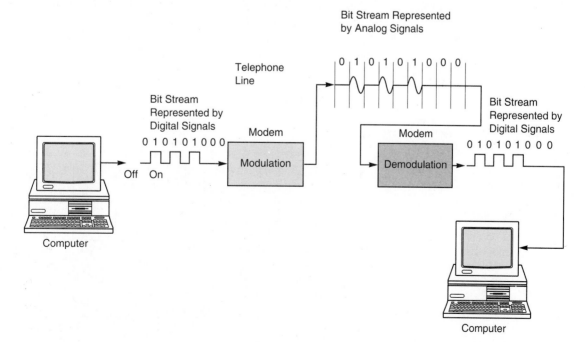

Serial versus Parallel Communication

Under **serial communication** a message is transmitted one bit at a time over a single communication channel. Communications between PCs and other computers through a modem and over telephone lines is normally done with serial communication.

Parallel communication is the simultaneous transmission of eight or more bits across a multichannel line (see Figure 14–2). Since all the bits that constitute a byte or character are transmitted simultaneously, the speed of parallel systems is often quoted in characters per second. Parallel transmission is faster than serial. Most PCs communicate with their printers in parallel mode.

Types of Communication Channels

The physical media over which communications are transmitted vary from copper wires to radio waves to glass fibers. Copper wires are the older technology; satellites and fiber optics are the newer technology.

Twisted Pair   A **twisted pair** are two insulated wires twisted around each other. This twisting reduces the interference from one wire to the other. Twisted pairs of wires can be combined with other twisted pairs into a large insulated cable. This is the telephone cable that you see strung along poles and it is the communication channel that is currently installed in homes to provide telephone service.

Coaxial Cable   **Coaxial cable** is a central insulated wire enclosed by a cylindrical conducting wire, both of which are enclosed with further insulation and a protective cover. Coaxial cable can conduct large quantities of information. In the computer world it is often used as a connection between remote terminals, such as IBM's 327X series of terminals, and mainframes. Coaxial cable is also used for transmission of cable TV signals to your home.

FIGURE 14–2
Parallel Transmission.
Since there are eight channels in this parallel transmission, a complete byte of eight bits can be transmitted in the time that it would take to transmit one bit with serial transmission.

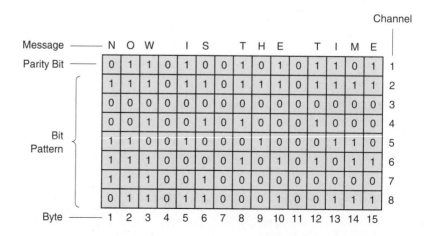

Microwave   **Microwaves** are electromagnetic (radio) signals in the radio frequency of about one billion cycles per second to twenty billion cycles per second. Microwaves are used as communication channels in line-of-sight ground transmissions and transmissions between ground stations and satellites. Microwave towers are often seen on top of hills and buildings. These stations must be in the line of sight with one another and must be approximately 30 miles apart. Since microwave transmissions are over radio waves they are subject to unauthorized interception.

Satellite   **Satellite transmission** uses geosynchronous satellites to relay microwave signals from one spot on the earth to a receiving location on the earth. Geosynchronous means that the satellite is in orbit at about 22,000 miles above the equator and traveling at the same rate as the rotation of the earth. Thus, it stays in the same location relative to a point on the earth. Satellites contain many communication channels that can receive and relay both analog and digital signals from stations on the earth. Satellites can send the signal back to a small geographic area, or spot, on the earth or they can send the signal to all of the earth's service that is in the line of sight from the satellite. Obviously, such signals can be intercepted. Thus, satellite transmission is often encrypted to forestall unauthorized interception.

Wireless Network   **Wireless networks** use infrared light or radio waves as communication channels to implement local area networks (LAN). Wireless LANs are often used in retail stores to monitor and manage inventory and to provide portable cash registers that are linked to the wireless LAN. Wireless LANs have several advantages. First, they eliminate the costs of running cable or wiring between stations on the network. Second, they provide location flexibility to LAN users since the device being used can be portable within the range of the LAN. Finally, wireless LANs are more reliable than cable or wire-based LANs. It has been estimated that up to two-thirds of problems with conventional LANs are due to cabling and connection problems.

Wireless LANs do have disadvantages. As with any light beam, infrared light is easily blocked or deflected. Thus, stations on an infrared-light LAN must be within the line of sight of each other or be placed where the light can be reflected off walls or ceilings to its destination. Thus, the portability of infrared LAN stations is quite constrained. Radio-based LANs must use radio waves, which are strictly regulated by the Federal Communications Commission, are subject to error-producing radio interference, and can be easily intercepted.

Fiber Optics   A major portion of communications is changing to fiber optic communication channels. **Fiber optics** uses a small strand of glass fiber, about the size of a human hair, to transmit enormous quantities of data by transmitting a pulsating light beam over long distances. One fiber can transmit 600,000 simultaneous telephone conversations. The same fiber can also transmit the entire Encyclopedia Britannica from Philadelphia to New York in 50 seconds. With these capacities it is little wonder that communication is moving rapidly to fiber optics. Already, all major cities in the U.S. are connected through long-distance fiber-optic cables. In fact, one common carrier, U.S. Sprint, uses only fiber-optic transmission. Several fiber-optic cables span both the Atlantic and Pacific oceans. Even though the capacity of fiber optics today is enormous, additional large increases in its ability to transmit messages are expected in the near future.

In addition to its advantage of large capacity, fiber optics has several other major benefits. It is completely insensitive to electromagnetic interference because it does not rely on electricity. It relies only on the transmission of light. Currently, it appears that fiber-optic cables are highly resistant to being bugged. This resistance to bugging is due to the fact that the cable emits no electromagnetic radiation that can be picked up and if you attempt to tap into the fiber in order to bug it, you will stop its light transmission, which can be detected instantly. Also, fiber-optic cable is relatively inexpensive and it has a low power consumption. Finally, it takes up much less space than any other type of cable for its transmission capacity.

Currently, there is a strong move among telephone companies not only to use fiber-optic cable for long-distance transmission but also to replace all twisted pair cable for telephone and other services in individual homes and businesses. In the future, perhaps by the year 2000, you will receive all your communications including telephone, computer communications, and cable TV over fiber-optic cables.

Common Carriers

A **common carrier** is a company that provides communication services to the general public and businesses. Examples of common carriers are AT&T, MCI, and U.S. Sprint. Common carriers are licensed and regulated by both federal, state, and local governments. Many businesses purchase their communication channels from common carriers. In fact, if you comply with the rules and regulations as promulgated by the appropriate government authority, common carriers cannot refuse to transmit your communications.

Broadband versus Baseband

In **baseband channels**, digital signals are transmitted over a communication channel without modulation. Remember that modems are used to modulate digital signals into analog or wave-form signals. Thus, baseband transmission does not use modems. The digital signals are transmitted directly over the communication channel. Baseband channels are widely used for local area networks of PCs. The distance of the transmission is limited to approximately two miles. Baseband communication channels can only transmit one signal at a time. Thus, when baseband is used on nonswitched networks there must be a method for sharing the single line that connects the devices attached to the line. We will discuss these methods below under Sharing Nonswitched Networks.

A **bandwidth** of a communication channel refers to the range of electrical frequencies that the communication channel can handle. In baseband the full bandwidth of the communication channel (that is, all frequencies) are used to transmit the single stream of digital on/off signals.

Broadband   In **broadband channels** the digital signals are modulated (changed into specific radio frequencies). Therefore, multiple streams of transmissions can occur over the same physical cable simultaneously, each occupying a different radio frequency. Broadband is used for transmitting large amounts of voice, video, and data over long distances. However, broadband transmission requires the use of modems.

Integrated Services Digital Network

Integrated Services Digital Network (ISDN) is an international standard for the digital transmission of voice, data, text, and images over common carrier networks. Note that the transmission is fully digital from end to end of the transmission line. ISDN promises to revolutionize communications. It provides two basic services:

1.   Basic rate interface (BRI) is a 144 kilobits per second service. This service is broken down into two 64 kilobits per second B channels that will carry voice, text, images, data, or video and one 16 kilobits per second D channel that carries control information. You could have the BRI service in your home under ISDN. Thus, you could carry on a conversation on one of the B channels while simultaneously communicating with your computer at 64 kilobits per second on the other B channel. ISDN provides substantially faster communications than do current phone lines. Currently, most PCs communicate over regular telephone lines at a maximum of 9.6 kilobits per second. The BRI service would be provided over two twisted pair channels.

2.   ISDN also provides a primary rate interface (PRI) service. PRI provides a 1.54 megabits per second service, which can be used as one high-speed channel or broken down into twenty-three 64 kilobits per second B channels and one 64 kilobits per second D channel.

Although the 64k bps service is substantially greater than the 9.6k bps provided by current telephone lines, it is substantially below the capabilities that most local area networks have. Local area networks transmit at greater than 10 megabits per second. A future service called broadband ISDN (BISDN) promises to increase ISDN transmission rates to 150 megabits per second.

ISDN service began to be implemented in a few locations in the U.S. in 1990. BISDN service is expected to start being available by 1993.

Other Channel Hardware

Multiplexers   As we have seen, some communication channels have tremendous transmission capabilities. Multiplexers are a way of dividing this large capacity among many users so that they can all use a single communication channel simultaneously. Without multiplexers, communication channels would sit idle probably 95 to 99 percent of the time. For example, a single channel that can carry one TV channel can also provide 1200 voice telephone channels. Very few users want to transmit the entire Encyclopedia Britannica from Philadelphia to New York in 50 seconds. Thus, huge channel capacities are divided through multiplexers.

A **multiplexer** merges many individual transmissions into a single high-speed transmission and reverses the operation on the receiving end. One type of multiplexer, a **frequency-division multiplexer**, simply divides the communication channel into multiple radio frequencies. Each frequency is then allocated to a particular user, such as a workstation (see Figure 14–3). Other multiplexers divide the transmission into small time slices. These are known as **time-division multiplexers**. Each transmitter is allowed one time slice in turn (see Figure 14–3). A **statistical multiplexer** is similar to a time division multiplexer, but it is a more intelligent device that allocates more transmission time to users that are sending and receiving larger volumes of communications (see Figure 14–3).

Front-End Processors   Mainframes and minicomputers have to communicate with several workstations at the same time. Routine tasks such as sychronization of signals and error checking can absorb a large proportion of the CPU's processing time. This often leads to degraded performance on more important jobs. In order not to waste expensive mainframe CPU time many systems have a small computer that is dedicated solely to the communication function. This computer is known as a **front-end processor**. It manages all routine communications with peripheral devices and workstations.

FIGURE 14–3
Multiplexing.
The multiplexers here are dividing a communication line among several computer users. However, multiplexers are available that divide one communication line, such as your home telephone line, between your personal computer and normal voice use of that communication line. With this voice/data multiplexer you can talk on your telephone at the same time that your PC is using the line for data communication.

Frequency-Division Multiplexing

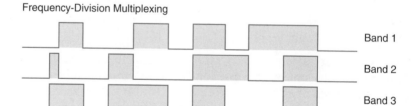

Time-Division Multiplexing

Statistical Multiplexing

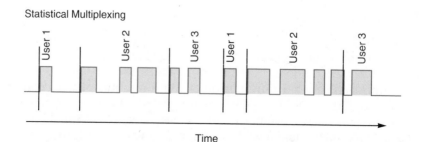

The flow of communications between computer devices is a stream of bits, represented by on/off line conditions. These bits are transmitted through various protocols and transmission modes at different speeds and in different directions.

Protocols

It is not enough simply to send raw communications from place to place. It's necessary to package the communication into blocks or "messages." The intervening communication hardware can then check for transmission errors and route each message to its correct destination.

A **communication protocol** is a set of rules governing information flow in a communication system. These rules define the **block format**, or **message envelope**, that packages each message to be transmitted. This envelope usually contains control characters to mark the message's beginning and end, as well as an address, so that data can be directed to particular devices. It might also contain characters used for error detection. Figure 14–4 shows a typical message envelope. A device that conforms to an error checking protocol operates without error, since it automatically retransmits any erroneous message. We will discuss protocols further when we cover Network Standards below.

Transmission Mode

As data is sent along a communication channel, the bit coding scheme used to represent a byte (a character of data) is typically the American Standard Code for Information Interchange. (ASCII was discussed in Chapter 12.) Two possible conditions, on and off, representing binary digits 1 and 0, respectively, are imposed on the line by the transmitter. The receiver monitors this train of signals and reconstructs the incoming byte. This can be done in two ways.

The simpler method, typically employed by personal computers, is **asynchronous transmission** (see Figure 14–5a). In this type of transmission the condition always goes off for one interval before a byte is sent, and always reverts to on for at least one interval at the end of each byte. This allows the receiver to synchronize with the transmitter at the be-

F I G U R E 14–4

A Message Envelope.

This protocol is IBM's widely used BISYNC.

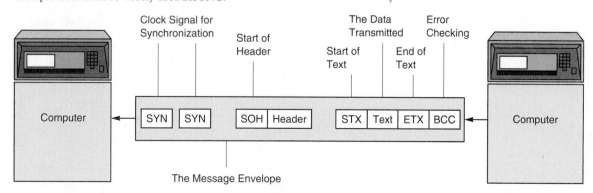

ginning of each byte and to start reading at the correct time. The two extra bits per byte increase the number of transmitted bits from eight to ten, but the real information content of the package, including the necessary parity bit, is only eight bits. Since 20 percent of the data transmitted are merely control information, this method is considered inefficient in terms of line usage. It is, however, easy to implement.

A more economical method, used by complex, high-speed devices, is **synchronous transmission** (refer to Figure 14–5b). With this method, the receiver's clock is synchronized with the sender for each transmission session. It is synchronized at the beginning of the transmission session and is allowed to run continuously. Therefore, it is not necessary to send signals at the beginning and end of each byte. However, if there are gaps in the data stream, they must be filled with "idle" bytes to maintain synchronization. At the beginning of the data stream a predetermined pattern of bits causes the receiver to synchronize its clock and start receiving the data. This type of transmission is often used between mainframes and terminals.

Transmission Speed

Data transmission speed is measured in **bits per second (bps)**. Sometimes the term *baud* is used interchangeably with bits per second. This is not strictly correct, since a baud rate is a telegraphic concept that is not necessarily applicable to computer data communications. Bits per second are often used as a measure of the transmission's speed of various communication devices, such as modems and networks. Just as clock speed

F I G U R E 14–5
Asynchronous and Synchronous Bit Streams to Transmit the Name Tom.
The difference between these two data transmission modes is that with asynchronous transmission (*a*) a start bit is transmitted before each byte. With synchronous transmission (*b*), a clock signal synchronizes the sender and receiver so that several bytes can be transmitted without sending a start bit before each byte.

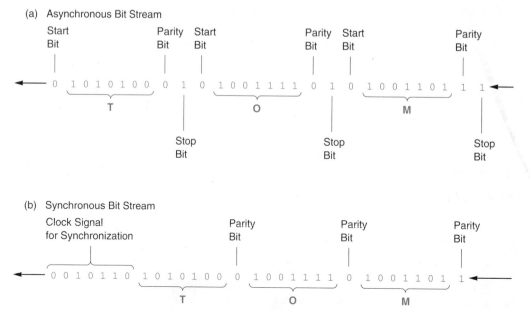

is a very elementary measure of CPU power bps is also a rudimentary measure for communication speed. For example, all communication devices have built-in error checking capabilities. When transmission errors occur the message is retransmitted. Thus, a device with a high transmission rate, say 4 megabits per second, may actually transmit communications at a much slower rate because it is unreliable and must retransmit erroneous messages, cutting down the effective transmission speed.

Transmission Direction

Data transmission can also be characterized by the direction that the communication channel allows. The three combinations of transmission directions are shown in Figure 14–6. A **half-duplex channel** can send and receive data, but only in one direction at a time. With a **full-duplex channel**, data can be sent and received at the same time. Full-duplex channels are used in computer-to-computer communications. A **simplex channel** allows data to be transmitted only in one direction. This channel is rarely used, since usually data must flow in both directions between a terminal and a CPU or between two CPUs.

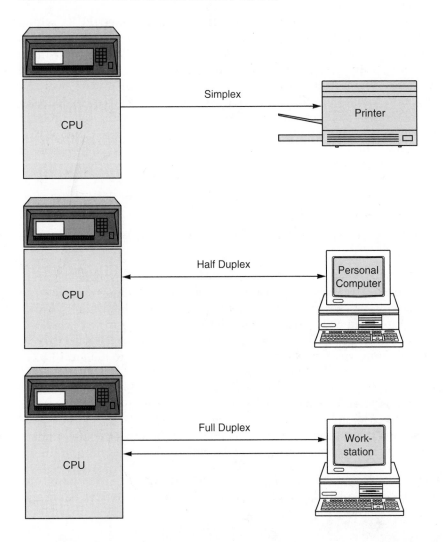

FIGURE 14–6
Simplex, Half-Duplex, and Full-Duplex Channels.

Data communication over regular telephone lines is normally done in half-duplex. When large-volume transmissions are required between CPUs, a full-duplex channel is usually established.

Networks

The first sections of this chapter dealt with the basics of communication, communication channels, and how communications are transmitted. In this section we will see how these basic characteristics of communications are used in actual computer networks.

Types of Networks

Switched Networks In a **switched network** a channel connection is made between the two devices communicating at the time the communication is initiated. For short line distances, say within a single firm's offices, this connection is maintained throughout the communication session. For long-distance communications, switched networks use a technique called packet switching. **Packet switching** divides the individual message into pieces (packets) and routes them to their destination, where they are put back together into a message. The individual packets may travel on different physical communication channels, but to the user it appears that a connection is made and dedicated to that user until the end of the communication session. Individual components of switched networks can use either a baseband or broadband communication channel.

Figure 14–7 illustrates a **digital private branch exchange (PBX)**, which is a type of switched network. A digital PBX is a private communications network installed in a firm. Today these PBXs operate in a digital manner. That is, all transmission of voice (telephone), data, text, images, and other types of communication are digitized to be transmitted over the network. In effect, these PBXs are digital computer networks. In addition to telephones, which convert your voice to digital signals, a number of CPUs, personal computers, faxes, and other devices can be linked to a digital PBX. The PBX can connect any two of these devices together on demand. This arrangement has several advantages.

1. The user can access many different computers from the same terminal or workstation.

2. A CPU can exchange data with any one of the other CPUs on the network.

3. A digital PBX can be used not only to link devices through communication lines but also to provide various translation services. The switching mechanism on the PBX, which is actually a computer, can change the format in transit to conform with the hardware requirements of the receiving device. Thus, devices that use different transmission protocols can be hooked to a digital PBX.

Digital PBXs are the direction in which within-firm data communication is going. With a digital PBX a company can hook many different devices together, transmit voice, data, images, and video over the same network, and maintain both inbound and outbound modem pools to provide for communication outside the PBX over analog transmission lines.

Nonswitched Networks **Nonswitched networks** can be either baseband or broadband. In a baseband nonswitched network all devices using the network share the same communication channel. Remember that when

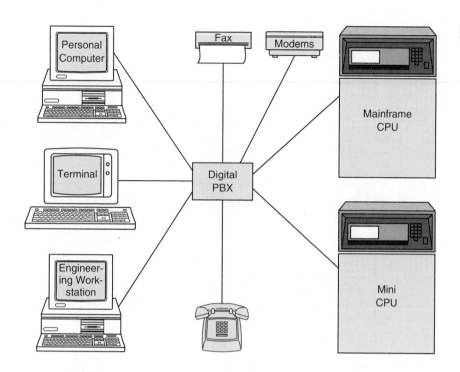

FIGURE 14–7
A Digital PBX (A Switched Network).

The digital PBX is a computer that acts as a switch to connect various devices.

baseband is used, the digital signal imposed on the communication channel occupies the complete bandwidth of the channel. Thus, only one device can use the channel at one time. Obviously some scheme for sharing this communication channel must be devised. We will discuss that in the next section on Sharing Nonswitched Networks.

There are two basic types of nonswitched baseband networks: a bus network and a ring network. A **bus** is an electrical or optical conductor (transmission medium) that acts as a single, high-speed, shared line for all devices connected to it. Thus, all the devices connected to the bus hear all the messages that are transmitted on the bus. The bus must be shared and each device must have the capability of detecting messages addressed to it. Figure 14–8 illustrates a bus network.

Note that on a bus network the failure of one of the devices connected to it in no way affects the operation of the bus network. One of the stations on the network could be completely destroyed and the network would continue operating, except if the bus itself was severed. Because of this inherent reliability of bus networks they are often used where high reliability is required and there is a potential for physical damage to the nodes on the network, for example, in military applications or in heavy industrial environments.

A bus is also used internally within computers to connect the microprocessor with other devices such as the disk drive, the keyboard, the video display card, and the parallel and serial ports. The basic concepts of a bus network and the bus within a personal computer are the same.

A ring network is illustrated in Figure 14–9. In a **ring network** each device is connected to another device through a continuous electrical or optical connection that goes from one device to another so that the com-

FIGURE 14–8
A Bus Network.

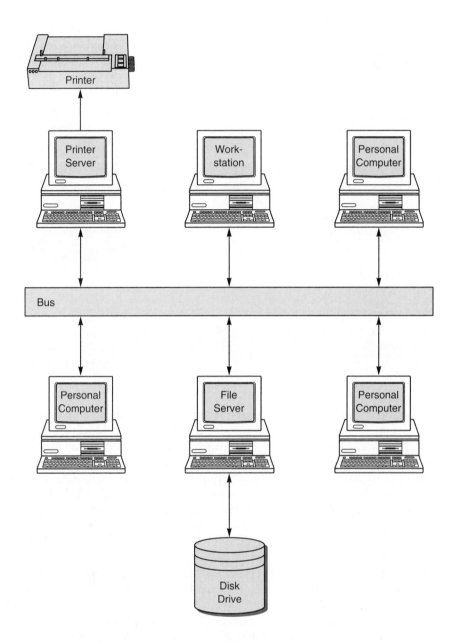

plete network forms a ring. Communications flow only in one direction around the ring, either clockwise or counterclockwise, but not both. In a ring network each device connected to the network has the responsibility of passing on every message that is not addressed to that device.

In this relaying of messages lies a disadvantage of ring networks: If one of the nodes goes down the complete network may fail. Obvious occurrences such as switching off a computer on the network are always taken care of in ring network hardware. The network interface card in a personal computer has the capability to continue passing on messages after the power is turned off for that personal computer. But what if the personal computer is turned off and there is also damage to the interface card or it malfunctions? Then the network fails. This would not occur on a bus network.

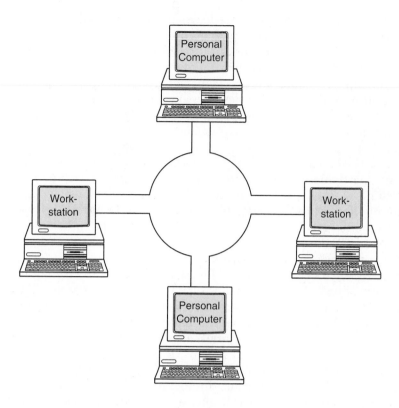

In theory, broadband nonswitched networks work identically to baseband nonswitched networks with one exception. Recall that when the communication channel is broadband, the channel can be divided into many individual channels represented by each radio frequency that the channel will carry. Thus, a broadband nonswitched network is like having several baseband nonswitched networks combined into one. Each frequency carried over the broadband channel operates identically to a nonswitched baseband network.

Sharing Nonswitched Networks

In a switched network any sharing of lines that occurs is transparent to the devices connected to the network (sharing long-distance lines on a switched network often occurs through multiplexing techniques, discussed earlier in this chapter). But on a nonswitched network in effect many devices, sometimes hundreds of devices, talk on the same shared line. Each device does have the capability of recognizing a message that is addressed to it, but how do we keep all these messages from bumping into and destroying one another? The method that a particular network uses to prevent these collisions between messages is called the network's **access method**. One way to illustrate these access methods is to use the analogy of human conversation. Let's assume we have fifty people in a room for a meeting. If they all talked at the same time over the communication media, in this case the air in the room, it's doubtful that any messages would be received. One way of imposing discipline on this conversation is to have a moderator who polls each person and asks if he or she has anything to say. In computer networks this access technique is called polling. Under **polling**, some master device, perhaps a mainframe computer, asks each device connected to the network in turn whether it wishes to transmit a message. If it does the line is open only for its transmission.

In our meeting we could allot each person five minutes to speak. When the five minutes is up the next person receives five minutes of time. This is equivalent to **time-division multiplexing**. Both polling and time-division multiplexing in a network are inefficient. In our human meeting analogy it would take a lot of time just to ask each person whether he or she had anything to say. The same is true of time division multiplexing, particularly if we had to wait five minutes for each person even though he or she didn't have anything to say. This obviously would waste a lot of time. Most networks today use one of the following two types of access methods, **carrier sense multiple access with collision detection (CSMA/CD)** or **token passing**. Either of these two access methods can be used with a bus or a ring network.

Although CSMA/CD, because of its long name, appears to be complicated, it is very simple. In fact, it operates identically to most group conversation among humans. Let's look at our meeting of fifty people again. One natural way of imposing discipline on this conversation is that when two or more people attempt to talk at one time, they all back off momentarily and one of them speaks. Thus, in human group conversation multiple people can begin speaking (access) at the same time. But we naturally sense the carrier (the air) through our hearing to determine if someone else is speaking as we begin to speak. If someone else is speaking a collision detection occurs. Thus, the term *carrier sense multiple access with collision detection* has evolved. This is identical to how the CSMA/CD access method operates. Any device connected to the network can impose a message on the network, but the device also has to listen to see if a collision occurred. If the collision did occur, the device retransmits the message until it gets through.

You can see one of the disadvantages of this access method. When the number of devices is large, the number of collisions that occurs increases very fast. This is what happens in group conversations among humans. If we had 100 people in the room all attempting to speak at the same time, we would have many collisions. Because messages have to be retransmitted when collisions occur, the CSMA/CD technique cannot guarantee how long it will take to transmit a message; as collisions increase the time to transmit a message also increases. In applications where transmission time is critical the CSMA/CD access method is at a significant disadvantage. In practice CSMA/CD is only used on bus networks.

Token passing is identical in concept to a technique that Native Americans have long used in their meetings. This technique employs a talking stick. A talking stick would work as follows in our meeting of fifty people. A piece of wood would be passed around the room. A person could only speak whenever he or she held the stick. The token in a network is analogous to the talking stick. A **token** is a series of bits that are continually transmitted around the ring or across the bus. A device can only transmit over the network when it receives a token that is marked "free." The device attaches its message to the token, the token is marked busy, and then the message is transmitted along with the token.

Token passing can be used on both bus and ring networks. There are several ways for a token ring network to deal with a personal computer attached to the network that is turned off or that is dead. Also, token ring networks can specify an upper limit time for transmission of a message since collisions and subsequent retransmissions do not occur.

Bridges and Gateways

A **bridge** is a device that connects two similar networks. For example, two different token ring networks can be connected with one another through a bridge. Thus, the PCs on one network can communicate with the PCs on the other network.

A **gateway** is a device that connects two different types of networks. For example, a gateway would connect a bus to a token ring network or it could connect a PC network to a network of mainframes.

Local Area Networks versus Wide Area Networks

A **local area network (LAN)** is a short-distance network that links computers and peripherals together. A local area network is usually confined to a distance of two miles or less and could be used by all those in a single building or a group of buildings within two miles of one another.

A **wide area network (WAN)** extends over a large geographical area, for example, over a whole state or country. Wide area networks are normally implemented over communication channels provided by common carriers. Bridges are used to connect LANs to WANs.

Value-Added Networks

Common carriers provide networks but a common carrier can only serve as a conduit for a communication. In other words, it's like a delivery truck that picks up the message and delivers it to the other end without changing it. **Value-added networks (VAN)** provide additional value by offering services other than the simple transmission of a communication. Some VANs provide electronic mail capabilities, such as MCI Mail or AT&T Mail. The most popular provider of a VAN is General Electric's GE Information Services (GEIS). This VAN provides electronic data interchange services for its approximately 8600 EDI*Express customers. EDI allows trading partners to transmit electronically all the data necessary to purchase and sell goods. We will discuss EDI in more depth below.

Network Hardware

We have already discussed much of the hardware associated with networks, including the communication channels and the devices that are hooked to a network, which are often called nodes on the network. These can include anything from a personal computer to a mainframe to a telephone. Two important network hardware items are the network interface card and servers.

Network Interface Card   A network interface card is inserted into a bus slot of a PC or workstation. It controls the receipt of and transmission of communications onto the communication channel, a bus or a ring.

When PCs communicate over a regular telephone line using a modem, the modem is connected to the serial port (often called RS232C interface). Thus, a PC can communicate to the outside world over its serial port. However, the serial port is much too slow for network communications. The network interface card not only provides much faster communication for networks, but also executes the access method used by the network, such as CSMA/CD or token passing. Some personal computers, such as the Macintosh, have the functions of a network interface card built into the PC and do not require a separate network interface card when they are connected to networks for which they are designed.

Servers   The concept of servers is central to most local area networks. In a network, a **server** is a device such as a PC that provides services to the other PCs in the network. Typical servers are file servers and printer servers. A **file server** is a high-powered personal computer with a large disk drive. This file server stores on its hard disk the data files and often the programs used by the other PCs in the network (its clients). Likewise, a **printer server** may be connected to a laser printer to provide high-quality printing for everyone on the network. The computer requesting the server to perform a task is called a **client**.

Local area networks are being used extensively to implement client-server computing. **Client-server computing** is a form of distributed computing where tasks are shared among devices (computers and peripheral devices) most suited to perform the task. These devices are usually connected to each other by a network. In client-server computing the tasks that must be performed in a typical business application can be separated into three categories: presentation, application logic, and server tasks. PCs, with their ability to provide colorful, graphic user interfaces, would be used to present (display) the application to the user. The application logic could be executed cooperatively on both the user's PC and other computers on the network. Various servers could provide database, printing, fax, expert system, or other services.

Network Software

A **network operating system** is control software that manages local area networks. This software typically resides on the network's file server. However, on a modest network it may reside on a user's PC. The network operating system is analogous to the operating system of a multiuser mainframe or minicomputer. It provides many services similar to those provided by a mainframe operating system: administering the network, providing backup and recovery capability, executing security routines such as password access controls, and monitoring the network usage through maintaining a log of user activities. A network operating system is not the same as a network interface card. The network interface card, a piece of hardware, is installed in each device connected to the network.

Network Standards

A **standard** is an acknowledged method of operation. In the communications field a standard refers to an acknowledged protocol for communications. One of the characteristics of communications, as you can see from this chapter, is the diversity of ways in which communications can be accomplished. We have different communication channel characteristics, different transmission processes, different types of networks, different ways that lines are shared, and so on. It is a wonder that any two devices can communicate with one another. To bring order out of this diversity there must be ways to bring together the various wiring schemes, protocols, and access methods so that a wide variety of devices from different manufacturers can communicate with one another. Standards attempt to produce this order.

Standards can arise when members of an accepted standards organization agree on a standard. Two important standards organizations are the American National Standards Institute (ANSI) and the International Standards Organization (ISO).

Standards can also be created through the dominance of a particular manufacturer or product in the market. For example, Lotus 1-2-3's spreadsheet file format has become a de facto standard for such files. IBM's dominance in the computer industry has produced several de facto standards.

In the network area there appears to be two major standards that are vying to dominate network management standards. First, there is IBM's **System Network Architecture (SNA)**. SNA is currently the most successful network architecture. It supports both peer-to-peer and tree-structured (hierarchical) networks. A hierarchical network may have a mainframe host computer serving as the network's control center. Beneath the host mainframe may be other mainframes, minis, and further on down the tree are workstations and personal computers. Most large IBM computer installations use SNA.

A further aspect of computer network standards is the ability or inability of the various computers in a manufacturer's complete line to execute the same software and to provide similar user interfaces to end-users. In March 1987, IBM introduced its **System Application Architecture (SAA)**, which is in effect an enhancement of SNA to provide the capabilities just discussed. SAA is a bold attempt to improve the connectivity and user friendliness of the various devices connected to a network. However, IBM has had great difficulty in making SAA a reality.

The second contender for the network management standard is **Open System Interconnection (OSI)**. OSI was established by the International Standards Organization (ISO). OSI is the only internationally accepted network standard that is designed to allow devices from different manufacturers to communicate with one another. Its goal is to provide connectivity between all devices on all networks. Several manufacturers, including Digital Equipment, Hewlett-Packard, and AT&T, have announced that their networks will comply with OSI standards.

In the past, large computer manufacturers such as IBM dominated the market and thus whatever they did tended to become a de facto standard. This situation has gradually been changing. As IBM's share of the computer market has declined it has been willing to form strategic alliances with other manufacturers and to comply more with standards that are agreed upon by national and international standards organizations. Thus, in the future we are likely to see the above network standards merge so that computers in a SNA network can work directly with computers that follow the OSI standard.

Electronic Data Interchange

Electronic data interchange (EDI) is the transmission of normal business transaction data between trading partners over a computer network. Transaction data include items such as purchase orders, shipping notices, invoices, and payments. It is important to note that EDI is not a network, it is an application of computer networks. The use of EDI is becoming a widespread business practice. Inventory control techniques such as just-in-time require that the time between placing an order and its receipt be minimized. The networks over which EDI is implemented are usually value-added networks, as we discussed above. In fact, GE's EDI*Express is one of the most widely used EDI networks.

An individual business can implement EDI through the use of any size computer from mainframes to personal computers. EDI software is available that will execute on any of these machines.

An international EDI standard has also been established by the International Standards Organization. This standard is EDIFACT (electronic data interchange for administration, commerce, and transport).

Management Implications

As we have seen in this chapter computer networking is diverse and complex. Many decisions must be made and pitfalls avoided if networks are to be used effectively. We conclude this chapter by discussing some of these decisions and pitfalls.

The Economics Favor Decentralized Processing

In recent years the cost/performance ratio of small computers (personal computers) has improved dramatically. Thus, distributed processing is often less expensive than centralized processing on mainframes. In fact, some companies are switching all or a part of their computer operations from mainframes to networks of PCs. This trend is called **downsizing** and it will accelerate in the future. Application 14–2 illustrates how Kodak has moved two strategic applications to a PC-based LAN.

The use of small computers may also reduce data communication costs because it allows more processing to be done at branch locations. Also, system reliability may be improved because if one computer crashes, its workload can be distributed to others. Finally, and probably most important, distributed processing allows the end users to interact directly with the computer. PC software is almost always more user-friendly than mainframe software. End users can solve many of their information processing requirements by themselves and yet networks tie them together with other individuals and databases in the firm.

Data Decentralization

When information processing is distributed the question of data storage tends to get more complex. With centralized processing the data are stored on the central mainframe. In distributed processing there are two types of data: local data and shared data. **Local data** are used only by the local node of the network such as a PC. It would serve no useful purpose to make these data available to the whole network. Thus, the data are simply stored locally, but it is still necessary to keep track of what is being stored and where. This is part of the database administrator's responsibility.

APPLICATION 14–2

Kodak Ports Two Strategic Applications to Run on LAN

By Caryn Gillooly

Eastman Kodak Co. has downsized two strategic business applications to run on an OS/2-based local-area network, enabling customers to submit orders via electronic data interchange and access data on any of the company's 80,000 products and parts.

The downsizing effort was mandated by upper management to migrate applications from expensive mainframe hosts to less costly departmental LANs. It has simplified access to product information, improved remote terminal response time by about 20% and provided Eastman Kodak with a competitive edge—all while cutting the overall budget.

"The company is moving to multiple business units, so data processing is moving to platforms it can afford to maintain," said Gus Holderer, manager of EDI planning and development for Eastman Kodak's Distribution Division.

In a span of just six months, Eastman Kodak set up an OS/2-based IBM Token-Ring Network at its headquarters here with 12 IBM Personal System/2 Model 80 servers running IBM's LAN Server network operating system, Holderer said.

Four of those PS/2 servers support a Microsoft Corp. SQL Server relational data base, providing remote users with access to information on product availability, prices, technical specifications, shipping dates, parts numbers and more.

The remaining servers are dedicated to handling network traffic and processing an estimated quarter million EDI transactions this year.

Resellers at remote OS/2-based workstations use Eastman Kodak-developed communications software and a modem to dial into the LAN via the GE Information Services value-added network.

Once connected to the servers, customers are presented with a menu of options, giving them access to price inquiries, order entry, order status or electronic mail. By accessing the price inquiry option, customers gain access to more than a gigabyte of product information from the local SQL Server data base.

The order entry option enables users to fill out an order worksheet, which supports an internally developed EDI format. Users then send that file over the public net to the LAN servers . . .

"This not only gives customers better response time, but it's much more user-friendly," said Barbara Balzano, lead systems analyst at Eastman Kodak.

Brad Blank, a consultant with Computer Task Group, based in Buffalo, N.Y., which helped develop the system, said one reason response times have improved is that SQL Server is designed to take advantage of the multiprocessing and multithreading features of OS/2. "It's as fast as a mainframe," Blank said. "SQL Server has handled our big data tables—some of which are a half-million records in size—very well. And we can update data across all the servers at the same time. . . ."

Given the success of the downsizing effort, Holderer said Eastman Kodak is committed to developing other LAN-based applications to respond more quickly to changing market conditions.

"In a LAN environment, you can move faster to develop applications for our business units," Holderer said.

Adapted with permission from *Network World* (March 25, 1991), pp. 2, 48, copyright March 25, 1991 by Network World Inc., Framingham, MA 01701.

Shared data may be stored in one of three ways. They can be stored on a central file server, they can be partitioned, or they can be replicated. Database management systems have the capability of handling each of these three treatments for shared data.

Central File Server   Under the central file server approach the database is stored on a high-speed disk connected to a PC that is in turn connected to the network. All users of the network who have authority to access the database can do so through the network.

Partitioning   With **partitioning** a particular kind of record is stored at the location that uses it the most. When another node (device) requests the record, the DBMS consults the data dictionary to determine the record's location and retrieves it from there. For instance, a bank may store a customer's account balance at the branch where the customer usually does business. On rare occasions the customer might execute a transaction at another branch. At such times the DBMS retrieves the data through the network. Since most data retrievals are done locally, communication costs of the network are minimized.

Replication   With **replication**, duplicate copies of the database are stored at all processing locations that need the data. Changes to the database are periodically copied to each of these locations. This approach is useful with small databases, for which it is cheaper to store multiple copies of the data than to use communication lines to retrieve individual records from distant locations. A large East Coast textile manufacturer uses replication in its distributed database. The database contains orders, customer data, production data, and warehouse information. It is periodically updated at all locations. Another example of replication is a local decision support system on a personal computer. The user may periodically replicate from the central database the portions of data that support his or her decision support system.

The Need for Expertise

Some firms make the mistake of assuming that to install and operate a network all they need to do is buy the network interface cards, the cabling, and the network operating system, install this hardware and software, and begin operating a network. In other words, stand-alone PCs are user friendly and networks are also user friendly. Thus, the same people who operate the PCs can maintain the network. Nothing can be further from the truth. Selection, installation, and maintenance of a network requires special expertise. When you move from stand-alone PCs to a network environment you take on most of the challenges that are characteristic of a mainframe/terminal environment, such as backup of files, security, access control, and network maintenance. A network of fifty PCs will require a full-time network administrator.

The Any-to-Any Myth

Some individuals erroneously believe that a network will allow the Apple Macintosh operating system to communicate directly with DOS, OS/2, or a mainframe operating system. They also believe that a network will allow Lotus 1-2-3 to directly access an EXCEL spreadsheet stored on a Macintosh computer or a spreadsheet stored on a VAX computer. Maybe in the future we will have these capabilities, but certainly today's networks do not allow any device or any application to automatically connect to any other device or application. Unless the compatible computers on the network are running common applications that are fully compatible at the application level, the connection of these computers over a network makes little sense. To use the network effectively you must have application software, such as dBASE IV, that is designed to operate on a network.

Standardization

Standardization is closely related to the topic just discussed. Since there exists a lack of standards between different computers, different operating systems, different networks, and different applications, a network user must be very careful to ensure that all the pieces of information systems technology that will be used in the network are compatible with one another. If there is any area where the term "let the buyer beware" applies, it is in the networking area.

Security

The dispersion of processing and files that is inherent in a network reduces the security of the information system. When all the processing is performed and the data is stored in one central location this location can be made very secure. Passwords, locks on PCs, and locked access doors when computers are not in use can all be used with networks to improve security.

Focus on Business Needs, Not Technology

It is certainly true that to understand networks and make intelligent decisions about networks a manager must have a basic knowledge of networking technology. However, when it comes to purchasing and implementing a network the manager must focus on business needs, not the technology. If the network doesn't support a business purpose it is a waste of the company's resources regardless of how well the network operates.

Summary

- There are two basic types of communications: computer to peripheral device and computer to computer.

- A communication channel is the physical line over which a communication is accomplished.

- Computers operate through the manipulation of digital signals. However, communications are often made through analog channels, such as telephone lines. Modems have to be used to convert the digital signal to analog, and then back to digital on the receiving end.

- Under serial communication a message is transmitted one bit at a time over a single communication channel.

- Parallel communication is a simultaneous transmission of eight or more bits across a multichannel line.

- A twisted pair is two insulated wires twisted around each other.

- A coaxial cable is a central insulated wire enclosed by cylindrical conducting wire, both of which are enclosed with further insulation and a protective cover.

- Microwaves are electromagnetic (radio) signals in the radio frequency of about one billion cycles per second to twenty billion cycles per second.

- Satellite transmission uses geosynchronous satellites to relay microwave signals from one spot on the earth to a receiving location on the earth.

- Fiber optics use a small strand of glass fiber about the size of a human hair to transmit enormous quantities of data by transmitting a pulsating light beam over long distances.

- A common carrier is a company that provides communication services to the general public and businesses.

- In baseband channels, digital signals are transmitted over a communication channel without modulation.

- The bandwidth of a communication channel refers to the range of electrical frequencies that the communication channel can handle.

- In broadband channels the digital signals are modulated (changed into specific radio frequencies) and thus multiple streams of transmissions can occur over the same physical cable simultaneously, each occupying a different radio frequency.

- Integrated Services Digital Network (ISDN) is an international standard for the digital transmission of voice, data, text, and images over common carrier networks.

- A multiplexor merges many individual transmissions into a single high-speed transmission and reverses the operation on the receiving end.

- A small computer that is dedicated solely to the communication function is often known as front-end processor.

- A communication protocol is a set of rules governing information flow in a communication system.

- Data transmission speed is measured in bits per second (bps).

- There are three combinations of transmission directions: half-duplex, full-duplex, and simplex.

- In a switched network a channel connection is made between the two devices communicating at the time the communication is initiated. This connection is maintained throughout the communication session.

- A digital PBX is a private digital communications network installed in a firm. It is a switched network.

- In a nonswitched network, all devices using the network share the same communication channel. Access methods are used to share the common communication channel.

- Although polling and time-division multiplexing are sometimes used, the two primary access methods are carrier sense multiple access with collision detection (CSMA/CD) and token passing.

- Under CSMA/CD access all devices connected to the common communication channel can send messages at any point in time. However, they must listen for a collision and if one occurs they must retransmit the communication.

- Under token passing a device must wait until it receives a free token. Then it attaches the communication to the token and marks the token as busy.

- A bridge is a device that connects two similar networks.

- A gateway is a device that connects two different types of networks.

- A local area network (LAN) is a short-distance network that links computers and peripheral devices, usually confined to a distance of two miles or less.

- A wide area network (WAN) extends over a large geographical area, perhaps a state or a whole country.

- Value-added networks (VANS) provide additional value by offering services other than the simple transmission of a communication.

- A network interface card is inserted into the bus slot of a PC or workstation. It controls the receipt and transmission of communications onto the communication channel, a bus or a ring.

- A server is a device such as a PC that provides services to the other PCs in the network. Typical servers are file servers and printer servers.

- Client-server computing is a form of distributed computing where tasks are shared among devices (computers and peripheral devices) most suited to perform the task. These devices are usually connected to each other by a network.

- A network operating system is control software that manages the network.

- A standard is an acknowledged method of operation.

- Standards are established when members of an accepted standards organization agree on a standard or through the dominance of a particular manufacturer or a product in the market.

- Currently, two major networking standards are vying to dominate the network management market, IBM's System Network Architecture (SNA) and the International Standards Organization's Open System Interconnection (OSI).

- Electronic data interchange (EDI) is the transmission of normal business transaction data between trading partners over a computer network.

- The economics of computing favor small computers and decentralized processing.

- When data are decentralized, they can be treated as local data or shared data.

- Shared data can be stored on a central file server. Also, they can be partitioned or replicated onto multiple computers.

- When a firm moves from stand-alone PCs to a network environment it takes on most of the challenges that are characteristic of a mainframe/terminal environment.

- It is a myth that any machine can be connected to any other machine over a network. Unless the compatible computers on the network are running common applications that are fully compatible at the application level, the connection of these computers over a network makes little sense.

- When purchasing network hardware and software, a firm must be sure that the items are compatible with one another.

- The dispersion of processing and files that is inherent in a network reduces the security of the information system.

- When it comes to purchasing and implementing a network the manager must focus on business needs, not the technology.

Key Terms

Distributed data processing (DDP)

Connectivity

Master-slave relationship

Peer-to-peer communication

Communication channel

Modulation

Demodulation

Modem

Serial communication

Parallel communication

Twisted pair

Coaxial cable

Microwaves

Satellite transmission

Wireless networks

Fiber optics

Common carrier

Baseband channels

Bandwidth

Broadband channels

Integrated Services Digital Network (ISDN)

Multiplexer

Frequency-division multiplexer

Time-division multiplexer

Statistical multiplexer

Front-end processor

Communication protocol

Block format

Message envelope

Asynchronous transmission

Synchronous transmission

Data transmission speed

Bits per second (bps)

Half-duplex channel

Full-duplex channel

Simplex channel

Switched network

Packet switching

Digital private branch exchange (PBX)

Nonswitched networks

Bus

Ring network

Access method

Polling

Time-division multiplexing

Carrier sense multiple access with collision detection (CSMA/CD)

Token passing

Token

Bridge

Gateway

Local area network (LAN)

Wide area network (WAN)

Value-added networks (VANS)

Server

File server

Printer server

Client

Client-server computing

Network operating system

Standard

System Network Architecture (SNA)

System Application Architecture (SAA)

Open System Interconnection (OSI)

Electronic data interchange (EDI)

Downsizing

Local data

Shared data

Partitioning

Replication

1. Explain the two basic types of data communication.

2. What are the differences between analog and digital communication?

3. What is the function of a modem in data communication?

4. What are the differences between serial and parallel communication?

5. What are the primary choices for the physical media over which communications are transmitted?

6. What are the advantages of fiber optics over other physical communication channels?

7. Explain the difference between broadband and baseband communications.

8. What is a common carrier?

9. Explain the basic capabilities of an integrated services digital network (ISDN).

10. What do multiplexers do?

11. Why are communication protocols necessary?

12. Explain the difference between asynchronous and synchronous data transmission.

13. How can data transmission speed, measured in bits per second, be misleading?

14. What are the differences between a switched network and a nonswitched network?

15. What is a digital private branch exchange?

16. Why do nonswitched networks but not switched networks have to be shared?

17. What are the differences between a bus and a ring network?

18. What are the primary access methods for sharing nonswitched networks?

19. Explain how carrier sense multiple access with collision detection and token passing are used to share a communication channel.

20. Explain the difference between a bridge and a gateway.

21. What are value-added networks?

22. What is a network interface card?

23. What are the functions of a server on a network?

24. How are standards set?

25. What are two major network management standards that are competing to become the dominant standard?

26. Explain the advantages of electronic data interchange (EDI).

27. Why do the economics favor decentralized processing?

28. Explain the terms shared data, local data, partitioning, and replication.

29. What is the any-to-any myth in communications?

30. How is security affected by the move from central processing to distributed processing?

Discussion Questions and Cases

1. Spreadout Incorporated has decided to connect its computers in twelve different states with a communication network. Elmer Ware, the president, is not sure how a communication network functions. Explain to him the important functions of a communication system and how they might relate to Spreadout's information systems operations.

2. Dublin Furniture is a medium-sized furniture manufacturing operation in Virginia with five plants scattered over five counties in the southwest part of the state. The company has one central mainframe computer. Each plant has access to the central computer through a variety of on-line terminals and workstations. For the last few months, manufacturing managers at the various plants have been building a case for distributed data processing. They argue that manufacturing resources planning (MRP-II) systems are becoming essential to effective manufacturing management. Their plans calls for a minicomputer to be purchased for each plant. Each plant would run its own MRP system. In addition, they argue that other applications could be distributed from the central mainframe to these minicomputers. For example, each plant could maintain its own personnel system. If you were chief executive officer of Dublin Furniture, would you approve the distributed data processing proposal?

3. Allied Innovators Incorporated has a computer problem concerning the communication of information among its worldwide operations. Each division takes care of its own processing needs with its own minicomputer or mainframe. Computer communications among the divisions, the divisions and their remote locations, and the divisions and corporate headquarters are handled overnight using common carrier lines. Allied Innovators' problem is twofold. First, certain divisions have began to receive defense contracts, making security an important issue. Second, the communication between divisions has increased significantly, and overnight communication is causing problems when information is needed quickly. What suggestions would you make to Allied Innovators to improve its communications and security?

4. The tax department of a regional certified public accountant (CPA) firm currently has twenty-five PCs that are used in a stand-alone mode by its tax professionals. The firm is considering networking these PCs and they have asked you to tell them how they could use a network. Furthermore, if they get a network they would like to know if they need to hire a network administrator to take care of the network. The tax department prepares tax returns for individuals and corporations. It also provides tax advice and planning. The tax returns are often prepared by an individual accountant and then reviewed by a supervisor, a manager, and a partner. The staff also has a tax library which they use to look up questions of tax law including IRS regulations and court cases. They also maintain on one PC a list of their clients with various information about those clients. How would you respond to their questions about this proposed network?

5. The Oakton Corporation has a chain of fifty retail lumber stores. At their corporate headquarters they have been operating a mainframe computer system for the past ten years. On this system they do all of their accounting work including accounts payable, payroll, and other applications. This system also provides substantial amounts of information through workstation terminals for the day-to-day management of the business and for long-run tactical and strategic planning and reporting. There are also numerous personal computers scattered throughout the organization, mostly used for local information processing and reporting tasks. Oakton is considering doing away with its mainframe computer operations and switching all the processing now done on the mainframe to a network of personal computers. What would you say are the advantages and potential pitfalls of Oakton's switch from mainframe processing to a client-server PC network?

INFORMATION SYSTEMS STRATEGIES

How to Avoid the Classic Blunders of Networking

By Michael Puttre

Fans of Rob Reiner movies might surmise that getting involved in a land war in Asia is one of the Classic Blunders of history. Veteran planners of networks will speak of opportunities for disaster on a similar scale.

But it is possible to avoid the Classic Blunders of networking. First of all, the experts have said, do not think of the network in terms of channels and multiplexers. Take a business-oriented approach. Remember that the network is being built to achieve a business goal. That goal should first be set out in a strategic planning process by senior management.

MIS [management information systems] must take that goal and, by applying technology, build a network that realizes it in an innovative way, insiders agree. As Mark Luczak, a management consultant at Cherry Hill, N.J.-based Infotron, pointed out, innovation is the term of the business man, not the technologist. "Forget about the technology," he said. "Old or new, it's how you use it to solve business problems."

Networking consultants have found that it is very easy to advise against selecting a poor network design, but it is important nonetheless. Simplicity is always best. "The correct model is to think of the network as the computer," advised Gene Shklar, director of marketing, Oracle's Network Products Division. "Managing and using the network should be no more complicated than for a single system."

Basics Overlooked

Something as basic as laying the network out in an oval or figure eight is oftentimes, needlessly, overlooked. Anthony Pompliano, president and chief executive of Metropolitan Fiber Systems, an Oakbrook Terrace, Ill.-based provider of fiber-optic network services, said that obvious route diversity reassures those who must run the business on the network. A side benefit is that a network blueprint that is clearly laid out will sit better with those who must approve it.

Each location on the network should be able to monitor the network and there should be a single point of control for network management. With that in mind, the network planner should always remember the Hinsdale fire, which offered a vital lesson—avoid a single point of failure. Also, network developers should never assume that rights of way will be available or that they are in the hands of friendlies.

Pompliano urges his planners to verify that the rights of way intended for use are in fact free to use and will remain that way. Digging a private conduit is the best way to ensure right of way, but for many companies, this is not a cost-effective option. Pompliano suggested leasing a conduit from an appropriate utility to avoid the likelihood of a company inadvertently leasing it from a competitor, which would jeopardize your right of way.

Advisors recommend that early in the design process, some time should be taken to visit the sites that will be served by the network. Walking through the building with the local corporate management and the building owner could help to locate physical attributes that might affect the network. Planners point out that entrances to buildings are important as are already available conduits and inner ducts. The local utilities should hand over information about the placement of their pipes, lines and cables. In addition, construction and congestion problems should be considered.

Every element involved must be examined in light of how it relates to the backbone, insiders have stressed.

Thinking of the network as a collection of commodities connected by lines of communication can ease planning headaches. Much hardware today already is considered among commodity items, and if industry trends are any indication, package software is fast becoming a commodity. Following that lead, each of these components should be able to plug and play with each other—analysts warn that network developers should exercise care in selecting these components.

Oracle's Shklar recommended that network planners work with vendors and systems integrators that are as unbiased as possible. MIS should remain skeptical of proprietary products and solutions on the basis that their proponents purport them to be an "emerging standard."

Although it is important to observe standards, many in the industry say that multiple standards will continue to exist for another 20 years or so. You do not want to get locked into an emerging standard that goes the way of Beta and the eight-track tape. Shklar advised network planners to select equipment that can be thrown out and replaced in the future. This way a company's network can be state of the art when the emerging standard changes.

While mixing and matching hardware and software, one thing to keep in mind is that the biggest cost items are the lines that support the network. Think about line optimization and keep an eye on tariffs. Warned Shklar: "Line rentals will kill you."

Balancing current network requirements with available line capacity is an ongoing process. Michael Filson, network consultant with Bull Information Services, said that in this balancing act, MIS has a tendency to fall one way or the other.

"People think communications lines are unlimited and they just keep adding terminals," he said. On the other hand, he also advised MIS not to overbuy bandwidth in anticipation of future growth as this amounts to a waste of resources and money. "A good network design should not last forever."

Once the line requirements for the network have been established, other planners warn that poorly configuring these lines can reduce network efficiency and lead to unnecessary costs. "Every location is different and needs to be studied separately," said Tony Campisi, manager of strategic marketing for Infotron. He indicated that response time, circuit load, communications protocols, tariffs, acceptable error rate and adequate back-up all figure into the calculation.

Configuring the lines is time consuming, although there are a number of tools available to automate the process. Infotron, for example, uses a proprietary planning tool as part of its network design services that reportedly shaves days off the time required to configure the network lines.

Delays Are Certainty

Do not underestimate the time required to build the network. People who build networks for a living cannot overstress this point. "We have built eight networks in eight cities and we still underestimate the time it takes," said Metropolitan Fiber's Pompliano. "At any given moment, something will come up which delays the network."

For Metropolitan Fiber, as well as for corporations building their own networks, city departments such as utilities, water and roads all conspire to ruin a timetable. When Metropolitan Fiber is late in getting their network up and running, it means that they are late in opening service to a new city. Each company knows what its own particular ramifications will be if the network's debut is delayed.

Assess the situation. Allow contingency time and build it into your schedule, pushing back the delivery date accordingly. While a shorter network gestation period sounds better than a longer one at proposal time, late delivery is worse. Besides, if things go according to plan and the network emerges earlier than anticipated, a network planner can always boast to superiors that the network was brought up ahead of schedule.

Users Make or Break

The deadliest trap is the one that is least technical. It is a matter of not knowing who the users (and potential future users) of a network are and what they do. Much had been said about the gulf that exists between users and MIS. Data processing is notorious for retaining the opinion that it "knows better." Not only can this result in a long lead time for applications as DP sets its own priorities, but it ensures that the users are never quite satisfied with the system, observers said.

In the past, this has not really been a problem from the networking point of view. "Users need to only be able to (complain)," recalled Michael Zisman, president and chief executive of Softswitch, Wayne, Penn., a network software company. "Now they can go out and requisition gear."

The huge drop in the dollar cost of computing power has shattered MIS's monopoly. It is not able to exert the kind of control over departments that it used to. "Users get (angry) and go out and buy things," said Zisman of the revolt. "It's Saturday morning, I've got my Visa card, and it's off to Businessland I go."

Department heads with disgruntled users and PC sign-off power can wreak havoc on a network. Although they go out and get what they need for their departments despite MIS, department heads will still go to DP and say that they want to be integrated. Since these people are not in collusion, they all go to different sources, seeking solutions. Then MIS is faced with integrating eight different LAN vendors, twelve different PC vendors, and a variety of different software vendors onto the network.

So get to know the users and involve them in the network planning process, observers advise. Design teams should "live" with users to get a first-hand feel for their requirements. Metropolitan Fiber sends an initial telemarketing group to a prospective city to get to know the ins and outs of prospective customers. The same principal applies to an internal network. There should be a constant flow of communication between MIS and those who must use the network. According to Bull's Filson, MIS should do most of the listening. "DP needs to get back to being a service," he said. "They have to involve the network users, the people with calluses on their fingers. Users don't ask (for) hard things to do."

There is a healthy dose of psychology in Filson's approach. For a system to succeed, the users must be convinced that it belongs to them. "If the network is their idea, they won't complain," he said. "If it's MIS's, they will complain and you can count on it."

Zisman agreed that smart MIS managers should be the architects and integrators of a network but that they cannot assume dictatorial powers. "MIS can't say, 'We're standardizing on X, you must use X.' The users will surely turn around and reply, 'X won't meet our needs.' "

Need Some Standards

While the network cannot be shoved down the user's throats, the users cannot be allowed free rein either. There must be some sort of standardization or the network will be byzantine and ultimately unworkable.

MIS should compose a short list of vendors that are compatible with the network. Inform the departments that they are free to go outside the list if they have special requirements, but that if they do they will not be integrated into the backbone. Furthermore, Filson noted that MIS can promote its vendor list by going out and getting site licenses for the software.

"That way you can tell the department heads that it won't cost them anything," he said. "They'll like that."

Finally, never underestimate the amount of expertise required to design and build a network. Also, do not assume that the required experience is available internally. Avail yourself of a consultant.

Discussion Questions

1. Why should you think of a network as a single computer? How does this approach simplify the network concept?

2. Is it realistic to think of network components as commodities? What advantages does this approach present?

Reprinted with permission from Fairchild Publications, *MIS Week* (October 2, 1989), pp. 21–28.

Four

Development of User Applications

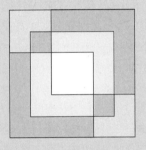

15

Information Strategy Planning

Typically, when an aircraft is built the primary builder, such as Boeing or Lockheed, designs and builds the structure of the aircraft while other components, such as the engine and the avionics (the electronics), are subcontracted to other firms to design and build. If you were managing this aircraft project would you allow each subcontractor to design and build its piece of the aircraft independently without some overall planning? Of course not. You might end up with engines designed for a fighter aircraft when you're building a passenger aircraft. Building an information system for a large system is just as complex as building an aircraft. Incredibly, though, many information systems are built without any overall planning. Allowing individual parts of a firm to build their own information system without strategic planning is analogous to building an aircraft without overall planning.

Information strategy planning is sometimes called information systems planning. Information strategy planning is also sometimes called strategic planning of information systems. The essence of **information strategy planning** is to align the information system with the firm's strategy. The goal is to create an information-based enterprise that supports the strategy of the business. Business systems are complex entities. We must use tools that assist in structuring these systems to support the firm's strategic objectives. In this chapter we will first look at the approaches to developing information systems and then look at the objectives of information strategy planning. Next the chapter introduces the information systems pyramid and looks at its components. Finally, the chapter introduces four information strategy planning methods.

Introduction

Approaches to Developing Information Systems

There are four basic approaches to developing information systems: ad hoc, data modeling, bottom-up, and top-down. Another way to look at these approaches is to see that they are approaches to information systems planning or lack of planning. It is important to note that these approaches are not mutually exclusive. Firms generally employ certain aspects of each approach.

Ad Hoc Approach

The **ad hoc approach** is directed toward solving a particular problem without considering other problems or the potential for integrating applications. Under this approach an analyst does not deal with the overall information requirements of the firm, but instead pinpoints only the trouble spots. In certain emergencies or in organizations undergoing rapid change, this approach might be important. However, it is inconsistent with the concept of planning an information system. Using this approach continually to meet additional demands for information produces a number of redundant and inefficient subsystems and databases that cannot be linked.

Data Modeling Approach

The **data modeling approach** attempts to develop a common database model that contains all the information necessary to support the operations of the firm and removes any data redundancies. It is important to note that the data modeling approach does not require that all of this information be stored in the same physical database. The database could be physically stored in several different locations, but it is planned so that it can be integrated. Emphasis is on establishing linkages within the database that allow common update, retrieval, and manipulation of data. An underlying assumption of this approach is that, since the analyst cannot anticipate all the information requirements of management, it is necessary to maximize the available data. Clearly the data modeling approach is important in any information strategy planning. The firm must know what data are necessary to support its strategy and activities. It is also clear that it is important to structure these data in such a way that access to them are enhanced and the problem of data redundancy is reduced. We will discuss this approach in this chapter under Information Strategy Planning Methods.

Bottom-Up Approach

The **bottom-up approach** focuses on the basic transaction processing requirements of the firm and implements systems to meet these needs. Typical transaction processing systems such as payroll, order entry, order processing, accounts receivable, and accounts payable are implemented. As management's demands on the information systems become more complex, steps to integrate the stand-alone transaction processing systems are undertaken. Later executive information systems and decision support systems may be built on top of these transaction processing systems.

When we look at how information systems have been developed in the past we see that the bottom-up approach is the predominant strategy used by firms. The advantage claimed for this strategy is that it allows the system to be developed in a logical, evolutionary, step-by-step manner. However, with no overall model of the information system there is no basis for incorporating features into each of the transaction processing modules that will facilitate integration as the information system evolves. Many of the transaction processing modules may have to be redesigned before they can be integrated with one another.

Application development by end users typically follows a bottom-up approach. One of the great dangers in application development by end users is that they will create a Tower of Babel, with systems that are redundant, do not integrate with one another, and are not well designed. In fact, one of the reasons why information strategy planning became more important during the 1980s is that it guides end-user development to support the overall strategy of the business.

Top-Down Approach

The **top-down approach** attempts to align information systems with business strategies and to involve top management in the information strategy planning process. This approach focuses on the strategies of the firm and the activities necessary to implement those strategies along with the data that the firm needs and the information technology available to implement an information system. By focusing on activities, data, and technology, a plan is devised that steers the information systems toward supporting the firm's strategies. This plan is sometimes called an information systems master plan.

As discussed above, none of these four approaches to developing information systems can work in isolation. There will always be cases where the ad hoc approach is required. Furthermore, no firm wants to stifle the creativity of end users that is inherent in the bottom-up approach. The overall data requirements of the firm must be modeled. The top-down approach of information strategy planning allows these other approaches to contribute to the goals of the firm. The information strategy plan is the glue that holds the information system together.

Objectives of Information Strategy Planning

Information strategy planning can produce several positive outcomes. In this section we will discuss seven of these benefits.[1]

Focus Information Systems on the Goals of the Business

In many organizations a communication gap exists between information systems personnel and top management. There are many reasons for this. Top management may be put off by the technical jargon that information systems people sometimes use. Systems in the past may have not met management's expectations or management simply may have a fear of information technology. Regardless of the reason for this communication gap, it results in information systems not being focused on the goals of the business. Information strategy planning requires senior executives to form an overall strategic vision for information systems. The plans that are developed in information strategy planning are the basis for the individual systems development projects whose development we discuss in the next two chapters. Thus, each system development project moves the information system closer to completing the strategic plan.

Redesign Business Processes

In the past, most information systems projects did not change the basic processes through which business was conducted. Often they only computerized processes that had been in use for many years. Today, there is considerable evidence that computer information systems can be the vehicle for radical transformation of the basic business processes. There is also much evidence that the expected productivity and competitive gains from information systems do not occur unless basic business processes are changed. **Re-engineering** is the use of information technology as a vehicle to radically redesign business processes to improve the delivery speed and the quality of goods and services. A major objective of information strategy planning is the re-engineering of business processes.

Involve Senior Management

Corporatewide information strategy planning that comes only from the information systems department is not likely to succeed. There are at

---

[1] The major concepts in this section are adapted from James Martin and Joe Leben, *Strategic Information Planning Methodologies*, 2nd Ed. (Englewood Cliffs, NJ: Prentice Hall, 1989), pp. 6–18.

least two reasons for this. First, information systems personnel simply do not have the business experience that top executives do. Second, information systems executives do not have the authority to make the rest of the organization conform to their information strategy plan. Figure 15–1 outlines the major reasons why top management involvement is necessary.

FIGURE 15–1
Why Senior Management Should Be Involved in Information Strategy Planning.
Reprinted from *Strategic Information Planning* (Englewood Cliffs, NJ: Prentice Hall, 1989), p. 9 with permission of James Martin and Joe Leben.

- Information is an extremely vital corporate resource. It affects productivity, profitability, and strategic decisions. Any resource that is important needs planning from the top.
- Where a *technical* group has planned corporate information resources, it has generally been unable to have the perspective of business managers or to understand the overall corporate information needs.
- The best laid plans of information systems designers have crashed on the rocks of corporate politics. Information systems, especially those that employ shared databases, tend to create political problems, often severe ones, and various factions will oppose them. Often, these problems can be solved only when top management has made it clear that it believes that advanced information systems are the way of the future and has signed off on a corporate information systems plan.
- Some of the methodologies for information strategy planning reveal anomalies, waste, and inefficiencies in the *corporate* organization and methods. In many cases the information strategy planning study has led to the reorganization of procedures and to corporate restructuring.
- Productivity in information systems development is vital. An appalling waste of development resources results from redundant uncoordinated application development and excessive maintenance and conversion activity. A top-down corporatewide information architecture is needed to lessen these.
- A formally structured corporatewide view of information processing is needed to set information systems priorities.
- Budgets need to be set for database development independently of application development.
- Orchestration is needed to make the various efforts fit together. Multiple *incompatible* fragments of databases and information systems cause excessive conversion costs and prevent senior management from obtaining the information it needs.
- An infrastructure needs to be planned for distributed systems. The separate database systems should be linked by a common network.
- The methodologies described of information strategy planning need the involvement of senior management and staff from user departments working with an overall directive from the top.

Control Diversity

Very powerful personal computers can be purchased by any department and many individuals in a firm. Nonprocedural languages enable end users to directly develop and maintain many of their own applications. However, without some **control of diversity** redundant applications and inconsistent, irreconcilable databases will be created. Failing to control end-user development is equivalent to building an aircraft without any overall plan. Neither the aircraft nor the information system will fly. The information strategy plan and especially its data model provide the framework to guide end-user development of applications.

Produce Consistency of Information

One of the most important objectives of information strategy planning is to produce **consistency of information**. Information can be inconsistent in several ways:

1. Various systems may have differing definitions of individual fields.

2. Even though the field definition may be the same, the way it is stored may differ. For example, the length of the field may differ, the number of decimal places may differ, or the field may be stored in character format in one system and numeric format in a different system.

3. Data may be processed immediately after an event occurs or at various time intervals, such as daily, weekly, or monthly. If the time of update differs between systems for the same data, different copies of the data may have different values. Thus, reports from different systems that should agree do not. This causes a great deal of confusion among management. They simply don't know which data is correct and in fact, usually assume that both copies are incorrect.

4. Update logic such as error checking may be different in different systems for the same data. Again we end up with inconsistent data from different systems because one system processes the data without change and the other system rejects the data.

With the proliferation of personal computers and application development by end users the occurrence of inconsistent data has increased dramatically. These inconsistent systems also make future integration of the system very difficult. A plan for the data (the data model) of a firm enables the systems development projects to be developed in a modular fashion. The data structures of the firm are stable and thus system developers can be sure what the input and output data of the system should look like. Stable data structures are also most important for quickly producing information retrieval programs and for supporting decision support systems that have ad hoc needs for data. These systems can be small or large, yet will be integrated with the overall strategic plan for information.

Defuse Corporate Politics

One of the major information systems problems in most firms is that end users perceive data that they create and maintain as their own. A basic underlying theme of information strategy planning is to make the enterprise information-based, where there is a plan for gathering and maintaining data so that they are not stored redundantly. This means that end users often must share their data with others in the organization.

The reluctance of end users to share data has killed many attempts by information systems personnel to develop a firmwide data plan. Valuable information is power. Managers and individuals within the firm are often reluctant to share it. However, with an information strategy planning approach top management is involved with the planning process. Their support for the information strategy plan and the data sharing that it requires can be the crucial political difference between success and failure in information strategy planning.

Enhance Information Systems Productivity

Productivity is a major concern, not only for firms, but for our society as a whole. Certainly, it is a concern of information systems professionals.

Systems that are developed without a strategic plan often fail or are mediocre in their benefits. Firms simply cannot afford to have redundant, inconsistent, and unproductive systems.

The information strategy plan allows information systems personnel to easily see which systems projects have a fast payback period and thus to select the projects that are most likely to be most productive. Information strategy plans can be very helpful in setting the implementation priorities for individual systems.

The Information Systems Pyramid

Before we look at the methods for information strategy planning, it is useful to see how information strategy planning fits within the information system function. Martin and Leben represent a firm's information system function as a pyramid. As shown in Figure 15–2, this pyramid has three sides representing the firm's data, the activities the organization carries out using data, and the technology that is used in implementing the information system. Figure 15–3 shows that the information systems function is directed from the top through the information systems strategy. The information systems pyramid can be viewed as a succession of layers that involve data activities and technology. At the top management strategy level the overall information strategy plan is created and maintained. This is the subject of this chapter. In the systems analysis layer logical models of individual systems that implement the information strategy plan are developed. These models describe what needs to be done, not how it is done. Thus, they are logical rather than physical. Systems analysis is the subject of Chapter 16 in this text.

In the system design layer of the pyramid information systems personnel design how a system will be implemented. At this level the data structures are designed, the individual application programs are designed, and the hardware to execute the system is selected.

At the implementation layer the individual system is implemented through the construction of physical databases and application programs and the installation of the system. System design and implementation are covered in Chapter 17 of this text.

Figure 15–4 describes some of the data and activities aspects of each level of the **information systems pyramid**. As mentioned above, activities also refer to the processes the organization carries out using data, such as processing orders and collecting accounts receivable. In this chapter we use the term activities in a broad sense to include both the processes necessary to create the information system and the processes that are carried out with the information system. They are both necessary to reach a firm's strategic goals.

Information Strategy Planning Methods

In this section we will discuss four information strategy planning methods: linkage analysis planning, critical success factors, technology impact analysis, and data modeling. Each method focuses on one or more sides of the information systems pyramid, i.e., data, activities, or technology. These planning methods are often referred to collectively as **information engineering**, although the methods used in systems analysis, system design, and implementation are often referred to as **software engi-**

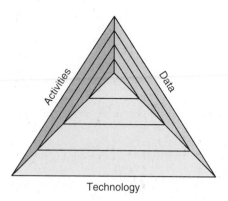

FIGURE 15–2
The Information
System Pyramid.
Reprinted from *Strategic
Information Planning*
(Englewood Cliffs, NJ:
Prentice Hall, 1989), p. 27
with permission of James
Martin and Joe Leben.

neering. Information engineering techniques rely heavily on easy-to-understand diagrams. These diagrams enable planners to get a grasp of the overwhelming complexity of many information systems. Relationships between data, activities, and technology can be revealed with these diagramming techniques.

Linkage Analysis Planning

Linkage analysis planning examines both the linkages within an organization and the external linkages that a firm has with customers, suppliers, and competitors in an attempt to formulate ways for the firm to gain a sustainable competitive advantage.

Linkage analysis planning was developed by Kenneth Primozic and Edward Primozic, both of IBM. It is particularly useful in assisting top-level executives to formulate a strategic vision for using information technology for competitive advantage. There are five major steps in a linkage analysis planning session:[2]

1. Examine the waves of information systems growth within the industry. The objective is to compare the firm's use of information systems technology with that used by competitors.

2. Compare where the firm stands on individual information technology experience curves with where competitors stand.

3. Examine the power relationships that currently exist within the industry and determine how these relationships may change in the future.

4. Examine the firm's extended enterprise. The extended enterprise consists not only of the firm but all other entities such as customers and suppliers with which the firm does business and interacts.

5. Identify opportunities to gain competitive advantage through the use of electronic channel support systems.

---

[2] *Ibid.*, p. 126.

F I G U R E 15–3
The Layers of the
Information System
Pyramid.
Reprinted from *Strategic
Information Planning*
(Englewood Cliffs, NJ:
Prentice Hall, 1989), p. 27
with permission of James
Martin and Joe Leben.

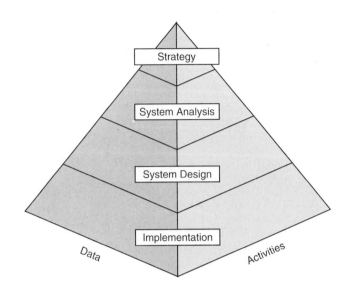

We will discuss each of these five steps below.

Waves of Information Systems Growth   Figure 15–5 illustrates five
waves of information systems growth that have either occurred or are beginning to occur. Batch systems were first introduced in the 1950s and
'60s, while people systems and home computers will become predominant in the 1990s. These systems will feature consumer databases, full
motion video, and touch screens. In this step of linkage analysis planning, the planners, consisting of top executives and information systems
executives, determine which of these waves of information systems
growth best represents where the firm currently stands.

F I G U R E 15–4
The Data and Activities Aspects of the Information System Pyramid.
Reprinted from *Strategic Information Planning* (Englewood Cliffs, NJ: Prentice Hall, 1989), p. 27 with permission of James Martin and
Joe Leben.

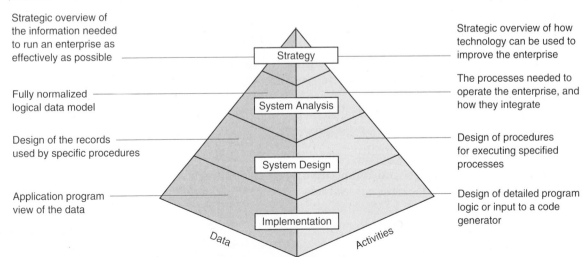

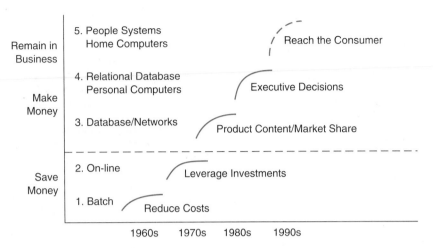

FIGURE 15–5
Waves of Information
Systems Growth.
Reprinted from *Strategic Information Planning* (Englewood Cliffs, NJ: Prentice Hall, 1989), p. 129 with permission of James Martin and Joe Leben.

Experience Curves   The basic concept behind **experience curves** (often also called learning curves) are that as individuals and companies use new information technology they learn how to use it more efficiently and effectively. Thus, a firm with more experience with a particular technology has a competitive advantage over those with less experience. Figure 15–6 illustrates some typical industry experience curves with various types of information technology. As you can see by the shapes of these curves, efficiency and effectiveness improve dramatically when a new technology is first implemented and then the improvement tends to level off with time. This is a typical learning curve pattern. After the firm determines where it stands in relation to the various waves of information systems growth, it uses experience curve analysis to determine how it stands compared to other competitors in learning how to use the technology of a given wave.

Industry Power Relationships   In this step all the players in an industry, such as manufacturers, consumers, retailers, and suppliers, are examined. A key objective is to determine where the **power relationships** lie in the industry. For example, the current industry power relationships may require a broker-wholesaler between the manufacturer and the retailer in the channel of distribution. The broker-wholesaler may serve as both a communication channel between the manufacturer and retailer, but also as a regional warehouse to enhance the delivery time between a retailer's restocking order and when that order is received. While doing linkage analysis planning, the manufacturer may find that a computer network can be substituted for the broker-wholesaler so that orders can be processed quickly and the goods delivered properly. Such a new system is an **electronic channel support system** because it is used to improve the distribution channels of the firm.

Another example of how computer technology has changed the power relationships of industry is the airline industry. Airline reservation systems gave those firms who were successful in implementing them substantial additional power over travel agents and also gave them substantial information that improved their competitive position in rela-

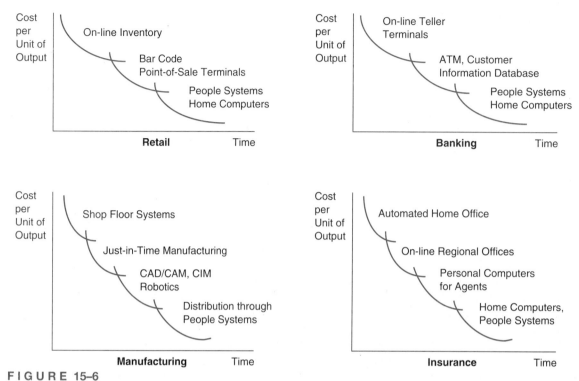

FIGURE 15–6

Typical Industry Experience Curves.

Reprinted from *Strategic Information Planning* (Englewood Cliffs, NJ: Prentice Hall, 1989), p. 132 with permission of James Martin and Joe Leben.

tion to other airlines. It is interesting to note today, during the airline shakeout, that those firms who have successful reservation systems, such as American and United, are those that are surviving. Those firms whose reservation systems were not successful, such as Pan Am and Eastern, have gone into bankruptcy. The examination of industry power relationships will help top management understand that the firm must operate as an extended enterprise and that information systems are necessary to facilitate such an operation.

The Extended Enterprise   Figure 15–7 illustrates the extended enterprise for an automobile manufacturer. As can be seen the **extended enterprise** includes not only the suppliers, but other firms, such as transportation dealers, auto insurance, auto financing, and consumers. To be competitive today firms must consider themselves to be part of an extended enterprise. In fact, one of the primary reasons that Japanese automobile manufacturers have been so successful is because of their tight links with suppliers and others in their industry.

   Information contributes greatly to the value of goods and services. Today, well over half the value added to goods and services comes from such items as product specifications and production techniques. These items of information must flow efficiently and effectively between firms and their suppliers. By viewing the firm as an extended enterprise, top management and information systems management can see where infor-

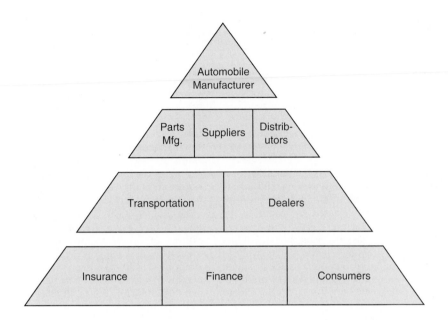

FIGURE 15–7
Extended Enterprise
for an Automobile
Manufacturer.
Reprinted from *Strategic
Information Planning*
(Englewood Cliffs, NJ:
Prentice Hall, 1989), p. 137
with permission of James
Martin and Joe Leben.

mation technology can enhance the flow of information and services to business partners and consumers.

Electronic Channel Support Systems   Channels of supply into the firm and channels of distribution for output to customers constitute the lifeblood of any firm. After having performed the steps in linkage analysis planning just discussed, the planners should be in a good position to recognize opportunities to build electronic channel support systems. An example of a firm that did this successfully is American Hospital Supply (now Baxter Healthcare) which supplies hospitals with various products. American Hospital Supply installed their computer terminals at nurses' stations. Thus, nurses could order products directly through these terminals. This system substantially enhanced American Hospital Supply's share of the market, while it reduced the supply inventory that hospitals must carry. However, the company subsequently lost its competitive advantage when it did not continue to innovate, thus allowing its competition to gain an advantage.

Linkage analysis is unique in its ability to bring top executives and information systems executives together to help create a strategic information vision. Linkage analysis focuses on waves of technology, the firm's experience with these technologies, the firm's competitive position within the industry, the firm's extended organization, and how the linkages within the firm's extended organization can be used to gain competitive advantages. Next we will examine critical success factors, a complementary approach to linkage analysis planning. Application 15–1 illustrates how The Progressive Corp. used information technology to improve its channel support system link to customers.

APPLICATION 15–1

Re-Engineering Puts Progressive on the Spot

By Julia King

Midnight, downtown Atlanta. A late-model sports car skids out of control on rainslicked Peachtree St. The teenage driver careens into a utility pole, making a perfect letter V of the hood of his car. Miraculously, he walks away from the accident unhurt.

Moments after the police arrive, a van driven by an adjuster from the driver's insurance company appears. Less than one hour later, the car has been towed to a garage, and the driver has been driven home with a check in his pocket to cover the costs of repairing his smashed but salvageable car, hiring a rental car and even replacing his $75 stone-washed designer jeans, which were torn at the knees during the accident.

While the accident described here is imaginary, the insurance company van is real. It is one of the most visible symbols of the largest IS [information systems] project ever tackled by The Progressive Corp.: a five-year, $28 million effort to automate claims processing.

Officials at the $15 million Mayfield, Ohio-based specialty insurer credit the 2-year-old system, dubbed Pacman (Progressive's Automated Claim Management), with averting a crisis and providing a springboard for national expansion into a new, much larger automobile insurance market.

"In terms of profitability and growth, [Progressive] is one of the best," says Gerald Lewinsohn, first vice president and insurance industry analyst at Merrill Lynch & Co.

Although Progressive calls the process "strategic redesign," Pacman is a textbook case of using re-engineering to take advantage of information technology.

Facing a Crisis

In 1986, company executives realized they had to make radical changes in how customers were serviced if Progressive was to survive cutthroat competition in the automobile insurance industry.

"Face it," says Bruce W. Marlow, Progressive's chief operating officer. "People just hate our product."

Progressive, which specializes in selling automobile coverage to drivers rejected or canceled by other insurers, saw that the answer lay in revamping its claims processing operations as well as adopting a companywide policy of responding immediately to all accidents, from a neighborhood fender bender to an interstate pileup.

It was clear, Marlow says, that only a complete rethinking of how the company did business could rescue it from "a crisis situation."

The process began in the claims department, which was largely paper-based and was run on a state-by-state basis. Some 175 claims offices across the country shuttled paperwork back and forth to company headquarters.

The goal was not only to reduce the flow of paper but also to shrink the number of days and even weeks between the time a claim was filed and the time it was paid.

Pacman was built around an IBM 3090 mainframe and Compaq Computer Corp. personal computers. More than 200 people spent 100,000 staff hours developing software and other projects during a two-year period.

Marlow says both Pacman and the immediate response program have dramatically changed the way Progressive claims adjusters do their jobs. Once confined to their desks for most of the day, adjusters now spend most of their working hours with current policyholders and prospective customers. Surprisingly, Marlow says, adjusters embraced their new jobs and more flexible hours.

What the company didn't foresee was what Marlow calls the "staggering ripple effects" the pro-

gram had on the rest of the company's 6,100 employees. Agents, reluctant to relinquish control over their own client base, at first were slow to turn over calls directly to claims adjusters. A second problem was how to instill a fast-response mentality into employees from other departments.

To help educate employees, the company spent an extra $1.3 million on training, including orientation and reference videos, computer-based training, a 40-hour live training class, two user manuals and a variety of support documentation.

Business Drives Process

Marlow's main advice to other companies is that senior management should bank on re-engineering taking longer than they would like. At Progressive, upper management began planning for changes in 1986. Actual implementation of the automated claims processing system and immediate response programs came three and five years after initial planning.

"When you're talking about fundamental changes in jobs, you have to give people time to get used to the idea," he says.

Marlow offers no hard figures on just how much the company has saved as a result of its strategic redesign. . . . But he notes that the immediate response program and automated claims processing system have helped launch Progressive from its $15 million niche business of selling nonstandard insurance to the $75 million market for standard automobile coverage.

"By taking a hard look in the mirror, we've launched ourselves into a marketplace that is six times the size of our current market," Marlow says.

Adapted with permission from *Computerworld* (July 15, 1991), p. 58, Copyright 1991 by CW Publishing, Inc., Framingham, MA 01701.

Critical Success Factors

Critical success factors are the few key areas where things must go right for the individual department or the firm to succeed. Figure 15–8 provides examples of critical success factors for several different industries. Note that these success factors are items that would not necessarily be picked up through linkage analysis planning. Thus, a critical success factor approach to information strategy planning is necessary along with other techniques. None of these methods are sufficient by themselves to perform good strategy planning. Most firms use a combination of techniques. The critical success factors technique was developed by John F. Rockart of MIT.[3] Figure 15–9 illustrates the major steps that must be completed to develop a list of critical success factors. Once these lists are completed, the planners can focus on how information technology can be used to support these critical success factors. Technology is one side of the information systems pyramid. We will see how technology is planned in the next section.

Automobile Industry
- Fuel economy
- Image
- Efficient dealer organization
- Tight control of manufacturing costs

Software House
- Product innovation
- Quality of sales and user literature
- Worldwide marketing and service
- Ease of use of products

Prepackaged Food Corporation
- Advertising effectiveness
- Good distribution
- Product innovation

Seminar Company
- Obtaining the best speakers
- Identification of topics
- Mailing list size and quality

Microelectronics Company
- Ability to attract and keep the best design staff
- Government R&D support
- Support of field sales force
- Identification of new market needs

Life Insurance Company
- Development of agency management personnel
- Advertising effectiveness
- Productivity of clerical operations

F I G U R E   15–8
Examples of Business Critical Success Factors.
Reprinted from *Strategic Information Planning* (Englewood Cliffs, NJ: Prentice Hall, 1989), p. 187 with permission of James Martin and Joe Leben.

Technology Impact Analysis

The fastest changing of the three sides of the information systems pyramid is technology. Failure to plan for changing technology can negate all the other potential benefits to be derived from information strategy planning. A significant new technology, if it is used effectively by a competitor early in its introduction, can remove all the competitive advantage a firm had planned on.

---

[3] John F. Rockart, "Chief Executives Define Their Own Data Needs," *Harvard Business Review*, March–April, 1979.

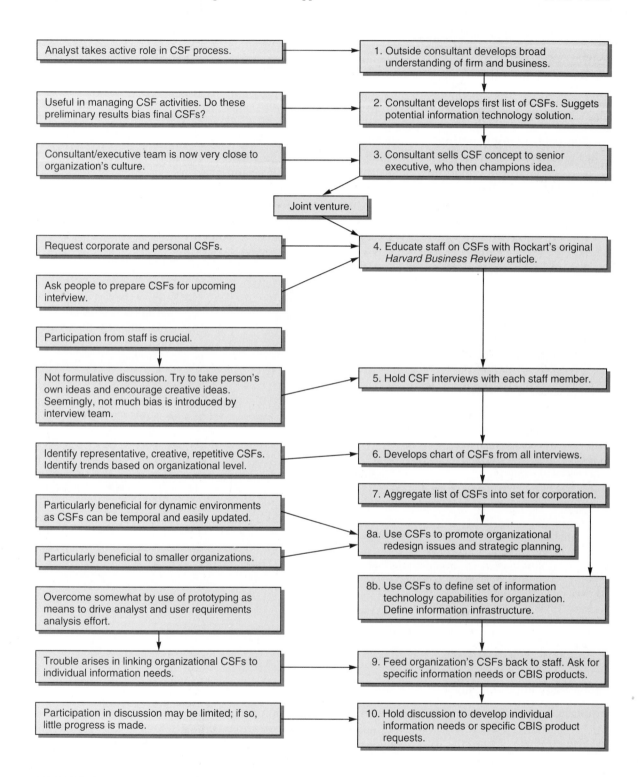

F I G U R E   15–9
Steps in Developing Critical Success Factors.

Reprinted from "An Assessment of Critical Success Factors," by Andrew C. Boynton and Robert W. Zmud, *Sloan Management Review*, Volume 25, Number 4, pp. 17–27, by permission of the publisher. Copyright © 1984 by the Sloan Management Review Association. All rights reserved.

Technology impact analysis develops an easy-to-understand diagram of current and expected information technology. One approach is to use an action diagram as illustrated in Figure 15–10. Action diagrams are read similar to outlines with the indented items being subsets of the item above. The three dots in a line item in an action diagram indicate that the item can be exploded to show additional detail beneath it. Computer-aided software engineering packages generally provide the capability to create and maintain action diagrams. The technology action diagram should be constantly updated and reviewed periodically by the planners to determine if new technology can be used to implement the firm's information strategy plan or if the information strategy plan needs to be changed because of new technology.[4]

Data Modeling

Data modeling identifies a firm's entire data needs and produces a plan that eliminates data redundancy, data inconsistency, and data inaccuracies. In firms that do not perform data modeling a situation arises similar to that illustrated in Figure 15–11. Each functional area of the business creates its own files. These files almost always contain data that are redundant with data stored in other functional areas, data that are inconsistent, and systems that cannot share data from one functional area to another. This is a major problem in most businesses today.

Data modeling produces a situation similar to that illustrated in Figure 15–12 where all functions within the business share an integrated database. The fact that it is integrated doesn't mean that all the data must be stored in one location. The data model is a conceptual, logical plan for the data. The actual physical storage of the data can be in different locations and in the files of different functions. But it is planned in such a way that it can be readily integrated and redundancy avoided.

There are many techniques for data modeling. An in-depth look at these techniques is beyond the scope of this textbook. Typically, a substantial portion of a database management systems course deals with data modeling. One of the techniques that is often used is entity-relationship diagramming. Most CASE tools support entity-relationship diagramming. Another technique that should be used is normalization of data.

The key to building data models is for the firm to store data on subjects rather than business transactions. Most firms now store data on business transactions, such as invoicing and accounts receivable collection. These transaction-oriented databases are primarily a result of the accounting influence on information systems. In the past, accountants have designed databases to support their needs while often ignoring the needs of the rest of the organization. Figure 15–13 illustrates how application systems can use subject databases. **Subject databases** store information about the subjects that a business deals with. Fundamentally, businesses deal with products, customers, parts, vendors, and so on. They do not deal with invoicing, accounts receivable, and other application systems. The application systems support the firm's dealings with

---

[4] Martin and Leben, p. 171–172.

the subjects, such as customers and vendors. Firms that organize their databases around subjects find that the basic underlying data they store supports most application systems they wish to develop. They also find that subject-oriented databases are much easier for decision support systems to use and that they support the ad hoc needs for information by the firm.

FIGURE 15–10
An Overview Action Diagram of Technological Changes.
Reprinted from *Strategic Information Planning* (Englewood Cliffs, NJ: Prentice Hall, 1989), p. 173 with permission of James Martin and Joe Leben.

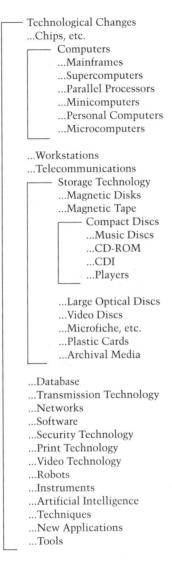

```
┌─── Technological Changes
│    ...Chips, etc.
│         ┌─── Computers
│         │    ...Mainframes
│         │    ...Supercomputers
│         │    ...Parallel Processors
│         │    ...Minicomputers
│         │    ...Personal Computers
│         └    ...Microcomputers
│
│    ...Workstations
│    ...Telecommunications
│         ┌─── Storage Technology
│         │    ...Magnetic Disks
│         │    ...Magnetic Tape
│         │         ┌─── Compact Discs
│         │         │    ...Music Discs
│         │         │    ...CD-ROM
│         │         │    ...CDI
│         │         └    ...Players
│         │
│         │    ...Large Optical Discs
│         │    ...Video Discs
│         │    ...Microfiche, etc.
│         │    ...Plastic Cards
│         └    ...Archival Media
│
│    ...Database
│    ...Transmission Technology
│    ...Networks
│    ...Software
│    ...Security Technology
│    ...Print Technology
│    ...Video Technology
│    ...Robots
│    ...Instruments
│    ...Artificial Intelligence
│    ...Techniques
│    ...New Applications
└    ...Tools
```

In summary, no firm should be without information strategy planning. As pointed out at the beginning of this chapter, to be without an information strategy plan is equivalent to building an aircraft without an overall plan. It is not likely that the information system will fly, much less that it will give the firm a competitive advantage. In the next three chapters we will examine how components of the information strategy plan can be implemented through the traditional approach of systems analysis, design, and implementation, and also through newer techniques, such as application development by end users.

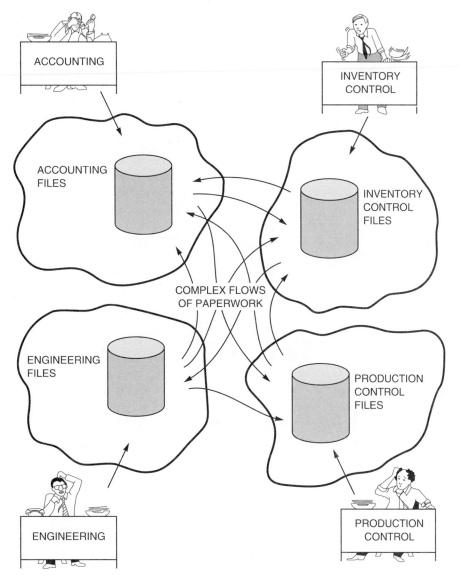

FIGURE 15–11
Confusion Due to
Lack of Data
Modeling.
Reprinted from *Strategic
Information Planning*
(Englewood Cliffs, NJ:
Prentice Hall, 1989), p. 71
with permission of James
Martin and Joe Leben.

Summary

- The essence of information strategy planning is to align the information system with the business strategy.

- There are four basic approaches to developing information systems: ad hoc, data modeling, bottom-up, and top-down.

- The ad hoc approach is directed toward solving a particular problem without considering other problems or the potential for integrating applications.

- The data modeling approach attempts to develop a common database model that contains all the information necessary to support the operations of the firm and removes any data redundancy.

FIGURE 15–12
A Firmwide Data
Model.
Reprinted from *Strategic
Information Planning*
(Englewood Cliffs, NJ:
Prentice Hall, 1989), p. 73
with permission of James
Martin and Joe Leben.

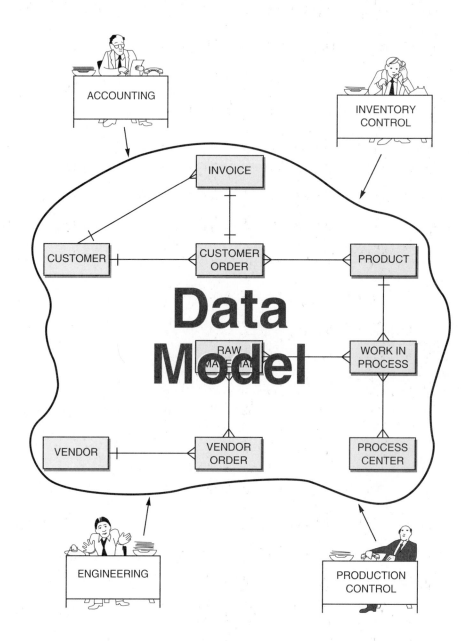

- The bottom-up approach focuses on the basic transaction processing requirements of the firm and implements systems to meet these needs.

- The top-down approach attempts to align information systems with business strategies.

- The objectives of information strategy planning include the following.

  1. Focus information systems on the goals of the business.

  2. Redesign business processes.

  3. Involve senior management in planning information systems.

  4. Control diversity.

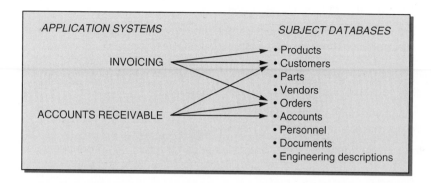

FIGURE 15–13
Application Systems
and Subject Databases.
Reprinted from *Strategic Information Planning* (Englewood Cliffs, NJ: Prentice Hall, 1989), p. 84 with permission of James Martin and Joe Leben.

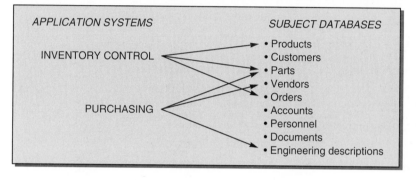

5. Produce consistency of information.

6. Defuse corporate politics.

7. Enhance information systems productivity.

- The information systems pyramid has three sides: data, activities, and technology. It also has four layers: strategy, systems analysis, system design, and implementation.

- Four popular information strategy planning methods are: linkage analysis planning, critical success factors, technology impact analysis, and data modeling. These planning methods are often referred to collectively as information engineering.

- Linkage analysis planning examines both the linkages within an organization and the external linkages that a firm has with customers, suppliers, and competitors in an attempt to formulate ways for the firm to gain a sustainable competitive advantage.

- Linkage analysis is performed in five steps:

1. Examine the waves of information systems growth within the industry.

2. Compare where the firm stands on individual information technology experience curves with where competitors stand.

3. Examine the power relationships that currently exist within the industry and determine how these relationships may change in the future.

4. Examine the firm's extended enterprise.

5. Identify opportunities to gain competitive advantage through the use of electronic channel support systems.

- Critical success factors are the few key areas where things must go right for the individual department or the firm to succeed.

- Technology impact analysis develops an easy-to-understand diagram of current and expected information technology.

- Data modeling identifies the entire data needs for a firm and produces a plan that eliminates data redundancy, data inconsistency, and data inaccuracies.

Key Terms

Information strategy planning	Linkage analysis planning
Ad hoc approach	Waves of information systems
Data modeling approach	Experience curves
Bottom-up approach	Power relationships
Top-down approach	Electronic channel support system
Re-engineering	Extended enterprise
Control of diversity	Critical success factors
Consistency of information	Technology impact analysis
Information systems pyramid	Data modeling
Information engineering	Subject databases
Software engineering	

Review Questions

1. What are the four basic approaches to developing information systems?

2. Compare the bottom-up approach to the top-down approach of developing systems.

3. What are the primary objectives of information strategy planning?

4. Outline some ways that information can be inconsistent.

5. What are the consequences of inconsistent information?

6. Draw and label the parts of the information systems pyramid. Explain these parts.

7. Describe four information strategy planning methods.

8. What are the steps in linkage analysis planning?

9. Why should information systems planners focus on the extended enterprise?

10. What is an electronic channel support system?

11. What are critical success factors and how can they be used in information strategy planning?

12. Discuss the importance of technology impact analysis to information strategy planning.

13. What does data modeling attempt to do for a firm?

14. What are subject databases and what are their importance to information strategy planning?

Discussion Questions and Cases

1. James Haskins is an accountant for the Elliott Corporation. He has worked for the firm for thirty years. For the past ten years he has prepared a series of reports that go to top management on a weekly basis. Three years ago he converted the gathering of data for these reports to a PC. Much of the data is stored in a database. However, he retrieves the data into a Lotus 1-2-3 spreadsheet and performs numerous calculations to produce the management reports. Currently, the Elliott Corporation is constructing a data model for the firm and James has been asked to provide a detailed description of the data he uses to produce the weekly reports. Thus far, he has refused to provide this description, stating that his system is working satisfactorily and that top management is perfectly happy with the reports they get each week. Thus, he sees no need to provide the description requested to information systems personnel. What course of action should the information systems department take?

2. Barbara Richardson is the chief information officer for Gateway Company. She has recently completed substantial reading in the information strategy planning area and is convinced that her company needs to implement an information strategy planning project. Barbara has discussed the concepts of information strategy planning with top management, but has run into a stone wall. The top executives generally make the following rationale: "We are busy with planning the products, the markets, the manufacturing, and the marketing strategy for the firm. The information strategy to support these efforts is your responsibility. We expect you to carry that out. You attend all the executive meetings; thus, you should know the strategy of the firm. So go do your job." How do you recommend that Barbara proceed?

3. The Seaboard Bank has developed its information systems over a period of twenty five years, primarily through a bottom-up approach. Applications are mostly stand-alone, although there are some ties between individual applications. Seaboard has not seen a need for a database management system since most applications were developed prior to the advent of reliable database management systems. These applications are currently operating satisfactorily. In fact, recently Seaboard implemented a new marketing strategy called Preferred Checking. The essence of Preferred Checking is that if a customer has a combined balance of checking, savings, credit card, home equity, and other accounts that exceed $10,000, then the customer gets several free items, such as free checking and free traveler's checks. This marketing campaign was highly successful. To implement it the information systems department had to build on top of its application systems the capability of pulling together information about customer accounts from the various applications so that

the combined balance of all accounts of a customer could be determined. They were successful in doing this. Thus, at this point Seaboard sees no need to do information strategy planning, implement subject-oriented databases, or use a database management system. If you were to take over as chief information officer for Seaboard today, would you change the approach of the information systems department? Why or why not?

4. You are the chief executive officer of a medium-sized large corporation. Ray Young, the managing partner of a large information systems consulting firm's local office, is a member of one of the civic organizations to which you belong. At a recent dinner meeting he discussed with you the concept of using information systems to restructure the basic operations of a firm. He called this process re-engineering. Ray said that several firms have used re-engineering to change their basic processes, many of which had been in existence for decades, to cut the time to market for new products. He also indicated that in most cases the cost of production and distribution were decreased. Ray would like to sell you a consulting engagement, whereby his firm re-engineers your basic processes. But you are not sure about the approach. It seems to you that the basic ways that you do business are logical and since your staff continually seeks ways to improve these processes, you doubt that they can be improved through additional applications of computers. Furthermore, re-engineering the basic processes of the business seems to you like a major undertaking that would take many years and would have substantial risks of failure. In fact, within five to ten years you expect to retire from your position. What approach would you take to Ray's proposal? Justify your approach.

INFORMATION SYSTEMS STRATEGIES

Visualizing Information Planning

By Bob Curtice and Dave Stringer

Has this ever happened to you? You're in a planning meeting with top business managers to brief them on the impact technology can have on the business. Your technical explanations are clear (after all, the information systems staff understood them). These same descriptions, however, are now being met with blank stares. You're frustrated, the executives are confused, and your plans for a new manufacturing system are looking dim.

Your effort is not at fault here; the way you package it is. How can you make clear to nontechnical managers the effect IS [information systems] technology can have on a firm? We're proposing strategic planning techniques that graphically show how information can impact an organization.

There are lots of planning methodologies out there. Typical ones get down to the gory details of functions and data and systems—important parts of technology planning, to be sure. But they only scratch the surface. While these methods get business managers *involved* in IS planning, they don't help them *understand* it.

Here's where IS chiefs can help. Technology managers can provide a big-picture view from which business executives can make informed decisions about future investments. Business managers are given the wherewithal to track, revise, shape and get up to their elbows in information technology planning.

Layouts at a Glance

The most effective strategic planning methodologies should provide comprehensive, graphical layouts of an organization's array of information at a glance. They should not only show where information is generated and needed by internal and external customers, suppliers, regulators and so on, but they should also depict where bottlenecks and opportunities exist.

The following are three such graphical planning methods:

■ **The information supply and demand matrix.** While other methodologies follow organizational boundaries, the information demand and supply matrix (see Figure 1) analyzes a business' information needs by function. This technique also points out how well IS is meeting those needs.

The information supply and demand chart pictured here represents the needs of a fictitious large manufacturing company, called Acme Manufacturing Co., but can be tailored to fit your organization.

The chart is structured as a matrix, with rows and columns. The columns should represent the six to 12 activities or high-level functions that collectively describe the processes of your business. For Acme Manufacturing, those functions include developing products and processes and managing finances.

There are always four rows in the matrix, characterizing the levels of management responsibility involved:

• Strategic functional level. Functions performed at this level are fundamental to the long-term performance and survival of the business and are integral to developing strategies and objectives as well as establishing new business directions. Examples for Acme include setting new product directions and long-term financing as well as developing marketing strategies.

• Planning and analysis functional level. Functions here establish how the company will meet long-term objectives as well as analyze internal and external events to determine their impact on achieving strategic goals.

• Control and monitoring functional level. Functions at this level ensure that the day-to-day business is carried out properly, efficiently and in line with plans.

• Operational functional level. Functions here execute the day-to-day routine transactions and activities that make up the business.

Nowhere on this chart is there a "managing information" function; managing information is something that occurs throughout the matrix (and organization).

Clearly, each level in the chart implies the need for different kinds of information technology support. Acme's technical and business management staff may find that there are many transaction-heavy on-line functions going on at the operational level. Therefore, an on-line transaction processing system may be appropriate here. Decision-support software, spreadsheets and the like may be the

right fit at the strategic level in which there are fewer users and more universal needs.

Moreover, graphically showing these levels encourages company executives to identify functions that are overlooked in other technology planning processes. For example, there may not be any activities identified at the strategic level having to do with managing people. Such critical observations force business and technology managers into in-depth discussions of what appears in the chart.

Three-Part Instruction

Each cell of the matrix has three pieces of information. First, it contains a list of the specific activities needed to perform all business functions; such a list appears at each functional level. In our example, in the planning and analysis category of the market products and services column, there is a list of activities such as determining market segments, constructing annual marketing plans and setting product prices.

Second, for each of these business activities, the matrix lists the information needed to carry it out effectively.

In this methodology, information needs are ascertained by an analysis of objectives, critical success factors, performance measures and knowledge of modern business practices. Other methodologies start with an analysis of the information and technologies users say they need. This analysis starts with the functions users perform, which in turn suggests to management the kind of information that's needed to do a better job.

For Acme Manufacturing, information needed to forecast demand includes customer orders by product, quantity and due date; marketing plans; historic demand forecasts; and planned promotions.

Thirdly, color coding is used to indicate how well information is currently supplied to each business activity.

Here, on a single chart, is a comprehensive picture of this business' activities, the information it requires and an assessment of how well that information is being supplied today. It serves as a basis for both management and IS to understand where problems with the quality and availability of information exist.

■ **The value matrix.** Strategic planning can also be done from a value perspective. The value matrix, set up like the matrix described above, shows senior managers where IS investments are likely to impact overall business strategy.

FIGURE 1

Information supply-and-demand matrix for Acme Manufacturing Co.
A technique for showing what the information needs of the business are by function and how well those needs are being met

	Develop products and processes	Produce products	Manage material	Market products and services	Manages finances
Strategic	Set new product directions / Long-range market needs / Competitive directions / Social/economic trends / Technology forecast / Strategic business plan		Determine sourcing strategy	Develop new product strategy / Develop marketing strategy	Set long-term financing strategy / Business plans / Economic forecasts / Capital expenditure plans
Planning and analysis	Analyze new product opportunities / Analyze new technology	Plan production schedule / Analyze production problems	Qualify new suppliers / Negotiate supplier contracts / Plan material requirements / Plan distribution requirements / Set stock levels	Determine market segments / Construct annual marketing plan / Set product prices / Forecast demand / Plan advertising and promotions	Prepare budgets / Analyze product costs
Control and monitor	Control development projects	Monitor production schedule / Control production quality	Monitor distribution performance / Control product quality / Monitor supplier performance	Monitor marketing plan / Report sales	Monitor budgets / Control foreign exchange exposure
Operational	Specify new products / Specify product process	Issue production work orders / Manufacture products	Process purchase requisitions / Process purchase orders / Receive material / Ship material	Conduct market reserch / Administer promotions / Arrange advertisements	Collect receivables / Prepare financial statements

Information is adequately supplied to the business function (not necessarily by computer)

Information is supplied but not adequately (inaccurate, late, incomplete or not usable)

Information is not supplied

Source: Arthur D. Little, Inc.

In the value matrix, planners assign a score to each cell. This score represents the value that the functions in that cell contribute to the firm's strategic business objectives. Thus, if a company's strategic objective is to improve its level of customer service, then cells with functions that concentrate on the operational aspects of logistics/materials management or the planning aspects of selling will receive a high value score.

One way to simplify the process is by using color to assign values to the cells. Different colors can indicate high value, average value or less than average value to the business.

The assessment of information quality (using the supply and demand matrix), combined with the value of business functions to strategic objectives (given by the value matrix), enable management to focus attention and priorities on those business areas that not only are needy but can also offer strategic benefits.

■ **The information supply architecture matrix.** Many managers have little grasp of the scope of systems, what business functions they support, how they interrelate or overlap and how newly developed systems fit into this picture.

The information supply architecture matrix (see Figure 2, p. 422) is intended to provide non-IS managers with this panorama. It uses a matrix with the same columns and rows delineated above, with each application system mapped out as a polygon. Each polygon overlaps cells containing functions supported by the application. One application may span many cells, and a cell may contain multiple applications. Connecting lines can be drawn between polygons to signify major interfaces between systems.

The information supply architecture is often prepared in two versions. One version depicts the current investment in applications, usually showing duplicate systems supporting functions and cells that have little or no systems support. The second version portrays a more planned state of affairs. Color coding can clue executives into the status of each application; it can tell whether the application is part of the current system, a new development, a modification and so on.

Such graphical portrayals of the IS environment form a clear and comprehensive picture without the need for technical jargon. Acme Manufacturing is not the only firm to capitalize on this kind of strategic planning methodology; real-life firms have made it work for them.

For example, following the use of such a graphical technique at the United Distillers Division of Guinness PLC in the UK, the company restructured the processing of 70,000 yearly export orders. Information now flows to a single customer administration executive, who handles all the activities involved in getting the goods to the customer. Benefits include lower order-processing costs, improved cash flow, enhanced customer service and growing market share.

Understanding, when communicated with pictures, enables executives and operating management to provide focus to the information management agenda. That's the kind of leadership and understanding IS needs if it wants to capitalize on today's information technology.

Discussion Questions

1. What advantages are there to a graphical approach to information planning?

2. Are the graphics displayed in this article too simplified to be of practical use? If so, how do you propose that they be changed?

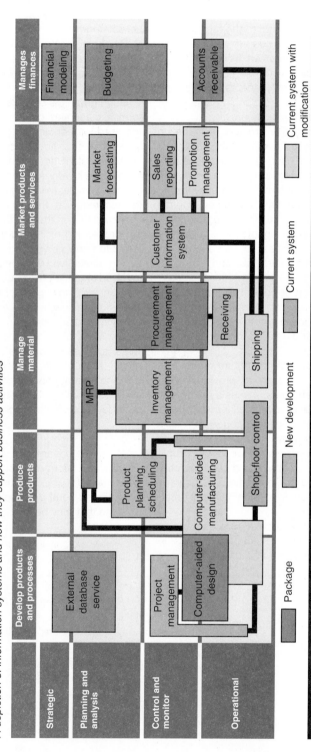

FIGURE 2

Information supply architecture for Acme Manufacturing Co.
A depiction of information systems and how they support business activities

Source: Arthur D. Little

16

Systems Analysis

Introduction

About six months ago, Tony, who owns and manages Tony's Pizza, decided to purchase a microcomputer and software to provide information he needs to manage his three pizza restaurants. He immediately contacted a computer salesperson and purchased the hardware and software, although he did not have a clear understanding of his information needs and how a computer would assist in meeting those needs. The computer salesperson reassured him by stating that "these microcomputers are so user friendly and flexible that you will have no difficulty using it. Hundreds of thousands of small-business persons just like you are using them to greatly increase their profits. In today's competitive world you just can't afford not to own one." Tony has become very disillusioned with computers. He has even hired a part-time computer consultant to help him use the computer. Thus far, his computer has been of little practical use to him. How could Tony have avoided this waste of his time and money?

Tony could have saved both time and money by doing some research before buying his computer system. If he had clearly understood his information needs and had selected software that met those needs, he would probably find his computer to be a very useful tool.

Application software is the most expensive aspect of information systems. The price of hardware has continued to decline because of technological advances. Unfortunately, software technology has not kept up with hardware advances. In fact, the cost of software continues to increase, primarily because software development is a labor-intensive process.

However, new approaches to the development of application software have resulted in significant time and cost savings for many firms. These approaches (discussed here and in Chapter 18) help businesses avoid some of the perennial problems of application software development, such as being overbudget and months or years late. They also help firms avoid some real disasters that have occurred in application development: systems that do not produce the output users want, systems that do not work at all, and systems that are out of date by the time they are operational.

If users are to avoid these pitfalls, they need to be thoroughly familiar with the latest approaches to application software development and purchase. They must be able to communicate with the systems analyst who is responsible for designing and implementing the system. If a system fails, users will lose, because it is their system and they are ultimately responsible for it. As Application 16–1 illustrates, user involvement is crucial to successful software development projects.

This chapter explores the first major step in systems development, systems analysis. First, it briefly discusses partitioning of systems, the process upon which good systems development is based. Then it describes the structured systems development life cycle, a procedure for developing complex systems. Next, it explains the steps in the structured systems analysis approach. Finally, it identifies the advantages of using structured systems analysis.

Partitioning of Systems

Systems analysis is a method for modeling and understanding complex systems. It is aimed at determining precisely what a new system must accomplish and how to accomplish it.

APPLICATION 16–1

Users Need a Larger Role in Software Development

By June Altman

The biggest single risk to any software development project is lack of user involvement, according to Jayne Hogan, a senior consultant in training and user services for Applied Information Development Inc.

Hogan maintains that 75 percent of delays in implementation of new applications are due not to coding or related problems, but to misunderstandings of requirements which result from inadequate user involvement. She said the net result of this problem is that "99 percent of all development projects are delivered late, over budget, and don't meet requirements."

In the class Hogan offers for both users and MIS [management information systems] employees, she illustrates her point by having the class design a child's toy based on a list of about a dozen requirements she gives them. At the end of the exercise, many toys have been designed but none are pre-cisely the toy that Hogan had in mind: a pinwheel. The exercise is meant to illustrate how specific requirements must be clear to achieve the desired results.

"If requirements aren't very clear and detailed, you're open to someone else's interpretation of the requirements," Hogan said. For example, "Saying I want fast response time is not good enough," Hogan said.

Such a requirement should be quantified, so that a test case can be written to prove whether the requirement has been met. Further, she advises, "Users need to be proactive; give MIS requirements, don't wait for them to draw them out."

Stresses Partnership

The relationship between users and MIS should be a partnership, she said. The role of MIS in such a partnership is to encourage and listen to users, not to make assumptions about what users want, nor to take on the responsibility of developing in a vacuum.

"I'm not saying MIS should sit on their hands during requirements development. They can offer suggestions; they can ask questions to clarify what a user wants."

Hogan, who draws her conclusions from years of experience both as a user and as a programmer analyst on the MIS side, said that after teaching her course for two years, she is beginning to see less resistance to the idea of an increased level of user involvement. "Now I'm getting more head-nodding," she said.

Any changes in a software-development project are far less expensive to make early on in a project, so the earlier users are involved—and the more often they are involved in every stage of development—the less costly any changes are likely to be.

Adapted with permission from Fairchild Publications, *MIS Week* (July 10, 1989), pp. 11, 12.

Perhaps the most important concept in systems theory that is used in the development of computer applications is the idea that any system can be partitioned into subsystems (or modules). Figure 16–1 illustrates a **hierarchical partitioning** of an information system into leveled sets of subsystems. In this figure, the accounting information system is partitioned into its various subsystems and then the payroll system is partitioned into four subsystems (modules). If a systems development project is to modify the reports produced by the payroll system, then the analyst draws a boundary around the module that produces output. This module is of primary interest in the development process.

Hierarchical partitioning is the key to the structured analysis, design, and programming of computer applications.

In fact, the term *structured* is closely related to hierarchical partitioning. *The American Heritage Dictionary* defines *structure* as the interrelation of parts, or the principal organization in a complex entity. In effect, a system is **structured** if it is hierarchically partitioned into subsystems, and the subsystems' interfaces with one another are defined.

FIGURE 16–1
Partitioning of a System.
This chart, called a structure chart, shows the hierarchical structure of a system.

Structured Systems Development Life Cycle

In **structured systems development**, analysts and programmers do three things: (1) partition complex systems into simple subsystems, (2) analyze, design, and implement the **interfaces** that exist between subsystems, (3) analyze, design, and implement the processes that go on within the subsystems. Figure 16–2 shows the subsystems of the payroll system. The arrows represent the interfaces or data flows between the subsystems, which are illustrated by circles. Systems analysts and programmers analyze, design, and build both the subsystems and the interfaces between them. Then they combine them to produce a complete payroll system. By first dividing a complex system into understandable and manageable subsystems; then designing, building, and testing each subsystem; and finally combining them, analysts and programmers can understand and produce very complex computer information systems.

Figure 16–3 illustrates the structured systems development life cycle. The **systems development life cycle (SDLC)** contains the steps analysts and programmers go through in building a computer information system. The structured systems development life cycle is much easier to understand than the older techniques that rely heavily on system and program flowcharts and lengthy verbal descriptions of systems requirements. The following example will be used to illustrate the SDLC procedure in this and the next chapter.

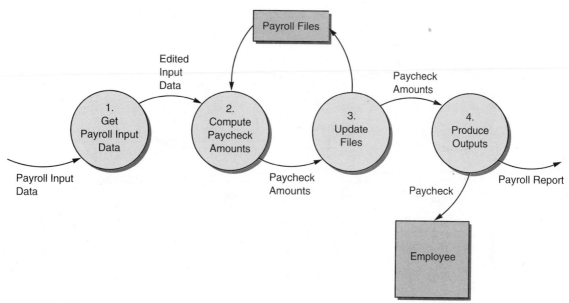

FIGURE 16–2
The Subsystems (Modules, Programs, or Processes) within the Payroll System.
This chart illustrates the lowest-level of Figure 16–1 and the data flows or interfaces between those modules. It also shows the files the modules use and the external entities that interact with this system (an employee who receives a paycheck).

Angelo Patti is the owner and manager of a large restaurant named Angelo's Pizza. Angelo is a very ambitious young man; he would like to have a chain of Angelo's Pizza restaurants. He feels that computers could be useful in managing both his current restaurant and a chain of restaurants. Angelo has an old college friend, Jose Wong, who established a computer consulting business after majoring in information systems. Recently, Angelo hired Jose to help develop the computer information system. After a brief feasibility study, Jose recommended that Angelo start with an information system containing the four subsystems shown in Figure 16–4.

In a **feasibility study**, the systems analyst performs many of the same steps that will be performed in the systems analysis phase, but much less thoroughly. The primary purpose of the study is to identify the objectives of the user's proposed system and to estimate whether or not the potential benefits of a new system justify the expense of a development project. The major inputs to the feasibility study are interviews and working documents from the users. The study produces a feasibility document that contains the following:

Feasibility Study

- Project name

- Description of the problem

- Statement of the critical assumptions on which the feasibility document is based

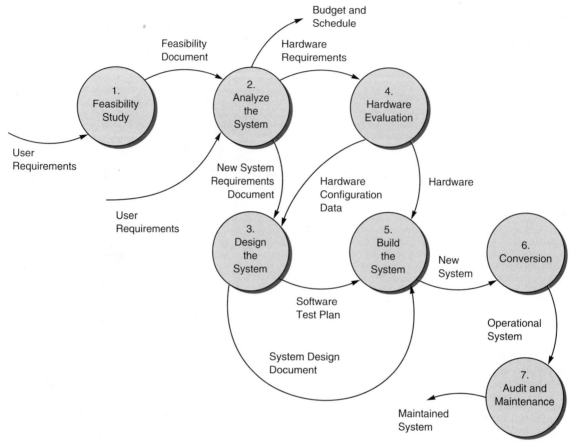

FIGURE 16–3
Structured Systems Development Life Cycle.
These steps should occur in any system development, whether it is a large, complex system or one simple program.

- Statement of the performance requirements of the system
- General description of the proposed system solution (this can be a new, modified, or existing system)
- Evaluation of the feasibility of the proposed system
- Possible alternative solutions

FIGURE 16–4
Information System
for Angelo's Pizza.

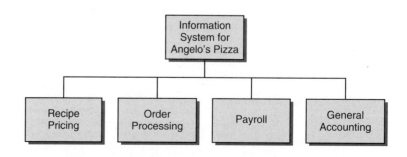

Figure 16–5 illustrates the phases within **structured systems analysis**. This figure is a partitioning of process 2 in Figure 16–3.

Figures 16–2, 16–3 and 16–5 are all **data flow diagrams (DFDs)**. Data flow diagrams are the primary tool used in structured systems development to graphically depict systems. You probably found that you could understand these figures without an explanation of data flow diagrams. This is one of their advantages; they are easy to understand because they are not cluttered with a lot of technical symbols.

Figure 16–6 illustrates the four symbols used in data flow diagrams. Contrast the simplicity of these DFD symbols with the **system flowchart** symbols shown in Figure 16–7. Although system flowcharting with this large variety of symbols is still done, many systems professionals are using data flow diagrams. Any information system can be graphically depicted using the four symbols of data flow diagrams, because only three things happen within an information system:

Structured Systems Analysis

FIGURE 16–5
Structured Systems Analysis.

Systems analysis has as its input the user requirements and feasibility documents. Its outputs include the hardware requirements, budget, and schedule for building the system and the new system requirements document.

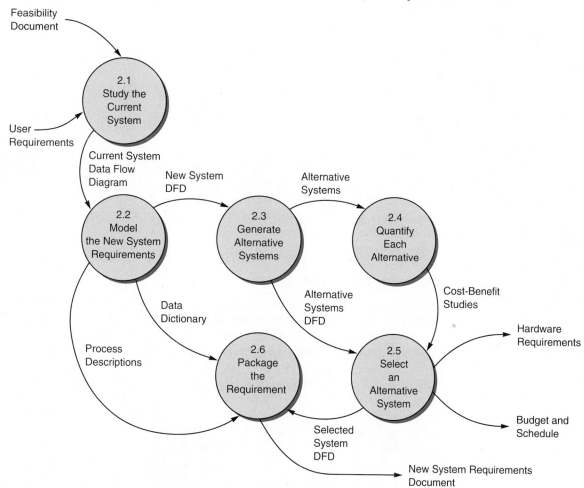

F I G U R E 16–6
Symbols Used in Data
Flow Diagrams.

Any information system,
no matter how complex
and large or how small
and simple, can be
graphically represented
by these symbols. They
are beginning to be
widely used by systems
analysts. Several
programs use these
symbols to draw data
flow diagrams with
computers. Some DFD
programs, like DFD Draw
from McDonnell Douglas
Automation Company,
run on the IBM PC.

Process or Data Transformation
A process that adds to, modifies,
or deletes data.

External Entity
A person, organization, or system that is
outside the boundary of the system
being studied. An external entity
is an originator or receiver of
data processed by the system.

Payroll
Input
Data

Data Flow
Data that flow into or out of
processes on a data flow diagram.
Data flows are sometimes called
interfaces.

Payroll File

Data Store
Any permanent or
temporary file of data.

- Data processing

- Data flows (input and output from processes)

- Data stores

The fourth symbol, the external entity symbol, is used to depict entities outside the system that interact with it.

A numbering system is also used in data flow diagrams. For example, the first digit of the numbers of the processes in Figure 16–5 is a 2, indicating that Figure 16–5 is a partitioning of the second process in Figure 16–3. Partitioning can be carried to as many levels as necessary, creating **leveled data flow diagrams**. In practice, it is rarely necessary to exceed five or six levels; they provide enough detail to show what occurs within the most complex of systems.

Study the Current System

The purpose of the first phase of systems analysis is to understand and document the user's current system. Usually, the user has a manual or a computer information system. Studying the system helps the analyst understand the user's information needs. Many of the processes performed by the current system will also have to be performed by the new one. The study relies on extensive interviews with user personnel and frequent reviews with users regarding the documentation that the analyst is creating. These reviews are called *walkthroughs*. The primary documentation tool used is a leveled set of data flow diagrams.

Figures 16–8 and 16–9 are the DFDs that Jose drew for the current order processing and recipe pricing systems of Angelo's Pizza. Note that the emphasis of the data flow diagrams in the flow of data.

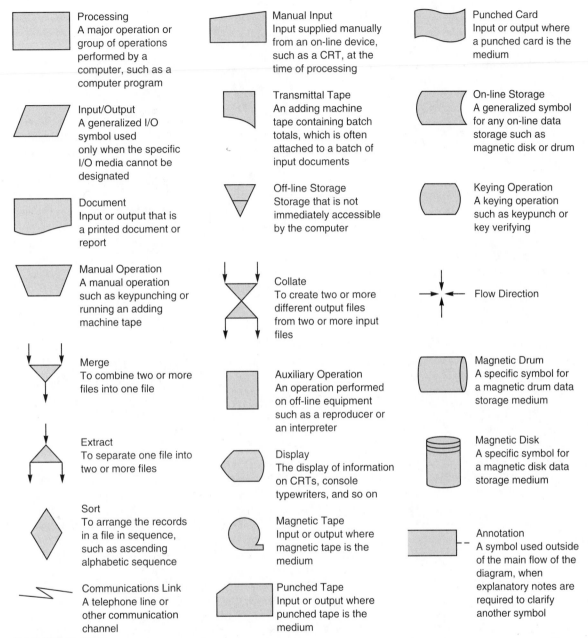

Processing
A major operation or group of operations performed by a computer, such as a computer program

Input/Output
A generalized I/O symbol used only when the specific I/O media cannot be designated

Document
Input or output that is a printed document or report

Manual Operation
A manual operation such as keypunching or running an adding machine tape

Merge
To combine two or more files into one file

Extract
To separate one file into two or more files

Sort
To arrange the records in a file in sequence, such as ascending alphabetic sequence

Communications Link
A telephone line or other communication channel

Manual Input
Input supplied manually from an on-line device, such as a CRT, at the time of processing

Transmittal Tape
An adding machine tape containing batch totals, which is often attached to a batch of input documents

Off-line Storage
Storage that is not immediately accessible by the computer

Collate
To create two or more different output files from two or more input files

Auxiliary Operation
An operation performed on off-line equipment such as a reproducer or an interpreter

Display
The display of information on CRTs, console typewriters, and so on

Magnetic Tape
Input or output where magnetic tape is the medium

Punched Tape
Input or output where punched tape is the medium

Punched Card
Input or output where a punched card is the medium

On-line Storage
A generalized symbol for any on-line data storage such as magnetic disk or drum

Keying Operation
A keying operation such as keypunch or key verifying

Flow Direction

Magnetic Drum
A specific symbol for a magnetic drum data storage medium

Magnetic Disk
A specific symbol for a magnetic disk data storage medium

Annotation
A symbol used outside of the main flow of the diagram, when explanatory notes are required to clarify another symbol

FIGURE 16–7
System Flowchart Symbols.
System flowcharts provide more information about how a system is physically implemented than do data flow diagrams. For example, the magnetic disk symbol may be used to indicate that a file is stored on magnetic disk. However, this complexity is unnecessary for good systems analysis. Good systems analysis focuses on what is done in an information system rather than on how it is done.

Jose also decided to partition process 3 in Figure 16–8 in order to gain a better understanding of that process. This lower-level DFD is shown in Figure 16–10.

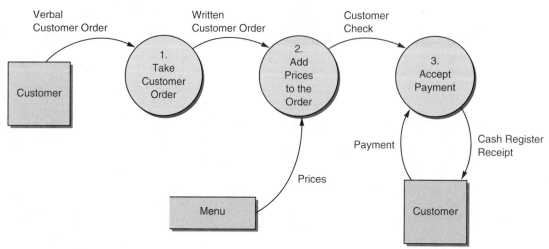

FIGURE 16–8
Current Order Processing System, Angelo's Pizza.
This data flow diagram focuses on what is done rather than on how it is done.

Model the New System Requirements

By now the analyst should be thoroughly familiar with the current system. His or her goal in defining the new system requirements is to describe what has to be done, not how it will be done. Of course, the

FIGURE 16–9
Current Recipe Pricing System, Angelo's Pizza.
Knowledge of computer hardware is not needed to draw this data flow diagram.

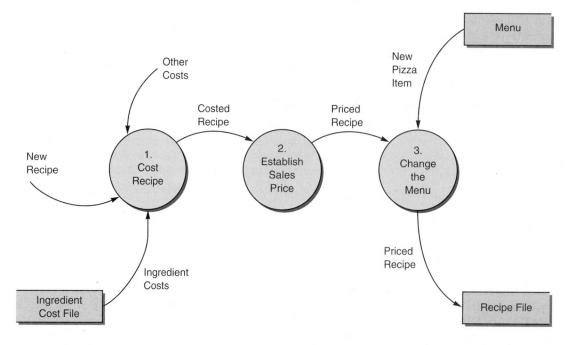

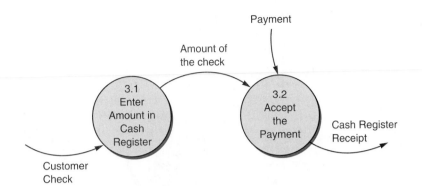

The inputs and outputs
here—customer check
payment, and cash
register receipt—are the
same as those for process
3 in Figure 16–8.

analyst will keep in mind some of the computer technology that could be
used in the new system. For example, Jose may feel that an electronic
spreadsheet could do Angelo's recipe pricing. But Jose is experienced
enough in computer information systems to know that all the computer
technology in the world will not help Angelo if he cannot define his information requirements.

As the first step in defining the information requirements for Angelo's
new system, Jose talked at length with Angelo about his needs, particularly about his business expansion plans. In summary, Angelo feels that
quick, efficient customer service is important. Most pizza is cooked to
the customer's order. Therefore, customers must wait for their orders.
Angelo is sure that decreasing the wait time for an order would increase
his competitive position, particularly with lunchtime customers. Also,
he would like to keep a name and address file on his customers, which
would be used for mailing promotional material to them. He may even
want to extend credit to selected customers.

After his discussions with Angelo, Jose believes that he can define a
system that not only would provide better information, but also would
improve Angelo's operations in processing customers' orders. In fact, he
feels that the system will be such a competitive tool that Angelo may
want to rename the restaurant Angelo's Hi-Tech Pizza!

In defining the system requirements, Jose will use structured specifications—data flow diagrams, a data dictionary, and process descriptions—to further define Angelo's information requirements.

Data Flow Diagrams Figures 16–11 and 16–12 are Jose's data flow diagrams for Angelo's new order processing and recipe pricing systems.
These DFDs do not differ substantially from those of the current systems
shown in Figures 16–8 and 16–9. This is typical. Many of the basic information and operational needs are the same regardless of how a system is
physically implemented. (A physical implementation is how a system is
actually performed in the real world. Manual systems and automated systems that use computers are different types of physical implementation.)

Another important point to understand about these two DFDs is that
neither indicates how the system is to be physically implemented. Either
system could be implemented many different ways on a computer. Or,
they could be performed manually! At this point it is not necessary to de-

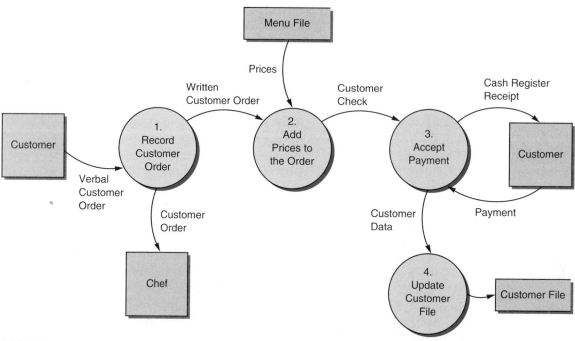

FIGURE 16–11
New Order Processing System, Angelo's Pizza.

cide how the systems will be physically implemented or to select computer hardware. Angelo's information and operational requirements are the only important considerations.

The points made in the preceding paragraph are crucial to your future success in applying computer information systems. Most failures in

FIGURE 16–12
New Recipe
Processing System,
Angelo's Pizza.

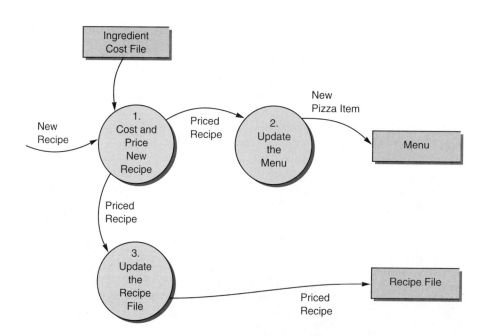

computer information systems occur because users buy computer hardware before they have a clear understanding of their information needs. Never buy computer hardware without first knowing how it will help you meet your professional, business, or personal objectives.

Data Dictionary   A **data dictionary** documents files and data flows. It contains information about and definitions of data used in a system. This dictionary gives you a single place to look up data definitions you do not understand. In addition, it may contain many other types of information and definitions, depending on the wishes of the analyst. For example, when considering a particular data flow, the analyst may include information such as frequency, volume, affected users, security considerations, and implementation schedule.

For instance, Jose made an entry in his data dictionary that looked like this:

```
Customer-Check=Date+Table-Number+[Item-
Ordered+Item-Price]+Sales-Tax+Total-Amount
```

In other words, the data flow called "customer-check" consists of the date, the table number, one or more items ordered with their item price, the sales tax, and the total amount. (The brackets indicate that there can be multiple items ordered and item prices.)

Data flows can be partitioned in the same way as data flow diagrams. For example, Jose defined *date* in the data dictionary as follows:

```
Date=Month+Day+Year
```

For the analysis to be complete, each data flow and data store (file) indicated on a leveled set of data flow diagrams must have a definition entry in the data dictionary. Data dictionaries are used to define data stores by specifying the data contained within each individual record.

May firms use computer-automated data dictionaries. Such dictionaries are needed in large and complex information systems because of the high volume of data that those systems store.

Process Descriptions   At some point, the partitioning of processes in leveled DFDs ceases. At this most detailed level of the data flow diagrams the processes are called **functional primitives**. But to be complete, analysts still have to specify the data transformations that go on within these functional primitives. These specifications are called process, or transform, descriptions. **Process**, or **transform, descriptions** document the internal workings of data processes.

There are three ways to describe the data transformations that occur within functional primitives on data flow diagrams. These are structured English, decision tables, and decision trees.

Structured English is plain English with a few restrictions. It is often called pseudocode because it is similar to computer program code. In fact, the syntax of structured English is restricted to the same basic patterns as structured programming. Figure 16–13 illustrates the allowable structured English patterns. Structured English process descriptions are easy to convert to structured computer programs.

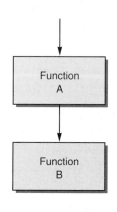

Simple Sequence Structure
(DO)

Do *A*
Do *B*

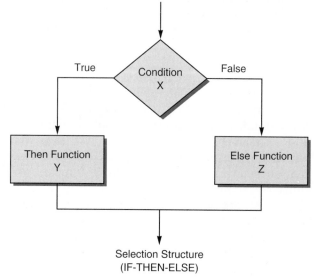

Selection Structure
(IF-THEN-ELSE)

If *X* is true
  Then,
   Do *Y*
  Else,
   Do *Z*

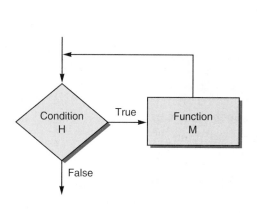

Loop Structure
(DO-WHILE)

Do *M* while *H* is true

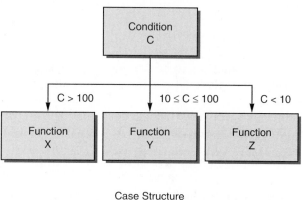

Case Structure
(SELECT-CASE)

Select the policy that applies:
Case 1 *C* > 100
    Do *X*
Case 2 10 ≤ *C* ≤ 100
    Do *Y*
Case 3 *C* < 10
    Do *Z*

FIGURE 16–13

Allowable Structured English Control Patterns.

These control patterns are useful for describing processes on data flow diagrams, and they are also useful in writing computer programs, as shown in Chapter 17.

On one of the lower-level DFDs, not shown in the text, Jose had a process called "approve customer credit." The structured English that describes the internal workings of that process is shown in Figure 16–14.

Decision tables allow large numbers of conditions to be concisely documented. Figure 16–15 illustrates a decision table for the same customer credit approval that Jose defined with structured English in Figure 16–14. Decision tables are read from top to bottom. In the example, four sets of conditions can occur. Rule 1 states that if the check is greater than fifty dollars and a bill is overdue by sixty-plus days, then Angelo refuses credit. The primary advantage of a decision table is that it allows many different combinations of conditions and their appropriate actions to be documented in a compact form.

The credit approval policy can also be documented with a **decision tree**, as shown in Figure 16–16. The decision tree is read from left to right, starting at Credit Approval Policy. Each branch illustrates a condition that can occur. Combinations of conditions lead to the actions on the right. For example, if the check is greater than fifty dollars and the customer is in good standing, Angelo extends credit (action 2). The decision tree is not as compact as a decision table, but most people find a decision tree easier to understand.

Generally, systems analysts use structured English for transform descriptions because it is much easier to write program code based on it. Decision tables and decision trees are used in the few situations where there are large numbers of conditions and therefore several different actions that could occur based on the combinations of conditions.

In this phase of the analysis (modeling the new system requirements), the analyst must have a good understanding of the information needs of the user. He or she develops a model of a system that will take data inputs and transform them into the information that the user needs. In doing this, the analyst relies heavily on the original feasibility study and user interviews. The output of this phase is a leveled set of data flow diagrams, process descriptions of functional primitives on the data flow diagrams, and a data dictionary. These specifications all serve to document the proposed new system.

```
IF the amount of the check exceeds $50,
     IF the customer has any bill more than 60 days overdue,
     THEN
          do not extend credit.
     ELSE (the customer has good credit),
          extend credit.
     ENDIF
ELSE (check is $50 or less),
     IF the customer has any bill more than 60 days overdue,
     THEN
          get manager's approval before extending credit.
     ELSE (the customer has good credit),
          extend credit.
     ENDIF
ENDIF
```

FIGURE 16–14
Structured English for Approval of Customer Credit, Angelo's Pizza.

When structured English process descriptions are put on a word processor, they can be modified and updated quickly for changes.

FIGURE 16–15
Decision Table for
Approval of Customer
Credit, Angelo's Pizza.
Although this decision
table shows only one
action for each rule,
decision tables can easily
document multiple
actions for each rule.

	Rules			
Conditions	1	2	3	4
1. Check > $50	Y	N	Y	N
2. Bill Overdue by 60 + Days	Y	Y	N	N
Actions				
1. Extend Credit			Y	Y
2. Refuse Credit	Y			
3. Get Manager's Approval		Y		

Generate Alternative Systems

In this stage of structured systems analysis, the analyst develops a number of configurations that will produce the required information. Most managements expect analysts to propose several options.

In developing alternative systems, analysts deal with the how and what of the system, that is, its physical aspects. For each option, some parts of the system may be manual and others automated. In terms of automated parts, there may be several ways to apply the computer. The output of this phase is several possible physical data flow diagrams. One method for indicating the alternatives is to simply mark on copies of the new system DFDs a proposed physical implementation of the system, as shown in Figure 16–17. For example, Jose is proposing that Angelo use Lotus 1-2-3 to cost and price new recipes.

FIGURE 16–16
Decision Tree for
Approval of Customer
Credit, Angelo's Pizza.
This figure shows two
conditions at each node,
but decision trees can
have more than two
conditions at each node.

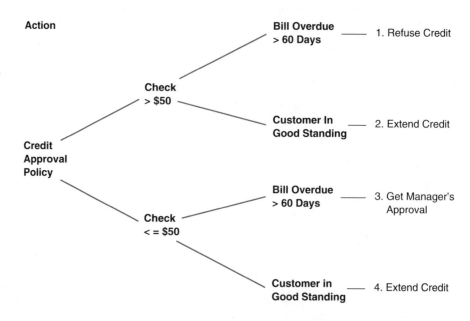

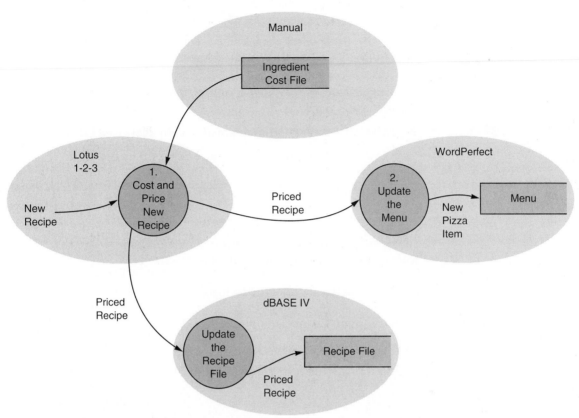

FIGURE 16–17
One Alternative for Implementing the New Pricing System for Angelo's Pizza.
Circles have been drawn around the various processes and files to show how they will be physically implemented.

Quantify Each Alternative

Each of the tentative new systems developed in the previous subphase
has costs and benefits associated with it. To determine these costs and
benefits, the analyst makes a tentative selection of hardware and software, if they are to be purchased. This is only a very general selection.
For example, the analyst might decide that the automated system will be
executed on a personal computer or minicomputer, or that it will be an
on-line system rather than a batch system. Analysts do not want to lock
themselves into a certain set of hardware or software at this point.

Both costs and benefits can be classified as tangible or intangible. Tangible costs include the following:

- Maintenance and operation

- Personnel

- Training and orientation

- Lease or purchase of new hardware and software

- Site preparation
- Design

Intangible costs include the following:

- Negative effects on employee morale, resulting in decreased productivity
- Negative effects on customers, resulting in decreased business
- Decrease in control of the information system by operating management
- Increased centralized control of the information system
- Increased specialization in information processing
- Increased potential cost for breakdowns or disaster when the information system becomes more centralized

Tangible benefits include the following:

- Reduced maintenance and operating costs
- Reduced personnel costs
- Reduced investment in hardware and software
- Reduced rental costs
- Reduced space requirements
- Reduced age of accounts receivable
- Increased inventory turnover
- Reduced investment in inventory

Intangible benefits include the following:

- Freeing operating management from information processing activities
- Improved control over information processing activities
- Improved decision making
- Increased emphasis on long-range planning
- Improved employee morale

It is not always possible or necessary to quantify all these costs and benefits. But if they exist, they should at least be identified.

Select an Alternative System

Management studies the alternative systems the analyst has developed, and costs and benefits associated with each, and then decides which option to implement. The data flow diagrams of the new system are very important tools in this phase. Since they are easy to understand, the analyst can readily employ them in presenting the proposed systems to management.

Package the Requirements

The final output of the structured analysis phase is integrated into a new system requirements document, consisting of

- an introduction containing the system's goals, objectives, and any background information that might be useful
- data flow diagrams depicting the major partitioning of functions and all the interfaces among the parts
- a data dictionary documenting each of the interface data flows and data stores (files)
- transform descriptions documenting the transformations that occur within each of the most detailed DFD processes through the use of structured English, decision tables, or decision trees
- input and output documents
- security, control, and performance requirements

Most systems analysts and users are beginning to see that the structured approach has significant advantages over other approaches to systems development. Among these are the following:

- Structured analysis requires a complete study of the user area, a study frequently omitted in other approaches.

- Structured analysis requires that the analyst partition what he or she has specified. The tools of other approaches—system and program flowcharts—are not well suited for partitioning. Partitioning is the key to many of the advantages of the structured approach.

- The structured system specification is very graphic and therefore easy to understand.

- The other approaches tend to focus on the physical aspects of the system hardware, vendor, operating procedures, and so on. By focusing on the logical aspects of data flows and data processes, the analyst can readily see the essential information flows and processes that are required in the new system.

- The structured approach produces highly maintainable systems not only from the standpoint of the analysis phase, but, as shown in the next chapter, also for design and programming purposes.

- Structured development documentation is cumulative. The documentation developed in any phase builds on the preceding documentation and serves as the basis for work in subsequent phases. For example, as shown in the next chapter, the DFDs, process descriptions, and so on developed in the analysis phase are also used in the program design and coding.

Advantages of Structured Systems Development

A system's **maintainability** is the ease with which it can be changed when there is a change in requirements. In the real world, requirements change often. Maintainability problems cause the demise of most systems and thus are very important to consider. The structured approach produces maintainable systems primarily because of its partitioned, or modular, approach to systems design.

Computer-Aided Software Engineering

Computer-aided software engineering (CASE) is the application of computers to the task of developing computer software. The term **software engineering** is often used as a synonym for software design and development. CASE tools provide the ability to create and maintain on a computer all the system documentation created during the system development life cycle. Documents such as data flow diagrams, data dictionaries, and structured English can be created and maintained by CASE tools. Figure 16–18 shows a data-flow diagram created on Excelerator, one of the most widely used CASE packages. Excelerator and most other CASE packages run on the IBM PC and its compatibles. Since drawings of data flow and other diagrams are a substantial part of system documentation, CASE tools require PCs that have good graphic capabilities.

FIGURE 16–18

A Data Flow Diagram Produced by Excelerator

Note that the symbols shown in this figure are slightly different from those in Figure 16–6. CASE tools and system analysts differ slightly in the shape of the four symbols used for data flow diagrams.

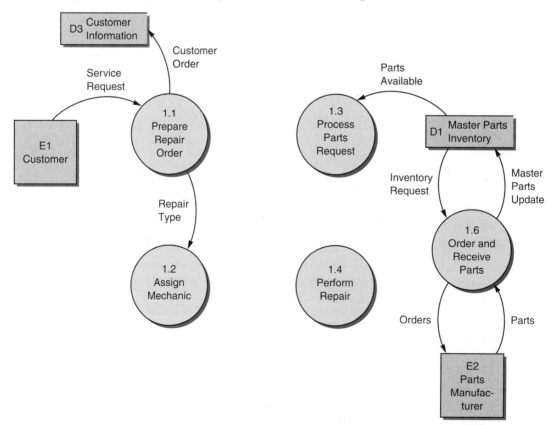

CASE tools currently have two other important capabilities. First, system analysts can use them to build executable prototypes of input and output screens. This enables users to evaluate these very important human/computer interfaces before computer programs are written. Thus, the programmer can be fairly confident that the screens will meet the users' needs.

Second, some CASE tools are capable of generating executable program code. Thus, CASE tools are becoming application generators that can automatically produce program code, such as COBOL, from the system documentation.

The program code is usually not complete, but it does provide a skeleton for the programs that can be modified and filled in by programmers. This capability certainly reduces the amount of manual coding necessary to produce an operational system.

CASE tools will become increasingly important in software development. They are the application of computers to the task of building software. CASE tools are to system analysts as word processors are to writers. They make the creation, organization, and changing of system documentation much easier. They also offer the capability of automating a significant portion of the programming process. However, just as with the introduction of any computer system, the introduction of CASE tools requires cultural and organizational changes if the system is to be successful. Application 16–2 illustrates this point.

Systems Analysis and Application Development Without Programming

In Chapter 11 we saw that programs can be developed with fourth-generation languages that require many fewer statements to accomplish the programs' requirements. Under the fourth-generation language classification are languages such as Focus, electronic spreadsheets, and application generators that generate most of the program code required for an application. All of these have in common the fact that they require much less programming (or in some cases no programming) to create an application. Thus, applications can be created and modified quickly. Many end users are employing these methods to build their own information systems applications. We will examine these methods in Chapter 18. However, at this point you may be wondering whether the system analysis approaches discussed in this chapter are useful for application development without programming. The answer to this question is not clear-cut; it depends on the situation. Here are some guidelines to use in deciding whether a structured system analysis is appropriate in a given situation:

1. Above all you must understand the inputs, data processes, and information outputs required of the system you are attempting to develop. If you are having difficulty understanding these, structured system analysis will help you.

2. As systems become larger and more complex, the partitioning capabilities of structured system analysis become most useful.

3. If you plan to implement the system by writing program code in a language such as BASIC or COBOL, structured system analysis is

CASE Veterans Say: Look Before You Leap

By Rosemary Hamilton

While some information systems shops are well on their way to a full-blown computer-aided software engineering (CASE) environment, other users are just beginning the journey. To those newcomers, users and analysts alike made this recommendation: Don't hurry to buy anything. . . .

In recent interviews, IS [information systems] managers and analysts said new users are making a big mistake if they look at a CASE implementation as a matter of selecting products. CASE is primarily a management issue requiring cultural and organizational changes before software tools can really be effective, observers said.

"People have to look at this as an information management issue and start implementing steps that will move them into that," said Lionel Brooks, a systems engineer in the information resource management department of New York Life Insurance Co., which is committed to IBM's AD/Cycle strategy for CASE. "If the corporate culture isn't in place, then you'll end up with big, expensive tools and not know what to do with them."

Emmanuel Ackerman, manager of data administration at De-

pository Trust Co., said he expects it will take years before his staff has fully adapted to a CASE environment.

"Taking a company through this, to grow into a formal methodology, is something that the experts say takes three to five years," Ackerman said. "You don't do it overnight. These are the problems of social evolution. This isn't just automating something."

In 1988, "we had no formal life cycle, no tools, nothing upper CASE," Ackerman said. "We became aware that CASE was coming down the road, so we asked, what did we need to do to get ready?"

The staff first evaluated what the goals were and what developers needed to get their jobs done. It then began evaluating published methodologies, including process-driven and data-driven methods. It ended up selecting the information engineering approach supported by Knowledgeware, Inc.'s. Information Engineering Workbench.

Now, the real work was under way.

"We have specialists on staff who are starting pilot projects with a straw methodology, and they are working some people through it," Ackerman said.

"We're seeing how well the users respond to it, how the development people respond, and we're measuring the impact on culture and structure."

Howard Fosdick, president of Fosdick Consulting, Inc., suggested that users first address the nonproduct issues, such as training and selecting a methodology. "For the first time in 30 years, we are getting away from writing code," he said. "Lots of companies structure teams based on this 30-year history. The organization has to change."

According to Vaughan Merlyn, chairman of CASE Research Corp., IS shops should first define standards for application development to replace the sometimes haphazard approaches used today. This step includes not only a software methodology but a staff structure that better reflects data management and standard development procedures.

Reprinted with permission from *Computerworld* (July 2, 1990), p. 27, Copyright 1990 by CW Publishing, Inc., Framingham, MA 01701.

more important. Changing program code is expensive. Structured system analysis helps to insure that you will not have to change your program code because you did not have a clear understanding of your information needs before writing the programs.

4. If you plan to implement the system with a flexible *fourth-generation language*, structured system analysis is less important and often not necessary. These fourth-generation languages, such as electronic spreadsheets and application generators, usually allow you to change a system much more quickly and with less expense than if it were programmed in a *third-generation language*, such as BASIC or COBOL. Fourth-generation languages are tools to develop systems without programming. They often allow you to quickly

develop an initial version of your system on a computer even when you have little understanding of your requirements. In effect, you can define your requirements and develop your system simultaneously in a trial-and-error fashion. This approach to developing systems is becoming very important.

Remember that the system development life cycle is still a most useful tool, even for application development without programming. The following steps must be performed in developing a complex system or a simple program:

1. Do a feasibility study.

2. Analyze your information requirements.

3. Design the system.

4. Evaluate hardware (if new hardware is required).

5. Build and test the system.

6. Convert to the new system.

7. Maintain the system.

It is a question of the degree to which these steps are done and how they are performed, not whether they are done. For example, if you are developing a simple electronic spreadsheet you should perform each of these steps. They may overlap, and some, such as the feasibility study, can be done in your head. In this case, the analysis, design, building, and testing many occur simultaneously.

Most difficulties in applying personal computers occur because users omit some or most of the steps in the system development life cycle. These steps have been developed and used over the years by professionals. They are also useful when people want to develop their own applications.

Summary

- Software development is the most expensive part of implementing a computerized system. A rational approach to systems analysis can help to minimize this expense.

- Systems analysis enables analysts to partition a complex system and focus on the interactions between its parts.

- The study of a large system is made possible through partitioning it into smaller, manageable parts.

- Structured analysis begins with a detailed analysis of the current system. Data flow diagrams are developed that depict the existing system.

- A new system is designed, based on the review of the current system and on new user requirements. The major tools used in this process are data flow diagrams, data dictionaries, structured English, decision tables, and decision trees.

- Several alternative ways to implement the system are generated. Since many different combinations may exist, it is necessary to compare the costs and benefits of the various options.

- Once an alternative is selected, various systems specifications are integrated into a complete package called the new system requirements document.

- Structured analysis is superior to other approaches in many respects. Its primary advantage is that it leads to the creation of systems that are easier to understand and maintain.

- Computer-aided software engineering (CASE) enables system analysts to create and maintain system development documentation with a computer. CASE also can generate program code.

- The system development life cycle (SDLC) is useful even when applications are developed without programming. It is a question of the degree to which the steps in the SDLC are applied and how they are applied, rather than whether or not they will be applied.

Key Terms

Systems analysis	Leveled data flow diagrams
Hierarchical partitioning	Data dictionary
Structured	Functional primitives
Structured systems development	Process or transform descriptions
Interfaces	Structured English
Systems development life cycle (SDLC)	Decision tables
	Decision trees
Feasibility study	Maintainability
Structured systems analysis	Computer-aided software engineering (CASE)
Data flow diagrams (DFDs)	
System flowchart	Software engineering

Review Questions

1. Why does the user need to be familiar with application software development?

2. Define systems analysis, and explain how it makes software development a more manageable task.

3. Explain the concept of partitioning.

4. List the elements of a feasibility document.

5. What are the differences in program and system flowcharts?

6. What is the essence of the structured systems development approach?

7. Describe the importance of data flow diagrams in structured analysis.

8. Differentiate between system flowcharts and data flow diagrams.

9. Explain the following terms:

   a. Data dictionary

   b. Transform descriptions

   c. Functional primitives

   d. Decision table

   e. Decision tree

   f. Structured English

10. Identify and describe the symbols used in data flow diagrams.

11. List the tangible costs and benefits that should be considered when selecting alternative systems.

12. Describe the components of a structured specification.

13. What qualities should a good structured specification possess?

14. Discuss the advantages of the structured approach over other approaches to systems development.

15. What is computer-aided software engineering?

Discussion Questions and Cases

1. Often, managers are reluctant to allow a systems analyst to "interfere" with their work. Some common objections are as follows:

   An outsider cannot understand the nature of the work within a short time period.

   We have been working like this for years. It's not broke. Why fix it?

   Interviews and questionnaires take a lot of time, and our personnel are already overburdened with production work.

   How would you respond to these objections?

2. Structured analysis and structured design are superior in many respects to other approaches to analysis and design. They do, however, suffer from certain drawbacks. Critically review structured techniques and identify their weaknesses.

3. Jane Montgomery is manager of systems development for White Motor Corporation, a large manufacturer of trucks. For the last five years, she has maintained a policy whereby newly hired individuals for the systems development group must have an educational background in either computer science, math, or industrial engineering. These employees are filling either programming or systems analysts positions. Jane believes that computer professionals must first understand hardware and software in order to perform their jobs properly. Furthermore, she feels that the development of application software requires a great deal of logical reasoning and design skill. Therefore, she believes that industrial engineers and mathematicians, as well as those with a computer science background, make good computer professionals. Several management-level individuals in user organizations have suggested that systems

development hire more individuals with backgrounds in user areas such as marketing, finance, personnel, and accounting. Jane's reply has been that it is the user's responsibility to convey to the systems analyst and programmer what he or she needs in an information system. It is the system analyst's and programmer's job to design, code, and implement the systems. She argues that these are two separate disciplines and that the advantages of specialization support her current hiring policy. Evaluate Jane's position.

4. Sam Jones is vice president of marketing for Giles Development Corporation, a large developer of condominiums, apartments, and single-family homes. Sam has requested that systems development begin work on a new marketing decision support system. This system will have the capacity of tracking historical sales, following demographic trends, and projecting sales trends. The primary objective of the system is to provide Giles Development with information that will help it decide what type of housing unit to develop in the future and where to locate the various types of units. Systems development has estimated that 40 percent of the effort in developing the system will be spent in the analysis phase. Sam is upset with this estimate. He feels that much less time should be spent on analysis and that systems development should quickly get into the design and implementation of the system. Do you agree or disagree with Sam's position? Explain your answer.

5. Frank Jones, a systems analyst for Kraco Corporation, a furniture manufacturer, has just completed the analysis phase of a systems development project for the marketing department. In the general design document, he proposed a number of options for implementing the new system. During a review of the design document, the review committee (which consisted of several marketing representatives) asked why he had wasted time developing several alternatives. The marketing vice president said to Frank, "We need only one system, not three." If you were Frank, how would you respond to the vice president?"

6. Joan Abby has been hired as a system analyst for the Datamax Corporation. Her primary job for the coming month is to develop a new computer system that will enable users in the accounting department to perform various payroll and monthly accounting functions. For several weeks, Joan has been conducting an extensive study to gain a thorough understanding of how the current system operates and interacts with its users. She has interviewed users and has spent time working on the current system. Joan feels the study of the current system is a necessary phase in structured system development. Her supervisor, however, disagrees with her. The supervisor feels the new system can be developed independently from the current system and has told Joan not to waste any more time. Whom do you agree with? Support your answer.

INFORMATION SYSTEMS STRATEGIES

Misuse of Power

By Vicki McConnell and Karl Koch

There is an abuse problem in corporate America today that nobody likes to talk about. Computers and information technology have been misused and underused by those who are ill prepared to use them. In addition, computer users have been abused by the manner in which technical systems are implemented. What most companies don't realize is that this dysfunctional relationship between users and technology is not a technological problem. It is a problem of poor leadership at all levels of business and information systems management.

The reality is that companies know a lot about a few aspects of implementing computer systems and a little about the rest. The knowledge base they have is poorly organized. Most businesspeople cannot point to one document in their corporate files that gives complete guidelines on how to go about implementing a computer system. Yet many organizations (dare we say *all*?) have voluminous records of implementations gone awry, of applications unused and underused and of the stated dissatisfaction of users.

To ease the implementation process, IS [information systems] and business managers need an inventory of what can go wrong, an organized methodology for implementing computer systems and information technologies and a rigorous argument for proper and effective procedures for implementing information technology.

What Can Go Wrong

The IS professional typically views the problems of computerization in terms of the technology rather than in terms of the business. That is, when an implementation falters or fails, it is seen as a missed opportunity to use the technology.

What has really happened, however, is a failure of the company to manage the relationship between its technology and its users.

Top business and IS management must set the criteria for technology use and implementation—that the technology serves the product or service of the business and that it serves the organization's human system. Executives also need to make sure that IS staffs are educated and trained in the business. When the technology invades every area of the business, the technician must be schooled in all areas of the business.

One of the best ways for an organization to educate its technical staff about the business is through a collaboration between technician and user during systems development. They can train each other in the business of the organization.

Action at All Levels

Computer implementations have their own set of management requirements. There are certain actions that must be taken at the operational, tactical and strategic levels of an organization's management if computer implementations are to work.

When the proper issues are addressed at all three levels, the implementation will succeed. When they are not, it will fail.

The operational requirements involve the setting of clear and stated expectations for the user. Two items must be included: what worker behaviors will change and what benefits the company will accrue from technology implementations.

Abuse occurs when user managers are unclear about the expectations they have of their employees (see Example 1). They either narrow their focus and expect too little of their users, or they fail to define the new behaviors they expect once the computer system is implemented. Only when user managers learn to set broad and comprehensive behavioral expectations for end-user staff will there be a more effective use of information technology (see "Great Expectations" below).

Setting the requirements for managing computer implementations is more difficult at the tactical management level of organizations. Firms everywhere are redefining the role of middle managers. Most of them are also seeking to eliminate layers of middle management. What is rarely recognized is that information technology is affecting this change because it provides many options for the way in which middle management can be handled and grouped. Top management must set the goal of changing the manner in which middle management functions. First, it needs to analyze the changes needed in middle management, then apply information technology as one tool in that change.

Middle managers will not necessarily be replaced by computers because the basic functions these people provide—consistency in the work and behavior of the firm—are important. Rather, a successful implementation of information technology can bring a whole new range of skills and capabilities to middle managers, such as the following:

- Decision thinking. The redefinition of planning. Rather than focusing on making decisions, the middle managers are more concerned with thinking toward a decision.
- Data interpreter. The supplier of new knowledge.
- Organizing responsibility. The new way to delegate. Focus on responsibility, not tasks.
- Front line. The new management style. Empowering and supporting those operational workers with customer contact.
- New knowledge skills. The real flattening of the hierarchy.
- Continuous learning. The ultimate challenge.

Always remember: Whatever is done to middle management will change the entire organization. Top IS and business management should not implement technical systems in middle management until they have analyzed the impact of automation on the quality of the organization's human interaction.

Technology cannot have this kind of effect on an organization without a driving vision of what the corporation intends to achieve in its business, with its technology and through its employees. That vision must exist at the strategic management level to direct the development and use of the corporation's technology. Automation will not disrupt strategic management of an organization. However, improper management of a technology implementation will (see Example 2).

Management at all levels must prepare its people and its organization for a future of constant technological pressures. This will be facilitated if management has a methodology for implementing computers and if employees know and value the concepts behind this methodology.

Controlling Corporate Change

There are dynamic ways of managing change that can help corporate leaders gain control over the future of the corporation in a world of changing technology. Top management must recognize that change is most effective when it is cyclical and iterative. People require time to practice the new forms of work. They must be cycled and recycled through the process of learning a change.

Change is also most effective when it is incremental and planned. In other words, people will respond positively when the change fits into the vision of the corporation and occurs in reasonable steps leading in that direction. Change is most effective when it leads to an openness to future change and creates a corporate climate that accepts and prepares for change.

To maintain control of the company's technological future, top management must do the following:

- Set common expectations regarding technology.
- Control technology through management of people.
- Recognize trends in technology development as they relate to the business.
- Recognize the need to organize the entire business to control its technology.

Creating a corporate climate that accepts changing technologies will require three executive management decisions. The first is decide who is in charge. The technology takes charge only when top management defaults on decision-making. Top management will be in charge of its technology when it decides to be.

The second decision is choose the battlefield. The true battle is not over technology; it is about the kind of business management wants and the kinds of employees management wants. Management will be in charge of technology when it develops its business and employees.

The third is kick the dependency habit. No business needs technology. Management will be in charge of its technology when it considers itself free to accept—or reject—any new technology. Management may choose more often than not to use new technologies, but this must be a choice made freely. Only a free choice leaves management in control.

The problems involved in implementing computer systems and information technology are only the symptoms of a larger issue: whether top management stays in control while constantly changing and upgrading its information technology. The answer lies in the values of the corporation. People must be valued above machines, the business above its technology. Then, the corporation must have a way to implement information technology that honors and supports these values.

Example 1:
Crossed Communications Lines

Want to know what can happen to a technology implementation when user managers have unclear expectations of their users? Read on.

An on-line inventory control system was implemented in a Midwestern farm equipment manufacturing company. The inventory control personnel who were going to use the system had little or no knowledge of basic computer terms and terminal operation. Before system implementation, they received no computer education and minimal training. As a result of management's failure to prepare users, the inventory control system was not fully operational for 10 months beyond the original start date, and the cost of the system skyrocketed from $250,000 to $1 million. The users were frustrated and angry because they did not receive proper support during the system's installation. They did not understand what management expected of them, nor did they know how to relate to the company's IS staff, who designed and implemented the system.

Example 2:
Fiascos

Technology implementations, when done correctly, should not disrupt strategic management of an organization.

But when done poorly, they certainly can, as the following examples show.

* An international fast-food chain introduced a computerized system for retrieving store operations information. The system was intended to move information up through the organization to senior management. Instead, the information jumped management levels and was sent directly to corporate headquarters. As a result, senior managers had much greater detail on store operations than the store managers had. This information was then used by some senior managers to reprimand store managers' performance.
* A major Midwestern manufacturer decided to computerize its production management systems. Approximately half of the affected employees were convinced that they would lose their jobs. They assumed cost cutting and staff reductions were the main reasons why management had instituted the change. The installation of the new system caused a number of employees to retire or quit. Those who stayed rebelled against the technology, causing a five-fold increase in the cost of the system and an extra seven months of installation time.
* A state bureau of motor vehicles computerized license plate records and sales information. During the planning phase, the administration solicited ideas and opinions of line workers and supervisors. Although their input was used, they got no feedback. They came to the conclusion that their participation was a waste of

time because management never listened to them anyway.

Great Expectations:
How Users Will Behave

Technology will be used effectively if managers know what kinds of behavior to expect from employees.

Managers can use the following categories to help them set behavioral expectations:

* **Productivity.** Once started on a specific computer task, how productive is the employee in a given time period?
* **Proficiency.** How much of a specific software application has the employee mastered?
* **Efficiency.** How well can the employee use all functions mastered in a given software application, moving from one task to another with ease?
* **Effectiveness.** How well can the person choose between options in mastered software applications?
* **Attitude.** Given past experience with computers, how positive is the employee's attitude toward present and future performance with the technology?
* **Quality.** How well can the employee perform according to corporate and work-group standards?

Discussion Questions

1. This article recommends that change be incremental. Yet many re-engineering advocates recommend radical change in basic business processes. Are these two views contradictory? Why or why not?

2. How are the topics of systems analysis and organizational change related?

Reprinted with permission from *Computerworld* (January 28, 1991), pp. 67–69, Copyright 1991 by CW Publishing, Inc., Framingham, MA 01701.

17

Systems Design and Implementation

You have just been assigned to write your first computer program. Your professor has given you the program's requirements, so you do not have to perform a systems analysis to determine them. Where do you start? How do you structure your program? What tools can you use to design the program? What is the best way to test it to be sure it works?

The previous chapter introduced the techniques for structured systems analysis of a proposed system. The specifications (data flow diagrams, process descriptions, and data dictionary) that were developed are the primary inputs for the structured design phase. Designing a new system with these structured specifications is a relatively easy process. However, for simple programs or programs for which the requirements are already known, designers often omit the analysis phase and begin with systems design. Figure 17–1 repeats the overview of the systems development life cycle so that you can readily see where design (process 3 in Figure 17–1) fits into the picture.

This chapter covers designing and building the new system. It also discusses conversion to the new system and describes the procedures for auditing and maintaining the new system.

Introduction

FIGURE 17–1
Systems Development Life Cycle.

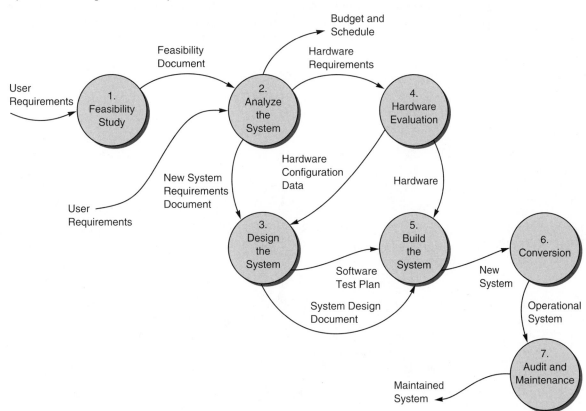

Design the System

Figure 17–2 is an overview of the structured design phase. **Structured design** is the process of designing the computer programs that will be used in the system. The system design document produced by the structured design phase is, in effect, a blueprint that the programmer follows in coding the programs. A plan for testing the programs is also produced during the design phase.

Only three activities are performed within structured design: (1) deriving the structure chart, (2) designing modules, and (3) packaging the design. When designers use structured analysis, they have less work to do in the design phase. In fact, a characteristic of structured analysis is that more work is done in planning the system and in the analysis phase than in the later stages of the systems development cycle.

The primary advantages of structured design are that it produces computer programs that (1) are more easily maintained, (2) can be tested module by module in a top-down fashion, and (3) can be more easily understood. All of these advantages occur primarily because the program is broken down into *logical modules* during the structured design phase. (Logical modules are individual parts of computer programs that are separate and identifiable.) Usually the systems analyst works on the design phase, although in some cases a systems designer does it. Sometimes systems designers are called programmer analysts since the process of designing the system requires both analyst and programmer skills.

Much of the work performed in designing a system is done with CASE tools. These tools are capable of drawing data flow diagrams and structure charts and maintaining a data dictionary. CASE tools will also have the capability of generating executable program code, as discussed in Application 17–1. Thus, CASE tools will take on the function of fourth-generation languages, i.e., to generate executable code.

FIGURE 17–2
Overview of the Structured Design Phase.

The objective of this phase is to produce a blueprint (the system design document) that will guide the building of the system.

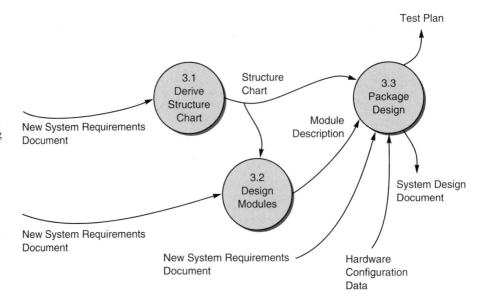

APPLICATION 17–1

CASE, 4GLs Define New Programming Environment

By Michael Puttre

As computer-aided software engineering (CASE) and fourth-generation programming languages (4GLs) become more widely used in applications development, the distinction between them is likely to blur, according to industry analysts. This will leave users to reconcile what they have come to regard as two distinct technologies. . . .

Boeing Computer Services, which provides internal systems support for Boeing Co., has noted a strong push from within the company toward CASE implementation. According to Jerry Christopher, manager of applications systems development, the automation capability provided by CASE has added "new vigor to old techniques."

Design analysis and requirements capturing tools let Boeing programmers deliver better-planned and more effective systems.

Boeing is also working with 4GLs for ad hoc sorts of applications. But Christopher views 4GLs

as appropriate only when requirements do not demand all the rigor of a CASE tool. And because he does not believe that 4GL and CASE functionality are on par, the role of the two development tools are separate at Boeing. "They are largely independent as far as I'm concerned," said Christopher.

Coming Together

That independence, however, may be short-lived in the marketplace. Last fall, IBM Corp. issued the bold statement that it had invented the 5GL—the fifth-generation language—with the introduction of AD/Cycle. While the specter of a next-generation language may cause some to squirm uncomfortably, advanced computer languages will have a major part to play in future applications development.

Since IBM had the privilege of defining the professional programming model for the '90s, that model became CASE. Consequently, users have been left to try to figure out how the 4GL and CASE worlds will come together in their businesses.

Numerous industry observers agree with IBM's contention that it will be absolutely vital to automate the software development process as much as possible. In that scenario, some portions of the CASE life cycle, by necessity, will be integrated with 4GLs.

According to a 1989 report published by ButlerBloor Computer Research and titled "4GLs: An Evaluation and Comparison," some of the larger 4GL vendors have or intend to add value to their 4GLs by integrating CASE tools with them. Software AG's Natural 4GL includes support for its Predict CASE tool for object-oriented programming. Oracle Corp. uses its CASE Dictionary, Designer and Generator tools extensively to support its SQL Plus 4GL.

As competition in the applications development tool market favors continued integration, it will become difficult to point to a particular product and say whether it is a CASE or a 4GL tool.

Adapted with permission from Fairchild Publication from *MIS Week* (February 26, 1990), pp. 22, 25.

4GLs With CASE Support

Product	Company	Major Operating Systems (Pending)
CA-DB:Generator	Computer Associates	MVS, DOS, OS/2, VMS (Unix)
Fastbuild	Sybase	DOS, VMS, Unix
Filetab-D	National Computing Center	MVS, DOS, VMS, Unix
Focus	Information Builders	MVS, DOS, OS/2, VMS, Unix
Ingres	Ingres	MVS, VMS, Unix (DOS, OS/2)
Natural	Software AG	MVS, OS/2, VMS
Powerhouse	Cognos	DOS, OS/2, VMS, Unix
Pro IV	McDonnell Douglas	MVS, DOS, OS/2, VMS, Unix
SQL family	Oracle	MVS, DOS, OS/2, VMS, Unix
SQL Toolset	Sybase	VMS, Unix (DOS, OS/2)

Source: ButlerBloor Computer Research, 1989.

Derive the Structure Chart

The primary tool used in structured design is the **structure chart**. A structure chart is a graphic representation of the hierarchical relationships between modules within a program or system. To create a structure chart, designers hierarchically partition into modules the tasks that a program must perform. Figure 17–3 shows a structure chart that hierarchically partitions the tasks that must be done when you go grocery shopping.

An example of a structure chart used for an information system is shown in Figure 17–4. When a program is designed in a structured way, the approach is often called **top-down design**. The figure shows that the program is broken down into independent modules, or subroutines, from the top down. The module at the top is called a control module, which in Figure 17–4 is the accounts receivable system. At the appropriate times, this module calls the three modules underneath to get the inputs from files, perform the processing, and write the outputs. Designers can continue subdividing modules into smaller parts, to simplify the program structure. Ideally, each module performs a single function.

By now you probably have noticed that this structure chart resembles a data flow diagram in concept. Although the two do not look similar, a structure chart is an exercise in hierarchical partitioning just as a data flow diagram is. All the advantages of data flow diagrams also apply to structure charts.

A data flow diagram documents what has to be accomplished; it is a statement of information processing requirements. A structure chart, on the other hand, documents how the requirements will be met in a computer program. The structure chart is the hierarchical partitioning of the programs that will be written for the system.

Since there is a close relationship between DFDs and structure charts, the structure chart can be derived directly from the DFD. To understand how this is done, you need to know more about structured design.

FIGURE 17–3
Structure Chart for Grocery Shopping.

This is a hierarchical partitioning of the tasks that must be performed in shopping for groceries. Tasks performed by computers can be partitioned in similar ways.

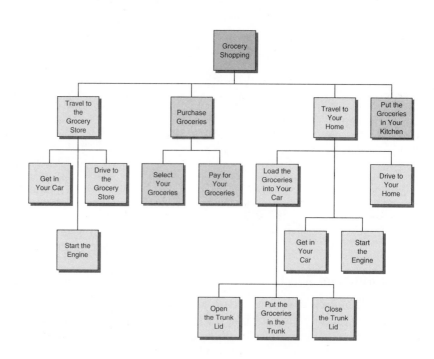

A design is structured if it is made up of a hierarchy of modules. Another requirement of structured design is that each of these modules or subroutines must have a single entry and a single exit back to its parent module. Each module should be as independent as possible of all other modules, except its parent. For example, in Figure 17–4 there should be no direct exit from the Determine Beginning Balance module to the Add Purchases module. Once the Determine Beginning Balance module has completed its processing, control of execution is passed back to the parent Compute Account Balance module. From there, control of execution can go back up to Perform Processing, or back down to any of the fourth-level modules. Control of execution passes along the connecting lines.

A third requirement of structured design is that within each module the code should be executed in a top-to-bottom fashion. There must not be any GO TO statements that cause the program statements to be executed in other than a top-to-bottom manner. This requirement, often called **go-to-less programming**, makes programs much easier to read. For example, how would you like to read a book that had a GO TO statement every few paragraphs, which caused you to go and reread previous paragraphs; then to go forward three pages and read something on that page; then to go back and finally transfer again to another page? You can see the problem with reading and understanding a program module that has GO TO statements. Program code with many GO TO statements is often referred to as **spaghetti code**.

There are also certain notational conventions used in structured design, as shown in Figure 17–5. By now you probably already recognize that the rectangular box is a module. A **module** is a bounded, named, and contiguous set of program statements often referred to as a **subroutine**. The line joining two modules is called a **connection**. This connection means

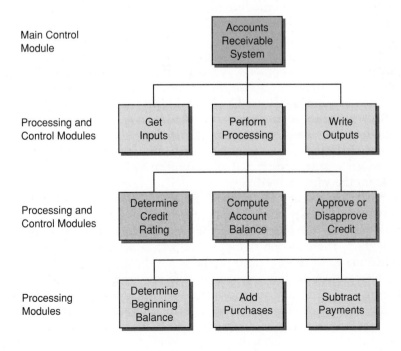

FIGURE 17–4
Structure Chart of an Accounts Receivable System.

An analogy can be made between a structure chart and the organization chart of a business. Top managers are at the top and those who do the detailed processing are at the bottom.

FIGURE 17–5
Notational
Conventions Used in
Structured Design.

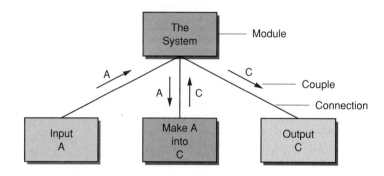

that the upper module has the capability of calling the lower module to begin execution. Finally, a couple is represented by a short arrow. A **couple** is a data item that moves from one module to another. For example, in the illustration, the system sends the data item A to the module labeled Make A into C, and then this module sends C back to the system.

Notice the general form of a structure chart. The input modules are on the left, processing modules in the middle, and output modules on the right.

Deriving structure charts from data flow diagrams is a straightforward task. Figure 17–6(*a*), Jose's DFD of the new order-processing system for Angelo's Pizza, can be used to illustrate how this is done. First, the central process in the DFD is identified. The **central process** is in the center of the DFD; therefore, it is usually not involved with getting input or generating output. Any process on the DFD can be selected as the central process; the choice is arbitrary. In this case, number 2 in Figure 17–6(*a*) is used. This process is placed at the top of the structure chart and called the system. Note that the top module in Figure 17–6(*b*) has the same inputs and outputs as process number 2 in Figure 17–6(*a*).

At the second level of the structure chart, one module is designed for each input stream, one module for the central process, and one for each output stream. A similar approach is used for each of the succeeding lower levels. For example, the second-level module Input Written Customer Order has one input stream (Get Verbal Customer Order) and one transform (Record Customer Order). A **transform** is a process (or module) that changes data into another form or into new data. For example, the module Record Customer Order transforms a verbal customer order into a written customer order. Note that the couples represent the flow of data to and from the various modules.

Another pattern in Figure 17–6 is that for each input process on the DFD, there is one two-part substructure (an input or get module and a transform module) on the structure chart. For each output process on the data flow diagram, there is one two-or-more-part substructure (a transform module and one or more output modules) on the structure chart.

One major advantage of deriving structure charts from DFDs is illustrated in Figure 17–6. The central part of the system, adding prices to the order, is isolated from the physical aspects of the input of the verbal customer order, the output of the cash register receipt, and the update of the

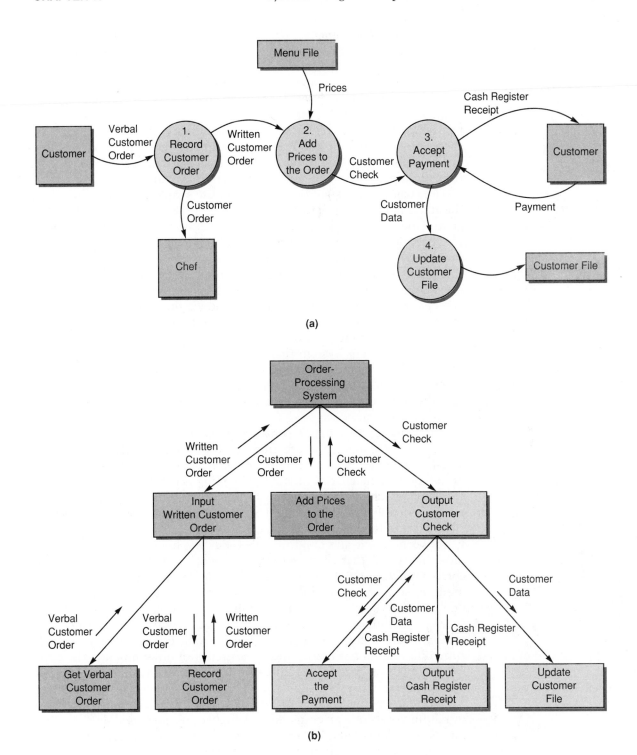

FIGURE 17–6

Deriving a Structure Chart for the New Order-Processing System for Angelo's Pizza.

Each module on this chart will be a separate subroutine in a computer program.

customer file. When changes occur in systems, the changes are very likely to affect inputs and outputs. The system has been hierarchically partitioned to isolate these inputs and outputs. Therefore, it is possible to make a change in this system by changing only one of these three isolated input or output modules. Remember that one of the primary advantages of the structured approach is the ease with which maintenance can be performed on the system. Many companies are now finding that they spend more money in maintaining existing systems than in designing and implementing new ones. Therefore, ease of maintenance is an extremely important consideration when a new system is being designed.

The structured design documented on the structure chart is based on the statement of information processing requirements, the data flow diagram. One might think that the structure chart is complete at this point. However, a few other things must be added. The designer has not indicated the flow of data between modules when errors occur. In fact, up to this point the designer has ignored error conditions altogether. In addition, programs need to process items other than computational items and character information in order to produce the ultimate output. The other primary type of data a program processes is *control data*. Control data are data the program uses solely for making processing decisions. For example, in any system that processes multiple file records, control data tell the program whether or not the last record on the file has been processed. Once the control data (sometimes called a switch) indicate that the last record has been processed, then end-of-job processing, such as totals, can commence.

Furthermore, two major considerations might cause a designer to change the module structure from that derived directly from DFDs. These considerations are coupling and cohesion. *Coupling* is a measure of the interdependence of modules. Coupling is central to the structured design approach. At the beginning of the discussion of structured design, we indicated that modules should be as independent of each other as possible. Naturally, there will be some coupling between modules, especially between parent and child modules. But the higher the coupling, the more likely it is that changes to the inside of one module will affect the correct functioning of another module. The designer's goal is to design modules so that one module can be easily modified without disrupting others. To do this, he or she must minimize coupling. If coupling is minimized, a module can be read through without having to look inside any other module, and the module being read can be completely understood. A module should not branch into the interior of other modules. In summary, a module's interfaces to the rest of the world should be minimized and stated explicitly.

Cohesion is a measure of the strength of association between the internal functions of a given module. A highly cohesive module has statements and data that are very closely related. For example, a payroll system program module that calculates weekly gross pay and also prints the payroll check is not cohesive. These are two separate functions and therefore should be partitioned into separate program modules. However, taken separately, each would probably be highly cohesive.

Cohesion and coupling are related concepts. If a module has high cohesion, then an attempt to break it into two or more modules would result in very high coupling between the resulting modules. One can use this criterion to decide whether or not a module has high cohesion. If simply attempting to break the module into two or more modules produces high coupling, then the original module should be left as it is since it has high cohesion. In other words, the statements or functions within the module are highly related.

Modules having acceptable cohesion perform only one allocated task or perform several strongly related tasks because they use the same data. Another clue to the cohesion of a module is its name. If the name involves multiple verbs and multiple objects (for example, calculate gross pay and federal tax withholding), then it probably has unacceptable cohesion. A module with a strong name, having one verb and one object, is likely to be strongly cohesive.

The examination of structure charts in this chapter assumes that they are to be applied when designing computer programs. But they are also useful in application development by end users, which is covered in depth in Chapter 18. When electronic spreadsheets or other fourth-generation languages are applied to complex problems, a structure chart can be used to organize and document the application. Unorganized and undocumented applications that are developed without programming are just as serious a problem as unorganized and undocumented programs.

In addition, some of the modules can be implemented in a system by acquiring application software and others by coding programs. Recall Jose's plan (in Figure 16–17 of Chapter 16) to implement Angelo's recipe-pricing system by using an electronic spreadsheet for one process (module) within the system.

Design the Modules

In the second subphase of the structured design phase, designers design the internal processing within each module. If the systems analyst developed a good structured English transform description back in the analysis phase, and if the structure chart closely resembles the data flow diagrams, then this subphase is easy to accomplish. Designers simply convert structured English to **pseudocode** by adding input and output statements as well as control-type statements, such as those that control processing when errors occur. The decision tables and decision trees developed in the analysis phase are also useful in documenting the internal design of the modules.

Some designers prefer to use program flowcharts to document the internal design of modules (see Figure 17–7). If flowcharts are used, they should be structured. In the previous chapter, the allowable control patterns of structured English were introduced. The same control patterns are allowed in structured pseudocode or program flowcharts. These control patterns have been reproduced in Figure 17–8 to refresh your memory. When drawing a structured flowchart, use only these patterns. Note again that there is no reason to ever use a GO TO type of control pattern in structured programming.

Long and complex program flowcharts are often difficult to follow even when drawn in a structured manner. Therefore, many designers adopt the structured English or pseudocode approach to documenting the

FIGURE 17–7
Program Flowchart
Symbols.

Program flowchart
symbols are much
simpler than those used
in system flowcharting.

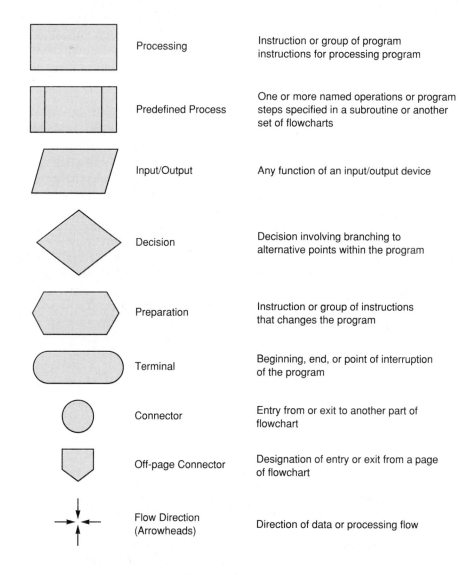

	Processing	Instruction or group of program instructions for processing program
	Predefined Process	One or more named operations or program steps specified in a subroutine or another set of flowcharts
	Input/Output	Any function of an input/output device
	Decision	Decision involving branching to alternative points within the program
	Preparation	Instruction or group of instructions that changes the program
	Terminal	Beginning, end, or point of interruption of the program
	Connector	Entry from or exit to another part of flowchart
	Off-page Connector	Designation of entry or exit from a page of flowchart
	Flow Direction (Arrowheads)	Direction of data or processing flow

processing that goes on within a module. Figure 17–9 shows a structured program flowchart and the same procedure documented in pseudocode.

Package the Design

In packaging the design, systems designers modify the design to fit the physical characteristics of the hardware and software configurations on which the system will be implemented. This physical environment can include such things as the program coding language, limitations of disk drives, and time restrictions. Thus far in the structured design process, designers have attempted to produce an ideal design, independent of the physical environment in which it will be implemented. In packaging the design, they modify it to fit the physical environment in such a way as to minimize deviation from the ideal design. They may have to do such things as combine modules to produce a system that makes efficient use of the machine resources (such as execution time and primary storage). How-

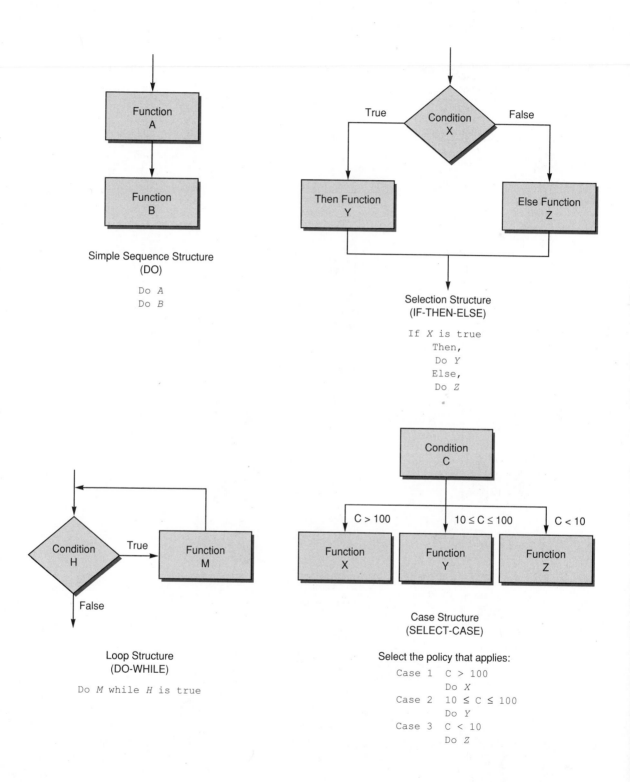

FIGURE 17–8
Allowable Pseudocode Control Patterns.

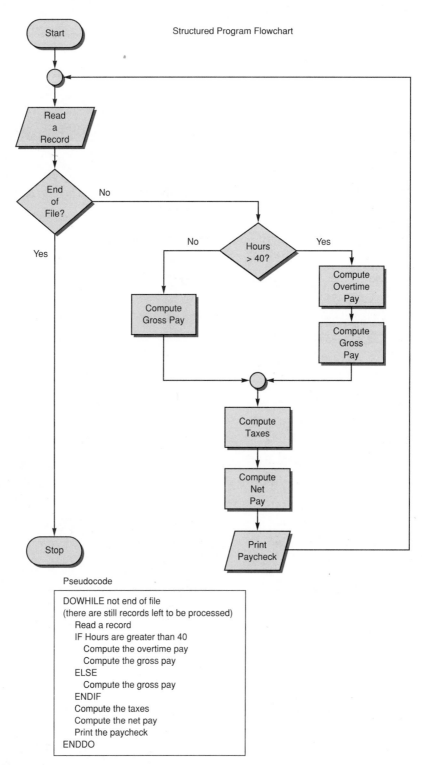

FIGURE 17–9

A Structured Flowchart and Pseudocode.

A program flowchart is a graphical way of representing the logic steps within a computer program. Some people find program flowcharts easier to follow than pseudocode.

ever, in the pursuit of efficiency, designers do not want to produce a system that compromises the modularity and therefore is difficult to modify.

Some analysts even go as far as to say that regardless of the physical environment, designers should first implement the system based on the ideal design, developed back in the module designing phase. Then, after the system is working, they can worry about modifying the system to improve efficiency. As Ed Yourdon, a systems analyst and design expert, states, "It is easier to make a working system efficient than to make an efficient system work."

This approach of implementing the ideal structured system is likely to be used more in the future. As hardware prices continue to decline, the efficiency at which a system uses a computer's resources is becoming less important. The human labor required to maintain and modify complex, nonstructured systems is a much more important consideration than how efficiently the system executes in a particular hardware environment.

The design packaging phase produces two primary outputs: the **test plan**, which documents a plan for testing the system before implementation; and the packaged design itself. The **packaged design** includes the structured specifications of data flow diagrams, data dictionary, structure charts, and module descriptions including pseudocode, structured English, decision tables, decision trees, and sometimes program flowcharts. In addition, the packaged design includes layout sketches that show how inputs and outputs are to appear on a video display or on paper.

Build the System

The primary activities that occur within the system building phase are coding, testing, and developing manual procedures. **Coding** is the process of writing a program (or module) in a computer language, based on the packaged design generated in the structured design phase. The task of coding the modules is often divided among several programmers in order to decrease the elapsed time necessary for coding. A well-structured and well-specified system helps ensure that each module is compatible with other modules even though they are written by different programmers.

Structured Walkthroughs

Before coding, many companies now perform a **structured walkthrough** of the design. In a formal structured walkthrough, the design documentation is made available to a review team of two to four people. These individuals review the design. Then, in a formal meeting, the designer presents the system design to the review team. As the designer "walks" the review team through the design, questions are clarified. Often significant improvements are made in the system design.

Structured walkthroughs are often also used to review the program code after a module has been coded. This process is called a **code inspection**. Here, the programmer walks members of a review team through the module's program code. During this process, the program code is checked for compliance with the module specifications and for other types of coding errors.

Top-Down Coding

Many firms that use structured programming advocate top-down coding. In **top-down coding**, the top module on the structure chart is coded and tested, then successively lower levels of modules are coded and tested. Many modules are coded concurrently. In fact, sometimes the coding phase overlaps with the systems design phase. However, the emphasis is on starting and completing the coding of the top modules first. Thus, coding of the higher-level modules can begin before the design of the lower-level modules is complete.

Top-Down Testing

After a module is coded, the first test to be performed is a **desk check**, which is a manual review of a module's logic. Both the programmer and the supervisor review the module. Desk checking also includes manually tracing hypothetical data (both valid and invalid) through the module's logic in order to verify that it will process the data correctly. For example, a payroll check for one million dollars or a requisition from inventory in excess of ten thousand dollars can be evaluated in terms of the logic and controls incorporated in the system.

A structured walkthrough of the program module code can be very useful at this point. Either formal or informal inspections of the code by other programmers often identify improvements that can be made in the program code.

After desk checking occurs, modules are compiled without execution. The compilation step almost always detects several deviations (compiler diagnostics) from the rules and syntax of the particular computer language being used. After these errors are corrected, the module is compiled and executed with test input.

When programs are structured, this testing can be done in a top-down fashion, as shown in Figure 17–10. Top-down testing is performed when enough modules have been coded (usually the top-level module and some of the second-level ones) to make the testing significant.

Program stubs are used to test these modules. **Program stubs** are dummy modules that are called by the parent module. They have input/output behavior that is sufficiently similar to the yet-to-be-coded real module that the parent module can be executed. Figure 17–10 illustrates testing with program stubs of the system depicted in Figure 17–6. The top module as well as one second-level one, the Input Written Customer Order module, have been coded. All the program stub modules perform input and output functions simulating the modules that are yet to be coded.

In addition, the program stubs write out a message, such as "output customer check has been called," each time the particular dummy module is called. This message provides a trace so that the programmer can identify when each program stub is called by the parent module. The ability to trace the program stubs called makes the debugging task easier. As modules are coded, they can be substituted for the program stubs. Then, in turn, if these modules call other modules that are yet to be coded, new program stubs can be inserted.

Top-down testing has significant advantages. The testing of the system can proceed in a top-down fashion as each module is coded. This

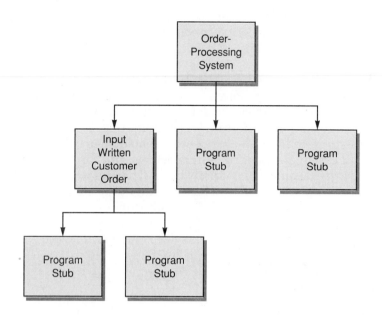

F I G U R E 17–10
Top-Down Testing.
Top-down testing allows
a programmer to test a
new system, using a
module-by-module
approach.

spreads the testing over a longer period of time, and avoids "crash" testing in a restricted time period after all the modules have been coded. In addition, errors are likely to be related to the most recently inserted module since modules inserted earlier have already been tested and corrected. Therefore, errors are much easier to isolate.

Preparation of **test data** is a very important step. Inadequate test data can be very costly later on because they can cause undetected errors (**program bugs**). Adequate test data are comprehensive, covering every type of valid and invalid input that could exist when the module is operational. Development of adequate test data usually requires that users participate, since they are most familiar with the various combinations of inputs that may occur. When the test data are used, every statement in the module should be executed, including logic that is seldom used; otherwise, the test will not be thorough. Software tools are available to identify the executed and unexecuted module statements. Given a set of test data, the expected output from the module's execution using these test data should be determined manually. In this way the programmer can ascertain whether the module's processing is valid.

After each coded module has been tested in a top-down fashion and then corrected, the modules are tested collectively as a system, using similarly comprehensive test data. Once the system has been tested with hypothetical data, the final test before implementation is to process real data at the volume levels expected when the system is installed.

System Documentation

System analysts and user personnel usually develop procedures concurrently with module coding and testing. A complete written set of manual procedures is developed that documents all manual processes to be performed by both user and data processing personnel in the actual operation of the system. The procedures cover such items as input preparation, control and balancing, error correction, and computer operator instructions. Collectively, these procedures form a critical part of the system's documentation.

Documentation is sometimes the most neglected aspect of the systems development life cycle. Firms frequently depend on a key individual or group of individuals to design and operate an information system. If these people rely on their memories for programming, systems, and operating information, and then they find other employment, the firm has to study and document the existing system before work can begin on modifying it or designing a new one. Rarely can anyone remember all the detailed design information of a complex computer information system.

Adequate documentation includes the following:

- All the specifications in the systems development life cycle
- Data flow diagrams and structure charts
- Data dictionaries
- Hardware specifications
- Performance specifications
- Job descriptions
- Procedure manuals

Chief Programmer Teams

Many firms organize their programming efforts into chief programmer teams. A **chief programmer team** consists of a chief programmer (who supervises the team), one or more programmers, a librarian, and a backup programmer. The backup programmer acts as an assistant to the chief programmer. The chief programmer and the backup programmer code the most important modules of a system while the other programmers in the team code the other modules.

The primary responsibility of the librarian is to maintain up-to-date documentation for the system the team is working on. Often, programmers do not enjoy doing the clerical and filing tasks that are necessary to maintain up-to-date documentation. With a library system, the documentation is centralized, rather than under the control of individual programmers, and is available to anyone on the team. The librarian's functions include maintaining copies of program listings, updating test data, picking up computer output, and maintaining up-to-date documentation in a secure file.

An important aspect of the management of a programming team is the measurement of its productivity. Measuring the output of programmers is difficult. Application 17–2 outlines one method of measuring programming productivity.

Conversion

In the conversion phase of the systems development life cycle, the user and systems personnel work closely together. In this phase, the firm converts, or changes, from its old information system to the new system.

Pinning Down the Benefits

By Andrew Topper

There is plenty said about computer-aided software engineering tools increasing staff productivity. But how do you track and measure the actual benefits?

Many companies use the number of lines of code produced per man-month as a basis. However, there are inherent problems with this measurement technique. In other words, more is not always better.

First of all, this metric is very dependent on the programming language used, be it third-generation, COBOL or assembler. A program written in COBOL that allows records to be added to a VSAM file, for example, will have significantly fewer lines of code than one written in assembler.

In addition, documentation may be written into the code, and you would not want to include that in the productivity metric. Also, this method often disregards the maintainability and performance of the finished code.

A better method might be to measure function points achieved per man-month. This measurement was developed by A. J. Albrecht at IBM, who defined a function point as a measurable, external aspect of a software system.

Albrecht listed the following five basic types of function points and then assigned a weight to each:

- Inputs to a program or system: 4 points.
- Outputs from a program or system: 5 points.
- User inquiries to a program or system: 4 points.
- File or database updates: 10 points.
- Interfaces to other programs or systems: 7 points.

Once you have added up all the function points of a program, you can start comparing function points per program in relation to how long it took to develop the program. You can also decipher how many function points are accomplished per week or month.

By applying these weights to specific programs under development, companies can track staff productivity as well as forecast how quickly they can develop programs.

In addition, by its very nature, this metric is independent of the language used and won't confuse documentation with actual code.

One company that has collected empirical data on the use of function points is Software Productivity Research Corp. in Cambridge, Mass. Based on national averages, the company defines a small system as having less than 100 function points; a medium system, 100 to 1,000; and a large system, more than 1,000 function points.

In addition, the average number of function points achieved per man-month for a small information system or commercial system is 12; medium is eight; large is four. The more complex the system, the fewer function points per man-month achieved.

Reprinted with permission from *Computerworld* (April 9, 1990), p. 63. Copyright 1990 by CW Publishing, Inc., Framingham, MA 01701.

The future success of the new system depends on how well it is accepted by user personnel. Any new system, especially one involving a computer, can be viewed as a threat to the security of the user personnel. Some resistance to change can be overcome if user personnel are meaningfully involved in the SDLC, and user involvement is possible for most phases of development.

A substantial training program may be required if the new system is significantly different from the old system. Often employees view training programs as a threat because they believe that evaluations made at the end of the program will be used against them. These people sometimes lack the self-confidence they need to return to school after many years of absence. The analyst must take these reservations into account when planning a training program. An orientation program should be prepared for all employees who will have contact with the system in any way.

Two potentially difficult personnel problems are the relocation of displaced personnel and adjustments to the organizational structure. If relocation is necessary, the personnel department should be involved in the process as soon as possible, since relocation may require a large adjustment on the part of the employee. Also, the employees should be kept fully informed of the changes so that rumors are reduced to a minimum.

Adjustments to the organizational structure also present human relations problems. Changes in supervisory positions or in relationships should be handled in a professional manner. New positions should be meaningful and not created simply to postpone the retirement of an older employee. Job enrichment and other personnel programs are appropriate in these circumstances.

The major physical changes involved in the conversion phase are site preparation and file conversion. Changes in hardware or work flow require changes in the physical location of the system or the personnel, or both. These must be well planned and coordinated. Inadequate site preparation will impair the performance of the system when it begins to operate.

Before conversion, files and data bases must be created for the system either through manual inputs (if the old system was manual) or through a combination of manual inputs and conversion of data from the old files. Conversion of files and databases is often time-consuming and costly, and it requires special programs. A critical point in this phase is the control of file conversion. File conversion programs must be thoroughly tested: new file listings must be manually reviewed for errors, and control totals must be balanced. Until file conversion has taken place, it is not possible to operate the new system.

The actual conversion of the complete system can be performed using four basic approaches: (1) parallel conversion, (2) direct conversion, (3) phased conversion, and (4) pilot conversion.

Parallel Conversion

Parallel conversion is illustrated in Figure 17–11. It is a widely used approach, consisting of operating both the old and new systems simultaneously until management is confident that the latter will perform satisfactorily. At that point, the old system is discontinued.

Parallel operation is often necessary, but it is very demanding on employees. They must operate two systems and then compare results. Because of this apparent problem, it might be viewed as desirable to minimize the time of parallel operation. However, the successful implementation of any new system requires sufficient testing to eliminate most major problems. In many situations, a parallel operation of several weeks or months is desirable.

Direct Conversion

When parallel conversion is not appropriate, the direct approach, illustrated in Figure 17–12, may be used. **Direct conversion** (sometimes referred to as cold turkey, or crash, conversion) consists of terminating the old system at the end of one workday and starting up the new system the next workday. This can be extremely risky, but it is gaining in popularity for the following reasons:

- With the parallel approach, demands of operating two systems may not allow enough resources to be allocated to the new system to

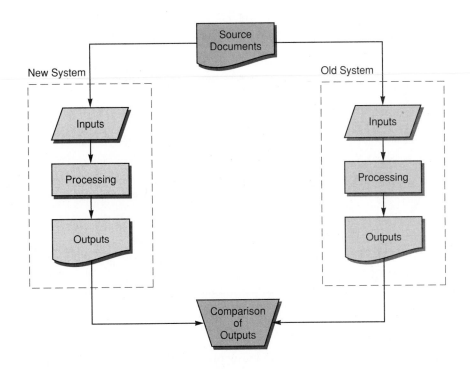

FIGURE 17–11
Parallel Conversion.

make it successful. Furthermore, employees may keep using the old, familiar system and not make a genuine effort to support and use the new system. The direct approach avoids both problems.

- With thorough testing of the system and training of personnel, the new system may operate at acceptable levels from its inception.

- In many cases, the risk of failure of the new system may be acceptable. For example, in most situations, reversion to the old system may be possible if failure occurs.

Phased Conversion

The third conversion approach is **phased conversion**, shown in Figure 17–13, in which the old system is gradually phased out and the new one is gradually phased in at the same time. This phase-in can be accomplished in a number of ways. For example, with a new accounts receivable system, all newly opened accounts can be processed by the new system while existing accounts continue to be processed by the old system. As accounts gradually turn over, the new system replaces the old. When the new system is operating satisfactorily, the accounts remaining on the old system are transferred to the new, and the old system is terminated. This approach has many of the same problems as the parallel approach, the primary one being the necessity of operating two systems simultaneously. In addition, two other significant drawbacks of phased conversion are as follows:

- The outputs of the two systems must be combined to gain a total picture.

FIGURE 17–12
Direct Conversion.

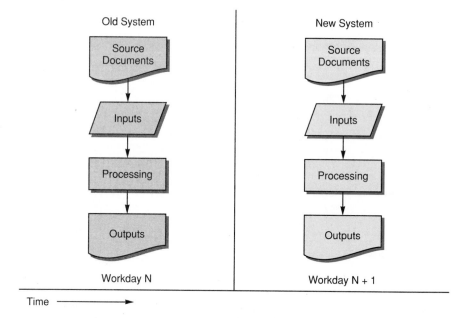

• A false sense of security may be created since backup by the old system does not exist for data being processed by the new system, except in the case of a total reversion to the old system.

Pilot Conversion

The pilot approach to conversion, shown in Figure 17–14, is often an excellent alternative. **Pilot conversion** consists of implementing the new system in only a selected portion of its ultimate implementation area (for example, in an organizational unit like a plant, branch, or division). If the system operates satisfactorily in the pilot implementation, it is then fully implemented. Within the pilot area, the system can be implemented by parallel, direct, or phased methods. The pilot method avoids many problems of the other three methods, but it does not test whether the system will operate satisfactorily under the increased volume of full implementation. Furthermore, in many cases it may not be possible to segregate an appropriate area for the pilot conversion.

After personnel and physical changes have been taken care of in the implementation stage, steps must be taken to phase out the old system. Although this may seem obvious, there are numerous examples of new systems being brought on-line without the old systems (especially manual systems) being terminated.

Postimplementation Audit and Maintenance

A frequently overlooked but necessary step in the systems development life cycle is the **postimplementation audit**. Two general areas are reviewed at this point. The performance of the new system is evaluated in terms of the objectives that were stated in the feasibility and analysis phases, and the systems development cycle is reviewed. The budgets and schedules that were developed in the feasibility and analysis phases can be used to evaluate the performance of the systems development team.

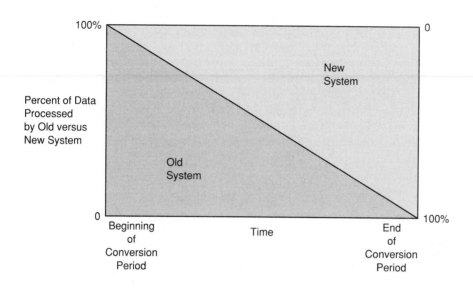

FIGURE 17–13
Phased Conversion.

For example, error rates and processing times can be compared with the rates in the design specifications of the system. User complaints can also be considered. Failure of the system to achieve the design specifications might mean that the expected benefits from the new system will never be realized. It also may mean that the system is not being operated according to the specifications.

Another aspect of evaluating the performance of the new system involves comparing the actual operating costs of the new system with the estimated costs. Significant deviations from the estimated costs lower the cost-benefit ratios of the new system.

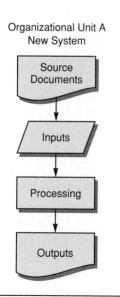

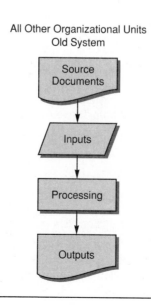

FIGURE 17–14
Pilot Conversion.

Who should conduct the audit? For small projects, the supervisor of the systems analyst is generally an appropriate choice. When a large project is reviewed, a team of systems personnel and managers who were not part of the project is appropriate. Internal auditors are frequently involved in the postimplementation audit of a large system. Sometimes outside people are brought in to conduct the audits. Their lack of personal connections, their broader experience, and their different view of the organization all contribute to a more objective review. Many companies also have periodic audits of systems in addition to the postimplementation audit.

The life span of an application system can be significantly extended through proper maintenance. Maintenance consists of promptly correcting any additional errors discovered in modules, updating the program modules to meet modified requirements, and maintaining the documentation to reflect system and module program changes.

Summary

- The documents produced during structured analysis are used extensively during systems design and implementation.

- A structure chart is a hierarchical diagram showing the relationship between various program modules. It is derived from data flow diagrams.

- Using the structure chart as a guideline, the systems designer designs the individual modules. The structured English statements written earlier may be used for documentation at this stage.

- The design is packaged and then modified to suit the hardware and software environment. In addition to the packaged design, a test plan is produced at this time.

- Structured walkthroughs are often used to review the packaged design as well as the program code.

- Coding and testing are done in a top-down manner. This means that the upper-level control modules are coded and tested before the detailed, lower-level modules are even written.

- Procedure manuals are generally written at the same time that coding and testing occur. These manuals form a critical part of the final system.

- Programming personnel are often organized into a chief programmer team. Many firms have found this to be an efficient structure.

- The conversion phase may involve many problems, such as user resistance, personnel relocation, and changes in the organizational structure. Careful planning is required at this stage.

- After the system has been converted, an audit is done to judge its performance against the original system objectives.

- Maintenance of a system consists of removing any additional program errors and changing the system to meet new information processing requirements.

Key Terms

Structured design	Structured walkthrough
Structure chart	Code inspection
Top-down design	Top-down coding
Go-to-less programming	Desk check
Spaghetti code	Program stubs
Module	Test data
Subroutine	Program bugs
Connection	Documentation
Couple	Chief programmer team
Central process	Parallel conversion
Transform	Direct conversion
Pseudocode	Phased conversion
Test plan	Pilot conversion
Packaged design	Postimplementation audit
Coding	

Review Questions

1. What is the difference between a structure chart and a data flow diagram?

2. Explain the following terms:

    a. Module

    b. Subroutine

    c. Connection

    d. Couple

    e. Coupling

    f. Cohesion

3. What makes a module cohesive?

4. How can you determine if a module is cohesive?

5. What is module coupling?

6. What is the relationship between coupling and cohesion?

7. Why are coupling and cohesion important to the user of information systems?

8. What are the outputs of the design packaging subphase?

9. Explain the concept of a structured walkthrough.

10. What is top-down coding?

11. How are program stubs used in testing?

12. What are test data? What qualities should they possess?

13. Why is documentation important to the users?

14. Describe the composition of a chief programmer team.

15. List the major problems that may be encountered during system conversion.

16. Discuss the four approaches to system conversion.

17. What is the significance of the postimplementation audit?

Discussion Questions and Cases

1. Omega Systems, a management consulting firm, is designing a new inventory control system for Nordener & Mufti, Inc., a distributor of petroleum products. The president of Nordener & Mufti feels that costs can be minimized by designing the new system so that it uses most of the existing hardware and software. The project manager at Omega does not agree. She believes that this would unduly restrict the design options and probably lead to the development of an inefficient system. Discuss the merits and demerits of both viewpoints and give your own opinion on the matter.

2. Despite the popularity of the top-down approach, some programmers are skeptical about its usefulness. One common complaint is that the top-level control modules cannot be coded unless the programmer knows exactly what takes place in the lower-level modules. Another problem is the difficulty of creating a simple hierarchy. Since some lower-level modules are called by more than one upper-level routine, the neat, inverted tree structure sometimes cannot exist. Maintenance is not as easy as the proponents of top-down design claim it to be. Most modifications made to a system were never anticipated at the time of original design. The top-down structure is therefore unable to accommodate these changes. Comment on the validity of these objections. If they are valid, does it mean we should abandon the top-down approach?

3. For each of the following cases, decide which of the four conversion methods you would use when switching to a new system. Justify each choice.
   a. An inventory reordering system at a fertilizer plant
   b. A military strategic surveillance system
   c. The book checkout system in your library

4. The systems development department for Gatt's Manufacturing Company has a policy whereby computer programs for new systems are written and tested by programmers. These programs are then put together into various subsystems. Once the subsystems have been written and tested, the whole system is integrated and tested by the user department. In the development of the last system, an integrated accounts payable/ purchasing system, a programmer did not properly code and test an error checking module that is used for month-end processing. At the end of the month, the program malfunctioned and brought the whole purchasing system to a halt. It took three weeks to correct the system because several programs had to be changed. A committee was formed to review the company's policies for designing and testing new systems. What design and testing strategy would have prevented this problem?

5. In the past year, the internal audit department of Flextix Corporation, a watch manufacturer, hired an EDP auditor. The auditor recently completed a review of the administrative accounting systems and a review of the systems development methodology that had been used to implement the systems. He noted that once the systems had been implemented, no postimplementation audit had been performed. He discussed his concern with the systems development director and the corporate controller. The director argued that the post-audit was a waste of time because he and the controller maintained close contact with all user problems. The director also said that it was the internal audit department's job to perform all auditing work in order to have an objective opinion on the status of a new system. The auditor argued that it was systems development's responsibility to perform the audit. Are postimplementation audits needed? If so, who should perform them?

6. Many of the Cobb Company's data processing systems were developed in the late 1970s, before widespread acceptance of the structured design and structured programming approaches. Although the systems are working properly at this time and they meet management's information needs, an increasing percentage of systems development's time is spent in maintaining existing programs. Currently, about 65 percent of the effort in systems development is concentrated on maintenance of these programs. In addition, in the past two years the internal audit department has hired two EDP auditors who specialize in auditing computer information systems. In performing their duties they must often review the code in these programs. They have found, however, that it is almost impossible to follow the logic of the code. Therefore, they have abandoned direct review of program code as an audit technique. Do you think that Cobb has a problem? If so, what is the nature and cause of the problem? What do you recommend to correct it?

7. Smith's is a regional department store chain located in the Middle Atlantic states. Smith's extends credit to all of its creditworthy customers and has a large number of outstanding accounts receivable. About 60 percent of Smith's sales are on credit. The company has had an on-line accounts receivable system for the past eight years. Recently, this accounts receivable system has been redesigned and recoded to use a database management system. In the design process, most of the input screens and output screens and much of the program logic were modified to better meet user and customer needs. The new system has been thoroughly tested and is now ready for conversion. The manager of systems development advocates using a direct conversion approach, but others in the organization prefer a pilot approach whereby two or three stores would be converted initially. The manager of systems development feels that direct conversion is the most appropriate for the following reasons: (1) the new system has been thoroughly tested, (2) employees can be trained in the use of the new system before conversion, and (3) employees are familiar with the use of an on-line accounts receivable system. Would you support either a direct or a pilot conversion, or some other method? Support your position.

Quality-Driven Software

By Raymond Falkner

Poor software quality is currently costing U.S. companies millions of dollars. This money is being spent on enormous amounts of rework to eliminate bugs and remedy requirement omissions in both existing and newly created systems.

Companies can stop this money drain, however, by establishing a quality culture. By first assessing the magnitude of the software quality problem and then targeting areas for improvement, firms can work to fight this waste.

Organizational-level measures are needed to get a big-picture perspective of how much a company is spending to provide quality software to users. One such method is called Software Cost of Quality (SCOQ).

The concept is simple: SCOQ is the total cost associated with controlling and providing software quality to users. Using a spreadsheet to measure costs in the following broad categories will provide a framework from which to begin the software quality effort:

- Prevention costs—the total of costs associated with preventing software defects, education and training, policies and procedures and product redesign before delivery. Each company will have its own unique set of subcategories. For example, a firm's education and training costs might include software-specific information systems management education, language training and so on.
- Appraisal costs—the sum of costs associated with measuring, inspecting, testing and auditing for software defects.
- Failure costs—the total of costs associated with correcting software system defects (for example, maintenance repairs), computer downtime and additional customer support.

Because some spending will always be required to produce and maintain quality software, the SCOQ will never be zero. Companies should target the SCOQ to be about 5% to 10% of the information technology budget.

Research on Japanese and U.S. companies has found that while the Japanese have an SCOQ of about 7% to 10% of the information technology budget, U.S. companies' numbers are 25% to 30%, with many insurance firms as high as 40%. That means tens of millions of dollars are being drained from some companies' bottom lines by poor software quality.

Besides indicating how much it is costing the company to provide quality software, the SCOQ lets IS [information systems] executives know if resources are concentrated on fixing software problems or preventing them. Unfortunately, studies have shown that most of the money is being spent primarily on correction rather than prevention. In fact, U.S. insurance companies' software quality costs typically break down this way: 7% to 8% are appraisal costs, 2% to 3% are prevention costs, and a whopping 30% are failure costs.

The numbers reflect the severity of the software quality problem, and as most IS managers have discovered, no single structured design or development methodology prevents quality problems from occurring. Not even a change in employee compensation programs has been proven to be sufficient to overcome poor quality. This is because producing quality software is an IS management problem.

Research conducted by W. Edwards Deming and other quality gurus found that only 15% of all manufacturing defects can be traced to individuals. In most cases, individuals are forced to execute poor processes that have product delivery, not quality, as their goal.

It is imperative that management shift the focus from getting things done fast to getting things done right. IS chiefs need to imbue their team with this quality ethic.

For IS managers, that means a three- to five-year software quality improvement plan that targets key management areas: measurements and reports, the software development process, IS organizational setup and software skills and technologies. The plan is a guide to follow during the shift to a quality culture and should result in a 50% reduction in a company's SCOQ.

Measurement and Reports

Software quality—defined as satisfying your customers in various software areas such as performance, reliability, serviceability, conformance and so on—can be measured. Systems-level quality measurements within the information technology organization are essential for real gains to be substantiated and monitored. Software quality measurement begins with a baseline that tells a company where it stands today so it can figure out where it wants to be tomorrow.

A key indicator of quality is customer satisfaction in terms of data accuracy, number of defects, error-free performance and the like. Customer satisfaction can be gauged via a customer satisfaction survey (see chart below).

Software defects are typically tracked by systems and reported in terms of systems reliability. Measures include pinpointing defects found within 90 days of delivery and mean time between failure. Productivity can be measured in terms of output, such as source lines of code or function points per effort month.

The results of these measures can be entered into a company database used for statistical analysis and quarterly reporting on trends. These figures can then be compared with internal objectives and the software quality improvement plan.

It is important that IS managers introduce a reporting process that clearly delineates the net causes and effects of software quality and productivity. Each report should be geared to its audience, with business managers knowing how overall software quality has changed and IS staff knowing how a specific system's quality has changed.

Metrics are not cure-alls, however, and they can actually work against quality if not focused properly. One company, for example, wanted to manage its maintenance budget better. It did so by keeping close tabs on programmers' lines of code and the ratio of maintenance and enhancement costs to production costs.

The result was code riddled with blank and extraneous lines (after all, programmers wanted to meet their quotas) and a maintenance nightmare. The two metrics intended to improve productivity and quality actually had the opposite effect because they took into account improvements only at the organizational level and not at the systems level.

If the company had instead measured output using function points and tracked maintenance productivity through the ratio of maintenance requests per full-time (or equivalent) worker, it would have achieved its desired results.

Development Process

A change in the software development process can further the creation of a quality culture. The existing software development process used by 95%

of all Fortune 1,000 companies consists of a structured process that dates back to the early 1970s. These processes are phase-driven and move sequentially from the requirements phase through design, construction, testing and implementation. Their advantage is project control; their disadvantage is a lack of customer satisfaction with software quality.

In the 1990s, the greatest change in software development (and quality) will occur as companies move from a software "product" orientation to a software "service" orientation.

Product-oriented software development works on the principle of unwavering requirements and the movement of software from one phase of development to another, obtaining all the appropriate sign-offs but with little user input.

Customers are involved only in requirements (within strict limits), and quality is judged by the correction of all previously identified defects as well as the ability of the development team to deliver the product as quickly as possible.

Service orientation has the customer as the driving force. Software development consists of multiple parallel activities, with requirements evolving from general to detailed. Customers are involved throughout the process and serve as the final determinants of whether the job is complete. Service-oriented software development has quality as its driving force.

Organizational Setup

Improving software quality will rely heavily on the people who construct software systems and not on machines. Computer-aided software engineering tools and automated aids help people in the process, but the correct organization and use of people determines the quality of the resulting product or service.

Companies have used a variety of organizational setups to determine and track software quality, but most have not worked. Quality assurance organizations, for instance, have had trouble in the past because they were deemed "inspectors" whose mission it was to uncover problems created by others.

Software maintenance staff members are often considered second-rate programmers or analysts charged with pacifying users and fixing problems created by developers. Developers are viewed as creative generalists who design, build, redesign, and rebuild to keep meeting floating requirements. This has led to poor quality, but enriching the work people do and not perpetuating stereotypes can turn this around.

A study conducted at a major communications company revealed that systems maintainers were surprisingly happier and more appreciated than any other information technology group in the company. Programmers, analysts and IS managers struggled to get themselves out of development and data centers and into maintenance. Why? Maintenance staffers didn't just work with code; they had close customer contact and were able to establish and manage schedules and satisfy their customers. They wanted to produce quality work and were allowed to do so. Interestingly, this company also spent less on maintenance and enhancements than the industry average, in spite of the poor quality of its development work.

Software Skills and Technologies

A quality culture relies on people who have the right quality orientation and the necessary skills and tools to create quality software. The trend toward new technologies has been slow to take hold in companies because of the retraining needed and resistance to change. However, new technologies must continue to be introduced to change the way systems are developed. New technologies allow active managers opportunity to enrich the IS "quality of work" environment and produce higher quality results.

The starting point has to lie in the retraining of managers, instilling in them a software quality ethic. Recognizing, communicating, rewarding and encouraging a quality ethic must be at the heart of every information technology organization. Most IS people want to produce quality work; managers must give them the means (skills and technology) and feedback (coaching) to do so.

Quality improvement requires a rethinking and revamping of human and technical processes. With millions of dollars—as well as the company's image as a quality provider of products or services—at stake, IS managers must personally lead

the charge. After all, isn't that what quality leadership is all about?

According to Quality Management Solutions, a software quality consulting firm in Acton, Mass., the most frequent causes of poor software quality are the following:

Incorrectly organized project teams.

Improper use of computer-aided software engineering methods and technologies.

Inadequately trained staff.

No tie between compensation and quality results.

Ineffective management measurement and reporting systems.

Outdated development processes.

Inappropriate levels of user involvement.

Destination: Quality

Starting on the road to a quality culture? Here are some stops along the way:

- Measure your Software Cost of Quality (SCOQ) to gauge what you've spent to produce and maintain quality software and whether you've spent it on prevention or correction. Remeasure every six to 12 months.
- Establish a baseline from which to work and improve.
- Institute a three- to five-year quality improvement plan that implements a systems-level measurement program, improves reports to management and IS staff, reorganizes project and departmental resources, introduces technologies to bolster IS skills and revamps development processes.
- Set a goal—typically a 50% reduction in the SCOQ.

Is your software satisfying users?

A key indicator of quality is customer satisfaction. The following is a prototype of a customer satisfaction survey.

User Satisfaction Survey

From the business user's perspective, please rate the following criteria in terms of satisfaction and importance. Use the following scale to answer each question...

Satisfaction	Importance
5-Completely satisfied	5-Extremely important
4-Very satisfied	4-Very important
3-Neither satisfied nor dissatisfied	3-Somewhat important
2-Mildly dissatisfied	2-Of minor importance
1-Strongly dissatisfied	1-Not important

	Satisfaction (answer 1-5)	Importance (answer 1-5)
1. Performance		
• Data accuracy	_____	_____
• Accessibility to current data	_____	_____
• Accessibility to historic data	_____	_____
• Timeliness of system response	_____	_____
• Completeness of system	_____	_____
2. Features		
• Flexibility for future modification	_____	_____
• Ability to query data by request	_____	_____
• Information summary capabilities	_____	_____
• Security capabilities	_____	_____
3. Reliability		
• Consistency of response time	_____	_____
• Extent to which system performs without error	_____	_____
• Minimal defects at delivery	_____	_____

System name _____ User name _____

Today's date _____ User title _____

Source: Quality Management Solutions

Discussion Questions

1. Are quality and getting things done fast incompatible goals? Why or why not?

2. What are the significant differences between a "product" and a "service" orientation to software development?

Falkner is founder and president of Quality Management Solutions, an Acton, Mass., consulting firm specializing in the quality of information technology software and services.

Reprinted with permission from *Computerworld* (April 29, 1991), p. 96. Copyright 1991 by CW Publishing, Inc., Framingham, MA 01701.

18

Application Development By End Users

Many information system experts believe that a large percentage of business applications can be developed by end users. User development is a major revolution in computer information systems, and it is already well under way. You should be prepared for it. How is this revolution being accomplished? What tactics and strategies are being used by those supporting this revolution?

Application development by end users means that the people who ultimately use application software, the **end users**, develop software without the assistance of programmers, and quite often without systems analysts. This approach is often called application development without programming.

There are three ways that end users can create or obtain application software without programming. One, end users can be given powerful but easy-to-use computer tools to create their own application software. These tools are often called *fourth-generation languages*. They are user-friendly computer software that enable end users to create application software in one-tenth the time required by typical third-generation languages such as BASIC, FORTRAN, and COBOL. Examples of fourth-generation languages are Lotus 1-2-3, dBASE IV, and FOCUS. Two, consultants or systems analysts can work directly with end users to generate application software through the use of fourth-generation languages that are too technical for users to employ without assistance. Three, preprogrammed application software packages can be purchased from outside vendors. (The purchase of application software is covered in Chapter 19.)

This chapter first examines some of the problems associated with the conventional application development approach. Next it discusses a variety of methods end users can employ to develop application software, and then it covers the blending of user development with conventional development. Finally, it examines the impact of user-developed software on the conventional information systems organization. In this area, it covers the concept of an information center and the changing roles of systems analysts and programmers.

While reading this chapter, keep in mind that application development by end users does not make obsolete the basic steps used in the systems development life cycle. Application development by end users only changes the degree to which those steps are performed and how they are performed, not whether they are done.

Problems With Conventional Application Development

Conventional application systems development is the process studied in the last two chapters. Figure 18–1 illustrates the conventional systems development life cycle using the structured approach. The disadvantages of using the conventional approach are discussed in the following sections.

Increasing Labor Cost

The conventional development cycle is a labor-intensive, time-consuming process. Creating data flow diagrams (for the old and new systems), drawing structure charts, and writing the programs are essentially manual processes, although recently CASE tools have been applied to assist in some of these tasks. The labor costs associated with systems analysis

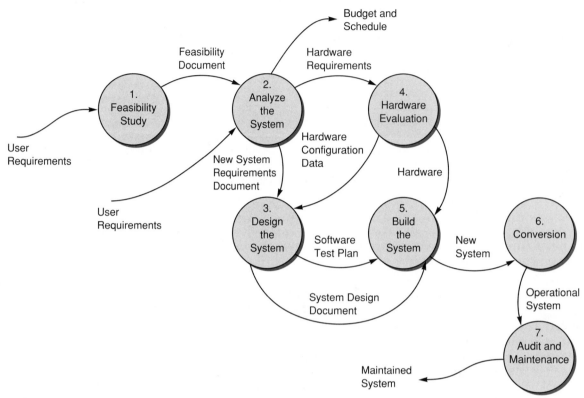

FIGURE 18–1
Structured Systems Development Life Cycle.

and programming continue to increase, while the price of computer hardware continues to decline. This relationship is shown in Figure 18–2. In the late 1970s, the cost of hardware was lower than the cost of labor for information systems organizations. This relationship between labor and hardware costs makes it economical to substitute hardware for labor.

With application development by end users, software is developed directly through the use of computers and fourth-generation languages, thereby eliminating most of the labor cost of programming and, to some extent, systems analysis. This approach may increase hardware costs because computers have to be used to execute fourth-generation languages. Also, these languages usually do not produce program code that executes as efficiently as program code written by programmers. However, these disadvantages are of little concern because of the dramatic decline in hardware costs. Application 18–1 illustrates how Alaska Air uses end-user computing to increase productivity.

Long Time Span Required for Application Development

A major disadvantage of the conventional approach is the often very long time span (months and sometimes years) required for the development of application software. Because of the dynamic nature of most businesses, the needs for the software (which were originally defined in the feasibility stage) may have changed substantially by the time the system is oper-

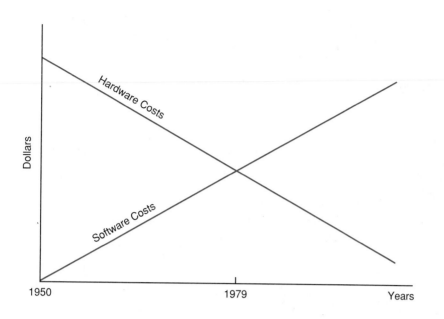

FIGURE 18–2
Software Costs versus
Hardware Costs.

As fourth-generation
languages become more
widely used, software
costs should begin to
decline.

ational. Therefore, the system is sometimes obsolete by the time it is implemented.

Slow Implementation of Changes

Closely related to the long time span for application development is the typically slow implementation of changes to the system. James Martin, a widely known information systems author and lecturer, has stated that the mere act of implementing a system changes the requirements for that system. In other words, after a system is implemented it will affect the user organization in unforeseen ways. Martin maintains that it is impossible to foresee all the effects of a new system on an organization's information needs. There will be requests for changes to the system immediately, as it is implemented, since the user cannot experience the

APPLICATION 18–1

Users Help Alaska Air Soar

by Julia King

Alaska Air Group, Inc. keeps information systems (IS) spending below 1 percent of the company's revenues by focusing on end-user computing. Employees in departments ranging from accounting to maintenance and flight operations are able to log onto the company's IBM mainframe com-

puter and access a wide variety of data. End users are also involved along with IS personnel in developing and customizing departmental software. All employees can access nearly all data directly, and 300 workers use Information Builders, Inc.'s FOCUS programming language. Many Alaska Air Group employees are given computer operations and applications

training. The company is moving its IS department away from data processing duties and more toward applications development and strategic projects.

Adapted with permission from *Computerworld* (Dec. 23, 1991), p. 16(1). Copyright 1991 by CW Publishing, Inc., Framingham, MA 01701.

new system until it is implemented. If systems are going to be successful, firms must be able to implement changes rapidly. This is often difficult to do with the conventional development cycle.

Work Overload

Maintenance of application software is a major concern. Most mature information systems organizations find that between 50 and 75 percent of their programming effort is in maintaining existing systems as opposed to programming new systems. If this trend continues, we may find situations in which almost all the programming effort within a firm is spent on maintaining existing systems!

Owing to the declining price of hardware, many new users have purchased computers. If these users depend on programmers to write the software for their computers, there will not be enough programmers to go around. In fact, for several years there has been an acute shortage of application programmers. If all of the new computer users are to get even minimal use of their hardware, we simply must find new ways of creating application software.

Prespecified versus User-Driven Computing

Martin has classified computing into two categories: prespecified and user-driven computing. In prespecified computing, most processing requirements are determined ahead of time. Therefore, formal requirement specifications can be created and the conventional development cycle can be used. In contrast, in **user-driven computing** users do not know in detail what they want until they use a version of it. They may modify the system frequently and quickly. Figure 18–3 summarizes the differences between prespecified and user-driven computing.

Today it is not entirely clear what percentage of business computing should be developed with the prespecified approach and what percentage with user-driven techniques. However, as users gain experience with the new tools that allow them to develop their own applications, user-driven techniques are certain to become the predominant approach. Martin states: "The requirements for management information systems cannot be specified beforehand and almost every attempt to do so has failed. The requirements change as soon as an executive starts to use his terminal. The point . . . is *not* that conventional application development . . . should be abandoned, but rather *it only works for certain types of systems.*"[1]

Methods for User Development of Application Software

Application development by end users became practical in the late 1970s and early 1980s owing to the availability of very powerful software. There are many of these fourth-generation tools. To be called fourth generation, a language should

- enable end users to develop software in one-tenth the time required by third-generation languages such as BASIC, COBOL, and FORTRAN

---

[1] James Martin, *Application Development without Programmers* (Englewood Cliffs, NJ: Prentice-Hall, 1982), 52.

FIGURE 18–3
Prespecified versus
User-Driven
Computing.
(James Martin,
Application Development
without Programmers,
© 1982, p. 55. Reprinted
by permission of
Prentice-Hall Inc.,
Englewood Cliffs, NJ.)

Prespecified Computing

- Formal requirement specifications are created.
- A development cycle such as that in Figure 18–1 is employed.
- Programs are formally documented.
- The application development time is many months or years.
- Maintenance is formal, slow, and expensive.

Examples: Compiler writing, airline reservations, air traffic control, and missile-guidance software development.

User-Driven Computing

- Users do not know in detail what they want until they use a version of it, and then they modify it quickly and often frequently. Consequently, formal requirement specification linked to slow application programming is doomed to failure.
- Users may create their own applications, but more often with an analyst who does this in cooperation with them. A separate programming department is not used.
- Applications are created with a fourth-generation language more quickly than the time to write specifications.
- The application development time is days or at most weeks.
- Maintenance is continuous. Incremental changes are made constantly to the applications by the users or the analyst who assists them.
- The system is self-documenting, or interactive documentation is created when the application is created.
- A centrally administered database facility is often employed. Data administration is generally needed to prevent chaos of incompatible data spreading.

Examples: Administrative procedures, shop floor control, information systems, decision support, and paperwork-avoidance systems.

- be user friendly, user seductive, and easy to learn and remember

- be appropriate for use by both end users and information systems professionals

This kind of software can be classified into the six categories illustrated in Figure 18–4. The following sections describe these categories (the last section covers both forms of application generators).

Personal Computer Tools

There are a wide variety of **personal computer tools** for end users. Electronic spreadsheets (Lotus 1-2-3 and Excel), database management systems (dBASE IV), and *integrated tools* (Framework, Enable, and Symphony) are all easily mastered by users (an integrated tool is a PC package that typically includes the functions of electronic spreadsheet, word processing, database management, and communications). The ideal first step for those who are new to computers is to learn one of these tools, preferably one of the integrated tools.

Query Languages and Report Generators

Query languages are usually associated with database management systems. They allow a user to search a database or file using simple or complex selection criteria. The results of the search can be displayed in detail or in summary format. For example, the query might state, "List all customer accounts that are thirty to sixty days overdue and have a balance in excess of a thousand dollars." This type of software is widely available today. Many of the packages also allow update of the database as well as data retrieval.

Report generators are similar to query languages except that they can perform more complex data processing tasks and can produce reports in almost any format. Generally, query languages are designed to be used without assistance from information systems professionals, whereas report generators sometimes require help from IS professionals, such as systems analysts.

Graphics Generators

Graphic output is becoming increasingly important to today's business management. **Graphics generators** allow users to retrieve data from files or databases and to display these data graphically. Users can specify the data they wish to graph and the basic format of the graph, such as pie, line, or bar.

Decision Support/Financial Modeling Tools

The most simple **decision support/financial modeling tools** are the two-dimensional electronic spreadsheets such as Lotus 1-2-3, which allow only rows and columns to be displayed. More capable decision support tools are available for large computers. Examples are System W DSS, Express, and Integrated Financial Planning System (IFPS). These tools allow the construction of complex business models that have more than two dimensions.

FIGURE 18–4
Categories and Examples of Development Tools.

Generally, the easier-to-use tools run on personal computers. But some of the mainframe application generators such as FOCUS and Nomad 2 are also very user friendly.

(Adapted with permission of *The James Martin Report on High-Productivity Languages*, published by Technology Insight, Inc., Marblehead, MA.)

1-2-3	Datatrieve	SAS Graph	CA-Stratagem	FOCUS	Application
dBASE IV	Easytrieve	Tell-A-Graf	Express	Fusion	Development
Excel	Inquire		IFPS	Ingres	Workbench
FOCUS	Intellect		SAS	Mapper System	DMS
Framework	Natural		SPSS-X	Natural	FOCUS
Harvard	Oracle		System W DSS	Nomad	Gener/OL
Graphics	QBE			Oracle	Line II
Quattro	QMF			SAS	Mantis
R:Base	RPG				Mitrol
SuperCalc	SQL/DS				Natural
Symphony					PacBase
					Rapid/3000
					Speedware
					Telon

Application Generators

Application generators can create an entire information systems application including input, input validation, file update, processing, and report generation. The user usually specifies what needs to be done and the application generator decides how it will be done. In other words, the application generator generates program code based on the user's requirements.

Many data processing operations are routine, and they tend to be performed in the same manner regardless of the application. For example, most applications communicate with terminals, update files, produce reports, and so on. These types of operations are preprogrammed in **generalized modules** included in the application generator. When these operations are required, the application generator retrieves the preprogrammed modules and modifies them slightly for the particular application's needs.

It is unlikely that everything a particular application requires can be generated by an application generator. Each application is likely to have certain unique requirements. Therefore, most application generators contain what are known as user exits. **User exits** allow a user or programmer to insert program code that takes care of these unique requirements of the application. User exit routines can be programmed in a variety of languages, such as BASIC, COBOL, and PL/1.

Most application generators are interactive. Sitting at a terminal, a user or a systems analyst responds to questions from the application generator. His or her responses define the application inputs, files, processes, and reports. The application generator uses these responses to generate code to execute the application. In a matter of hours, an experimental **prototype** of the application may be up and running. This allows the user to experiment with the new application and make modifications if necessary. Table 18–1 lists some application generators that are suitable primarily for information systems professionals.

Table 18–1 provides examples of the tools just discussed. The packages are classified into those suitable for end users and those that require professional help. A package is classified as suitable for end users if a typical end user can learn how it works in a two-day course and can return to using it after several weeks of not working with it. The package should be easy to start using so the user can gain confidence in his or her ability to use the package quickly. The user can learn more sophisticated applications after gaining more experience.

Category/Product	Vendor	Environment	Suitable for End User	Analyst
Personal Computer Tools				
dBASE IV	Ashton-Tate	IBM PC	x	x
Excel	Microsoft Corp.	IBM PC	x	x
Harvard Graphics	Software Publishing	IBM PC	x	x
1-2-3	Lotus Development	IBM PC	x	x
R:Base	Microrim	IBM PC	x	x
Paradox	Borland International	IBM PC	x	x
Query Languages and Report Generators				
Datatrieve	DEC	DEC	x	x
Easytrieve	Pansophic Systems	IBM, IBM PC	x	x
Intellect	AI Corp.	IBM, Honeywell	x	x
RPG-III	IBM	System 38, AS/400	x	x
QBE	IBM	IBM	x	x
QMF	IBM	IBM	x	x
SQL/DS	IBM	IBM	x	x

Table 18–1

Leading Fourth-Generation Language Products

Notice that some of the application generators run on IBM compatible personal computers. This allows users to employ the same language on both mainframes and PCs. When IBM PC is indicated, the software will run on all IBM PC compatible computers.

Category/Product	Vendor	Environment	Suitable for End User	Analyst
Graphics				
SAS/Graph	SAS Institute	IBM PC, DEC, DG, Prime, HP, Sun, Apollo	x	x
Tell-A-Graf	Issco	IBM, DEC	x	x
Decision Support and Financial Modeling				
Express	Management Decision Systems	IBM, Prime	x	x
System W	Comshare, Inc.	IBM, DEC	x	x
Application Generators Suitable for End Users				
FOCUS	Information Builders	IBM, IBM PC, Wang, HP, Tandem, DG, DEC	x	x
Nomad	MUST Software	IBM, IBM PC	x	x
Oracle	Oracle Corp.	IBM, IBM PC, DEC, DG, Harris, Unisys, HP, Honeywell, Prime, NCR, Wang, Macintosh, Next	x	x
SAS	SAS Institute	IBM, IBM PC, DEC, DG, Prime, HP, Sun, Apollo	x	x
Application Generators for IS Professionals				
DMS	IBM	IBM		
Application Development Workbench	Knowledgeware	IBM, IBM PC	*	x
Mantis	Cincom Systems	IBM, DEC, Wang, NCR, IBM PC	*	x
Mark V	Informatics General	IBM	*	x
Natural	Software AG	IBM, DEC	*	x

*Subset may be suitable for end users.

Adapted with permission of *The James Martin Report on High-Productivity Languages*, published by Technology Insight, Inc., Marblehead, MA.

Figure 18–5 shows how Nomad, an application generator, generates the report in Figure 18–6. Note that only a minimum amount of information must be included in the commands to produce a report. Nomad can easily produce much more complex reports than the one shown in Figure 18–6. Individuals experienced in writing programs in COBOL, BASIC, or FORTRAN are pleasantly surprised at how simple it is to produce meaningful reports with a language such as Nomad.

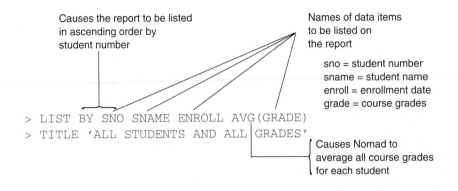

Causes the report to be listed in ascending order by student number

Names of data items to be listed on the report

sno = student number
sname = student name
enroll = enrollment date
grade = course grades

```
> LIST BY SNO SNAME ENROLL AVG(GRADE)
> TITLE 'ALL STUDENTS AND ALL GRADES'
```

Causes Nomad to average all course grades for each student

F I G U R E 18–5
A Nomad Report Request.

When a firm attempts application development by users, three types of development usually evolve:

Types of Application Development

1. The traditional development cycle, as illustrated in Figure 18–1. This is often used for applications whose requirements can be prespecified and are likely to remain stable over a reasonable period of time.

2. A fourth-generation language used as a prototyping tool. The systems analyst and the user quickly generate a **skeleton application program**, which serves as a model for the application. The end user interacts and experiments with this prototype and thereby refines the system's requirements. After the final requirements have been defined, the application is programmed in a conventional fashion. Quite often, parts of the prototype code can be used directly in the conventional programming process.

3. A fourth-generation language used to develop the entire application. Programmers are usually not used with this approach. The prototype itself becomes the application software.

Blending User Development With Conventional Development

PAGE 1

STUDENT NUMBER	STUDENT NAME	ENROLLMENT DATE	AVG GRADE
	ALL STUDENTS AND ALL GRADES		
76	PAUL BRAXTON	SEP 78	2.0
92	ANITA MACDONALD	SEP 78	3.5
167	BRAD WHITLOCK	SEP 79	2.3
198	ANN DISCALA	SEP 79	3.1
436	JOSEPH PANE	SEP 78	3.1
466	MARTHA LEVIN	SEP 79	3.3
468	GARY ZANDER	SEP 78	no grade

F I G U R E 18–6
The Report Produced by the Nomad Report Request in Figure 18–5.

The sequence of this report could be changed by simply saying "by sname" instead of "by sno" in Figure 18–5.

The second approach is more likely to be successful in applications that process very high volumes of data because of hardware efficiency considerations. The basic model of the application is developed by using an application generator, but the final application program is written in a traditional programming language to produce code that reduces processing time and storage space. However, in many business data processing applications the processing volume is not very high and the number of times the program is run is very low. For example, some programs are used only one time. Such applications are likely to use the third type of application development. Also, the third type of application development is more likely to be used whenever the application must be operational in a very short period of time and when the requirements are likely to change frequently.

Also note that the efficiency at which a particular program runs, that is, machine efficiency, is becoming less and less important because of the declining cost of hardware. Therefore, one of the primary reasons for using application development types 1 and 2 is declining in significance. Some would even argue that for most business information systems applications, machine efficiency is not a significant consideration. In the 1990s most business application development will be done using the third approach.

Table 18–2 illustrates the effects of these three types of application development on the various steps of the application development cycle. Note that when application development is done without professional programmers, the cycle is radically modified and compressed in time. The development process becomes a quick, informal, and interactive process. The user, directly or with the aid of a systems analyst, creates and modifies his or her own applications.

Database Administration

By now you may be thinking that application development by users results in isolated users creating their own redundant data files, which leads to chaos. How can firms have users from various departments create their own files containing redundant and uncoordinated data which cannot be accessed by other legitimate users? For example, data in a payroll system are often used by both the payroll department and the personnel department.

The solution to this potential problem is effective **database administration**. Databases are essential to the effective use of application development by users; thus the role of the database administrator becomes very important. He or she must ensure that the data contained in the database are sufficient to meet the needs of various users and that one or more users cannot modify the data in such a way as to destroy their usefulness to other people. Does this mean that each user is constrained in the ways that the data can be used because of the needs of other people in the firm? Certainly not. A user can extract portions of the database and set these data up in his or her own files. The data can then be modified and manipulated in any way that the user sees fit, without harming the data in the database.

	Type 1 Conventional Application Development	Type 2 Application Generator Used as a Prototyping Aid Followed by Programming	Type 3 Application Development without Professional Programmers
Requirements Analysis	A time-consuming formal operation, often delayed by long application backlog.	The user's imagination is stimulated. User may work at a screen with an analyst to develop requirements.	The user's imagination is stimulated. User may develop his/her own requirements, or work with an analyst.
System Specification Document	Lengthy document. Boring. Often inadequate.	Produced by prototyping aid. Precise and tested.	Disappears.
User Sign-off	User is often not sure what he/she is signing off on. User cannot perceive all subtleties.	User sees the results and many modify them many times before signing off.	No formal signoff. Adjustment and modification is an ongoing process.
Coding and Testing	Slow. Expensive. Often delayed because of backlog.	The prototype is converted to more efficient code. Relatively quick and error-free.	Quick. Inexpensive. Disappears to a large extent.
Documentation	Tedious. Time-consuming.	May be partly automated. Interactive training and HELP response may be created on-line.	Largely automatic. Interactive training and HELP responses are created on-line.
Maintenance	Slow. Expensive. Often late.	Often slow. Often expensive. Often late.	A continuing process with user and analyst making adjustments. Most of these adjustments can be made very quickly—in hours rather than months.

T A B L E   18–2
Effects of Types of Application Development on the Application Development Cycle.
(James Martin, *Application Development Without Programmers*, © 1982, pp. 66–67.
Reprinted by permission of Prentice-Hall, Inc., Englewood Cliffs, NJ.)

End-User Development and CASE

Many of the application generator tools used by programmers and analysts to assist users through rapid prototyping are the same as (or very similar to) the application generators used in computer-aided software engineering (CASE). The underlying concept of using computers to assist in the creation of software is the foundation of both CASE and application development by end users. CASE tools are changing the methods that analysts and programmers use to create software, and fourth-generation languages are allowing end users to develop software. These two methods of creating software are tending to merge, with end users creating the relatively simple software and programmers and analysts creating the larger, more complex systems. However, programmers and analysts work directly with users and create rapid prototypes of these complex systems so that users can provide immediate feedback on their reactions to the prototypes.

Some Cautions about Application Development by End Users

As with most new approaches to solving problems, application development by end users is not without its potential pitfalls. Users are often not aware of or do not follow important software development standards, such as adequate documentation, built-in controls and edits, and proper testing. For example, let's assume that Jennifer West developed a complex real estate investment spreadsheet application for her firm. She did not document the application because she knew in detail how it worked, since she developed it. Furthermore, she was the only one to use the spreadsheet. The spreadsheet required the input of twenty-three pieces of data, and she did not build in any edits to check whether each data item was within a reasonable range. Jennifer had no problem using the spreadsheet. However, a year after completing the spreadsheet she left the firm and her replacement, Emily Warren, had to spend many hours figuring out how to use the spreadsheet. Also, the spreadsheet was designed to use a loan amortization calculation of only fifteen or thirty years. When Emily entered a loan term of twenty-five years, the spreadsheet appeared to work properly, but in reality the information it produced was erroneous. The firm was led to invest in a large real estate venture in which they lost a substantial sum of money.

Another potential drawback of application development by end users is that it may not make sense for a highly paid professional or manager to spend a great deal of time developing software that a lesser-paid programmer or analyst could perhaps develop more economically. In essence, the professional or managerial user must decide whether to develop the software or delegate the software development to a computer professional, even though he or she will have to spend a great deal of time explaining the software requirements to the developer. Obviously, the answer to this question depends on the facts of each software development project. The decision is even more difficult if you, as a professional or managerial user, like to work with computers. In effect, you may ignore your job as accountant, manager or whatever as you spend a great deal of time developing software.

Firms that have successfully applied application development by end users are aware of these problems. They establish standards for end-user software development and they manage software development by end users with the goal of preventing these pitfalls. Application 18–2 outlines some of the concerns that others have about end-user programming.

Information Centers

If application development by end users is to succeed, it must be coordinated and managed. The purpose of an **information center** is to manage the support for application development by end users. Its primary objective is to encourage and accelerate the use of new software tools. The rea-

APPLICATION 18–2

IS Sounds Cautionary Note on End-User Programming

by Karen D. Moser

Although the industry has been calling for a revolution in end-user programming tools, the movement may turn out to be a minor uprising, many analysts say.

A battery of graphical, point-and-click programming tools—Borland International Inc.'s Object-Vision, Oracle Corp.'s OracleCard and Software Publishing Corp.'s Info Alliance—have recently debuted to rave reviews. These tools are tempting users with the promise of inventing their own software and courting information systems (IS) departments with the prospect of reducing the longstanding applications backlog.

Hype and strong initial customer demand for these products is expected to set off a wave of introductions, but many analysts predict the category will remain a niche market. "It is not going to boom the way these [companies] would like—it's not another spreadsheet market," said Nancy McSharry, manager of PC software research at International Data Corp., a market-research firm in San Jose, Calif. "I would be surprised if, combined, [the products] sold 150,000 units in 1990." The reality is that while many of the tools facilitate development, they are too difficult to use and require too much training to be popular among end users.

"There aren't any end-user tools, not really," said Steve Morse, information systems officer for Manufacturers Hanover Trust Co., a New York investment bank. Most end-user programming solutions take a radically different approach from the way users typically think about solving business problems, demanding a completely new skill set for users, he said.

At many companies, these tools are finding a home—not with end users, but with programmers.

"We use some of the tools available, but they are used by programmers," said Bill Hartz, a New York consultant to a major Wall Street investment bank. The tools can provide a head start on application design, but a programmer typically must use C to do further customization or to hammer out problems that crop up with printer or network drivers, Hartz explained.

IS professionals and programmers are also hesitant to encourage end users to dabble in applications development out of a concern for efficiency and security.

"IS shops are not doing a big job of supporting end-user tools," said Brian Proffitt, a development tools strategist for IBM in Boca Raton, Fla. "They are intimidated by it because more people are trying to use these tools, and [IS] is afraid of what kind of disaster will crop up." Common problems include end users losing data from a corporate database or corrupting data, Proffitt said.

While most developers would be happy to channel their energies to visionary projects rather than programming drudgery, they are skeptical about how much work the new tools will actually let them offload.

"I wouldn't care to know how to push a button to generate a reservation, and [users] shouldn't care how to create an application," said Rock Blanco, vice president of information systems for Garber Travel Service Inc., a Boston-based travel agency.

One compelling benefit of end-user programming tools, Blanco said, is to let end users make a prototype of the application interface, reducing programmers' work load and alleviating the high fees associated with programming services.

Proponents of end-user programming such as Sheldon Laube, chief information officer for Price Waterhouse, a New York accounting, auditing and management-consulting services firm, argue that it is a natural evolution from the macro language that is now a key component of spreadsheets.

To ensure that users can successfully embrace this type of product, however, a number of critical training and support factors have to be in place.

For example, Price Waterhouse requires that end users participate in 40 hours of continuing education a year. Currently, the company offers corporate training classes in Lotus Development Corp.'s Notes work-group package, and Laube plans to launch classes in both Asymetrix Corp.'s ToolBook and Borland's ObjectVision.

To meet the needs of end users after they've completed initial training, Price Waterhouse also maintains a specially trained technical support staff. Once these mechanisms are ready to handle end-user programming, Laube plans to distribute programming tools to approximately 1,000 employees.

sons that application development by end users should be managed are as follows:

- To encourage the rapid adoption of application development by end users

- To assist end users in their development efforts

- To prevent redundancy in application creation

- To ensure that the data used in the various applications are coordinated and not redundant

- To ensure that data are not simply created and stored in isolated personal files

- To ensure that the systems created are controlled and can be audited

Figure 18–7 illustrates a typical organization for an information systems department that has an information center. The **technical specialists** at the information center are experts on the various software tools and can assist in training end users to utilize the tools. In a smaller organization, the information center usually relies on technical specialists from the software vendor. For example, if a firm is using FOCUS and a technical problem occurs, the company gets in touch with a specialist at Information Builders, the FOCUS vendor. The **end user consultants** work directly with users in creating applications. Since application development by users is often done on PCs, the end-user consultants must have expertise in PCs as well as mainframes and minis.

The user consultants also work closely with the database administrator. They do so to ensure that data used in both conventionally developed applications and user-generated applications are coordinated and not redundant. Figure 18–8 lists the functions typically performed by an information center.

FIGURE 18–7
Organization of an Information System Department That Has an Information Center.
Information centers began to be implemented in the early 1980s.

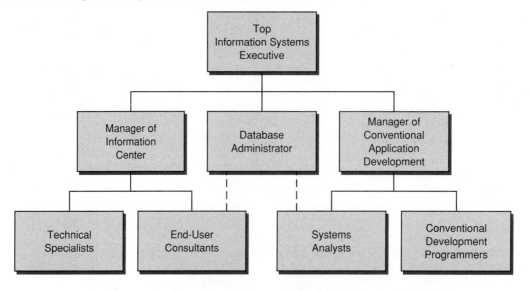

The advent of software that enables application development by end users causes the roles of systems analysts and programmers to change. If fourth-generation software is to be used effectively, systems analysts must recognize that there are many ways to create a new application. In the requirements analysis or feasibility study phase, the systems analyst must realize that there are many tools, any one of which may be appropriate for solving the end user's problem. The tools for obtaining new applications are as follows:

Changing Roles of Systems Analysts and Programmers

- Systems analysts using a conventional systems development cycle

- End users purchasing an application software package

- End users generating their own applications without outside help

- End users working with systems analysts or information center consultants to generate the application

- Systems analysts and end users generating a prototype, experimenting with the prototype, and then coding the application in a conventional manner

---

By the End-User Consultants:
- Training the end users to employ the tools and create applications
- End user encouragement, education, and selling
- Generation of applications (without programmers) in conjunction with end users
- Generation and modification of prototypes
- Specification of changes to prototypes that may be needed to make them into working systems
- Consulting on end user problems
- Determining whether a proposed application is suitable for Information Center development, and selecting the software and methods
- Demonstrations of Information Center capabilities to users, including senior management
- General communication with senior management
- Communication with conventional application development
- Linking to the data administrator(s) in defining and representing data
- Maintaining a catalog of available applications and databases
- Coordination to prevent duplicate or redundant application development

By the Technical Specialists:
- System set-up and support
- Dealing with technical and software problems
- Selection of languages and software and the versions of those which are used
- Assistance in choosing techniques or software for a given application (the job of the Techniques Analyst)
- Communication with vendors
- Monitoring system usage and planning future resources
- Charge-back to users
- Tuning or reorganizing an application for better machine performance
- Auditing system usage and application quality

FIGURE 18–8
Functions of an Information Center.
(James Martin, *Application Development without Programmers*, © 1982, p. 306. Reprinted with permission of Prentice-Hall Inc., Englewood Cliffs, NJ.)

Many systems analysts trained in conventional application development find it difficult to change their roles. Perhaps the best way for a systems analyst to encourage the use of these new software tools is to

- Search constantly for more effective and efficient ways of creating applications

- Avoid the use of programmers whenever possible

- Take on a consultant role and encourage end users to employ the software themselves, rather than do it for them

Those of you who have planned a career in programming may be quite disturbed by the material covered in this chapter. It would be easy to imply that the demand for programmers would decrease drastically and perhaps even disappear as application development by end users continues to increase, which it most certainly will do. However, there will continue to be a large demand for programmers, for the following reasons:

- The explosion in the use of computers has created a large demand for application software developed both through conventional programming and through end user development.

- There will continue to be a significant proportion of all applications that are prespecified and are therefore well suited to the conventional development cycle.

- Systems software such as operating systems and database management systems, as well as application software created for sale by vendors, are likely to continue to be developed using conventional programming because of hardware efficiency considerations. There is a large demand for programmers in this area. In fact, the most highly skilled programmers work for software vendors.

Summary

- The conventional process of developing applications has several disadvantages:

- The high cost of programming expertise makes it very expensive

- The time span for program development is usually very long

- Program maintenance absorbs much programmer time, to the detriment of new system development

- Computing can be classified into two categories: prespecified and user-driven.

- User-driven systems can be created through the use of five techniques:

    - Personal computer tools

    - Query languages and report generators

    - Graphics generators

    - Decision support/financial modeling tools

    - Application generators

- When application development by end users is employed, three types of application development usually evolve:

- Conventional application development cycle

- Prototyping with a fourth-generation language and subsequent coding with a conventional language

- Total systems development with a fourth-generation language

- Database administration is needed when end users develop their own applications. It ensures that data redundancy is minimized and that shared data resources are properly used by all.

- Many of the tools used in application development by end users are the same as those used in computer-aided software engineering.

- If application development by end users is not well managed, software may be redundant, poorly documented, and not properly tested.

- The application development efforts of end users can be coordinated by an information center. This center assists end users in developing their own applications.

- With more and more end users creating their own applications, the roles of systems analysts and programmers are changing.

Key Terms

Application development by end users

Application generators

Generalized modules

End users

User exits

Prespecified computing

Prototype

User-driven computing

Skeleton application program

Personal computer tools

Query languages

Database administration

Report generators

Information center

Graphics generators

Technical specialists

Decision support/financial modeling tools

End user consultants

Review Questions

1. What is application development by end users?

2. Which is more important for an IS organization, labor costs or equipment costs?

3. How does the time span of conventional application development affect a system's utility?

4. Discuss the work overload on programmers and its implications.

5. Distinguish between prespecified and user-driven computing.

6. What is a query language?

7. Describe the basic purpose of a report generator package.

8. Why are graphics packages becoming important for business people?

9. Explain the concept of an application generator.

10. What is the difference between a third-generation language and a fourth-generation language?

11. How does a report generator differ from an application generator?

12. Briefly describe three basic types of application development.

13. Discuss the role of the DBA in a user-driven information systems environment.

14. Why is it important to have an information center to manage application development by users?

15. Discuss the changing roles of programmers and systems analysts.

16. What are some of the possible pitfalls of application development by end users?

Discussion Questions and Cases

1. Many large computer installations prescribe standard languages, like COBOL or C for all programs to be executed on their equipment. This practice results in consistency, but it can lead to certain problems. Based on the material discussed in this chapter, what problems would arise in this kind of environment?

2. Which of the six user development methods would you use for each of the following applications? Explain the reasons for your choices.
   a. Sales forecast by territory
   b. Manufacturing process control
   c. Customer billing and accounts receivable
   d. Mailing list
   e. Course registration at a university
   f. Portfolio management

3. Frances Shields, the systems development manager of the Carmel Corporation, has been inundated with requests to develop applications. In reviewing the file of unfulfilled requests, Frances began to wonder how many more requests for systems development services users might have that have not been made known to her. Frances has been reading about this invisible, or shadow, backlog of requests, and she does not know what to do. As much as Frances would like to maintain control over systems development, she knows that she will one day have to let users begin developing some applications. What are some alternatives that Frances should consider in allowing users to create their own computer application systems?

4. About two years ago, the JDF Corporation established an information center. Since then, the company has strongly supported application development by end users. Consequently, many users are actively engaged in developing their own applications, both for personal computers and for the mainframe. Recently, the internal audit department performed an audit of JDF's users application development approach. The audit report contains some disturbing findings. The auditors found numerous instances of the same data being stored several different times,

both on the mainframe and on personal computers. In addition, they found that essentially the same application software had been created several times. For example, the home appliances division and the home electronics division had both created marketing analysis systems using a mainframe program generator. Although these two systems are not identical, they are very similar. Based on their findings, the auditors have recommended that the corporation reassess its commitment to application development by users. Do you agree with the auditors that their findings are a serious problem? What recommendations do you have for the JDF Corporation?

5. Thomas Wesley is vice president of information systems for a major U.S. corporation. He came to the company when it installed its first computer system twenty years ago. Thomas has never been convinced that application development by end users is a reliable way to produce computer applications. He would prefer that all computer applications be produced by programmers in his department. What advantages does application development by end users have that might change Thomas' mind? What arguments would Thomas use to refute those advantages?

INFORMATION SYSTEMS STRATEGIES

MIS, End Users Begin to Merge, but Differences Persist

By Leslie Goff

There are still profound differences between end users and MIS [management information systems] departments even though they may be more closely aligned than ever in their purchasing plans, as well as in their satisfaction with system service, support and performance.

Even though MIS has begun to demonstrate a better understanding of workers' needs and business processes when designing end-user systems, it does not consider a common user interface or ease-of-use high priorities, while end users, on the other hand, rank these as top needs.

At the same time, while end users have become more concerned with multivendor connectivity and networks, their approach to computing still tends to be tactical, or "How can I solve this immediate problem now?" MIS has a broader, long-term strategic view of its company's information resources.

The two groups continue to come closer together, however, an illustration that the "battle between MIS and the users is probably as much rhetoric as reality. MIS and users are not often in disagreement over their most important needs or technology priorities," according to a study of MIS executives and departmental managers at 840 companies by The Sierra Group Inc., Tempe, Ariz.

"The prevailing wisdom was that the two groups hated each other," said Marty Gruhn, vice president of The Sierra Group. In reality, she added, their relationship is based on a dichotomy: "Users still believe in mother and apple pie, and MIS has been around the block already."

This dichotomy can explain most of the differences between users and MIS, including the ease-of-use issue. The study found that, based on overall needs, both groups consider ease of use a priority, but users ranked it number one by a significant margin. Similarly, a common user interface, including windowing and graphical capabilities, is far more important to users than to MIS, even though both groups have included it on their long-term agendas.

"It comes from heritage," Gruhn said. "How many years have you been around computers, and how easily can you adapt to different interfaces? Users just don't want to have to learn how to use 10 different packages. MIS is much more technically competent. They can go from one interface to another and just accept that that's the way it is."

By the same token, users are more concerned with industry standards for multivendor connectivity than is MIS. For example, Open Systems Interconnection (OSI) standards rated a 4.7 in importance from users, but only a 3.8 from MIS, which considers proprietary vendor issues, such as IBM Corp.'s SNA (Systems Network Architecture) and SAA (Systems Application Architecture) more important.

"Again, MIS is more technically competent," Gruhn said. "They can take three cans and string them together and rig something up. Users see standards as the delivery vehicle."

The tactical and strategic differences between the two groups are most apparent in terms of their connectivity plans. Both groups have exhibited strong demand for file servers, but users, who are installing local area networks mainly to achieve PC-to-PC connectivity, are more biased toward file server solutions. The study found that 78 percent of users plan to increase their budgets for purchasing file servers, compared with only 63 percent of MIS organizations.

MIS is concentrating on what the Sierra Group called "second-generation networking," or interconnecting PCs into logical workgroups via minicomputers and LAN servers. Although MIS demand for PC-oriented connectivity solutions is high, the study said, MIS shows a stronger growth rate for mainframes and networks.

"This underscores the salient strategies of these two audiences," the report said. "Most MIS organizations are moving toward a two-tiered computing model that ties existing PCs to the mainframe via networks. Conversely, departments are intent on maintaining their autonomy by purchasing more discrete desktop products and lashing them together through networks into workgroup solutions." Further, the study said, users "have yet to discover the implications of forthcoming enterprise architectures."

Gruhn said this state of affairs is likely to change, and that both groups will continue to exert increasing influence on the other. Users will become more enterprise-oriented as a result of two inevitable events.

First, she said, a user will put in a system and for one of many reasons it will crash, driving home the fact that computing is more than just feeding in data and seeing what pops out, and prompting the realization that "computing is where you're going, not where you are."

Second, as MIS achieves interconnection between departments and workgroups, users will begin to see the benefits of sharing and accessing common information. They will begin to understand that things like SAA are strategically important for them to get what they want, Gruhn said.

MIS organizations, likewise, will over time champion more user causes, such as the common interface and ease-of-use issues, Gruhn said. "Given enough push for long enough, users can influence MIS's perception of the world."

Discussion Questions

1. What are the root causes of the differences between users and IS departments?

2. What steps would you propose that management take to increase the cooperation between users and IS departments?

Satisfaction with Existing Systems: Users Vs. MIS

		Service	Support	Performance
Mainframes	Users	8.1	6.5	7.4
	MIS	8.1	6.9	7.8
Minicomputers	Users	7.7	6.6	7.3
	MIS	8.0	6.6	7.5
PCs	Users	8.0	7.3	8.2
	MIS	7.8	7.0	7.7
LANs	Users	8.3	8.0	8.0
	MIS	7.6	7.1	7.4
File servers	Users	8.3	7.8	8.3
	MIS	7.2	7.2	7.4

Source: The Sierra Group Inc.

Reprinted with permission of Fairchild Publications from *MIS Week* (August 7, 1989), p. 25.

19

Computer System Evaluation and Acquisition

Introduction

The Boston Insurance Company is a medium-sized property and casualty insurance company. All of its policy and claims processing is performed on large mainframe computers. The computer information systems it uses are the latest, state-of-the-art on-line systems. The company is heavily dependent on these systems, both for transaction processing and for management information. Yet it does not own a single computer! Neither does it employ systems analysts or programmers! How could this be?

Today, companies and individuals have access to many types of computer systems, and they can choose to purchase those systems or acquire access to them in other ways. Users have become increasingly involved with the evaluation and acquisition of computer hardware and software. Often managers serve on user committees that are responsible for selecting a computer system. Even when the information systems function is not a routine responsibility of the manager, he or she often becomes involved with selecting a computer system because of the computer's impact on his or her department.

This chapter first discusses how various computer systems are evaluated, including the very important area of evaluating purchased software. Next it covers methods for evaluating the costs versus the benefits of a computer system. Then it examines the methods for financing computer systems. Finally, it explores the various sources for information systems equipment and services. It should be noted that the techniques covered in this chapter are useful in evaluating and acquiring any size computer system from mainframe to personal computer.

Conducting An Evaluation of a Computer System

Approaches to acquiring computer hardware and software have changed over the years. Available hardware and software was much more limited in the past. Purchasing a particular manufacturer's hardware usually locked the buyer into that company's software and utility programs since they were sold as a package. This practice was known as **bundling.** Hardware components of different manufacturers were usually incompatible. **Plug-compatible** hardware units (units produced by other manufacturers that directly replace hardware units produced by major manufacturers such as IBM) did not exist. Therefore, the process of acquiring a computer was very informal. Decisions were based on a review of the manufacturer's specifications, what competitors were doing, other computer users' recommendations, or the desire to buy from a favorite manufacturer. Today, sophisticated computer users employ a more structured approach. The range of systems and costs within the computer industry is simply too broad for an unstructured evaluation to be successful.

As illustrated in Figure 19–1, the evaluation process has five primary steps:

1. Feasibility study
2. Systems analysis
3. Development of a request for proposal
4. Proposal evaluation
5. Vendor Selection

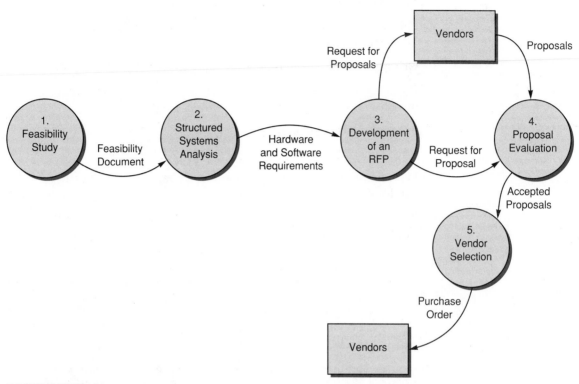

FIGURE 19–1
Steps in Evaluation and Purchase of Computer Hardware and Software.
Determining your hardware and software requirements through structured systems analysis is an important step. Many firms have purchased inappropriate hardware and software because they did not first determine their requirements.

Although the evaluation steps are discussed sequentially, the actual process can be highly iterative, and the steps can overlap. Steps 1 and 2 were discussed in Chapter 16; therefore, this section begins with step 3, which is the first task to be completed when purchasing hardware or software.

Development of a Request for Proposal

The **request for proposal (RFP) document** puts the requirements for the equipment and software in a form that vendors of hardware and software can respond to. It serves as a communication tool between the potential buyer and the vendor. It is sent to each vendor that is asked to propose hardware and software for the system. Among the areas it should cover are the following:

- A description of present and proposed applications, including for each application its processing mode (batch or interactive), input/output volumes, data flow diagrams, file descriptions (including size), database characteristics, and how often the application will be run

- Reliability requirements

- Backup requirements

- Vendor service requirements

- Outline of any specific hardware or software features required, such as printer speed or disk capacity

- Criteria for evaluating proposals

- Plans for a vendor demonstration of hardware and software to the buyer

- Implementation schedule

- Price constraints

- List of any specific questions about the characteristics of the vendor's hardware and software

- Procedures for clarifying the RFP and submitting the proposal, including the person to contact for RFP clarification and the scheduled date for submitting the proposal.

The RFP is sent to each prospective vendor, along with an invitation to bid. The buyer should expect a notification from each vendor as to whether it will bid or not.

Proposal Evaluation

The fourth step in the evaluation and purchase of a computer system is to evaluate the vendors' proposals. This evaluation involves viewing hardware and software demonstrations, determining the performance characteristics of the systems using various evaluation techniques, and examining other criteria in proposed systems.

Hardware and Software Demonstration   In the first phase of proposal evaluation, vendors demonstrate their proposed systems to the potential users. Usually only a few vendors are invited to demonstrate. They generally present the major features of their proposals orally. The complete system may be demonstrated at the buyer's location, if the system is easily portable. If not, the buyer may visit the vendor's facility for the demonstration. The vendors' presentations enable several of the buyer's employees to gain an understanding of the features of the various proposals. However, most buyers use more substantial techniques to evaluate these proposals than merely listening to oral presentations, watching demonstrations, and reading proposals.

Evaluation Techniques   Performance evaluation of computer hardware and software is a major tool used in the selection of new equipment. For each proposal, the buyer would like to know the performance characteristics (job run–time, throughput, idle time, response time, and so on) when executing current and planned applications, but obtaining such information is impossible. Planned applications have not been developed, and current applications may not execute on the various equipment involved without program modification. However, techniques are available to assist the buyer in obtaining approximate performance data. Performance evaluation techniques fall into two categories. Traditional techniques provide gross measures of a system's performance characteristics. Current techniques provide the buyer with much more reliable and extensive measures of a system's performance.

Tradition Techniques   The traditional techniques of performance evaluation compare performance characteristics such as number of bits processed in each operation by the CPU, primary and secondary memory access time, millions of instructions per second (MIPS) executed by the CPU, the clock speed of the CPU, and an average time for a mix of instructions. All are gross measures of computer performance, with only limited usefulness—and then only when the various computers have similar internal organizations. These techniques ignore the effects of software on system performance.

Another traditional technique is the **kernel program**, which is a small sample program executed on each proposed computer. In some cases the kernel program is not actually executed, but the run–time is derived on the basis of instruction execution time. This approach may be helpful in standard mathematical applications, but it is not very useful for business systems since software and input/output effects are ignored.

Current Techniques   Several more reliable techniques are benchmark programs, work load models, simulation, and monitors. **Benchmark programs** are sample programs or test jobs that represent at least a part of the buyer's primary computer work load. They include software considerations and can be current application programs or new programs that have been designed to represent planned processing needs. The buyer can design these programs to test any characteristic of the system. For example, the benchmark might test the time required to recalculate a spreadsheet or the average response time for inquiries from terminals when the system is also executing a **compute–bound** batch job. (A compute–bound job requires large amounts of CPU time and relatively little input and output.) Terminal inquiries during the test can be handled manually, or a tape or disk unit can be set up to simulate them. Figure 19–2 illustrates benchmark tests that can be used to evaluate a database management system.

Work load models are computer programs that accurately represent the buyer's planned computer work load. The model programs require the same mix of demand for computer resources that the buyer's application programs will require. For example, if the buyer's total work load is expected to contain 15 percent high–CPU–demand work, 10 percent compilation, 30 percent terminal input/output, and 45 percent batch input/output, the work load model programs should contain the same mix. Work load models differ from benchmark programs in that the latter usually do not accurately represent the buyer's complete planned work load.

Simulation techniques have been used extensively to evaluate complex alternative systems when it is not possible to analytically determine which alternative is preferable. For example, a computer simulation can be used to determine which aircraft would be the best purchase for an airline, given its present fleet, its expected route structures, and its passenger demand. Simulation is equally applicable to the evaluation of alternative computer systems.

F I G U R E 19–2
Benchmark Tests for a
Database Management
System.

Tests like these can
produce valuable data on
which to judge various
software.

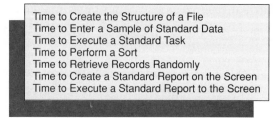

Time to Create the Structure of a File
Time to Enter a Sample of Standard Data
Time to Execute a Standard Task
Time to Perform a Sort
Time to Retrieve Records Randomly
Time to Create a Standard Report on the Screen
Time to Execute a Standard Report to the Screen

Simulation packages can simulate almost any computer system. Input to these packages includes descriptions of expected work loads, files, input/output volumes, and the vendor's equipment. The simulation program then simulates the running of the user's described work load on the described equipment. Simulating the equipment of different vendors is accomplished by changing the equipment description input. Validity of the simulation greatly depends on how accurately the simulation models the equipment and the buyer's anticipated work load. Since a valid simulation can be difficult to achieve and perhaps more difficult to recognize by people inexperienced in simulation, it should be used only by sophisticated computer buyers.

Monitors are hardware or software devices that monitor the operation of a computer and provide operating statistics such as idle time of the CPU and average job execution time. Software monitors are programs that periodically interrupt processing to collect operating statistics. They are part of the operating system and therefore have access to all operating system data. Hardware monitors are devices attached to the hardware component being monitored. They collect data on whatever characteristic is being measured.

Monitors are used primarily in the evaluation and **fine tuning** of existing computer systems, rather than in the selection of new systems. Employed as a fine-tuning tool, they can indicate where bottlenecks occur within the system. For example, the CPU may not be fully utilized while jobs are waiting in queue, because input/output channels are operating at capacity.

For most firms, a combination of benchmarking and work load models is the best technique for evaluating performance. Often vendors already have the results of several benchmark runs, which the buyer can use. The extent to which benchmarking and work load models are used depends on the size of the computer being purchased. Personal computers are often purchased without the buyer using either technique. Benchmark tests for personal computer hardware and software are regularly published in such journals as *PC Magazine* and *PC Week*.

Other Evaluation Criteria   The final phase of evaluating proposals is to examine the specific equipment, software, and general criteria of each proposed system.

Equipment Criteria   Many technical criteria should be considered in selecting computer equipment. Some examples are as follows:

• Time the CPU takes to execute a mix of instructions

• Primary memory size and its read/write speed

- Storage device characteristics

- Disk drives (including disk access time, data transfer rate, capacity, and whether removable or fixed)

- Tape drives (including capacity, transfer rate, and recording density) .

- Video display

- Time to write to the screen with scrolling

- Time to write to the screen without scrolling

Software Criteria   In software, the primary areas of concern are operating systems, compilers, and application programs. Operating systems have a major impact on the efficiency of computer processing. Some of the features that should be evaluated are as follows:

- Multitasking capabilities

- Job management features

- Availability of a graphical user interface, like the Macintosh interface

- Availability of utility programs

- CPU time and primary storage space overhead required by the operating system

- Quality of the operating system's documentation

In terms of the program compiler, the user should determine whether the major compiler to be used is available and if it is well supported by the vendor. In mainframe business information systems, COBOL is the primary compiler, but many fourth–generation languages such as FOCUS are now being used. On minicomputers and microcomputers, the primary languages are Report Program Generator (RPG), BASIC, and C, although there is a trend toward the same languages being used on all sizes of computers.

The main concerns with application programs are the availability, capabilities, and reliability of necessary application programs. Users may want to purchase application software and make minor modifications to adapt the programs to their particular needs. In such a case, the extent of the documentation and the ability of the programs to be modified are considerations. The reliability and capabilities of application software can usually be best determined by consulting current users. The evaluation of purchased software is covered in more detail later in this chapter.

General Criteria   General criteria to be evaluated when selecting computer systems include vendor support, compatibility, and modularity. Vendor support is crucial to the success of a computer system in a variety of areas, including the following:

- Personnel training

- Repair and maintenance

- Installation
- Preinstallation testing
- Hardware backup arrangements

Vendor support is generally adequate among large, established computer vendors. However, there are many new firms in the minicomputer and PC industry, and in some cases their support is minimal. In addition, even with large computer vendors, repair and maintenance services may be slow and expensive for users located in rural or remote areas.

Compatibility can be divided into two parts: hardware and software compatibility. Users should know how compatible a potential vendor's hardware is with the hardware of other vendors. Compatibility enables a buyer to consider other vendors for certain components of the system. For example, since many companies sell remote terminals and PCs, the buyer could realize substantial savings by purchasing them from small computer vendors. In addition, some computer manufacturers specialize in less expensive, plug–compatible units that replace the major components (the CPU, for example) of the large vendors' systems. However, the use of mixed systems (plug–compatible units) can increase management problems because it is difficult to assign responsibility for hardware failures when a system contains units from two or more vendors.

The primary concern about software compatibility is whether the user's existing software will execute on the proposed system. In addition, the user should determine whether the new software is compatible with other computer systems, both from other vendors and from the proposed vendor. If the compatibility of proposed new software is limited, this can be a major restriction to a buyer who later wants to change systems. Vendors often offer families of computers (such as the IBM 4381, 3090, and 9000 series). Transition from one member to another of these families is very easy since peripheral equipment and operating systems are compatible throughout the line.

A final general criterion that a user should evaluate is **modularity**. The modularity of a computer system is its ability to add capacity or components to the system. It allows for growth without changing systems. For example, additional main memory or disk units can be added when processing requirements dictate such expansion. The capability is crucial if the user's information processing requirements are expected to increase.

Evaluation of Purchased Software   System software is almost always purchased from a vendor or supplied as a package along with the hardware. There is also a trend toward purchasing application software instead of developing it in-house. (Application 19–1 illustrates this trend.) This section discusses the evaluation of purchased software. In-house development was covered in Chapters 16, 17, and 18.

Purchasing application software packages has several advantages:

- Software development is labor intensive. Therefore, it is becoming increasingly expensive. Costs per user can be cut by spreading development and maintenance costs over many users.

APPLICATION 19–1

Store-bought vs. Home-Cooked

By Sheryl Kay

In analyzing the buy vs. build question, information systems executives agree that certain unique business applications will necessitate creating software in-house regardless of time or monetary considerations. Commercial packages, however, increasingly are finding a place in corporations as IS [information systems] professionals seek measures to cut costs while maintaining a high level of service to users.

Commercial packages are particularly good for generic types of applications. . . . For example, horizontal business applications, such as accounting, payroll and human resources, are easily and efficiently addressed with packages. . . .

When figuring the economics of developing an accounts-receivable system in-house for one of its 12 divisions, Equifax, Inc. in Atlanta calculated that it could outfit the entire company with a packaged system for the price of writing software for just two divisions. According to Mary Delashmit, director of product systems support, a system from Management Science America, Inc. would run $1.2 million, as opposed to internal development costs of $560,000 per division.

Delashmit sees other advantages as well: "We are provided with support, training and user groups, all of which we'd have to coordinate on our own had we developed in-house."

As a Rule

Some companies adopt the policy of purchasing software whenever possible. At North Carolina Baptist Hospital/Bowman Gray School of Medicine, in Winston-Salem, N.C., such a policy has been in place since June 1989, when Ernst & Young put together a strategic IS plan for the hospital.

According to Bob Peddycord, director of systems programming, a survey conducted by Ernst & Young found that the hospital's users had a good feeling for packages. In fact, four of the hospital's major systems, including patient billing and accounting, had been purchased from the outside.

"Given the magnitude of the patient accounting system, had we replaced it with something developed in-house, it would have taken us several years rather than the one [year] it will take us," Peddycord explains. Even in terms of personnel expenses, he adds, in-house development costs would have far exceeded the cost to install purchased software, "so it's time and money saved." . . .

Some pitfalls lay on the buying path. Although vendor–provided maintenance and upgrades may be viewed as positives in purchasing software, they can also be construed as negatives. Since both functions are at the discretion of the vendor, if a user company changes its operating procedures the canned software may no longer be suitable if the vendor cannot provide for those new needs.

Of course, a user may not be able to find a suitable commercial product in the first place. The narrower the scope of a business or an application, the less likely a company will be able to identify an outside offering that fits its needs. In-house development, then, is far from extinct.

Still a Need for In-House Work

"No one knows a company or its operations as well as the requester or the data processing services provider," observes Chuck Newton, president of Newton-Evans Research Co. in Ellicott City, Md. This is why, Newton concludes, companies will continue to develop in-house systems at a total cost of nearly $11 billion in 1990.

Newton reminds IS executives that in-house development may mean a longer lead time before the system is in full production—if ever. In-house projects, he says, fall prey to endless tweaking by IS employees, who just don't seem to want to let go. "You can go anywhere in the country where development is done by MIS, and you'll always hear, 'Yes, the system is 90% completed, but we'd still like to do this and this,'"Newton says.

Advances in technology will help to improve that process. For instance, developing systems using computer-aided software engineering (CASE) saves time and money and, in many instances, produces a superior end result. CASE, however, will also benefit commercial development efforts, driving down costs that could be reflected in lower package prices. "It will be interesting to see who adopts this approach most emphatically, first—the vendors or corporate MIS,"says North Carolina Baptist Hospital's Peddycord.

Bill McNee at Gartner Group concurs. In addition to CASE tools, the advent of relational database technology, SQL and open systems simplify applications development in-house. "In the mainframe world, proprietary is dead," McNee says. He predicts an accelerated trend toward buying "applications shells"— packages that will sit on top of these open environments and allow the corporation to customize the system according to its own specific needs.

Kay is a Tampa, Fla.-based free-lance writer specializing in emerging technologies and human resources.

Reprinted from *Computerworld* (February 26, 1990), pp. 67,70. Copyright 1990 by CW Publishing, Inc., Framingham, MA 01701.

- Purchased software is often better documented than software developed in-house.

- Purchased packages are often very flexible. They can be adapted to fit specific user needs without modifying programs.

- Applications can be implemented faster since the long lead time involved in software development is eliminated.

- The risk of large cost and time overruns of in-house development is reduced.

    Among the disadvantages of purchased software are the following:

- Purchased software is not likely to meet the needs of the user as closely as software developed in-house.

- Certain uncontrollable risks are assumed when software is purchased. For example, the vendor may go out of business, or may fail to maintain and update the software.

- With purchased software the expertise in the application program is outside the user company, whereas with in-house development, that expertise is also in-house.

    There are many sources for application software. To find out what packages are on the market, the buyer should consult **software directories** such as those published by International Computer Programs, Ziff-Davis Publishing, or Datapro.

    The overall approach to evaluating software packages is very similar to evaluating hardware. The primary factors are as follows:

- Does the package meet the user's needs or can it be modified at a reasonable cost?

- What are the initial and yearly costs of the package?

- How efficient is the package? How much of each computer resource (run-time, primary storage, and secondary storage) does the package require?

- Will additional hardware be required?

- What are the operating system requirements of the package?

- How satisfied with the package are other similar users?

- Is the package well documented?

- Can data be easily entered, manipulated, and corrected?

- Are there easy-to-use query facilities for displaying the data contained in the system's files?

- Are thorough backup facilities and procedures provided?

- Are screens and menus easy to access and use?

- What on-line help is available?

- What level of computer expertise is required from the user?

- Are there user groups for the software?

- Does the vendor provide the user's employees with extensive training for using the package?

- Is local support offered, and is a hotline available?

- Is the vendor viable? What is the vendor's financial status? How long has it been in business?

- Does the package appear to be viable over the long run? Can it accommodate changes in hardware and operating systems as well as changes in the user company's needs?

- Are the performance claims of the vendor specifically guaranteed by the terms of the contract?

- Does the vendor provide a free trial period? Is this period sufficiently long, given normal implementation time spans?

- Does the package provide adequate data editing, audit trail, and other control features?

Vendor Selection

In most cases, more than one computer system or software package can meet a user's needs. A widely used method for ranking competing systems is to assign points based on the degree to which each system meets important criteria, and then to total the points to obtain a ranking (see Figure 19–3).

System Characteristics	Maximum Points	Points Assigned System			
		A	B	C	D
Hardware					
Memory size	20	10	15	20	10
Disk access time	10	10	8	5	10
Disk capacity	20	20	5	15	10
Modularity	30	30	20	25	15
Compatibility	30	30	10	15	20
Software					
Operating system	30	20	15	25	30
Ease of use	60	35	30	35	50
Application programs	40	30	40	20	25
Compatibility	30	30	30	25	25
Vendor support	40	20	30	35	40
Cost	50	30	40	40	50
Benchmarking results	50	50	40	45	30
Total	410	315	283	305	315

FIGURE 19–3
Outline of a Point Ranking System.
The maximum points are assigned, based on the relative importance that the buyer feels each system characteristic should have. Usually a team of two to four people independently rank each system being considered.

With this method, the difference among vendors on one or two factors can override the total score based on the ranking. For example, vendor support could be so poor that it precludes the purchase of an otherwise outstanding system. Communicating with the vendors about the point ranking system can be an effective tool for helping them respond more effectively to the RFP.

Another widely used method to select hardware and software is the **checklist**. The checklist specifies all the important characteristics of the required computer system. Figure 19–4 illustrates a checklist for acquiring a personal computer system.

Cost–Benefit Analysis

The cost–benefit analysis of a proposed computer system is not a trivial task. This is particularly true when a company is considering its first computer installation, since no internal data exist on which projected costs and benefits can be based. Historically, many companies have tended to overestimate benefits and underestimate costs of computer installations. This tendency has been fostered by computer salespeople, who quite naturally tend to emphasize benefits and deemphasize costs. It is easy for company management to become euphoric about push-button answers to information problems, especially when competitors or business associates have installed computers. To avoid this tendency, a realistic cost-benefit analysis should be completed regardless of the difficulty involved. Potential costs and benefits can at least be identified even if they cannot be estimated with a high degree of accuracy.

Costs are usually separated into two categories—nonrecurring and recurring. **Nonrecurring costs** are initial costs not expected to arise again after installation of the system. Examples include hardware and installation costs. **Recurring costs**, on the other hand, are expected to occur continually throughout the life of the installation. Examples include operator salaries, forms, data entry, and the like. The terms costs and benefits refer here to cash flows, not to an accrual concept. A capital budgeting model, which discounts cost-benefit cash flows back to their present values, should be used to compare costs to benefits.

Nonrecurring Costs

Perhaps one of the most difficult aspects of estimating the costs of a computer system is identifying all potential costs. To aid the process, nonrecurring costs can be classified in five categories. First is the cost of computer hardware. This is classified as a nonrecurring cost if the hardware is purchased, but if the hardware is rented or leased, the cost is recurring. Due to decreasing costs of hardware, many companies are now purchasing it. Aside from the cost of the basic computer configuration, there are costs of installing communication lines and equipment, office equipment for the computer staff, and so on.

The second area of nonrecurring costs is software costs. Systems software, the operating system, compilers, and the like, are usually purchased. Application software can be purchased or developed in-house. Often, software costs are also recurring due to annual lease payments required by the software vendor or periodic additions of application programs. Software costs are likely to be the largest nonrecurring costs, regardless of whether software is purchased or developed in-house. The costs of in-house software development are easy to underestimate. For this reason, most companies prefer to purchase most, if not all, of their software.

A third category of nonrecurring costs includes personnel and organizational costs. New personnel may have to be hired and trained, and al-

FIGURE 19–4

Checklist for Acquiring a Personal-Computer System

Checklists are very valuable to those interested in acquiring a personal computer or any other computer or software. With so many variables involved in the decision, a checklist is a practical way of assuring that all important factors are considered.

When considering the computer needs of your organization, begin by determining what applications are required. Based on the requirements of the software you choose, you can then make hardware decisions.

The following checklist is intended to aid you in selecting these PC components. First, it provides you with a list of features and capabilities to consider when selecting software. It then goes on to address hardware requirements, including vendor-related considerations.

Software

1. What problem(s) are you trying to solve?

   _____
   _____
   _____
   _____
   _____
   _____

2. What types of application software do you need?
   _____ Electronic spreadsheet
   _____ Word processing
   _____ Budgeting
   _____ Project planning
   _____ Project management
   _____ Graphics
   _____ Database management
   _____ Query languages
   _____ Electronic mail
   _____ Scheduling
   _____ Statistical
   _____ Inventory
   _____ Communications
   _____ Access to subscribed-to databases
   _____ Industry-specific packages
   _____ Custom software
   _____ Other _____

3a. Is integrated software, allowing the transfer of data between packages, needed?
   _____ Yes
   _____ No

3b. If yes, which packages need to be integrated? Check all that apply.
   _____ Spreadsheet
   _____ Word processing
   _____ Subscribed-to databases
   _____ Data downloaded from mainframe
   _____ Other

4. Are error-checking capabilities for uploading and downloading data needed?
   _____ Yes
   _____ No

5. What level of sophistication is the user? The package? (1=High; 3=Low)

	User	Package
Package A	_____	_____
Package B	_____	_____
Package C	_____	_____

6. Is hard copy documentation necessary?
   _____ Yes
   _____ No

7. Is on line help required?
   _____ Yes
   _____ No

8. What is the development history of the software (i.e., have there been several releases, indicating product evolution)?

   _____
   _____

9a. Is it important that the software be compatible with your existing microcomputer software or with other software of interest?
   _____ Yes
   _____ No
   _____ Doesn't matter

9b. Who will supply the interface programs that may be needed?
   _____ Vendor
   _____ Corporate staff
   _____ Individual user

10. What types of communication support do you need?
   _____ PC to PC
   _____ Asynch
   _____ Bisynch
   _____ SDLC
   _____ Local area network
   _____ PC to dedicated word processor
   _____ None
   _____ Don't know

11a. Is the software installed and guaranteed?
   _____ Yes
   _____ No

11b. Is it supported through a "hot line"?
   _____ Yes
   _____ No

12a. Is education available?
   _____ Yes
   _____ No

12b. Is it provided by the vendor?
   _____ Yes
   _____ No

13. What operating system does the software require?
   _____ OS/2
   _____ MS-DOS
   _____ PC-DOS
   _____ Windows
   _____ Unix (Xenix, etx.)
   _____ UCSD p-System
   _____ Vendor specific
   _____ Other _____

continued

14. What are the hardware requirements of the software?

Memory _____ K

Microprocessor:

_____ Z80/8080/8085
          8086/80286/80386/80486/
          80586
_____ 6502/6509
_____ 68000/68030/68040/68050
_____ Vendor Specific
_____ Don't know

Diskettes:

_____ 3½
_____ 5¼

Number of disk drives:

_____ One
_____ Two

Hard disks:

_____ Yes
_____ If "Yes," what capacity?

_____

_____ No

Printer:

_____ Dot matrix
_____ Letter quality
_____ Laser
_____ Graphics ink jet

Video Display:

_____ Alphanumeric
_____ CGA
_____ EGA
_____ VGA

Hardware

1. Do you need to be able to expand the memory on your system?

_____ Yes
_____ No

2. Do you need to be able to add peripherals?

_____ Yes
_____ No

3. Do you need a color display?

_____ Yes
_____ No

4a. Do you need graphics capability?

_____ Yes
_____ No

4b. If yes, do you need color graphics?

_____ Yes, immediately
_____ Yes, later
_____ No

5a. Do you need modems?

_____ Yes
_____ No

5b. If yes, what kind?

_____ Direct connection
Speed _____ bps
_____ Acoustic coupler

5c. Will you need intelligent auto-dial capabilities?

_____ Yes
_____ No

6. Will the vendor install the hardware you purchase?

_____ Yes
_____ No

7. Is the hardware maintenance available through the vendor?

_____ Yes
_____ No

8. How long will it take for the system to be delivered?

_____ One to three weeks
_____ Three to six weeks
_____ Over six weeks

Vendor

1. Are you buying hardware from:

_____ A local supplier
_____ A mail-order supplier
_____ Direct sales force

2. How long has the hardware vendor been in the computer business?

_____ Less than one year
_____ One to five years
_____ Five to ten years
_____ More than ten years

3. Is the vendor financially stable?

	Software Vendor	Hardware Vendor	Single Source Vendor
Yes	_____	_____	_____
No	_____	_____	_____

4. Is this a new venture for the hardware vendor?

_____ Yes, first venture in microcomputers
_____ No, part of extensive product line

5. How many hardware service locations are available?

_____ 1
_____ 2 to 10
_____ 11 to 50
_____ 51 to 100
_____ Over 100

6. Is the hardware vendor:

_____ Local
_____ Nationwide

7. How many microcomputer systems has the vendor installed?

_____ None; this is first
_____ Less than 100
_____ 100 to 500
_____ 501 to 1,000
_____ 1,001 to 10,000
_____ More than 10,000

8. Does the vendor supply and support a full line of peripherals?

_____ Yes
_____ No

9. How long will it take to get service?

	Software	Hardware
Less than 24 hours	_____	_____
24 to 48 hours	_____	_____
More than 48 hours	_____	_____

10. How many hours of free consultation time does the vendor provide? _____

11. Does the vendor have a toll-free technical hot line? _____

most certainly there will be costs associated with relocating personnel. The cost most often overlooked in this area is the temporary decline in organizational efficiency. Change is often not readily accepted, and morale and efficiency may decline during the implementation period. Considerable resources are often spent to minimize the disruptive effects of the change to new computer-based systems.

A fourth category of nonrecurring costs includes all aspects of preparing the site for computer equipment and personnel. These are space, air conditioning, power requirements, fixtures, fire protection, backup sites, and so on.

Conversion costs are the fifth category of nonrecurring costs. They include such things as the creation of new data files and the cost of parallel operations. Normally, extensive overtime costs are incurred during the conversion phase because it is necessary to operate the old and new systems simultaneously and to resolve problems in the new system. In addition, temporary personnel may be necessary to handle the increased work load.

Recurring Costs

Recurring costs include such things as hardware rental payments, maintenance, personnel costs, insurance, electricity, and space occupancy costs. Maintenance is often included in the hardware rental payment but can usually be identified separately. The option of performing one's own maintenance or buying vendor maintenance is always available when equipment is purchased.

Personnel costs are the largest portion of recurring costs. In addition to computer operator personnel, a system and programming staff is usually necessary to maintain and update software. The latter positions usually are those of systems analysts, systems programmers, and application programmers. Personnel costs also include salaries of information systems supervisory and management personnel, data input and control personnel, and any additional user staff necessary under the new system.

Conversion to a computer-based system tends to concentrate a firm's information resources. Destruction of all or part of the information systems operation can represent a substantial—even fatal—loss to a company. Therefore, insurance, including business interruption insurance, is a necessary recurring information systems cost.

Finally, space occupancy costs should not be ignored even if the space is owned. Normally, an opportunity cost is associated with the space, since alternative uses for it may be available.

Benefits

Benefits of a proposed computer installation are usually more difficult to estimate than costs. Some benefits, such as elimination of the cost of certain operations, are tangible and therefore relatively easy to estimate. However, others are highly intangible, such as the increased customer goodwill resulting from prompt shipment of orders.

Many companies install computer-based systems even though cost projections exceed benefit projections. These companies are willing to invest the excess costs. They want to enhance their expertise with computers to gain a competitive advantage, and as a result this benefit of a computer installation is very difficult to quantify.

A major benefit often cited for computer installation is the resultant savings in clerical costs. However, these savings usually occur slowly over a period of time, and the increase in computer-related staff usually offsets the savings in clerical costs. It is usually difficult, if not impossible, to justify a computer installation solely on the basis of such savings.

An important benefit, and one of the most difficult benefits to quantify, is the increase in the timeliness and reliability of management information that a computer system produces. The system can often provide information that simply was not available at an acceptable cost using a manual system.

Computer-based systems can reduce working capital requirements for a given level of sales through better accounts receivable and inventory control. Better monitoring of accounts receivable and faster billing can accelerate cash flows and reduce bad debts. One area in which computers have been applied most successfully is inventory control. Sales forecasting and just-in-time inventory techniques can significantly reduce inventory levels.

Computers can substantially increase labor productivity. An example in this area is computer-based labor and job scheduling. Many manufacturing firms now use computers for their day-to-day scheduling of both machines and labor.

For most companies, customer service improves when a computer-based system is installed. Orders can be processed more quickly, customer inquiries can be handled more expeditiously, and customer records, such as accounts receivable, tend to be more accurate.

An often overlooked benefit of computer systems is that they allow for expansion. Growth of a business often overwhelms a manual system, whereas most computer systems have sufficient processing and storage slack to permit substantial expansion. Furthermore, additional processing and storage hardware can normally be added at a reasonable cost. However, this is not always the case. The capacity of a computer system to expand is a critical variable that should be evaluated during the selection process.

Making Estimates

In all cases, cost and benefit quantities are estimates. Since these are future costs and benefits, they cannot be measured directly. Some estimates are highly reliable; others may be off the mark considerably. At least three techniques are used for coping with the inexactness of computer system cost-benefit analysis.

One technique is to quantify only the costs and benefits that can be quantified reliably. Those difficult to quantify are simply identified as potential costs or benefits that cannot be quantified.

A second technique is to attempt to quantify almost all costs and benefits and develop three estimates for each one—a most likely, a pessimistic, and an optimistic estimate. This technique at least suggests the potential divergence of actual from estimated costs and benefits.

The final technique, the expected value approach, is in theory the preferred approach for dealing with estimate variability. With this technique, one develops a probability distribution for each cost-benefit estimate. This distribution is an estimate of the probability that costs and benefits will actually attain a certain magnitude. Based on these distributions, one can derive the expected value of costs and benefits as well as the estimated probability that benefits less costs will attain a certain magnitude.

Users may choose from three financing alternatives for acquiring computer systems: purchase, rental, and lease. Usually all of these are available from manufacturers or their representatives, and rental and lease arrangements can also be made through a third party. Many companies rent or lease computer hardware and software.

Financing Alternatives

Purchase

The primary advantage of purchasing equipment is the potential cost savings if the equipment is kept for its useful life, normally three to six years. Furthermore, the purchaser can take the investment tax credit and depreciate the asset for tax purposes. The rental or lease payment is also tax deductible.

Although purchasing equipment generally results in lower overall costs, the buyer assumes the **risk of obsolescence**, and does not have the **flexibility** of canceling the arrangement. Furthermore, purchasing requires capital that may be better utilized elsewhere.

Another consideration when acquiring computer equipment is maintenance. If the equipment is rented, the manufacturer usually provides maintenance services. If the equipment is purchased, the company has several maintenance alternatives:

- Purchase a maintenance agreement that provides for all maintenance, parts, and labor.

- Pay for maintenance on a per-call basis, as required.

- Have the company's own employees maintain the equipment.

Most personal and mini-computer hardware is purchased. Mainframes are often rented or leased.

Rental

Under the rental option, the company rents the equipment on a monthly basis directly from the manufacturer or a third party. Most agreements have a minimum rental period, such as ninety days. After the minimum period, the user can cancel the agreement with short notice—one to two months. This flexibility is perhaps the major advantage of renting. However, the value of this flexibility is often overestimated since the user may have a large investment in training, preparation, and implementation.

Rental agreements generally provide for 176 hours of use of the equipment per month (8 hours per day x 22 average work days per month = 176 hours). Using the equipment for more than eight hours a day may require an additional rental payment, although at a reduced rate.

Renting is the most costly approach in terms of overall cash flow. However, the user does not need the large capital outlay required in purchasing equipment. In addition, the risk of obsolescence and the responsibility for maintenance are borne by the manufacturer. In some cases, renting the equipment may produce a greater continuing contact with, and support from, the manufacturer than purchasing it will.

Leasing

Leasing is a compromise between purchasing and renting. Typically, leasing costs less than renting but more than purchasing. Most risks of obsolescence can be transferred to the lessor through an option to purchase the equipment at the end of the lease. Moreover, leasing is not as flexible as renting because the lessee is locked in until the lease expires—typically after five years. However, sometimes the lease can be terminated early through the payment of a termination charge.

Lessors are often third-party, independent leasing companies. The lease agreement may provide a maintenance contract and does not usually charge for operation beyond 176 hours per month. Leasing offers substantial cost savings over renting for the user who is willing to forego the additional flexibility that renting offers.

The ultimate choice of financing involves a trade-off between risks of obsolescence, flexibility, and costs. These trade-offs are illustrated in Figures 19–5 and 19–6. The flexibility variable has become less important because computer systems themselves are now designed to be much more flexible. They can be upgraded through additional primary storage, secondary storage, or attached CPUs.

Sources Of Information Systems Equipment And Services

Information systems equipment and services are widely available. The computer industry is intensely competitive, and this has been a major factor in the rapid technological advancement of the industry. Suppliers are innovative and they continually look for unfilled customer needs.

FIGURE 19–5
Costs versus Risk of Obsolescence Trade-Offs of Financing Alternatives.

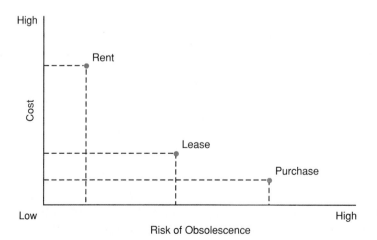

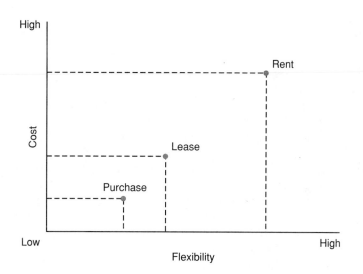

FIGURE 19–6
Costs versus
Flexibility Trade-Offs
of Financing
Alternatives.

This competitive atmosphere can result in substantial cost savings for the buyer. This section discusses the major equipment and service options available.

Computer Manufacturers

Many manufacturers produce complete lines of computer systems, including mainframes, minis, and personal computers. IBM dominates this market with more than a third of the information processing sales. IBM was late to enter the computer market. When it introduced its IBM 650 computer in the mid-1950s, Sperry-Univac was already established. However, IBM quickly became dominant, and successfully defended its market share against strong competitors such as RCA, General Electric, and Xerox, all of which have dropped out of the mainframe business.

Other producers of large computers include Unisys, Amdahl, Cray Research, Honeywell, Hewlett-Packard (HP), AT&T, Digital Equipment Corporation (DEC), and Control Data Corporation (CDC). These manufacturers tend to specialize, often in areas that IBM historically has not covered well. Cray Research specializes in very large supercomputers that usually have scientific, military, or space applications. Control Data Corporation also specializes in scientific computers. Hewlett-Packard, DEC, and Honeywell tend to specialize in engineering and scientific applications.

Personal computers are now used extensively in both large and small businesses. IBM also dominates this market with the IBM PS/2 series. There are, however, a host of other PC manufacturers including Apple, Compaq, Radio Shack, and almost all the mainframe and minicomputer manufacturers. There are also a very large number of mail-order PC manufacturers. Some of the most widely known are Dell Computer Corp., Northgate Computer Systems, and Gateway 2000. Medium-sized and large companies usually purchase personal computers directly from the manufacturer. Small firms buy them from mail-order and local retail computer stores and local offices of computer manufacturers.

Software Vendors

In the early 1970s, court decisions required hardware manufacturers to sell their hardware without also requiring the customer to purchase the manufacturer's software. This unbundling produced a new market for companies that do not manufacture computers but do produce computer software. Since hardware and software no longer come as one package, the user is free to purchase software separately.

In addition, the advent of personal computers have spawned a large number of software vendors for these machines. Purchasing software from software vendors often affords significant price and performance advantages. The complete range of software, including application programs, application generators, database management systems, utility programs, and operating systems, is available from these vendors. In the application programs area, a software vendor often has specialized programs, such as a package for project scheduling, that are not available from the computer manufacturers.

In the past, much of the hardware and software sold in the United States originated here. However, as illustrated in Application 19–2, hardware and software sources and markets will be international.

Sources of PC Hardware and Software

Although the sources discussed in this section are for personal computers as well as mainframes and minis, there are some special considerations when buying personal computer hardware and software. Since the market in number of units for PC systems is much larger than for minis and mainframes, there tends to be considerably more information available about PC systems. Books, articles, and magazines related to personal computers are readily available. Magazines such as *PC Magazine* and *PC Week* carry reviews of both hardware and software. These are an important source of information in purchasing PC systems. The advertisements for software and hardware in these magazines are also good sources of information about products and their prices. Magazines and journals serving professional groups such as engineers, accountants, and bankers often publish articles describing personal computer applications in their own areas of expertise.

There are several ways to acquire personal computer hardware and software. Franchise retail chain stores such as Computerland and Entre are major outlets as are personal computer superstores, such as CompUSA. Because of their large sales volumes these stores are able to support a staff of technical advisors and maintenance personnel. They carry a wide variety of PC products. Many dealers in office equipment offer business-oriented hardware and software. Electronics stores also participate in the personal computer business.

Many colleges and universities have discount agreements with computer vendors that allow their students, staff, and faculty to purchase PC hardware and software at substantial discounts. If you are a student be sure to check whether your school has such agreements before you purchase PC hardware or software.

There are also many mail order suppliers of PC systems. A mail order hardware or software product tends to be less expensive than one bought from a store. But the buyer does assume some extra risk of purchasing a

APPLICATION 19–2

Going with Globalization Thrust

By Mitch Betts

Globalization will be more than just a buzzword in the 1990s. It will be the primary force that shapes the U.S. Electronics and computer industries as companies increasingly look offshore for their competition, market opportunities and capital.

That was the sweeping conclusion of "Electronics 90: The New Competitive Priorities," a study released last week by the professional services firm Ernst & Young and *Electronic Business* magazine. The study was based on a survey of chief executive officers from 744 companies in the computer, software, communications, semiconductor and electronics sectors.

The survey found that more than 30% of the CEOs expect that foreign companies will be their top competitors by mid-decade, compared with only 13% today.

Software Scare

Even in the software industry—long dominated by the U.S.—executives are concerned about emerging competition from the Far East. "To the extent that there will be offshore competition, I expect it to come from Japan," said Jon A. Shirley, outgoing president of Microsoft Corp., in an interview published in the study.

While almost all of the CEOs considered the U.S. to be their primary market, most executives said they believe that foreign markets will become increasingly important in the next five years, the survey stated.

"Virtually every executive in this industry will need to understand the issues of international distribution and sales, strategic partnering with foreign companies, recruiting foreign personnel and managing currency rate exposure," said Stephen E. Almassy, national director of Ernst & Young's computer industry services.

The surveyed executives view Western Europe, Japan and the Pacific Rim as the key markets to exploit, but they are already finding foreign sales a challenging mission. While more than 60% of U.S. electronics firms have sought to establish sales in Japan, nearly one-third have failed, according to the survey....

G. Steven Burrill, national director of Ernst & Young's high-technology industry services, said the survey "demonstrates unequivocally that corporate leaders in high technology no longer think in terms of domestic markets or domestic technology developments."...

High-Tech Trends

In addition to globalization, the study identified the following trends for the high-tech industries during the 1990s:

• Seventy percent of the CEOs named customer service as a top area of focus for their companies in the coming five years.

• More than 86% of the industry CEOs expect strategic alliances to play an "extremely important" role in their companies' business strategies over the next five years.

• Half of the CEOs expect their own companies to be acquired or merged in the next five years.

• No consensus developed about what role the U.S. government should play in boosting the competitiveness of high-tech industries.

• The possibility of a recession is by far the most serious economic concern of all electronics companies. The second biggest economic issue was the federal budget deficit.

product without testing it. However, most mail order houses allow a thirty-day trial period in which the purchaser can return the product and obtain a full refund. Although mail order houses usually offer less personal support than local dealers, they invariably have toll-free hotlines so that you can contact a technical assistance person directly from your office. Sometimes, though, these toll-free lines are busy when you most need assistance. If you are purchasing a standard software product such as Lotus 1-2-3 or a widely used piece of hardware such as a PC-compatible computer, you can save substantial amounts of money through mail order without assuming any undue risk. This is particularly true if you already have some expertise in the hardware or software that you are purchasing.

Service Bureaus

Service bureaus are companies that provide computer processing services on an as-needed basis. They generally charge for the services at an hourly rate. Service bureaus are a primary source of computer services for small businesses, and they routinely handle standard applications, such as payroll and accounts receivable. Either the service bureau or the customer provides the programs.

Using a service bureau can reduce costs. It also provides the opportunity to test programs before installing a new computer, and to arrange backup services for a company that owns its own computer. Service bureaus also handle data entry or temporary processing overloads.

The main disadvantage of service bureaus is that companies may lose control over data. This could result in serious security problems. Related to the question of data security is the problem of data file ownership. Users of service bureaus or time-sharing services (discussed in the next section) should be sure that they retain all rights of file ownership, including access and use. Another potential problem with service bureaus is lengthy processing turn-around, since the user does not have control over the processing schedule.

Time-Sharing Services

Time-sharing services provide the user with access to a computer through a remote terminal located at the user's place of business. The CPU and secondary storage are located at the site of the time-sharing service. Execution of user programs is initiated through commands issued at the terminal. Turn-around is very fast because programs are executed under a multitasking operating system that rotates among programs, allowing each program a CPU time slice. Thus, many independent users can gain access to a computer system at the same time.

The characteristics of a typical time-sharing system include the following:

- Each user has access to the computer system through one or more terminals, typically a video display device with hard-copy print capability.

- Data and instructions arrive at the CPU simultaneously from many users, and the system services all users concurrently by giving each small slices of CPU time on a rotating basis.

- Each user feels that he or she is the sole user of the system.

- Each user's data files are stored by on-line, direct-access storage devices at the central computer site, and are protected by password access systems. Thus the user has immediate access to data.

- Users can have their own private application programs, or they can use the public programs provided by the time-sharing service.

Time-sharing in commercial firms is usually limited to jobs with small amounts of input and output, such as statistical programs and financial planning models. However, time-sharing is ideally suited for scientific jobs since they usually have small input/output amounts and relatively more computation.

Time-sharing has the following advantages:

- The user has immediate and continuous access to the computer, and the response is immediate.

- Small jobs often cannot be handled by service bureaus because it takes too much time to process and transport them to and from the service bureau. These jobs are often easily handled by time-sharing systems since they allow immediate access.

- For the casual user of computers, time-sharing is often less expensive than other modes of access to computer services.

- The user has access to a wide variety of standard and utility programs stored on the time-sharing computer system.

The disadvantages of time-sharing include the following:

- The potential for data loss or for unauthorized access to a user's data is increased since data are stored at the central computer site. A time-sharing user should closely evaluate the installation's data control procedures.

- Time-sharing is usually more expensive than service bureau processing and may be more expensive than using personal computers.

- Input/output capabilities of most time-sharing services are limited; therefore, it is impractical to process jobs requiring large I/O capabilities with time-sharing.

Computer Lessors

As mentioned earlier, a potential computer user can lease hardware rather than purchase it. Many companies specialize in leasing computers. Generally the user can lease a computer for substantially less than it would cost to rent one. However, the lessee gives up flexibility since leasing is a long-term commitment.

Peripheral Hardware Manufacturers

Much of the peripheral hardware in a computer system can be acquired from vendors other than the CPU manufacturers. Components such as tape drives, disk drives, and printers are plug-compatible with the hardware produced by the computer manufacturers. In fact, some companies produce CPUs that can replace widely used CPUs such as IBM computers. Such equipment can be significantly less expensive. However, the user may encounter service and maintenance problems when dealing with more than one vendor. When equipment fails, it may be difficult to pinpoint which vendor's equipment is responsible.

Information Systems Consultants

Certified public accountant (CPA) firms and management consulting firms both provide information systems consulting services. Almost all of the management advisory service work that CPA firms provide is in the area of information system consulting. Consultants can be invaluable to the new user and to experienced users who are making major changes in their systems. Equipment salespeople are not always accurate in their performance claims. **Information systems consultants** can help the user evaluate these claims and choose a satisfactory system.

Outsourcing

Under **outsourcing** a company turns over a significant part of its information systems function to an external organization, such as a facilities management vendor. A **facilities management vendor** specializes in managing, staffing, and operating computer information systems for user organizations. This may include all aspects of the information system including computer operations, programming, and systems analysis. Many information systems consultant organizations such as Andersen Consulting and Electronic Data Systems (EDS) also provide facilities management services. Outsourcing contracts are typically long term, from five to ten years. Outsourcing became very popular during the late 1980s. Some of the reasons for its popularity are as follows:

1. Some firms feel that their expertise is in their core business area, not in information systems. Thus, they feel an outside organization that specializes in information systems can better manage that function.

2. Outsourcing may be substantially less expensive than an in-house information systems function. In the 1980s, firms became especially cost conscious because of international competition and debt burdens due to leveraged buyouts.

3. In-house systems may have become obsolete over time and are incompatible with new information systems technology.

4. The information services provided by outsourcing vendors have been proven reliable over time. Thus, a substantial portion of the risk in developing and maintaining complex information systems is reduced.

5. Outsourcing vendors operate in a competitive marketplace. Thus, they have a large incentive to provide the best service to the contracting firm. Otherwise, the firm will change outsourcing vendors.

6. The time and cost of recruiting and retaining technical information systems staff is eliminated.

Outsourcing does have several disadvantages, including the following:

1. It may be difficult to use information systems for competitive advantage if the information systems function is outsourced. For example, how can a company be sure that its new competitive information systems technology, which is executed by an outsourcing vendor, is not being shared with its competitors?

2. Vendors may submit low bids in order to obtain a contract to perform information systems services. Once the organization is locked in, the fees may increase. It may be difficult to change outsourcing vendors.

3. The lifeblood of a business is its information—information about customers, products, sales, employees, production costs, and so on. It may not be wise to turn this information over to an outside organization.

4. Outsourcing a portion of the information systems function may have devastating psychological consequences on the remaining information systems staff. This staff may feel that top management views their past efforts as a failure.

The key to a good outsourcing relationship with an outsourcing vendor is a good contract. These contracts may be as long as 200 pages and may last as long as ten years. Thus, a great deal of thought must enter into them. They must be in detail to cover what the responsibilities of the outsourcing vendor are. They must also provide flexibility for changes in the environment. Information systems technology can change substantially in a ten-year period. Firms can change through growth, loss of markets, mergers, acquisitions, and divestitures. It is most important to specify how conflicts between the contracting parties are to be resolved.

Outsourcing is likely to be a significant factor in future information systems. It is not new—companies have been outsourcing part or all of their information systems functions through service bureaus, time-sharing services, purchase of software, and facilities management vendors since the 1950s. What is new is the increase in the amount of outsourcing that is being done.

Summary

- Generally, users are heavily involved with the evaluation and acquisition of computer hardware and software. A major portion of the business of most management consulting firms is the evaluation and installation of computer information systems.

- The primary topics in this chapter were system evaluation, cost-benefit analysis, financing alternatives, and sources of information systems equipment and services.

- A system evaluation consists of the following steps: feasibility study, structured systems analysis, development of a request for proposal, proposal evaluation, and vendor selection.

- Three financing alternatives are available: purchasing, renting, and leasing. The trade-offs among the three options primarily involve considerations of costs, capital availability, risks of obsolescence, and flexibility.

- The buyer or user of computer information systems has a wide choice of sources for information systems equipment and services. Among them are the following:

- Computer manufacturers

- Retail computer stores

- Software vendors

- Service bureaus
- Time-sharing services
- Computer lessors
- Peripheral hardware manufacturers
- Information systems consultants
- Outsourcing vendors

Key Terms

Bundling	Software directories
Plug-compatible	Checklist
Request for proposal (RFP) document	Nonrecurring costs
Kernel program	Recurring costs
Benchmark programs	Risk of obsolescence
Compute-bound	Flexibility
Work load models	Retail computer stores
Simulation techniques	Service bureaus
Monitors	Time-sharing services
Fine tuning	Information systems consultants
Vendor support	Outsourcing
Compatibility	Facilities management vendor
Modularity	

Review Questions

1. What are the five primary phases of the computer system evaluation process?

2. What areas should be covered in a request for proposal?

3. What are some current techniques a buyer can use to evaluate a computer system's performance?

4. Distinguish between a benchmark program and a work load model.

5. How can simulation be employed to evaluate computer systems?

6. Describe and evaluate the usefulness of monitors.

7. What are the primary criteria with which a computer system should be evaluated?

8. Discuss the importance of compatibility as a criterion for evaluating a computer system.

9. What are the major kinds of nonrecurring costs of a computer system?

10. What are the financing alternatives available to the computer user?

11. What are the available sources of information systems equipment and services?

12. Are monitors used more in the selection of new systems or in the evaluation of existing systems? Why?

13. What is modularity and why is it important in selecting a computer system?

14. List four criteria for equipment that should be considered in vendor selection.

15. What is meant by compatibility in computer systems? Why is it an important consideration?

16. List six software criteria in the selection of a computer system.

17. What is outsourcing? What are it's advantages and disadvantages?

Discussion Questions and Cases

1. Janet Smith, owner and manager of a small business that produces delicate instruments for engineering purposes, has decided to acquire a computer system. She plans to use it for accounts receivable, accounts payable, payroll, and work-in-process control. Her company deals with few customers and suppliers. Most orders are large and designed to customer specifications. Janet, who is also an engineer, has managed operations firsthand, usually relying on her own observations for control. Her management philosophy is that no reports are as beneficial as "seeing it for herself." She has always been fascinated with gadgets and computer technology. Based on the information presented, should she acquire a computer system? Why or why not?

2. The Cascade Company has completed a review of five different proposed computer configurations. Based on the review, the five different configurations have been rated on a scale of one to ten (ten being the most desirable rating). The results of this rating appear in the following table. Examine the table and determine which configuration should be selected for the Cascade Company. Justify your choice.

		Configuration Rating				
Characteristic	Weighting Factor	A	B	C	D	E
Hardware						
Memory size	0.9	10	9	8	7	5
Disk Access time	0.5	10	10	6	9	8
Disk capacity	0.8	9	8	10	7	9
Modularity	1.0	8	7	10	9	8
Compatibility	1.0	10	9	10	10	10
Software						
Operating system	0.9	6	10	8	7	10
Ease of use	1.5	10	10	9	10	10
Application programs	0.4	10	5	5	9	8
Compatibility	0.9	6	9	8	5	10
Vendor Support	1.0	2	9	6	9	8
Cost	1.2	7	10	8	7	9
Benchmarking results	1.1	10	8	10	7	10

Curtis Company operates in a five-county industrial area. The company employs a manual system for all its record keeping except payroll, which is processed by a local service bureau. Other applications have not been computerized because they could not be cost-justified. However, the company's sales have grown at an increasing rate over the past five years. With this substantial growth rate, a computer-based system seems more practical. Consequently, Curtis Company recently engaged a management consulting firm to conduct a feasibility study for converting its record-keeping system to a computer-based system. The consulting firm reported that a computer-based system would improve the company's record-keeping system and still provide material cost savings. Therefore, Curtis Company decided to develop a computer-based system for its records. Curtis hired a person with experience in systems development as manager of information systems. His responsibilities are to oversee the entire systems operation with special emphasis on the development of the new system. Describe the major steps that will be undertaken to develop and implement Curtis Company's new computer-based system. (Adapted from CMA Examination, June 1976, Part 5, No. 4.)

4. American Chemical is a large chemical company headquartered on the West Coast. About two years ago American decided that it needed a new computer-based accounts payable system. After doing a feasibility study and developing a requirements document, the company decided to purchase an accounts payable package from a large and reputable software house. Based on demonstrations of the system and on subsequent evaluations, it was decided that the package should be modified to fit American's specific needs. A contract was developed with the software house to make the necessary modifications. About eight months later, it became apparent that the software house was not going to be successful in making these modifications. By this time, American had invested several hundred thousand dollars in the package, but the software house could not get the package to execute after the modifications. In an attempt to salvage its investment, American hired another software development firm to try to straighten out the mess. This attempt was unsuccessful as well. Primarily because of this disastrous experience, the director of information systems for American Chemical instituted a policy which stated that before an outside software package is purchased, the package must meet American's needs close enough that no modification will be required, or alternatively, American Chemical must be able to change its way of doing business to fit the way the package operates, without modification. Evaluate this policy.

5. Carolina Manufacturing is considering installing a manufacturing resources planning system. Carolina has had extensive experience in the use of computers, having installed its first computer-based system in the late 1950s. In addition, Carolina has a great many manufacturing experts on its staff. However, no one working for the company has had experience with MRP systems. The director of manufacturing and the director of information systems currently disagree on how to gain the necessary MRP experience to implement this system. Angela Battle, the director of information systems, advocates hiring an outside consulting firm to guide the company in the implementation of the MRP system. Consulting rates in the area are $125 per hour, and it is expected that the total consulting fee would be approximately $150,000. Jim Johnson, the director of manufacturing, feels that it would be much better for Angela to hire someone with MRP experience to join the information systems staff. Such an individual could be hired for about $65,000 per year, which includes fringe benefits. Which approach do you think Carolina should take?

Outsourcing Without Guilt

By Paul Clermont

Nothing is sacred about information technology anymore. Tough times and cutthroat competition are causing many companies to examine spending across the board—including in information systems areas. Organizations are willing to make radical changes to stay competitive, so it's no surprise that many are scrutinizing the outsourcing of information technology management activities.

The impetus to analyze outsourcing options often comes from top management. Senior business managers want to know why information technology activities are being performed in-house when outside organizations might be able to handle them more economically.

To senior executives, outsourcing sounds like a blessing. They view internal information technology organizations—justifiably or not—as spending too much on things that take too long to get done and, even then, don't seem to work very well.

These executives have no doubt heard of outsourcing's generic benefits: economy, service quality, predictable cost and quality, flexibility, making fixed costs variable and freeing up human and financial capital. However, they may be less aware that these benefits do not necessarily accrue in equal measure for every organization. Some companies will successfully capture major benefits from outsourcing, while others will not. Still others will talk themselves out of even trying and will leave the potential benefits on the table.

A Trio of Strengths

For companies to derive value from outsourcing, they need to do three things well:

- Segment the range of information technology activities into pieces that can potentially be outsourced.
- Use sound business-based analysis to identify those segments it makes the most sense to outsource.
- Treat the outsourcing relationship as a partnership, using the procurement process as a test of the vendor/user working relationship.

By segmenting a company's information technology activities, it is easier to decide which pieces are ripe for outsourcing.

Information technology activities can be segmented along technology-based lines such as transaction processing, desktop computing, network management and so on. In these cases, the outsourcing decision is primarily focused on processing—that is, whether the company wants to own and operate mainframes, voice networks and other technologies.

Information technology can also be further segmented according to the area of the business being served. For example, an airline may use superficially similar on-line transaction processing systems for its reservations and its accounts payable, but the appropriateness of outsourcing each of those activities is vastly different.

Outsourcing does not have to be an all-or-nothing proposition to be worthwhile. Companies that have rejected outsourcing may have made the mistake of looking at their information technology as a monolith. These companies might have seen the value of farming out some activities, but when they lumped those outsourceable pieces together with others that were deemed impractical to outsource, they concluded it made no sense to handle the project out of house.

Segmenting is important because outsourcing has never been applied to the whole enchilada. Even outsourcing pioneers such as Eastman Kodak Co. have retained considerable information activity in-house. And General Motors Corp. is again conducting some information technology activity in-house rather than through its systems integrator subsidiary, Electronic Data Systems Corp.

By separating technology activities, companies can make sure they match an out-sourcer with the appropriate job. In that way, they'll get the skills and knowledge of a specialist for each area they want to outsource. Segmentation gives companies a real base from which to make an outsourcing decision.

Once you've segmented information technology activities into manageable pieces, you can decide, through a business analysis, which of those pieces (if any) should be outsourced.

One area companies will not want to abdicate to an outside organization is the executive management role in technology direction setting. Such a strategic task is best kept in-house.

Outsourcing segments make sense under the following business conditions:

- Outsourcing makes sense when there is little opportunity for the company to distinguish itself competitively through the quality of its information technology processing operations. The competitive value may instead lie in applications and database operations.

  Kodak focused its initial outsourcing effort on operations: mainframe processing, telecommunications and personal computer support. Application development and support both stayed in house.

- Outsourcing makes sense when there is limited opportunity for the company to distinguish itself competitively through the quality of its applications. "Commodity" applications such as credit card processing and payroll are classic examples. Automatic Data Processing, Inc. has built a successful business in processing payroll using its proprietary application.

  These examples are likely candidates for having their application development and support as well as their hardware platform outsourced. This frees up resources for IS [information systems] activities with a larger potential payoff—for example, customer service or manufacturing planning systems.

  Too facile a business analysis in this case could be dangerous, however. Speed-based competition has given new importance to such areas as logistics and distribution, even though these activities were considered strategically neutral only a few years ago.

- Outsourcing makes sense when the predictability of uninterrupted information technology service is not of great importance. When predictability is paramount, the extraordinary sense of urgency is not fully communicable to a financially independent outsider. Airline reservations and catalog shopping systems come to mind, as do some of the high-value transactions that financial institutions often process on fault-tolerant computers.

- Outsourcing makes sense when it does not strip the company of critical technical know-how that is key to future IS innovation.

  One example is computer-integrated manufacturing. Today's scheduling applications and shop-control applications are almost commodities, so it is not critical for most companies to maintain a pool of skilled people to build such applications.

However, systems that integrate these applications with robots and flexible machining centers are not only far from being commodities, but they are also potential competitive weapons. Any company fortunate enough to have such skills in-house should think hard before letting them go in the interest of short-term economy.

- Outsourcing makes sense when existing information technology capabilities are limited and ineffective. Why commit the time, money and management attention to internal IS changes when the other evaluation factors mentioned above indicate you should outsource? On the other hand, if information technology is well managed and productive, there may not be much immediate financial value for a vendor to add.

  This list needs refinement and tailoring for each individual organization. Regardless, the overall theme here is business linkage. Without a sound business impetus, there may be little reason to devote scarce resources to providing certain information technology activities internally. It make little sense to outsource when your own high-quality performance can make a competitive difference.

Create the Partnership

With the business analysis done and outsourceable information technology activities identified, companies need to put related outsourceable segments together in packages to which vendors can respond. These packages should be reasonably self-contained.

Buyers then need to evaluate vendor's bids according to a number of dimensions. Technical competence to deliver should be the basis on which to start negotiations; the real challenge is to evaluate the softer partnership aspects of the deal.

One such "soft" criteria is that the vendor must have a feel for the customer's business and exhibit appropriate consulting and people skills when dealing with the customer's staff.

Another issue is the buyer's understanding of a vendor's pricing and how that compares with internal costs. An outsourcing vendor will quote his full cost plus profit. This will exceed the internal cost of providing information technology only in theory; in practice, it usually will not because the vendor applies the disciplines of line management to the customer's staff activity.

Before consummating a deal, companies need to analyze whether the vendor brings a clear advantage to the table. This means understanding the cost/quality trade-offs. Can you live with five-second response time during peak hours? Is next day repair of PCs in remote offices OK? These are valuable questions to answer whether or not you're considering outsourcing; outsourcing deals just make the cost of higher service levels far more explicit and visible.

A vendor's promised service levels must be measurable, and there needs to be a clear basis for determining when the intent, rather than just the letter, of the agreement has been met. The basic ideas of statistical quality control are helpful here because they focus on overall performance levels as well as on defects.

For example, in dealing with on-line response time, occasional responses of more than five seconds are of much less concern if the average is holding at three seconds. IS should be concerned only if the average begins to steadily creep upward.

Finally, the cultures must be compatible enough to let both parties feel good about living together for the next few years. To create the necessary comfort level requires a joint effort of the vendor and client staff involved in the outsourcing deal. Good vendors will anticipate questions and provide good answers.

Few organizations have the luxury of ignoring the outsourcing option in today's cost-and service-conscious business environment. Companies will still come to a wide variety of conclusions about how much of the option they should pick up.

The important point is to arrive at answers through a business-driven process. Doing so is beneficial for everyone, including outsourcing vendors that will significantly aid their cause by helping potential clients perform a sound analysis.

From the vendor's viewpoint, a customer who buys less than the possible maximum and understands just why he bought it will be a good multi-year partner. From the customer's viewpoint, a vendor that understands and contributes to the decision process will be a good partner.

Without a partnership being based on sound business thinking, outsourcing will fail sometimes spectacularly but more often, quietly.

Discussion Questions

1. Would it ever be advisable for a firm to outsource an application that gives them a competitive advantage? Provide an example.

2. What are some of the disadvantages of outsourcing?

Reprinted from *ComputerWorld* (September 9,, 1991), pp. 67–68. Copyright 1991 by CW Publishing, Inc. Framingham, Ma 01701.
Clermont is a principal at Northeast Consulting Resources, Inc. in Boston. He consults on IS strategies planning and its link to business.

20

Information Systems Control and Security

Many information systems do not have effective controls, and attempts to implement such controls are often thwarted by accidents or intentional fraud. In the area of computer fraud alone, the U.S. Department of Commerce estimates that only one out of every hundred cases is ever exposed. Furthermore, many of these cases are uncovered purely by accident. In one survey the average loss per case of computer fraud was $1,090,000. During a recent year, people perpetuating computer fraud in the banking industry took about twenty-four times as many dollars per crime as their counterparts in other types of white collar bank crime. Events of this nature make information systems controls and security a popular and important topic in the computer field.

This chapter first examines the need for control and security and then it looks at the characteristics of computer system controls. Next, it explores the general controls that apply to all computer applications. Finally, it covers controls for specific computer applications.

Information and data are the lifeblood of a business. Today, most information and data are processed and stored by computer systems. Companies realize the value of data and information and thus spend considerable resources to protect this valuable asset. Although control and security of computer-based systems have been important since their beginnings in the 1950s, the threats to these systems have steadily increased over time. Also, the nature of computer-based systems has certainly changed over time. Currently, information systems resources are widely dispersed through the use of PCs, minis, and mainframes that are either stand-alone or networked together. Computers can be accessed in many ways. Thus, the challenge of providing effective control and security has increased. In this section we discuss some of the basic reasons why control and security are important.

Information Integrity

Information integrity is a quality of information that has not been compromised by accidental or malicious destruction, alteration, or loss. Important business decisions rely on information stored and retrieved from computer systems. Large amounts of money can be lost if the information does not have integrity. Control and security techniques help to ensure that information is not either accidentally or intentionally destroyed, altered, or lost. Information integrity is the primary reason for control and security. If the information does not have integrity, the other reasons for control and security are not important.

Computer Crime

A **computer crime** is the use of a computer to commit an illegal act. Criminals have discovered that the computer can be used for competitive advantage and they continually come up with new and ingenious ways to commit computer crime. For example, recently a company had an excessive number of long distance calls on its phone bill. They discovered that calls were being placed by people who called the company's 800 toll-free number and then used the transfer to extension feature of the

Introduction

The Need for Control and Security

company's voice mail system. After the transfer, they would dial 9 to get an outside line and place a long distance telephone call. The company's long distance calls were restricted but these calls went through because they were placed by the voice mail system, not by a telephone extension.

Computer crime can be classified into five different categories:

1. Theft of data or services such as the unauthorized use of a computer through hacking.

2. Financial crimes, including using a computer to alter information for financial gains. These crimes are often called fraud or embezzlement.

3. Software piracy, the illegal copying and use of copyrighted software.

4. Property theft, the theft of computer hardware and software.

5. Vandalism, the destruction of computer hardware, software, or data through any technique, including infection by computer viruses.

Computer crimes result in direct monetary losses by the company that is a victim of these crimes. There is also another loss associated with computer crime, which can be substantial. This loss is the loss of customer confidence in the firm when the crime is publicly revealed. The fact that a company is a victim of a computer crime often leads customers to believe that the firm is sloppy in its business practices. Two types of computer crime, computer viruses and espionage, have become so widespread that they will be discussed separately below.

Computer Viruses

Computer viruses, a new form of computer sabotage, were developed in the late 1980s. These viruses are computer programs designed to replicate themselves and spread to other computer systems. Once they infect a computer system, their actions can range from the relatively harmless, like displaying the message "Gotcha" on workstation screens, to the very destructive, like erasing all the computer system's disk files.

Viruses can spread from computer to computer through network connections or through shared storage media among computers. Some of the most notorious virus attacks have spread quickly (in a few hours) all over the country through national computer networks. Such attacks have consumed many hours of computer and human time in efforts to purge computer systems of the virus.

Writing a computer virus program is an easy task for a skilled programmer, especially a system programmer. Although writing and intentionally spreading a virus program is reprehensible and illegal, we can expect to have computer viruses around for the foreseeable future.

The analogy with biological viruses is most appropriate. Even the protections against computer viruses are called vaccines. These vaccines are programs that monitor a computer system to detect and purge a system of a virus before it does damage. There are vaccines available for all types of computers. But unfortunately, as with biological virus vaccines, computer virus vaccines do not protect a system against all viruses, particularly new ones. Thus, backup of critical computer files is a very important protection against virus attacks.

The following is a list of precautions that businesses should take to protect themselves against computer viruses:

1. Inform all personnel of the virus problem, the danger, and company policy regarding information integrity.

2. Utilize a "quarantine" computer (a stand-alone computer with no hard disk) to screen all outside software that is to be used in the firm. Periodically check all software in use for file size and data changes. Most vaccine programs perform these steps automatically.

3. Stop the transportation of executable program files from work to home and back.

4. Make sure that program and data files are not mixed on disks. Program and data files should be kept in separate directories.

5. Prohibit employees from downloading and using bulletin board programs unless they are thoroughly tested and checked for viruses before their use.

6. Use write-protection devices on all executable program files. Viruses insert themselves into executable files. The use of write-protection devices prevents this insertion from occurring.

7. Place virus protection software (vaccines) on all computer systems to prevent, detect, or identify and remove viruses from the systems.

8. Back up all computer files on a routine basis. There is no guarantee that the backup will be virus free. But at least the firm will have a copy of all its program and data files in case the virus erases these from the computer's disks. Virus removal techniques can be used to remove the virus if it exists on the backup copy.[1]

Computer viruses can wreck havoc with a computer system. Any business that is not taking steps to protect itself from computer viruses is taking a very large risk. Fortunately there are relatively inexpensive ways to decrease the risk dramatically. Perhaps the most important are routine backups and the use of a virus vaccine on all computer systems. The vaccines are effective and are relatively inexpensive.

Industrial Espionage

Industrial espionage is spying on a business to gain confidential data and information. This confidential information is usually trade secrets, technical expertise, or strategic and tactical plans. Such information is increasingly being stored on computer systems. For example, during the Persian Gulf war a British Air Force general left his automobile parked at a new car dealer while he was shopping for a car. In the trunk of his auto-

[1] Maher, John J. and James O. Hicks, Jr., "Computer Viruses: Controller's Nightmare," *Management Accounting*, October 1989, pp. 44–49.

mobile was a portable computer containing the allies' plans for the Persian Gulf Campaign. The computer was stolen from his automobile. However, within a few hours the computer was recovered, but there was no way of knowing whether or not an Iraqi agent had copied the files contained in the portable computer. Although this is not industrial espionage the same sort of thing can easily happen to a business.

Two primary factors are causing the rampant increase in industrial espionage. First, most countries now expect that future competition among nations is going to be economic arena rather than military. Knowing what your competitor is doing is of obvious value.

This leads to the second reason for the increase in industrial espionage. With the end of the Cold War, countries both in the West and in the former Communist bloc have very large espionage infrastructures that are underemployed. Military espionage, although still occurring, is not as important as it was during the Cold War. Foreign intelligence agents have refocused their Cold War spying activities into the industrial arena. For example, during 1988 and 1989 the French exterior security organization attempted to hire employees of Texas Instruments, IBM, and other U.S. firms to provide industrial information for pay. Also, the two primary espionage agencies in the U.S., the CIA and the National Security Agency, have admitted that they are considering "putting more effort into gathering industrial information."[2]

In summary, the companies of the world have a great deal of valuable information that is stored and processed by computers. This information is often transmitted over networks to other computers. The control and security of this information is an extremely important endeavor for any business that wishes to survive into the future as illustrated in Application 20–1.

Characteristics of Computer System Controls

The underlying concept of control does not change when a firm starts using computer information systems. Many controls utilized in manual information systems are also used in computer information systems, but their methods of application and appearance are often very different.

Computer system controls have the following characteristics:

- They are more formal and extensive than manual system controls. Extensive formal controls are needed for computer systems because most computer processing is performed in a mode invisible to humans. Therefore, it is not possible for personnel to detect unexpected errors during processing, as they often can in manual systems.

- They must be specifically designed into the system. For example, documentary evidence is lacking in computer processing. Input can be combined with other input and transformed to such an extent that the trail between input and output is lost. If audit trails are not designed into a computer system, they do not exist. **Audit trails** provide the ability to trace inputs to sporadic outputs and to trace outputs and to trace outputs back to inputs.

---

[2] Alexander, Michael, "Industrial Espionage Within U.S. Runs Rampant," *Computerworld*, March 4, 1991, p. 64.

APPLICATION 20–1

High-Tech Boom Opens Security Gaps

By Michael Alexander

Corporate America is embracing technology as never before, putting personal computers into the hands of every white-collar worker and stitching computer systems into international networks.

Yet many information systems security experts fear that what may be good for business may be even better for computer outlaws and make it easier for them to commit new sorts of crimes.

Although technology has made many corporations more competitive, it has also made them more vulnerable to attack from employees and outsiders, said Dan White, partner and regional director of information security services at Ernst & Young.

The rapid adoption of distributed systems, electronic data interchange, local-area networks and other technology has outpaced the capacity of most companies to secure them against attack, White said.

Telecommunications networks, especially those that cross international boundaries, are also more vulnerable to electronic industrial espionage, according to Noel Matchett, president of Information Security, Inc., a security consulting firm based in Silver Spring, Md.

"Every time valuable information is transmitted on unprotected circuits, there is the possibility it is being intercepted by competitors," Matchett said. "Frequently, transmissions are routed over satellite, microwave and even cellular phone circuits, making theft of information undetectable."

Networks of all types, not just for computers, have proliferated out of control, creating "a lot of security problems" and augmenting the number of potential points of unauthorized entry into company computer systems, White said. "The networks are without end points, and most IS [information systems] managers do not even know how extensive their networks really are," he added.

Many foreign competitors are also being aided by their nations' intelligence organizations in carrying out this electronic eavesdropping, according to Matchett, who previously worked for the National Security Agency on computer security issues. "They are actively participating in it; there is even tasking for certain information for their countries' businesses".

Calculating losses as a result of electronic industrial espionage is a difficult task because unauthorized access to databases is rarely discovered and there is no immediate evidence of theft, he said. However, Matchett said he believes that the losses may reach into the billions of dollars per year.

Investigating and prosecuting crimes that cross national, legal and cultural boundaries will also be difficult, if not impossible, said Raymond Humphrey, director of corporate security at Digital Equipment Corp.

"There are no walls around a hacker, who can conceivably start his or her activity in Australia and leap across national boundaries to the U.S.," Humphrey said.

• They must be incorporated early in the design process. It is expensive and often very difficult to install controls after a system has been implemented.

• The control of maintaining good system documentation is critical because the processing steps and information stored in computer files are invisible. Thus, computer systems do not have a **backup procedure** of examining documents and interviewing clerical personnel to determine processing steps, as manual systems do.

• Good control is necessary because information files are often centralized. Loss of computer files would force many of today's firms out of business, at least temporarily.

• They can be much more effective than controls in manual systems. Once a control is implemented in a computer program, it is performed with nearly 100 percent reliability. No manual control can be that reliable. The key to control is to utilize the power of the computer creatively.

- As in manual systems, the controls in a computer system can overlap. Thus, strong control in one area can compensate for weak control in another.

- Often people's attitudes toward security of computer systems are not what they should be. For example, people usually do not consider a computer password as the equivalent to a vault key. They may not realize that a company can lose much more through illegal access to its computer than it can through illegal access to its vault.

The American Institute of Certified Public Accountants provides a taxonomy of computer controls in its audit and accounting guide, *The Auditor's Study and Evaluation of Internal Control in EDP Systems*. The classifications used in that guide have been adapted to provide the overall structure of this chapter. The primary categories of controls are general and application.

General Controls

General controls are the overall managerial controls applied to all software, hardware, and personnel involved in the information system. They include management, system development, hardware and system software, access, and miscellaneous controls.

Management Controls

The computer-based information system is a complex, valuable resource. It is subject to the same kinds of management control devoted to other important company resources. **Management controls** include an information system master plan, the segregation of functions, the selection and training of personnel, written systems and procedures, and a budget and user billing system.

Information System Master Plan   The information system master plan outlines the overall strategy for implementing a firm's information system. A good plan lists the order in which each component is implemented and includes implementation dates. It clarifies objectives and provides a sense of ordered progress to the development of the information system. Without a master plan, the information system is likely to become a hodgepodge of incompatible computer programs. Master plans also help to control the duplication of effort that often occurs in PC environments.

Segregation of Functions   **Segregation of functions** is the principle of dividing duties among employees so that collusion among two or more employees is needed for a fraud to be successful. For example, a firm might give one employee control of cash received, and another employee the duty of entering those receipts on the computer. If the same employee held both duties, he or she could steal the cash and change the computer records, so the firm would not know the cash was missing! Segregation of functions is critical in computer systems because in an uncontrolled computer environment, it is easy to change data or program files and not leave a trace of the change.

An effective central information systems organization is segregated from users and has control over the data and program files. However, it never has the authority to originate inputs or correct errors in them, unless the errors originate in information systems.

The structures of a small, a medium-sized, and a large information systems organization are shown in Figures 20–1, 20–2, and 20–3, respectively. A typical firm's job functions are identified in each figure.

To prevent collusion among employees, it is most important to segregate the duties of systems and programming personnel from the duties of equipment operators. Systems and programming personnel know the details of program logic, record layouts, and file structures. If they also have the ability to enter a program in a production job stream or to operate the equipment, they can easily and surreptitiously modify production programs or data files.

In a system controlled with segregation of functions, the programmers, analysts, and equipment operators do not have direct access to production programs or data files. A librarian is responsible for cataloging, custody, and security of program and data files. These files are issued only to authorized personnel and only when they are needed for authorized tasks. Programmers use copies of production source programs and data files to make and test changes; they never use actual production files. (The review and control of program changes are discussed later in this chapter.)

Programmers, analysts, and equipment operators also do not have access to the input/output controls, such as batch control totals or master file field totals. If they had access to such totals, they could conceal fraudulent modifications by changing an application's input/output controls. In small and medium-sized firms, these input/output controls are usually maintained in the user organization. However, there is a trend, especially in large firms, toward establishing an additional control group within the information systems organization. This approach allows the firms to exercise more uniform control over all information systems applications.

Equipment operators do not have access to application documentation, except that needed to perform their duties. Otherwise, they may be able to modify programs and data files, especially if they have some knowledge of programming. Information about specific applications is provided to equipment operators only if they need to know it to run the job. The operating system gives instructions to the operator through the operator's video display console each time a job is run. Operators do not need to know program logic, record layouts, or file structures. They also do not need to correct errors in application programs (this is the responsibility of the systems and programming staff).

With the control features described here, those best able to modify program and data files—the systems analysts and programmers—are isolated from the equipment, production programs, production data files, and input/output controls. The equipment operators, although they have access to the equipment, are isolated from the program documentation, the input/output controls, and the program and data files, except when jobs use a particular program or data file. These controls substantially decrease the risk of fraud and make it easier to detect fraud if it occurs.

Another way to control fraud is to rotate duties and make vacations mandatory. Rotating duties is accomplished by rotating personnel among

FIGURE 20–1
Small Information
Systems Organization.

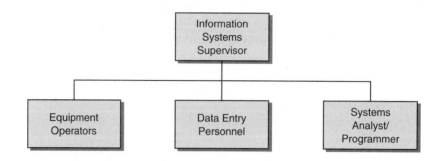

FIGURE 20–1
Small Information
Systems Organization.

shifts or by rotating the scheduled run-time of applications among shifts. If employees are covering up a fraud through their daily job activities, moving them to other jobs or requiring them to take vacations prevents them from engaging in the cover-up activities. Thus the fraud may be discovered. Rotation of duties is easier to accomplish among low-level personnel like operators and control clerks. However, high-level personnel can be required to take vacations.

Much of what is discussed in this section applies to mainframe and minicomputer installations. But how do you handle segregation of functions in personal computer installations, where one person may be the user, operator, and programmer? Quite often personal computer programs are purchased, not programmed by the user. Therefore, unauthorized changes to programs are unlikely. However, very little can be done to provide further segregation of functions in microcomputer systems. The other controls discussed in this chapter must be relied on more heavily to compensate for the inability to segregate functions.

FIGURE 20–2
Medium-sized Information Systems Organization.

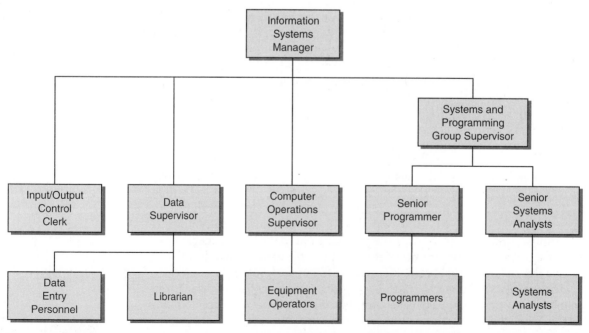

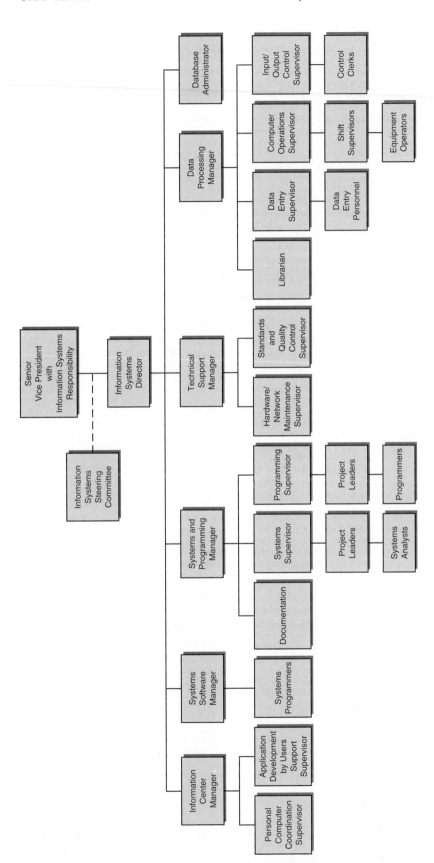

Selection and Training of Personnel　Ultimately, the success of any information system depends on the skills of the people who operate it. The basic skills required for different information systems functions vary widely. For example, programming demands exactness, abstract reasoning, and an ability to work with minute details successfully. A programmer does not need advanced interpersonal skills, since successful programming requires very little interaction with other people. On the other hand, a systems analyst must be able to interact with managers to determine their information needs and sometimes to tactfully convince them that their needs are different from what they seem. These tasks require advanced interpersonal skills. In addition, analysts often work with abstract concepts, and they must be generalists who work well with uncertainties. A working knowledge of computer capabilities, quantitative methods, accounting, information theory, organization theory, competitive strategy, and other disciplines is necessary for successful systems analysis.

Matching basic human characteristics and skills with a job's requirements is essential, especially for positions that are difficult to control and therefore lend themselves to fraud. One example of such a position is that of the systems programmer. Systems programmers are usually the most highly qualified programmers. Since they maintain the operating system programs, they have indirect access to all of the installation's application programs and data. In addition, they have access to security programs, such as password systems. Therefore, systems programmers must have a high level of integrity and trustworthiness, as well as skill. Employee bonding and security investigations are often used to select people for these sensitive positions.

Training information systems personnel differs from training most other employees. Since information systems knowledge is rapidly changing and highly technical, many companies rely heavily on outside sources for training. Among these sources are hardware vendors, software vendors, software houses, universities, and organizations that specialize in technical information systems training. Information systems personnel tend to spend more time in training than other personnel because of the rapid technological changes in their field.

Written Systems and Procedures　To maintain effective control over information systems operations, standard procedures must be established. (Many of the controls discussed in this chapter are procedures, or they depend on the regular execution of procedures to be effective.) Once established, procedures must be written and maintained. Otherwise, they are unlikely to be followed. Without enforced written procedures, people tend to regress to using practices that process data with the least inconvenience to them. This regression normally produces a lapse of control.

Budget and User Billing System　A firm's information system is a valuable economic resource, representing a large investment. In the early stages of a company's conversion to a computer system, the computer system is often treated as a free resource to user organizations. This usage encourages otherwise reluctant users to develop computer applications and to employ idle computer capacity. Although this approach can be defended for new installations with excess capacity, eventually users must be charged for information systems services if the installation is to be cost-effective.

System Development Controls

System Development Controls can be divided into three areas: system development cycle, system documentation, and program change controls.

System Development Cycle Controls   System development cycle controls are included in the systems development methodology covered in Chapters 16 and 17 of this text.

System Documentation Controls   Documentation is the primary vehicle of communication about the system among systems analysts, programmers, users, management, and auditors. Much of the documentation is initiated during the systems development cycle. In fact, it is impossible to develop a large, complex system without it.

Analysts and programmers tend to get their jobs done while developing minimal permanent documentation. This lack of documentation inevitably becomes very expensive to the company when program modifications are needed or when the systems analyst or programmer who knows the system leaves the firm. There is no doubt that tight implementation schedules contribute to documentation deficiencies. Often, however, programmers simply consider it a boring chore to go back and document an elegantly designed program after coding.

Many information systems organizations have found that assigning the responsibility of documentation to a documentation specialist, or a librarian of a chief programmer team, is the best solution to the documentation problem. The specialist does not originate the documentation. This is the responsibility of systems analysts, programmers, users, and others. However, the specialist does ensure that documentation meets firm standards; that it is updated when the system is modified; and that he or she maintains custody over the documentation. Such custody prevents access to the documentation by those who have no need to know about the system.

Documentation standards appear in several forms. *System documentation* provides an overview of the system and includes the following:

- A system description
- Data flow diagrams and flowcharts showing the flow of information through the system and the relationships between the processing steps, inputs, programs, and outputs
- Specifications that governed the design and implementation of the system
- Input screens and forms and their descriptions
- Output layouts and descriptions
- Data structure diagrams

- Control descriptions
- Program change authorizations and their implementation dates
- Audit trail descriptions
- System backup procedures
- A data dictionary
- System structure charts

Program documentation provides information about individual programs and normally includes the following:

- A narrative description of the program
- Program structure charts
- Structured English, program flowcharts, decision tables, and decision trees that document the details of program module logic
- Source statement listings
- Program test data listings
- A testing log
- Images of job control language and other control records
- Input/output formats and distribution
- Copies of program change request forms, the authorization for changes, and their implementation dates
- Instructions for the computer operator
- File retention procedures
- A description of error detection and control features

Operations documentation provides computer operations with the instructions needed to run a computer-based application efficiently. For each program, it includes the following:

- A brief description of the system
- Setup instructions
- Input keying procedures
- Input and output balancing procedures, and control and distribution procedures
- Operating notes that explain program console messages and actions required of the operator
- Recovery and checkpoint-restart procedures
- Emergency instructions
- Normal and maximum run-times

- Hardware and operating system requirements

User documentation includes the following:

- A narrative description of the system

- Data flow diagrams and system flowcharts

- Instructions for interacting with the system through a video display to input data and respond to queries

- Instructions covering the proper completion of any input forms

- Description of control procedures and indication of the person or position responsible for each procedure

- Error correction procedures

- Computer output balancing and checking procedures

Library documentation includes the following:

- Backup procedures

- Retention procedures

- Restrictions on file access and file checkout procedures

- File labeling procedures

- Procedures for maintaining a log or an inventory of each physical file

Program Change Controls Having uncontrolled ability to make changes in production application programs can be the equivalent of having direct, uncontrolled access to a company's cash. For example, a programmer can change an order entry program to send regular shipments of inventory to friends. At the same time, he or she can prevent the accounts from being invoiced and updated. In any system in which checks are produced by computer, the possibilities for fraud are nearly endless.

In a payroll application, one programmer was caught stealing from his fellow employees. He changed the program module that produced annual tax withholding (W-2) forms so that his W-2 withholdings were overstated, and the total withholdings of other employees were understated by the same amount. To prevent other employees from becoming suspicious, the programmer had each employee's withholdings for the year understated by only one dollar. The company, however, had approximately two thousand employees. Upon filing his federal tax return, the programmer was thus able to claim a refund for two thousand dollars in excess withholdings. This fraud went undetected for several years, until a shrewd employee found that the withholdings reported on his W-2 form did not balance (by one dollar) with the total of withholdings reported on his weekly paycheck stubs.

Prevention of fraud is not the only rationale for controlling program changes. **Program change control** makes it more likely that authorized program changes will be made promptly, that they will be tested thoroughly before implementation, and that production programs will not be disrupted by haphazard changes.

In a controlled system, changes to both application and system programs are based on written authorizations, as illustrated in Figure 20–4. Authorizations are approved by the user and by someone in an appropriate level of management.

F I G U R E 20–4
Program Change Control.

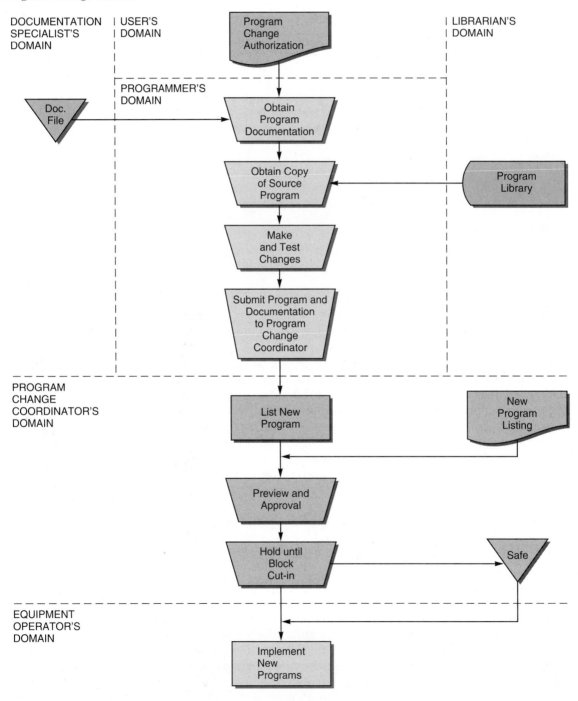

Programmers are not able to change production programs directly. To make a change, a programmer obtains an electronic copy of the production source program from the librarian and the program documentation from the documentation specialist. He or she then makes program changes to the copy (these changes do not affect the original). After testing the changed program, the programmer submits it to a program change coordinator, along with authorization and evidence of the testing. The program change coordinator is the manager of systems and programming, a committee, or any responsible individual from systems and programming.

The program change coordinator reviews the new program and its supporting documentation, and approves or disapproves its implementation. As a basis for this review, the coordinator directly lists the new program. The coordinator does not use a program listing submitted by the programmer, because changes may have been made to the program after the programmer listed it. The coordinator may also run a source **code comparison** between the current production source program and the new source program. The output of the source code comparison is a complete listing of all changes from the current to the new source program.

After the new program is approved, the program change coordinator holds it in custody until a *block cut-in* date. Block cut-in is a procedure whereby all program changes are collected (batched) and implemented into the production program library at a predetermined time (for example, once a week). Block cut-in improves control over program changes by allowing all changes to be traced to specific block cut-ins. Operations implements the new programs at a block cut-in, when it receives the programs from the program change coordinator.

An additional program change control is the implementation of software that monitors and records read and write accesses to the production program library. The software records and reports such statistics as time of access, the device from which access is made, and the user identification of the individual accessing the library. Ideally, write accesses occur only at block cut-in. However, emergency program changes are sometimes necessary. To maintain control, emergency changes are implemented only by the operations staff. Operations makes copies of the old and new source programs and delivers them directly to the program change coordinator. This procedure allows the coordinator to review each change after its implementation.

Hardware and System Software Controls

Vendors build control features into computer hardware and systems software. These controls are separate from those exercised by application programs or people. The controls discussed in this section are not necessarily incorporated into all hardware and software. Therefore, one criterion for selecting new hardware or software is its vendor-supplied control features.

Hardware Controls   *Parity checks* are a basic hardware control. Data are represented in the computer as binary digits. When a character is moved or stored internally in either the CPU or secondary storage, a redundant bit (parity bit) is added to the bits that represent the character. Parity bits detect equipment malfunctions that cause the alteration of a bit within a byte during processing. Figure 20–5 illustrates parity bits. The parity bit causes the number of on bits within a byte to be even in an even parity computer or odd in an odd parity computer. For example, if a computer is designed with even parity, the occurrence of a byte with an odd number of on bits indicates a parity error.

In a *redundancy check*, two hardware units perform a task independent of each other. The results of the two operations are then compared to make sure they are the same. If they are not identical, an error has occurred. For example, in some disk drives, two independent read heads read each record, and the disk unit compares the results for discrepancies that signal read errors.

Write-read checks are similar to redundancy checks. As data are written on magnetic tape, the tape passes through the write head, then immediately through a read head. The data are read and compared to the characters that should have been written. A difference indicates that an error has occurred. Write-read checks are available on a variety of data storage devices.

Validity checks monitor the bit patterns of bytes to determine whether the combination of the on and off bits represents a valid pattern within the character set of the computer.

Write suppress features   Various hardware and software devices protect tapes and disks from being written to either accidentally or maliciously. All of these devices make the media read only, thus the media cannot be written to. Of course, writing to a disk or tape destroys the existing information on that storage media. The older reel-type tapes have write protection rings that must be inserted into the reel before it can be written to. Floppy disks have a write protection notch that can be used to physically prevent the disk from being written to. In addition, both floppy disks and hard disks can be protected through the **write suppress feature**, which is available in most operating systems. In the PC- and MS-DOS operating systems, this write suppress feature is activated through the attribute (ATTRIB) command. The write suppress feature is an important control to prevent viruses from inserting themselves into executable files and also to prevent viruses from erasing important files.

Echo checks verify that a device has been activated to carry out an operation it was instructed to perform. For example, when the computer is ready to transmit data to the printer, it transmits a signal that activates the printer. If the printer is ready, it sends an echo signal back to the computer. If the printer does not send the echo signal, the computer postpones transmission and signals the operator that the printer needs attention.

FIGURE 20–5
Even Parity Check. (Courtesy of IBM Corporation.)

Note that the C row bit is on when it is necessary to make the number of on bits in a byte (column) even.

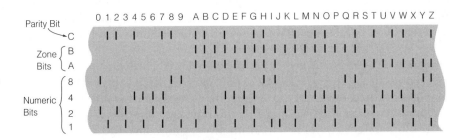

Preventive maintenance checks help avert hardware failures. Periodically, components are examined to detect, adjust, and repair faulty parts. Vendors offer customers preventive maintenance service. The object is to repair components that are near failure before they actually fail. At the same time, necessary adjustments and cleaning are accomplished. A good preventive maintenance program can significantly reduce hardware failure.

Today's computer hardware is substantially more reliable than earlier hardware. If the other elements in a computerized information system were as reliable as the hardware, we would have highly reliable systems.

System Software Controls System software consists of the operating system, which is designed to control and manage computer resources during the execution of application programs. The operating system functions as a manager. It has several built-in control features. For example, it provides password protection for access to files, and it processes file header and trailer labels. The first record on a file is a *header label*. It contains information about the file, such as the file name. The file name is read by the computer to verify that the correct file has been read. The last record of a file is a *trailer label*. It contains control information, such as a count of the number of records in the file. Operating systems automatically execute the control features inherent in header and trailer labels.

Access Controls

Access controls limit access to program documentation, program and data files, and computer hardware to authorized individuals. Authorization is given only to individuals whose jobs require it. Many of the controls discussed earlier also help control access. For example, the segregation of functions within the information systems organization and between users and the information systems organization augments access control.

Program Documentation Access to program source documentation is restricted to individuals whose jobs require it—normally, the programmer assigned to a particular application and his or her supervisors. The assigned programmer needs access to the documentation only when working on the application. At all other times the documentation is in the custody of the documentation specialist, if there is one, or the systems programming manager.

Program documentation is a valuable resource. Even experienced programmers find it difficult to make fraudulent program changes without access to program documentation.

Program and Data Files The librarian exercises primary control over access to program and data files. There are two kinds of libraries. One is a manual library, which consists of a separate room or a fireproof vault in which are stored magnetic tapes, disk packs, floppy disks, and any other removable storage media. This library is accessible only to authorized library personnel, specifically excluding programmers, systems analysts, and equipment operators. In a manual library, the librarian maintains physical control over all removable files when they are not being processed. In addition, accountability records are maintained for each file. These records include the following information:

- Date the file was created

- Serial or volume number of the magnetic tape reel, cassette, or disk on which the data are stored

- Names of logical files stored on the physical volumes (cassettes, reels, or disks)

- Date the file is to be scratched (reused)

- Person currently holding the file, and the file's location

- Backup file's remote storage location

The librarian's authorization for release of the files to operations is based on each shift's schedule of jobs to be processed. However, an individual file is not released until it is called for by the operating system. Individual files are returned to the library when processing is complete.

The other type of library is set up through system software. In advanced information systems, most program and data files are stored online. Access to these files is obtained through remote terminals or batch programs. Control is maintained through password schemes, device authorization tables, and data encoding.

Password schemes require users to enter a predetermined set of characters to gain access to a part of the information system. The three-level password scheme is the most common control used in computer libraries. First, the user logs onto the system by entering a unique user identification code. The system then asks the user to enter a password in order to gain access to the system. Finally, to access an individual file, the user is asked to enter the file name. Password systems can also require separate passwords to read or write to each file. This feature allows individuals to read a file with the read password and prevents them from changing the file without a write password.

Password control schemes depend on the password being kept secret from unauthorized personnel. Passwords should be changed regularly to maintain their secrecy. In all password-controlled systems, written records of passwords are kept to a minimum. For example, printers do not print passwords because their discarded output could be used to obtain passwords. In addition, the system keeps a record of each invalid password that is input, the terminal or workstation from which it originated, the user's identification code, and the time it was used. Invalid passwords are monitored to isolate attempts to gain unauthorized access to files through trial and error.

One federal government system containing sensitive information records erroneous passwords, and then goes one step further. It allows the user three opportunities to enter the correct password within thirty seconds. If the user fails, the system assumes that an unauthorized attempt to access the system is occurring and cancels the user's identification code. The user is completely excluded from the system until he or she obtains a new identification code.

A *device authorization table* lists the files to which each device (terminal or workstation) can gain access for reading and for writing, and the time of day access can be gained. When used with a password system, a device authorization table provides additional file security. For example, this system may specify that a terminal in manufacturing cannot gain access to the accounts receivable file, even if the user of that terminal enters the password of the accounts receivable file.

For particularly sensitive data, an encryption approach can be used. In a **data encryption** approach, data are stored on the file in coded form. The data cannot be used unless the code is broken. Software that encodes and decodes data is available for purchase.

Technically, anyone may access an on-line data file using regular telephone lines from anywhere in the world, if that person knows the valid telephone number, user identification code, and password. Microcomputers have compounded the security problem. It is now possible to write a program instructing a microcomputer to follow a trial-and-error scheme to gain access to a computer system and its files. Therefore, sensitive data should be accessible only from hard-wired terminals or workstations, over leased telecommunications lines or through a dial-back procedure for terminal connections. With a *dial-back procedure,* the individual attempting to connect a terminal gives the phone number from which he or she is dialing. A computer operator (or a computer) verifies that the phone number is a valid location from which to connect to the system, and then establishes the connection by dialing the user back. Application 20–2 illustrates how several companies promote data security among their computer users.

Computer Hardware   Access to computer hardware in the central computer facility is controlled by limiting it to those who are authorized to operate the system. In a controlled system, users, analysts, and programmers are not allowed to operate this equipment. Otherwise, the risk of unauthorized changes is too great. Limiting hardware operation to equipment operators is often called a *closed-shop approach*: access is limited by using a "locked door"; work is passed to and from the equipment facility through a "window."

Of course, users must be able to operate personal computer hardware. But its use can be limited to certain persons through locks on the PC and/or locks on doors to the room in which the PC is located.

Miscellaneous Controls

Control groups, internal audit reviews, and file backup are three additional general controls. They help ensure the proper use of management information systems resources.

Control Group   The **control group** is separate from computer operations, and it maintains input/output controls. It logs all batches of input, records batch **control totals**, and reconciles batch control totals to intermediate and final output control totals. After the control group has verified that processing was completed successfully, it distributes the output to authorized users. The control group also provides quality control by maintaining logs of various types of errors and their sources.

Password: User Awareness

By Michael Alexander

In the weeks leading up to Friday, Sept. 13, the computer security troops at Metropolitan Life Insurance Co. launched a widescale campaign to alert computer users to the impending dangers of the Jerusalem, Friday the 13th and other computer viruses that were set to go off on that fabled unlucky day.

With 18,000 personal computers in-house and about 11,000 laptops in the field, Met Life had plenty of reasons to worry. However, when the day ended, only two PCs had been infected.

It is an extraordinary success story—one that is often overlooked these days when viruses are as common as colds but far more damaging. The main reason so few machines were hit was Met Life's ongoing computer security awareness program, says Fran Smyth, assistant vice president of information systems risk management at Met Life.

New York-based Met Life is one of a growing number of corporations that have orchestrated formal computer security awareness programs to instruct computer users on how to safeguard the integrity and confidentiality of corporate information.

Computer security awareness is a "topic whose time has finally come," according to Cathy Weyhausen Englishman, a member of the technical staff of the computer security group at AT&T Bell Laboratories in Murray Hill, N.J.

There has been "a dramatic change" in the number of companies introducing computer security awareness programs in recent years, but the topic of discussion is still "the new kid on the block," Englishman says.

The key to a successful awareness program is to develop a multimedia campaign with a theme that fits the company's culture, she says. "You may want to plan a year at a time and maybe have four themes during the year," she says.

Increasingly, companies are turning to security units or councils, populated with users and managers from a variety of key organizations within the companies, to promote computer security awareness and help ward off viruses as well as other problems.

There are 40 members of the information systems security council at Eastman Kodak Co. in Rochester, N.Y. The council's mission is to create posters, flyers and other media and host computer security awareness seminars, says John Welsh, director of the IS [information systems] security service at the company. The council consists of "a mix of people, not just those who are totally focused on computer operations," Welsh says. "We are also linked to our technology development organization to get the security oar in the water as soon as new things are being developed in the company."

Most companies have basic security policies or building blocks in place before establishing a council, Welsh says. The basics, typically endorsed by senior management, cover a gamut of security issues, from limiting data access to authorized users to reminding users how often data should be backed up.

Getting the endorsement from management for the council's efforts is critical, he says. "The endorsement itself is what prompts most people to turn to us and say, 'Please come to talk to us about this,' " he says.

Corporations are using many techniques to promote computer security awareness, including the following:

• **Posters**. "Reflect your theme in different ways—recognize that people are attracted by different approaches," Englishman advises. "One person might love a cartoon, while another thinks that that is making light of the situation."

• **Booklets and flyers**. Publications for users may emphasize various aspects of security, such as how to protect against getting a virus and how to determine when a PC has been infected. The booklet or flyer will have greater impact if it is addressed and sent to each employee by internal mail rather than by merely dropping them on desks, Englishman adds.

• **Videos**. There are a variety of off-the-shelf, 10- to 15-min. videotapes that address computer security. There are enough of them out there that you can find ones that reflect your theme. Larger companies often opt to create their own videos. "Video is the state of the art," Englishman says. "If you don't have a video you don't rate because that is how you communicate nowadays."

• **Articles in company newsletters**. They may discuss computer security or publicize upcoming events organized to promote security.

• **Employee "trinkets."** Englishman advocates giving employees items such as pens, stickers and antistatic screen cloths—with a security message attached.

There are several reasons for the growing interest in fostering computer security awareness in a full-fledged program, several corporate computer security chiefs say. First, the spread of personal computers and local- and wide-area networks in recent years has spawned a concern that corporate information is not as well protected as it once was when it resided in the data center.

Senior management is also taking a closer look at security because of both corporate and personal liabilities that may ensue if valuable information is lost or falls into the wrong hands.

"Computer security is directed very much toward the standard of 'due care,' which says whatever is appropriate or available in the same industry," Englishman explains. "Management is held responsible for at least implementing that level of security."

Met life has been touting security to users for more than eight years, but it was not until it set up a "security awareness unit" about three years ago that the effort was formalized, Smyth says.

"There are five people in the unit, and they are charged with keeping aware of new developments, techniques, programs,

products and with creating an ongoing awareness program," Smyth says.

Reprinted from *Computerworld* (October 7, 1991), pp. 89–90. Copyright 1991 by CW Publishing, Inc., Framingham, MA. 01701.

Internal Audit Review   During the information systems development process, periodic external reviews are conducted on the work completed to date and on the plans for completing the project. Once a system has been implemented, it is subject to periodic review by an **internal audit group** or by an external group.

The professional association of internal auditing, the Institute of Internal Auditing (IIA), publishes several books about information systems control and auditing. In addition, the Association of EDP Auditors has been formed. One of its activities is the Certified Information Systems Auditor program. This program provides certification of auditors who pass an examination, have adequate experience, and meet continuing education requirements.

File Backup   Chapter 21 will discuss the **physical security** of computer systems from human-caused and natural disasters and interruptions. It is not cost-effective, or even possible, to prevent all threats to computer systems. One must assume that computer operations will be interrupted at times. In fact, accidental destruction of a portion of a file may occur frequently. Destruction of a complete installation, however, is unlikely. In either event, the installation can be protected by an interruption recovery plan with the following components:

- Offsite backup storage of program and data files, documentation, and supplies. Often, local banks provide storage services in their vaults.

- Backup hardware sites. A backup site can be another company with similar equipment that has agreed to provide backup on a reciprocal basis. Other possibilities include service bureaus and the equipment vendor.

- A set of documentation outlining the procedures to be followed during an interruption.

- Business interruption insurance.

Backup data files can be a natural by-product of normal processing. Updated files stored on magnetic tape are backed up by retaining the old (parent) master file and transaction file used in creating the new updated (child) master file. If the new file is destroyed, it can be recreated by simply rerunning the file updating run that originally created it. This procedure, called **grandparent-parent-child backup**, is shown in Figure 20–6.

Files and databases stored on a direct-access storage device and updated in place are more difficult to back up. The contents of such files and databases should be periodically written (dumped) onto magnetic tape or another removable storage media, such as floppy disk, and stored.

The degree of backup needed is related to the potential loss involved. In a mission-critical situation—for example, in an airline reservations system—it may be necessary to back the system up completely with an additional, independent system. Each of the two systems has its own hardware, software, and personnel. Both systems are updated with each customer reservation transaction. Either system can carry on the reservation processing if the other system goes down.

Application Controls

Application controls protect specific applications in the installation, such as accounts receivable. They are divided into input, processing, and output controls.

Input Controls

Input controls provide reasonable assurance that inputs are authorized, converted to machine-readable form correctly, processed as intended, and free from errors. These controls include input authorization, data conversion, data editing, error handling, and data communications.

Computer information systems have four basic types of inputs. Each is subjected to appropriate input controls:

FIGURE 20-6
Flow of Files in
Grandparent-Parent-
Child Backup.

Vertical dimension
illustrates the flow of
grandparent-parent-child
master files in processing,
and horizontal dimension
illustrates the flow of
these files for backup
storage.

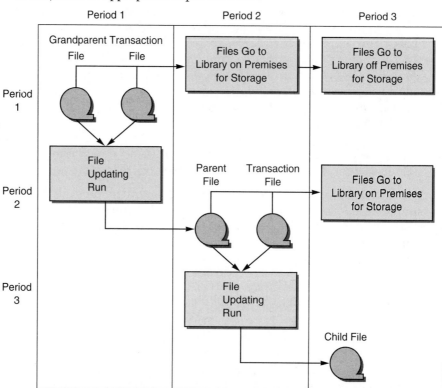

- *Information retrieval inputs* request the computer to display, either on hard copy or on video display screens, the information it has stored or can produce.

- *Transaction inputs* result directly from the firm's transactions and are normally the largest volume of input. For example, transaction inputs can be computer-generated purchase orders based on inventory stock levels.

- *File maintenance inputs* are all changes to files other than transactions. They are made less frequently than transaction inputs, but they can have more permanent and far-reaching effects. For example, a change in the price of a widely sold product affects many individual invoices and accounts receivable.

- *Error correction inputs* correct errors resulting from the three previous inputs. Perhaps the primary control problem in this area is making sure that errors are corrected promptly and that the corrections are authorized properly.

Input Authorization   In batch systems, transaction inputs are typically based on a source document. For example, credits to accounts receivable can be based on cash receipt documents. In an effective system, the flow of source documents to data conversion is strictly controlled. Whenever possible, documents are batched. The user or the originating department and the input/output control group compute batch control totals and maintain them. Authorization signatures are appropriate in many cases, such as on an approval for payment of an accounts payable voucher. Other control devices, such as prenumbering source documents, restricting their storage, and logging their transmittal between organizations, increase control of input authorization. Control is also increased if the people authorized to make each type of input are identified, and if procedures for identifying and validating the source of each input are installed. In an interactive on-line system, input authorization is usually based on access controls such as passwords. Passwords used in this way are often called electronic signatures.

Data Conversion   Data conversion often takes two steps: (1) transcribing the data to a source document, and (2) keying data onto a machine-readable medium. The transcription step is eliminated if possible, because one of the best ways to reduce errors in data conversion is to eliminate manual conversion. In a retail system, one way to avoid transcription is to install point-of-sale cash registers that automatically capture sales and inventory transaction inputs.

The primary data conversion control is batch control totals. Figure 20–7 illustrates batch control. The originating department batches source documents in limited numbers. Batches can consist of natural logical groupings of documents, such as a day's transactions or the source documents from an organizational unit. However, they do not have to be based on any logical grouping.

Batch control normally consists of a total of a quantity field, such as the total hours worked by employees in a given batch of time cards. If

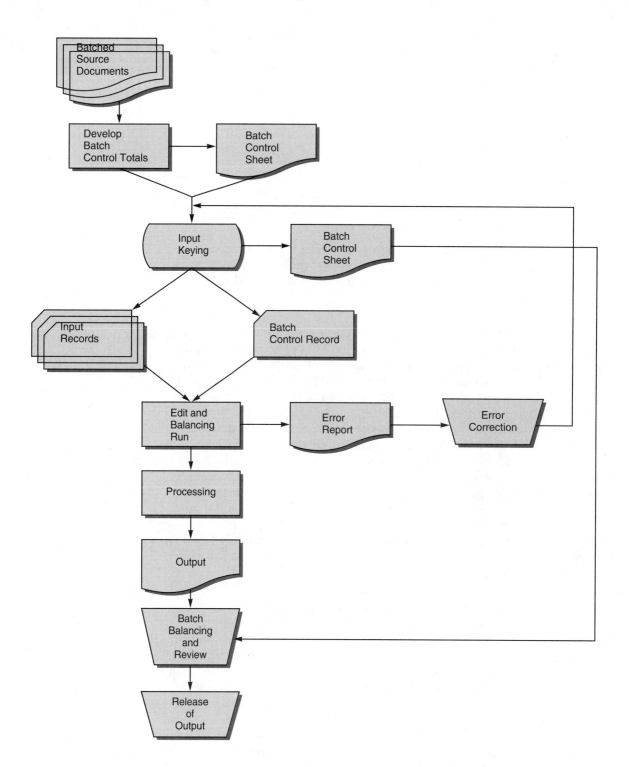

FIGURE 20–7
Batch Control.

there is no quantity field, hash totals can serve for batch control. A **hash total** is a summation of a nonquantity field—for example, the sum of the first three digits of the social security numbers on the payroll file maintenance inputs that update employee names. Hash totals have no meaning except for control purposes.

Batch control totals are keyed into a separate batch control record for each batch. Before further processing, a balancing and edit program verifies whether each batch of inputs balances.

Batch control totals can also be used in on-line real-time systems. The computer can assign each transaction to a batch number. Balancing is done after processing has occurred.

Data Editing   Many of the errors that occur while data are being collected and converted can be detected before processing by using the computer to edit input. For batch input, these edits are often performed by a separate edit and balancing program.

Real-time interactive input or batched input entered through on-line terminals or workstations located where the data originate can be edited and corrected on-line. As each input record is entered, it is edited, and the terminal operator is notified immediately if an error occurs. The advantage of this on-line editing procedure is that errors can be corrected immediately by the person who made them or who has the information to correct them. On-line editing is more reliable than batch editing.

The edit techniques normally found in well-designed edit routines and programs are as follows:

- **Anticipation checks**, which check for expected conditions, including nonblank fields and an input record for each master file record. For example, on employee time card records in a payroll system, the hours worked are expected to be nonblank. (If no hours were worked, a zero is expected in the field.) Furthermore, each employee in the master file is expected to have a time card input record for each payroll processing period.

- Limit or **reasonableness checks**, which verify that data items are within reasonable limits. For example, in a payroll system, hours worked per week are expected to never be negative and never exceed seventy-two. An accounts payable system for a milling company might check invoice input by computing a price per pound for grain invoices and verifying that the price is within established limits. There are many possibilities for reasonableness checks. This technique is limited only by the systems analyst's imagination.

- **Arithmetic proof checks**, which verify the results of other computations. One example is a check to see that the debits total equals the credits total for general journal inputs. Batch control total verifications are another commonly performed example of arithmetic proof checks.

- **Numeric and alphabetic checks**, which ascertain that numeric input record fields contain only numeric characters and that alphabetic fields contain only alphabetic characters.

- **Invalid code checks**, which verify codes contained in input records to ensure that they are valid. Examples are checks of department codes or sales territory codes. Each type of input record usually has a unique record code that enables the system to identify the type of input. For example, all accounts receivable payment records may have a record code of 5. These codes must be verified before a record is edited, since most other edit checks depend on the type of input record received.

- **Sequence checks**, which are made on all input to sequential processing programs to verify that the input records are in ascending sequential order by the record key field. In another form of sequence checking, the input records are expected to be in a certain sequence. For example, an airline reservations system may require that the reservation agent's identification be input before the customer's reservation data.

Error Handling　　Once they are detected, errors must be corrected. Simply listing errors on an error list or file and sending them to the user department to be corrected are insufficient. In the rush of day-to-day operations, the user department may ignore the lists or give them a low priority. Another tendency is to correct errors that are easy to correct, and to leave errors that require more intensive investigation. The most elegant and creative error detection system will fail if errors are not corrected.

Techniques used to control the **error handling** process are as follows:

- A cumulative error list or file is used. It contains not only the error detected in the current processing run, but all errors detected in previous runs that have not been corrected. Cumulative error lists are produced from the file of uncorrected errors.

- The responsibility for correcting errors is often given to a senior individual in the user department. This individual is likely to correct errors carefully because he or she has a direct interest in the system's integrity. Data originators, who can be in nonuser departments, may not be as careful. In any case, the individual responsible for error correction should be thoroughly familiar with the application system, since proper interpretation and correction of errors often requires considerable skill.

- The editing of real-time input is carefully monitored. Real-time input allows the advantage of on-line editing, but it also presents some error handling disadvantages. For example, how can a company control the situation in which an operator deliberately or inadvertently fails to correct an error displayed on the video display screen? At least two control approaches are possible. First, the input system can be designed to refuse additional input until the error is corrected. Second, a record of all errors and their corrective entries can be made. This list can then be reviewed periodically to ensure that errors are being properly corrected.

- All error corrections are set up to flow through the same edit procedures that control original input.

Data Communications   The communication of data between departments and from one processing step to another must be controlled, whether this communication is accomplished by documents, input transmittals, magnetic tape, or telecommunications. In the case of documents or input transmittals, batch control totals are the primary instrument of data communication control. For tape or telecommunications record counts, hash totals or field totals effect the control. Each time the data are processed, totals are taken and compared with the control totals to ensure that data have not been altered or lost.

In addition, some companies implement data encryption devices for the transmission of sensitive data over telecommunications channels, although this is not always effective. It is fairly easy to intercept transmitted data, especially data transmitted over microwave channels. However, data transmitted over fiber-optic cable are practically immune to unauthorized interception. Encryption provides protection, but some codes are easily broken.

Processing Controls

Even if a system has well-designed input controls, some errors can slip by, or additional errors can be created during processing. Therefore, controls that increase the integrity of processing are essential. Most **processing controls** are very similar to input controls:

- Run-to-run control totals, such as **record counts** and critical quantity totals, are verified at appropriate points in the processing cycle. These controls detect operator errors—such as mounting the wrong version of the master file—when control totals do not balance.

- Reasonableness checks are incorporated into processing programs. Although most errors of this type are detected and corrected during input, errors (or intentional unauthorized changes) can be created during processing. Incorporating these checks into processing programs also provides additional assurance that errors detected by input editing are actually corrected.

- Controls are included to detect operator errors such as processing the wrong file. External file labels or, more important, an internal file labeling system that allows the computer to verify file identifications automatically can prevent these errors.

Output Controls

Output controls are executed by the control group. They help ensure the accuracy of computer results and control the distribution of output. They include the following:

- Output control totals are reconciled with input and processing totals before information systems releases the reports.

- The computer console log or the job execution stream on the computer output is reviewed to detect any unusual interrupts or processing patterns that may affect the validity of the output.

- Job control language listings are checked to ensure that no unauthorized programs were executed during processing.

- Output reports are visually scanned to make sure that they look correct. Critical input transactions are compared individually with output reports to ensure that changes were made correctly. Other techniques, such as statistical sampling, are sometimes used to review output.

- Copies of output reports are delivered to authorized recipients only. An integral part of a system's documentation is a list of all system output and the recipient of each copy.

- The use of accountable documents (for example, blank check stock) is verified by comparing computer-generated counts to actual usage recorded from preprinted sequence numbers on the documents.

Auditing Information Systems

The auditing of information systems consists primarily of checking to assure that the information systems conform to the information systems controls discussed in this chapter. As we noted earlier, an individual system does not have to have all the controls covered in this chapter. Strong controls in one area can offset weak controls in another area. In most information system audits, the auditors are interested in assuring that the data and information have integrity. In fact, normal audit procedures are not designed to detect computer crime. Those that do detect computer crime require more work on the part of the auditor and thus are more expensive.

In the typical information systems audit the auditor is concerned with substantiating the information produced by the system. In this process the auditor performs two types of tests: compliance tests and substantive tests. In **compliance testing** the auditor is concerned with reviewing the information system to be sure that it complies with good information systems controls. The auditor is looking to identify the strengths of a system's controls and its weaknesses.

Once the control strengths and weaknesses are identified, the auditor can judge how good the controls are. If the controls are good, and therefore reliable, the auditor doesn't have to do as much substantive testing. In **substantive testing** the auditor is attempting to verify the integrity of information produced by the system. Obviously, if good information systems controls are in place and are followed, then the information produced has more integrity. If information systems controls are poor, the data have less integrity and the auditor must do considerably more direct verification of the information produced by the system. This verification process consists primarily of tracing outputs back to their constituent inputs to verify that the data were processed correctly into information.

Audits of information systems can have different focuses. Some audits are focused on data integrity; some are focused on physical security; others are focused on information systems controls. Within information systems controls, the focus can be on general controls or controls for individual system applications.

Information systems audits are often performed by the internal audit staff of a company. The Institute of Internal Auditors has traditionally taken the lead in developing techniques for both the control and audit of information systems. Information systems audit has become a recognized career area. The EDP Auditor's Foundation administers an exam and grants the Certified Information Systems Auditor (CISA) designation. The CISA exam is covered in more depth in Chapter 24.

Audits of information systems, particularly control and security audits, have also become lucrative businesses for public accounting firms (external auditors). Some firms have established separate groups that are typically called computer assurance services groups. These groups not only audit information systems controls but also perform consulting engagements, advising clients on the controls that should be implemented for their particular information system.

Summary

- Information and data are the lifeblood of a business. Today, most information and data are processed and stored by computer systems. Companies realize the value of data and information and thus spend considerable resources to protect this valuable asset.

- Information integrity is a quality of information that has not been compromised by accidental or malicious destruction, alteration, loss, or error.

- A computer crime is the use of a computer to commit an illegal act.

- Computer crime can be classified into five different categories:

    1. Theft of data or services such as the unauthorized use of a computer through hacking.

    2. Financial crimes, which includes using a computer to alter information for financial gains. These crimes are often called fraud or embezzlement.

    3. Software piracy, the illegal copying and use of copyrighted software.

    4. Property theft, the theft of computer hardware and software.

    5. Vandalism, the destruction of computer hardware, software, or data through any technique, including viruses.

- Computer viruses are computer programs designed to replicate themselves and spread to other computer systems. Once they infect a computer system their actions can range from the relatively harmless to maliciously destructive.

- Industrial espionage is spying on a business to gain confidential data and information. This confidential information is usually trade secrets, technical expertise, or strategic and tactical plans.

- Users can make significant contributions to the application of controls in computer systems. Although computer controls often fail to detect crime and errors, they can be far more reliable than manual control systems if they are used creatively.

- Computer controls may be classified as general controls and application controls.

- General controls are the overall managerial controls applied to all software, hardware, and personnel involved with the management information system.

- Management controls include activities such as planning the information systems development process, segregating functions, selecting and training personnel, writing systems and procedures, and establishing a budget and a user billing system.

- System development controls ensure that application systems are developed and documented in accordance with prescribed standards.

- Control over equipment and systems software is a crucial area of general controls.

- It is necessary to restrict access to documentation, programs, and data files related to production programs.

- Internal audit organizations, control groups, and file backup help ensure the proper use of management information systems resources.

- Application controls protect individual system applications, such as the payroll application and the manufacturing requirements application. These controls are divided into input, processing, and output controls.

- Input controls help ensure that inputs to the system are authorized, converted and processed correctly, and free from errors. Processing controls increase the integrity of computer processing. Output controls help ensure the accuracy of computer results and control output distribution.

- Auditing information systems consists primarily of checking to see if systems conform to information systems controls.

Key Terms

Information integrity	Control totals
Computer crime	Internal audit group
Computer viruses	Physical security
Industrial espionage	Grandparent-parent-child backup
Audit trails	Application controls
Backup procedure	Input controls
General controls	Hash total
Management controls	Anticipation checks
Segregation of functions	Reasonableness checks
System development controls	Arithmetic proof checks
Documentation standards	Numeric and alphabetic checks
Program change control	Invalid code checks
Code comparison	Sequence checks
Write suppress feature	Error handling
Preventive maintenance checks	Processing controls
Access controls	Record counts
Password schemes	Output controls
Data encryption	Compliance testing
Control group	Substantive testing

1. What is information integrity?

2. What are the five categories of computer crime?

3. What are some ways to prevent the spread of computer viruses?

4. Why is industrial espionage a more common problem today?

5. Outline and discuss the characteristics of controls in a computer-based system.

6. What are the general controls of computer-based systems?

7. Many computer frauds are executed through unauthorized changes to computer programs. How can program changes be controlled? Do program change controls differ for small and large information systems organizations?

8. Why should the systems analysis and programming functions be segregated from the equipment operating function?

9. In regard to billing users for computer services, what is the normal evolutionary process through which most firms go?

10. What are the elements of good systems documentation?

11. How do hardware and system software controls differ?

12. Identify two different ways to set up a file library.

13. How do companies protect themselves from unexpected interruption of computer services? Explain this in terms of hardware, software, and computer-based files.

14. Indicate what type of general control each of the following represents.

    a. Construction of hash totals

    b. Parity checks

    c. Documentation

    d. Rotation of duties

    e. Passwords

    f. Segregation of functions

    g. Trailer labels

15. What are the application controls of a computer-based system? How do they differ from general controls?

16. What are the four basic types of input to computer-based systems?

17. How is the data conversion process controlled?

18. Discuss the types of edit techniques that can be incorporated into computer programs.

19. Once detected, how should errors be processed and handled?

20. Why are controls over computer output needed?

21. What is the difference between compliance testing and substantive testing in an information systems audit?

Discussion Questions and Cases

1. The Smith Company is in the process of computerizing several of its accounting applications. It has three programmers, and it wants you to allocate the programming among them to maximize internal control and minimize fraud. The programs will perform the following functions.

   a. Maintain general ledger

   b. Maintain accounts payable ledger

   c. Maintain accounts receivable ledger

   d. Print checks for signature

   e. Maintain cash disbursements journal

   f. Issue credits on returns and allowances

   g. Reconcile bank account

   Allocate programs to the programmers in the best way. Justify your allocation. How does your answer relate to segregation of duties?

2. Documenting information systems applications is an important step in the design and implementation of any computer-based system. Documentation provides a complete record of information processing applications. However, documentation is a phase of systems development that is often neglected. While documentation can be tedious and time-consuming, the lack of proper documentation can be very costly for an organization.

   a. Briefly identify and explain the purposes proper documentation can serve.

   b. Briefly discuss the basic types of information that should be included in the documentation of a data processing application.

   c. What policies should be established to regulate access to documentation data for the following four groups of company employees?

      1. Computer operators

      2. Internal auditors

      3. Production planning analysts

      4. Systems analysts

   Adapted from CMA Examination, December 1977, Part 5, No. 2).

3. The North Face Company is considering implementing an accounts payable computer system. Top management has instructed the information systems department to design a system that maximizes efficiency and minimizes potential fraud. The following proposal for the system has been delivered to you for your evaluation. All purchase orders are sent directly to the information systems department biweekly from the purchasing department. After their batch delivery, the price, quantity, and other pertinent information are processed directly to the accounts payable disk file. When the receiving department notifies purchasing that an order has been received, information systems pays the vendor on the basis of data input from the purchase order. No editing run is implemented because the information systems staff is excellent and because editing is considered too costly. In addition, purchase orders are used to update the

inventory file biweekly. The staff analyst who constructed the system feels that it is efficient and can save the company quite a few dollars because it reduces the need for historical master files.

a. List the areas of weakness in this system.

b. Present a data flow diagram of a revised accounts payable system that maximizes internal control and minimizes the potential for fraud. Utilize the concepts presented in this chapter of grandparent-parent-child files, transaction files, error files, edit runs, and input hash and batch totals.

c. Does the revised flowchart utilize the concept of an audit trail?

d. What other source documents should be utilized in this system?

4. Joe Hagen was the lead programmer for the demand deposit accounting system in the Southeastern Banking Corporation. He also programmed applications for wire transfers of money. Joe devised a scheme to defraud the bank of one million dollars. He inserted code in the demand deposit accounting system that would increase his account by one million dollars whenever a check for twenty dollars was processed through the account. Joe wanted to be out of the country when his scheme was executed, so he scheduled his annual vacation in a foreign country. Just before leaving for the airport, he stopped at a local drug store and cashed a check for twenty dollars. Joe knew that it would take approximately twenty-four hours for the check to clear the bank and to trigger the transfer of money to his account. By that time he would be out of the country.
Upon arriving at his destination, Joe waited for a day and then initiated a wire transfer from his account to a foreign bank account. A few days later, Joe called from the foreign country to say he liked his vacation so well that he had decided to resign from his job and take an extended vacation. The bank never heard from Joe again. But it did discover the fraud approximately six months later. What could have been done to prevent this computer crime?

5. Winchester and Company is a large international management consulting firm specializing in computer-based systems. Recently, a large bank in a southeastern city became concerned over the security of its automated teller machines. The bank has twenty of these machines scattered over the city. The bank hired Winchester and Company to determine if there were any security weaknesses in these automated teller machines. As a part of its review of the automated teller machine system, Winchester asked two of its employees to break into the system by nonphysical means and steal as much money as they could. After discussing the plan with the bank management, they approved the operation. Over a period of two days, the two Winchester staff members managed to steal eight thousand dollars from the bank's automated teller machines. If you were on Winchester's staff and were assigned this task, how would you attempt to break into the system? How do you think the Winchester staff employees managed to steal the eight thousand dollars?

6. Leslie Long is in charge of computer security for Dominion First Securities, a large stock brokerage firm. Dominion has offices in most of the medium-sized and large cities in the eastern half of the United States. Dial-up access allows each office to use a central mainframe computer located in New York. Leslie is very concerned that the firm's computer system is vulnerable to invasion by nonauthorized users. Is such an attack possible? If so, what steps can Leslie take to protect the system against nonauthorized use?

INFORMATION SYSTEMS STRATEGIES

How to Ensure Network Security

By David Coursey

If some morning a man named Tom Ellis shows up unannounced at your data center, consider the possibility that your job may be about to abend. For if Ellis, a security specialist with Arthur Andersen appears, you've probably already had your share of abends, system crashes, pirated passwords and other nightmares.

"It's very seldom that MIS [management information systems] directors are the ones who call us in. More often than not it's some senior management person who has some concern about information systems security—either because an event has happened or there is a concern he or she may be exposed," Ellis said.

This isn't the kind of introduction Ellis likes, but it is how he meets MIS executives whose CEOs have lost faith in their ability to protect the company's data assets. He'd prefer to meet the MIS staff first and solve problems before they become critical.

"Most of the better MIS directors recognize they have a need to call in specialists that deal with information systems security," Ellis said.

Ellis is a partner and director of information systems risk management services in the Dallas office of Arthur Andersen. One of his specialities is the security audits, something MIS executives need to be familiar with and should be doing regularly on their own.

Here are the steps to take in auditing your own organization and consequently developing a security plan:

* Decide what security means:

Security is something many MIS executives take for granted, concerning themselves with it only when a problem occurs. Many MIS departments don't have people trained to deal with such problems or to prevent them, said Dorothy Houston, a district security manager with AT&T, based in Warren, N.J.

Like Andersen Consulting, AT&T offers customers a broad range of security services but goes a step further—offering promotional material and videotapes based upon those the telecommunications giant uses in-house.

The concept of security is a broad one and may have different meanings to the auditors and MIS executives involved. At one level, security only relates to physical access to the data center or to machines themselves.

More commonly, Ellis said, security is perceived as protection against unauthorized access to sensitive information assets. In a broader context, security is associated with the safeguarding of the integrity of data assets against any risk, whether errors, omissions, unauthorized changes, disaster, loss of competitive advantage through disclosure or other risks.

"Only by understanding the objectives of a security audit can an MIS director anticipate the scope of the review and be responsive to the audit's findings," Ellis said.

AT&T's Houston said all levels of an organization must be responsible for information security. Smart MIS executives recruit senior executives and lines-of-business managers and users to participate in the security review, partly because they have information the MIS executive may not have and partly to generate support for proper security measures.

Jeff Marinstein, vice president of Contingency Planning Research, a Jericho, N.Y., disaster planning and risk management consulting firm, said security is an important part of a successful risk management program.

"The hope of this is not to slap in a security software program or a retinal eye scanner but to develop a comprehensive system of physical and logical security. It's important to understand why this is being done and to communicate it to all employees," Marinstein said.

Marinstein said it is important for users to understand why security measures are in place and for managers to develop a security policy, with appropriate punishments for violators.

"People who five years ago didn't have access to corporate information now own and are responsible for it on a personal computer. And many companies haven't stopped to consider this," Marinstein said.

* Look for problems that really exist:

You've read all about viruses and other external threats to a corporation's data assets. If the content of computer and popular magazines is to be believed, dealing with these issues will relieve all of a corporation's security headaches.

Don't believe it.

"It's gotten a lot of play, and it is exciting to read about people who hack their way into networks and do damage. And while there are some occasions when significant networks have been brought down, my experience in working with clients is a virus problem is indicative of some other more basic problems," Ellis said.

"The problem is not that these hackers are so smart they can weasel their way through any system. That's not true at all. Sometimes it's the users or companies that aren't smart enough to know they have to protect themselves."

Houston recommends MIS executives look at the vulnerability of information or systems to loss. After the vulnerabilities are defined, it is possible to recommend appropriate solutions.

• Don't overlook the obvious:

Most data loss and other problems are caused not by viruses or other external threats but by human mistakes and failures. Poorly designed systems live up to the work that went into them—or lack of it—and cause problems as a result.

Ellis cited the example of a large retail client that tried to implement a large point-of-sale system. "Nothing more than cash registers to capture sales information and transmit it to the host. They did a very poor job of implementing the system and as a result lost thousands of sales transactions a day," Ellis said.

The chain reaction that followed screwed up customer billing statements, affected cash flow and ultimately created tremendous chaos—all because MIS executives hadn't covered the basic issues of program quality and data security when the system was created and installed.

Another example is a client who spent $100 million designing a new system. "They didn't do any coding, testing or implementation. They spent $100 million and did such a poor job they had to scuttle the whole project and start over again.

"Those are problems that are much more pervasive than the outside threat problem," Ellis said. "Errors and omissions in the basic methodology, putting controls into the basic system before it goes into production, is the most important step in eliminating problems later."

Many companies when they choose to conduct a security audit do it entirely in-house. Others seek outside assistance or contract the work entirely to an outsider such as Ellis or AT&T's Data Security Services organization.

• Decide how important the information is:

Whatever method is chosen, Ellis recommends the process begin with a preliminary security review. Its objective is to determine how important information systems are to a company's overall performance.

This is something senior managers, MIS executives and information systems staff should already know. But understanding how important each application is to the overall success or failure of the business allows security needs to be kept in proper perspective.

AT&T's Houston recommends that each application and system be rated according to criticality to the business.

• Determine the potential loss:

In a multiple CPU environment, for example, a processor used only for testing would not require the layers of security needed for an on-line transaction processing system. That sounds simple, but developing such knowledge allows security to be assigned quite specifically and cost-effectively, reducing the tendency to paint with too broad a brush.

At the same time, a mission-critical system, such as an airline reservation system, has the potential to take the company down with it. MIS executives should be clear on the value of each system to their organization.

• Determine the cost to correct the problems:

Correction can take a variety of forms. Some systems have to be completely redesigned, Ellis said. But often additional security can be added through hardware or software purchased from outside.

"You shouldn't just look at the cost of hardware or software changes," Houston said. "Information systems include people and machine costs. Employee training needs to be figured in as well, from the information center out to the end-users."

• Compare the cost of solving the problems to the loss potential:

Houston said the cost of data loss must be weighed against the cost of solving the problem. In the examples above, a CPU with no critical applications might be relatively unprotected, but adding security features might cost more than the value of the potential loss. On the other hand, a mission-critical system could justify huge investments intended to prevent even greater losses.

If the potential loss is greater than the cost of solving the problem, develop an implementation plan.

Marinstein said this is one of the basic principles of all risk management. "We should not spend more to protect an asset than we could to replace it," he stated. "it is easier to schedule spending on avoiding a potential loss than it will be to recover or replace that loss when it occurs unexpectedly."

If the potential loss is less than the implementation cost, accept the risk. Some companies require managers to document why a risk is acceptable, which could be a useful document to have your senior executives file in the event of problems.

Marinstein said it is often possible to reduce a risk at much lower cost than eliminating it completely. In doing so, overall systems security may be improved as well.

A cost-effectiveness analysis might determine that rewriting mainframe code at a time cost of, say, $10,000 would be less expensive than having the system generate billing errors that would cost $50,000 to solve.

Ellis said integrated systems are inherently more risky than machines that are not connected to anything else. The more interconnected a system is and the more parts depend upon each other, the more likely a failure or breach in one area is to ignite problems systemwide.

Still, business necessity appears to be moving MIS toward even greater connectivity and greater risk for companies that don't properly manage that risk.

Likewise, systems that are more complex make it difficult for users or administrators to recognize when a problem has occurred. Giving users a great access to sensitive information, especially through EDI technology, increases the risk associated with that access.

"End-user computing is becoming increasingly popular and useful but may expose sensitive corporate databases to corruption if not properly protected.

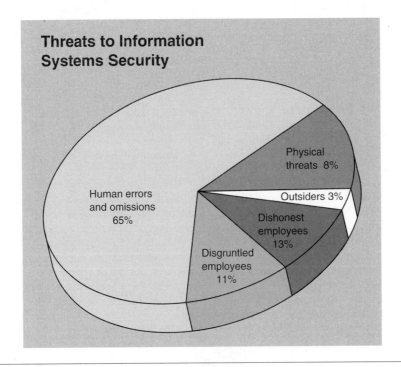

Threats to Information Systems Security

Human errors and omissions 65%

Physical threats 8%

Outsiders 3%

Dishonest employees 13%

Disgruntled employees 11%

MIS executives should recognize their role in protecting corporate databases and balance this concern against the need to allow access to databases by users," Ellis said.

Discussion Questions

1. Does information security have any relationships to information systems ethics or to law?

2. If you have a personal computer, how long has it been since you backed up your hard disk? If your hard disk were to fail, what steps would you take to recover?

Reprinted with permission of Fairchild Publications from *MIS Week* (November 27, 1989), pp. 26, 32.

PC Security Precautions

Do	Don't
Maintain an inventory of computer hardware and software, including all serial numbers.	Forget cards installed in machines or peripherals when making an inventory of your equipment.
Make sure there is adequate, secure storage for media containing sensitive information when not in use.	Use public-domain software from bulletin boards and associates.
Make sure the copyrighted software is used only in accordance with the licensing agreement for that software.	Forget to protect against static electricity in the work area.
Determine whether sensitive information is shredded or recycled when no longer needed.	Give network users access to more directories than they need to do their jobs. A workstation virus could damage any server directories it can access.
Determine whether to store copies of vital data off-site.	Process a critical function on your PC without preparing to process it in an alternate location.
Determine if your PC has multiple users and whether it should have a user log and assigned administrator.	

This chart is based on recommendations contained in the booklets "Desktop Computer Security Guidelines" and "Computer Virus Awareness and Prevention" available from AT&T and designed for distribution to users. Call 1-800-447-0012 for information.

Five

Information Systems, Management, Society, and You

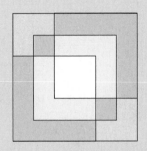

21

Information Resource Management

Computer information systems are often large and complex. With the advent of minicomputers and personal computers, computer systems are being dispersed to a large number of points at far-flung locations. Computer technologies such as electronic mail, decision support systems, personal computers, application development by users, computer networks, and computer-integrated manufacturing are causing monumental changes in the conduct of business activities. Managers who successfully manage these technologies will be winners in the competitive business arena.

Management of the information systems resource has seen significant changes in recent years. In the 1960s and 1970s, information systems managers gradually increased their power and influence within most organizations. Typically, they moved from managerial positions within another function, such as accounting, to vice-presidential positions within the information systems function. These managers were looked upon as experts in information processing, and they held the keys to the computer resource. In recent years, distributed data processing and application development by users have resulted in a challenge to the power of the information systems manager. With users directly purchasing hardware and either purchasing or creating software, many see the role of the information systems manager changing to that of a consultant, an advisor, and a coordinator. However, centralized computer facilities will continue to exist, especially for large databases that support many users concurrently. The challenge of administering centralized databases and communication networks with distributed computing will continue to provide information systems managers with a crucial role in the management of business organizations.

This chapter first discusses the structure of the information systems function. It then looks at managing system development. Finally, it covers the management of system operations, including system maintenance, data processing (DP) operations, the physical security of computer operations, and managing end-user-computing.

This examination of the management information systems function is broken down into two major areas: the location of the information systems function within the structure of the organization, and the internal structure of the information systems function itself.

The Organizational Location of Information Systems

Typically the information systems function is located in one of two areas in an organization. The chief information systems executive may report to the vice president and controller as depicted in Figure 21–1, or he or she may report directly to the president as vice president and chief information officer, as depicted in Figure 21–2. There are advantages and disadvantages to both of these organizational locations for the information systems functions.

The **controller**, being the chief financial officer in a corporation, is looked upon as the primary provider of financial management information. In addition, functions in the controller's areas such as payroll, accounts payable, and accounts receivable are often the first applications to

FIGURE 21-1
Chief Information
Systems Executive
Reporting to the Vice
President/Controller.

This organizational
location for the chief
information systems
executive often occurs in
small and medium-sized
firms.

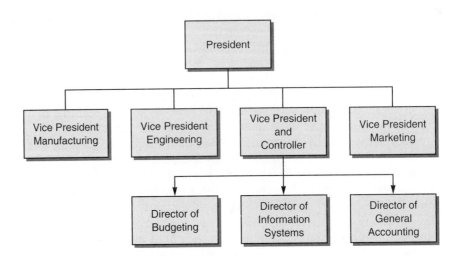

be computerized. Therefore, the information systems function often originates and matures within the controller's organization. The primary disadvantage of having the chief information systems executive report to the controller is that the computer resource may be dominated by and used primarily to solve problems within the accounting area. Therefore, other functions such as marketing, engineering, and production applications of the computer may be neglected. The primary advantages of having the chief information systems executive report to the controller are that accounting is an information-oriented discipline and accountants are well trained in the area of control. These skills of accountants may produce a computer system that is well controlled and easy to audit.

Many large, mature information systems organizations are separate and have a chief information officer who is a vice president and reports directly to the president, as illustrated in Figure 21-2. This location for the information systems function helps ensure that each functional area receives unbiased attention from the information systems department. Today, with computers penetrating many aspects of all functions, it is particularly important that the chief information systems executive be a member of the unbiased vice presidential level of management.

FIGURE 21-2
Chief Information Systems Executive Reporting to the President.
In large firms and in firms in which the information systems function has been developed to its full potential, the vice president for information systems normally reports to the president

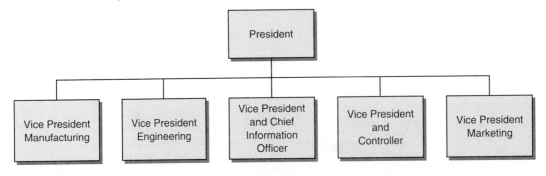

The Internal Structure of Information Systems

The organization of the information systems function itself varies from firm to firm, particularly between small and large firms. Figure 21–3 depicts a typical information system organization in a large firm. In small organizations, many of the functions identified in this figure are consolidated or do not exist. For example, a small firm may purchase all of its software, so it has no need for the systems and programming function and the systems software function.

As shown at the manager level of Figure 21–3, six distinct functions should be carried out within information systems or arranged through outside sources. A specific information systems organization chart may look quite different from Figure 21–3. However, the major functions that an information systems organization is concerned with are covered in the figure.

The **information center** is responsible for coordinating and supporting application development by end users. The people in the center are technical experts on the software that users typically employ without programming, such as Lotus 1-2-3 and FOCUS. They act as consultants to assist the user in application development without programming. Since the personal computer is used in this effort, the coordination of personal computing is often carried out by the information center. The personal computer has brought several challenges, including managing the personal computer. The responsibilities of the personal computer coordination group are listed in Figure 21–4.

The **systems software department** installs and maintains system software such as operating systems and database management systems. The people in this department are technical and very highly skilled programmers who rarely deal directly with users.

Application software is developed by, or selected and purchased with the help of, the **systems and programming department**. The people in this department interact heavily with users as they develop user applications.

The **technical support staff** is in charge of maintaining hardware and establishing data processing standards. These **standards** are very much like the procedures for the data processing function. They include such things as program, data, and application naming conventions, procedures for maintaining the integrity of communication systems, and guidelines that govern the content of user procedure manuals.

The **data processing operations department** manages the day-to-day operations of the computer hardware. Employees of this department also monitor the processing of computer jobs and assist when human intervention, such as mounting tapes, is required.

A function that is relatively new in most large information systems organizations is that of **database administration (DBA)**. The DBA department is responsible for coordinating the database and providing for data security.

The information systems **steering committee** is made up of high-level managers from each function within the business, including marketing, accounting, information systems, manufacturing, and so on. Its purpose is to guide the overall direction of information systems. For example, the steering committee decides the priorities for implementing specific ap-

FIGURE 21–3
Large Information
Systems
Organizations.

As computer information
systems have become
more important to
organizations, the
information systems
organization itself has
grown in size and
influence. Within the
information systems
organization, the area
that is growing most
rapidly is the information
center with its personal
computer coordination
and support of
application development
by end users.

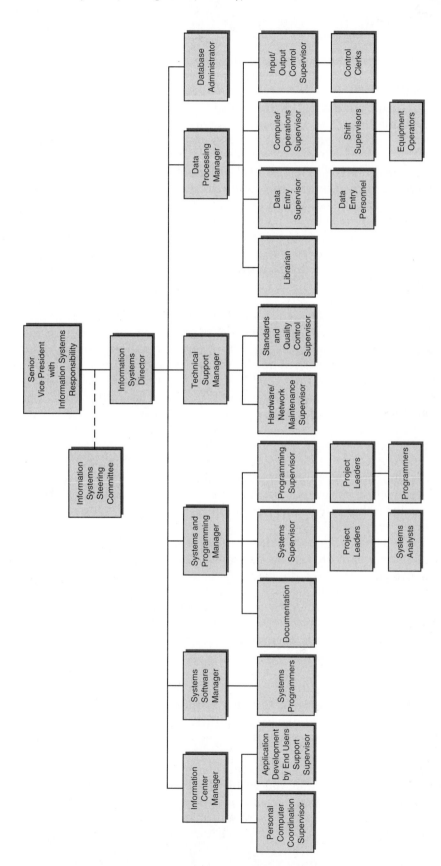

- Standardizing hardware purchases
- Standardizing software purchases
- Providing PC access to mainframe databases
- Preventing the redundant development of software
- Preventing the redundant creation and storage of data
- Assuring that data stored on personal computers are secure
- Providing personal computer training
- Maintaining the firm's in-house "personal computer store" where users can try out a wide variety of PC hardware and software

FIGURE 21–4
Responsibilities of the Personal Computer Coordination Group.

Personal computer coordination groups originated in the early 1980s. The information processing that is performed through personal computers and application development by users is 75 percent of the total information processing of firms.

plication systems. Much of the high-level planning for information systems is either performed or approved by the steering committee. Ideally, the steering committee provides the broad perspectives and guidance necessary to ensure that the information systems resource supports the objectives of the business as a whole.

Managing System Development

Perhaps the most important aspect of managing the system development effort is the **system development methodology** used. Previous chapters discussed the structured approach to system development, system prototyping, and application development by users. A structured methodology, blended with system prototyping and application development by users, should be used to develop any new system.

Another aspect of managing system development is the process by which development efforts are controlled. Most system development organizations use a project management approach. Under the **project management approach**, each application development of significant size is assigned to a project development team. This team is usually headed by a senior systems analyst, or sometimes by a user department manager, who has system development experience. Sufficient resources in the form of programmers, systems analysts, hardware, and software are assigned to the team to complete the project. As illustrated in Application 21–1, the team approach to management is being applied to all areas of information systems management.

Each project is assigned its own financial budget and time schedule. The financial budget performance is tracked by periodic reports which compare actual expenditures to budgets. Schedule performance is managed and controlled through a project schedule performance tool such as **program evaluation and review technique (PERT)**, **critical path management (CPM)**, or **Gantt charts**. PERT and CPM are scheduling methods that use networks consisting of activities that consume resources and take time, and events that mark the beginning and end of each activity. These methods allow the minimum amount of time in which a project can be completed and the critical path to be determined.

Gantt charts are the most conceptually simple of the scheduling techniques. Figure 21–5 illustrates a typical Gantt chart. Planned times for the various tasks are shown with blue bars; the actual times are shown

APPLICATION 21–1

Teamwork Takes Work

By Carol A. Norman and Robert A. Zawacki

Ask information systems managers whether they believe their organizations can have employee-to-supervisor ratios of 40 to 1, and chances are they'll say, "Impossible! Service quality will suffer! How can I have this ratio and add value to the business, which is what the CEO wants me to do?"

IS [information systems] managers can have it all—quality service, added value and a leaner management layer—but it requires a management philosophy that encourages taking risks and empowering people as well as an organizational structure that puts that philosophy into practice.

IS groups in certain large companies are experimenting with the use of self-directed work groups, a team management approach that gives IS individuals the skills to handle change and make better business and technology decisions. Because they broaden their expertise, these IS individuals become more productive, motivated and satisfied with their jobs.

While still in pilot stages at most firms, self-directed work groups have the potential to improve IS effectiveness throughout a company. Because team members are expected to manage, evaluate and improve the group's work environment, IS staff members such as programmers and systems analysts learn skills that can ease interactions with business units and ensure effective system implementations.

For example, a systems analyst who has been trained in negotiation and conflict resolution would have not only the technical expertise to deliver a program but also the change management skills that are needed to make its implementation palatable to business users.

Who Does What?

Unlike a traditional organizational setup in which a supervisor is the prime decisionmaker, self-directed groups typically spread the decision-making among individual team members.

The IS manager of old becomes a team consultant or a team member, or he leaves the group or company. Manager attrition and turnover during the life of the work group account for much of the cuts in management salary overhead.

As a consultant, this person acts primarily as a group facilitator and team mentor as well as coordinator working with leaders in traditionally managed groups. For example, he may be called in by the group to give his opinion on a potential hire or advise a group member contemplating a move from maintenance into software development or a business unit.

The team then becomes responsible for scheduling work, vacation and leaves, negotiating task assignments, training, hiring replacements and appraising individuals' performance. Each team member is empowered to make commitments for which the entire team is accountable.

Less Trial and Error

For new IS staff members, the group can shorten the company policy and technology learning curve. A mentor can guide the new members through the intricacies of the organization as well as tell them who the IS experts are for questions on maintenance, networks and so on. There's less trial and error involved; the person becomes an effective part of the IS group more quickly.

Furthermore, broadening an IS individual's responsibilities fulfills his high need for achievement and enables him to value his work more. In fact, with the kinds of non-technical decision-making skills developed in this participatory management setup, team members are likely candidates for leadership roles in traditionally managed groups.

Self-directed work groups are not the latest quick fix or *One Minute Manager*. They are usually part of a hybrid company—one in which the majority of groups (and thinking) are hierarchical. Many self-directed work groups take years to reach maturity, with only about 75% of pilot projects ever getting that far. Twenty-five percent fail or are on their way to failure because they lack the vision, planning and staff buy-in vital to their existence.

Fall short on any one of these elements and the consequences are not good. One IS self-directed work group pilot, for instance, had top management behind it and support from employees but no business unit acceptance. That work group is no longer functioning.

All involved in the project must understand that while the concept of self-directed IS work groups is attractive, it is not one without costs. Expect, for example, to double your IS training budget in the first 12 to 18 months as team members come up to speed on the duties once relegated to the former group supervisor. Furthermore, the majority of these costs will not go to technological training but to "soft" management-type courses.

Hard to Get Used To

Self-directed work groups will also take their toll on employees. Some staff members will not get used to the fluid makeup of such groups and will quit or move on to more structured environments within the organization.

Getting self-directed work groups to work takes work.

IS managers and group consultants must help employees understand that a self-directed work group is a risky proposition and that they may become frustrated. For those individuals unable to handle this pressure, IS must ensure the existence of "safety nets"—feedback mechanisms and clear career options—to make the risk less threatening.

Feedback is solicited from team members as well as the business organization at large. IS measures satisfaction with the work group through questionnaires in which work group individuals rate satisfaction with each other and their consultant.

Business units also get into the act by rating such service staples as reliability, responsiveness, competence, access, courtesy, communications, credibility, security and understanding of the business unit. These assessments happen throughout the life of the self-directed work group—typically at inception, six months 12 months, 18 months and so on.and so on.

IS group feedback is gathered at a group review process that occurs every 30 days. The group uses these review sessions to access team effectiveness and job satisfaction. Individual performance appraisals and feedback happen on a yearly basis. If a performance improvement program is in place for an individual, feedback can occur every 60 days.

Career Motivation

Along with feedback, a clear career path has been found to be a primary motivator for IS professionals. That's why organizations with self-directed IS work groups on their minds need to ensure they have a career track in place. Because the upshot of these groups is a reduction in management layers, the business management track may not be as viable an option as it once was. A technology track must exist that delineates the technical, business and management competencies needed to move from position to position in IS.

This track usually contains levels that are roughly comparable in salary and status to the traditional business management track.

When implemented correctly, self-directed work groups have tremendous potential. They can increase team productivity while increasing employee satisfaction and developing leadership skills; heighten technical preparedness for new products, services and business; increase IS service quality to business units; treat team members as major contributors in the process; and develop a successful self-directed work group model that can be applied to other aspects of the business.

These are benefits your chief executive officer can relate to.

Norman is a principal systems specialist in the customer support group at Digital Equipment Corp. in Colorado Springs and a member of a self-directed work group. Zawacki is a professor of management and international business at the University of Colorado in Colorado Springs.
Reprinted from *Coputerworld* (April 1, 1991), pp. 77, 78. Copyright 1991 by CW Publishing, Inc., Fromingham, MA 01701.

with gray bars. The chart shows that for project A, task A–1 was started on time and completed before schedule. Task A–2 was started before it was scheduled and has not yet been completed, although more than the planned time has elapsed. A Gantt chart can be a valuable measurement tool in a complex project. It aids in scheduling and coordinating, and provides a visual means of evaluating progress. Since preparing a Gantt chart does not require extensive effort or data, the potential benefits generally exceed the cost.

Several good project manager software packages are available for personal computers, such as the Harvard Project Manager and the Primavera Project Planner. The Primavera package schedules up to ten thousand tasks, assigns resources to tasks, tracks costs, and produces reports, Gantt charts, and PERT charts. Computer-based tools such as these allow the project manager to quickly see the impact of schedule and resource changes.

In addition to managing system development, the director of information systems is responsible for managing the operation of information systems. This task involves overseeing system maintenance, data processing operations, and the physical security of the system.

Managing System Operations

Now

Project A	Programming Group		Week Ending Oct. 6, 19___	Week Ending Oct. 13, 19___	Week Ending Oct. 20, 19___	Week Ending Oct. 27, 19___	Week Ending Nov. 3, 19___	Week Ending Nov. 10, 19___
	Task A-1	P	▓▓░					
		A	▓▓					
	Task A-2	P		░▓▓	▓▓			
		A		░▓▓	▓▓			
	Task A-3	P				▓		
		A						
	Task A-4	P					░▓	░
		A						
	Task A-5	P						░
		A						
Project B	System Design							
	Task B-1	P	▓▓░					
		A	▓▓					
	Task B-2	P		▓▓	░			
		A	░▓	▓				
	Task B-3	P				░▓	░	
		A				▓		
	Task B-4	P					░▓	░
		A						
	Task B-5	P						░
		A						

FIGURE 21–5
Gantt Chart.

Gantt charts are easily understood tools that allow managers to quickly visualize the schedule for a project. Inexpensive personal computer plotters allow firms to quickly produce these charts.

System Maintenance

System maintenance is the correction of errors discovered in programs and the modification of programs to satisfy changed user requirements or conditions. Changes in programs are often also necessary when new hardware is introduced. System maintenance has become a challenge for many information systems organizations. In many cases it consumes 70 to 80 percent of the systems and programming resources. Such situations leave few resources for developing new systems. Methods for decreasing the cost of system maintenance are of paramount concern to information systems managers.

As with managing system development, the adoption of a structured system development methodology greatly enhances the ability to manage system maintenance. Efficient and effective system maintenance requires an understanding of the program to be modified. Programming personnel must be able to effect the change by changing the program statements in a confined and isolated area of the program. If a change requires modification in many different areas of the program or system, then system maintenance becomes an almost impossible task. As explained in previous chapters, structured methodologies produce modular programs. Each module is as independent and self-contained as practical. Therefore, changes are likely to affect only a restricted area of one module.

Often organizations have programs that meet their needs but are difficult to maintain because they are nonmodular or they use unstructured code. These organizations may hire firms that specialize in rewriting programs to restructure these programs in a modular form that follows structured programming standards. Some programs are rewritten manually, but COBOL programs are often restructured using other programs that do not require human intervention. Rewriting can often extend the life of a program for several years.

Active data dictionaries also simplify system maintenance by restricting both the number and location of program changes. **Active data dictionaries** allow data to be defined in one location. The data definitions are then used by all programs that process those data. The programs use each data item by referring to a data name, such as ZIP–CODE for an address zip code. The physical format of the data, including their type (character or numeric) and their length, must be known to each program that uses them. Thus, the physical format definition of a data item is also stored in the active data dictionary. The term *active* is used since each program actively uses the data dictionary for data definitions.

To illustrate the system maintenance advantages of an active data dictionary, consider the recent U.S. Postal Service's change from a five-digit zip code to a nine-digit zip code. Many firms have hundreds of programs that use the zip code data item. To search through all these programs, locate where the format of zip code is defined, and make the change from five to nine digits would be a monumental task. With an active data dictionary, only one change is necessary, and that change is made to the dictionary. None of the programs that use the data dictionary for data definitions must be manually changed. They may have to be recompiled, but recompilation is an automated process.

Requests for changes in programs originate with users and should be made on a formalized change authorization form. On this form the user identifies the program or system to be changed and outlines the changes desired. This form requires authorization signatures, which must be obtained before the changes are made. Authorization signatures are typically required from user management and from the systems and programming manager, and are sometimes required from the data processing steering committee. Figure 21–6 shows a change request and authorization form.

Actual changes to programs must be well managed and controlled. (Control of program changes is discussed in depth in Chapter 20.) After the changes have been made, the system is thoroughly tested using the same set of tests used when the system was developed. The tests are modified to reflect changes and are then run before the changed system is implemented.

Data Processing Operations

Managing data processing operations is much like managing any production shop within an organization. Management is concerned with maintaining sufficient capacity to process the computer jobs. Users of the

FIGURE 21–6
Change Requests in an Authorization Form.

The authorization and documentation of changes made to systems are crucial to well-maintained systems. Without such documentation, fraudulent changes could easily occur, or the system could be changed until no one really knows what the system does.

REQUEST FOR SYSTEM MODIFICATION

User Name:

Department:

Telephone No.:

System Name:

Module(s) to be changed (if known):

Please describe the change(s) desired and explain the reasons thereof:

Signature	Approved	Rejected	Comments
Requestor	☐	☐	
Dept. Manager	☐	☐	
IS Liaison Officer	☐	☐	
Manager, Systems and Programming			

resource are charged for the resources they use. Personnel are hired, managed, and sometimes dismissed, and the machines are maintained in operable condition.

Processing capacity may be limited by any number of factors including primary storage size, secondary storage size, CPU power, number of terminals, and so on. Any of these can become a **bottleneck** that limits the capacity of the computer system. Data processing management monitors these resources and determines if one is likely to become a bottleneck in the future. Additional resources usually can be obtained at a reasonable price if the potential capacity bottleneck is identified promptly. **Software monitors** such as IBM's system management facilities help determine the usage levels of various system resources. For example, managers can determine the percentage of time various terminals are used and the time of the day they are used. They can also determine if the CPU is running close to its maximum capacity at any given point during the day. Trends of system resource utilization enable managers to project when various resources will be used at their capacity and, therefore, when expansion should be planned. Hardware monitors are also sometimes used to detect bottlenecks and to determine utilization levels for various devices. Figure 21–7 shows the output of a hardware monitor used to control resource usage.

An effective way to ensure that the computer resource is used efficiently is to charge users for their use of the various computer resources including CPU time, disk space, tapes, printing, and so on. Under a **user billing system**, the DP operations department is set up as a service center to the rest of the firm. Its services are available to anyone in the firm who is willing to pay for those services. Rates for the services should be similar to the rates charged if the user contracted for data processing services outside the firm with, for example, a service bureau.

Physical Security

In many companies today the information systems resource is a crucial asset. Even a temporary loss of this resource through fire, sabotage, or other disaster can be costly. You will likely soon learn firsthand the need for contingency planning, with backup of files. After you have worked for several days on an electronic spreadsheet, program, or word processing file, you will accidentally lose or erase it. Each term, one or more of my students indicate that they have lost their boxes of disks. Typically, many days of work are stored on those disks, and they have not been backed up. One such experience usually teaches the importance of planning for disasters. Imagine the cost to a large business if it lost all its files in a fire and no file backups had been made!

File backup (discussed in more depth in Chapter 20) is a technique for recovering from a disaster after it occurs. This section examines physical security that helps prevent disasters from occurring. It covers five areas within physical security: entry, sabotage, fire, natural and environmental disaster, and power controls.

Entry Control   A well-designed entry control system controls entry to the computer facility. Only operations personnel are allowed to enter the computer facility itself. Programs and data that are manually delivered to the computer room are passed through a window. (Most programs and data today are transmitted electronically to and from the computer, and thus require input data and program change control rather than entry control.) **Entry control** is usually done through locked doors to the computer room. These doors are opened through various means, such as a plastic card with a magnetic strip similar to a credit card, or a combination of both a plastic card and a memorized entry code.

Plastic cards and keys can be lost or misplaced, and thus may be used by someone other than the person authorized to use them. Providing 100 percent positive identification of each person entering a computer facility is difficult. Firms have tested, and are using, a wide variety of techniques and machines to provide positive identification. One machine examines the pattern of each person's fingerprints. (You cannot misplace your fingerprints!) But it has been found that a photocopy of a person's fingerprints can trick the machine into unlocking the door. Another machine works similar to the fingerprint machine, except each person has to kiss the machine! Lip prints also uniquely identify a person. But aside

FIGURE 21–7
Sample Hardware Monitoring Report.

This is a graph displaying eight different variables that are being monitored. Each variable can have values from 0 to 100 percent. The number of dots from the center of the graph illustrates the magnitude of each variable. For example, the CPU is active 78.5 percent of the time, while the CPU is busy only 10.5 percent of the time. Notice that the CPU Active and CPU Wait times add up to 100 percent. The CPU Only Busy and CPU Plus Any Device Busy time add up to the 78.5 percent time that the CPU is active. When the CPU is active it is either executing the operating system (which is called the supervisor) or it is executing a particular application program called a problem. Therefore, the total of the Supervisor State and Problem State times is 78.5 percent, the same as the CPU Active time percentage.

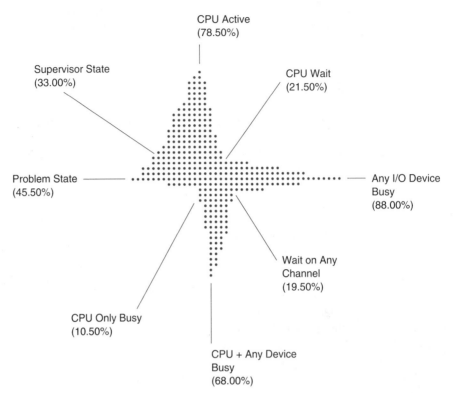

from its obvious drawbacks, this machine can also be misled by a photo-copy of a person's lip prints. A third machine shines light into each person's eyes and identifies him or her based on the retinal patterns within the eyeballs. Although this technique is harmless, employees probably would not accept it. Eventually, though, machines that are highly reliable in identifying individuals will be developed.

Sabotage Control Physical sabotage of the hardware, programs, and data is prevented to a large extent through passwords and by physical entry controls over the computer facility itself. In addition, firms that specifically design a secure computer facility usually provide **sabotage control** by constructing the computer room to bombproof specifications. When computers were first used in the 1950s and 1960s, it was common to have large glass windows in the walls of the computer center so that a firm could show off its computer facilities. A saboteur could have easily tossed a bomb through those windows.

Fire Control The most likely physical threat to a computer facility is fire. The best **fire control** procedure is to store backup copies of data and programs at another location and to arrange for emergency use of alternative computer hardware in case of a fire. In addition, many computer centers use a fire suppression gas known as halon. The halon is released by fire and smoke detection systems, and it is effective in suppressing fires. The primary disadvantage of halon is that it is very expensive. An accidental release of the gas may cost a firm several thousand dollars just to replace the gas. Other, less expensive gases are available, but they are impractical because they are poisonous to operations personnel. Halon is a nonpoisonous gas.

Natural and Environmental Disaster Control   Natural and environmental disasters should be considered when choosing, the site for a computer room. **Disaster control** provides protection against such catastrophes as floods, hurricanes, bursting pipes, and so on. Water can destroy the sensitive electronic equipment in a computer room. Fire control water sprinklers on floors above the computer room are an environmental hazard that is sometimes overlooked. Water leaking down through pipe holes and other crevices onto computer equipment, tapes, and disks can be very damaging. For this reason, the floor above the computer room should be thoroughly sealed to prevent water leakage.

Power Control   Large computer systems should have uninterruptible and controlled power systems. Plugging such computer systems directly into electrical lines is not a good idea. If the power goes off, even momentarily, the data and programs stored in semiconductor primary storage are lost because semiconductor storage is volatile. Furthermore, power spikes (increases in the current voltage) can heavily damage a computer system. Power spikes are often caused by electrical thunderstorms. Some computer centers guard against these types of power spikes by shutting down computer operations during electrical thunderstorms. However, in many situations shutting down the computer during electrical thunderstorms is not a viable alternative.

Many organizations use power supply systems to provide **power control**. These systems consist of batteries and backup generators. The batteries are continuously charged by the incoming electrical service, and the computer draws its power from the batteries. The computer is insulated by the batteries from the electrical service lines, and can thus avoid power spikes. In the case of a power outage, the batteries are sufficient for a short duration. Long power outages are covered by the backup generator system.

Personal computers can be protected against power spikes and electrical noise with inexpensive devices that shut the power off when these electrical disturbances occur. Uninterruptible power systems can also be purchased for PCs, but they are expensive.

Managing End-User Computing

Many of the concepts of managing end-user computing were covered in the latter sections of Chapter 18. You may want to go back and review these sections at this point. In this chapter we will cover some of the concepts surrounding the primary issue in end-user computing: How do you divide the responsibilities for end-user computing between the end user and the central information systems organization? In the early days of personal computers and end-user computing there was very little control in management of end-user computing. In fact, some argued that end-user computing should be managed with a laissez-faire approach; that is, end users should be free to purchase and use whatever personal computer hardware and software they deemed necessary without any management from the central information systems organization. The arguments for a laissez-faire approach revolved around the contention that end users best knew what hardware and software suited their tasks and that to control end-user computing would stifle the creativity and innovation of end users.

Most experts today would agree that a laissez-faire approach to end-user computing is the prescription for a disaster consisting of duplicate systems, incompatible systems, and corrupt and lost data. Thus, in addition to the support and consulting that the central information systems organization should provide to end users, as discussed in Chapter 18, the central information systems organization and end users must arrive at some division of the responsibilities for end-user computing. There are potential negative consequences if the central information systems organization dominates end-user computing and there are also negative consequences if end users dominate end-user computing. Figure 21–8 lists some of the possible implications of excess dominance by either group.

The particular responsibilities that information systems and users will have depends on the individual organization. However, we can list the minimum responsibilities of each group. Central information systems should have responsibility for the following:

1. Large multiuser databases

2. Information center consulting

3. Implementing and maintaining the network

4. Procedures to compare the costs of internal development of systems projects versus outsourcing

5. A list of preferred hardware and software and their suppliers

6. A guide and detailed checklist for the questions that should be asked when purchasing any hardware or software

7. A inventory of all information systems hardware and software

8. A plan for the career paths of information systems professionals throughout the organization

9. An information systems master plan that outlines the strategic plan for information systems development[1]

As a minimum users should have the following responsibilities to fully participate in all information systems development and maintenance efforts that affect them: To receive, review, and approve all expenditures of funds for information systems that are being developed or are in operation for the user departments' benefits.[2]

As organizations become more dependent on computer systems, managing information system resources become more critical. Many of you will be involved in varying degrees in information systems resource management.

[1] McFarlan, Warren F. and James L. McKenney, "The Information Archipelago—Governing the New World," *Harvard Business Review* (July–August 1983), p. 98.
[2] Ibid., pp. 98–99.

IS dominates	User dominates
Too much emphasis on database hygiene.	Too much emphasis on problem focus.
No recent new supplier or new distinct services; too busy with maintenance.	Information systems claims lack of control. Explosive growth in number of new systems and supporting staff.
New systems always must fit data structure of existing system.	Multiple suppliers delivering services. Frequent change in supplier of specific service.
All requests for service require system study with benefit identification.	Lack of standardization and control over data hygiene and system.
Standardization dominates; few exceptions.	Hard evidence of benefits nonexistent.
Information systems designs and/or constructs everything.	Soft evidence of benefits not organized.
Benefits of user control over development discussed but never implemented.	Few measurements and/or objectives for new systems.
Study always shows construction costs less than outside purchase.	Technical advice of information systems not sought or, if received, considered irrelevant.
Head count of distributed minis and development staff growing surreptitiously.	User buying design, construction, maintenance services, and even operations from outside.
Information systems specializing in technical frontiers, not user-oriented markets.	User building networks to own—not corporate—needs.
Information systems spending 80% on maintenance, 20% on development.	While some users are growing rapidly in experience and use, other users feel nothing is relevant because they do not understand.
Information systems thinks they are in control of all.	No coordinated effort for technology transfer or learning from experience between users.
Users express unhappiness.	Growth in duplication of technical staffs.
Portfolio of development opportunities firmly under information systems control.	Communications costs rising dramatically through redundancy.
No strong user group exists.	
General management not involved but concerned	

FIGURE 21–8

Possible Implications of Excess Dominance of Systems Development and Use by Central Information Systems or User.

APPLICATION 21–2

A Conservative Road to Success

By Rosemary Hamilton

Picture grocery shopping with an automated shopping cart, a device now being piloted at some supermarkets. A computer screen attached to the cart can flash sale messages and advertisements to shoppers as they travel through the store.

This may be one of the latest devices in retail automation, but information systems executives at The Stop & Shop Companies, based in Braintree Mass., have their doubts about it. They are waiting for the so-called video cart to prove that it would truly help customers rather than distract them.

This opinion exemplifies the way Stop & Shop's top IS [information systems] executives do their jobs. They show a practical, no-nonsense approach to managing IS at the largest supermarket chain in New England. The company runs 117 grocery stores as well as 130 Bradlees general merchandise stores. The ultimate aim of IS, addressed by a combination of in-store and back-room automation, is to create a store environment in which customers like to shop, says Robert Manson, vice president of information sys-

tems. The goal is to implement systems and devices that make all aspects of shopping, from finding items to having credit authorized, quicker and easier for the customer.

"We look at these things [such as video carts], and we are aware of them," adds Bruce Hannon, vice president of information services. "But we don't experiment on customers."

This conservative philosophy guides not only management of the store but the corporate data center as well. Late last year, the firm completed an $18 million IS rehaul that included a new data center, which runs a partial lights-out operation, and an upgrade of its mainframes. However, the firm did not select IBM's newest generation, the Enterprise System/9000, because a 3090J model suited its purposes. Hannon says he expects the 3090 to handle the job for three years.

Also, the executives are not interested in shifting gears to jump on all the latest IS trends, such as downsizing. Manson says the company has long maintained a balance between centralized and decentralized computing. The main data center handles corporatewide issues

such as networking and payroll while individual stores handle support for their specific functions.

However, Stop & Shop has also played the innovator. It was one of the first food retailers to implement point-of-sale scanning devices on a chainwide basis in the early 1980s. Since then, it has continued to add in-store devices, from systems managing the pharmacies and video rental centers of its "superstores" to handheld radio frequency devices used to collect inventory data directly from store shelves.

Richard Norris, a senior consultant at Arthur D. Little, Inc. in Cambridge, Mass., says the company keeps a low profile when it comes to retail automation. "They have not been particularly visible in their use of IS to further their business," he says. . . .

This approach has apparently paid off. While it is difficult to measure the exact impact IS has had on the health of the company, it has long maintained a clear market lead in New England.

Reprinted from *Computerworld* (February 4, 1991), pp. 51, 55. Copyright 1991 by CW Publishing, Inc., Framingham, MA 01701.

Sometimes, we start to believe that to manage information systems we must stay on the cutting edge by adopting all the latest technology. It is important to remember that many firms are successful with a more conservative approach as illustrated in Application 21–2.

Summary

- In recent years the role of the information systems manager has changed as users have become more actively involved in data processing.

- The information systems function may be located within the controller's organization where the controller is considered to be the primary provider of information. On the other hand, many organizations treat information systems as a separate function with a vice president who reports directly to the president.

- A structured system development methodology should be used. Normally system development is carried out using the project management approach for project control.

- If a structured methodology is used for system development, program maintenance becomes an easier task. However, all changes must be authorized and properly documented in order to prevent confusion and chaos.

- Active data dictionaries substantially reduce the number of program changes that must be made when the format of data changes.

- Operations should be constantly monitored to detect bottlenecks and inefficiencies. User billing should be used to ensure efficient use of resources.

- Physical security of the computer system is a major responsibility of systems management. Procedures should be implemented for both the prevention of disasters and recovery from disasters like fire and flooding.

- Determining the responsibilities of central information systems versus end users is one of the key questions in the management of end-user computing.

Key Terms

Controller

Information center

Systems software department

Systems and programming department

Technical support staff

Standards

Data processing operations department

Database administration (DBA)

Steering committee

System development methodology

Project management approach

Program evaluation and review technique (PERT)

Critical path management (CPM)

Gantt charts

System maintenance

Active data dictionaries

Change authorization form

Bottleneck

Software monitors

User billing system

Entry control

Sabotage control

Fire control

Disaster control

Power control

Review Questions

1. What developments are causing a change in the role of the information systems manager?

2. What are two possible locations for an information systems department within the firm? How do they differ?

3. Identify the major functions within an information systems organization.

4. Explain the project management approach. List some of the tools that may be used to control a project.

5. What are the primary factors that managers of systems maintenance must be concerned with?

6. Why is it important to have formal change authorization procedures?

7. List several factors that could limit processing capacity.

8. What is user billing? What is its advantage?

9. Briefly describe the idea of entry controls.

10. What controls do you use to control for the threat of fire?

11. List some of the major natural disasters that may threaten a computer installation.

12. How can you prevent damage due to irregularities in the power supply?

13. What are the minimum responsibilities of central information systems and of end users in the management of end user computing?

Discussion Questions and Cases

1. As president of Hi-Tek Inc., you must decide whether the manager of the information systems department should report to the controller or directly to you. Which alternative do you choose? Why? If you think that neither of these arrangements is suitable, what do you suggest instead?

2. Assume that you are redesigning the mainframe computing facilities of a company located on the eleventh floor of a downtown office building. What physical security features must be built into the new design? Give reasons to justify the cost of these security features.

3. The Cancun Corporation recently acquired a fourth-generation software package that allows end users to quickly write their own programs to produce ad hoc management reports from the corporation's database. The package was so successful that people in user departments began implementing their own systems without the aid of the systems development department. The head of the systems development department began to worry that users might not be aware of the ramifications of not specifying new systems according to an established system development methodology. She also thought that information stored in the various systems might be redundant. Should the applications development be controlled? If so, what are some possible solutions to controlling the applications developed by end users?

4. Jim Brown was a cost accountant for The Southern Pines paper processing plant and made extensive use of a popular spreadsheet program. He created several programs for analyzing overhead accounts, and everyone in the cost accounting department used the programs. The policy of the firm was for the cost accounting manager to review the logic of all spreadsheet programs before the spreadsheets were used for everyday reporting.

One day a vice president of the company approached Jim and asked him to make a change in a spreadsheet program format. Jim made the change without approval, and accidentally also changed a cost calculation formula. The vice president used the erroneous information in a company bid, and the bid was lost because the calculation of the cost estimate was too high. The following week, the cost accounting manager noticed the faulty spreadsheet calculation. Subsequently, both Jim and the vice president were fired. What controls should have been in place that would possibly have prevented this situation?

5. Thomas Incorporated has a large centralized computer operations facility. The computers are operated on a seven-day-a-week, twenty-four-hour-a-day basis. Ray Harper is a computer operator in the facility. Ray is considered by operations management to be its most valuable computer operator. He is highly experienced and very loyal to the company. Whenever a problem arises, he can be counted on to diligently work toward its solution. In fact, Ray is so dedicated that during the past five years he has not taken a vacation. From the standpoint of the company, do you see any problem with the fact that Ray has declined a vacation in the past five years?

INFORMATION SYSTEMS STRATEGIES

Measure for Measure

By Howard Rubin

The awareness of and need for information systems measurement is reaching a feverish level, yet the mortality rate for most measurement programs is about 80%. These failures can be traced to betting the whole program on a single metric and then trying to figure out what to do with it.

IS [information systems] input—investments in tools, techniques, people, environment, architecture, the workplace—has no meaning unless it is connected to business outcomes—improved quality, shorter cycle times, increased shareholder value, enhanced customer satisfaction and so on.

Good metrics answer the question: What is the value of (add here any technology you like) to the business? Effective measurement programs take concerns in both IS and the business as their basis.

To evolve to business-oriented measurement, an organization typically goes through three stages of measurement evolution:

■ **Stage 1: Internal IS measurement.** At this stage, IS organizations focus on designing a meaningful measurement program from a technical vantage point. IS develops operational definitions for IS performance at the organizational, application and project level. In this way, it can define key measures for assessing its technical and software processes in terms of quality, productivity and impact on customer satisfaction.

Typical measures at this stage include productivity-oriented I/O ratios, defect and/or failure densities and intensities, software process maturity ratings and technical quality.

■ **Stage 2: Linking to the business.** At this point, the IS organization focuses on linking these key technical indicators to business performance.

For example, the IS organization should be able to make assertions about its performance in business terms: "If we show a productivity increase of N% this year, the business will be able to lower product costs by Y% or produce Z new products and revamp M old products."

A shift in measurement occurs at this stage, going from output/input to outcome/input. Typical measures include functional quality and those metrics used in Stage 1.

■ **Stage 3: Business-oriented measurement.** At this stage, the IS organization can directly express changes in its performance. The measurement focus shifts to outcome—business value, cycle time, quality, profitability, shareholder value, process improvement and yield.

Measurement Dashboard

What kinds of measures should a company implement throughout these three stages? IS can set up a measurement program based on 10 metric categories that provide a reasonable universe for measuring an IS organization, its projects and its applications. Each category is a gauge that shows current performance, baselines, directional trends and target improvement areas.

These 10 gauges form a "dashboard" from which a company can gather all the information it needs to measure the IS organization. The IS department can select from these 10 the individual metrics appropriate for what it is trying to measure.

Just as a car's gauges can range from simple colored lights to detailed gauges calibrating units of temperature for water, oil and other factors, these dashboard gauges can vary in the level of detail they track and amount of information they convey.

For example, an IS director may want a general gauge to view organizational performance at the product or application level, while a project manager might need a cluster of detailed gauges for assessing internal project performance at the process level.

In the following list, gauges 1 through 9 are the more technical metrics typically used during Stage 1 of a company's measurement evolution. Gauge 10 takes a company through Stages 2 and 3.

1. **Productivity metrics.** These measure the software delivery rate and ability to support software.
2. **Quality metrics.** These measure the technical quality of the software produced and maintained, the software's functional quality in the context of meeting business needs and the quality of the software engineering process as practiced by IS.
3. **Delivery metrics.** These measure the organization's ability to meet time and cost commitments.
4. **Penetration metrics.** These measure the extent to which tools and techniques have been successfully disseminated.
5. **Work profile metrics.** These measure the effort and elapsed time it takes for work to progress through life cycle stages.
6. **Demand metrics.** These measure request backlogs and the IS organization's ability to service them.
7. **Technology assimilation metrics.** These measure the organization's ability to adopt and assimilate promising new software engineering technology.
8. **Work distribution metrics.** These measure the balance between maintenance and development.
9. **Capability metrics.** These measure the ability of the IS organization to manage, measure and improve itself.

10. **Business-oriented metrics.** These link IS functions to the success measures used by the business to gauge business performance.

All of this good stuff sets the stage for a shift from the current output/input view of IS measurement to a more meaningful outcome/input view.

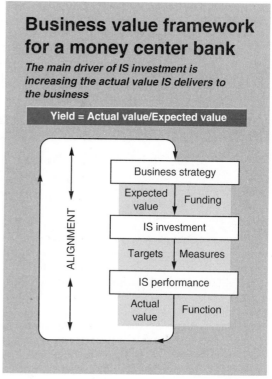

Business value framework for a money center bank

The main driver of IS investment is increasing the actual value IS delivers to the business

Source: Howard Rubin Associates, Inc.

Business Measurement

To measure IS in business terms, companies need to build a business value framework for figuring out what IS yields. Yield is the actual value delivered to the business vs. what the business expected the benefits to be. Increasing the yield of IS to the business is the main driver of IS investment in an organization.

Yield is calculated using the following equation: Yield = f (delivered value/expected value × customer satisfaction). This equation translates into "yield is a function of the ratio of delivered value to expected value weighted by customer satisfaction (0% to 100%)."

That's how it looks; here's how it works. At the start, the customer specifies the project's business value in quantifiable terms (expected value). At the end of the project, the customer states the value as delivered (actual value). Yield is this ratio of actual value to estimated value.

However, yield must be adjusted for customer satisfaction, which ranges from 0% to 100%. Therefore, while a delivered product can be almost exactly what the customer requested (0.9), if the customer was only 50% satisfied with the process that created the product, yield is 0.9 × 50%, which equals 0.45.

A money center bank, for example, wanted to assess IS contribution to its business—in other words, its IS yield. It set up a framework that showed the relationship between business strategy, IS investment and IS performance. Using the framework provided the bank with a clear path to implementing business-oriented measurement.

The bank's framework indicated multiple aspects of IS alignment at the institution. There is alignment between the business strategy and IS investments in projects and infrastructure, align-

ment between IS investments and actual IS performance and alignment between IS performance and the business strategy. Alignment can be measured thusly: alignment = f (strategy, capacity, capability, technical performance).

IS performance has three other measurable components besides alignment: capability, capacity and technical performance. These key indicators can be measured as follows:

- IS capability = f (process maturity, skills, tools, technology, tool use, knowledge).
- IS capacity = f (productivity, staff availability, backlog of old work).
- IS technical performance = f (productivity, quality, cost of quality, meeting commitments).

The point here is the alignment, capability, capacity and technical performance are dependent on a number of functions IS can measure. These key indicators are so intertwined, however, that

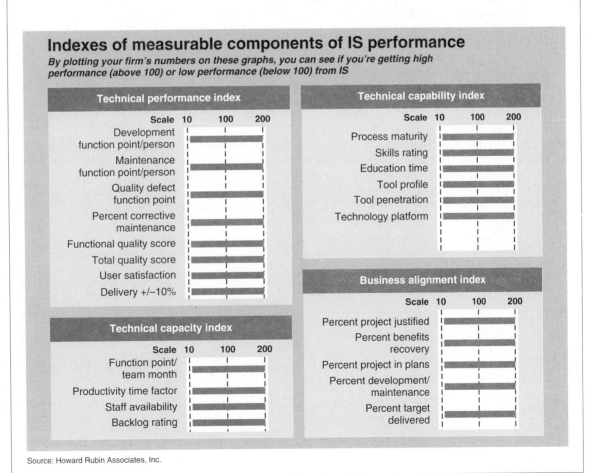

Indexes of measurable components of IS performance

By plotting your firm's numbers on these graphs, you can see if you're getting high performance (above 100) or low performance (below 100) from IS

Technical performance index

	Scale	10	100	200
Development function point/person				
Maintenance function point/person				
Quality defect function point				
Percent corrective maintenance				
Functional quality score				
Total quality score				
User satisfaction				
Delivery +/−10%				

Technical capability index

	Scale	10	100	200
Process maturity				
Skills rating				
Education time				
Tool profile				
Tool penetration				
Technology platform				

Technical capacity index

	Scale	10	100	200
Function point/team month				
Productivity time factor				
Staff availability				
Backlog rating				

Business alignment index

	Scale	10	100	200
Percent project justified				
Percent benefits recovery				
Percent project in plans				
Percent development/maintenance				
Percent target delivered				

Source: Howard Rubin Associates, Inc.

even if an organization is an exemplar of technical performance and has outstanding capability and ample capacity, it will not contribute any business value unless it is aligned to the business. Alignment channels IS energy into useful work.

Create Indexes

To make these abstract "equations" real, they can be turned into indexes (see chart): technical performance index, technical capability index, technical capacity index and business alignment index. These are analogous to a consumer price index or market basket and contain those items that should be measured.

The scales work this way: For each index component, the 100 point represents the 1980 industry benchmark. A 10-point movement to the right or left of this point indicates one standard deviation from the 1980 value. Numbers above 100 indicate high performance; numbers below 100 indicate low performance.

While the indexes shown indicate industry performance, an individual company can use them to start tracking its rate of improvement.

Viewing these indexes together creates a first approximation framework for assessing the value of IS to the business: Business value = f (alignment, capability, capacity, performance).

Roughly translated, this measure means the business value of computing is a function of being able to channel performance, capability and capacity into the right work categories through proper alignment. The interpretation of the indexes is that superior performance, capability, capacity and alignment translate into high business value for IS.

True productivity can then be measured as the change in business value resulting from an investment that impacts alignment, capability, capacity and technical performance.

This framework forces a realistic connection between IS actions and business outcomes. It also provides a basis for adding value to many of the measures being used today by establishing the links between the five key business indicators: technical performance, capability, capacity, alignment and business value.

Finally, it provides a context for IS investment analysis and assessment of the impact of investments on each indicator.

The companies that will win the competitive battles of the 1990s and beyond are those that leverage their technology investments to create new possibilities and major changes in the economics of doing business.

The IS mission is (and will continue to be) to provide increasing value to the business. Business-oriented measurement is the entry point for those ready to take on the challenge.

Discussion Questions

1. Do you think it is wise for a business to measure its information systems organization to the depth discussed in this article?

2. Discuss how you would specifically operationalize some of the measurements covered in this article.

Rubin is chairman of the department of computer science at Hunter College in New York. He is also a Nolan, Norton & Co. research fellow and president of consulting company Howard Rubin Associates, Inc., in Pound Ridge, N.Y.
Reprinted from *ComputerWorld* (April 15, 1991), pp. 77–78. Copyright 1991 by CW Publishing, Inc. Framingham, MA 01701.

22

Managing International Information Systems

Today, business is conducted in a global environment. Many firms, both domestic and foreign, have international operations. In some ways international information systems and their management are more important than domestic information systems. Because of the distances involved and the unreliability of mail service and other traditional means of communication, a well-managed international network can be the key to fast and reliable global communications. Application 22–1 illustrates how global communications can even be beneficial to small firms, in this case law firms.

Many issues confront managers of international information systems, such as the problems of working with different cultures and skill distributions. In this chapter we will first discuss business reasons for global information systems. Then we will describe strategies for managing international information systems, and finally, we will cover several issues that confront managers of international information systems.

Introduction

APPLICATION 22–1

Stretching the Law

By Barbara Wierzbicki

As corporations become more global in their operations, the professional services that support corporations are finding that they also need to widen their horizons.

Lex Mundi, a worldwide non-profit membership organization founded in 1989, allows its member law firms to expand without incurring the overhead associated with maintaining foreign offices.

The key to providing effective support for clients with far-flung interests isn't in trying to learn everything yourself but rather in cultivating a network of sources who can tell you what you need to know when you need to know it, founder Steve McGarry says. McGarry handled legal matters in 60 countries during his 10-year career as in-house counsel for Houston-based NL Industries, Inc.

From its small office in Houston, Lex Mundi connects more than 105 law firms and 8,000 attorneys in nearly 200 offices worldwide. In terms of staffing and technology, the group operates on a shoestring. Administration is handled by McGarry and one secretary. They work with several personal computers, a laser printer and a facsimile machine. Still, members say the information-sharing provided by the consortium helps them immensely when their clients need answers on how to proceed in foreign parts.

The core member service is referral. The group maintains 10 databases containing the resumes of its lawyer members, noting their areas of specialization and interest. This resource, members say, expedites research to make fast local connections for clients. It also fosters the formation of far-reaching personal networks.

Recently, for example, McGarry received a query from a member in Paris asking if any Lex Mundi members were likely to be interested in forming a special committee on global transportation issues. Turning to one of the databases built around a customized version of Borland International's Paradox database management system, McGarry found the names of 250 lawyers who spend more than 90% of their time dealing with global transportation affairs.

The ability to make that kind of connection in so little time really helps to level the playing field for small law firms, says Gerard Bruyninckx, an attorney at Trenite van Doorne in Rotterdam, Netherlands. According to Bruyninckx, U.S. companies with client interests in the Netherlands have traditionally relied on large New York or Chicago law offices with established branch locations in that country. With Lex Mundi, however, he sees the possibility of more collaboration among local firms in the two countries.

Wierzbicki is a free-lance writer in Apple Valley, Minn.
Copyright 1990/91 by CW Publishing, Inc., Framingham, MA 01701
Reprinted from *Computerworld* (October 1, 1990), p. 93.

Business Reasons for Global Information Systems

Table 22–1 lists the primary reasons why a business would establish a global information system. A review of this table reveals that many of these reasons are the same for both international and domestic systems. Flexible operations and joint resources are important to domestic firms as well as international firms. However, some of these reasons are unique to international business. Such things as having global customers, global products, and having to reduce risks associated with currency conversions only apply to international firms.

T A B L E 22–1
Business Reasons for Global Information Systems

1. Global consumers/customers	Firms that serve traveling customers—airlines, hotels, rental car, and credit card companies—find it necessary to have worldwide customer databases. A similar requirement is increasingly being imposed by corporate customers with global operations that more and more are demanding integrated worldwide services.
2. Global products	The product is either the same throughout the world (e.g., Coca-Cola) or is assembled from subsidiaries throughout the world (e.g., security, currency exchange, or real estate). Information systems can provide the ability to manage worldwide marketing programs.
3. Rationalized operations	Different subsidiaries build different parts of the same product based on availability of skills, raw materials, or favorable business climate. For example, a computer manufacturer might build software in the U.K., monitors in South Korea, and circuit boards on the west coast of the U.S. Information systems are used to coordinate the operations.
4. Flexible operations	Operations are moved from a plant in one country to a plant in another. For instance, a computer vendor moves production of personal computers between plants in response to labor strife or raw material shortages. Common systems exist across plants, which facilitates the move.
5. Joint resources	National subsidiaries may share certain facilities or people. For instance, the European subsidiaries for a petroleum company jointly own tankers or storage tanks. A material resource system is implemented to track the location of joint resources.
6. Duplicate facilities	A chemical company uses nearly identical plants to produce gases in different countries. Software supporting that production facility can be readily shared.
7. Scarce resources	A chemical firm requires that high-cost gas compressors be available in case of breakdowns in its identical worldwide plants. High costs prohibit storing them at each facility. A parts logistics system coordinates the compressors' use and distribution.
8. Risk reduction	Risks associated with currency conversions, multiple global markets, and multiple traders are alleviated. For instance, a petroleum company develops a global system for bidding on crude oil contracts, or a multinational bank implements a global risk management system for currency trading.

| 9. Legal requirements | Information requirements mandated by laws in one or more countries are consolidated. For instance, financial or environmental regulations imposed on a subsidiary may necessitate corporatewide information requirements if the subsidiary intends to sell or use products manufactured elsewhere. |
| 10. Economies of scale for systems | One corporatewide system is used to reduce data center requirements, duplicate development activities, and maintenance resources. |

Reprinted by special permission from B. Ives and S.L. Jarvenpaa, *MIS Quarterly*, March 1991, p. 40. Copyright 1991 by the Society for Information Management and the Management Information Systems Research Center at the University of Minnesota.

Strategies for Managing International Information Systems

As we will discuss in more depth later in this chapter, information system strategy must be linked to corporate strategy. Thus, the strategies for international information systems management closely follow the basic models of global business strategy. Bartlett and Ghoshal outline four basic global business strategy models: a multinational strategy, a global strategy, an international strategy, and a transnational strategy.[1]

With a multinational strategy, the firm operates in a decentralized manner. Each foreign subsidiary has a great deal of autonomy. Under a global strategy, the firm operates in a centralized fashion with the central headquarters largely controlling what goes on in each country. Using an international strategy, the headquarters of the firm attempts to stay on the cutting edge of innovations and diffuses these innovations quickly throughout the firm to maintain a competitive advantage. Finally, with a transnational strategy the firm uses a combination of the preceding three strategies. Local flexibility is maintained, but with overall direction from the central firm. Rapid diffusion of innovation is maintained throughout the firm.

Ives and Jarvenpaa identify four approaches for managing international information systems.[2] These approaches correspond closely to Bartlett and Ghoshal's four basic models of global business strategy. They are:

1. **Independent information systems operations** (corresponding with a multinational strategy).

2. **Headquarters-driven global information systems operations** (corresponding with global strategy).

3. **Intellectual cooperation in global information systems** (corresponding with an international strategy).

4. **Integrated global information systems** (corresponding with the transnational strategy).

---

[1] C. A. Bartlett and S. Ghoshal, *Managing Across Borders: The Transnational Solution* (Boston: Harvard Business School Press, 1989).

[2] B. Ives and S. L. Jarvenpaa, "Applications of Global Information Technology: Key Issues for Management," *MIS Quarterly* (March 1991), 33–49.

Independent Information Systems Operations

Firms that have an independent information systems strategy allow their foreign subsidiaries a great deal of autonomy. **Common systems,**—systems that are used throughout an organization—between subsidiaries in the firm are few. Under an independent information systems strategy, central information systems personnel have very little contact with their counterparts in the foreign subsidiaries. Since the subsidiaries' systems are not integrated, this strategy has the potential to severely impede an international business strategy. Exchange of data between subsidiaries and the parent can be difficult.

Headquarters-Driven Global Information Systems

Some firms impose corporatewide information systems on their subsidiaries. There is currently a trend toward more use of common systems. The big advantage these systems have is that global information systems strategies are easier to implement than when each subsidiary is allowed to develop systems independently. Data transfers between subsidiaries and central organizations are greatly facilitated. However, there may be an adverse reaction from foreign subsidiaries to the imposition of these common systems by the central corporation, particularly when representatives of the central corporation are from a foreign country.

Intellectual Cooperation in Global Information Systems

The goal of this form of global information systems management is to allow foreign subsidiaries the flexibility to meet local needs and yet to disseminate innovations from the central organization. However, instead of management requiring these innovations, as in the headquarters-driven information systems operation, the local subsidiaries are encouraged to adopt the innovations through intellectual arguments. The atmosphere is one of joint innovation between units of the corporation worldwide. Personnel are often interchanged between subsidiaries and the central organization. Innovations are diffused through idea sharing and discussions.

Integrated Global Information Systems

Bartlett and Ghoshal argue that the transnational strategy (which corresponds to integrated global information systems) will supersede the previous three strategies of multinational, global, and international. The reason for this, they say, is that the transnational approach will enable firms to be globally efficient, diffuse innovations rapidly, and quickly respond to local needs.

Feeney et. al[3] have outlined the characteristics of an integrated global information systems strategy. These include: multinational teams for information systems development and database design (these teams assure that data can be shared across the worldwide organization); following international standards, such as open systems interconnect standards;

---

[3] D. Feeney, M. Earl, and H. Stephenson, "Information Technology and Global Strategies: From Tradeoffs to Simultaneities," Oxford Institute of Information Management Working Paper, Templeton College, Oxford, England, 1990.

global databases and data dictionaries; and two-way innovation flowing between the parent and subsidiaries and also between subsidiaries. Although it is doubtful that any firms have yet attained an integrated global information systems strategy, many firms feel that this is the direction in which they should be moving.

Huff identifies ten issues that face global information systems managers. These include the **linking of information systems to corporate strategy, telecommunications, applications development, operations, hardware technology, standards, skill distributions, data issues, cultural differences,** and **vendor issues.**[4] These issues are discussed in the following paragraphs.

Critical Issues for Global Information Systems Managers

Linking Information Systems to Corporate Strategy

Global information systems must be tied to the corporate strategy. In fact, using global information systems is a primary method by which management can attain its global strategy. Tying global information systems strategy to the corporate strategy is just as important as the tie between domestic information systems strategy and corporate strategy. Ives and Jarvenpaa list the following key issues to be addressed when linking international information systems to business strategy:

- "Understand each business unit's global business strategy."

- "Determine the appropriate global information systems management approach or information systems strategy to align with the global business strategy."

- "Identify the fundamental objective or objectives driving the global information systems strategy and global information systems applications."

- "Classify and prioritize applications based on their contributions to global business strategy."

- "Assign responsibility for developing and implementing the global information systems strategy."

- "Assist senior management to understand the potential impacts of global information systems on corporate strategy."[5]

Telecommunications

Since the distances are so great and because of the often unreliable international mail service, an effective global telecommunications network is perhaps the centerpiece of global information systems strategy for most corporations, as illustrated in Application 22–2. However, developing a

---

[4] S. L. Huff, "Managing Global Information Technology," *Business Quarterly* (Autumn 1991), 71–75.
[5] B. Ives and S. L. Jarvenpaa, 42.

APPLICATION 22-2

Global Information Officers Entering IS Picture

By Alice Laplante

When Unum Life Insurance Co. in Portland, Maine, acquired a British insurance firm last year, senior information systems managers were challenged to develop a new set of skills: building a technically progressive IS [information systems] operation that works in harmony with U.S. standards yet fits the needs of the foreign subsidiary. The company's answer: a decentralized "team" management style.

As more U.S. corporations grow international in scope, top IS executives are beginning to broaden their backgrounds to master a dramatically different systems scenario. What this means is that senior IS managers are finding that they must take a more team-oriented, cooperative approach to solve complex technological and organizational issues.

The difficulties of this transition are documented in a paper by Jerry Kanter and Richard M. Kesner of Babson College in Wellesley, Mass. Titled "The CIO/GIO as Catalyst and Facilitator: Building the Information Utility to Meet Global Challenges," it examines the issues facing the global information officer.

Companies unable to optimize their IS resources on a global scale will find themselves at a significant competitive disadvantage, according to Kanter, executive director of the Center for Information Management Studies at Babson.

Some of the problems that skilled global information officers are expected to address are the following:

- Duplication of high-cost systems development efforts at multiple sites.
- Implementation of systems incapable of connecting to each

other or to the main data center without hassle and expense.
- Inability of IS to serve the strategic business needs of a worldwide organization in a timely manner.

Because of the newness of the global information officer role, these professionals face managerial and organizational challenges: They must balance the need for some sort of global IS game plan with a decentralized and flexible management style, Kanter says. As a result, most U.S. multinational firms have given foreign IS subsidiaries a wide degree of autonomy in making key technology decisions.

This is the case at Merrill Lynch & Co. in New York, says Howard P. Sorgen, first vice president and director of information technology. Utility functions such as telecommunications, data centers and centralized applications development activities are done out of central IS in New York, which also sets standards for appropriate hardware and software to be used by Merrill Lynch offices worldwide. Everything else is left up to the individual site.

"We provide our overseas locations with an appropriate degree of entrepreneurial freedom," Sorgen says. "They are much more closely attuned to the local market and can therefore ensure that a technological solution fits the business needs of that particular site."

Technical obstacles are also something global information officers will have to face in the global IS world.

Telecommunications is particularly critical: With the quantity and quality of vendors and services varying so widely from one country to another, it can be difficult to put a worldwide telecommunications network in place. In addition, global information offi-

cers can't assume that technologies available here will be available overseas, says Sheldon Laube, the national director of information technology at Price Waterhouse in New York.

"Things we take for granted, like quality phone service, can be extraordinarily difficult to get in South America and some parts of Europe," Laube says. Basic hardware and software can be difficult to purchase in certain countries, he adds. "You can standardize on systems here that are well beyond what the technology and infrastructure of other countries can support."

Emerging communications technologies such as videoconferencing help the global information officer keep in touch with and manage a diverse scattering of international IS groups. Most U.S. multinationals are putting sophisticated videoconferencing systems in place and make extensive use of electronic mail and voice mail to communicate across geographic and time barriers.

Stepping-stones

The following six components are essential if a senior IS executive is to successfully move into the global arena, say Jerry Kanter and Richard M. Kesner, authors of a working paper on the global information officer published by Babson College:

- A team-oriented approach to management that rules through consensus, with a sensitivity to the diverse peoples and cultures that make up a global IS organization.
- An appropriate IS structure that balances centralized architecture and standards policy with autonomous local activity. Heading this IS structue, the global information officer should report to

the senior executive officer of the corporation and sit as a peer on the executive council and participate fully in strategic business decisions.

- A firm grasp of existing computer and telecommunications technologies as well as a vision of how emerging technologies can benefit the business.

- A commitment to total quality management, which focuses on excellence in both individual and team performance.
- A willingness to turn to resources outside IS for guidance and support on critical decisions.
- A desire to become an agent of change for human resources as

well as technological concerns within the organization.

LaPlante is a free-lance writer based in Palo Alto, Calif.
Copyright 1990/91 by CW Publishing, Inc., Framingham, MA 01701. Reprinted from *Computerworld* (August 19, 1991), p.70.

global information systems network is not easy. Most telecommunications in foreign countries are controlled by companies owned by each country's government. These are often known as PTT organizations (post, telephone, and telegraph), since they are public utilities that provide all three of those services. Standards for telecommunications often differ between countries. Also, the telecommunication rules by which information systems managers must play differ by country. Finally, telecommunications costs in foreign countries can be much higher than in the United States. This is particularly true in Europe where networks are likely to involve two or more countries.

Applications Development

Acquiring or developing software to be used internationally can present some unique challenges. Many countries have local content rules that require software to be purchased or partially developed locally. Purchased software that is designed to be used in the United States and Europe may not have the language capabilities to be used in Asian countries, for example. Acquisition and development of software requires that representatives from all the countries where it is to be used be included on the development team.

Operations

Computer operations in foreign countries can be a challenge. Quite often the computer operations personnel are members of militant labor unions which, in some countries, may go on strike frequently. A strike in a country that is key to an information systems network can paralyze the complete network. Even routine computer maintenance may be a problem because of the difference in time zones. For example, normal 1:00 A.M. maintenance in New York can be in the middle of the afternoon in Tokyo, preventing communication between the two sites at that time of day because of the computer being down for maintenance.

Hardware Technology

Vendor support for certain types of hardware may be lacking in some countries. In addition, some countries have severe restrictions on the import of computer hardware to protect their local computer hardware industry. Until recently Brazil was such a country. Because of import restrictions it was very difficult to use hardware not manufactured in Brazil. The country recently relaxed its restrictions on import of computer hardware.

A serious problem in some parts of the world is the total disregard for software copyrights. Software, particularly PC software, is routinely copied and often these copies are sold on the market at drastically reduced prices. Such behavior, which does not violate local legal or ethical norms, can present severe ethical problems for international companies and in some cases legal problems. Ives and Jarvenpaa[6] list the following key hardware and software issues that global information systems managers must address:

- "Determine the number and locations of regional data centers."

- "Ensure 24-hour system availability and support for global applications operating from global data centers."

- "Select vendors who can provide support in dispersed locations."

- "Select hardware and software appropriate for shared data or processing requirements."

- "Expect delays and incompatibilities from vendors operating outside their own home markets."

- "Anticipate a reduced set of hardware and software alternatives."

- "Identify reliable local information technology distributors and service providers."

Standards

Integrating multicountry information systems can be a real challenge because of the lack of international standards for hardware, software, and communications. Over time this problem will be partially alleviated through the move to open systems standards. But we are far from having open systems today.

Skill Distributions

Individuals in some foreign countries, particularly those in Europe and Asia, have a very high level of computer skills. However, there are many countries in the world where the range of communications and computer skills that are available in the developed world simply do not exist. Even between developed countries the skill levels and aptitudes of the work force may differ. For example, studies have shown that Germans are excellent project managers, while French systems analysts tend to be stronger in theoretical areas such as data modeling, and North American systems analysts are stronger at system implementations. These differences in abilities may be due to differing emphases in educational systems, in addition to cultural differences. Information systems professionals must take these skill differences into account when deciding on the makeup of project teams. Application 22–3 provides some additional observations on skill distributions.

---

[6] *Ibid.*, 43.

National Flavors in the Global Stew

By Scott Kramer

Just because a company operates globally does not automatically mean that it loses its national accent. According to a number of consultants who have dealt with multinational firms rooted in various countries, there are some noticeable differences in the way that multinationals handle information systems, and these differences seem connected with their geographic origins.

"If you look across Europe, you'll see information technology following the mind-set of each respective country," says Brad Power, managing associate at Index Group, Inc. in Cambridge, Mass. "For example, Germany and Sweden are great at engineering and manufacturing, so that's where they are strong in automation."

U.S.-based corporations, some consultants say, frequently tend to be faster off the mark in adopting technology and, possibly as a result, less careful about assessing environmental impact. "Americans are more inclined to go for a technological risk to give them a big advantage," says David Stringer, international practice director at Arthur D. Little, Inc.'s Information and Telecommunications Management Practice in London. "In Europe, we're not getting into that game."

Ira Magaziner, an international business consultant based in Bristol, R.I., and co-author of *The Silent War*, a book about global competition, has noted a difference in the amount of preparation devoted to business process changes related to technology implementation. "In Germany, Japan and some other countries such as Sweden," he says, "more emphasis is placed in understanding the change in work organization clearly; there is more of an emphasis on changing work flows prior to implementation. That way, they get more out of it."

Location can influence business attitudes, Power says, and there are certain differences that carry through not only into business but also into use of information systems by business.

"When it comes to systems in general, any European [company] has to work across borders," Power says. "The U.S. first thinks about the U.S., while overseas is an afterthought." Furthermore, he says, European firms are used to designing systems to accommodate country-by-country variations. U.S. firms are just learning how to do this and still tend to think of Europe as a single market. For example, if a bank in New York needs to add a foreign currency for exchange rates into a computer system, it might entail a change in the system's architecture. A similar European institution, however, would probably already have a flexible system for diverse monetary arrangements. The U.S. thinks homogeneously, while Europe takes a more open-ended, heterogeneous approach, he says.

This openness to diversity manifests itself, according to Magaziner, in Europe's eagerness to embrace nonproprietary systems. "Unix is catching on quicker in Europe than it is here in the United States," Magaziner notes. "We talk a lot about it, but we're slower in moving toward actual adoption."

Kramer is a free-lance writer based in Irvine, Calif.
Copyright 1990/91 by CW Publishing, Inc., Framingham, MA 01701. Reprinted from *Computerworld* (October 1, 1990), p. 93.

Data Issues

One of the primary issues that has been discussed extensively in the literature is transborder data flows. Some countries have laws that restrict the personal data (such as personnel data) about their citizens that may be stored outside the country. These transborder data flow laws generally do not allow data to be stored in a foreign country whose privacy laws are less restrictive than in the citizen's home country. For example, data concerning German citizens could not be stored in the U.S. if U.S. privacy laws are more lax than the German laws. However, in practice most companies have found that restrictions on transborder data flows are often vague. Thus, companies who work directly with the appropriate regulators can satisfactorily meet the requirements of the laws concerning transborder data flows.

Cultural Differences

Cultural differences can be a major impediment to integrated international information systems. Perhaps the biggest problem is the language difference. This is particularly true when attempting to use software developed in the United States or Europe in an Asian country. In fact, the ASCII coding structure, because of its limit of eight bits in a byte, has restricted the internationalization of computer software. ASCII can only represent 256 different characters, plenty for Western languages, but far too restrictive for all the languages of the world. There is currently a move to develop a 16-bit character coding structure, which will be called UNICODE. The 16-bit capacity of UNICODE will allow up to 65,536 different characters. Such capacity will allow sufficient room for the many characters of such Asian languages as Chinese, Japanese, and Korean.

Cultural differences go far beyond just language differences. Many actions that are correct in our culture may be totally inappropriate in another culture. Application 22–4 illustrates this point with some examples.

Lack of attention to cultural differences can increase the likelihood that users will reject a software package because of the "not invented here" syndrome. In comparison to the American economy, many foreign economies pay much more attention to the protection of an individual's right to a job. Therefore, the introduction of computer systems that threaten jobs can be considerably more difficult than in the United States.

Ives and Jarvenpaa[7] list the following key cultural issues:

- "Identify critical systems applications or skills competencies (or weaknesses) possessed by foreign subsidiaries."

- "Provide opportunities for global organizational learning related to these areas of unique competency."

- "Recognize the sensitivity of foreign subsidiaries to imposed solutions and seek mutually acceptable alternatives."

- "Seek new ways to sensitize managers sent abroad (or brought to the U.S.) to cultural, religious, and political differences."

Vendor Issues

When choosing hardware and software for foreign locations managers must recognize that the level of vendor support may be substantially less in a foreign country. In the U.S. it is easy to phone a hotline to get vendor support when hardware or software difficulties occur. This may be impossible in certain foreign countries. Often, the vendor does not have a local hotline, particularly in less-developed countries. A vendor's product may be available in a country, but only through locally licensed representatives. These local representatives may not be as reliable as the parent company in the United States.

---

[7] *Ibid.*, 45.
[8] *Ibid.*, 44.

APPLICATION 22-4

A Cautionary Multicultural Tale

By Nell Margolis

Seventeen years ago, when the phrase "multinational corporation" was newly in vogue, a business scholar made a startling suggestion and told a harrowing tale.

The suggestion went beyond "contrarian" to the very rim of weird: While his fellow writers on the international business scene focused earnestly on the potential problems of irreconcilable currencies, disparate legal systems and the hardship of telephone communication across time zones, this particular writer dismissed fiscal, legal and temporal agility as necessary but insufficient.

The truly successful multinational players, he said, would be those who mastered the nuances of the various cultures into which their new ways of doing business might lead them.

To illustrate his point, he recounted the following story. As I recall it, the tale was true, but names had been deleted to protect the mortified:

A major U.S. manufacturing company based in a Midwestern state won a hotly contested, highly lucrative contract with an equally august South American firm. With the deal announced, the details hammered out and the champagne corks already popped, the U.S. company sent one of its senior executives down to the new partner's headquarters to sign the final papers—an act that both parties saw as purely ceremonial.

Keenly aware of the significance of the deal to both companies, the U.S. executive—let's call him U.S.—and his South American counterpart and personal host—let's call him S.A.—prepared for several days of high corporate splendor. S.A. packed the days with educational presentations and entertaining side trips.

In addition, as he would have done for the highest ranked dignitary, he arranged for lodging in a grand hotel and hosted an endless round of sumptuous meals at his dining club.

And that's where things began to go south. U.S., knowing that back in the heartland, he would have put an honored guest at ease by inviting him to his home for a big dinner with the family, wondered why the same courtesy wasn't accorded him. It began to gnaw at him that S.A. was apparently holding him at bay. And U.S. wasn't altogether skilled at hiding his feelings.

S.A. was baffled by U.S.' increasingly obvious lack of appreciation for the gala visit on which so much attention had been lavished. Rooted in a formal and deeply religious culture, S.A. would never have considered the idea of taking U.S. home to meet his family, much less to dine with them. To do so in his world would have been not only the height of business discourtesy but also an insult of huge proportion to the family whose home he would have defiled by merging it with business. As U.S. went from ungrateful to insolent, S.A. went from baffled to furious. And S.A. wasn't altogether skilled at hiding *his* feelings . . .

By the time the contract-signing ceremony rolled around, the two "ambassadors" were no longer on speaking terms. Partnership was out of the question. The South American contract eventually went to a European conglomerate.

Could this happen today? You bet, says British management consultant John Mole—now more than ever. The consultant who took his prescient pen in hand 17 years ago might be staggered to see the legal, fiscal and, heaven only knows, technological changes that have whipped the

world into a global marketplace virtually overnight. But when it comes to lack of cultural awareness, he wouldn't find the world much altered.

Sure, it's been a while since we've tried to sell the Chevy Nova in Spanish-speaking countries, where the car's name means "Won't Go"—but just five days ago, a Washington lawyer told me a story about a colleague of his who, dispatched to a recently open Eastern European country to seed business relations, prepared for everything except the fact that the phone books would be written in a language he couldn't read. Yes, Mr. Mole, we still need your observations.

Even more, we need your book. Mole's *When In Rome—A Business Guide to Cultures & Customs in 12 European Nations*, is out in a first U.S. paperback printing just in time for Europe '92—and, just in time for holiday shopping. Smart CEOs will buy in bulk and attach a copy to each employee's holiday greeting card.

With little time spent on academic analysis, Mole cuts to the chase after cross-cultural clues. He walks the reader through the various components of the European Community, throwing out tips under such headings as Labor Market, Teams, Meetings, Upward Mobility, Communication, Women, Etiquette, Socializing, Punctuality and Language.

Mole got his information, he says, from interviews with some 200 practicing business managers, "most of them expatriates."

Their mistakes could save you a few.

Margolis is *Computerworld's* senior editor, industry.
Copyright 1990/91 by CW Publishing, Inc., Framingham, MA 01701. Reprinted from *Computerworld* (November 18, 1991), p. 94.

Managing global information systems is certainly a challenge. However, many of these challenges are also a component of domestic information systems. For example, there can be large cultural differences between different regions and between different ethnic groups in the United States. Managing cultural and ethnic diversity is certainly a skill that managers here must learn in order to operate effectively. Most of the other issues discussed above have applications to domestic information systems also. Vendor support in rural areas of the United States, for example, is certainly not as high as in urban areas. Likewise, telecommunications may be more difficult in rural areas. Thus, these issues are just more severe in an international context than they are in a domestic context. A company that manages these issues well domestically is also likely to be able to handle these issues in the international market.

Summary

- In some ways international information systems and their management are more important than domestic information systems. Because of the distances involved and the unreliability of mail service and other traditional means of communication, a well-managed international network can be the key to fast and reliable global communications.

- Bartlett and Ghoshal's four basic global business strategy models are a multinational strategy, a global strategy, an international strategy, and a transnational strategy.

- Ives and Jarvenpaa's four approaches for managing international information systems are:

    1. Independent information systems operations (corresponding with a multinational strategy).

    2. Headquarters-driven information systems operations (corresponding with global strategy).

    3. Intellectual cooperation in global information systems (corresponding with an international strategy).

    4. Integrated global information systems (corresponding with the transnational strategy).

- Huff identifies ten issues that face global information systems managers. These include the linking of information systems to corporate strategy, telecommunications, applications development, operations, hardware technology, standards, skill distributions, data issues, culture, and vendor issues.

- Global information systems must be tied to the corporate strategy. In fact, global information systems is a primary method by which management can attain its global strategy.

- Many countries have local content rules that require software and hardware to be purchased locally or to be partially developed locally.

- Computer operations in foreign countries can be a challenge. Quite often the computer operations personnel are members of militant labor unions which, in some countries, may go on strike frequently.

- Vendor support for certain types of hardware may be lacking in some countries. In addition, some countries have severe restrictions on the import of computer hardware to protect their local computer hardware industry.

- Integrating multicountry information systems can be a real challenge because of the lack of international standards for hardware, software, and communications.

- Individuals in some foreign countries, particularly in Europe and Asia, have a very high level of computer skills. However, there are many countries in the world where the range of communications and computer skills that are available in the developed world simply do not exist. Even between developed countries the skill levels and aptitudes of the work force may differ.

- Some countries have laws that restrict the personal data (such as personnel data) about their citizens that may be stored outside the country.

- Cultural differences can be a major impediment to integrated international information systems. Perhaps the biggest problem is the language difference. This is particularly true when attempting to use software developed in the United States or Europe in an Asian country.

Key Terms

Independent information systems operations

Headquarters-driven global information systems

Intellectual cooperation in global information systems

Integrated global information systems

Common systems

Linking of information systems to corporate strategy

Telecommunications

Applications development

Operations

Hardware technology

Standards

Skill distributions

Data issues

Cultural differences

Vendor issues

Review Questions

1. What are the major business reasons for having a global information system?

2. Identify and discuss the differences in the four basic global business strategies.

3. Identify and discuss the differences in the strategies for managing international information systems.

4. Relate the basic global business strategies to the strategies for managing international information systems.

5. Identify the major issues that global information systems managers must address.

6. What are the major managerial concerns in the international telecommunications area?

7. Identify the key hardware and software issues that global information systems managers must address.

8. How do European privacy acts affect transborder data flows?

9. What impact can unionization of DP departments have on DP operations?

10. What are common systems?

11. What are some cultural issues that managers should be aware of?

12. What should managers do to address cultural issues?

Discussion Questions and Cases

1. Arguments can be made that affiliates of multinational companies should be allowed to develop their own information systems without any direction from corporate management. Provide some arguments for and against this approach.

2. IBM produces and sells computers in all the EEC countries. As a part of the harmonization of standards implicit in Europe '92 several heads of IBM divisions in Europe would like to remove the Spanish consonant ñ (pronounced like the *ny* in *canyon*) from the keyboard and character set of computers sold throughout the EEC countries. The head of IBM's Spanish operations has declared that this will not happen as long as he is an executive with IBM. What are the arguments for and against removing the ñ from the character set of computers produced and sold within the EEC?

3. The countries of Eastern Europe, because of the former communist system, are currently at a competitive disadvantage with the economies of Western Europe, Japan, and the United States. Some companies in these new free-market economies are very interested in using information systems for a competitive advantage. They feel that the use of information systems can perhaps give them a head start in gaining competitive advantage over Western European countries. Do you think Eastern European countries can gain a competitive advantage through using information systems technology? Why or why not?

4. The Bell Software Company writes custom business application software for its clients. They would like to reduce the costs of writing this software. Thus, they have explored the possibility of hiring programmers in India to code some software for them. What do you think are some of the advantages and disadvantages of this approach? Should Bell Software have some of their programming done in India? If they do, what are some of the ways that they can go about doing this?

5. Some countries have erected tariff barriers to protect their information systems and computer industries. For example, Brazil has prohibited the import of some computers in order to protect its own local computer manufacturers. Also, at various times the United States has accused Japan of "dumping" memory chips into the United States market at below production costs. What are the arguments for and against protecting the domestic computer and information systems industries through trade barriers in a developed country or in a developing country?

6. Some countries provide substantial governmental subsidies to their computer industry. These may range form research funding to direct grants for producers of computer hardware and software. For example, Japan's Ministry of International Trade and Industry (MITI) provides funding for the Japanese Fifth and Sixth Generation Projects. These projects are attempting to produce computer systems that process vague or incomplete data, are based on optical techniques, perform neural computing, use parallel processing to process huge databases, and perform advanced artificial intelligence tasks. Is this subsidy a barrier to international trade? Regardless of whether or not you feel that government subsidies are a barrier to international trade, do you feel that governments should or should not provide these subsidies? Justify your answer.

INFORMATION SYSTEMS STRATEGIES

Information Must Conform in a World Without Borders

By Janet Fiderio

Ask Hans Huppertz about the importance of information sharing in global corporations, and he'll tell you that it is necessary to forget most of what you learned in geography class. "Global companies can't afford to operate as a series of independent geographic segments," says Huppertz, director of corporate information systems at Dow Chemical Corp. "They need to operate as a single global entity."

Dow makes 50% of its sales outside the U.S. and has manufacturing facilities scattered throughout Europe, Central America, South America and the Pacific Rim. While many Dow subsidiaries have their own manufacturing facilities and can react quickly to local markets, the need for corporate headquarters to coordinate and monitor activities is vital.

"We want to get the product as close to the customer's place of operation as possible," Huppertz says, "but we also need to remember the needs of our customers, and many of our customers are global customers."

Global customers, according to Huppertz, are companies such as Ford Motor Co., which may order products in Latin America, Canada, the U.S. and Europe and expect the specifications of those products to be the same no matter where they are sold. "In the past, each [facility] had its own specifications for dealing with the local customer," Huppertz says. "If you work, however, with a global customer—no matter if the customer is in Brazil or the Netherlands or the U.S.—it's the same customer, and it wants the product to be identical in terms of specifications."

To meet the challenge, Dow had to rethink its IS [information systems] network. "We are now tying our computer systems closer together so we can service our global customers on a global basis," Huppertz says. "We're also trying to make information available across all functions. In the past, a lot of the data we had was captive within independent operating units."

Unification and standardization of information are becoming key priorities for many companies these days as it becomes clearer that international competitiveness requires coordination on a scale that cannot be achieved with isolated outposts.

"U.S. companies are beginning to realize they can't treat their foreign operations as 'also-rans' or 'stepchildren,'" says Susan Welch, president of Waltham, Mass.-based IMC Systems Group, Inc., a manufacturer of international trade management software. Welch is also a former import manager for Zayre Corp. Integrating these operations into corporate strategy and the corporate information flow is imperative if the companies are going to grow internationally, she says.

Information and telecommunications systems become more critical than ever when you start expanding into foreign territories, says Arthur Fairclough, director of import/export control at Unisys Corp.

Unisys opened its first overseas subsidiary in 1988, Fairclough says, but today it has overseas factories, OEM vendors and sales and service personnel in hundreds of locations, including Japan, Korea, Taiwan, the UK and France. Coordinating the activities of that many sites requires rapid communication and good information sharing, he says, and for that, "We rely totally on our systems."

Developing systems that are going to be invested with that kind of power is not just a matter of technical wizardry, however. As Bill Ledford, director of financial reporting systems at R.J. Reynolds Tobacco International, points out, international systems require a special kind of diplomacy.

R.J. Reynolds, which has manufacturing facilities in such locations as Puerto Rico, Canada, Ecuador, Germany, Korea, the Canary Islands, Malaysia and Hong Kong, uses a system called the Tobacco International Consolidation and Reporting System, or TICRS, to help management keep track of international activity.

TICRS, which incorporates electronic mail and McCormack & Dodge's General Ledger 3.0, is not only a mixture of internally developed and commercial software, according to Ledford, but also the result of a great deal of human networking between the development team and the staff members of overseas facilities. "We involved the people offshore since they were the ones who would make the thing work or not," Ledford says. "Before we put that software in, we talked to them and said 'Here's what we're thinking about doing, give us your opinion of it.' "

Ledford and his team spent much of their time demonstrating the Input/Interface package—proprietary menu-driven software that lets foreign offices request reports from company headquarters and download profit and loss information as well as balance sheet and cash flow data throughout the month to corporate headquarters. They can also use the package to create a local database and run trial balances.

"We took it out and demonstrated it to them, " Ledford explains. "We couldn't even hook it up to the mainframe because we didn't have the interface for the McCormack and Dodge system ready, but we took it out and said 'Here's what it looks like, here's how it operates, what do you think? We still have time to change it.' "

When it came time to install the system on the IBM System/36s, 38s and Application System/400s used at 12 of the company's facilities, Ledford sent two people to each location to install the software and train the staff—one systems person and one finance person.

"We found that this worked very well," Ledford says. "As a side benefit, you get to know the people out there, and now we've got both systems and finance people who have been to these offshore locations who probably never would have gotten there any other way."

Another added benefit is that the foreign staff now has names of people at corporate headquarters whom they feel comfortable contacting when things go wrong. Having a personal contact reduces feelings of isolation. "That pays a lot of dividends, and we feel good about that," Ledford says. "We constantly get phone calls from these people. The question may have nothing at all to do with the system, but they know us so they call, and we'll scramble around here and find someone who can help them."

World Has To Be Involved

Dow's Huppertz also makes the point that building a system on this scale takes coordination between those who provide the technology and those who will use it. "This is not the kind of thing you can do in one location and hope to roll it out to the whole world. The world has to be involved to make it successful," Huppertz says.

Dow uses project teams that consist of both users and IS staff. Project teams work closely together and are located in one building. If, for example, a module for use in a French subsidiary is being designed, a member of the French staff who understands that facility's requirements is a member of the project team. That professional resides in the U.S. during the development cycle.

"When it is time to implement the new software, these people go back to their homeland and take part in the implementation process," Huppertz says. "The biggest mistake we could make today is trying to build [systems] in the isolation of the IS department."

A major component of Dow's strategy for global information exchange is its proprietary order chain system. After almost two years of development, pilot modules are scheduled for implementation during the next two months in the U.S., Europe and Canada. When completed, the system will be able to track the status of any order worldwide, from the time it is placed to the time the order reaches its destination.

One of the benefits of such a system, Huppertz says, is that it allows the company to communicate with customers in the same product language around the globe. "If we sell a product here or on the other side of the world, we have the same product code for that product," he asserts. "You can't have different codes and different names for your product."

Smooth trafficking of orders to widely dispersed manufacturing locations and the ability to capture information about orders on inventories in standardized forms were two major objectives that led Unisys to develop its Consolidated Backlog System.

This integrated system for order management, inventory management and invoicing, which runs on four Unisys A/17s in Detroit, can be accessed by sales personnel at all of the company's sites.

If, for example, a French sales representative wishes to place an order for a mainframe system, he enters all system specifications into the central system, which then breaks the order into its component parts and sends each to the appropriate manufacturing location.

The company also relies on its own proprietary E-mail system to keep dialogue open between corporate headquarters and distant personnel. "The most important point in the international environment is communications," Fairclough says. "The better you can communicate, the more efficient your business will be. The fax machine has been a great invention. The telephone obviously helps. But in terms of the time differences and getting things understood, global E-mail is a big asset to running a business properly."

At another computer maker, Harris Corp., E-mail is both a bridge across cultures and a symbol of the kind of diversity that multinational companies must accommodate. "We have Banyan Mail, CC:Mail, Profs, HPmail, HPdesk and Vaxmail all connected via [products from] Softswitch," says Karl McCalley, vice president of systems. Harris generates approximately one-third of its sales overseas and expects that share to jump to 50% by 1994. Manufacturing facilities in Malaysia, Kuala Lumpur, India, Taiwan, South Korea and Ireland communicate over a dedicated network consisting of T1 lines and 56K bit/sec. lines to Europe and the Far East so that they can report their production and capacity to the home office in Melbourne, Fla.

Each facility keeps its own database, which the central office queries weekly. All facilities share a common planning formula. Manufacturing facilities report their capacity, and marketing offices report demand. All reports come into the home office in a common format. Using these reports, an integrated central planning engine combines demand and capacity forecasts to produce factory schedules and order acquisition schedules, which Harris communicates back to the field.

Few companies are staking quite as much on global networking, however, as Visa International. More than 49% of Visa's transactions were generated outside the U.S. in 1989 and, by 1993, the company expects more than 60% of a projected $700 billion in sales to be generated outside the U.S.

Power Behind the Drive

The engine supporting this expansionary drive is Visa's global network and sophisticated electronic transaction processing system, Visanet, which operates as a giant switch, connecting its member banks with customers worldwide.

Visanet's three data centers service five regions with more than 330 access points internationally. The data centers—in San Mateo, Calif.; McLean, Va.; and London—house IBM 3090 mainframes to handle the heavy transaction load.

At the San Mateo facility, the switching and authorization systems run on an IBM 3090, while clearing and settlement services run on an IBM 1090. Development work is done on an Amdahl Corp. machine. A 3090 in London and another 3090 in McLean fulfill more processing obligations. In September, a fourth processing center in Yokahama, Japan, will be operating using two IBM 4381s.

"Each facility is linked to a specific member base as well as being interconnected," says Michael Massey, senior vice-president of international operations and the person responsible for overseeing Visanet. "In other words, the center in London communicates with both the McLean facility and the San Mateo facility." When Yokahama comes up, it too will communicate with the other facilities.

Visa uses T1 circuits, which span both the Atlantic and Pacific oceans, as well as the continental U.S. "We use the local telephone companies as well for the local connects that need to be made between member institutions and our local data centers, and we also use satellite links," Massey says. While most of Visanet's connections are leased lines, the company has dial-up lines and Switched 56 service available as a backup.

The result of this massive network is that Visa headquarters gets reports of regional activity every day. "All the systems are interconnected, so, for example, when our clearing and settlement system finishes running this evening, we will know the total dollars that went through the system. Then that is totaled," Massey says. "We know how many authorization transactions went through London, how many went through the West Coast and also the dollar amount when we go to clear and settle."

This trend information is also fed into daily, weekly and monthly reports that are sent to those responsible for ongoing market trend analyses. Visanet also lets the company's development team send system enhancements and emergency changes electronically through the network to each facility. "We don't have to mail tapes to actually enhance our systems," Massey says. "The system developers can do that through the facilities here."

Easier Said Than Done

Setting up a network outside the U.S. is not always easy.

According to Massey, establishing systems and networks in some areas of the Middle East, Latin America and Africa, where local Postal Telephone and Telegraph authorities (PTT) are not as developed, may mean longer lead times to get service.

Once established, however, those links are usually reliable. And if they're not, Massey is prepared. "Once those lines are established," he says, "they're connected to what we call our Advanced Network, and they get the same monitoring as our major trunks between carriers."

The Advanced Network is actually Network Corp.'s IDNX Network, a fully automated monitoring system that warns operators when lines drop below specifications and reroutes traffic automatically when a link goes down. "IDNX alerts the operator that he has a potential problem. But at the point that the system has determined that degradation has reached a threshold level, it automatically switches to a backup route. The operator has to do nothing," Massey says. IDNX monitors all of Visanet's links, from the long-haul T1 to the local lines provided by the Bell operating companies in the U.S. and PTTs in foreign countries.

Massey could order international lines through AT&T or other long-haul carriers, who will do all the negotiating with foreign telephone companies for him, but he says that doing it yourself is worth going the extra mile. "There are some service bureaus that say, 'Give us your orders, and we'll handle everything,' but we stay very close [to our service providers], because what happens in the middle of the night if our folks have telephone problems?" Massey asks. "We want to make sure that there's a relationship established with the local companies so that we don't have to go through a third party."

In some countries you may have a choice of vendors, and in other countries, you may be negotiating with a government-owned facility. "Regardless, you still sit down, establish a relationship," Massey says. Not only do Visa's staff members make personal contacts with foreign service providers, but they also establish service objectives that are measured each month.

"I spent a great amount of time in Japan over the last three months working with the local service providers, negotiating and understanding what they can and cannot do," Massey says. "When you come up with something that they can't perform as well as you may find in the U.S., you work to find an alternative."

Telecommunications networks and information systems are the glue that hold corporate global business strategies together.

In order for that glue to hold, the IS manager needs to be on the spot, whenever and wherever strategies are being formed or impacts are going to be felt.

"The IS manager must be involved in developing the business strategy and the way information management and technology will support that strategy," says Donald Marchand, dean of the School of Information Studies at Syracuse University. "If it requires redefining how R&D and manufacturing interact and what technologies they use to design products, he or she has to be there right at the planning stage."

The role that information systems play in managing complex shipping and logistics activities and in tracking the resulting import and export requirements can't be overstated.

IS, claims Susan Harris, corporate logistics manager at Intel Corp. in Santa Clara, Calif., is essential in helping her manage Intel's transportation and finished goods warehousing network. Harris is responsible for the movement of materials from the supplier to Intel's facilities, from one Intel facility to another and then from the final finished goods warehouse to the customer.

To track activities in Intel's U.S. and foreign facilities, the company is currently installing a new version of its sales and marketing system. The company plans to implement the system during the next four to five years and include a shipping module that will be used by the logistics department.

According to Harris, there's no way for organizations to get around installing integrated systems. When manufacturing, sales, purchasing, tracking and reporting systems are integrated, she says, you can respond more quickly to your customers.

"Think in terms of the fact that you're establishing a worldwide shop floor, and each of the workstations needs to be connected—just as you would do with a shop floor that's contained by four walls," Harris says.

Tracking Details

Another concern of corporations that trade extensively across U.S. borders is how they can keep track of a dizzying assortment of laws and import/export requirements when moving products.

According to Arthur Fairclough, Unisys Corp.'s director of import/export control, keeping track of import requirements can be complicated and time-consuming because corporations have to comply with U.S. customs laws.

"You have to properly classify the goods for the correct payment of duty, and you have to comply with country-of-origin markings on goods and any other laws that the government happens to introduce," he says.

Fairclough and his staff use a third-party product called Import Statistics from Waltham, Mass.-based IMC Systems Group, Inc. to help them keep a corporate record of company imports with the import transaction, the duty paid and other statistics from the tip to the freight payments. Unisys also uses the package to match imports against exports for the duty drawback provision of the customs law.

Discussion Questions

1. Using the strategies for managing international information systems discussed in this chapter, identify which strategy is used by each of the firms discussed in this article. Justify your answer.

2. What, in your opinion, is the most important aspect of global information systems? Why?

Fiderio is a Gilsum, N.H.-based freelance writer.

Reprinted from *Computerworld* (October 1, 1990), pp. 91–96, with permission of the author, Janet Fiderio.

23

Information Systems and Society

What has produced the most change in our society during this century? The automobile? The airplane? No, not the computer. The answer is, none of these. People produce change. Humans, like you and me, are behind the major developments in new hardware and software. The founders of Apple Computer were two college students in their early twenties. They revolutionized the computer industry. People also apply computers. If necessary, they can change the impact of computers on society. But first they must know what those impacts are likely to be.

The assumption throughout this book has been that the application of computers will enhance both an individual's work and his or her personal life. Most would agree with this assessment, although some would say that these enhancements have been slow in coming and that the computer has not yet produced the revolution it promised. However, any revolution, even one that enhances people's lives, produces changes. Changes have both positive and negative consequences. Dislocations occur, and the changes must be adjusted for.

This chapter looks at what impacts computer information systems may have on society and at some of the challenges that these systems pose for society. It first examines the potential impact of computer information systems, then explores the areas of automation and artificial intelligence. Next, it considers the privacy questions associated with computerized information and the significant effects that personal computers are having on people's lives. Finally, it explores the serious problem of computer crime.

Introduction

Computer information systems could change the way human society functions. They may result in a growing information revolution, a tendency for people to consider working at home, and a variety of system control problems.

The Potential Impact of Computer Information Systems

The Information Revolution

Information is wealth. Although some would say that the computer has caused information to be wealth, information has always been wealth. For example, if you have information about where an interstate highway interchange is to be built before others know the location, purchasing land in that area is almost certain to increase your wealth. The computer is simply a new source of significant amounts of information. Those who can afford to buy a computer and who have the skills to use it will be better able to acquire information than those who cannot use the technology. Will the computer revolution produce two new classes in society, the information rich and the information poor?

Electronic newspapers have been proposed and some are available now. By simply connecting your personal computer through regular telephone lines to the newspaper's large computer, you would have the ability to retrieve any news item. In addition, you could retrieve articles from past newspapers—perhaps up to several years old—through keywords. You could even select only news articles that were of interest to you. In effect, you could make your own newspaper! For example, you could simply enter the name of your favorite sports team and retrieve all articles about the team, if that were all you wanted to read. But in reading traditional newspapers, people acquire a broad spectrum of information. Would the ability to select reading material tend to make the human knowledge base more narrow?

Already **information services** such as The Source and Dow Jones News Retrieval allow you to retrieve a wide variety of information, including electronic news. Figure 23–1 shows the Dialog database, which may be accessed with a remote terminal. It contains information on a large number of subjects, ranging from accounting to zoology. These types of services allow you to retrieve stock market quotes, order airline tickets, and order various merchandise. With such a service, you could save money (and thereby increase your wealth) by having the computer search for the least expensive airline fare when you plan to travel.

Some people suggest establishing an information assistance program, similar to current fuel assistance programs, for the disadvantaged. Otherwise, those people will become further disadvantaged because they cannot access the information that personal and business computers provide. Should an information assistance program be developed? To provide such a plan is a political decision. However, this question illustrates the degree of impact that some feel the computer revolution may have on society.

If society reaches the point at which people do a significant amount of their shopping through electronic means, work at home on a personal computer connected to an office computer, and receive most of their entertainment as well as their religious and educational instruction through cable TV, some significant questions arise. Can humans all re-

FIGURE 23–1
A Robot.

treat into their electronic cottages and still function as a society? Possibly not. Many would argue that a democratic society requires frequent **face-to-face contact** among its citizens. Further, an electronic society provides very great threats to privacy, as discussed later in the chapter. These threats decrease personal freedom and increase the ability of others to manipulate and monitor an individual's personal life.

Working at Home

Personal computers, personal copiers, fax machines, and existing telephone lines have made working at home possible for many employees, as illustrated in Application 23–1. This work at home phenomenon is often called **telecommuting**. Even President Bush has encouraged working at home because the reduction in commuting will conserve energy and reduce pollution. The types of jobs that are suitable for telecommuting have the following characteristics: The tasks are clearly defined, the work outputs are measurable, close interpersonal communication with other workers is not vital to the job, the work can be transported to and from the office, the employee is an independent worker, and the employee has a good working knowledge of the devices, such as PCs, used in telecommuting.[1]

Telecommuting has several advantages for employees:

1. The commuting time saved allows time for other pursuits.

2. The employee can work at his or her own pace.

3. Expenses for commuting and some wardrobe and dry-cleaning costs are eliminated.

4. Telecommuting is often advantageous for physically handicapped persons.

5. Even though they are working, employees may be spending more time with their families.

Among the advantages of telecommuting for employers are the following:

1. The pool of talented recruits is drastically increased. The geographical area in which workers can be recruited is much greater if they don't have to commute. This is true even if the employee has to commute to the office one or two days per week. Even those who live close to the company often find telecommuting more attractive.

2. Companies that offer telecommuting may be viewed as more receptive to employee needs, thus they may have better employee relations.

3. Because of lack of interruptions and employees' increased job satisfaction, they may be more productive.

4. Since employees are working in their homes the office space costs for the employer can be reduced.

---

[1] Burden, Kevin, "The Viability of Telecommuting in IS," *Computerworld*, November 26, 1990, p. 85.

APPLICATION 23–1

Telecommuting Is On the Rise; MIS Acts as Facilitator

By June Altman

Telecommuting is becoming increasingly popular, with estimates as diverse as 100,000 to 2 million people working at home during part of the work week, but MIS [management information systems] professionals are more likely to be facilitators of this option than participants in it.

This is the reverse of five years ago, when MIS professionals were among the first workers to do their jobs from home. At least one expert said he thinks one of the primary reasons MIS is not more heavily represented among the growing number of telecommuters is the trend toward moving MIS professionals into the user community and away from heads-down coding.

However, a number of factors are making telecommuting a more attractive option for employers, so that eventually every department in a company, including MIS, will have more work-at-home arrangements in the near future. These factors include the increased availability of such inexpensive communications equipment as fax machines, and the increased need of companies to control such overhead costs as office space.

Even broader issues—such as the air pollution caused by huge numbers of automobile commuters—are leading such bodies as the state of California to consider work-at-home programs. US West and IBM Corp. are among the other companies that have sanctioned telecommuting programs.

Gil Gordon, publisher of Telecommuting Review, a newsletter based in Monmouth Junction, N.J., said that he expects the percentage of the American workforce that works at home at least two days a week to grow from 0.1 percent today to between 5 and 10 percent within five years. . . .

Thomas E. Miller, vice president and director of the Home Office Research Program at Link Resources, Inc., New York, put the total number of telecommuters in the United States at nearer to 2 million. Of these, 6 percent are computer analysts and programmers and another 6 percent are computer engineers and scientists. He noted that estimates are imprecise, however, because many companies that do not formally allow employees to work at home informally permit such arrangements. . . .

Both Gordon and Miller said that large companies are generally more resistant to work-at-

home programs than are smaller companies.

"Small companies perceive work at home as an opportunity to expand without additional real estate, secretaries and office equipment, and to attract people they might not otherwise get," Miller said.

Among the large companies that have become involved with work-at-home programs is US West, which now has about 400 employees participating. Buck Benham, chairperson of the company's Flexible Work Arrangement Group, said participants include a wide range of employees, including engineers, systems analysts and program analysts.

The company considers one of the major benefits of the program to be its impact on retaining certain employees who might otherwise leave. For example, Benham said the company estimates it saved $50,000 in training expenses for a replacement for one highly experienced electrical engineer who was planning to leave but decided to stay because of the work-at-home option.

Adapted with permission of Fairchild Publications from *MIS Week* (October 23, 1989), p. 34.

Telecommuting also has its critics. These individuals point out several disadvantages of telecommuting:

1. Telecommuting employees may retard their career development. An employee who is working at home may be forgotten when promotion time comes. Furthermore, promotion to supervisor and manager roles requires good interpersonal skills. When one is working alone at home it is difficult to develop these skills.

2. It may be difficult to measure productivity. In the past managers have associated activity with productivity. When an employee is working at home it is difficult to gauge activity. On the other hand, this may be an advantage since high rates of activity doesn't

necessarily mean high productivity. Telecommuting may force managers to devise new ways of measuring productivity that are based on true output.

3. Work space may be duplicated, particularly when employees work both at home and in the office.

4. Security problems may occur. Sensitive data may have to be transmitted or carried to and from home and could be intercepted or lost during transportation in an automobile. The home is not as secure an environment as the office. Data could be more readily copied in an unauthorized manner at home.

5. The interpersonal contact that many people need for creative thought, direction, and clarification is reduced or eliminated with telecommuting.

6. Employees may find the distinction between home and work blurred. The sanctuary of going home and leaving the cares of work behind may be lost.

In summary, would you really want to work for a company for which you did all of your work at home through electronic means? Off the top of your head, you might answer with an enthusiastic yes. No doubt such an arrangement would have many advantages. You could live almost anywhere you wanted and spend more time with your family. But working where you have direct contact with other people also has significant advantages. The social interaction and exchange of ideas, triumphs, and so on among co-workers is a significant contributor to the mental well-being of most individuals. Consider the fact that most surveys show that the most common way to meet a marriage partner is at work.

In any case, in the very near future you may have a chance to decide whether to work at home or at a traditional workplace. If a significant number of people decide to work at home, there will be noticeable impacts on society. However, most individuals will probably quickly become bored with working at home and will prefer at least a portion of their work to be in a workplace.

Control Problems

To illustrate another potential problem that computers and the emerging communication technology can cause, consider the **electronic shopping** systems such as QUBE. The QUBE systems has been tested in Columbus, Ohio. It is a combination of a cable TV system and computer technology that allows viewers of any TV program to respond electronically to such things as surveys and orders for merchandise. Some have said such a system could produce instant responses to surveys, allow shopping by electronic mail, and even allow instant electronic democracy in which voters could respond to an issue through their QUBE terminal systems. Such proposals are questionable, however. For example, how would researchers know who is pushing buttons in a survey? Is it an adult or a three-year-old child who just happens to be watching the program and likes to push buttons?

Picture the presidential candidates stating their positions in a TV debate. After the debate is over, the voters push their buttons and elect the president! This, of course, is absurd. The control problems would be horrendous. Consider the real-world case of a very conservative married couple who subscribe to the QUBE system. They began receiving sexually explicit materials through the mail. To their amazement they found that their four-year-old child had ordered the materials by pushing the appropriate button while watching a cable TV program. Since the parents were the cable TV subscribers, the materials were shipped in their names—and they ended up on the mailing lists of places dealing with such materials. What if your five-year-old turned on your personal computer and started transferring your bank account funds? Many of these problems have solutions, but as yet the problems still exist.

Displacement of Humans

In the early days of computers, in the 1950s, many people were concerned that computers were going to displace large numbers of people from their jobs, particularly those in clerical occupations. They worried that as clerical functions became automated, there would be no need for people with clerical skills. This did not occur to the extent predicted. In general, more jobs were created than were lost, although the new jobs often call for different skills, such as programming and systems analysis.

Automation

In general, managements use computers to generate more information. They do not use them to generate the same amount of information as before and thereby reduce the labor force. However, this is beginning to change. Computers are being used to control robots that are quickly replacing human workers on assembly lines in industry (see Figure 23–1). In some factories in Japan, the whole production line is automated on certain shifts. The only humans at the factory are security guards. The robots even have the capability of repairing themselves whenever they break down. For example, when a drill bit breaks, the machine simply replaces it from a bin of replacement bits. These factories do require maintenance personnel during the day shift.

Office automation is likely to reduce the need for typists, clerks, and other office personnel. Before personal computers, computers were primarily used for high-volume tasks. Many of the day-to-day tasks were still done manually. Personal computers are rapidly changing this.

If automation, through computers, does displace significant numbers of workers from their jobs, will society support the retraining of these workers? Will there be enough alternative jobs? It seems there will. There is always something to be done, regardless of how many tasks are performed by computers and machines. And usually these remaining jobs and new jobs are more interesting. The computer often does the dull and routine jobs such as assembly line and clerical work. The bottom line, though, is that anytime a human can be replaced with a machine at a cheaper cost, society as a whole benefits because the standard of living rises.

Artificial Intelligence

Artificial intelligence is a computer application in which the computer makes decisions or judgments that appear to require human intuition, reasoning, and intelligence. One type of artificial intelligence that is beginning to see practical use is the expert system. **Expert systems** attempt to provide the same judgmental advice that human experts such as doctors provide. In the areas in which they have been successful, these systems can equal and often surpass the best judgments made by humans. For example, they have been applied to the diagnosis of illnesses. Given the symptoms of a patient, the expert system may ask more questions, request additional laboratory tests, and eventually arrive at a diagnosis that is as good as or better than that of the best doctors in very limited areas of medicine. One approach to developing these expert systems is to model the thought processes that a physician goes through when he or she makes a diagnosis. This not only results in an artificial intelligence system, but also provides interesting insights into how humans reason and make judgments.

Will these systems ever replace experts such as doctors, lawyers, engineers, accountants, and information systems consultants? Certainly some of these expert systems may make better judgments than the least competent people in these areas, but most professionals will use the systems as tools. A medical diagnosis expert system could assist doctors greatly in narrowing down the possibilities of the diagnosis for a particular patient.

Will the professionals accept these systems, which may seem to diminish the human experts' importance to society? I think they will. Most true professionals are always looking for ways to improve their productivity and the quality of the service they provide to their clients.

One final danger of these expert systems is that people may think the systems are infallible since they are computer based. Nothing can be further from the truth. These systems are models of the human judgment process, and many human judgment imperfections are also a part of expert systems. Professionals, such as doctors, must continue to know enough about their fields to recognize when the computer-based expert system is providing answers or diagnoses that are unreasonable.

Export of White-Collar Jobs

Earlier in this chapter we discussed the fact that many employees are now working at home. These employees are often in jobs such as programming, technical writing, research, and data input. If these jobs can be performed at home 30 miles from the office, possibly they can be performed 2,000, 5,000, or 12,000 miles from the office, in other countries where wage rates are substantially lower. In fact, in the future it may be easier to export white-collar jobs than it is to export blue-collar jobs. The primary cost difference between working 30 miles from the office and 12,000 miles from the office is the communication costs—and these costs are rapidly decreasing. Most of the highly educated people in the world speak English. In fact, many white collar tasks for U.S. companies are already being performed in foreign countries. For example, computer programs are written in India and the second edition of this textbook was keyed into computer typesetting equipment in Korea.

From a purely economic standpoint, the **export of white-collar jobs** has the same advantages in international trade as the export of blue-collar jobs. It can be shown conclusively that the world as a whole benefits when goods and services are purchased from people, companies, or countries that can produce them at the lowest costs. We all, obviously, end up with less expensive goods and services. Our challenge will be to keep our skills at a level where we can continue to lead the world in providing goods and services that the rest of the world is willing to buy.

Automation, artificial intelligence, and the export of white collar jobs will increase the need for retraining and continuing education. In the past, individuals could spend approximately the first twenty-one years of their life gaining an education that prepared them for a career and could expect to stay in this career throughout their working lives. This is likely to change dramatically. We will find that we must continually update our skills. Computer systems will automate some skills out of existence. Other skills will become uneconomic because individuals in other countries working for lower wages can perform these skills using computers and telecommunication lines. Thus, to be successful we must continually learn new skills. Some have predicted that up to half of our working life will be spent learning new skills. The first twenty-one years of our lives should be spent in learning the basic common skills of our first career and learning how to learn. The ability to learn new skills quickly may be the most important skill that we learn.

Computers and Individual Privacy

Computer information systems do pose a threat to the privacy of individuals. How this threat is handled, particularly through legislation, may determine how readily people accept computer information systems.

Potential Problems

If I were asked by a totalitarian regime what would be the best way to provide almost total surveillance over the country's population. I would suggest establishing a pervasive **electronic funds transfer system (EFTS)** and eliminating paper, coin, and check money as much as possible. I would also recommend installing two-way cable TV systems with centrally located computers as a part of the cable system, and perhaps a computer in each home. You may be wondering what this combination of systems has to do with surveillance. In fact, people appear to be headed in the direction of using such systems. Think for a minute—what actions can you perform in our society, or in any modern society, without spending money? You cannot travel, you cannot buy food, and you cannot rent a motel room. You can do very little without spending money. If every time you spent money you gave the merchant, the airline, or the gas station a plastic card, your transaction could be recorded through a communication system to a central database. Your funds would be electronically transferred from your account to the merchant's account. The computer could easily record the time of the transaction, the day, where you are, and other surveillance information. In fact, it could keep a record of all your movements and all your purchases. Through the cable TV system others could know what programs you are watching on TV and when you watch them. Other people could easily obtain a great deal of information about almost all your actions and know approximately where you are at any time.

You may be thinking that such a situation could never occur in the United States. Certainly the technology is available for these systems and the society is moving rapidly toward these capabilities as electronic funds transfer, two-way cable systems, home electronic shopping, and other systems are implemented. Consider one actual case. In Columbus, Ohio, where the QUBE system was installed, a local movie theater owner was taken to court over an allegedly pornographic movie that was shown at his theater. Currently, the test that the Supreme Court applies to determine whether a movie is pornographic or not is whether or not it goes beyond the moral values and standards of the community in which it is being shown. In this case, by coincidence the same movie had recently been shown on the local QUBE system. So the theater owner's defense lawyer summoned the records from QUBE to determine who in the community watched the allegedly pornographic movie on the cable network. This was a brilliant move by the lawyer. If a significant number of people watched the movie, including supposedly outstanding citizens, then the movie did not go beyond the community's moral values. But do you want judges, lawyers, and jurors reviewing the records of what you have watched on cable TV? Is this an **invasion of privacy**? Fortunately, the judge in this case had the good judgment to keep all names confidential. The case against the theater owner was dismissed.

Another privacy problem is the large amount of data concerning individuals that are stored in many different databases throughout the country. Are these data being used in ways that could potentially harm the individuals whose personal characteristics are stored in these databases? Are the data being sufficiently protected from unauthorized uses?

If you have ever applied for a life or health insurance policy you know that you must often submit information about your health history, including information from your personal physician and information gathered through medical tests. This information is often stored in a medical database to which most insurance companies in the country have access. Of course, you must give permission to the insurance company gathering the information to store that data in the medical database. But most people routinely give this permission. Data stored in this medical database that indicate that you have a chronic health problem might not only prevent you from getting health and life insurance in the future but also might prevent you from getting a particular job. The company may not want to hire you if you are likely to have health problems that could decrease your productivity and could also increase the company's cost for group health insurance.

You might be thinking that this is not a problem for you since you don't have any chronic health problems. But there is a project underway that might change your mind: the human genome project. This is a massive project (three billion dollars) to map the gene structure of a "normal" human being. This project is well under way and is expected to be complete by the year 2005. It has obvious major benefits. We will know what genes cause all inherited diseases and tendencies toward certain illnesses, such as cancer and heart disease. Some of these defective genes have already been discovered. It is likely that a large proportion of the population has some "abnormal genes." Doctors will be able to determine if you have genes that predispose you to certain types of illnesses and in many cases eliminate the defective gene or treat you to avoid the disease.

It is also obvious that life and health insurance companies and even some employers would like to have this information about you. Already, some genetic tests are the basis for rejection of life insurance policy applications. Would you want these data stored in a computer database? What controls over access to such data would you want? The safeguards are certainly not there today. In fact, if we fail to come up with adequate privacy safeguards for gene data, it may be politically impossible to continue with the human genome project. Such a delay would result in continued human suffering that could be avoided with completion of the project. Congress is currently working on legislation to provide privacy in this area.

Certainly, in the future our society will have to make important decisions about the safeguarding of personal data stored in computer databases. Some of these decisions have already been made through legislation, which we cover in the next section.

Privacy and Security Legislation

From the examples just given, you can see some of the problems related to privacy. Through two-way cable systems, computers could constantly monitor individuals' financial transactions and the entertainment and goods people purchase. In addition, governmental agencies and private businesses maintain large databases with information that concerns private individuals. Substantial legislation has been passed that addresses the privacy issues of these databases and other security issues.

In the nongovernmental, or private, area, the major legislation was the **Fair Credit Reporting Act** of 1970. Many lending agencies and credit bureaus maintain records concerning your credit worthiness and your financial transactions. The act helps you ensure that this information is correct. First, you have a right to access the data stored about you, and second, you have a right to challenge the data in order to correct any inaccuracies. However, the institutions still have the right to maintain the information concerning you—it just has to be correct, and they must allow you access to it.

Perhaps the greatest effect of privacy legislation has been on the operations of the federal government. Several acts cover this area. The first, the **Freedom of Information Act** of 1970, allows individuals to access any information about them that is stored in a federal government database or file.

The **Educational Privacy Act** applies to educational institutions that are funded by the federal government. These include almost all educational institutions because almost all receive at least some federal funds. The act states that a student's educational records may be accessed by both the student and his or her parents, and that information can be collected only by certain authorized individuals and distributed to only certain authorized individuals and agencies. The rights provided for under this act may be waived by the student.

The **Privacy Act of 1974** applies only to federal government agencies and provides that

1. information collected for one purpose cannot be used for other purposes unless the individual gives consent;

2. there must be no secret collections of data; and

3. individuals must have a right to access and correct erroneous data.

Agencies collecting information are responsible for ensuring its accuracy and protecting against its misuse.

The **Right to Financial Privacy Act** of 1978 addresses a threat to privacy that exists within financial institutions. Currently every check and credit card transaction that you make is recorded on microfilm by your bank and stored for five years. Before the Right to Financial Privacy Act, governmental investigative bodies such as the IRS and FBI could access these microfilm records and examine them without your knowledge. As has been shown, a great deal of information can be collected from these financial transaction records. The act provides that if an investigative body wishes to access your personal financial data stored at a financial institution, you must be notified. This notification provides you with an opportunity to challenge the access in court.

The **Electronic Communications Privacy Act of 1986** prohibits private citizens from intercepting data communications without authorization. Government agents must get court orders to intercept electronic communications. However, this act does not cover telephone conversations over portable phones. Anyone nearby with simple radio equipment can pick up these conversations. But, telephone conversations over cellular telephones are protected under this act.

The **Computer Matching and Privacy Act of 1988** regulates the computer matching of files that is often performed by federal and state organizations. This matching of computer files attempts to locate individuals who are delinquent on loan guarantees or have failed to report income for tax purposes, and to determine eligibility for federal and state programs, such as welfare.

Lack of computer security has privacy implications as well as computer crime implications. We will cover some cases of computer crime later in this chapter. Several laws address computer security and fraud. The **Computer Fraud and Abuse Act of 1986** applies to interstate computer crimes and to computer systems used by the federal government and federally insured financial institutions. This act makes it a felony to gain unauthorized access to "federal interests" computers with intent to alter, steal, or destroy data if the victim suffers a loss of at least $1,000 or if the files are medical records.

The **Computer Security Act of 1987** requires periodic computer security training for operators of sensitive federal computer systems. In addition, the act requires that any federal organization that operates a sensitive system must establish a plan that assures the security and privacy of the system.

Some of the federal privacy legislation does not apply to state institutions and private organizations, especially those that do not operate in interstate commerce. So many states have passed their own privacy and security legislation. The provisions of the state laws are usually similar to the provisions of the federal acts. Only two states do not have legislation dealing with computer crime.

Computer Monitoring

Computer monitoring is the use of computers to directly monitor, supervise, and evaluate employee performance. The use of computers to monitor employees has become a highly controversial practice. It has productivity, social privacy, and psychological implications. Computer monitoring can be categorized into three different types:

1. Those that focus on performance, such as measuring use of computer time, the content of telephone conversations, or measuring keystrokes.

2. Those that focus on employee behavior, such as measuring the use of resources, testing an employees' predisposition to error, or tracking worker location via identification badges.

3. Those that focus on employee characteristics, such as their truthfulness or the state of their health.[2]

A computer monitor is simply a set of computer programs and some type of sensor that detects the performance to be measured. They have several capabilities:

1. Monitor without interfering in any way with the performance of the work being done. The measurement scheme can be entirely invisible to employees and customers and yet generate and record vast amounts of incredibly detailed work measurements.

2. Count the number of keystrokes produced per minute.

3. Count the number of transactions and errors made in a given period of time.

4. Alert a supervisor when a worker isn't connected to the system or when a workstation is turned on or off.

5. Compare actual performance to productivity standards.

6. Randomly listen in on conversations made over the phone, record where the call goes, who made the call, when it occurred, and how long it lasted.[3]

Almost anyone who works directly or indirectly with the computer can be monitored. Currently it is estimated that approximately ten million workers are monitored electronically in the United States. By the

[2] Grant, R. and Higgins, C., "Monitoring Service Workers via Computer: The Effect on Employees, Productivity, and Service," *National Productivity Review*, Spring 1989, pp. 101–112.

[3] Susser, Peter, "Electronic Monitoring in the Private Sector," *Employee Relations*, Spring 1988, pp. 576–580.

year 2000 this number is expected to be thirty million. In the past, computer monitoring was concentrated primarily in the data processing, insurance, airline, and telecommunication industries. Today it has expanded to include technical and professional workers such as pharmacists, stockbrokers, and nurses. Taxi drivers, truck drivers, and others find themselves being monitored by electronic systems mounted on their vehicles.[4]

Certainly employers have the right to monitor employees' work for performance evaluation purposes. However, do they have the right, is it ethical, is it good employee relations, or does it even make economic sense to use computers to monitor employees constantly and to collect such detailed statistics? Those who favor computer monitoring justify it with several reasons. Among them are:

1. The computer is not biased and has no favorites. Thus, the performance evaluation is objective.

2. Computer monitoring often provides instant feedback on performance, allowing employees to quickly adjust their work habits and improve productivity.

3. Computer monitoring may provide substantial cost savings. Individuals whose performance is not up to par can be replaced or transferred to other tasks.

4. Employees learn quickly whether or not they are suited for a particular job. Thus, they will not spend a good portion of their careers in a job for which they are not suited.

5. Problems in employee performance can be detected early and additional training that corrects problems can be given to the employee.

Those who oppose computer monitoring argue the following:

1. Workers who are subjected to computer monitoring constantly feel pressure to perform and thus are more likely to succumb to stress-related illness.

2. Worker productivity may actually decrease. To meet the goals of the measurements being made, workers may cut off customers on the phone line, enter incomplete data, etc.

3. Computer monitoring may cause supervisors to focus on quantitative measures of performance that the computer can produce rather than qualitative measures that the computer cannot measure. Qualitative factors such as how a customer is treated on the phone may be much more important than how long it takes to process the customer's order.

4. Constant monitoring violates an employee's sense of dignity and privacy.

---

[4] Grant and Higgins, pp. 101–112.

Computer monitoring is a reality. However, many companies have decided not to use it in any way, as illustrated in Application 23–2. For those that do use computer monitoring, two very crucial things must be done. First, computer monitoring has the potential to be a disaster for employee relations. Thus, when implementing a computer monitoring system a company should hire an outside consultant who has had extensive experience in implementing these systems and avoiding the employee relations problems that can occur. Second, the measures of productivity must be measures of true productivity. You can be sure that whatever you measure, employees will focus on maximizing that measure. For example, if the measurement in a telephone order entry operation is the number of orders processed per hour, then the order entry operators are going to attempt to process as many orders as they can. Customers may be cut off or treated in an abrupt manner to maximize the number of orders processed. Certainly, such treatment of customers will not benefit the company in the long run.

APPLICATION 23–2

How to Motivate Workers: Don't Watch 'Em

By Aaron Bernstein

Electronic eavesdropping is a tempting tool for boosting office productivity. Airlines, insurers, and telecommunications companies, among others, often clock every second that workers spend on computers or on the phone with customers. From a handful a decade ago, the number of monitored employees has reached 10 million, says the federal Office of Technology Assessment.

But now, the search for quality is abridging this trend. Federal Express, Bell Canada, USAA, and Northwest Airlines, among other major employers, are finding that too much speed spoils service.

Handle Time

They have begun to stress quality over quantity, or to end monitoring entirely. The result seems to be happier customers and employees. Proponents also say that a focus on quality does as much as monitoring to keep productivity high and rising. "A lot of people ask, which do you want, quality or quantity?" says Rebecca Olson, head of customer service for Federal Express Corp.'s southern region. "We found that you can have both, though it took a while to sink in."

FedEx was among the first to see this. In 1984, it was worried about United Parcel Service Inc.'s move into overnight deliveries. Management realized that it could save money by slicing just one second off the average time its 2,500 customer-service agents spent on each call. So, FedEx began to monitor the average "handle" time per call—and made beating the clock 50% of an agent's performance review.

Two years later, the strategy came home to roost. Employees griped that limiting each call to 140 seconds created too much stress—and made them cut off customers before questions were answered. "The management was sending out mixed messages," says Paula Biffle, who has worked as an agent in FedEx's Memphis office since 1983. "We became confused about what they wanted."

A new system cleared that up. Today, a supervisor listens in on a random call twice a year. Afterward, the discussion with the agent focuses on quality: The length of calls isn't mentioned. Both employees and executives say that service has improved—without hurting speed. The average call even dropped to 135 seconds, although that has crept up in recent years as the company added new services.

Other companies are following FedEx's lead. In 1989, Bell Canada, concerned about quality and union unhappiness over monitoring, ran a six-month experiment. Ontario operators were monitored as a group, instead of individually, on how fast they handled calls. Management also stopped disciplining workers whose average handle time rose above the standard 23 seconds. Now, "if we see a problem with the group average, we ask employees if they know the cause and work with them to get it back down," says Carol M. Stephenson, Bell Canada's head of operator services in Ontario.

The test was a success. Productivity stayed up. Nearly 70% of the 2,400 operators involved said their service improved, and 75% liked their job more. All 5,000 Bell Canada operators work this way now—thanks to a company that saw waste in too much haste.

Another important area of the computer's impact on society is **computer crime**. Several sensational computer crimes have been uncovered. Most experts, however, maintain that the computer crime discovered thus far is only the tip of the iceberg; most of it remains hidden. As discussed in the chapter on control of computer information systems, a computer system that is not well controlled provides almost unlimited opportunities for a person wanting to steal funds or goods and conceal the theft. The amount of money taken in an average armed robbery is very small compared with the amounts taken through computer theft. Yet those who perpetrate a computer crime often are not prosecuted when they are caught.

Very few of the known computer crimes have been uncovered by auditors. Certified public accountants maintain that it is not a part of their responsibility in an audit to uncover crime since to do so would require procedures that are prohibitively expensive. However, most people feel that the detection of fraud is a part of the auditor's responsibility. Somehow this inconsistency must be resolved. As auditors become more competent in computer technology and use that technology as an audit tool, more computer crime may be uncovered by auditors.

The following three cases illustrate three typical computer crimes and describe how they were discovered.

Computer Crime Cases

Equity Funding

The management of Equity Funding Life Insurance Company used the computer to perpetrate a major fraud against investors and creditors. The company generated bogus insurance policies with a total face value of over two billion dollars. These policies were then sold to reinsurers. Computer programs were rigged so that the auditors could not easily access the files of the nonexistent customers. The fraud was finally exposed when a former employee disclosed it, and the stockholders lost enormous amounts of money.

Pacific Bell

A teenager retrieved passwords, user manuals, and other confidential documents from the trash cans outside the Pacific Bell phone company's office. He then proceeded to steal equipment from supply centers. Using his knowledge of the company's computer system and a remote terminal, he altered accounting records to show the theft as a bona fide use of equipment. The fraud was not discovered until an accomplice turned himself in.

Wells Fargo

Two employees of Wells Fargo Bank collaborated with an account holder to make fraudulent deposits to his account. Using the computerized interbranch settlement system, the bank employees would make an offsetting entry to another branch's account. This entry would be rolled over every ten days so that no actual payment was demanded from the other branch. The criminals withdrew $21.3 million before the fraud was discovered, which happened when they made an improper entry.

Computer crimes often are not prosecuted or are not prosecuted effectively. There are many reasons for this, some of which follow:

1. The justice system is not qualified to prosecute computer crimes. Lawyers and judges have little training in computer systems and they find it difficult to trace evidence of the crime through a computer system. Even where they do have this training they have difficulty in presenting this highly technical material to juries who do not have expertise in the computer area.

2. Computer crime is white-collar crime. Both lawyers and the public are less willing to prosecute white-collar criminals than they are crimes of violence. The following quote illustrates the problem: "Why should a prosecutor take a white-collar computer crime case when he doesn't know what a computer is? He can't find a law he is familiar with to prosecute and in the same 65 days of work it takes to prosecute the average white-collar crime he can convict a murderer, two rapists, and three armed robbers."[5]

3. Corporations may not report computer crimes because they fear the negative publicity. This publicity may lead customers to lose confidence in the corporation's ability to manage. Other reasons why corporations do not report computer crimes are the fear of repeated attacks by copycat criminals, the possibility of countersuits from the accused, and the expense and difficulty of prosecution. Some have estimated that up to 95 percent of computer crimes are never reported.

4. Computer laws do not address computer crimes committed by minors. A significant percentage of computer hackers who break into computer systems are minors.

Personal Computers

Personal computers have been explored in other sections of this book. However, it would be useful to examine here some of the impacts they are likely to have on society. Earlier this chapter indicated that access to personal computer technology may differentiate between those who can use information to produce wealth and those who cannot.

One significant question is, will we lose many of our current mental skills as the computer performs these tasks for us? For example, most of the math that engineers learn in college and use in their day-to-day work, and all basic mathematical functions, can be performed by the computer. Children are using the computer to complete their mathematics homework in elementary and secondary schools. Will this dependence on the computer cause us to lose our math skills?

Perhaps a more significant question is, does it make any difference if we lose a skill that we can purchase for a few hundred dollars or less? As we have advanced over the centuries, we have lost many skills that were absolutely necessary to our survival in earlier times. There are very few

---

[5] Savage, J. A., "Loopholes, Apathy Open Gates to Hackers," *Computerworld*, August 8, 1988, p. 1.

people today who have the necessary skills to survive through hunting and food gathering in a Stone Age fashion, without the use of modern firearms. This question of loss of skills is an important controversy. Some say it will not make any difference; others are very concerned about the loss of mental skills.

On a more positive note, there is no question that personal computers are going to make our lives more productive and take away some of the more boring tasks that we now have to perform. These electronic tools are going to become much more **user friendly**. In fact, many people already find them very easy to use.

Summary

- Information is wealth, and computers assist people in obtaining this wealth. Those who do not possess knowledge about the computer might end up being poor because they lack the information necessary to compete with others.

- Personal computers, personal copiers, fax machines, and existing telephone lines have made working at home possible for many employees. This work-at-home phenomenon is often called telecommuting.

- Although automation does take away jobs temporarily, in the long run it creates more jobs. Moreover, it helps to raise the society's standard of living.

- Artificial intelligence aids experts in making better-informed decisions in areas such as medicine and engineering. These systems, however, do not replace human intelligence; rather, they complement it with the computer's immense memory and fast speed.

- Computers and communication technology may make it much easier to export white-collar jobs.

- The computer can potentially be used to monitor most people's actions, thus robbing individuals of privacy.

- A privacy problem is the large amount of data concerning individuals that are stored in many different databases. An example of such data is personal medical data. Recognizing this threat to the public's basic freedom, Congress has enacted several acts to protect the privacy of U.S. citizens.

- Computer monitoring is the use of computers to directly monitor, supervise, and evaluate employee performance. The use of computers to monitor employees has become a highly controversial practice. It has productivity, social privacy, and psychological implications.

- Computer crime is a growing threat to society. The average amount taken in a computer fraud is many times greater than in a traditional robbery. Unfortunately, auditors have had little success in detecting computer fraud. And computer crimes are often not prosecuted.

- The advent of personal computers could cause us to lose some of our basic skills. On the other hand, the personal computer will make life much more interesting by performing many of our routine chores for us.

Key Terms

Information services

Face-to-face contact

Telecommuting

Electronic shopping

Artificial intelligence

Expert systems

Export of white-collar jobs

Electronic funds transfer system (EFTS)

Invasion of Privacy

Fair Credit Reporting Act

Freedom of Information Act

Educational Privacy Act

Privacy Act of 1974

Right to Financial Privacy Act

Electronic Communications Privacy Act of 1986

Computer Matching and Privacy Act of 1988

Computer Fraud and Abuse Act of 1986

Computer Security Act of 1987

Computer monitoring

Computer crime

User friendly

Review Questions

1. Explain the phrase "information is wealth."

2. What are the advantages to the employee and employer of working at home? What are the disadvantages?

3. Discuss some control problems that may be encountered when using data communication technology.

4. In the long run, how does automation create more jobs than it eliminates?

5. Is it possible for an artificial intelligence system to replace a human mind? If not, what functions can such a system perform?

6. Describe how computer technology could be used to monitor the actions of an individual.

7. How does computer technology constitute a threat to individual privacy?

8. What rights do you have under the Fair Credit Reporting Act of 1970?

9. List the major provisions of the Computer Fraud and Abuse Act.

10. What is the likely effect of personal computers on our basic mathematical skills?

11. Why are victims of computer crime often reluctant to report the crime?

12. How could Pacific Bell have prevented the computer fraud perpetrated against it?

13. What are the arguments for and against the use of computers to monitor employee performance?

Discussion Questions and Cases

1. "Computerization will ultimately lead us to the point where we will only have to push buttons for everything. There will be no room for creativity or original thought." Discuss this statement.

2. Expert systems are based on models of human thought processes. In what ways is such a system superior to traditional computer programs? Identify and justify some applications of artificial intelligence other than those discussed in this chapter.

3. Legislation and case law on the subject of computer crime is in its infancy. Discuss some of the problems a court would face when trying a case of computer fraud. Why is it difficult to use precedents from traditional criminal law?

4. The Fairfax Company is in the process of developing a new computer-based accounting system. This new system will result in the loss of ten clerical positions in the accounting department. Overall, though, the company will not experience a reduction in personnel owing to the new system. New positions will be created both in systems development and in accounting. However, these new positions will require different and higher-level skills than the current clerical personnel have. With three of the employees, retraining for the new positions is feasible. The other seven are long-time employees of the company and most will reach retirement age in approximately ten years. Management has decided that retraining these employees would not be feasible. Furthermore, even if it were feasible it is doubtful that any of these employees would want to go through the retraining. If you were the manager making the decision about the future of these seven employees, what would you do?

5. Carolyn Short is a programmer for the Appalachian Tire Company. The main language used in Appalachian's computer information system is COBOL. To help reduce the application backlog, the computer center management recently began purchasing personal computers for some user departments. It also started thinking about buying application productivity tools for prototyping and for managing systems development. Management has assured Carolyn that COBOL would still be used as the main language, and that she would have plenty of work to do. Carolyn is worried, though, that her current skills in COBOL may not be needed in the future if COBOL is eventually replaced by a high-level language that non-programmers could easily use. Is Carolyn justified in her worries that she could be replaced? What should Carolyn do?

6. Midland Brokerage, a regional firm in a Virginia city, has recently discovered that an employee has used the computer to embezzle seventy-five thousand dollars from the firm. The firm's management has decided to handle the case in the following manner. It will confront the employee with the evidence it has concerning embezzlement. If the employee will return to the firm a substantial portion of the seventy-five thousand dollars, the management will agree to dismiss the employee without calling in law enforcement officers, and the case will be closed as far as the firm is concerned. The management will also agree to handle the dismissal as a normal resignation, and the firm will give the employee favorable recommendations for any new job that he might pursue. The firm's primary rationale for this approach is that it cannot afford the adverse publicity that would ensue if the embezzlement were publicized in the newspaper. Public questions over the security of investors' funds might cause the firm to lose customers. Evaluate the firm's approach.

7. To what extent do you believe that Congress should regulate the storage of data that pertains to individuals?

8. Insurance companies argue that they must have knowledge of pre-existing medical conditions of health and life insurance applicants. Otherwise, a

reverse-selection process would occur; many individuals would wait to apply for such insurance until it was highly likely that they would collect on the policy. After all, if you had a terminal case of cancer, with no insurance, it would be nice to have an insurance company issue you health and life insurance at normal rates. However, when the human genome project is complete, gene tests could reveal that you have a high likelihood of having an often terminal case of cancer in the future. Should insurance companies be allowed to use gene test results? If so, how do you propose that those with abnormal gene tests obtain insurance? If not, how do you propose that insurance companies protect themselves from reverse selection? Should potential employers be allowed to use gene test results? Outline the major points of legislation (if any) that you feel should be passed in the area of medical data privacy.

9. What do you consider the major ethical, employee relations, and productivity problems (if any) of using computers to monitor the performance of employees?

INFORMATION SYSTEMS STRATEGIES

How the Good Guys Finally Won

By Steven Levy

Larry Seiler does not consider himself a troublemaker. Not even a gadfly. But one day when he called up his electronic mail he read a message that stunned him. The Lotus Development Corporation was preparing to ship a product called Lotus Marketplace: Households. The most important component of this software—CD ROM package was a listing of names and personal data, including estimated income, of more than 120 million Americans. Including, almost certainly, Larry Seiler.

The 35-year-old computer consultant–engineer was incensed at what he considered an intolerable invasion of his privacy. He called Lotus to verify the information and found that, yes, Marketplace: Households was indeed headed toward the pipeline. So he wrote a letter to Lotus Development Corporation, taking advantage of Lotus's offer to remove his name from Marketplace. He gave Lotus CEO Jim Manzi a few things to think about while he was at it. Here is a flavor of his prose:

"If you market this product, it is my sincere hope that you are sued by every person for whom your data is false, with the eventual result that your company goes bankrupt . . . . I suggest that you abandon this project while there is time to do so."

Lotus thought so much of Seiler's suggestion that the company did just that. On January 23, 1991, Lotus and its partner in the enterprise, a billion-dollar personal-data company called Equifax,

aborted Marketplace after Lotus had put an estimated $10 million into the project. It seems that Seiler's opt-out request was one of approximately 30,000 that Lotus had received in the brief period since the product announcement in August of 1990. In addition, consumer groups and privacy advocates were declaring war on Marketplace. It was, said Manzi, "an emotional fire storm," one that would be difficult—and expensive—to extinguish. So, to the astonishment of Larry Seiler, who never expected such an easy win, Lotus and Equifax killed the product.

According to the statements of Manzi and his counterpart at Atlanta-based Equifax, former IBM executive C. B. (Jack) Rogers, Jr., the whole muck-up was largely the result of a flawed perception of the product—folks just didn't understand how harmless it really was, nor how it would help them.

But the truth is that the misperception was on the part of Lotus Development Corporation. Marketplace was doomed from the beginning, one of a series of bizarre missteps by Lotus in the Macintosh market. Instead of delivering the product that people have been expecting from Lotus since the introduction of the Mac—a killer spreadsheet—the company ventured into the treacherous territory of privacy issues in the electronics age.

To Market, to Market

It began in early 1989, Dan Schimmel, chief developer of Marketplace, considered it a natural extension of Lotus's ventures into CD ROM technology.

A wonderful aid to small businesses—desktop direct mailing. Previously, the process had been, by and large, limited to big institutions. Lotus Marketplace would change that.

The Lotus product was essentially a HyperCard front end to a package of shiny discs holding names, addresses, marital status, age groupings, and estimated buying habits of almost every American with plastic in his or her pocket—and their families. Users could tool around with the data until a list was produced that met the characteristics they were looking for—elderly, apartment-dwelling cat owners in Toledo, or rich foreign-car buyers with children in a suburb of Seattle. It was to be a classic case of the personal computer delivering the leverage of the big shop to the desktop. Lotus would use its software-design skills and marketing expertise to move the product; Equifax would provide the information from its vast stores of data held on millions of Americans.

But there was a fly in this ointment: the nature of direct-mail marketing and personal-information databanks. Basically, they rely on the unwitting compliance of the people whose names and demographic profiles—often including revealing credit information—are being sold. Consumer advocacy groups have griped about the process for years, but those who profited from the industry insisted that when people understood the process, they had no complaints.

"We felt from the get-go that privacy was an issue we would address," says Schimmel. Lotus decided not to offer two kinds of data that would set off alarm bells in consumer advocacy circles: phone numbers and credit ratings. But other safeguards were required. To Figure out what these would be, Lotus and Equifax took surveys, ran focus groups, and used as a consultant Dr. Alan Westin, a Columbia professor who is recognized as the grand guru of privacy issues.

The scheme that emerged made Marketplace into an obstacle course for its users, all in the service of protecting the public. When you paid $695 for Marketplace: Households, you would essentially be buying a useless box. To get the good stuff— the disc with the names—you were supposed to send Lotus proof that you were a legitimate business. Along with the discs, you would receive stern admonitions about their use. The information itself was limited—though it did list names, addresses, marital status, sex, race, and dwelling type, really personal stuff like income and life-style data were not tracked to individuals, but to nine-digit zip code areas. And even if you wanted to, you couldn't search the disc by name.

Finally, a metering system was to charge you each time you printed out a list of names. Some of the names were dummies, and if you sent an objectionable mailing to those addresses—stuff like pornography—Lotus planned to cut you off at the knees.

Marketplace Confidential

Was this enough for the privacy advocates? No. Most privacy-oriented groups are working to impose more restrictions on the direct-mail industry—how could they embrace something that would extend circulation of personal information from a relatively small number of companies to millions of potential junk-mail producers?

So naturally, the groups, spearheaded by the Computer Professionals for Social Responsibility (CPSR), objected. They complained about some data coming from credit records, a gray area of the law. And they raised a fuss about insufficient notice for those who wanted to opt out. But Lotus had expected complaints from the privacy people—they even figured, says one source, that the controversy would be good publicity for the product! What Lotus didn't figure on was the very ground of privacy opinion shifting from underneath it.

"In the past two and a half years [since Marketplace was first conceived], public attitudes about the use of information underwent a significant change," says privacy expert Alan Westin. "Previously, people thought that the only ones who cared were the 'privacy nudnicks.' But in 1990 I came out with a major survey—done by the Louis Harris polling firm—which revealed that it was not only the highly educated people who were concerned, but everyone across the board." Indeed, 71 percent of the respondents thought that consumers have lost all control over the use of their personal information by corporations. It was logical to think that Marketplace would be regarded as one more threat to an already beleaguered right to personal privacy.

This news came too late for Lotus and Equifax. The problem was that with privacy concerns high, Marketplace was a natural jumping-off point for the media to discuss the question of whether personal information should be sold in the first place.

By being framed in the middle of this controversy, Marketplace suffered. "No matter how many privacy protections are built in, if the concept itself sounds formidable, you never get to explain," says John Baker, senior vice president of Equifax. As it turned out, negative publicity began rolling in, from places like the *Wall Street Journal*. Marketplace's image was tarnished and the stain threatened to spread to the reputations of the companies involved.

Tales from the Encrypt

Compounding this problem for Lotus and Equifax was another potential rat's nest. The privacy protections in Marketplace were contingent on preventing the user from free access to the names and information on the disc, so you couldn't do things like search for specific names, or copy the information into a database and pass it on to the local porno distributor. But it is not at all clear that Lotus had adequately protected the data.

Dan Schimmel of Lotus denies that this ever became an issue, but according to Alan Westin, "questions were raised by Equifax and me whether we would be able to look at the public and say that Marketplace has adequate security. If you don't have it, you won't be able to keep your promises—then it's not a security problem, it's a confidentiality problem." Already, some critics were vowing not only to crack the program and announce their results, but to distribute the procedure on cracker bulletin boards so anyone could do it.

Apparently Lotus felt that its confidential data-compression scheme would be adequate to keep all but the most skilled security experts from cracking the program. But Equifax wasn't blindly accepting Lotus's assurances. According to John Baker, if the product had gotten close to shipping, Equifax was ready to use a "tiger team" of computer wizards to crack a beta copy. If the Equifax team did the trick, Marketplace would have required sophisticated encryption—which would have increased costs and incurred delays in implementation.

The Net Result

The final straw for the product, though, was probably the direct onslaught of negative response characterized by Larry Seiler's letter. It was a real problem for Lotus to accommodate thousands of people suddenly opting out, especially since the product was on CD ROM and could not be easily recalled once it was sent out. But even more demoralizing for Lotus was the viciousness of the responses, many of which were sent directly to Jim Manzi's electronic mailbox.

Amazingly, this deluge came not as the result of an organized campaign, but from a grass-roots movement spurred by the ease of communication on computer networks. Concerned citizens would collect packets of information on the product and, with the ease of computer mail, send the data packages to dozens of friends. Who would send it to their friends.

This chain-letter-style communication is best seen in the circulation of Larry Seiler's missive. Besides sending it to Lotus, he posted it on an electronic forum, allowing people to copy it and send it to friends on other interconnected networks. As a result, the letter was seen by thousands of people. Within days, more than 100 people sent personal responses to Seiler. The responses came from as far as Saudi Arabia.

Sure, some of the remarks made about Marketplace on the computer nets weren't totally accurate. But generally, mistakes were quickly corrected by subsequent postings made by more meticulous critics. For many readers, it was an educational process—not only about Marketplace, but about the ready availability of personal information to those willing to pay for it.

And true to Alan Westin's survey results, people didn't like it. A lot of them hated it. In light of that, and of the fact that these people reflected the feelings of the public at large, Lotus and Equifax had to face up to destiny and pull the plug on Marketplace. The product wasn't the core business of either company, and it was drawing bad press and bad feelings. (Lotus was particularly concerned that many of the angry responses were from its spreadsheet customers.) Trying to save it would have required adjusted opt-out procedures and possibly even a rewrite for encryption—thus lowering the expected payoff for an investment that was far from a sure thing. (An earlier, less controversial variation of the product, which offered lists of businesses rather than consumers, was selling dismally.)

The Lesson

Is there a lesson? Lotus's Dan Schimmel doesn't draw any big conclusions from the experience—he just says the timing was wrong. But I think more than that was wrong.

Lotus is supposed to be a company that understands how personal computers empower people and improve their lives. In this case, it missed the boat. Though Marketplace ostensibly decentralized and made more accessible direct-mail marketing, a formerly elite activity, the product's eventual effect would decrease the power of individuals, specifically their ability to maintain privacy. The consequences are more than extra junk mail and the potential for misuse. By packaging us on CD ROM and selling us, Marketplace dehumanizes us.

Larry Seiler recognized this immediately, as did the thousands who opted out of Marketplace. Along with the consumer advocates and the media, they made Marketplace into a lightning rod for dissatisfaction about the use of personal data. And as Alan Westin puts it, "You don't stand up in a storm and hold a lightning rod unless you're a masochist."

Discussion Questions

1. Will privacy issues become more important in the future? Why?

2. What are the major mistakes made by the developers of Marketplace? Could these mistakes be overcome and a similar product marketed?

Macworld columnist Steven Levy is writing a book on artificial life.
Reprinted from *Macworld* (June 1991), pp. 69–89, with permission of Sterling Lord Literistic, Inc. Copyright © 1991 by Steven Levy.

24

Information Systems and You

Susan has tentatively decided that she would like to pursue a career in computer information systems. She feels that computers are going to become increasingly important in the future. Being practical, she agrees with the advice that it is easier to ride a horse in the direction in which it is traveling than to make it go in a different direction. But she has a nagging doubt. You see, Susan is really a "people person." She likes dealing with people and she is afraid that computer careers are technology and machine oriented. Are there careers for people-oriented individuals, like Susan, in computer information systems?

Most people realize that computer information systems have had and will continue to have a significant impact on their lives. Many experts agree that this impact is just beginning. Computers will be even more pervasive and useful in the future. This chapter first examines the effect of computers on professional careers, then explores the various information systems careers available. It also looks at the several professional associations and certification programs associated with information systems. Finally, it discusses two suggested models for information systems education.

Introduction

Very few careers, if any, will not be affected by computers. Business professionals rely heavily on computers for their record-keeping and information needs. Those who know how to use computer technology effectively will be at a competitive advantage. As discussed in the previous chapter, artificial intelligence, or expert systems, will even affect the most prestigious careers such as medicine, law, and accounting. These and other careers are based on information or expert knowledge. Computer systems may be able to provide much of this expert knowledge more effectively and at a lower cost.

Most business professionals will find that computers relieve them of many of the boring, time-consuming, and repetitive details of their jobs. This will leave the more exciting, challenging, and interesting aspects of a professional career for people to master. You will probably be much more productive in your career than your predecessors. But regardless of how sophisticated computer systems become, some areas of knowledge and action will always require human discretion.

Many experts have said that we are entering the **information age** because of computer information systems. A greater percentage of the work force will be employed as **information workers**. Large amounts of information will be almost instantly available to decision makers. It is important that they understand not only the information technology but also the decision models, such as just-in-time, linear programming, and others, on which computer information systems rely. A decision maker must be able to decide whether the information supplied by the computer or the action recommended by the computer is reasonable. Business professionals cannot simply turn the decision making over to the computer without understanding what is going on.

In summary, the computer will provide a great deal of information, but users must still understand the underlying process. Otherwise, the actual intelligence behind these systems, the human mind, will lose control. People must continue to exercise creative thinking and control. The

The Effect of Computers on Professional Careers

computer is simply a very powerful tool that must be used effectively if professionals want to maintain their competitive advantage.

Information Systems Careers

The largest impact of the computer revolution will be on information systems careers. The Bureau of Labor Statistics has predicted that the number of jobs for all information systems professionals will increase substantially from 1986 to the year 2000. The increases in specific fields are as follows:

- Systems analysts—an increase of 76 percent
- Programmers—an increase of 70 percent
- Computer operators—an increase of 48 percent

The number of information systems specialists recruited is expected to be greater than that of any other professional group. And, as illustrated in Application 24–1, there is room for information systems personnel to grow and have a major impact on firms.

The primary reason for this increase is the declining cost of hardware and therefore, the increase in the number of computers. Once businesses and other organizations acquire computers, they want them to perform specific jobs. These jobs take software, which in turn usually requires programmers and systems analysts. Someone must also operate the computer and service it.

This forecasted large increase in jobs in the information systems area does not mean these jobs are recessionproof. In the midst of the recession of 1982, the job market dried up for entry-level programmers without experience. There was an oversupply of these people. At the same time, the market was still very good for programmers who had three to four years of experience.

Figure 24–1 illustrates the relationships among the main careers in information systems.

Programmer

As discussed in previous chapters, there are two types of **programmers**: application and systems. Systems programmers write and maintain system software such as operating systems, compilers, utilities, and database management systems. These individuals usually have a degree in computer science. They often work for computer manufacturers and software development firms. Most large computer systems require a few systems programmers, whereas most medium-sized and smaller ones do not employ a full-time systems programmer.

Most jobs in programming are for application programmers. These people write and maintain computer programs that perform jobs specified by the user, such as inventory control, accounts receivable, accounts payable, airline reservations, marketing analysis, and personnel information systems.

It is possible to obtain a job as an application programmer without a four-year college degree. Individuals who obtain their programming education in technical schools and community colleges often become appli-

Experiencing Life at the Top

By Amy Cortese

Tracking Merrill Lynch & Co.'s minute-to-minute stock performance on a personal computer in his corner office overlooking Manhattan's financial district, DuWayne Peterson does not look like your average information systems chief. Indeed, he is not.

Known as the million-dollar man because of his seven-figure salary, Peterson has accomplished what many IS [information systems] executives are still striving for—entry into the inner circle of top management.

"You couldn't be in a better position" in this industry, acknowledges the 58-year-old Peterson. But he stresses that his job goes beyond that of the typical IS chief.

As executive vice-president, operations/systems and telecommunications at the nation's largest retail brokerage house, Peterson oversees 12,000 employees and a budget of just over $1 billion.

As testament to his important role at Merrill, he is an *ex officio* member of the Executive Committee, along with the chairman, president and a handful of other executive vice-presidents.

Peterson seems to have the right balance of technical and business savvy, colleagues say.

"DuWayne is very much a senior business executive, at the top of the organization. With a firm like Merrill Lynch, that's what you need," says Bruce Turkstra, Merrill's senior vice-president of global IS.

"He has good political sense and social sense," adds Gerry Eli, director of global IS. "He fits right in with upper management."

Peterson cites three success factors for aspiring IS executives: a solid track record of performance, good communication skills and the ability to translate technology into business terms. "The key is establishing credibility with management," he says. "The compliment I always get is that I make it sound so easy. You have to take the mystery out of it." . . .

Damage Control

As Wall Street continues to undergo brokerage industry contractions, Merrill has been one of the hardest-hit firms, because of its freewheeling expansion during the boom years of the 1980s. Peterson's charter has been to control costs while continuing to deploy technology to Merrill's strategic advantage.

In light of layoffs and budget cuts, some might resent Peterson's large salary, but colleagues defend it. "He deserves every penny of it. He's added 10 to 100 times more than that to the firm," Turkstra says.

Peterson says that his status gets him "a lot of notoriety," but colleagues describe him as first and foremost a family man. No doubt he has helped inspire two of his three children to become involved in the business: One is in telecommunications at Procter & Gamble Co., another in the computer center at Pacific Bell. . . .

Peterson's management philosophy? "I like to hire the best people I can get my hands on, give them the authority and the tools they need to get the job done—then let them have some fun," he says.

Subordinates agree. "DuWayne has a unique ability to let his people show initiative while establishing a vision," Turkstra says.

Eli characterizes Peterson's informal, entrepreneurial style as "more California." "He sets goals and expects everyone to live up to expectations," he says.

Where do you go from the top? Peterson says he will finish out his working life at Merrill. "I'd like to retire eventually, maybe do some consulting," he says. But when that time comes, he says, "You stop and take stock of your life. This business moves so fast."

cation programmers. Many of them, however, have college degrees in computer science, information systems, mathematics, or a host of other areas. Most employers prefer that application programmers not only have training in the computer area, but also have education or experience in their application area. For example, it is helpful to a programmer writing application programs in the accounting area to have accounting expertise; or in the marketing area, to have marketing expertise. Therefore, many employers seek application programmers who have a broad, business-oriented degree with a major in information systems, and who have taken all the other general business courses, including accounting, finance, economics, business law, marketing, management, and management science.

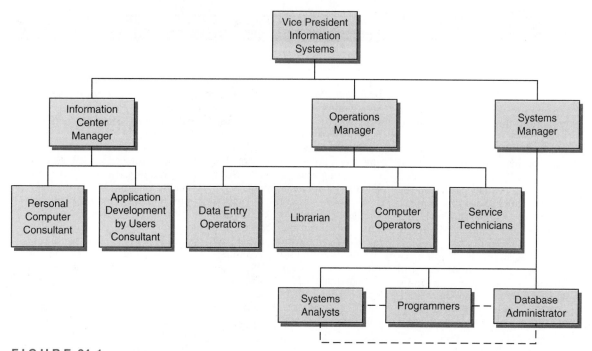

F I G U R E 24–1
The Information System Department.
College graduates entering the information systems field usually start in the information center or the systems
department. Both types of consultants within the information center are currently high-visibility positions with a lot of
exposure to different end-user applications.

Although the demand for programmers is projected to remain large,
new programming tools, such as application generators, could decrease
the demand for programmers. In addition, application development by
end users without programmers is likely to become much more preva-
lent in the future.

Systems Analyst

A systems analyst may be compared to an architect. The **systems analyst**
analyzes and designs application systems. In carrying out this responsibility, the analyst is heavily involved with the systems development life
cycle from analysis through implementation. Often the analyst is looked
upon as an intermediary between the users and programmers. Most analysts do not perform programming, and they do not have to be highly
skilled programmers. However, the analyst should be familiar with several different business-oriented languages. Some firms have positions
known as **programmer/analysts**. In these firms, the systems analyst performs both programming and analysis functions and therefore must be
competent in programming as well.

It is more important that systems analysts have competence in the application area in which they are working than in programming. The analyst must deal directly with users and must understand their
applications in order to design a new system. For these reasons, an ana-

lyst sometimes has a formal education in areas such as marketing, economics, accounting, or management. But the best combination is to have an education in one of these application areas plus an information systems education. In fact, systems analysts often are employed by and report to the user organization rather than the information systems function. They analyze and design new systems and then turn the specifications over to the information systems organization for programming.

Whereas programmers often work with machines and program code, systems analysts work directly with people (end-user personnel and programmers) most of the time. A good systems analyst has highly developed communication skills. Listening, persuasion, teaching, and consulting skills help ensure success for a systems analyst.

The job outlook for systems analysts is bright. They can initially pursue a career in systems analysis, and then decide whether to remain in the information systems organization or to move into management in the application area in which they are trained, such as finance, accounting, or marketing. They are usually actively recruited by end-user organizations because of their computer expertise. Even if end users develop many of their own applications in the future, they will need individuals with the expertise of systems analysts to guide them in the use of new software such as application generators and database management systems.

EDP Auditor

A subspecialty of the auditing field is EDP auditing. An **EDP auditor** has computer expertise and thus can assist traditional auditors both in the review of computer controls and in the production of audit information through the use of computers. Currently, EDP auditors are in high demand. Some people think that in the long run traditional auditors will acquire the necessary computer expertise and EDP auditors will no longer be needed. This probably will not happen. It is very difficult for one individual, an auditor, to maintain a high level of expertise in computer technology, auditing, and accounting at the same time. Furthermore, computer technology will continue to advance. In the foreseeable future, organizations will continue to need EDP audit specialists who keep abreast of the latest computer technology and the methods for controlling application systems based on that technology.

Data Processing Operations

Data entry operators, librarians, and computer operators work in the field of data processing operations. A **data entry operator** keys data from source documents into computer-readable form, usually disk storage. Job openings in this area are expected to decline in the future. This is owing primarily to source data automation, in which terminals, cash registers, and other devices capture data at the point of an event or transaction. Data entry operators generally have only a high school diploma. They do not need advanced education at the college level. The primary skill required is good typing.

A **librarian** is responsible for storage of computer programs and data files. These files are stored on tape or disk. The job entails keeping records of the use and storage of these files, and operating equipment that tests the storage media (such as tape and disk) to ensure that data are stored without error. A high school diploma is sufficient for this job.

Computer operators run the computer equipment. Most have only a high school diploma. However, the operator must be familiar with the equipment and must be able to operate various types of equipment, such as printers, communication equipment, tape drives, disk drives, plotters and CPUs. This requires some technical training. In addition, the operator must be able to convey to programmers and sometimes to systems analysts and users the nature of problems that occur in the execution of computer jobs.

Database Administrator

A **database administrator** is responsible for the design and control of a company's database. This is a management position. Medium-sized and larger firms have several individuals in the DBA's department. Database administrators must have a high level of technical database experience. They also must be able to communicate effectively with various user groups since their primary responsibility is meeting the often conflicting needs of users. The major duties of the DBA are designing databases; developing data dictionaries; designing and implementing procedures that will ensure the accuracy, completeness, and timeliness of data stored in the database; mediating and resolving conflicts among users' needs for data; and advising programmers, analysts, and users about the efficient use of the database.

Information Systems Consultant

An **information systems consultant** is very much like a systems analyst. This individual may be employed within an organization's information department or by outside management consulting firms or CPA firms. The consultant's role ranges from helping a user develop an application to performing a complete analysis, design, and implementation of a system.

A consultant employed by a firm in its information center may hold a specialized position either as a personal computer consultant or as an information center consultant. Personal computer consultants coordinate usage and assist users in applying personal computers. Information center consultants may also assist PC users, but generally their efforts are directed toward helping users retrieve and manipulate data stored on mainframe databases. As personal computer hardware and software become more powerful, the jobs that these two types of consultants do are likely to merge. They both are currently aimed at assisting the end user in developing applications without programming.

Consultants who work for outside consulting firms are more likely to be involved in the complete development of a system. Often they are employed as an alternative to developing a system in-house.

Many information systems consultants, particularly those employed by outside consulting firms, hold advanced degrees such as a master's in business, information systems, or accounting. To be a successful consultant requires a special set of skills and experience, including maturity, an ability to communicate effectively, a high level of technical knowledge both in computer systems and in computer applications, and the ability to recognize problems and come up with solutions quickly without getting bogged down in the details.

Information Systems Manager

All the information systems careers discussed here have management positions. Usually a person starts out in one of the careers and then moves up to a management position in that area. In addition to needing technical expertise, **information systems managers** need the management skills that are universal to all management positions. These include the ability to communicate both orally and in written form; the ability to plan, organize, and implement; and human relations skills, which are necessary in the supervisory function of management. Almost all information systems managers have a college education. Application 24–2 covers some of the other factors that are important to success as an information systems manager.

Professional Associations

Several professional associations serve the field of computer information systems. Most have as their primary purposes the continuing education of computer professionals and the exchange of ideas. Some also offer professional certification programs. Many of these associations welcome student members. In fact, some, such as the Association for Computing Machinery, have local student chapters on many campuses.

AFIPS

The **American Federation of Information Processing Societies (AFIPS)**, 1815 North Lynn Street, Arlington, Virginia, 22209, (703) 558-3600, is a federation of information processing societies. Among the societies represented by AFIPS are the Data Processing Management Association, the Association for Computing Machinery, the Institute of Electrical and Electronic Engineers (IEEE), the American Statistical Association (ASA), and the American Institute of Certified Public Accountants (AICPA). The primary activities of AFIPS are to sponsor the yearly national computer conference and exposition, and to represent its constituent professional societies in a similar international group called **International Federation of Information Processing Societies (IFIPS)**.

DPMA

The **Data Processing Management Association (DPMA)**, 505 Busse Highway, Park Ridge, Illinois, 60068, (312) 825-8124, was founded as the National Machine Accountants Association. Its name was changed to DPMA in 1962. The association holds monthly meetings at its local chapters, holds an annual data processing conference, sponsors an annual information systems education conference, publishes a monthly journal called *Data Management*, and sponsors various educational programs. This is a business-oriented data processing association. Its membership is made up largely of practicing business data processing professionals. However, there are also more than four hundred student chapters of DPMA.

APPLICATION 24–2

CIO Careers More Lucrative, but Risky

By Clinton Wilder

If you are a chief information officer, the good news is you can make more money during the next few years—perhaps more than you ever thought possible. The bad news is you are much more likely to get fired.

The rapid elevation of the information systems function has made the profession both more lucrative and more volatile, said Thomas J. Friel, a Menlo Park, Calif.-based managing partner at executive search firm Heidrick and Struggles, Inc. at *CIO* magazine's recent Perspectives conference.

Salaries for top IS [information systems] talent have the potential to double or even triple over the next few years, Friel said, but executives may have to switch companies to attract them. "Insiders, many of whom have labored faithfully for years in IS, will not be automatically promoted," he said.

Many prominent IS executives have switched companies and in-

dustries during the past few months. . . .

What makes an IS superstar who can command the big bucks? According to Friel, the key is simply "leadership and the proven ability to use technology to make money."

Texas Instruments, Inc. IS Chief John W. White, who shared a career-oriented panel with Friel, had a slightly different view. He said the critical success factor is using information technology to reduce cycle times in product development, distribution logistics or virtually any business process.

White also contended that rotating through non-IS functions is an important path to successful IS leadership and should be done early in one's career. "I think you need to move around and develop a broader base of experience," he said. . . .

Friel likened the ongoing evolution of IS management to that of financial management in U.S. companies since World War II. The chief financial officer position

gradually evolved from nonexistent to the vice president level and then to the executive suite. Now, he noted, companies are required by the Securities and Exchange Commission to have the position as a signatory to financial statements, and the CFO job can be a path to chief executive officer.

Following the same pattern, Friel predicted that more CIOs will become CEOs in the years ahead. "Along with the trauma of increased pressure on CIOs, there is also the opportunity to move up and out of the position," he said. "For those who can adapt and make money by applying technology, the future is very bright indeed."

ACM

The **Association for Computing Machinery (ACM)**, 11 West 42nd Street, New York, New York, 10036, (212) 869-7440, has as its primary objective the advancement of the science and art of information processing. It is the largest technical, scientific, and educational computing organization. Many of its members are computer science faculty members at universities. The ACM has many **special interest groups (SIGs)**. For example, ACM members who have a special interest in small computers are members of SIGSMALL. Other special interest groups are database, computer science education, and programming languages. Active ACM chapters are located on many college campuses and in most cities.

ASM

The **Association of Systems Management (ASM)**, 24578 Bagley Road, Cleveland, Ohio, 44118, (216) 243-6900, was founded in 1947 and is a national organization. ASM publishes a monthly journal called *Journal of Systems Management* and has local chapters in most cities. It holds an annual conference. Its membership is made up largely of systems analysts and information systems managers.

SIM

The Society for Information Management (SIM), 111 East Wacker Drive, Suite 600, Chicago, Illinois, 60601, (312) 644-6610, was founded in 1968. Its members include information systems managers, business systems analysts, and educators. The SIM holds an annual conference and also sponsors an annual International Conference for Information Systems Education. The latter has in recent years become an important event, at which papers and ideas are exchanged among business information systems educators.

EDP Auditors Foundation

The **EDP Auditors Foundation**, 455 Kehoe Blvd., Suite 106, Carol Stream, Illinois, 60188, (312) 653-0950, is a professional association of auditors who specialize in EDP auditing. It has local chapters in all major cities and holds an annual conference. In addition, it publishes a journal called *The EDP Auditor*. One important activity of this foundation is sponsorship of the Certified Information Systems Auditor exam. This exam is discussed in the next section.

Professional Certification Programs

Several professional certification programs are offered in the information systems area. Students who plan careers in information systems should take the exams relating to their career interests. The best time to sit for these exams is during the senior year or shortly after graduation, since the tests are based on material learned in an undergraduate program.

CDP and CCP

The **Certificate in Data Processing (CDP)** examination and the **Certificate in Computer Programming (CCP)** examination are administered by the **Institute for Certification of Computer Professionals (ICCP)**, 2200 East Devon Avenue, Suite 268, Des Plaines, IL, 60018, (312) 299-4227. This organization is nonprofit and was established in 1973 with the purpose of testing and certifying computer professionals. As with AFIPS, the ICCP is made up of several constituent societies. The CDP examination originated with the DPMA but was turned over to the ICCP in 1974. Candidates for the CDP exam must have at least five years of professional experience in information systems. The exam consists of five sections: data processing equipment, computer programming and software, principles of management, quantitative methods, and systems analysis and design. The CCP is also a five-part exam and is designed to test the knowledge and skills required of a senior-level programmer.

CISA

The **Certified Information Systems Auditor (CISA)** exam is administered by the EDP Auditors Foundation, 455 Kehoe Blvd., Suite 106, Carol Stream, IL, 60188, (312) 653-0950. This is a multiple-choice exam that covers the following general areas:

- Application systems controls

- Data integrity

- Systems development life cycle

- Application development

- Systems maintenance

- Operational procedures controls

- Security procedures

- System software

- Resource acquisition

- Resource management

- Information systems audit management

In addition to passing the exam, the applicant must have a minimum of five years of practical experience in EDP auditing in order to become certified.

Information Systems Education

Two professional organizations have been active in designing **model curriculums** for information systems education. Both the ACM and the DPMA have published model curriculums. Outlines of these curriculums are shown in Figures 24–2 and 24–3. As these figures show, the course titles of the two curriculums differ substantially. The primary difference between the two models is that the ACM curriculum has a more theoretical and conceptual basis, whereas the DPMA model curriculum is more practical and applied in nature. Another difference is that the DPMA model curriculum emphasizes that information systems education should be housed within colleges of business.

FIGURE 24–2
DPMA Model Curriculum for Computer Information Systems.
This curriculum is oriented toward undergraduate information systems programs in business colleges. (From *The DPMA Model Curriculum for Undergraduate Computer Information Systems*, copyright 1985, Data Processing Management Association Education Foundation. All rights reserved. Reprint permission granted.)

List of Courses

Core Courses

CIS/86-1	Introduction to Computer Information Systems
CIS/86-2	Microcomputer Applications in Business
CIS/86-3	Introduction to Business Application Programming
CIS/86-4	Intermediate Business Application Programming
CIS/86-5	Systems Development Methodologies: A Survey
CIS/86-6	Data Files and Databases
CIS/86-7	Information Center Functions
CIS/86-8	Systems Development Project

Elective Courses

CIS/86-9	Advanced Office Systems
CIS/86-10	Computer Graphics in Business
CIS/86-11	Decision Support and Expert Systems
CIS/86-12	Artificial Intelligence in Decision Making
CIS/86-13	Advanced Business Applications Programming
CIS/86-14	Computer Control and Audit
CIS/86-15	Distributed Intelligence and Communication Systems
CIS/86-16	Programming Languages: Procedural, Nonprocedural, and Fourth Generation
CIS/86-17	Computer Hardware, System Software, and Architecture
CIS/86-18	Information Resource Planning and Management

Continued

CIS/86-19   Systems Development Project with Information Center Techniques
CIS/86-20   CIS Communication, Reporting, and Documentation Techniques

Business Support Courses

BUS-1   Financial Accounting Practices
BUS-2   Managerial Accounting Practices
BUS-3   Quantitative Methods in Business
BUS-4   Principles of Management
BUS-5   Principles of Marketing
BUS-6   Principles of Finance
BUS-7   Organizational Behavior
BUS-8   Production and Operations Management
BUS-9   Business Policy

FIGURE 24–3
ACM Model Curriculum for Information Systems.
The ACM model curriculum has been implemented at both the undergraduate and the graduate levels.

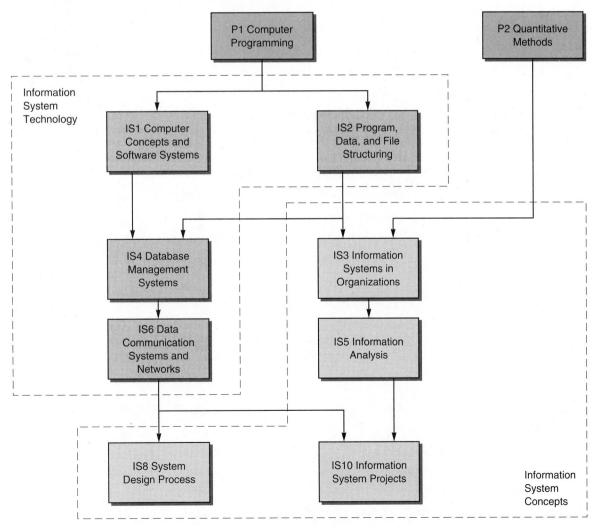

It is rare that an information systems curriculum at a specific university or college exactly matches either of these two curriculums. Model curriculums are designed to be just that—models that are modified to fit the particular needs of a particular university or college. You do not have to follow these model curriculums exactly to receive a good information systems education.

Summary

- Most business professionals will now have to rely on computer-generated information to perform effectively in their jobs. However, in order to make informed and responsible decisions they must also understand the processes used by the computer in generating the information.

- The Bureau of Labor Statistics has predicted a large increase in information systems jobs during the 1980s and 1990s. Careers in information systems may be categorized as follows:

  Programmer

  Systems analyst

  EDP auditor

  Data processing operations

  Database administrator

  Information systems consultant

  Information systems manager

- Many professional associations serve information systems personnel. Some prominent ones are as follows:

  American Federation of Information Processing Societies

  Data Processing Management Association

  Association for Computing Machinery

  Association of Systems Management

  Society for Information Management

  EDP Auditors Foundation

- Several professional certifications exist in the information systems area. The Certificate in Data Processing, Certificate in Computer Programming, and Certified Information Systems Auditor are widely recognized qualifications for EDP personnel.

Key Terms

Information age	Programmer/analysts
Information workers	EDP auditor
Programmers	Data entry operator
Systems analyst	Librarian

Computer operators

Database administrator

Information systems
  consultant

Information systems managers

American Federation of
  Information Processing
  Societies (AFIPS)

International Federation of
  Information Processing
  Societies (IFIPS)

Data Processing Management
  Association (DPMA)

Association for Computing
  Machinery (ACM)

Special interest groups (SIGs)

Association of Systems
  Management (ASM)

Society for Information
  Management (SIM)

EDP Auditors Foundation

Certificate in Data Processing
  (CDP)

Certificate in Computer
  Programming (CCP)

Institute for Certification of
  Computer Professionals
  (ICCP)

Certified Information Systems
  Auditor (CISA)

Model curriculums

Review Questions

1. Why is it important to understand the decision models used by computers?

2. What is the primary cause of the increase in demand for information systems specialists?

3. Distinguish between an application programmer and a systems programmer.

4. What kind of educational background is needed for a career as an application programmer?

5. Why would the use of application generators decrease the demand for programmers?

6. What is the difference between a programmer and a systems analyst?

7. Describe the functions of an EDP auditor.

8. Why is a librarian necessary in the data processing department?

9. Distinguish between a database administrator and a data processing manager.

10. What skills are needed for a career as an information systems consultant?

11. Briefly describe each of the professional associations discussed in this chapter.

12. What is the purpose of the CDP examination?

13. What do the initials CISA represent?

14. What are the primary differences between the model curriculums suggested by the ACM and the DPMA?

Discussion Questions and Cases

1. Some experts argue that tools like application generators and easy-to-use computer languages will greatly reduce the need for programmers in coming years. Does this mean that programming jobs will be the next victims of automation? Why or why not?

2. If you decide to build a career in the information systems area, which professional associations would you like to join? How would they contribute to your professional development?

3. Professions such as medicine, law, and accounting have strict state licensing requirements for practitioners. Why is there no such requirement in the information systems profession? Is such a requirement likely to be imposed in the future?

4. The Abbett Company is considering a policy which would require that all of its computer professionals, including EDP auditors, have an appropriate professional certification. Individuals within the systems development department could hold either the Certificate in Computer Programming or the Certificate in Data Processing. EDP auditors would need to be Certified Information Systems Auditors. Abbett management believes that this policy would build a spirit of professionalism among computer personnel. Managers feel that this is now lacking, and to some extent accounts for the high staff turnover the company has experienced in these areas in the past. Do you think this is a good policy?

5. Campbell Manufacturing Company is a large, diversified manufacturer of industrial and consumer products located in the northeast. Campbell is considering a policy of encouraging employees in end-user departments to transfer to the information systems department for a minimum period of two years, and encouraging employees in the information systems department to transfer to end-user-type jobs in marketing, finance, personnel, and so on, also for a minimum of two years. Campbell's management feels that this cross-training will be very useful in the future, especially as end users begin to develop applications themselves. Do you think this is a good policy? Would you be willing to make such a transfer if you were an employee?

6. A personnel officer of the Computer Consulting Company was interviewing and looking at the resume of a prospective employee. He noticed that the interviewee held a bachelor's in accounting and a master's in information systems, was a CPA, and had had five jobs working with computers over the last eight years. The personnel officer stated to the interviewee, "Your resume looks impressive with your education and certifications. You have also worked with some major companies and have had many duties that indicate that you perform well. But I still have one question: Why do you change jobs so often, if I may ask?" The prospective employee replied that he was always looking for a challenge, since new computer technology is always being developed. He commented, "Your firm seems to be on the leading edge of this technology in the systems development field." The personnel officer was not quite satisfied with the answer; he wondered whether he should hire someone who had switched jobs every one or two years. Should he hire this person?

INFORMATION SYSTEMS STRATEGIES

The Rising Value of Versatility

By Alan Radding

Patricia Gilmore believes in being ready for any situation. "My aim has always been to have a staff that can program on anything for anything," she says.

That philosophy has been put to the test in recent months at Coleman Co., where Gilmore is director of MIS [management information systems]. Making do with less has become a way of life at the Wichita, Kan.-based sporting goods manufacturer since a leveraged buyout led to across-the-board staff reductions, including a 59% cut in the information systems staff.

The reductions came at a critical time for the IS department, Gilmore says. The company is on the verge of a major shift to personal computers and PC networks—a move that's in the budget for 1991.

Because she can't count on adding staff or even acquiring new tools during this period of extreme belt-tightening, Gilmore is depending on her existing staff to perform in a dramatically changed working environment. "Everyone's job is changing a lot," she says. "There will be fewer people in IS operations and more PC support and LAN support." Programmers who previously worked on the mainframe systems will now be doing PC applications, too.

Gilmore says she is confident that her remaining staff will rise to these challenges, chiefly because adaptability has always been one of her main hiring criteria. She has made a point, she says, of seeking people with a strong grasp of systems methodologies and changing technologies, steering clear of specialists and, instead, hiring graduates from four-year, degree-granting computer science programs.

Coleman's situation is far from the exception. Companies everywhere are either tightening their belts or trying to get into condition in case that need arises. The impact of this new emphasis on trimmed-down fitness is being felt in IS, as it is in every other department. At the same time, new technologies are pushing both high-level computing and IS staffs deeper into business areas.

As a result of these dual pressures, U.S. business and the IS function are both going through periods of transition. Unfortunately, it is easier to distinguish what is being left behind than where these trends are all heading.

It is an oversimplification to say IS is changing from the centralized mainframe to distributed PCs and that staff members should prepare to shift their skills and focus accordingly. "In some companies, that is happening, but not everywhere. There is no one answer," says Steve Joffe, vice president at Paramus, N.J.-based Source EDP.

At Spalding Worldwide Sports in Chicopee, Mass., a number of changes are already under way. The focus of development is shifting away from COBOL, says Bard White, Spalding's director of MIS. Instead, the company is "bringing in more commercial packages and doing more client/server stuff on a PC."

Everyone on the systems staff is required to learn PCs, DOS and PC packages, he says, and telecommunications and networking skills are in heavier demand than ever before.

But these changes don't mean that traditional mainframe-oriented COBOL programmers are going to find themselves suddenly stuck with obsolete skills. Upkeep of existing COBOL code will provide work for a long time to come. Furthermore, there are many large companies that are far from ready to make a wholesale switch.

Burlington Industries in Greensboro, N.C., isn't ready for a big move, even though the company is moving toward a more diversified mixture of platforms.

"We need to go from the PC to the midrange to the mainframe. Networking, particularly local-area networking, is growing in importance," says E. Ritchie Fishburne, director of corporate IS. That's only part of the picture, however. "We also have 20-plus years of programming in place and need people to maintain those systems," Fishburne says.

Adaptability an Asset

At many places, the major change will be that, like Gilmore, IS managers will soon place more emphasis on adaptability as a job qualification. According to Thomas Lodahl, chairman of Cognitech Services Corp., an Easton, Conn., consulting firm that deals with IS-related human resources issues, COBOL programmers of the future will need to know computer-aided software engineering, C, C++, object-oriented programming and Unix, and they will have to deal with core systems in which network hooks are as important as the basic code.

Even companies that are moving in the direction of mainframes for the first time aren't planning to settle for plain vanilla mainframe programming skills.

Highland Superstores, Inc., a 100-store consumer electronics chain based in Plymouth, Mich., is converting from an IBM System/38 to a mainframe to accommodate its rapid growth. Highland is seeking programmers who understand DB2 and SQL and are capable of functioning as business analysts, says George Buick, vice president of distribution, warehousing and IS.

It is not just the hiring expectations that are changing: so are the settings in which IS staff members can expect to work. Although head counts in many central IS departments are flat or shrinking, overall demand for IS professionals is not diminishing as much as those figures and all the talk about user programming would indicate.

Instead, IS staffs only seem to be getting smaller because IS professionals are being drawn into business areas.

"LANs and PCs are pushing IS professionals into the user groups," Joffe says. Furthermore, many consultants and recruiters say that when these systems professionals become ensconced in business areas, they may become harder to identify because of title shifts that de-emphasize their technical orientation and emphasize their support function. A systems analyst assigned to a marketing department may, for example, wind up carrying a business card that says "marketing analyst."

And that's not even the farthest reach of the integration trend. J. Daniel Couger, professor of IS and management science at the University of Colorado in Colorado Springs, says many IS professionals are now being hired directly into business departments. More than half of Couger's last graduating class took that route, he says.

It is true that some users are beginning to perform functions that used to belong to IS professionals, but most observers say this is a case of cooperation, not replacement.

If you are concerned about efficiency, it makes no sense to have users operating on their own, Buick says. It's true, he adds, that "if you have an astute user, he can use SQL to query the database on his own." The question is whether you really want him to. Buick says he thinks not: "It sucks up cycles if you let the users run amok." Instead, Highland channels requests through its IS analysts, who use the same advanced tools to "knock out the requests four to five times faster," he reports.

The increase in educated requests from users who could do for themselves in a pinch is one rea-son why demand is expanding so rapidly for technically skilled analysts. By the end of the century, this job category will be growing at a faster annual rate (72%) than that of programmers (60%) in part because of the broader scope of the analyst function, says Brenda Wallace, an economist at the U.S. Bureau of Labor Statistics.

These projections represent the continuation of a trend that has already begun, says Richard Wonder, national director at the IS Division of Robert Half International, Inc. in Menlo Park, Calif.—"a collapsing of functions, with more programmer/analysts than pure programmers or pure analysts," he says.

This new breed of programmer/analyst, Wonder says, will write code where necessary, do systems analysis and write documentation, aided by new tools that accommodate this combination of jobs.

Wonder is most worried about the pure coder who has no experience with or interest in higher-level languages or business issues. "The ones who should be most concerned are COBOL programmers without any business skills," he says.

Joffe, however, says that the person who should be most concerned is the nontechnical analyst—one who does not have programming skills at any level. For individuals of this type, he says, the handwriting is on the wall: "He'd better become technical or become a user."

IS shops are already looking for interdisciplinary types. "I need someone who is not afraid to code but is also not afraid to do analysis," says Steve Crapser, manager of systems development at Kendall Healthcare Products Co. in Mansfield, Mass. Crapser can usually find one or the other, he says, but the combination is hard to come by.

"Technical skills are a given. We expect people to be state of the art and to maintain that level," says Donna McNamara, director of human resources at the Corp. Technology Group of Colgate Palmolive Co. in Piscataway, N.J.

It's what can be layered on top of those technical skills that really makes the difference, says McNamara—things such as the ability to listen to clients, understand their needs and communicate with them; the ability to think like a businessperson; and the ability to work as part of a team that includes business and financial people as well as systems professionals.

Personal Skills a Plus

Other IS directors echo McNamara's insistence on a combination of technical and business/personal skills. Their message is clear: Neither skill set is enough by itself anymore.

"The IS person must understand the business and then know where to get the technology to solve the problem," says Christina Kucharyszyn, manager of IS staffing at Glenview, Ill.-based Kraft General Foods, Inc. She warns prospective IS staff members at Kraft to be prepared to spend as much as 95% of their time working with users.

To find these people, many firms are paying a premium—at least for certain skill combinations—despite corporatewide efforts to keep costs down.

Gilmore has found it imperative to "hang onto key people," despite the intense pressure to cut costs. As a result, she has been "fairly generous with salary increases," even as she moves people into the end-user PC networking environment.

At Spalding, White pays a premium for the combination of technical skills and business knowledge. But, he adds, "the closer you get to the end user—the pure PC person—the softer the salaries get."

If the IS staff is increasingly involved with the user, then who is doing the routine or specialized work of IS? Often, the departments are turning to outsiders—independent contractors who come either with a highly specialized skill or as a general reinforcement to take over routine programming chores during peak periods.

The use of independent contractors, like outsourcing itself, has become an accepted option, but there is no major upswing in the use of consultants, Wonder reports. Contractors are used mainly as a short-term solution.

At Highland, for instance, Buick is able to keep his IS staff stable at about 100 people, despite going through an IBM System/38-to-mainframe conversion that requires rewriting every application, by turning to independent contractors. At times, the population of his IS shop has reached 200 people, half of them independent contractors. "We hold the [permanent] head count at 100, because that's the appropriate long-term level," he notes.

"The real value of consultants is when you are doing a conversion. Otherwise, we prefer permanent staff," Crapser says. Kendall went through a major conversion to IBM Application System/400s and used contractors extensively but has since minimized the use of outsiders.

Even Alan Bugh, vice president of MIS at Wilson Sporting Goods Co. in River Grove, Ill., brings in contractors for some projects, although he doesn't like using them. "These are not very exciting projects—things like IMS-to-DB2 conversions," he explains.

"If the project is going to last, say, 18 months, then I'll hire, but if it's just for three or four months, then I'll use a contractor, Fishburne notes.

Despite the dim economic outlook, corporate imperatives to reduce expenses and the increasing use of programmer productivity tools, growth in IS staffs is inevitable, because demand for information continues to skyrocket.

"There continues to be growth because there is such a demand—more and more projects. We never make as much progress as we'd like to," says Garland Gunter, director of MIS at Cincinnati-based Lenscrafters, Inc.

Discussion Questions

1.　Why are both technical skills and business skills important to an information systems professional?

2.　Is it as equally important for business computer users to have computer skills as it is for information systems professionals to have business skills?

Radding is a free-lance writer based in Newton, Mass., specializing in business and technology.

Reprinted from *Computerworld* (November 26, 1990), pp. 61–64, with permission of Alan Radding.

Glossary

Gaining familiarity with information systems terms is necessary for your understanding of information systems. The many differing definitions of information systems terms that exist are often a barrier to understanding the subject. Thus, the American National Standards Institute (ANSI) has attempted to standardize the definitions of information systems terms through publication of the *American National Standard for Information Systems—Dictionary for Information Systems*. When possible, definitions from this source are used here.

This glossary uses three different sources for its definitions. The source of each definition is noted in parentheses following the definition. Definitions not followed by a source notation have been compiled by the author.

The source notations used in this glossary are as follows:

- (ANSI) A definition that has been reproduced with permission from *ANSI X3.172-1990, American National Standard for Information Systems—Dictionary for Information Systems*, Copyright 1990 by the American National Standards Institute. Copies of this standard may be purchased from American National Standards Institute, 11 West 42nd Street, New York, NY 10036.
- (IBM) A definition that has been reproduced with permission from *Dictionary of Computing*, IBM Publications C-20-1699-8 (1991), Copyright 1991, by International Business Machines Corporation.
- (ISO) A definition that has been reproduced from the *International Organization for Standardization's Vocabulary—Information Processing, ISO 2382*, with permission from the American National Standards Institute. Copies of

this standard may be purchased from American National Standards Institute, 11 West 42nd Street, New York, NY 10036.

Access To read, write, or update information, usually on secondary storage such as a disk.

Access arm In a magnetic disk unit, an arm on which magnetic heads are mounted. (ISO)

Access controls The controls that limit access to program documentation, program and data files, and computer hardware.

Access time The time interval between the instant at which a call for data is initiated and the instant at which the delivery of data is completed; access time equals latency plus transfer time. (ISO)

Accounts payable system A computer system that helps provide control over payments to suppliers, issues checks to those suppliers, and provides information necessary for effective cash management.

Accounts receivable system A computer system used for billing customers, maintaining records of amounts due from customers, and generating reports on overdue amounts.

Accuracy (1) A quality of that which is free of error. (ISO) (2) A qualitative assessment of freedom from error, with a high assessment corresponding to a small error. (ISO)

Acoustic coupler A type of telecommunication equipment that permits use of a telephone handset as a connection to a telecommunication line for data transmission by means of sound transducers. (IBM)

Action construct A construct in a program where a single action is performed.

Ada A general-purpose high-level *procedure-oriented language*, originally developed under the aegis of the U.S. Department of Defense to provide a means, independent of proprietary *machine languages*, for implementing *embedded systems*; it features *structured programming*, *data structures* with *strong typing*, *multitasking*, and facilities of object-oriented *programming*. (ANSI)

Address (1) A character or group of characters that identifies a register, a particular part of storage, or some other data source or destination. (ISO) (2) To refer to a device or a data item by its address. (ISO) (3) See **relative address**. (ANSI)

Algorithm Synonym for **Program.**

Alphabetic character A letter or other symbol, excluding digits, used in a language. (IBM)

Alphanumeric Pertaining to a character set that contains letters, digits, and usually other characters, such as punctuation marks. Synonymous with alphameric. (ANSI)

American National Standards Institute (ANSI) An organization consisting of producers, consumers, and general interest groups, that establishes the procedures by which accredited organizations create and maintain voluntary industry standards in the United States. (IBM)

Analog computer A computer that processes analog data. (ISO)

Analog data Data in the form of a physical quantity that is considered to be continuously variable and whose magnitude is made directly proportional to the data or to a suitable function of the data. (ISO) (ANSI)

Analyst A person who defines problems and develops algorithms and procedures for solution of the problems. (ISO)

Anticipation check A control based on the fact that certain fields in an input record should always be nonblank or that an input record is expected for each master file record.

APL (A Programming Language) A high-level, general-purpose programming language for mathematical applications that simplifies notations and the handling of arrays. (ANSI)

Application A specific use of a computer to perform a business task.

Application controls Controls applied directly to the individual computer application: (1) input controls, (2) processing controls, and (3) output controls.

Application development by users The development of application programs by users, with only limited support from programmers and system analysts.

Application generator A software system that generates computer programs based on the user's needs. Actually, an application generator consists of a large number of precoded modules that perform various functions. The user merely specifies the functions needed for his or her application and the system invokes the appropriate modules and runs them.

Application program A program written for or by a user that applies to the user's work, such as a program that does inventory control or payroll. (ANSI)

Application programmer A programmer who writes and maintains application programs. Contrast with **System programmer**.

Application software See **Application Program**

Application systems Computer programs written to perform specific business tasks.

Archival storage Storage not under direct control of the computer on which backup information and old records are kept.

Arithmetic assignment The assignment of the results of an arithmetic operation to a numeric variable.

Arithmetic logic unit A part of a computer that performs arithmetic, logic, and related operations. (ISO)

Arithmetic operator A symbol that represents the performance of an arithmetic operation like addition, subtraction, multiplication or division.

Arithmetic proof checks A control that verifies the results of mathematical operations.

Array An arrangement of data in one or more dimensions: a list, a table, or a multidimensional arrangement of items.

Artificial intelligence (AI) The capability of a device to perform functions that are normally associated with human intelligence, such as reasoning, learning, and self-improvement. See also **Expert systems, Knowledge base**. (ANSI)

ASCII (American National Standard Code for Information Interchange) The standard code, using a coded character set consisting of 7-bit coded characters (8 bits including parity check), that is used for information interchange among data processing systems, data communication systems, and associated equipment. The ASCII set consists of control characters and graphic characters. (ANSI)

Assemble To translate a program expressed in an assembly language into a computer language equivalent. (ISO)

Assembler A computer program that is used to assemble. Synonymous with assembly program. (ISO)

Assembly language A computer-oriented language whose instructions are symbolic and usually in one-to-one correspondence with computer instructions, and that may provide other facilities such as the use of microinstructions. Synonymous with computer-dependent language. (ISO)

Assignment The placement of a certain value in a variable.

Assignment statement A program statement that performs some computations and assigns the resulting value to a variable.

Asynchronous transmission A data transmission method in which each byte is transmitted separately.

Attribute A characteristic or property held by an entity.

Audit trail The capability to reconstruct processing steps and trace information back to its origins.

Backup copy A duplicate of data or programs used to restore the original if it is lost or destroyed.

Backup file A file that contains redundant copies of programs and data which are used to reconstruct current files in case current files are partially or totally destroyed.

Backup procedure A control procedure that provides additional evidence about the integrity of stored information.

Base register In the central processing unit, a register that is used as a reference point to specify all other storage locations for the program.

BASIC (Beginner's All-Purpose Symbolic Instruction Code) A procedural algebraic language originally designed for ease of learning with a small instruction repertoire. (ANSI)

Batch An accumulation of data to be processed. (IBM)

Batch-direct The processing method in which changes and inquiries to the file are batched and processed periodically under a direct-access file organization method.

Batch processing (1) The processing of data or the accomplishment of jobs accumulated in advance in such a manner that the user cannot further influence the processing while it is in progress. (ISO) (2) The processing of data accumulated over a period of time. (ANSI) (3) Loosely, the execution of computer programs serially. (ANSI) (4) Pertaining to the technique of executing a set of computer programs such that each is completed before the next program of the set is started. (ANSI) (5) Pertaining to the sequential input of computer programs or data. (ANSI)

Batch-sequential processing The processing method in which changes and inquiries to the file are batched and processed periodically under a sequential file access method.

Batch-serial execution A method of data processing in which each program is executed in the order in which it was read into the system and only one program is executed at a time.

Batch total The sum resulting from the addition of a specified numeric field from each record in a batch of records which is used for control and checking purposes. See **Control total** and **Hash total**.

Baud A unit of signaling speed equal to the number of discrete conditions or signal events per second. Synonymous with bits per second (bps). (ANSI)

Benchmark program A sample program that is representative of at least part of the buyer's primary computer workload and that is executed on alternative computer configurations to provide information useful in making a computer acquisition decision.

Bidirectional printing The ability of a printer to print onto the paper when the carriage is moving either to the right or to the left. This speeds up printing because it eliminates carriage returns, during which no printing can take place.

Binary (1) A condition that has two possible values or states. (2) A number system whose base is two.

Binary digit In binary notation, either of the characters 0 or 1. (ISO)

Binary representation A number system that uses only the digits 0 and 1, rather than the ten digits in the decimal system. This system is used to represent electronic computer design since its two digits are used to represent the two conditions (on and off) that are present in electronic components.

Binary search A method of searching for a particular record (or value) in a sequential file (or list). The file must be in either ascending or descending order by the record key that is being searched for. First, the file is split into two halves. Since the file is in sequential order by record key, the half that contains the desired record can be determined by comparing the record key in the center of the file with the record key that is being searched for. The half that contains the desired key is then split in half, and the process continues until the required record is found.

Bit (1) In the pure binary numeration system, either of the digits 0 and 1. (ISO) (2) See **Check bit, Information bit, Parity bit, Sign bit.** (ANSI)

Bit mapped A system in which each possible dot of a cathode ray tube display is controlled by a single bit of memory.

Block (1) A string of records, words, or characters that for technical or logical purposes are treated as a unit. (ISO) (2) A collection of contiguous records that are recorded as a unit, and the units are separated by interblock gaps. (ANSI)

Block format The format of each individual message sent through a communication system. The block format includes control characters to mark the beginning and end of the message, and error detection characters.

Bootstrap A program used to start (or boot) the computer, usually by clearing the primary memory, setting up various devices and loading the operating system from secondary storage or read-only memory.

Bottleneck A slowdown in one part of the system that can cause the whole system to operate below capacity.

Boundary The area that separates one system from another.

BPI Bits per inch. (IBM)

BPS Bits per second.

Branch (1) In a network, a path that connects two adjacent nodes and that has no intermediate nodes. (ISO) (2) A set of instructions that are executed between two successive branch instructions. (ANSI)

Branching The transfer of execution to a nonsequential statement.

Break A key on most keyboards that is used to tell the computer that the current operation is to be aborted.

Bridge A functional unit that interconnects two local area networks that use the same logical link control procedure, but may use different medium access control procedures. (ISO)

Bubble sort A method of sorting the elements of an array. In a bubble sort, each element is compared with the next element, and if they are out of order, they are switched.

Bubble storage A nonvolatile memory device that stores data by polarizing microscopic bubbles in a crystalline substance.

Buffer area An area in primary memory in which data are stored temporarily after they are retrieved from secondary storage or before they are placed in secondary storage. The data may be modified by a program while they are in the buffer.

Bug A mistake or malfunction. (ANSI)

Bundling The selling of hardware and software together as a package.

Burst (1) In data communication, a sequence of signals counted as one unit in accordance with some specific criterion or measure. (ANSI) (2) To separate continuous-form paper into discrete sheets. (ANSI)

Bus A communication link that connects the central processing units to its peripheral devices.

Bus network A network configuration that provides a bidirectional transmission facility to which all nodes are attached. A sending node transmits in both directions to the ends of the bus. All nodes in the path copy the message as it passes. (IBM)

Byte (1) A binary character string operated upon as a unit and usually shorter than a computer word. (ISO) (2) A group of eight adjacent binary digits representing one EBCDIC character. (IBM)

Cache memory A special buffer storage, smaller and faster than main storage, that is used to hold a copy of instructions and data in main storage that are likely to be needed next by the processor, and that have been obtained automatically from main storage. (ISO)

CAD Computer-aided design or computer-assisted design. The term covers a wide range of systems that function as tools to expedite mechanical and electronic design.

Calculate To perform one or more arithmetic functions including addition, subtraction, multiplication, and division.

Calculator A device that is especially suitable for performing arithmetic operations, but that requires human intervention to alter its stored program, if any, and to initiate each operation or sequence of operations. A calculator performs some of the functions of a computer but does not usually operate without frequent human intervention. (ISO)

Call To cause a module to begin execution.

CAM Computer-aided manufacturing or computer-assisted manufacturing.

Capacity The amount of data that can be stored on a disk, most often expressed in kilobytes (1,024 bytes) or megabytes (1,048,576 bytes). Because most disks use some area for storing format and location information, capacities are usually given as both unformatted and formatted.

Card punch An output unit that produces a record of data in the form of hole patterns in punched cards. (ISO)

Card reader (1) An input unit that reads or senses the holes in a punched card, transforming the data from hole patterns to electrical signals. (ISO) (2) An input device that senses hole patterns in a punched card and translates them into machine language. Synonymous with punched card reader. (ANSI)

Cartridge (1) For tape, one of the ways that recording tape is packaged. Cartridges include two tape reels and a set of guide rollers inside a shell that looks like a fat audio cassette. (2) For disks, cartridges are plastic shells that hold removable hard disks.

Cassette A package for magnetic tape similar in appearance to a standard audio cassette, but filled with tape optimized for digital recording.

Cathode ray tube (CRT) A vacuum tube in which a beam of electrons can be moved to draw lines or to form characters or symbols on its luminescent screen. (IBM)

CD-ROM High capacity read-only memory in the form of an optically read compact disc. (IBM)

Central processing unit (CPU) Deprecated term for processing unit. (ANSI)

Chaining (1) A method of storing records in which each record belongs to a list or group of records and has a linking field for tracing the chain. (IBM)

Channel (1) A functional unit, controlled by the processor, that handles the transfer of data between processor storage and local peripheral equipment. (IBM) (2) A path along which signals can be sent (e.g., data channel, output channel). (ANSI)

Character A member of a set of elements that is used for the organization, control, or representation of information; the elements may be letters, digits, punctuation marks, or other symbols. (ISO)

Character check A check that verifies the observance of rules for the information of characters. (ANSI)

Character data Data on which arithmetic calculations are not done.

Character printer A device that prints a single character at a time. (ISO) (2) Synonymous with serial printer. (ANSI)

Character set An ordered set of unique representations called characters (e.g., the 26 letters of the English alphabet, Boolean 0 and 1, the set of symbols in the Morse code, and the 128 ASCII characters). (ANSI)

Character string assignment The assignment of a literal value to a string variable.

Check bit A binary check digit (e.g., a parity bit). (ANSI)

Checkpoint (1) A specified point in time or in the course of a processing activity at which a record is made of the state of a system including the transactions in process at that particular point. (ANSI) (2) A point at which information about the status of a job and the system can be recorded so that the job step can be later restarted. (IBM)

Chief programmer team An organizational structure often used for programming projects. The team is a small group consisting of a chief programmer, assistant programmers, a librarian, and a backup programmer. It works independently on a programming task with very little supervision.

Chip (1) A minute piece of semiconductive material used in the manufacture of electronic components. (ANSI) (2) An integrated circuit on a piece of semiconductive material. (ANSI)

Circuit board See **Printed circuit board**.

Classify To identify an item of data with a certain category. For instance, a sales transaction may be classified as cash or credit.

Client server The model of interaction in distributed data processing in which a program at one site sends a request to a program in another site and awaits a response. The requesting program is called a client; the answering program is called a server. (IBM)

Client-server networks A computer network in which certain nodes have been designated servers to other nodes on the network. These servers may perform operations such as printing or data base management. The client nodes depend on the server nodes to perform this specified server function.

Clock/calendar A hardware and software feature that automatically sets the time and date when the computer is started or rebooted.

Clustered system A data entry system in which several keyboards are connected to one or two magnetic tape drives.

COBOL (Common Business-Oriented Language) A programming language designed for business data processing. (ANSI)

CODASYL Conference on Data Systems Languages. (IBM)

Code (1) A set of rules that maps the elements of one set, the coded set, onto the elements of another set, the code element set. Synonymous with coding scheme. (ISO) (2) A set of items, such as abbreviations, that represent the members of another set. (ANSI) (3) Loosely, one or more computer programs, or part of a computer program. (IBM) (4) To represent data or a computer program in a symbolic form that can be accepted by a processor. (ISO) (5) To write a routine. (ANSI)

Code inspection A review of program code by a review team. In the inspection, the programmer walks the reviewers through the code, and the reviewers check the code for compliance with design specifications.

Column A vertical arrangement of characters or other expressions. Contrast with **Row**. (ANSI)

Command (1) A control signal. (ANSI) (2) An order for an action to take place. (ANSI) (3) Loosely, a mathematical or logical operator. (ANSI) (4) Synonymous with order. (ANSI)

Common carrier In the USA and Canada, a public data transmission service that provides the general public with transmission service facilities; for example, a telephone or telegraph company.

Communication protocol A set of rules governing the flow of data through a communication system.

Communications adaptor A part that electrically or physically connects a computer or device to a data communications network. (IBM)

Compare To examine two pieces of data to determine whether they are equal or one is greater than the other.

Compatible Pertaining to computers on which the same computer programs can be run without appreciable alteration. (IBM)

Compile (1) To translate a computer program expressed in a high-level language into a program expressed in an intermediate language, assembly language, or a machine language. (ISO) (2) To prepare a machine language program from a computer program written in another programming language by making use of the overall logic structure of the program, or by generating more than one computer instruction for each symbolic statement, or both, as well as performing the function of an assembler. (ANSI)

Compiler A computer program for compiling. Synonymous with compiling program. (ISO)

Compiler diagnostics Errors detected in a computer program during its compilation.

Compile-time diagnostics Error diagnostics that are produced when a program is compiled.

Compressed format A data format that eliminates unnecessary blanks between data values.

Compressed printing A method of reducing the horizontal distance between dots in a dot matrix printer. This method prints characters that are narrower than, although the same height as, those processed by noncompressed printing. The compressed format thus prints more characters per inch.

Computer A device that consists of one or more associated processing units and peripheral units, that is controlled by internally stored programs, and that can perform substantial computations, including numerous arithmetic operations, or logic operations, without human intervention during a run. A computer may be a stand-alone unit or it may consist of several interconnected units. (ANSI)

Computer-assisted instruction (CAI) A computer application in which a computing system is used to assist in the instruction of students. The application usually involves a dialog between the student and a computer program which informs the student of mistakes as they are made. (IBM)

Computer center A facility that includes people, hardware, and software, organized to provide information processing services. Synonymous with data processing center, installation. (ANSI)

Computer crime A crime committed through the use of software or data residing in a computer. (ANSI)

Computer fraud Illegal use of computer facilities to misappropriate corporate resources, including unauthorized changes to both software and hardware systems.

Computer graphics (1) Methods and techniques for converting data to or from graphic displays via computers. (ISO) (2) That branch of science and technology that is concerned with methods and techniques for converting data to or from visual presentation, using computers. (ANSI)

Computer-integrated manufacturing (CIM) The integration of computer operations, communications, and organizational functions for total factory automation. (IBM)

Computer operator An employee who monitors the performance of the CPU and storage devices, and who performs most of the human functions necessary to keep the system running.

Computer output microfilm (COM) A technique for converting and recording data from a computer directly to a microform. (ISO)

Computer program A sequence of instructions suitable for processing by a computer. Processing may include the use of an assembler, a compiler, an interpreter, or a translator to prepare the program for execution, as well as the execution of the program. The sequence of instructions may include statements and necessary declarations.

Computer service technician A trained technician who is responsible for the repair and maintenance of hardware devices.

Concatenation The process of joining together two or more literals to form a single literal.

Concentric tracks Circular tracks that have a common center.

Concurrent (1) Pertaining to processes that take place within a common interval of time during which they may have to alternately share common resources; for example, several programs are concurrent when they are executed by multiprogramming in a computer having a single instruction control unit. (ISO) (2) Contrast with **Consecutive, Sequential, Simultaneous**. (ANSI)

Connection A link between two modules showing which module calls the other.

Connectivity The capability of a system or device to be attached to other systems or devices without modification. (ISO)

Consecutive (1) In a process, pertaining to two events that follow one another without the occurrence of any other event between them. (ISO) (2) Contrast with **Concurrent, Sequential, Simultaneous**. (ANSI)

Console The part of a computer used for communication between the operator or maintenance engineer and the computer.

Constant A data item with a value that does not change. (IBM)

Consultant In electronic data processing, an information systems expert who assists users in developing and debugging their own applications.

Control The process of comparing actual results to planned results.

Control data Data that are used by the program solely for making processing decisions.

Control group A group of employees that is separated from computer operations, and that maintains input/output controls and reviews output before it is distributed to users.

Control program A computer program designed to schedule and to supervise the execution of programs in a computing system. (ISO)

Control statement A statement that regulates the order of execution in a program (e.g., an IF statement).

Control total A sum, resulting from the addition of a specified field from each record in a group of records, that is used for checking machine, program, and data reliability. Synonymous with hash total. (IBM)

Control unit (1) A subsystem contained within the transformation process of every information system. A control component selects, interprets, and executes programmed instructions so that the system can function. In total, it controls the actions of a system. (2) The part of the central processing unit that decodes program instructions and directs the other components of the computer system to perform the task specified in the program instruction.

Conversion (1) The process of changing from one method of data processing to another. (IBM) (2) The process of changing from one form of representation to another (e.g., to change from decimal representation to binary representation). (IBM)

Copy protected Disks or tapes that have been recorded in a way designed to prevent the data on them from being copied but still allow the data to be read and used.

Counter A variable used to keep track of the number of times a loop has been executed. Its value is increased (or decreased) by one every time the loop is traversed.

Couple A data item that moves from one module to another.

CPM (Critical Path Method) A project scheduling method that uses networks to determine the sequence of activities that must be completed on time to avoid delays in completion of the total project. This sequence of activities is called the critical path.

CRT display See **Cathode ray tube (CRT)**. (ANSI)

Cursor A movable, visible mark used to indicate a position of interest on a display surface. (ANSI)

Cursor key A key that, when pressed, causes the cursor to move in a designated direction. Arrows engraved on the keys indicate direction of cursor movement; up, down, right, left or home (top left corner of screen).

Cycle An interval of space or time in which one set of events or phenomena is completed. (ANSI)

Cylinder (1) In an assembly of magnetic disks, the set of all tracks that can be accessed by all the magnetic heads of a comb in a fixed position. (ISO) (2) The tracks of a disk storage device that can be accessed without repositioning the access mechanism. (IBM)

Daisy wheel A print element for several popular printers consisting of a plastic or metal disk with spokes radiating from the center portion (like the petals on a daisy flower). At the end of each spoke is a circular area with a typeface impression on it.

DASD Direct access storage device. (IBM)

Data (1) A representation of facts, concepts, or instructions in a formalized manner suitable for communication, interpretation, or processing by humans or by automatic means. (ISO) (2) Any representations such as characters or analog quantities to which meaning is, or might be, assigned. (ANSI)

Database A collection of interrelated data, often with controlled redundancy, organized according to a schema to serve one or more applications; the data are stored so that they can be used by different programs without concern for the data structure or organization. A common approach is used to add new data and to modify and retrieve existing data. (ANSI)

Database administrator The person responsible for coordinating the database and providing for data security.

Database machine A computer dedicated entirely to the use of a database management system.

Database management system A computer program that stores, retrieves, and updates data that are stored on one or more files.

Data block A set of data values processed as a whole.

Data cartridge See **Magnetic tape cartridge**. (IBM)

Data communication (1) The transmission and reception of data. (ANSI) (2) The transfer of data between functional units by means of data transmission according to a protocol. (ISO)

Data definition The process of creating a schema by identifying and describing data elements and their relationships that make up the database structure. (ANSI)

Data definition language A language used to define the relationship between the logical and physical views of a database.

Data dictionary A dictionary that defines the meaning of each data item stored in a database, and describes interrelationships among the items.

Data editing Synonymous with editing.

Data entry The process of entering data into a computer system in order to communicate with it.

Data entry operator An employee who keys data from source documents into computer-readable form like disk or tape.

Data flow diagram A graphic representation of the movement and transformations of data within an organization.

Data independence A lack of dependence between the physical structure of data storage and the structure of application programs.

Data integrity (1) The state that exists when data are handled as intended and are not exposed to accidental or malicious modification, destruction, or disclosure. (ANSI) (2) The preservation of data for their intended use. (ANSI)

Data item The smallest element of data stored or used by a program.

Data management The function of controlling the acquisition, analysis, storage, retrieval, and distribution of data. (ANSI).

Data manipulation language A language used to define operations on a data base such as retrieval, sorting, and updating of records.

Data processing The capture, storage and processing of data to transform them into information that is useful for decision making.

Data redundancy The situation in which identical data are stored in two or more files.

Data set The major unit of data storage and retrieval, consisting of a collection of data in one of several prescribed arrangements and described by control information to which the system has access. Synonymous with **File**. (IBM)

Data structure diagram A graphical representation of the logical relationships between various data files.

Data switch A device that is similar to a telephone exchange, and that can establish a data communication link between any two devices connected to it.

Data type The category to which a data item belongs (e.g., numeric, alphabetic).

Debug To detect, to locate and to eliminate errors in computer programs. (ISO)

Decimal number system A number system whose base is ten, and that represents numbers in terms of the powers of ten (in units of tens, hundreds, and so on). This is the number system normally used in the United States.

Decision making The process of selecting one course of action from two or more alternatives, based on the values of one or more variables.

Decision model A set of rules that are used in making a choice between two or more alternatives.

Decision support system (DSS) An integrated set of computer tools that allows a decision maker to interface directly with computers to create information useful in making semi-structured and unstructured decisions.

Decision table A table of all contingencies that are to be considered in the description of a problem, together with the actions to be taken for each set of contingencies. (ISO)

Decision tree A graphic representation of all contingencies to be considered, together with the actions that must be taken for each one of them.

Default format A data format automatically assigned by the computer, if the programmer does not specify one.

Default option An implicit option that is assumed when no option is explicitly stated. (ANSI)

Demand listing A report generated only when a user requests it, typically used to fill irregular needs for information.

Density See **Recording density**. (ANSI)

Desktop publishing The use of personal computer application software to integrate text, charts, and pictures and to design, display, and print high-quality documents comparable to typeset documents printed by professional publishers. (IBM)

Destructive process A process that destroys the existing value of a variable it is operating on.

Device controller A part of the central processing unit that manages communications between the central processing unit and peripheral devices.

Diagnostics A set of routines used to detect program errors and system malfunctions or to carry out standard performance tests. Errors and failures are detected by comparing the results with known correct results.

Dial-up terminal (1) A terminal on a switched line. (IBM) (2) A terminal that is connected to the computer by dialing the computer system over a telephone line. See **Hard-wired terminal**.

Digital computer A computer that consists of one or more associated processing units and that is controlled by internally stored programs and operates on data stored in digital form; it may be a stand-alone unit or it may consist of several interconnected units. (ANSI)

Digital optical disk Synonym for optical disk. (ISO)

Digitize To convert voice or other patterns to digital signals so they can be processed and stored by a digital computer.

DIP switches A collection of small switches on a dual in-line package (DIP), used to select options on circuit boards without having to modify the hardware.

Direct access (1) The capability to obtain data from a storage device or to enter data into a storage device in a sequence independent of their relative position, by means of addresses that indicate the physical location of the data. (ISO) (2)

Contrast with **Sequential access**. (IBM) (3) The file organization that enables a record to be located and retrieved by the central processing unit without a large amount of searching.

Direct-access storage device (DASD) A device in which access time is effectively independent of the location of the data. (IBM)

Direct conversion A method of converting to a new information system, such that the old system is discontinued one workday and the new system is started the next day.

Direct file organization A file organization that allows direct access to a record without sequentially examining a large number of other records.

Disaster controls Controls that minimize the risk of loss due to natural disasters like flooding and hurricanes.

Disk See **Digital optical disk**, **Fixed disk**, **Flexible disk**, **Hard disk**, **Magnetic disk**, **Nonremovable disk**, **Optical disk**. (ANSI)

Disk controller card A printed circuit board that interfaces disk storage drives to the central processing unit of a personal computer.

Disk drive A device that houses a disk or diskette while it is in use. The disk drive contains a motor and one or more magnetic heads to read and write data on the disk.

Diskette Synonymous with **Floppy disk**.

Display (1) A visual presentation of data. (ISO) (2) To present data visually. (ANSI)

Distributed database A database that resides on two or more separate computers simultaneously. The database may be either partitioned between the two computers or replicated at both locations.

Distributed data processing The concept of distributing the load of data processing through the installation of minicomputers at a company's remote locations, so the local data processing needs are handled by the remote location's own local computer.

Document (1) A medium and the information recorded on it that generally has permanence and that can be read by user or machine. (ANSI) (2) To record information to provide support or proof of something.

Documentation (1) The aids provided for understanding the structure and intended uses of an information system or its components, such as flowcharts, textual material, and end-user manuals. (ANSI) (2) A collection of documents that support and explain a data processing application.

Documentation standards Specific procedures for system documentation including flowcharting conventions, coding conventions, and documentation revision procedures.

DOS Disk operating system.

Dot matrix printer A printer or a plotter that prints characters or line images that are represented by dots. Synonymous with matrix printer. (ISO)

Double-density diskette A diskette manufactured with technology that allows it to hold twice as much data as diskettes manufactured at the standard density.

Double-sided diskette A diskette that provides two surfaces on which data may be written by the computer.

DO WHILE construct In a program, a construct in which an operation is repeatedly performed as long as a certain logical condition remains true.

Downloading The process by which information from within a database, stored in a remote mainframe or minicomputer, is brought down to a personal computer for manipulation.

DP operations department Management information systems personnel who are responsible for managing the day-to-day operations of data processing facilities.

Drum printer An impact printer in which a full character set, placed on a rotating drum, is made available for each printing position. (ISO)

Dump (1) Data that have been dumped. (ISO) (2) To write at a particular instant the contents of storage onto another data medium for the purpose of safeguarding the data. (ISO)

Duplex transmission Data transmission in both directions at the same time. (ISO)

Duplication check A check based on the consistency of the results of two independent performances of the same task. (ANSI)

EBCDIC (Extended Binary Coded Decimal Interchange Code) A coded character set consisting of eight-bit coded characters. (ANSI)

Echo check (1) A check to determine the correctness of the transmission of data in which the received data are returned to the source for comparison with the originally transmitted data. Synonymous with loop check. (ISO) (2) A hardware control that verifies that a device has been activated to carry out an operation it has been instructed to perform.

Edit To prepare data for a later operation. Editing may include rearrangement or addition of data, deletion of unwanted data, modification of data, format control, code conversion, and application of standard processes such as zero suppression. (IBM)

Edit directed I/O Input or output of formatted data.

Editor A program through which text can be entered into the computer memory, displayed on the screen, and manipulated as the user chooses. An editor is an aid for writing a program. It is also the central component of a word processor.

EDP auditor An auditor who specializes in auditing computer-based information systems.

Electronic disk Software that permits extra primary memory to be used as if it were a disk drive by simulating disk drives within the system's RAM.

Electronic funds transfer system A computerized system that can transfer money from one point to another immediately, using data communication lines.

Electronic mail The transmittal of messages between computer users over a data communication network.

Electronic shopping The process of selecting merchandise and ordering it through a remote terminal installed in one's home.

Embedded pointer Within a record, a field that contains the address of a related record.

Encoding Storage of data in coded form. The data may not be accessed by a user who does not know the code.

Encryption The conversion of programs or data into a secret code or cipher.

End users Individuals who ultimately use application software.

Entity A subject on which data are kept in an information system.

Entry controls Controls over entry to areas in which computer equipment such as central processing units and storage devices are installed.

Erasable storage A storage device onto which different data can be written at the same storage location. (ISO)

Ergonomics The science of designing computer hardware and software so that humans find them easier and more comfortable to use.

Error handling Procedures for detecting errors in input data, and for ensuring that those errors are corrected before the data is processed.

Error message An indication that an error has been detected. (ANSI)

Error recovery The ability of a system to continue operating normally after the user has made an input error.

Exception report A report generated only if an activity or system gets out of control and requires human attention.

Executable statement A program statement that instructs the computer to perform a certain action.

Execution The running of a computer program.

Execution path The specific set of program instructions used by the computer.

Execution time (E-time) (1) Any instant at which a program is being executed. (IBM) (2) The time during which an instruction in an instruction register is decoded and performed. (IBM)

Execution time diagnostics Error diagnostics that are produced when a program is executed.

Executive Information System An information system that provides for the communication of summary and detail information to executives.

Expansion board A printed circuit board that accommodates extra components for the purpose of expanding the capabilities of a computer.

Expansion slot A slot for installing additional expansion boards that perform functions not provided by the computer's standard hardware.

Expert systems (ES) Systems that provide for solving problems in a particular application area by drawing inferences from a knowledge base acquired by human expertise (ISO).

Expression A variable, constant, function, or any combination of these elements separated by arithmetic or relational operators.

Extract (1) To select and remove from a group of items those items that meet a specific criteria, for example, to obtain certain specified digits from a computer word as controlled by an instruction or a mask. (ANSI) (2) To remove specific items from a file. (IBM)

Facilities management vendor A firm that specializes in managing, staffing, and operating computer installations for its customers.

FAX The use of a telephone system for the electronic transmission and receipt of hard copy images. (ISO) Synonymous with facsimile, telefax.

Feasibility study The first step in the systems development life cycle. At this step the systems analyst identifies the objectives of the present system and determines whether an attempt to develop a new system would be cost-effective.

Fiber optics A branch of optical technology concerned with the transmission of communications by light beams through thin cables of extremely pure glass.

Field On a data medium or in storage, a specified area used for a particular class of data; for example, a group of character positions used to enter or display wage rates on a screen. (ISO)

File (1) A set of related records treated as a unit (e.g., in stock control, a file could consist of a set of invoices). (ISO) (2) A collection of related records.

File activity ratio The proportion of master file records that are actually used or accessed in a given processing run of the file or during a given period of time.

File area On a disk, the area available for storage of files containing data or programs.

File directory The disk area allocated to hold a directory that names and indicates the area occupied by each file and the available space on the disk.

File layout The arrangement and structure of data or words in a file, including the order and size of the components of the file. (ISO)

File maintenance inputs In files, all changes that are not originated by transactions.

File protected Pertaining to a tape reel with the write-enable ring removed. (IBM)

File protection ring A plastic ring that must be inserted into a reel of magnetic tape before the tape can be written on. (An alternative is a no-write ring which prevents the file protection ring from being inserted and therefore prevents files from being written on when it is inserted in a reel of tape.)

File protect notch A cutout on the upper right corner of a floppy disk used to prevent accidental destruction of data.

File query The retrieval of some specific information from a file.

File volatility ratio The proportion of additions and deletions to a file in a given period of time.

Fine tuning The process of removing bottlenecks and reallocating work among system resources, in order to obtain maximum output from the given resources.

Fire controls Controls that minimize the risk of losses from fire. These include both emergency procedures and preventive measures.

Fixed disk A disk that is permanently mounted in its disk drive, or the disk and drive combination.

Fixed-length record A record having the same length as all other records with which it is logically or physically associated. Contrast with **Variable-length record**. (IBM)

Fixed-point constant Synonymous with **Integer constant**.

Flag (1) An indicator or parameter that shows the setting of a switch. Synonymous with switch indicator. (ISO) (2) Any of various types of indicators used for identification (e.g., a word mark). (ANSI) (3) A character that signals the occurrence of some condition, such as the end of a word. (ANSI) (4) Synonym for sentinel. (ANSI)

Flat file A file containing only fixed-length records of equal length.

Flexible disk A flexible magnetic disk enclosed in a protective container. Synonymous with **Floppy disk**. (ISO)

Floating parameter A variable within the definition of a user-defined function. It has no meaning outside the function definition.

Floppy disk A data storage medium that is a 3½-, 5¼-, or 8-inch disk of polyester film covered with a magnetic coating.

Flowchart (1) A graphical representation in which symbols are used to represent such things as operations, data, flow direction, and equipment for the definition, analysis, or solution of a problem. Synonymous with flow diagram. (ISO) (2) See **System flowchart**.

Font A family or assortment of characters of a given size and style (e.g., 9 point Bodoni Modern). (ANSI)

Format To put the magnetic track and sector pattern on a disk. A disk must be formatted before it can store any information. Formatting completely erases any previously stored data.

FORTRAN (FORmula TRANslation) A programming language primarily used to express computer programs by arithmetic formulas. (IBM)

Fourth-generation language A flexible application development tool such as electronic spreadsheets, query languages, and application generators that allow users to develop applications by describing to the computer what they want rather than programming the computer in a how-to, step-by-step fashion.

Front-end processor A computer configuration in which minor jobs or communication tasks are handled by a mini central processing unit, allowing the main central processing unit to handle all batch jobs and programs the front-end processor (minicomputer) cannot handle.

Function A preprogrammed set of statements that may be called by a one-line reference and returns one single value to the calling program.

Functional area An organizational unit of a business corresponding to its major duty or activity such as engineering or finance.

Functional information system A set of application systems that satisfy the information needs within a functional area of a business.

Functional primitive The lowest level of a data flow diagram, in which the actual processing of data is described.

Functional reference A call to a function at some point in the program. The call is made by giving the function name and a value for its parameter(s).

Gantt chart A graph in which activities are plotted as bars on a time scale.

General controls Overall managerial controls applied to all software, hardware, and personnel involved in the information system.

Generalized module A precoded module that performs some commonly used function. It may be used by many different users for a variety of purposes.

Giga (G) When referring to storage capacity, two to the thirtieth power, 1,073,741,824 in decimal notation. (IBM)

Gigabyte One billion bytes.

Grandparent-parent-child backup A file backup system in which the current version of the file and the two previous versions are always retained.

Graphics The making of charts and pictures. (IBM)

Graphics language A computer language that may be used to retrieve data from files or databases and display them graphically.

Hacker (1) A computer enthusiast. (ANSI) (2) A computer enthusiast who uses his or her knowledge and means to gain unauthorized access to protected resources. (ANSI)

Half-duplex In data communication, pertaining to an alternating, one way at a time, independent transmission. (ANSI)

Half-inch tape The big reels of tape used with mainframes and minicomputers.

Hanging separator At the end of a PRINT statement, a symbol that causes the next PRINT statement to continue writing on the same output line.

Hard copy (1) In computer graphics, a permanent copy of a display image that is portable and can be read directly by human beings; for example, a display image that is recorded on paper. (ISO) (2) A printed copy of machine output in a visually readable form; for example, printed reports, listings, documents, and summaries. Contrast with **Soft copy**. (IBM)

Hard disk A rigid magnetic disk. (ISO)

Hard error An error in disk data that persists when the disk is reread.

Hardware Physical equipment as opposed to programs, procedures, rules, and associated documentation. (ISO) Contrast with **Software**. (ANSI)

Hardware monitor A machine device that monitors usage and performance of various computer system devices.

Hardware study An analysis of hardware requirements for an information system. It normally leads to a tentative selection of equipment.

Hard-wired terminal A terminal that is directly wired to the computer. See **Dial-up terminal**.

Hash total The result obtained by applying an algorithm to a set of data for checking purposes (e.g., a summation obtained by treating data items as numbers). (ANSI)

Head A device that reads, writes, or erases data on a storage medium. (ANSI)

Header (1) The top part of a report, including the column headings. (2) The first record in a file. It contains descriptive information concerning the file.

Header label A file label or data set label that precedes the data records on a unit of recording media. (IBM)

Header value A special value specified before a loop is executed. It tells the program how many times the loop is to be performed.

Hexadecimal representation A number system used to represent data internally in a computer and for memory dumps. The digits of a hexadecimal number represent powers of sixteen.

Hierarchical network A distributed system design in which a superior/subordinate relationship exists between distributed computer installations.

High-level language A programming language that does not reflect the structure of any particular computer or that of any particular class of computers. High-level languages are primarily designed for, and are syntactically oriented to, particular classes of problems. (ANSI)

Hollerith card A punch card characterized by 80 columns and 12 rows of punch positions. (ANSI)

Horizontal network A distributed system design in which each local installation is equal and has the capability of communicating with all other installations. Synonymous with ring network.

Host computer (1) The primary or controlling computer in a multiple computer installation. (IBM) (2) A computer used to prepare programs for use on another computer or on another data processing system; for example, a computer used to compile, link edit, or test programs to be used on another system. (IBM)

Human factors The positive and negative behavioral implications of introducing electronic data processing systems into the workplace.

Hybrid network A ring-structured communication network in which each node on the ring is also the center of a star network.

Hypermedia A method of presenting the information in discreet units or nodes that are connected by links. The information may be presented using a variety of media such as text, graphics, video, animation, images, or executable documentation. (IBM)

Hypertext A way of presenting information on-line with connections between one piece of information and another called hypertext links. (IBM)

IF-THEN-ELSE construct In a program, a construct in which either one of two possible courses of action is taken, depending on whether a certain logical condition is true or false.

Immediate-direct processing The immediate processing of transactions and inquiries with direct access files.

Immediate mode A mode of processing under which transactions are processed to update the master file shortly after they occur.

Impact printer A printer in which printing is the result of mechanically striking the printer medium. (ISO)

Implementation In the systems development cycle, a phase in which coding, testing and manual procedure development are done.

Index A list used to indicate the address of records stored in a file. This index is much like an index to a book.

Index file A file used to indicate the address of records stored on secondary storage devices.

Indexed sequential access method (ISAM) A file organization in which records are stored sequentially, yet direct access may be made to individual records in the file through an index of records' absolute addresses.

Inference engine In artificial intelligence, the components of an expert system that apply principles of reasoning to draw conclusions from the information stored in a knowledge base. (ISO)

Infinite loop In a program, a loop that has no exit. The computer keeps performing the loop indefinitely unless some external action is taken to stop the program.

Information (1) In information processing, knowledge concerning such things as facts, concepts, objects, events, ideas, and processes, that within a certain context has a particular meaning. (ISO) (2) Data that has been processed so that it is meaningful to a decision maker to use in a particular decision.

Information bit In telecommunication, any bit generated by the data source and not used for error control by the data transmission system. (ANSI)

Information center In an organization, a service department that assists users in developing their own computer applications.

Information retrieval (IR) Actions, methods, and procedures for recovering stored data to provide information on a given subject. (ISO)

Information system A formalized computer system that can collect, store, process, and report data from various sources to provide the information necessary for management decision making.

Information system consultant An individual who assists users with various problems using problem-solving methods that range from simple troubleshooting to complete system design and implementation.

Information system manager A management information systems professional who is responsible for managing the entire electronic data processing department, or some part of it.

Information system master plan An outline of the overall strategy for implementation of the information system.

Information workers People who create, process, and use substantial amounts of information as a normal part of their jobs.

In-house development The process in which a firm produces its own application software.

Initialize To assign an initial value to a variable, before beginning a specific process. Counter variables are often initialized to zero before they start counting the number of loops executed.

Initial program load (IPL) The initialization procedure that causes an operating system to commence operation. (IBM)

Ink-jet printer A nonimpact printer in which the characters are formed by the projection of a jet of ink onto paper. (ISO)

Input controls Controls that ensure that all inputs are authorized, are accurate, and are properly converted to machine-readable format.

Input data (1) Data being received or to be received by a device or a computer program. (ANSI) (2) Data to be processed. (ANSI)

Input mask A form displayed on a cathode ray tube to guide the keying of input.

Input/output statement A program statement that causes the computer to either read input data or produce output.

Input unit A device into which data may be entered for use by a data processing system. Synonymous with input device. (ISO)

Inquiry (1) A request for information from storage; for example, a request for the number of available airline seats, or a search for information from a file. (IBM) (2) A request for information from another system. (IBM)

Instruction In a programming language, an expression that specifies one operation and identifies its operands, if any. (ISO)

Integer constant A constant number that does not contain a decimal point or a fractional part.

Integrated circuit A device that contains transistors that are deposited photochemically on a chip of silicon material. These devices have greatly increased the speed of computers while sharply reducing their size.

Integrated package A personal computer package that typically includes the functions of electronic spreadsheet, word processing, database management, and communications.

Intelligent terminal (1) Synonym for programmable terminal. (IBM) (2) A terminal that contains a microprocessor and is therefore capable of performing some data processing by itself without recourse to the central computer.

Interactive Pertaining to a program or system that alternately accepts input and then responds. An interactive system is conversational, that is, a continuous dialog exists between user and system. Contrast with batch. (IBM)

Interactive data entry The process of entering data directly into the computer through a data entry terminal.

Interface (1) A shared boundary between two functional units, defined by functional characteristics, common physical interconnection characteristics, signal characteristics, and other characteristics, as appropriate. The concept involves the specification of the connection of two devices having different functions. (ISO) (2) A point of communication between two or more processes, person, or other physical entities. (ANSI)

Internal storage (1) Storage that is accessible by a processor without the use of input/output channels. It includes main storage, and may include other kinds of storage such as cache memory and special registers that can be accessed by the processor. (ISO) (2) Synonym for processor storage. (IBM)

International data transfer The movement of data across national boundaries through data communication networks.

Interpreter A program that translates a high-level language—such as BASIC—into a machine language so it can be used in the computer. An interpreter is slower and less efficient than a compiler, but easier for programmers to use.

Interrupt A suspension of a process, such as the execution of a computer program, caused by an event external to that process, and performed in such a way that the process can be resumed. Synonymous with interruption. (ISO)

Inverted file (1) A file whose sequence has been reversed. (ANSI) (2) In information retrieval, a cross-index file in which a keyword identifies a record; the items, numbers, or documents pertinent to that keyword are indicated. (ANSI)

I/O Input/output. (ANSI)

ISO International Organization for Standardization. (ANSI)

Jabber In local area networks, transmission by a data station beyond the time interval allowed by the protocol. (ANSI)

Job (1) A unit of work that is defined by a user and that is to be accomplished by a computer. Loosely, this term is sometimes used to refer to a representation of a job; the representation may include a set of computer programs, files, and control statements to the operating system. (ISO) (2) A collection of related programs, identified by appropriate job control statements. (IBM)

Job control language (JCL) A problem-oriented language designed to express statements in a job that are used to identify the job or to describe its requirements to an operating system. (ANSI)

Job queue A line of programs awaiting their turn for execution.

Kernel program A sample program of small size executed on alternative computer configurations to provide information useful in making a computer acquisition decision.

Key (1) An identifier within a set of data elements. (ISO) (2) One or more characters, within a set of data that contains information about the set, including its identification. (ISO) (3) To enter information from a keyboard. (IBM)

Key-to-disk data entry The process of recording data on disk before inputting them to the computer.

Key-to-diskette data entry The process of recording data on diskettes before inputting them to the system.

Key-to-tape data entry The process of recording data on magnetic tape before inputting them to the computer.

Key verifier In key punching, a machine that verifies that data have been key punched correctly.

Keyword In a programming language, a special word that tells the computer which operation to perform.

Kilobyte (K) When referring to computers, 1,024 bytes of memory that store 1,024 characters of data or programs. Therefore, 256K of tenth power, or 1,024—because of the binary nature of computer memory will hold 256 times 1,024, or 262,144, characters of data. In terms of computers, K is a power of two—two to the memory. In contexts other than computers, the word kilo or the symbol K indicates 1,000.

Knowledge base In artificial intelligence, a database that contains information about human experience in a particular field of knowledge and data resulting from solution of problems that have been previously encountered. See also **Expert systems**. (ANSI)

Knowledge engineer In artificial intelligence, a person who extracts knowledge from a domain expert and organizes it for a knowledge base for an expert system. (ISO)

Label (1) An identifier within or attached to a set of data elements. Synonymous with tag. (ISO) (2) In programming languages, an identifier that names a statement. (ANSI) (3) A record that identifies a volume on tape, disk, or diskette or that identifies a file on the volume. (IBM)

Language In relation to computers, any unified, related set of commands or instructions that the computer can accept. Low-level languages are difficult to use but closely resemble the fundamental operations of the computer. High-level languages resemble English.

Language translator A general term for any assembler, compiler, or other routine that accepts statements in one language and produces equivalent statements in another language. (IBM)

Laser printer A high-quality nonimpact printer that is capable of producing a wide variety of type fonts.

Laser storage A memory device that makes use of laser beams for storing data. These laser beams form microscopic patterns to represent characters on various surfaces.

Leasing A contract arrangement which binds the user of a system to rent it over a relatively long period of time. Leasing typically costs less than a rental arrangement.

Left-justify To line up characters such that the first nonblank character in each line is on the left margin.

Letter quality Printed output that appears to have been typed on a typewriter.

Leveled data flow diagram A hierarchically partitioned data flow diagram. Each level describes in more detail the data flows shown in the level above it. Increased partitioning at lower levels keeps the diagrams of manageable size.

Librarian A management information systems employee who is responsible for the storage of program and data files. These files are normally stored on tape or disk.

Library (1) A file or a set of related files, for example, a set of inventory control files in stock control. (ANSI) (2) A repository for demountable recorded media, such as magnetic disk packs and magnetic tapes. (ANSI) (3) See **Program library**. (ANSI)

Library routine A proven routine that is maintained in a program library. (ANSI)

Light pen An input device that allows the console operator to choose among alternatives. When a menu is presented on the screen, for instance, a number of choices are given to the operator, each with a box next to it. The operator positions the light pen at a box representing his or her choice and then presses the entry button on the pen. The pen contains a light sensor which returns a signal that indicates to the computer which choice the operator has made.

Limit or reasonableness check See **Reasonableness checks**.

Linear search A sequential search of the elements of an array for the purpose of locating a particular value.

Line feed The action of advancing the paper in a printer or the cursor on a screen to the next line.

Line printer A device that prints a line of characters as a unit. (ISO)

Linkage editor A program for creating a load module from one or more object modules or load modules or by resolving cross references among the object modules and possibly by relocating elements. Synonymous with linker. (ANSI)

Link edit To create a loadable computer program by means of a linkage editor. (IBM)

Linking Synonymous with link editing.

List (1) An ordered set of data items. (ISO) (2) To print or otherwise display data items that meet specified criteria. (ANSI) (3) Synonym for chained list. (ANSI)

Literal Synonymous with **String constant**.

Lithium battery An easily removable battery that lasts from 12 to 18 months and is normally used to power clock/calendars in personal computers.

Load (1) To enter data or programs into storage or working registers. (ISO) (2) To bring a load module from auxiliary storage into main storage for execution. (IBM)

Load module A module that is the output of a linkage editor and that is in a form

suitable for loading into main storage for execution. (ISO)

Local area network (LAN) A data network located on the user's premises in which serial transmission is used for direct data communication among data stations. (IBM)

Local data Data that are used by only one computer in a distributed data processing environment.

Logical model In a system, a model that emphasizes what is to be done, rather than who or what is to do it.

Logical record (1) A record independent of its physical environment. Portions of one logical record may be located in different physical records or several logical records or parts of logical records may be located in one physical record. (ANSI) (2) A record from the standpoint of its content, function, and use rather than its physical attributes; that is, a record defined in terms of the information it contains. (IBM)

Logical view The representation of the data in a database in a format that is meaningful to the applications programmer and end user.

Logoff The procedure by which a user ends a terminal session. (IBM)

Logon The procedure by which a user begins a terminal session. (IBM)

Loop (1) A set of statements that are repeatedly performed during program execution. (2) To repeatedly perform a set of statements during program execution.

Loop check Synonym for echo check. (ISO)

Loop variable A variable used as a counter in a FOR-NEXT loop. It keeps track of the number of times the loop has executed.

Machine cycle The time required by the central processing unit to perform one machine operation.

Machine language An artificial language whose elements are machine instructions. Synonymous with computer language. (ANSI)

Machine operation The smallest unit of processing done by a computer (e.g., adding 0 to 1).

Macro instruction A set of program statements that may be invoked simply by a one-line reference to the set.

Mag tape The shortened form of the term magnetic tape.

Magnetic disk A flat circular plate with a magnetizable surface layer on one or both sides of which data can be stored. (ISO)

Magnetic drum A circular cylinder with a magnetizable layer on which data can be stored. (ISO)

Magnetic ink character recognition (MICR) The automatic recognition of characters printed with ink that contains particles of magnetic material. (ISO)

Magnetic storage A storage device that uses the magnetic properties of certain materials. (ISO)

Magnetic tape A tape with a magnetizable layer on which data can be stored. (ISO)

Magnetic tape cartridge A removable storage device that consists of a housing containing a belt-driven magnetic tape wound on a supply reel and, in some cartridges, a take-up reel. (IBM)

Magnetic tape drive A device for moving magnetic tape and controlling its movement. Synonymous with magnetic tape transport. (ISO)

Mainframe (1) A large computer, usually one to which other computers are connected in order to share its resources and computing power. (ANSI) (2) A large computer system.

Maintainability The ease with which maintenance of a functional unit can be performed in accordance with prescribed requirements. (ISO)

Maintenance Correction of errors discovered in programs, and updating of the programs to satisfy changed requirements.

Man-machine boundary The line of demarcation between manual operations and computerized functions.

Management controls Control mechanisms that ensure proper management of electronic data processing facilities in accordance with organizational objectives.

Management information system (MIS) (1) The total flow of information within an enterprise that supports the decision-making functions of management at all organizational levels of the enterprise. (ANSI) (2) A system for providing information for decision making; an automated system that uses a computer to process data.

Manual input (1) The entry of data by hand into a device. (ANSI) (2) The data entered as in (1). (ANSI)

Mass storage Storage having a very large storage capacity. (ISO)

Master file A file that is used as an authority in a given job and that is relatively permanent, even though its contents may change. Synonymous with main file. (ANSI) (ISO)

Matrix printer Synonym for dot matrix printer. (ISO)

Megabyte A total of 1,048,576 bytes of memory. A megabyte is often thought of as 1 million bytes, but it is actually 1,048,576 bytes, since it is 2^{20} bytes.

Memory (1) All of the addressable storage space in a processing unit and other internal storage that is used to execute instructions. (ISO) (2) Main storage, when used in reference to calculators, microcomputers, and some minicomputers. (ANSI)

Memory dump The process of printing the contents of primary storage.

Memory module Extra memory chips that may be added to the basic hardware of a personal computer in order to expand primary storage.

MICR Magnetic ink character recognition. (ANSI)

Microcoding (microprogramming) The technique of placing programs in hardware devices (like read-only memory). This is often used for systems programs like operating systems.

Microcomputer The smallest of computer systems.

Microfiche A sheet of microfilm capable of containing microimages in a grid pattern, usually containing a title that can be read without magnification. (ANSI)

Microfilm (1) A high-resolution film for recording microimages. (ANSI) (2) To record microimages on film. (ANSI)

Microform A medium such as microfiche, or microfilm, that is suitable for recording microimages. (ANSI)

Microprocessor chip The microprocessor chip contains the circuitry of the central processing unit—the portion of the computer that does the calculating and executes the program. It is mounted in one socket of the central processing unit board of a personal computer.

Microsecond One-millionth of a second. (IBM)

Millisecond One-thousandth of a second. (IBM)

Minicomputer A midsize computer generally used in midsize or smaller organizations by several users at the same time.

Minimal BASIC A basic set of commands recommended by the American National Standards Institute for inclusion in any version of the BASIC language.

MIS Management information system. (ANSI)

Mnemonic symbol A symbol chosen to assist the human memory; for example, an abbreviation such as mpy for multiply. (ISO)

Modem (modulator-demodulator) A functional unit that modulates and demodulates signals. One of the functions of a modem is to enable digital data to be transmitted over analog transmission facilities. The term is a contraction of modulator-demodulator. (ISO)

Modularity The extent to which a system is composed of modules. (ANSI)

Module (1) In programming languages, a self-contained subdivision of a program that may be separately compiled. (ANSI) (2) A packaged functional hardware unit suitable for use with other components. (ANSI)

Monitor (1) A device that observes and records selected activities within a data processing system for analysis. Possible uses of monitors are to indicate significant departures from the norm, or to determine levels of utilization of particular functional units. (ISO) (2) Software or hardware that observes, supervises, controls, or verifies operations of a system. (IBM) (3) A cathode ray tube for viewing computer output.

Monitor program A computer program that observes, regulates, controls, or verifies the operations of a data processing system. (ANSI)

Motherboard A printed circuit board onto which other printed circuit boards connect.

MS-DOS (Microsoft Disk Operating System) An operating system used on personal computers, especially the IBM PC and its compatibles.

Multimedia Material presented in a combination of text, graphics, video, animation, and sound. (IBM)

Multimedia system A system capable of presenting multimedia material in its entirety. (IBM)

Multiplexing In data transmission, a function that permits two or more data sources to share a common transmission medium so that each data source has its own channel. (ISO)

Multiprocessing (1) A mode of operation that provides for parallel processing by two or more processors of a multiprocessor. (ISO) (2) The processing of a single program by two or more central processing units.

Multiprogramming (1) A mode of operation that provides for the interleaved execution of two or more computer programs by a single processor. (ISO) (2) The capability of a computer central processing unit to execute two or more programs concurrently.

Multitasking A mode of operation that provides for concurrent performance, or interleaved execution of two or more tasks. (ANSI)

Nanosecond One-thousand-millionth of a second. (IBM)

Natural language processing A program that attempts to understand natural languages, such as English, through the application of artificial intelligence.

Nest (1) To incorporate one or more structures of one kind into another structure of the same kind; the structure may be a loop, a subroutine, or a set of statements. (ISO) (2) To place subroutines or data into other subroutines or data at a different hierarchical level so that the subroutines can be executed recursively and the data can be accessed recursively. (ANSI)

Network A configuration of data processing devices and software connected for information interchange. (IBM)

Network data structure The data structure that allows a many-to-many relationship among the nodes in the structure.

Neural networks Artificial intelligence systems that are designed to learn to solve a problem based on a pattern of previous cases. These systems attempt to mimic the actions of the neurons in animal brains.

Node (1) In a network, the point at the end of a branch. (ISO) (2) The representation of a state or an event by means of a point on a diagram. (ANSI) (3) In a tree structure, a point at which subordinate data items originate. (ANSI)

Nonexecutable statement A statement that does not cause the computer to perform any action. It merely informs the computer or a human reader about the format, characteristics, and nature of various data and processes.

Nonimpact printer A printer in which printing is not the result of mechanical impacts with the printing medium. (ISO)

Nonprogrammable decision A decision related to an ill-defined or unstructured problem.

Nonrecurring costs The initial costs that are not expected to arise after the initial installation of a computer system.

Nonremovable disk A disk or diskette that is permanently installed in a device. Synonymous with **Fixed disk**, **Hard disk**. (ANSI)

Nonvolatile storage In a computer system, primary or secondary storage that does not lose the data stored in it when the electrical power is interrupted.

Numeric Pertaining to data or to physical quantities represented by numerals. Synonymous with numerical. (ANSI)

Numeric/alphabetic checks Controls to ensure that input record fields that should contain only numeric characters do not contain alphabetic characters or vice versa.

Numeric data Numbers on which arithmetic calculations will be performed.

Numeric variable A variable that can only assume numeric values.

Nybble Four bits.

Object code A machine language program that has been produced from a higher-level language through the compilation process. It is called object code since its production is the objective of compilation or translation.

Object module A set of instructions in machine language produced by a compiler from a source program. (IBM)

Office automation The integration of office activities by means of an information processing system. This term includes in particular processing and communication of text, images, and voice. (ISO).

Off-line Data or a device that is not under direct control of the computer. Normally a human must place an off-line reel of tape on a tape drive before the computer can access data stored on it.

Off-line storage Storage that is not under the control of a processing unit. (ANSI)

On-line (1) Pertaining to the operation of a functional unit when under the direct control of a computer. (ISO) (2) A computer system, peripheral device, or file, such as a terminal or disk drive, that is in indirect communication with the central processing unit.

On-line direct access system A computer system that has several terminals in direct communication with the central processing unit which is in turn in direct communication with direct access files.

On-line storage Storage under the control of the central processing unit. (ANSI)

On-line system A system in which the input data enters the computer directly from the point of origin or in which output data is transmitted directly to where it is used. (IBM)

Open systems (1) Computer hardware and software that can interact without modification with hardware or software obtained from other vendors. (2) In general systems theory, a system that interacts with its environment by accepting inputs and producing outputs.

Operand (1) An entity on which an operation is performed. (ISO)

Operating system Software that controls the execution of programs; and that provides services such as resource allocation, scheduling, input/output control, and data management. Usually, operating systems are predominantly software, but partial or complete hardware implementations are possible. (ANSI)

Operational decision A decision on how to carry out specific tasks effectively and efficiently.

Operator A symbol that indicates the performance of a mathematical operation such as division, multiplication, addition, or subtraction.

Opscan Synonymous with **Optical scanner**.

Optical character recognition (OCR) Character recognition that uses optical means to identify graphic characters. (ISO)

Optical disk A disk that records information and reads it back using light (laser beams).

Optical reader A device that reads handwritten or machine-printed symbols into a computing system. (IBM)

Optical scanner (1) A scanner that uses light for examining patterns. (ISO) (2) A device that scans optically and usually generates an analog or digital signal. (ANSI)

Order (1) A specified arrangement, which in contrast to a sequence need not be linear; for example, the ordering of a hierarchy of items. (ANSI) (2) To place items in an arrangement in accordance with specified rules. (ISO)

Order processing system A computer system that initiates shipping orders, keeps track of backorders, and produces various sales analysis reports.

Origination The creation of raw data as a result of a business event or transaction.

Output The information produced by a computer.

Output controls Controls that help ensure the accuracy of computer results and the proper distribution of output.

Output device Synonym for **Output unit**. (ISO)

Output unit A device by which data can be conveyed out of a computer. Synonymous with **Output device**. (ISO)

Outsourcing The purchase of information system services from an outside vendor.

Packaged software A program designed for a specific application of broad, general usage, not adapted to any particular installation.

Packed decimal format A format in which each byte in a field except the rightmost byte represents two numeric digits. The rightmost byte contains one digit and the sign. For example, the decimal value +123 is represented as 0001 0010 0011 1111. Contrast with unpacked decimal format. (IBM)

Packet In data communications, a sequence of binary digits including data and control signals that is transmitted and switched as a composite whole. (ISO)

Page In a virtual storage system, a fixed-length block that has a virtual address and is transferred as a unit between real storage and auxiliary storage. (ISO)

Page printer (1) A device that prints one page as a unit; for example, COM printer, laser printer. Synonymous with page-at-a-time printer. (IBM) (2) Contrast with **Character printer**, **Line printer**. (IBM)

Paging (1) The transfer of pages between real storage and auxiliary storage. (ISO) (2) An allocation technique by which main storage is divided into page frames. A computer program need not be located in contiguous page frames in order to be executed. (ANSI)

Paint To draw directly on a video screen, as opposed to writing programs that create images.

Palette The overall selection of colors or shades available in a graphics display system.

Parallel conversion A method of converting to a new system whereby both the old and the new systems operate concurrently until management is satisfied that the new system will perform satisfactorily.

Parallel port A connection through which data are transmitted eight bits at a time (or in parallel). Generally used with printers.

Parallel processing (1) The concurrent or simultaneous execution of two or more processes in a single unit. (ANSI)

Parameter A constant value supplied by the user to the program. The execution of the program is in some way modified based on the value of this parameter.

Parameterized application package Prewritten application programs that the user can modify to suit his or her own requirements. The modification is done by specifying values for certain parameters.

Parity bit A binary digit appended to a group of binary digits to make the sum of all the digits, including the appended binary digit, either odd or even, as predetermined. (ISO)

Parity check A redundancy check by which a recalculated parity bit is compared to the predetermined parity bit. (ISO)

Partitioning Decomposing a data flow diagram into smaller, more detailed diagrams.

Pascal A block-structured high-level computer language named after a French mathematician and scientist, Blaise Pascal.

Password (1) In computer security, a string of characters known to the computer system and a user, who must specify it to gain full or limited access to a system and to the data stored within it. (IBM) (2) In systems with time-sharing, a one- to eight-character symbol that the user may be required to supply at the time he or she logs on the system. The password is confidential, whereas the user identification often is not.

Patch To make a temporary or expedient modification of a program in order to locate and correct an error. (ISO)

Payroll program A computer program that prepares checks to pay employees and maintains payment information.

Payroll register A report that provides a recapitulation of payment transactions for each employee and serves as an important part of the audit trail of the system.

Payroll system A computer system that assists in the preparation of salary checks, maintains payment records, and provides management reports related to payroll activities.

Peripheral equipment A functional unit that provides services external to a processing unit. Synonymous with peripheral device. (IBM)

Personal computer A computer small enough to be placed on a desktop and designed to be used by one person who possesses very little, if any, programming knowledge.

PERT (Program Evaluation and Review Technique) A scheduling method using networks consisting of activities that consume resources and take time, and events that mark the beginning and end of the activities. This method allows the minimum amount of time in which a project can be completed, and the critical path, to be determined.

Phased conversion A method of converting to a new system whereby the old system is gradually phased out and the new gradually phased in at the same time.

Physical file A collection of records that are physically located contiguous to one another.

Physical implementation The way a system is actually performed in the real world. Manual systems and automated systems (such as computers) are different types of physical implementation.

Physical record (1) A record whose characteristics depend on the manner or form in which it is stored, retrieved, or moved. A physical record may contain all or part of one or more logical records. (IBM) (2) Records that physically exist. Contrast with **Logical record**.

Physical view Representation of the data in a database in terms of physical characteristics like location, field length, and access method.

Picosecond One-trillionth of a second. One-thousandth of a nanosecond. (IBM)

Pie chart A chart that shows the relative values of various quantities as wedge-shaped sections of a circle.

Pilot conversion A method of converting to a new system in which the new system is introduced in some selected departments. If it functions satisfactorily, then it is extended to the whole organization.

Pixel The smallest dot that can be displayed on a screen. The word is derived from a contraction of the term picture element. All screen images, including both text and graphics, are made up of combinations of pixels. The more pixels per screen, the finer the images that can be drawn.

Planning Part of the process of management decision making. Planning involves identifying the alternatives from which to choose, selecting the criteria to be used in choosing an alternative, and selecting the

plan of action to be implemented for the problem.

Platter The actual metal (or other rigid material) disk that is mounted inside a fixed disk drive.

Plotter An output device, driven by the computer, that moves a pen across a sheet of paper to create a multiple-line pattern.

Plug-compatible A hardware unit produced by one manufacturer that can directly replace units produced by another manufacturer.

Pointer (1) A data element that represents an address or location of a related stored record in a file. (ANSI) (2) An identifier that indicates the location of a data item. (ANSI)

Point-of-sale (POS) data entry Immediate entry of sales transactions to the computer through a cash register that is connected to the computer.

Polarize To cause a magnetic substance to contain a positive or negative charge.

Polling A process by which the central processing unit addresses different terminals in turn to check if they have any input data for transmission to the central processing unit. A single line links all these terminals to the central processing unit.

Port An input/output connection for interfacing peripherals and computers.

Portability (1) The ability to transport equipment manually. (IBM) (2) The ability to run a program on more than one computer without modifying it. (IBM) (3) The ability to move programs from one computer to another without modification.

Postimplementation audit A process that usually consists of two steps: an evaluation of a new system using the objectives stated during the systems investigation phase, and a review and evaluation of the systems development cycle.

Power controls Controls that prevent damage to the system from voltage fluctuations and power breakdowns.

Precision The number of digits a number is allowed to have.

Prespecified computing Electronic data processing applications for which processing requirements can be determined ahead of time and programmed in the conventional manner.

Primary key In a record, a field whose value uniquely identifies the record. For instance, identification number may be a primary key for a file or database pertaining to students at a university.

Primary storage Within a central processing unit, the storage that stores the program while it is being executed, the data the program is using, and all or part of the operating system. Primary storage is often also called memory, internal storage, core storage, and random-access memory.

Printed circuit board A laminated plastic board, about one-sixteenth of an inch thick, onto which wiring is electroplated. This wiring connects components and sockets which are fastened to the board. The sockets receive chips.

Printer A device that writes output data from a system on paper or other medium. (IBM)

Print spooler Software that allows a memory area to hold output to be printed, enabling the user to simultaneously perform other tasks on the personal computer.

Procedure-oriented language A problem-oriented language that facilitates the expression of procedures as an explicit algorithms; for example, FORTRAN, ALGOL, COBOL, PL/I. Synonymous with imperative language. (ANSI)

Process (1) A course of events defined by its purpose or by its effect, achieved under given conditions. (ANSI) (2) To perform operations on data. (ISO)

Process control Automatic control of a process, in which a computer system is used to regulate the usually continuous operations or processes. (ISO)

Process descriptions A description of the data transformations that occur within the most detailed processes on a data flow diagram.

Processing controls Controls that increase the integrity of processing.

Production The jobs, programs, or files that are actually used in the daily tasks of an information system.

Program A set of instructions for the computer to follow.

Program bug An error in a computer program.

Program code The instructions used in a computer program.

Program documentation The documentation relating to individual programs.

Program library An organized collection of programs or parts of programs, and possibly other information pertaining to their use. (ISO) (2) Synonym for partitioned data set. (IBM) (3) A file containing the production copies of both application and systems programs.

Program module A small identifiable unit of program statements that performs one program task.

Program stubs Dummy modules that are called by the parent module during the testing phase. They allow the parent module to be tested before the lower-level modules are written.

Programmable decision A decision that is made within the guidelines of an established policy.

Programmable read-only memory A read-only memory into which data or programs can be written by an external programming device.

Programmer A person who designs, writes, and tests computer programs. (ANSI)

Programmer/analyst An information systems professional who performs both programming and systems analysis functions.

Programming The designing, writing, and testing of computer programs. (ISO)

Programming language An artificial language that is designed to generate or to express programs. (ISO)

Programming Language One (PL/1) A programming language designed for use in a wide range of commercial and scientific computer applications. (ANSI)

Prompt A symbol presented on the cathode ray tube screen to tell you that the operating system or program is ready to accept a new command or line of text.

Proprietary That which is exclusively owned by an individual or corporation, such as a patent.

Protect To safeguard data from unauthorized changes or destruction.

Protocol A set of codes that must be transmitted and received in the proper sequence to guarantee that the desired terminals or computers are hooked together and can "talk" as desired.

Prototype An experimental version of a computer application.

Pseudocode A description of program logic using English language sentences instead of the statements of a computer language.

Punched card A card punched with hole patterns. (ISO)

QUBE system A combination of cable TV and a computer system; it allows viewers to respond to broadcast messages through a keyboard.

Queries Requests for information from a file.

Query language A high-level computer language used to retrieve specific information from a database.

RAM See **Random-access memory (RAM)**.

RAM disk See **Electronic disk**.

Random Something that occurs in no particular order.

Random access An access mode in which specific logical records are obtained from, or placed into, a mass storage file in a manner independent of the locations of other records. (ANSI)

Random-access memory (RAM) Storage whose contents can be read and modified directly without searching. Random-access memory is normally used for primary storage.

Random addressing Synonymous with direct addressing.

Randomizing A technique by which the range of keys for an indirectly addressed file is reduced to smaller ranges of addresses by some method of computation until the desired address is found. (IBM)

Read-after-write A mode of operation that has the computer read back each sector written to the disk, checking that the data read back are the same as those recorded. This slows disk operations, but raises reliability.

Read-only memory (ROM) Synonym for **Read-only storage (ROS)**. (ISO)

Read-only storage (ROS) A storage device whose contents cannot be modified, except by a particular user or when operating under particular conditions; for example, a storage device in which writing is prevented by a lockout. Synonymous with fixed storage. (ANSI)

Read/write head A magnetic head capable of reading and writing. (ISO)

Real constant A constant that may contain a decimal point with or without a fractional part.

Real storage The main storage in a virtual storage system. Physically, real storage and main storage are identical. (ISO)

Real-time information Information about ongoing events that reflects the status of these events in a completely up-to-date manner.

Real-time processing The manipulation of data that are required or generated by some process while the process is in operation; usually the results are used to influence the process, and perhaps related processes, while it is occurring. (ANSI) (ISO)

Real-time system A computer system with the capability of immediately capturing data concerning ongoing events or processes and providing information necessary to manage these ongoing events.

Reasonableness checks Program controls that monitor the values of input data and make sure that they are within proper limits. For instance, a reasonableness check would trap a time card that showed 150 hours worked in one week.

Record (1) A group of related data elements treated as a unit. (ISO) (2) A collection of adjacent data fields relating to some specific entity. Analogous to a file folder in a manual file.

Recording density The number of bits in a single linear track measured per unit of length of the recording medium. (ANSI)

Record layout The arrangement and structure of data or words in a record, together with a definition of the order and size of the component elements of the record. (ANSI)

Recurring costs The costs expected to continually arise throughout the life of the computer's installation.

Redundancy check A check that uses one or more extra binary digits or characters attached to data for the detection of errors. (ISO) (2) A control imposed by the performance of a task by two hardware units independent of each other.

Reengineering The complete redesign of the basic business processes of a firm using information technology.

Register A storage device that has a specified storage capacity. (ISO)

Relational data model A logical view of a database; it treats all data as if they were stored in the form of tables.

Relational operator A symbol that represents the performance of a comparison operation between two quantities or values. For instance, "is greater than" is a relational operator.

Relative address An address calculated as a displacement from a base address. (ANSI)

Relevance The usefulness of data for decision-making purposes.

Reliability A quality held by that which is dependable and can be trusted.

Remote Pertaining to a system, program, or device that is accessed through a telecommunication line. (IBM)

Remote job entry (RJE) Submission of a job through an input unit that has access to a computer through a data link. (ISO)

Removable disk A disk drive in which the disk itself can be removed; in particular, a hard disk drive using disks mounted in cartridges.

Report Management information printed on a hard-copy medium like paper.

Report generation The production of information output.

Report generator A high-level language that can be used to produce reports in almost any format.

Report program generator (RPG) A programming language specifically designed for writing application programs that meet common business data processing requirements. (IBM)

Request for proposal A document that specifies the requirements for equipment and software to be purchased.

Reserved words Words in a program that have a special meaning for the compiler. The user may not use them for any other purpose.

Resident Pertaining to computer programs that remain on a particular storage device. (ISO)

Resident supervisor That part of the operating system that is used most often, and is continuously stored in primary storage.

Resolution The fineness of detail that can be shown in a display. Commonly, resolution for computer displays is stated as the number of possible lines across the image and the maximum number of possible dot positions in each line. For example, the IBM-PC has a maximum screen resolution of 640 dots across by 200 lines.

Resource Any facility of the computing system or operating system required by a job or task, including main storage, input/output devices, the processing unit, data sets, and control or processing programs. (IBM)

Resource allocation The assignment of the facilities of a computer system for the accomplishment of jobs; for example, the assignment of main storage, input-output devices, or files. (ISO)

Resource management Synonymous with **Resource allocation**.

Response time (1) The elapsed time between the end of an inquiry or demand on a computer system and the beginning of the response; for example, the length of time between an indication of the end of an inquiry and the display of the first character of the response at a user terminal. (ISO) (2) The elapsed time between submission of a command on a remote terminal and the completion of that command as evidenced by a message on the terminal screen or printer.

Retrieve To move data from secondary storage to the central processing unit so that it may be processed.

Reverse engineer To derive a computer system's or program's design specifications directly from the program code.

Right-justify To line up characters such that the last nonblank character in each line is on the right margin.

Rigid disk A hard, flat, circular plate coated with magnetic material, used as a secondary storage device.

Ring network configuration A communication network in which several central processing units are connected in a circular pattern. Each computer can communicate with either one of its neighbors in the circle.

RJE Remote job entry. (ANSI) (ISO)

ROM See **Read-only memory (ROM)**.

Rounding The process of replacing a number with the closest possible number, after dropping some of its decimal digits.

Routine A program, called by another program, that may have some general or frequent use. (ISO) (2) A computer program.

Row A horizontal arrangement of characters or other expressions. (ANSI)

RPG See **Report program generator (RPG)**.

RS-232C (serial) port A personal computer input/output port through which data are transmitted and received serially, one bit at a time. It can be used in conjunction with modems, printers or other serial devices.

Run (1) A performance of one or more jobs. (ISO) (2) A performance of one or more programs. (ISO)

Sabotage controls Controls that reduce the risk of sabotage in electronic data processing operations.

Scan (1) To examine every reference or every entry in a file routinely as part of a retrieval scheme. (ISO) (2) To examine sequentially, part by part. (ANSI)

Scheduled listing A report that is produced at a regular interval like a week, a month, or a year.

Schema The logical structure of a database.

Scratch To erase data on a volume or delete its identification so that it can be used for another purpose. (IBM)

Scratch file A temporary work file. (IBM)

Search The examination of one or more data elements of a set for one or more elements that have a given property. (ISO)

Secondary storage (1) In Series/1, processor storage beyond the first 64 Kb. (IBM) (2) Synonym for auxiliary storage. (IBM)

Sector A predetermined angular part of a track or a band on a magnetic drum or magnetic disk that can be addressed. (ISO)

Seek A movement of the disk read/write head in or out to a specified track.

Segment A term often used as a synonym for record in a database management system.

Segregation of functions Dividing up the work load among employees such that the work of one becomes a check on the work of others.

Self-documenting A characteristic of a computer language whose statements are easy enough to understand that English descriptions of the program steps are not necessary.

Semantic error An error in the logic of the program, as opposed to syntax errors.

Semantic gap A lack of correspondence between a problem definition and the computer code written to solve it.

Semantics (1) The relationships of characters or groups of characters to their meanings, independent of the manner of their interpretation and use. (ISO) (2) The relationships between symbols and their meanings. (ANSI)

Semiconductor A solid crystalline substance, such as silicon, that has a conductivity greater than good insulators but less than good conductors such as metal.

Semiconductor storage Storage that uses integrated electronic circuits on semiconductor material to represent bits of data. See **Chip**.

Sentinel value Synonymous with **Trailer value**.

Sequence checks A control that verifies that input records are in ascending order by record key field.

Sequential (1) Pertaining to a process in which all events occur one after the other, without any time lapse between them. (ISO) (2) Contrast with **Concurrent**, **Consecutive**, **Simultaneous**. (ANSI)

Sequential access (1) An access method in which records are read from, written to, or removed from a file based on the logical order of the records in the file. (IBM) (2) Contrast with **Direct access**. (IBM)

Sequential construct In a program, a construct in which two or more operations are performed in sequence.

Sequential file organization A file organization with all records typically ordered in ascending order by record key.

Serial processing (1) Pertaining to the sequential or consecutive execution of two or more processes in a single device such as a channel or processing unit. (ANSI) (2) Contrast with **Parallel processing**. (ANSI)

Server In a network, a data station that provides facilities to other stations; for example, a file server, a print server, or a mail server. (ISO)

Service bureau A company that provides batch computer processing service on an as-needed basis and charges for the service based on an hourly rate.

Shared data Data that are used by two or more computers concurrently in a distributed data processing system.

Sign bit A bit or a binary element that occupies a sign position and indicates the algebraic sign of the number represented by the numeral with which it is associated. (ISO)

Simplex transmission Data transmission in one preassigned direction only. (ISO)

Simulate To build a model or imitation of something that occurs in the real world, such as a business, weather system, or aircraft. Simulations that are built on computers are mathematical models.

Simulation The representation of selected characteristics of the behavior of one physical or abstract system by another system; for example, the representation of physical phenomena by means of operations performed by a data processing system; or the representation of operations of a data processing system by those of another data processing system. (ISO)

Simultaneous In a process, pertaining to two or more events that occur within the same interval of time, each one handled by a separate functional unit; for example, in the execution of one or more programs, several input/output operations handled by input/output channels, input/output controllers, and associated peripherals may be simultaneous with one another and with other operations handled directly by the processing unit. (ISO) (2) See also **Concurrent**, **Consecutive**, **Sequential**. (ANSI)

Skeleton application program A simple program developed as a model for an actual application. The skeleton program includes only the most essential capabilities needed in the actual application. Synonymous with **Prototype**.

Soft copy An image on a video or other electronic screen, as opposed to hard copy on paper.

Soft error An error in reading data from the disk that does not recur if those same data are reread.

Soft-sectored Disks that mark the beginning of each sector of data within a track by a magnetic pattern rather than by a physical hole in the disk.

Software Programs, procedures, rules, and any associated documentation pertaining to the operation of a system. (ANSI)

Software directory A reference book that lists a large number of software packages and describes their major characteristics.

Software monitor A software system that monitors the performance of various system devices.

Sort (1) To segregate items into groups according to specified criteria without necessarily ordering the items within each group. (ISO) (2) To arrange a set of items according to keys that are used as the basis for determining the sequence of the items (e.g., to arrange the records of a personnel file into alphabetical sequence by using the employee names as sort keys). (ANSI)

Sort key A key used as a basis for determining the sequence of items in a set.

Sound synthesizer An acoustic device that when connected to a computer can produce many different musical sounds.

Source code A program written in a higher-level language than machine language. It is called source code because it is the starting point or source in the compilation process to produce object code.

Source data automation The capture of data in computer-readable form at the place and time of an event.

Source document A form containing data that are being keyed into a computer system.

Source language A language from which statements are translated. (ANSI)

Source program A computer program expressed in a source language. (ISO)

Specification form A form used to specify computations, input file format, and report format in the report program generator.

Specification statement In a program, a passive statement that describes data characteristics to the computer but does not make the computer perform any action.

Spindle The center shaft of a disk.

Splitter In a local area network, a passive device used at a node to interconnect more than two branches. A splitter neither amplifies nor regenerates data signals. (ANSI)

Spooling (Simultaneous Peripheral Operation On-Line) The use of auxiliary storage as a buffer storage to reduce processing delays when transferring data between peripheral equipment and the processors of a computer. (ISO)

Spreadsheet A program that allows the user to create a large, two-dimensional table on the computer's screen, and to manipulate the data in the table in many different ways.

Stand-alone Computer hardware or software that operates in an independent and separate manner.

Standard An acknowledged guideline or norm against which performance is measured.

Star network configuration A communication network in which several microcomputers are connected to one central processing unit.

Statement (1) In programming languages, a language construct that represents a set of declarations or a step in a sequence of actions. (ANSI) (2) In computer programming, a symbol string or other arrangement of symbols. (ANSI) (3) Synonym for **Instruction**. (ANSI)

Statistical multiplexor A multiplexing device that allocates transmission time to different terminals in proportion to their volume of data input/output.

Storage The process of retaining data, program instructions, and output in machine-readable form.

Store (1) To place data into a storage device. (ISO) (2) To retain data in a storage device. (ISO)

Stored program A set of instructions that resides in the computer's memory and may be executed without human intervention.

Strategic decision making The process of making decisions at the upper or strategic level of the organization. These decisions affect the future of the organization and are made in an environment of uncertainty. Strategic decisions involve establishing goals, policies and long-term resource allocations.

Streaming tape A tape-recording method used only to make backup copies of information from hard disks. Streaming tapes record data blocks close together, leaving too little room to be able to start and stop between blocks.

String A sequence of elements of the same nature, such as characters, considered as a whole. (ISO)

String constant A constant composed of alphabetic, numeric and special characters, enclosed within double quotes.

String variable A variable that can take on as a value any string of alphabetic, numeric, and special characters.

Structure chart A graphic representation of the hierarchical relationships between various modules.

Structured That which is highly organized.

Structured analysis A system analysis methodology used in structured systems development. A structured analysis moves from a study of the existing system to its logical model. Then the logical model of the new system is created and developed into a new physical system.

Structured design Development of the logic of program modules and their interfaces.

Structured English A tool used for describing program logic in English-like terminology. It uses the vocabulary of English combined with the logical constructs of a programming language to make the logic understandable to human beings.

Structured programming In computer programming, an approach that restricts the flow of control to three basic constructs: sequence, loop, and conditional.

Structured system development A system development methodology based on three major principles: partitioning into small modules, specification of interfaces between modules, and specification of processes within the modules.

Subroutine (1) A sequenced set of instructions or statements that may be used in one or more computer programs and at one or more points in a computer program. (ISO) (2) A routine that can be part of another routine. (ANSI)

Subschema The logical view of the part of a database that is of interest to a particular application.

Subscript A variable whose values uniquely identify individual elements of an array. Synonymous with **Index**.

Substrate The material a disk is made of beneath the magnetic coating. Hard disks are generally made of aluminum or magnesium alloys (or glass, for optical disks), while the substrate on floppy disks is usually Mylar.

Subsystem (1) A secondary or subordinate system, usually capable of operating independently of, or asynchronously with, a controlling system. (IBM) (2) A part of the total system. All subsystems combine to comprise the system.

Summary file A file containing data extracted and summarized from other files.

Supervisory program A computer program, usually part of an operating system, that controls the execution of other computer programs and regulates the flow of work in a data processing system. Synonymous with executive program, supervisor. (ANSI) (ISO)

Surface The top or bottom side of a disk platter.

Symbolic language A programming language that expresses addresses and operation codes of instructions in symbols convenient to humans rather than in machine languages. (ANSI)

Synchronous transmission A data transmission method in which a long stream of bytes is transmitted without interruption. This method is economical for complex, high-speed equipment that processes large volumes of data.

Syntax (1) The relationships among characters or groups of characters, independent of their meanings or the manner of their interpretation and use. (ANSI) (2) The structure of expressions in a language. (ANSI) (3) The rules governing the structure of a language. (ANSI)

System People, machines, and methods organized to accomplish a set of specific functions. (ANSI)

System analysis (1) In system development, the systematic investigation of a real or planned system to determine the functions of the system and how they relate to each other and to other systems. (IBM) (2) The evaluation of the set of alternatives in a system with a set of criteria.

System analyst A person whose responsibility is to analyze, design, and develop information systems.

System and programming group Management information systems personnel who develop or acquire applications software systems.

System command Operating system commands issued by the user to facilitate the creating, editing, and execution of programs.

System development controls Control procedures to manage the system development, system documentation, and program maintenance functions; controls relating to the system development cycle, systems documentation, or program changes.

System development life cycle The different phases that a typical computer-based

information system goes through in its development and use.

System documentation The documentation of the system that provides an overview of the system's features.

System flowchart A flowchart providing an overall view of the inputs, processes, and outputs of a system.

System maintenance The process of correcting errors discovered in programs and changing the programs to satisfy changed user requirements or conditions.

System network architecture (SNA) A data communication system used to connect various IBM devices.

System programmer A programmer who plans, generates, maintains, extends, and controls the use of an operating system with the aim of improving the overall productivity of an installation. Contrast with **Application programmer**. (IBM)

System unit The part of a personal computer that contains the central processing unit.

Systems software A set of programs that controls the use of hardware and software resources. These programs allocate system resources to application programs, based on their needs and their priorities.

Table (1) A two-dimensional data structure used as a logical model in relational database management systems. (2) An array of data elements, each of which may be unambiguously identified by means of one or more arguments. (ISO)

Tactical decision making The process of making decisions at the middle or coordinating level of the organization. The decisions are made primarily to reach the present goals of the organization. A common decision on this level involves resource allocation for the present needs of the organization.

Tape drive See magnetic tape drive. (ANSI)

Technical support staff Management information system personnel who are responsible for maintaining hardware and establishing data processing standards.

Telecommunications Any communication between two computers, or devices with embedded computers, in various locations. Telecommunication differs from networks in that it takes place over long distances and is usually carried out over phone lines, radio waves or a satellite transmission apparatus.

Temporary storage In computer programming, storage locations reserved for intermediate results. (ANSI)

Terminal (1) A point in a system or communication network at which data can either enter or leave. (ANSI) (2) A device, usually equipped with a keyboard and display device, capable of sending and receiving information. (IBM)

Test data Hypothetical data used to test a new program for errors. Test data should be comprehensive enough to cover all possible types of valid and invalid inputs so that program performance may be observed under all circumstances.

Third-generation language A programming language such as FORTRAN, COBOL, Pascal, or BASIC that requires you to instruct the computer in a procedural, step-by-step fashion.

Third party A company other than the user or the computer system manufacturer.

Thrashing In virtual storage systems, a condition in which the system can do little useful work because of excessive paging. (IBM)

Throughput A measure of the amount of work performed by a computer system over a given period of time, for example, number of jobs per day. (ANSI)

Timeliness The speed with which data are provided to the user for decision-making purposes.

Time sharing (1) An operating technique of a computer system that provides for the interleaving in time of two or more processes in one processor. (ANSI) (2) A method of using a computing system that allows a number of users to execute programs concurrently and to interact with the programs during execution. (IBM)

Time-sharing service A service firm that rents out computer time to its customers. The customer typically accesses the central processing unit through a remote terminal located at its place of business.

Top-down approach A system development approach that calls for the development of an integrated information system based on the objectives of the business.

Trace (1) A record of the execution of a computer program. It exhibits the sequence in which the instructions were executed. (ANSI) (2) To record a series of events as they occur. (IBM)

Track An invisible magnetic circle pattern written on a disk as a guide to where to store and read the data.

Track density The measurement of how closely tracks are packed on a disk, specified as tracks per inch (TPI). Most fixed disks have a track density in the hundreds or thousands.

Tractor feed A mechanism with a train of feed pins on each side that fit into the pinholes of continuous paper stock. Line advance commands from the computer then cause the paper to advance.

Trailer label The last record in a file on magnetic tape. It contains control information such as a count of the number of records in the file.

Trailer value A special data value that signals the end of a set of data. Synonymous with **Sentinel value**.

Transaction A business event such as a sale to a customer. In information systems, the term transaction is often used to refer to any change made in a computer file.

Transfer rate For a disk or other peripheral device, the rate at which information is transferred from the device to memory, or vice versa.

Transform description A description of how data are to be processed at the lowest levels of a data flow diagram.

Translation The generation of object code from source code.

Translator A computer program that translates from one language into another language and in particular from one programming language into another programming language. Synonymous with translating program. (ISO)

Tree data structure A hierarchical data structure characterized by a top node called a root and nodes having a one-to-many relationship.

Turnaround document A document that can be sent out to human users and can also be read by the computer when it is returned. The remittance advice on a punched card that comes with utility bills is a common example of a turnaround document.

Turnaround time (1) The elapsed time between submission of a job and the return of the complete output. (ISO) (2) The elapsed time between submission of a batch job and the availability of output.

Turnkey system A complete system in which all hardware and software have been installed and debugged. In theory all you have to do is turn a key.

Two-dimensional Allowing only rows and columns.

Universal product code (UPC) A bar-coded symbol printed on the package of a consumer product. This is detected by an optical reader and is used by the computer to identify and price the product.

Update To modify a master file with current information according to a specified procedure. (IBM)

User Anyone who requires the services of a computing system. (IBM)

User affirmation The process of asking the user if he or she will enter further data. This is used when executing programs that require interactive data entry.

User-defined function A function defined by a programmer, as opposed to a built-in function.

User-defined words In a program, words that have been defined by the programmer to have specific meaning.

User-driven computing Electronic data processing applications for which users do not always know what information they will need and when. It is often necessary to modify the programs on short notice in such systems.

User-friendly systems Software systems that make it easy for non-computer-oriented people to use computers.

Utility program A computer program in general support of the processes of a computer; for example, a diagnostic program, a trace program, a sort program. Synonymous with service program. (ISO)

Vacuum tube A glass-covered instrument used to regulate the flow of electrons through the circuits of early computer systems.

Validation Tests to determine whether an implemented system fulfills its requirements. (ISO)

Validity checks Hardware controls that monitor the bit structure of bytes to determine whether the combination of the on and off bits represents a valid structure within the character set of the computer.

Value added network (VAN) A communication provider who provides services beyond those of a common carrier. For example, communications may be converted by the VAN from the protocol of one device to the protocol of another.

Variable A quantity that can assume any of a given set of values. (ANSI)

Variable-length record (1) A record having a length independent of the length of other records with which it is logically or physically associated. Contrast with **Fixed-length record**. (IBM) (2) Pertaining to a file in which the records need not be uniform in length. (ANSI)

Vendor support Services provided by the seller of a hardware or software system. These typically include training, repair and maintenance, installation, testing, consulting and backup arrangements.

Verifiability The ability to confirm the accuracy of data. Accuracy may be confirmed by comparing with other data of known accuracy or tracing back to the original source.

Virtual drive The use of a drive name (a letter of the alphabet on the personal computer) to refer to part of a disk drive. Virtual drives are often used for large-capacity hard disks.

Virtual storage The storage space that may be regarded as addressable main storage by the user of a computer system in which virtual addresses are mapped into real addresses. The size of virtual storage is limited by the addressing scheme of the computing system and by the amount of auxiliary storage available, and not by the actual number of main storage locations. (ISO)

Voice recognition system A hardware or software device that can interpret the patterns of an individual's speech, thereby enabling voice input to a computer.

Volatile storage A storage device whose contents are lost when power is cut off. (ISO)

Walkthrough A step-by-step review of the documentation or other work produced by a systems analyst or programmer.

Wide area network (WAN) (1) A data communication network designed to serve an area of hundreds or thousands of miles; for example, public and private packet switch networks and national telephone networks. (IBM)

Winchester disks Hard disks that use a technology similar to an IBM model that had the "Winchester" code name. These disks use the read/write heads that ride just above the magnetic surface, held up by the air dragged by the turning disk. When the disks stop turning, the heads land on the surface, which has a specially lubricated coating. Winchester disks either must be sealed or have a filtration system, since ordinary dust particles are large enough to catch between the head and the disk.

Window In computer graphics, a predefined part of a virtual space. (ISO)

Word A character string or a bit string considered as an entity. (ISO)

Word processing system A computer system that stores and processes text data. These systems typically include powerful editing and text formatting capabilities.

Word size A measure of the amount of data the central processing unit can process simultaneously.

Working storage Synonym for **Temporary storage**, working space. (IBM)

Work load model A set of one or more computer programs that are representative of the buyer's planned computer work load. These are typically executed on alternative computer configurations to provide information that is useful in making an acquisition decision.

Workstation (1) A functional unit at which a user works. A workstation often has some processing capability. (ISO) (2) A terminal or microcomputer, usually one that is connected to a mainframe or to a network at which a user can perform applications. (IBM)

WORM Write-once-read-many; usually in the context of optical disks. (ANSI)

WORM optical disk Write once read many optical disk. (ANSI)

Write To make a permanent or transient recording of data in a storage device or on a data medium. (ANSI)

Write-enable ring A device installed in a tape reel to permit writing on the tape. A tape mounted on a tape unit without the ring in position is protected; writing to the tape cannot occur. (IBM)

Write-once As applied to optical disks, technologies that allow the drive to store data on a disk and read them back, but not erase them.

Write-protect notch A cutout in one corner of a diskette that is optically scanned to allow writing on a disk. If the notch is covered with tape, the drive will not write on the diskette; thus, it is write protected.

Write-read checks A control similar to redundancy checks. As data are written on magnetic tape or disk, they pass through a read head, which reads the data and compares them to the data that should have been written.

WYSIWG (What-you-see-is-what-you-get) A capability of a text editor or word processor to continually display pages exactly as they will be printed. (IBM)

Index

A

AACSB. *See* American Assembly of Collegiate Schools of Business
Abstract material, value of, 25
Access controls, 264–65, 551–53
  information and privacy issues, 63–64
  See also Security
Access method
  network interface card for execution of, 380
  for nonswitched networks, 377–78
Accounting information systems, 131–39
  applications, and subject databases, 415
Accounts payable, 135–37
Accounts receivable
  sales management systems support for, 131–32
  system components, 133–35
Accuracy, 67–68
  of stored and disseminated data, 61
ACM. *See* Computing Machinery, Association for (ACM)
Active data dictionary, 344, 345, 583. *See also* Data dictionary
Activities
  in a business cycle, 119
  finance, 119
  spending, 119
Activity ratio, and efficiency of file processing methods, 323
Address
  cylinder, 313
  physical, 312, 318, 319
  relative, 312
  sector, 313
  track, 313
Ad hoc approach to planning, 397
AFIPS. *See* Information Processing Societies, American Federation of (AFIPS)
Airline reservation systems, 405–6
American Assembly of Collegiate Schools of Business (AACSB), 14
American Civil Liberties Union, 62
American Hospital Supply, 101

American National Standards Institute (ANSI), 283, 381
American Standard Code for Information Interchange (ASCII), 306, 371, 608
Analog communication versus digital communication, 364–65
ANSI. *See* American National Standards Institute (ANSI)
Anticipation checks, 559
Apollo System (United Airlines), 8, 101
Application
  autonomy, advantages of, 172
  behavioral science, 82
  black-box concept, 32
  competitive advantage, 91, 154
  computer-aided software engineering (CASE), 14
  decision support systems (DSS), 164–66
  development life cycle, 493
  efficiency, 492
  electronic data interchange (EDI), 363–64
  end users, 483–99
  forms, 206
  Fraud Detection System, 183
  generalized modules, 489
  globalization, 106
  inventory control, 450–51
  maintenance, 486
  networks, 48
  open systems, 34
  order processing, 129
  personal computers, 161
  privacy issues, 62–63
  prototype, 489
  risk taking, 111
  software, 262, 264
  technology, 14
Application controls, 556–62
Application development
  cycle of, 493
  by endusers, 483–99
  for international use, 605
  time span of conventional and fourth-generation language use, 484–85
Application generators, 269, 488–91

Application programmers, 264, 644–46
Applications
  Epson America, Inc., 75
  Federal Express, 103
  GTE, 108
  Light*Link network, 114
  Xerox Corporation, 43
Application software, 262, 264
  cost of, 424
  loading on a personal computer, 266
Argyris, Chris, 165–66
Arithmetic-logic unit, 221, 227
Arithmetic proof checks, 559
Artificial intelligence, 11–12, 152, 168–71, 625
ASCII. *See* American Standard Code for Information Interchange (ASCII)
Ashby, Ross, 35
Ashby's law of requisite variety, 35
ASM. *See* Systems Management, Association of (ASM)
Assembler for machine language code output, 279
Assembly language, mnemonic, 279
Asynchronous transmission of data, 371–72
ATMs. *See* Automatic teller machines (ATMs)
AT&T Mail, 379
Attributes, relational model, 349–50
Audio-response output devices for computers, 252
Audio text systems, 200
Auditing, careers in, 647
Audits
  and computer crime, 633
  of information systems, 562–63
Audit trail, 68
  in computer systems, 538
  loss of, on magnetic media, 237
Automatic teller machines (ATMs), 103
Automation, 624
  office, 4, 192–211
Autonomy
  and expert systems use, application, 172

PHOTO CREDITS